WAR AND PEACE

CW01432878

MICHAEL KEATING
MATT WALDMAN
(*Editors*)

War and Peace in Somalia

*National Grievances, Local Conflict
and Al-Shabaab*

HURST & COMPANY, LONDON

First published in the United Kingdom in 2018 by
C. Hurst & Co. (Publishers) Ltd.,
41 Great Russell Street, London, WC1B 3PL
© Michael Keating and Matt Waldman, 2018

Second impression, 2020
All rights reserved.
Printed in India

The right of Michael Keating and Matt Waldman to be identified as the
authors of this publication is asserted by them in accordance with the
Copyright, Designs and Patents Act, 1988.

A Cataloguing-in-Publication data record for this book
is available from the British Library.

ISBN: 9781787380189

This book is printed using paper from registered sustainable
and managed sources.

www.hurstpublishers.com

CONTENTS

v

CONTENTS

vi

CONTENTS

THE HUMAN DIVERSITY OF CONFLICT: WOMEN, MEN AND YOUTH

UNDERSTANDING AND RESPONDING TO AL-SHABAAB

CONTENTS

FOREWORD

*His Excellency, The President of The Federal Republic of Somalia,
Mohamed Farmaajo*

The hearts of Somalis are heavy with grief. For too long, Somalis have used violence to achieve their goals or to resolve their differences. Too many lives have been lost. Too many dreams have been destroyed.

The time has come for Somalia to put an end to violence. This will require a truly national effort to rebuild our country, restore trust in one another, and repair the deep cultural and historical bonds that draw us together as a nation.

It will require confidence and determination to succeed. We must use the force of arms to fight violent extremists, and to defend innocent men, women and children, who suffer the brunt of this war. This battle must be led by Somalis, but we need the sustained commitment and support from the African Union, United Nations and key international partners.

It requires all of us, including the Federal Government of Somalia, to learn from experience and acknowledge where we can do better. We must not engage in or tolerate corruption or injustice. We must address grievances and work to ensure respect for the human rights of all Somalis. Where military action is necessary, it must be respectful of civilians and in accordance with the law.

For many Somali leaders, achieving peace will require a change of mindset and way of thinking. Across the country, we must seek to resolve conflicts, avoid confrontation, to find and build on shared values, and even be prepared to engage in dialogue with those we see as adversaries. We must also talk and listen to all those Somalis who are affected by the decisions of those who hold power.

My Government is committed to this agenda and to restoring hope to Somalis, including by crafting a national reconciliation plan to which all stakeholders can contribute.

Peace can never be achieved if we do not fully understand the causes, complexity and dynamics of the many conflicts that blight our nation. That is why I commend the work of the United Nations, supported by the Government of Norway, and all of the Somali and international researchers and experts who contributed to this portfolio. A greater understanding of the challenges we face today will enable us to chart the path to a more peaceful and prosperous future.

PREFACE

Michael Keating, Special Representative of the United Nations Secretary-General for Somalia and Head of the United Nations Assistance Mission in Somalia

In recent years, Somalis have increasingly turned to political dialogue to thrash out their differences. Progress is often precarious and unpredictable, characterized by clan-based calculations and deals among powerful actors. To achieve sustainable peace and establish a functional state, this dialogue needs to be more inclusive and address many grievances and disputes around the country.

Political dialogue has nevertheless delivered results: a provisional constitution, the establishment of Federal States, an Upper House of Parliament that represents the country's regions and not just its clans, an electoral process in 2016 that was limited but more inclusive than any since 1969, transitions of central power, a national development plan, and agreement on the national security architecture.

Those who use violence to advance their goals jeopardize this arduous political journey, and threaten the safety and well-being of all Somalis. Most obviously, Al-Shabaab has chosen that course.

Like other Somalis, members of Al-Shabaab hold views about basic issues such as the nature of the state, foreign involvement, the administration of justice, and the role of women in society. But they use large-scale violence, terror, coercion and intimidation to advance their agenda.

The consequence is that thousands of Somali men, women and children have been killed and injured, up to one in four Somalis have been internally displaced, and millions have lost their livelihoods.

Regrettably, it is not only extremists who generate violent conflict in Somalia. The country is blighted by a multiplicity of local and regional conflicts, often over land, resources and power. Too often adversaries turn to force to advance their interests.

Those who have power—whether political, military, social or economic—often abuse it in ways that create or perpetuate grievances and injustices that fuel conflict. Mistreatment, misrule, corruption and marginalization sow the seeds for violence.

The resulting insecurity has compromised progress in every sphere, hampered Somalis' extraordinary entrepreneurial skills and undermined confidence in the future of the country. Somalis are among the poorest people in the world. Young people have limited opportunities. Half the population faces chronic food insecurity and live in conditions that are unacceptable in the twenty-first century.

Resolving conflict and reducing levels of violence are therefore the greatest challenges facing Somalia.

International actors are implicated in many ways, motivated variously by their own security priorities, strategic interests, and rivalries. But blaming the country's woes on external actors is inadequate. It is up to Somalis, both men and women, to forge their own pathway to peace.

The role of the United Nations is to support Somalis in this task and enable them to assume greater control over their own destiny. The UN does this by facilitating dialogue, providing strategic and technical advice, promoting norms and rights-based approaches, supporting the emergence of accountable institutions, sharing global experience, and mobilizing the support of international actors, governmental and civil society. Our role is also to help create space for processes which are best pursued exclusively by local actors.

But the most basic ingredient for conflict resolution and state-building is the willingness of Somalis, especially those with power, to choose dialogue over violence. This is essential in order to prevent further conflict and achieve lasting peace.

Achieving peace also depends on a political and practical strategy to resolve conflict and address the drivers of violence. This strategy must be Somali-led and owned. It should draw upon the cumulative experience and knowledge of experts and practitioners, Somali and international. It is in that spirit that we share this collection of papers.

INTRODUCTION

Michael Keating and *Matt Waldman*

This volume is part of an Initiative of the United Nations Assistance Mission in Somalia (UNSOM), overseen by Michael Keating and directed by Matt Waldman.[1] The Initiative has been implemented with the support of the Government of Norway and in consultation and collaboration with the Federal Government of Somalia. The Initiative has several key goals. Above all, it is intended to serve as a resource for the government, and to ensure that national, international and UN policy-making is well informed, up-to-date and improves the prospects for peace. The Initiative seeks to contribute to an informed debate within Somalia about how to reduce violence. It is also hoped that the Initiative will contribute to the establishment of diverse, multidisciplinary communities of practice, whose expertise could help to generate a more peaceful future for Somalis.

The first phase of the Initiative aims to support high-calibre research, analysis, thinking and writing on key issues relating to peace and reconciliation in Somalia and to promote wider collaboration between the UN, government and civil society. As such, the Initiative involves experts, academics, researchers, analysts and peacebuilding practitioners, most of whom have years, if not decades, of experience working on Somalia or in the field of conflict resolution. They were invited to produce concise briefing papers on issues of their choice, taking into account gaps in knowledge or common misunderstandings, their particular expertise, and the potential, in any given area, for action that contributes to peace and reconciliation. They were asked to provide a deeper understanding of the conflict, and set out policy and practical steps that should be taken to reduce violence, promote reconciliation and increase the prospects for peace. To that end, many contributors have carried out field research in Somalia and neighbouring countries, including surveys, in-depth interviews, and focus group discussions, in addition to extensive desk research and analysis.

The resulting papers, most of which were written during the first half of 2017, are contained in this book. They follow a standard format, and the summary and recommendations sections of each paper have been translated into Somali and are available on request.² Given the diverse professional backgrounds of the authors, and different means of research, the papers vary considerably in methodology and approach. The papers were not censored and do not reflect the view of the United Nations. In fact, some of them contain criticism of the UN, government and other national and international actors. We believe that a frank, open and multidisciplinary discourse is essential for acquiring a deeper and clearer understanding of the conflict. Effective support for conflict resolution in Somalia depends on such an understanding.

* * *

Somalis have endured violent conflict for three decades. The cost of the violence, whether in terms of the human and psychological harm, the social impact, economic damage, political implications, or the lost opportunities, has been incalculable. Loss, suffering and uncertainty are a daily reality for millions of Somalis. Every clan, every community and every family has paid a price.

The hopes and aspirations of Somalis depend on action to address the violence. Somalia desperately needs a more coherent, determined and effective approach to conflict resolution. Without peace, it will be difficult if not impossible to build a functional state that can generate revenues and deliver basic services, especially justice, healthcare and education, for its long-suffering population. Without stability and the rule of law, Somalia's huge potential for commerce and entrepreneurship will be hampered, and investment will remain limited.

The starting point for progress is genuine commitment among Somali leaders to end violence and resolve differences through peaceful and inclusive dialogue. Without such will, no amount of knowledge, capacity building, or international involvement will succeed.

Securing this commitment will not be easy. Citizens and political leaders across Somalia routinely call for peace and reconciliation, but their actions, too often motivated by clan, factional and personal interests, fall short of what is required. A genuine resolve among Somali leaders to promote the safety and well-being of all Somalis, regardless of their differences, and to act in the interests of society as a whole is essential.

Successful conflict resolution in Somalia also requires a shared understanding of the country's many conflicts. We hope the papers in this volume contribute to such an understanding. Efforts to resolve any given conflict require an awareness of its history, causes, dynamics and implications. They must also draw on a deep understanding of the parties involved in and affected by the conflict: their motivations, beliefs and perceptions, as well as their core interests and concerns.

Given the diversity and complexity of Somalia's conflicts, the legacies of mistrust, and the weakness of institutions, there can be no one-size-fits-all approach to conflict resolution. There should be careful consideration of which actors are best placed to engage, and the approaches they should use to help prevent, resolve or mitigate conflict. This, in turn, requires an appreciation of the different interrelated strands of violent conflict in Somalia today.

The most lethal and destructive conflict is the armed insurgency conducted by Al-Shabaab against the state. This will require a multi-pronged approach. A key element will be effective operations carried out by national and foreign security forces, acting in a professional, disciplined and coordinated way.

The success of the African Union Mission in Somalia (AMISOM) and Somali troops, at great human sacrifice, in expelling Al-Shabaab from the main population centres has resulted in the group adapting its military tactics and broader modus operandi. Al-Shabaab exploits the weakness of government and uses coercion, intimidation and persuasion to undermine state authority at every level.

Progress against Al-Shabaab will depend not just upon military and counter-terrorist operations but also on a broader political strategy. This political strategy should include engagement with a wide range of Somalis in order to promote involvement in peaceful politics, challenge extremist interpretations of Islam, and discourage the use of violence or coercion. The strategy must prioritize efforts to address the issues that Al-Shabaab exploits, especially corruption, the abuse of power, the absence of the rule of law, and lack of educational and job opportunities for young people. It should seek to curtail abuses by security forces.

Furthermore, the strategy cannot succeed without more effective efforts to resolve the many conflicts on which Al-Shabaab thrives, often by aligning itself with the weaker of two or more local adversaries.

Over years, in many parts of Somalia, conflicts have arisen between factions, communities, clans and sub-clans, often relating to disputes over land, power, resources and revenues. The origin of many conflicts predates the emergence of the federal state but some, such as the conflicts in the cities of Galkacyo or Dhusamareb, have been exacerbated by the federal state-building process.

Conflicts draw on deep-seated grievances generated by past atrocities, land grabs, forced displacement and misgovernance. Violence has been reinforced by discrimination, marginalization, the oppression of minorities, and the abuse of human rights. The perpetrators have often benefited from impunity. Certain actors on all sides have perpetuated or aggravated conflict for their own gain or advantage.

These conflicts and grievances are being accentuated by profound demographic changes and intense pressures on Somali society. Nearly half of the population is under 15 years of age. The use of new technologies and social media is booming. Rapid, unplanned urbanization is being accelerated by environmental degradation, weather-related shocks and internal displacement. Long-established traditions and livelihoods are in jeopardy, traditional social structures are under strain and the roles of young men and women are changing. Social and cultural expectations of boys and men have evolved as a result of decades-long cycles of violence and insecurity. Limited opportunities for young men to fulfil these expectations in a peaceful way has increased their tolerance of violence and vulnerability to extremism.

Differences and disputes in Somali society are not new. But over years of conflict, and in the face of these pressures, Somalia's traditional dispute resolution mechanisms, especially the clan system and customary law known as *xeer*, are being eroded.

A national strategy and framework for peace and reconciliation is therefore urgently required. The strategy should benefit from experience in Somalia and around the world, support local capacities for conflict resolution, and incorporate mechanisms for establishing truth and accountability. The strategy should seek to ensure that local reconciliation efforts identify and utilize sources of leverage and influence, while also developing resilience to threats posed by spoilers, and actors with vested interests in the war economy.

In most cases, peace and reconciliation efforts should be led by local actors, not just by power brokers but by community leaders, business, women and youth. Civil society and non-governmental organizations have a crucial role to play. National or international actors must therefore do more to enable and support these efforts, while recognizing that direct involvement can sometimes complicate or even undermine progress.

Major regional disputes have often been dealt with by Mogadishu and the diplomatic community by brokering bargains between power holders. These agreements often involve the allocation of official positions, whether in government, the security forces or civil service, and the sharing of resources and security assets between clan elders and power brokers, especially those who have coercive capacity. But power-sharing agreements that are reached without the involvement and agreement of those who are affected by them will be fragile and potentially unsustainable.

The key to achieving the peaceful resolution of many disputes is to ensure that all those who have a stake in peace—including young people, women, minorities, businesses and professional groups—are consulted and have a say in decision making. Politicians and power holders must be open to consultation, and support the creation of safe spaces and channels for inclusive dialogue.

The role of women as both agents and resolvers of conflict has been underestimated. Conflict resolution and reconciliation processes in Somalia are dominated by powerful men. Women align with family, clan, and factional interests as much as men do—but they have a major potential role in resolving conflict that has been overlooked, including through distinctive contributions, collective action, and strategic thinking.

Somali disputes are best resolved by Somalis. As illustrated by papers in this volume, some of the most successful mediation efforts in the country have benefited from having limited or no foreign involvement.

There are cases, however, that involve powerful actors or that relate to federal issues, state formation or cross-border concerns that may benefit from the involvement of the United Nations and international partners. This could involve logistical, facilitation or diplomatic support for inclusive dialogue. The United Nations, in particular, is entrusted by the UN Security Council to use "good offices" to support the Federal Government of Somalia's peace and reconciliation process.

Where appropriate, input could be provided in areas such as process design, mediation, capacity building and confidence building. Support might also relate to securing political or diplomatic backing for a process, managing spoilers, and the implementation or monitoring of agreements.

Somali conflict resolution efforts will benefit from coherent and sustained international and regional support for the stabilization of the country and a comprehensive approach to security. Key partners include the African Union, Intergovernmental Authority on Development and the principal financial investors in Somali security, including the European Union, United Kingdom, United States, Gulf states and Turkey. Their willingness to cooperate on plans and priorities agreed by the Somali leadership, both in the Federal Government and Federal Member States, will be a key determinant of success.

For many years, there has been a high degree of unity in the UN Security Council about the need for peace and reconciliation in Somalia. The challenge is to leverage that unity to encourage and enable Somali politicians and power brokers to resolve their differences, as well as to protect Somalia from the effects of rivalries between international actors.

The international community should be more deliberate in the way it uses its financial, development and humanitarian assistance with a view to addressing long-standing grievances, reducing the displacement and marginalization of certain groups, encouraging the peaceful resolution of disputes that arise in the course of the federal state building process, and consolidating political agreements.

Indeed, looking ahead, *conflict prevention* should be a major priority for Somalia. Several major decision-making processes should be approached from a "do no harm" perspective, and should prioritize the avoidance of conflict. In fact, they should be seen as opportunities for strengthening reconciliation.

The most important such process is perhaps the revision of the provisional federal constitution which governs the respective powers of the President, Prime Minister, Upper House and House of the People, as well as of the Federal Government and Federal Member States. Consequential decisions will need to be made about resource and revenue sharing between the Federal Government and Federal Member States; the electoral model and strengthening political accountability; building professional national security forces; agreeing and strengthening the justice and corrections system; and developing the national educational curriculum.

These decisions require genuine dialogue with all Somali stakeholders, whose views, concerns and aspirations must be taken seriously. If mishandled, and perceived as illegitimate, such processes could further divide Somali society. If handled well, they could form the foundation stones of a more stable and prosperous future.

The United Nations is committed to peace and reconciliation in Somalia. This volume complements the findings of the Consultative Conference on National Reconciliation held in Mogadishu in June 2017 and a Colloquium

INTRODUCTION

on Peace and Reconciliation held in Mogadishu in February 2018. We hope the volume serves as a resource in the development of the Federal Government's national reconciliation strategy and framework, and that it contributes to the emergence of a collaborative network of experts, practitioners and officials. We will continue to work with international partners and the Somali government at the national and state levels to promote inclusive dialogue and to advance the prospects for peace.

Mogadishu, January 2018

OVERVIEW

The following section provides a brief overview of the papers in this volume. It attempts to highlight some of the authors' key points in a single paragraph for each paper. The observations are therefore necessarily simplified. However, it is included in order to make readers aware of the wide range of topics and issues that are addressed and to enable them to identify particular papers of interest.

Papers are divided into the following eight sections: (1) Addressing the Past: Impunity, Illegitimacy and Exclusion; (2) Understanding Local Conflict and Developing Effective Responses; (3) Promoting National Peace and Reconciliation; (4) The Human Diversity of Conflict: Women, Men and Youth; (5) Understanding and Responding to Al-Shabaab; (6) International Aspects of Al-Shabaab; (7) Engaging with Al-Shabaab; and (8) Aid, Business and Reconciliation.

1. *Addressing the Past: Impunity, Illegitimacy and Exclusion*

Every month, hundreds if not thousands of Somalis are directly affected by violence. But, as Jutta Bakonyi argues, the conflict has a powerful impact on the everyday experience of Somalis in many other ways. People have been routinely forced to move to find safety; at the same time, fighting or road-blocks have severely constrained their ability to travel, limiting economic and employment opportunities. Certain clans have faced discrimination or exclusion. Interestingly, the Union of Islamic Courts (UIC)—and initially Al-Shabaab—were originally seen as providing some level of security, order and justice. Yet, over time their behaviour came to be seen as brutal, arbitrary and in defiance of tradition and values, which undermined their legitimacy. Bakonyi argues for action to enhance the legitimacy of the central government and federal governments, especially through the deployment of disciplined security forces and establishment of mechanisms to resolve disputes fairly and impartially.

Large-scale clan-based killings and forced displacement during the 1988–1992 civil war have left a legacy of grievance and division that plagues modern-day Somalia. Crimes committed in that period, argues Lidwien Kapteijns, lie beneath current territorial and political fractures—and ongoing violence in places such as Gaalkacyo and Laascaanood. Falsified clan histories and hate narratives were developed to incite and justify violence, sustain discrimination and avoid accountability—and they pose a major obstacle to reconciliation efforts. The key will be to recognize the role of clans in understanding the conflict, yet not to oversimplify clan agency or overestimate the power and validity of clan identities. Looking ahead, there is a strong case for the acknowledgement of past atrocities and a process of accountability for those who are responsible.

Tobias Hagmann and Mohammed Mealin Seid argue that all parties to the conflict have committed violations of international law but with few legal consequences. This is not merely a human rights issue. Continued impunity, they say, hampers state-building, especially efforts to build a functioning justice system or to tackle corruption. Impunity fosters grievances, including through benefiting dominant clans, which causes weaker clans to turn to Al-Shabaab or other armed groups. Achieving stability requires efforts to record past crimes, secure restitution for victims, and establish mechanisms for accountability.

The civil war in Somalia severely affected the diversity of Somalia's cities. Having once been inclusive, they became dominated by certain clans, causing some groups to feel excluded from rights, resources, power or political life. As Ken Menkhaus and Ismahan Adawe point out, this has generated grievances which have the potential to undermine stability and could ultimately lead to violence. As loci for social services, business opportunities, employment and politics, cities serve critical social, political and economic functions in Somalia, which is only underscored by increasing urbanization. Taking steps to monitor and protect urban inclusivity could help strengthen Somalia's social cohesion and reduce the likelihood of violence.

Lack of inclusion in Somali society has a profound effect on the vulnerability of certain groups. According to the UN Somalia Accountability Project, certain groups, especially the Rahanweyn clan and Bantu Somalis, were severely, and disproportionately, affected by the droughts of 1991–1992 and

2011–2012. It is highly likely that they have also borne the brunt of the 2016–2017 drought. They are the victims of structural inequalities in Somali society that limit social and economic opportunities. Analysis shows that members of marginalized clans are more vulnerable to violence. In such circumstances, they turn to more powerful clans, external military forces or Al-Shabaab for protection, thus magnifying conflict. Looking ahead, interventions of any kind, such as those related to humanitarian or peacebuilding issues, should be informed by analysis of the political economy of different elements of Somalia's society.

2. Understanding Local Conflict and Developing Effective Responses

Local conflict in Somalia often has local drivers. As research by the Garowe-based Peace and Development Research Center (PDRC) shows, in arid rural areas of Somalia conflicts often derive from disputes over access to and control over water sources and grazing lands, on which half of the population depends for its livelihood. The situation is exacerbated by, on the one hand, the expansion of demand for such resources, from new settlements, a growing population and a higher head of cattle and, on the other hand, the depletion of such resources through overuse and environmental deterioration. In urban areas, "land-grabbing" after the collapse of the central government remains a persistent source of conflict, especially in the absence of effective mechanisms of conflict resolution or law enforcement. The allocation of power and resources according to clan affiliation can lead to politically motivated conflict, a situation compounded by rapid urbanization. Both rural and urban disputes, which are increasingly interconnected, have the potential to spiral into cycles of violence through revenge killings and inter-clan or inter-communal escalation. Clan and community elders and religious leaders have traditionally played a key role in the resolution of disputes, through applying *xeer*, Somalia's traditional customary law. But such mechanisms, argues PDRC, are no substitute for addressing the root causes of conflict and establishing the rule of law.

Some observers believe that underlying conflicts have been exacerbated by the process of state formation and federalization, through reviving disputes over political representation, boundaries and rights over land and resources. This is borne out by analysis of conflict dynamics conducted by Najum Mushtaq and the Life and Peace Institute in Lower Shabelle in South-West State, Galmudug and Hirshabelle. In Lower Shabelle, Al-Shabaab exploits

Biyamal–Habar Gedir rivalry by co-opting clan militias who bear grievances against the FGS. The formation of Galmadug from Galgadud and Mudug regions, while Mudug is claimed by Puntland, is said to have contributed to violence in the city of Galkayo. The armed group Ahlu Sunna Wal Jama'a (ASWJ), which is based in Galmadug, continues to be at odds with the new Galmudug administration. Meanwhile the formation of Hirshabelle state was beset by disputes over clan representation. Overall, Mushtaq presents a compelling case for ensuring that along with the ongoing process of state-building, attention is given to addressing local drivers of conflict.

In an in-depth field study, Abdullahi Odowa of the Hargeisa-based Observatory of Conflict and Violence Prevention (OCVP) describes the role of traditional peacemaking in the Sanaag region of Somaliland. The civil war in Somaliland entailed devastating inter- and intra-clan violence and political power struggles which caused the death and displacement of thousands. Over several years peace initiatives were led by clan elders and community leaders, using *xeer*. According to Odowa, initiatives were largely successful because of the political will to make them succeed and the spirit of reconciliation; the way they worked upwards from grassroots level, and the fact that they were locally funded, with minimal government interference. He notes, however, that there has been inadequate implementation of agreements, insufficient memorialization of victims, and that such initiatives do not bring about fair and effective governance. Looking ahead, he emphasizes that processes of local reconciliation are fragile and therefore vulnerable to external intervention. He argues they must be locally owned, free from fixed agendas or deadlines, and work from the bottom up.

Community-based Sharia courts emerged in Mogadishu in 1992 in response to the collapse of the state. Ahmed Ibrahim argues that the courts operated as centres of conflict resolution and reconciliation, and had a level of success because they operated on the basis of accepted cultural and religious norms. He argues that in general Western observers tend to take an over-simplistic, dichotomous view of Islam in Africa, seeing it as being either traditional or radical. Without thorough analysis, they have assumed that the Mogadishu courts fell into the latter category. However, his extensive field research suggests that the courts reflected the moral outlook of the communities they served and their views of legitimate authority and justice. The lesson, in Ibrahim's view, is that the international community should not overlook the symbiotic relationship between traditional and religious institutions. Religious scholars could have a positive role to play in the administration of justice.

OVERVIEW

The paucity of data on local conflicts in Somalia makes analysis of peace-making initiatives difficult. Using what information there is available, UN analyst Galymzhan Kirbassov conducted quantitative analysis, from which he makes several propositions about what factors determine the success of peace initiatives. He sees an inverse correlation between the intensity of violence and fatality rate, and the likely duration of peace, meaning that the more destructive the violence, the shorter a peace agreement is likely to hold. A military imbalance between the parties also reduces the likely duration of peace. However, enforcement by a credible and capable third party emerges as a critical determinant of sustainable peace—a point of obvious relevance to those engaged in supporting processes of local reconciliation.

Local conflicts in Somalia have many sources, and the extraction of natural resources carries a risk of igniting new conflict or exacerbating old feuds. Mohamed Abdi Omer and Mohamed Farah Hersi of the Hargeisa-based Academy for Peace and Development (APD) have investigated the case of a mining concession granted by the Somaliland authorities to a Chinese company for the extraction of beryllium at a site in the Awdal region of Somaliland. This has generated strong objections from communities that believe they will be deprived of the economic and employment benefits of the mine, pastoralists who have concerns about the mine's ecological impact, artisan miners who fear they may be put out of work, and local government, which feels it has been cut out of the arrangement. The concession has also catalysed inter-clan conflict about the potential beneficiaries. The case underscores the need for clear thinking about laws and policies relating to resource-exploitation, in order to maximize the potential benefits for communities and minimize the likelihood of conflict.

Abukar Sanei and Mohamed A. Omar of the Mogadishu-based Centre for Policy Analysis & Research (CfPAR) oversaw interviews of 114 Somalis about how local conflicts should be resolved. Notably, four in ten of those interviewed said they were not aware of any reconciliation activities in their area. Most expressed support for a broad range of measures to resolve conflicts, including power-sharing and the integration of militias into national security forces. Approximately one third of those interviewed expressed support for the formation of a truth and reconciliation commission, and over half thought that civil society actors, including elders or non-government organizations, should take a leading role in resolving local disputes.

The role that international actors play with respect to local conflicts is critical. Najum Mushtaq and the Life and Peace Institute argue that AMISOM has played an essential role in enabling the FGS to meet critical milestones in the state formation process. Yet, AMISOM forces have had less success in achieving sufficient stability for dialogue and reconciliation to take place, and in reducing the threat from Al-Shabaab. The paper points to Somali mistrust of foreign forces and the practice of AMISOM's national contingents allying with local clan forces and other armed actors, which complicates local conflict dynamics. Significantly, the May 2017 London Security Pact defined international support for the establishment of capable Somali national police and security forces. Yet, while critical, the authors argue that this is no substitute for a broad-based peace and reconciliation process.

Adam Day of the Centre for Policy Research in UN University Tokyo addresses the question of what the UN could do to support reconciliation at the local level. He conducted research into UN efforts in a wide range of settings, to mitigate or resolve identity-based, resource-driven or politically-motivated local conflict. He develops nine recommendations, making the case that the UN should: (1) take a whole-of-mission approach to mapping local conflict, drawing on a broad range of expertise; (2) ensure process design takes into account structural drivers of conflict, institutional factors and individual leaders, and avoids inadvertent adverse effects; (3) incorporate effective and appropriate communication with communities; (4) take into account the gendered causes and impact of conflict, and the gendered dimensions of peacebuilding; (5) develop targeted approaches to young men; (6) build the negotiating capacities of the parties; (7) provide timely support and resources for confidence-building measures; (8) partner with other actors, especially national and local government; and (9) build links to national level reconciliation efforts.

3. *Promoting National Peace and Reconciliation*

Rivalries and tensions in Somalia exist on several levels: within and between Federal Member States (FMS); between FMS and the FGS; and in the wider region. For this reason, Aden Abdi and Alexander Ramsbotham of Conciliation Resources argue that reconciliation should be incorporated into all reform and state-building efforts, including initiatives that relate to decentralization, federalism and the constitution. A comprehensive and inclusive framework for national reconciliation should be developed. Within this framework, they argue, there should be mechanisms to hold leaders accountable, including for past crimes, for which a truth and reconciliation commission should be established. They say that the application of *xeer* helped to build peace in Somaliland and argue that it could play an important role in promoting national reconciliation.

Joakim Gundel describes how violence in Somalia is underpinned by land, resource and identity conflicts, and the grievances of "minority" groups that have been victimized. Echoing Abdi and Ramsbotham, he thinks that Somalia should, with international backing, launch a truth and reconciliation process. This process, organized by an independent facilitation committee, should be established from the ground up, using participatory action research methodologies. It would progress from the district to the federal state level, to the national level, and would ultimately result in a new Somali constitution.

If a national reconciliation process is initiated, what lessons can be drawn from other countries that have gone through processes of transition? Thania Paffenholz, Constance Dijkstra and Andreas Hirblinger of the Inclusive Peace and Transition Initiative draw lessons from Afghanistan, the Democratic Republic of Congo (DRC), Mali, and Yemen. The paper cautions against excluding armed actors from political processes, while acknowledging that their inclusion needs to be carefully managed. The paper suggests that processes should go beyond elites and closely reflect the demands of the population, warning that mechanisms for decentralization or federalization can easily be manipulated by certain groups for their advantage. Finally, the paper argues in favour of a broad-based and inclusive constitutional process, with popular participation.

Abdurahman Abdullahi "Baadiyow" also argues for a national reconciliation process which recognizes and addresses the mass violence of Somalia's past. He distinguishes between apolitical and political conflict, and diagnoses four sources or types of conflict, all of which are interconnected. First, a state–society conflict, generated by tension between a traditional society and a modern state; second, a power struggle among the non-Islamist ruling elite; third, an ideological clash between non-Islamist and Islamist elites—between clannism and Islamism; fourth, a resulting civil war, in which clans are instrumentalized by elites. In Baadiyow's view, reconciliation must begin with constitutional and legal reforms that synthesize modernity and tradition. The second phase will be to establish constructive dialogue among Somali elites to achieve better governance and a new political culture. The third phase will be to reconcile the clans using traditional mechanisms and transitional justice that is consistent with Islam, which begins with the documentation of human rights and consultation with clan elders.

Reconciliation that is truly national must involve both Somalia and Somaliland. As the Centre for Humanitarian Dialogue (HD) explains, talks have taken place between Somalia and Somaliland since 2012 but have faced considerable challenges and unsatisfactory levels of implementation. They say the political stalemate will be resolved by the agreement of some form of mutually acceptable political association or official recognition of Somaliland as an independent state. HD argues there should be a framework for dialogue, which involves clear facilitation, technical and material support, together with political will and leadership on the part of the parties. International backing should be coherent and a coordination body could provide advice and support to the process in the periods between talks, facilitate additional discussions or assist with implementation of whatever is agreed by the parties.

4. The Human Diversity of Conflict: Women, Men and Youth

Judith Gardner, with the Life and Peace Institute, challenges the conventional understanding of the roles of men and women in the Somali conflict. Her research suggests that women are involved in intra- and inter-clan conflict in many different ways, including in financing, mobilization, logistics, intelligence, and active fighting. The roles they take at any given point are closely connected with clan affiliation and the current situation of the clan. It seems kinship and clan are often exploited for elite interests. However, women have also taken action to end conflict. In Kismayo, women have worked for peace through a range of means, including persuasion, mobilization, fundraising, organizing demonstrations, or advocacy. The findings underscore the importance of women's full and meaningful involvement in peacebuilding.

Other research bears out some of these points, including that undertaken by a Somali female researcher, whose name has been withheld for safety reasons, and Stephen Harley. Based on direct engagement with six women in Al-Shabaab who are or were married to Al-Shabaab fighters, they find that such women were accorded privileges by the group. They were able to run their own businesses, use smartphones and travel freely. They also assisted in Al-Shabaab operations, gathering intelligence or fundraising. The women are apparently seen within Al-Shabaab as serving the important functions of producing the next generation of Al-Shabaab fighters and inculcating them and others with Islamist thinking.

According to Hamdi Mohamed with ASAL Consulting, women in Somalia have long held important roles, negotiated their space, and exercised considerable influence in their communities. This has been achieved through creative and effective ways, even in traditional nomadic families and communities. *Xeer*, Somalia's customary law, plays an important role in regulating disputes in Somali society, but generally excludes women from daily political life. The more recent "clannization" of politics, represented by the "4.5 formula" (by which seats in Parliament were allocated to certain clans), is believed by women to have entrenched gender inequalities and contributed to new ways in which women are disenfranchised, especially those in urban areas who are not familiar with the kinship system. Women have taken steps to challenge this situation, such as when, after finding that no women were members of the five clan delegations in the Arta Peace Conference in 2000, they established a "sixth clan" and insisted that they be allowed to participate. Women have served as informal mediators, taken a key role in the survival of family and kin in conflict situations, and taken leading positions in civil society organizations. Mohamed argues there should be a far deeper, nuanced appreciation of the peacebuilding roles of women in Somalia, including recognition of the importance of their informal contributions.

Sahro Ahmed Koshin at SIDRA Institute also explores the role of women in peacebuilding through a survey of 152 people in Galkayo (South and North) and Kismayo. Notably, 71 per cent of respondents felt that Somali women have an important role in peacebuilding and conflict prevention and resolution. Respondents saw social and cultural norms as hindering women's involvement, including stereotypes about women being intrinsically emotional or physically weak. The biggest factors preventing women overcoming these hindrances were seen as lack of education and lack of access to finance. 39 per cent of respondents felt that women were not properly valued or included by their clans, and 30 per cent said they were seen as not capable of building peace. However, 68 per cent of respondents thought these attitudes were changing in a positive way. Over half of respondents were not aware of UN Security Council Resolution 1325 on women, peace and security and only one in ten thought that key partners placed a high priority on women's involvement in peace and security. The paper emphasizes the importance of new efforts to promote women's inclusion in peacebuilding, including through wider skills development and education.

Few studies have focused solely on the experience of young men, who are the predominant perpetrators and victims of violence in Somalia. This is the focus of pioneering field research by Judy El-Bushra, Judith Gardner and Adan Abokor, with the Rift Valley Institute, in nine areas of Somalia and in Kenya.

Somali men face high expectations: they are to protect the well-being of the family, kinship group and clan, and, among other things, demonstrate self-discipline, courage, humanity and generosity. They are exploited by older elites and are under pressure to support their clan or sub-clan, sometimes by taking up arms. They often face daily physical insecurity, although levels of vulnerability are often tied to class or ethnic background. While young men are often judged by negative stereotypes or perceived as security threats, the study suggests that in fact they weigh risks, seek to live by moral values, strive for an education and try to fulfil family responsibilities by generating an honest income. The study argues that among other things more should be done to improve youth leadership development and educational opportunities for both men and women.

These findings are echoed by field research carried out in Baidoa, Kismayo, and Hargeisa by a team of researchers and practitioners at Transparency Solutions. They found that young people in Somalia are looking for ways to contribute meaningfully to their society but feel frustrated and disenfranchised by the lack of opportunities available to them. Although young people constitute around two-thirds of the population of Somalia, youth unemployment may be as high as 80 or 90 per cent in some areas. Transparency Solutions' research suggests that efforts to support youth involvement in peace and reconciliation would need to overcome negative attitudes of older generations, lack of funding for such work, limited inclusivity, lack of positive role models, and security concerns. Strikingly, 75 per cent of respondents in Kismayo and Baidoa said that insecurity deterred their involvement in youth activities. Some 40 per cent of respondents felt that youth unemployment and associated poverty help to explain why young people join militias or radical groups, and many pointed to the attraction of a sense of belonging and self-worth. In addition, over half of respondents from Kismayo and Baidoa believed that extremists exploited the religious devotion and lack of education among young people. The study argues that two areas for positively engaging young people are sport, supported by 56 per cent of respondents, and social media, used by over 60 per cent of respondents on a daily basis. With the right support and investment, these areas could offer possibilities for young people to fulfil their potential, act as agents of change and contribute to social reconciliation.

5. Understanding and Responding to Al-Shabaab

Al-Shabaab is a complex, multi-faceted phenomenon which requires in-depth study in different locations. Catherine Besteman and Daniel Van Lehman

18

write about the group's policies and activities in the Jubba River Valley, based on research with 41 people who were either recently displaced from the Valley or have relatives living there. They describe how, since the collapse of the Siad Barre regime in 1991, powerful militias tied to major clans have vied for control of the Valley, often exploiting and predating marginalized groups, especially the farming communities known as Somali Bantus. Al-Shabaab has done likewise, extorting considerably higher levels of harvests, "taxes", and remittances from Somali Bantus than from Somalis from the major clans. Likewise, the group imposes far stricter constraints on movement and forcibly conscripts more boys from the Somali Bantus than from other Somalis. Al-Shabaab also imposes more stringent penalties for non-compliance with their rules, sometimes resulting in eviction from long-held farmland. This marginalization demonstrates that a just and sustainable peace in Somalia will depend on far more effective efforts to protect the rights of Somalia's oppressed populations.

Such predatory behaviour raises the question of the motivations and drivers of Al-Shabaab. Roland Marchal explains how Al-Shabaab has consistently opposed foreign troops in Somalia, which he describes as a nationalistic position that resonates with the wider population. He describes how Al-Shabaab has insisted on the implementation of Sharia in the areas it controls, which has gained a level of support among Somalis as it helps to solve practical problems. The application of Sharia has led to brutal and uncompromising action to secure its implementation. Yet, to have any chance of succeeding, it was necessary for Al-Shabaab to reject clan affiliations, which appeals to many young Somalis. Within its ranks Al-Shabaab provides space for members of clans that have been marginalized and mistreated. For fighters, Al-Shabaab offers the opportunity to take revenge against what are seen by some as aggressor forces. Others have joined because their friends had already joined or because there were guaranteed economic advantages. Ultimately, Marchal argues, Al-Shabaab is a Somali politico-military organization that is capable of flexibility in its vision and operations when its survival or popularity is at stake. Significantly, Somali viewpoints are not always antagonistic to Al-Shabaab, which, if nothing else, throws light on some of the mistakes or weaknesses of its enemies—the FGS and international presence.

Richard Barrett of the Global Strategy Network also turns to the issue of Al-Shabaab's motivations, especially the issue of why fighters join the group and why they quit, based on analysis of over 100 interviews with individuals currently and previously in Al-Shabaab. He concludes that a majority seek a sense of belonging and purpose, influenced by Al-Shabaab's claim to be acting in defence of Islam. Younger members are attracted by the opportunity for adventure, prospects of economic security, and because of the encouragement of friends who have already joined. Fighters often leave because life in the group, and the treatment of its members, are harsher than expected, or they find that the group does not abide by its religious principles, especially in its brutality and use of arbitrary detentions. Family members can sometimes persuade members of Al-Shabaab to leave the group but the practical difficulties and dangers of desertion constitute a major deterrent. Interestingly, six Al-Shabaab leaders were interviewed who suggested that the group was fighting a political rather than ideological battle, and that its members had little interest in Al-Qaida's global agenda.

On the basis of research in seven Somali cities, Hussein Yusuf Ali concludes there are five main causes of youth radicalization. First, weak governance and state fragility, which provide openings for Al-Shabaab. Second, a sense of political injustice, especially due to the marginalization of certain clans and groups, under-representation of Islamists, and the political exclusion of youth. Third, socio-economic injustice: respondents viewed officials, politicians and businessmen as corrupt, avaricious and benefiting at the expense of the population, especially young people. Clan-based discrimination was seen as reinforcing socio-economic inequalities. Fourth, corruption in the court system: justice was seen as being available to the highest bidder, generating profound grievances. Al-Shabaab exploits this by offering what are described as efficient and non-corrupt "courts". One respondent mentioned that a judge in Mogadishu had even advised him to seek justice in Al-Shabaab courts. Finally, the foreign military presence: respondents expressed misgivings about the presence of foreign forces, compounded by corruption or abuses by foreign troops and Somali soldiers or police. Looking ahead, the author argues for governance reform, an AMISOM exit strategy, measures to boost youth employment, and consideration of the potential for negotiations with Al-Shabaab.

Considerable media attention has been devoted to Al-Shabaab's previous ability to recruit foreigners. However, reinforcing Hussein Yusuf Ali's argument, Mohamed Haji Abdullahi "Ingiriis" emphasizes that the group's primary source of recruits is young Somali men. He makes the point that many factors help to explain an individual's decision to join the group, and that a single individual is usually multi-motivated. Ingiriis especially highlights the role of economic exclusion, political marginalization, and indoctrination, compounded by clan grievances. Ingiriis cautions against relying on military means alone to defeat Al-Shabaab, an approach that he considers as largely unsuccessful since 2007.

What does Al-Shabaab deliver in the areas it controls? Roland Marchal notes that beyond securing an area that it controls, Al-Shabaab's non-military activities vary from place to place depending on the context, especially the population's attitude towards the group. Marchal considers three areas of activity: *dawa* (preaching) and education, organizing civil society, and the administration of justice. He notes that Al-Shabaab uses religion to enhance its legitimacy and as a means of social control. The group promotes religious education in Quranic schools, and exalts dogmatism and righteousness, which undermines tolerance and open-mindedness. On taking control of a community, Al-Shabaab will declare that Sharia, rather than *xeer*, will be applied. It therefore tends to disempower elders, while sometimes promoting and manipulating the role of other groups such as women, teenagers and traders. The group enforces harsh rules of behaviour, but they are predictable. It also establishes courts that are generally considered to be non-corrupt and whose judgements are enforced. Marchal asks whether the FGS has the ambition and imagination to exceed what Al-Shabaab delivers in terms of public goods.

Richard Barrett points out that Al-Shabaab's call for global jihad has limited local appeal and the group therefore tries to deliver what appeals to Somalis: dispute resolution; religious principles to overcome patronage and corruption; and the promotion of national interest over clans or foreigners. However, he says the group has lost territory and that in many areas it depends on cooperation from clan elders. Fear pervades the higher echelons of the movement and it has faced a challenge from the establishment of a branch of IS in north-east Somalia. The group's narrative of uniquely operating above clan politics is challenged by the election of President Farmaajo who won with cross-clan support. As Barrett says, "Where Al-Shabaab is in control, it offers justice through Sharia courts, though not always in strict accordance with Sharia law; it raises taxes and levies, though not always according to the rules it espouses; it delivers aid, though not always without favouritism; it provides education, though not always imparting the skills that are most needed; it mediates between clans, though not always impartially; and it does not deliver these services evenly across all areas under its control." In addition, the group argues against foreign influence on the FGS, but it too is subject to foreign influence. Barrett adds that Al-Shabaab exerts less energy in delivering services, than in disrupting the FGS from doing so.

Al-Shabaab competes for positive media coverage, for which Mary Harper says it has developed a public communications operation that is versatile, resilient and often able to seize the initiative. In her field research, many respondents said they thought Al-Shabaab messaging was more compelling than FGS and international counter-messaging. The group produces high-quality media products, targets local, national, and international journalists, and is rigorous and persistent. "No other group or individual connected with Somalia engages with the author as directly, reliably and efficiently as Al-Shabaab," Harper says. However, Al-Shabaab threatens journalists who do not do the group's bidding and is engaged in producing highly distorted stories and projecting power and success for the vastly expanded number of Somali websites, many of which are unreliable. Yet, the author says counter-narrative efforts are sometimes equally misleading. While many Somalis see through Al-Shabaab propaganda, the less educated are perhaps more impressionable. The author argues for a more home-grown, hands-off response to Al-Shabaab propaganda.

Stig Jarle Hansen, Linnéa Gelot and members of the ISHA human rights group consider how Al-Shabaab messaging can be best countered, drawing on field research in Mogadishu and Baidoa focusing on the area of Bay/Bakool. They found that lack of security, opportunity, and justice, combined with clan conflicts, create conditions that Al-Shabaab can exploit. "Radicalism *is* lack of education, employment, and justice!" said one respondent. In Bay/Bakool the group is seen as having semi-territorial control, in other words, a fairly regular presence despite intermittent deployments or patrols by FGS and AMISOM forces, and many local people carry out tasks for the group out of opportunism or concern for their safety or property. Respondents expressed concerns about unprofessional conduct by Somali or Ethiopian forces. There are reports of those who surrender being summarily executed, tortured or disappeared by Somali or Ethiopian forces. Some elements of these forces are alleged to sell munitions to Al-Shabaab or even arrange security pacts. Respondents said that efforts to counter and prevent violent extremism (CVE-PVE) should avoid oversimplification by defining individuals as either good or bad, and that reconciliation should start at household level, given the strong influence of family and close relatives over former, current or potential fighters. Respondents reported wide-ranging female involvement in Al-Shabaab, as noted above by Judith Gardner and others, for which targeted programmes should be developed. The authors point out that local sheikhs and elders do not always work against radicalism, and that CVE-PVE efforts should seek to work more closely with such leaders.

6. *International Aspects of Al-Shabaab*

The alliance between Al-Qaida and Al-Shabaab is widely acknowledged—but what exactly is the nature and strength of the relationship, what sustains it and what are its prospects? Tricia Bacon and Daisy Muibu observe that cooperation between the groups is limited and irregular but that the relationship has proven durable despite the loss of leaders on both sides and the emergence of IS in north-east Somalia. The resilience of the relationship is attributed to several factors: Al-Shabaab's links to Al-Qaida's affiliate in Yemen, which may have enhanced Al-Shabaab's military expertise; Al-Qaida's ability to help Al-Shabaab with raising funds; Al-Shabaab's oath of allegiance or *bayah* to Al-Qaida; and the trust and predictability of the alliance, reinforced by ideological and personal ties between some leaders. The relationship is used by Al-Shabaab leaders to justify measures to enforce unity, control its rank and file, and avoid defections to IS. Importantly, the relationship is flexible, giving Al-Shabaab leaders access to assistance and jihadi prestige, while retaining a high degree of autonomy. The authors conclude that, "on the whole, Al-Shabaab operates autonomously and focuses on its local agenda, while paying occasional lip service to broader global jihadist causes."

The research organization Sahan Africa assesses the threat posed by Al-Shabaab both in Somalia and to the Horn of Africa. Sahan describes Al-Shabaab as a composite insurgency, which has skilfully exploited local grievances through aligning itself with disaffected clans or minority groups. Sahan notes that in 2016 it stepped up its efforts to co-opt clan leaders through coercion and incentives, even establishing a new Council of Clan Leaders. At the same time, Al-Shabaab has increased attacks using Improved Explosive Devices (IED) against Somali government and AMISOM forces, and carrying out complex attacks on locations in Mogadishu used by political elites. According to Sahan, since 2010 Al-Shabaab has sought to establish itself in the Horn of Africa, initiating insurgent activities in six countries of the region and conducting attacks in five of them. In 2013 Al-Shabaab's then-leader, Godane, established two transnational military wings: one focusing on Kenya, Tanzania, and Uganda; the other focused on Ethiopia. Al-Shabaab's regional unit, Jaysh Ayman, has carried out a campaign of attacks in northern Kenya, while its affiliate Al-Hijra is said to have established a range of networks and operational cells, including in Kenya's prisons. Al-Shabaab's security and intelligence branch, the Amniyat, was implicated in the 2013 Westgate Mall attack and has been involved in planning attacks against Ethiopia.

Among other things, Sahan calls for greater security cooperation between the countries of the region in order to counter the regional threat.

Given Al-Shabaab's expanded regional presence, to what degree does Al-Shabaab draw on non-Somali foreign fighters to sustain its operations? Tricia Bacon and Daisy Muibu explain that regional recruits mostly come from Kenya, followed by Tanzania and Uganda. These fighters generally occupy rank and file military roles, and increase the group's ability to operate and recruit in the region. Such fighters increase the effectiveness of local propaganda, now produced in Swahili to target Muslims in Kenya and elsewhere in the region. Foreign fighters from Yemen are said to have brought prestige and improved the group's expertise in explosives. However, the influence of foreign fighters has generally been limited to tactical and operational, rather than strategic, issues. "Leadership positions are overwhelmingly, if not exclusively, held by Somalis," the authors say. In addition, the number of foreign fighters joining Al-Shabaab from outside the region has diminished over the past six years, since the group's purges of such fighters between 2011 and 2013, and the emergence of the Islamic State and other extremist groups in Iraq and Syria. Looking ahead, foreign fighter influence within the group is likely to remain limited given that many of its activities are acutely local and its strength often depends on managing and exploiting clan conflict. Given that foreign fighters are more likely to be hardliners than an average member of Al-Shabaab, the authors wonder whether the diminution of their influence could have a positive effect on the group's posture towards reconciliation.

Addressing another angle of overseas recruitment, Joshua Meservey explores the degree to which members of the Somali diaspora are susceptible to recruitment by Al-Shabaab and why. He describes how recruitment among the diaspora has been carried out through a decentralized peer-to-peer model. His research suggests that most such recruits tend to be young, male, and born to parents who emigrated from Somalia or who came with their parents at a young age ("the 1.5 generation"). We might anticipate that such individuals are alienated in Western societies, but in fact they tend to be relatively well educated, with language skills, good prospects, and networks of friends. This suggests that perhaps the factors "pulling" recruits to Al-Shabaab may be more influential than "push" factors. It seems many recruits were attracted by ideological arguments, which blend religious justifications, nationalist reasoning, and anti-Western rhetoric. Meservey posits that perhaps such individuals never fully assimilated the mainstream values of their home countries of birth or upbringing. He argues that Western governments should seek to delegitimize Al-Shabaab's worldview, including through working with religious leaders, while also promoting the values of their own societies.

7. Engaging with Al-Shabaab

Harmonie Toros, working with Krypteia, considers the potential for negotiations with Al-Shabaab. She points out that the idea should be taken seriously given that modern terrorist campaigns are five times more likely to end through political engagement as opposed to military defeat. Several actors have had repeated formal and informal interactions with the UIC and then Al-Shabaab at different points, which the author analyses. The UIC engaged in two sets of political talks, which were hampered by lack of support from regional powers and from hard-line military factions, respectively. Al-Shabaab also engaged in talks with humanitarian actors regarding the response to the famine of 2011. Separately, the FGS has declared an amnesty for Al-Shabaab members who "defect" but its attitude to negotiations is unclear. Interestingly, international observers interviewed by the author regarded some core purported Al-Shabaab goals as consistent with the wishes of most Somalis, especially ending foreign interference in Somali politics and achieving non-corrupt governance and justice in accordance with Islamic principles. Some elders expressed the view that Al-Shabaab should be brought into a broader dialogue process, which they believed should be Somali-led but with international and regional backing, perhaps supported by elders and business actors. The prospects for talks are limited. Al-Shabaab's leaders have consistently rejected talks and international officials are reluctant to contemplate negotiations until pro-government forces have achieved greater strength on the battlefield. Until then they are willing to support talks with commanders who might desert with their fighters. The author warns, however, that battlefield strength might not be achieved by the FGS and AMISOM, and that greater success in encouraging "defections" of moderate factions could leave a body of committed hard-line fighters that may be difficult to defeat militarily and with whom it is impossible to negotiate.

Somali attitudes towards the conflict and its resolution are undoubtedly crucial factors in formulating policies on peace and reconciliation. Joanne Crouch and Abdi Ali of Saferworld conducted 71 key informant interviews with Somalis on this issue in Mogadishu, Kismayo and Nairobi, as well as indirectly in Gedo and Baidoa. Respondents expressed concerns about Al-Shabaab's indiscriminate and excessive use of violence, considered inconsistent with Islam, and its restrictions on freedom of speech and movement. However, respondents spoke positively about Al-Shabaab's strict enforcement of rules and their impartial resolution of disputes. They also compared Al-Shabaab favourably to the government in terms of reducing clan influence over politics or the allocation of resources, and in terms of minimizing corruption in "tax" collection, but noted the group's failure to provide social services. Support for Al-Shabaab was said by respondents to be sustained due to the persistence of injustice, inequality and mistrust of the government, combined with youth unemployment. Many respondents believed that military forces from neighbouring states were advancing their interests and saw AMISOM as an obstacle to peace. Three-quarters believed that a military approach was necessary but that the current approach was not succeeding and was causing suffering for civilians. Nearly all believed that reducing youth unemployment and improving governance were essential. Strikingly, three-quarters of respondents also expressed support for a negotiated solution to the conflict, but doubted Al-Shabaab would be willing to engage. The authors argue that the Somali Government should explore the feasibility of negotiations and seek to identify what forms of Al-Shabaab behaviour or political beliefs might be open to change.

Clearly, an important issue is whether Al-Shabaab leaders have any interest in dialogue or negotiation. Anneli Botha and Mahdi Abdile, with the Network for Religious and Traditional Peacemakers, interviewed 17 mid-level Al-Shabaab leaders, who showed remarkably high levels of interest in engagement. 80 per cent of respondents considered negotiations "extremely important"; 90 per cent also considered national reconciliation to be extremely important; and remarkably, half of leaders interviewed said they would participate in a political process. However, the leaders insisted on "conditions" for negotiations, which are perhaps better considered as political demands, which appear to be quite far-reaching. All respondents insisted on the withdrawal of foreign forces and a general amnesty for Al-Shabaab members. Over two-thirds of respondents believed that negotiations should lead to: the formation of security forces that comprise forces of all parties; the full implementation of Sharia (the meaning of which is not entirely clear); the formation of a new government consisting of all parties; and securing the employment of Al-Shabaab members. Most respondents believed any political process should exclude foreign actors, although two-thirds were open to the involvement of Middle Eastern countries, and one-third were open to the involvement of the United Nations. The findings should be treated with caution, but suggest that there may be more interest in negotiations on the part of Al-Shabaab leaders than has generally been assumed.

8. *Aid, Business and Reconciliation*

In recent years, Somalia has witnessed an increasing range of activities involved in state-building and peacebuilding. If these efforts are to succeed they will require cooperation among and between national and international actors. Dominik Balthasar and Anja Osei of Swisspeace conducted a survey and used network analysis to assess forms, patterns and levels of cooperation. Their analysis suggests that networks remain sparsely connected and that a decentralized core of international organizations is surrounded by less connected national counterparts. AMISOM emerges as important to coordination among international actors; whereas the FGS and FMS emerge as central to networks of cooperation between international and national actors. The authors find that connections between international and national actors are fragmented, informal and relatively sparse (with 1.5 per cent of all possible connections being realized). Overall, the findings suggest that there is considerable scope and potential for greater cooperation among and between international and national actors. The authors argue that increased collaboration could enhance the prospects for peace and reconciliation in Somalia, given that denser networks contribute to the flow of information, trust-building, and more effective problem-solving.

Network analysis is also used by Mircea Gherghina, Sandra McNeill and Khadir Abdi of Transparency Solutions to reveal the dynamics and intricate relationships between business, political elites and armed actors in Somalia. In a pilot study the authors analyse the network of a prominent business actor with interests in Somalia, Somaliland and elsewhere in East Africa. The analysis highlights the importance of connections to prominent figures in politics or security, corroborating the view that power in Somalia is heavily concentrated in individuals rather than institutions. The analysis also shows a high level of interaction between state and business actors, which has several explanations. Businesses need government support or approval for their activities, such as through contracts or licensing. Separately, business actors often develop a wide range of relationships, including with armed actors, which can be useful for officials in helping to bring about talks to resolve outbreaks of violence. Such cooperation is mutually beneficial, as instability often adversely affects business production, supply lines or sales. State–business interaction is also explained by high levels of information-sharing, which again is in each party's interests, especially where the information relates to security threats. The authors conclude that network analysis may be useful for mapping networks of influence that may be of more direct relevance to peace and reconciliation, such as youth, clans or spoilers.

It is widely acknowledged that businesses in Somalia do not always act in a way that supports peace and reconciliation. Some politico-business networks prioritize their own interests rather than the interests of the state or the population. Businesses use militias and pay protection money to Al-Shabaab. However, as Bahar Ali Kazmi and Faisa Abdi Loyaan of Creative Alternatives Now point out, businesses are forced to operate in very difficult circumstances, with pervasive insecurity, weak institutions, and limited rule of law. The authors argue that many business leaders see themselves as apolitical and socially responsible. They also describe how businesses contribute to employment, seek to expand skills and education, and are sometimes involved in providing social assistance. There is considerable potential, the authors argue, for businesses to contribute to peace and reconciliation, as well as development, through greater cooperation with Somalia civil society.

ADDRESSING THE PAST

IMPUNITY, ILLEGITIMACY AND EXCLUSION

LOOMA DHAMA

POLITICAL INCLUSIVITY
IN THE SOMALI URBAN CONTEXT

Ken Menkhaus and *Ismahan Adawe*

Authors

Dr Ken Menkhaus is Professor of Political Science and Chair of the Political Science Department at Davidson College, and a specialist on the Horn of Africa. He is the author of over 50 articles, chapters, and monographs on Somalia.

Ismahan Adawe is an independent consultant based in Nairobi with experience as a civil servant in the Federal Government of Somalia and as an analyst on development and refugee return issues.

Summary

Lack of inclusion in negotiations, power-sharing, and access to rights and resources in Somalia's main cities has been an unresolved driver of conflict since the civil war erupted in 1988. Progress has been made in inclusivity in negotiations and power-sharing, but a dominant, exclusionary, pastoral-based logic of *u dhasheey* or "rights by blood" to Somalia's major cities remains an impediment to peace. Different Somali cities vary today in their degree of cosmopolitanism, but all are at best only partly inclusive, with one dominant clan tending to monopolize the security sector and control of government revenues and other rents. Ethno-hegemony in major cities is deeply problematic and a source of enduring grievances, especially when these cities serve as a regional or national capital where all Somalis expect to enjoy full citizenship rights.

This paper calls for the creation by Somali stakeholders of an "urban inclusivity index"—a basket of indicators measuring degrees on inclusion and exclusion to full rights and access to resources in Somalia's main cities—as a tool to monitor progress in expanding cosmopolitanism in Somali urban areas. More fully inclusive cities will serve as a powerful engine of peacebuilding and economic recovery, and will advance goal number 11 of the UN Sustainable Development Goals—"Make Cities Inclusive, Safe, Resilient, and Just."

Introduction

Lack of inclusivity in Somali negotiations, power-sharing arrangements, and/or rights and access to resources, especially in urban centres, has been a major preoccupation of Somali constituencies, and a major source of grievances and occasional armed conflict. The claim of lack of inclusivity has also sometimes been a convenient tool for spoilers to reject a peace accord or foment violence. To cast a political process or outcome as *looma dhama*—"not inclusive"—is to delegitimize it.[1]

This paper explores the role of inclusivity in Somali elite bargains and political settlements, and how inclusivity—treated as a universal concept in the peacebuilding literature—may need to be contextualized in the Somali setting to fully appreciate its importance in Somali discourse and politics.[2] The paper focuses principally on the question of ethnic or clan inclusion/exclusion, while recognizing that there are many other types of exclusion, most notably along gender lines, that merit attention. We focus specifically on inclusion and exclusion with regard to rights and access to resources and security in major Somali cities. This emphasis on inclusion in cities is based on the observation that one dangerous legacy of the Somali civil war has been enduring degrees of exclusion in major cities, and on a theory of change that posits that cities that exhibit greater levels of inclusion or cosmopolitanism help to consolidate peace.

Research Findings on Inclusive Peace

Inclusion is increasingly understood to be a necessary though not sufficient condition for consolidation of post-war peace. In a recent study of post-civil war outcomes, Charles Call reached the conclusion that "political inclusion, including but not limited to power-sharing arrangements, is highly correlated with consolidation of peace."[3] Call's findings reinforce a conclusion reached by seminal World Bank World Development Report 2011, which concluded that a critical step for breaking the cycle of conflict and fragility is confidence-building, which rests on "inclusive-enough coalitions" that minimize the potential for spoilers to emerge.[4]

Inclusive-enough coalitions are reached through elite bargaining, which, if successful, produces political settlements.[5] Not all political settlements are inclusive; some can be very narrow power-sharing arrangements, or exclusionary deals imposed on weaker groups, and can thus produce "limited access orders" that are vulnerable to instability.[6]

Di John and Putzel argue that "the ultimate test of inclusiveness needs to be anchored in the distribution of rights and entitlements, which are the outcome of the settlement."[7] This is a critical observation applied to the Somali context, where more attention has been paid to inclusive bargaining processes and formal power-sharing in government, and less to inclusive rights and entitlements, especially in major Somali cities.

Looma Dhama: *Inclusivity and Exclusion in Somali Politics and Discourse*

Inclusiveness is a matter of great concern in all post-conflict political settlements. But it is a particular preoccupation in Somali negotiations and systems of representation, reflecting the country's pastoral heritage and its recent history.

Inclusion and Exclusion in Somali Pastoral Tradition

Accounts of Somali traditional negotiations and conflict management celebrate the highly inclusive "pastoral democracy" of clan assemblies, or *shir*, which provide opportunities for all clan elders to actively participate.[8]

While Somali *shir* are built around the principle of clan inclusivity, rights of access to land and settlements in traditional Somali settings have historically been more exclusive. In pastoral settings, clans lay claim to specific rangeland, wells, and settlements on the basis of identity, or rights by blood—*jus sanguinis*, or in Somali *u dhasheey*. Other clans can access and use this territory only by negotiation, use of force, payment, or, when under real distress, adoption into the host clan (*shegad*). In a primarily pastoral setting, monopoly claims by clans on land constituted the rules of the game that all communities understood, and a source of "rent" when others sought access to or through it.

Inclusion and Exclusion in the Barre Era and the 1988–1992 Civil War

Before the civil war, larger cities in Somalia were understood to be "cosmopolitan" areas where all Somalis had full rights to live, own property, run businesses, and hold positions in civil service. Often, cities had neighbourhoods that were understood to be enclaves of particular clans, but all had rights to live in the city. This was true not only in the capital Mogadishu but in provincial cities as well.

Over the course of Siad Barre's 20-year reign, however, the regime became an increasingly narrow clan coalition, and hence less and less inclusive. Privileged clans under Barre's rule came to dominate key positions in the government and military, and enjoyed privileged opportunities to control and divert state resources, and engage in large-scale land grabs, especially in irrigated riverine areas. This left a legacy in which some urban and agricultural zones were rendered multi-clan without being cosmopolitan. To the extent that empowered clans came to build businesses, own farms, or hold positions of power in high value cities and riverine areas, they were viewed as "settlers" rather than citizens, and their claims to land and rights a source of contestation.

The civil war period of 1988–92 produced widespread ethnic cleansing, and Somalis fled to their clan's home areas for protection. This transformed some previously cosmopolitan cities into mono-clan urban areas. The fact that the capital city Mogadishu itself became the domain of a single clan family created a nettlesome problem for national reconciliation and political normalization.[9] Land-grabbing (*dhul boob*) produced a new wave of settlers.[10] The prevailing ethos of the era was that of the victor's peace, captured in the expression *waan taabsadey*, or "I touched it"—a term used to lay permanent claim to any resource one came into possession of during the war.

Due to 25 years of communal clashes, insurgency and counter-insurgency, recurring humanitarian crises, and most recently refugee returns, one tenth of Somalia's population—1.1 million people—are internally displaced persons (IDPs). Almost all of the country's IDPs are concentrated in urban centres.

Their presence and growing numbers in these cities add urgency to the question of inclusion and rights of citizenship in major Somalia cities. Most of the IDPs are from poor, low-status, southern Somali agricultural communities, such as the Digil-Mirifle and Somali Bantu. As they flow into the crowded slums that pass for IDP "camps" in urban areas, they are changing the demographics of these cities in ways that challenge exclusivist clan claims to cities. The presence of the IDPs is generally tolerated by host communities because they serve as a useful pool of cheap labour. But they are treated as guests with limited rights, who "belong" to distant home territories. This exclusionary discourse targeting IDPs is one of the most sensitive and potentially explosive issues in Somalia today, especially as the IDPs are likely to remain permanent residents in cities dominated by certain clans.[11]

Inclusion and Exclusion in the Current Somali Context

Inclusion in Negotiations

Over the past 20 years, national-level political negotiations have come to reflect a political settlement based on the principle of proportional representation as expressed in the 4.5 formula (a power-sharing arrangement which gives equal quota to the four "major" clans, and a half-point to a cluster of "minority" clans). The 4.5 formula, however, only provides the roughest level of relative parity between major clan-families in talks. It can be manipulated or used in bad faith to marginalize or freeze out rivals, and even when used in good faith it does little to ensure inclusiveness. That goal requires extensive negotiations within clans, so that all sub-clans and clans are adequately represented. Even then, destabilizing exclusion can occur, either when individual leaders (with spoiler capacity) are left out, or when factions and movements (such as Damal Jadiid, Ahlu Sheikh, or Ahlu Sunna Wal Jama'a) are under- or over-represented.

Inclusion in Governance Structures and Power-sharing

Somalia and international observers are exceptionally attentive to inclusion and exclusion in the composition of national and regional administrations, especially at the cabinet level. Newly declared administrations or cabinets are scrutinized to see not only which individuals are selected, but which clan and sub-clans were empowered or snubbed. The task of forming a perfectly balanced cabinet that satisfies all constituencies is impossible. Because cabinets typically involve a small number of positions, and because cabinet positions are highly unequal in terms of power and control of resources, the best an administration can hope for is an "inclusive enough" coalition that does not provoke defections or sabotage.

Federalism has helped to devolve but not resolve issues of power-sharing from the Federal Government to Federal Member States. As these regional states increase their revenues and power, their degree of inclusiveness will become a matter of greater importance. If not made more inclusive, federalism runs the risk of replicating ethno-hegemony at the subnational level. Federal Member State states that treat some Somalis as de facto "immigrants" with limited or no rights as citizens reinforce this problem.

Inclusion and Exclusion in Somali Cities

Where inclusion and exclusion appear to matter the most in Somali politics—especially for average Somali citizens—is the question of rights to live and access resources in Somalia's main urban centres. Claims by clans to entire cities on the principle of "rights by blood" are deeply problematic misapplications of a logic that was designed to manage pastoral land rights. Indeed, a case can be made that the single greatest conflict driver in Somalia today, and the most dangerous fault-line in the precarious political settlement undergirding the FGS, is the unresolved question of who may claim full, or at least partial, rights in which cities.

Defining a Cosmopolitan City

In an ideal post-conflict urban setting, *u dhasheey* discourse would have little political traction, and Somalia's main cities would meet, or at least come close to meeting, criteria that define a cosmopolitan or inclusive city. A basket of indicators to measure different aspects of urban inclusion could include:

- The right to reside in any part of the city.
- The right to move freely in any part of the city regardless of lineage identity.
- The right to be treated as a resident, or *degan*, and not a guest (*galti*) or settler.
- The right to enjoy the same level of security as residents from politically dominant groups.

- The right to enjoy the same level of access to justice, conflict resolution, and mediation of disputes as residents of politically dominant groups.
- The right to reclaim, own, buy, and sell property.
- The right to operate a business.
- The right to compete fairly for employment opportunities at all levels.
- The right to work in the security sector.
- The right to compete for civil service positions.
- The right to hold political office.
- Freedom from protection rackets or any other arrangements involving a quid pro quo with a more powerful host community.

In reality, none of Somalia's cities meet this standard, and most fall far short of it. But some come closer than others. Not all Somali cities need to aspire to cosmopolitan status. Some towns are small and provincial enough that they are understood to be the domain of one or two clans. By contrast, the capital city, Mogadishu, must aspire to be as cosmopolitan as possible, if the government seated there is to have any chance of claiming to represent the entire population. The question gets more difficult when applied to those many cities in between the capital and the provincial—regional capitals, or major commercial hubs, for instance, like Kismayo, Galkayo, Beled Weyn, Baidoa, Bosaso and Merka.

Access and rights in urban areas are a major preoccupation in Somalia for several reasons. First, major cities are the site of one of the most valuable and contested assets in Somalia—urban real estate. Second, cities are the location where most government-controlled "rent" opportunities exist—from foreign aid, customs revenues, large contracts, and other accoutrements of the state. Third, cities are the locus of the most profitable business opportunities. Finally, cities are the site of the highest quality social services, whether provided by the private, non-profit, or public sectors. All this makes access critical. But the high value of urban areas also fuels chauvinistic discourse among some Somalis who claim a city belongs exclusively to their clan.

The Spatial Logic of Inclusive and Exclusive Cities

No city in Somalia today is completely exclusionary. All reflect some degree of arrangements to accommodate or tolerate the presence of Somalis from clans that are not dominant in or indigenous to the city.

1. Green Lines—Divided Cities

This category of Somali city is only minimally inclusive. The city is divided by a green line into two or more clan-based areas. Very little crosses the green line—traded goods typically must be off-loaded from one truck to another. Though divided cities appear to be, and often are, volatile and prone to armed clashes, they also possess a logic of minimal interaction and minimal competition that, at least in the short term, can reduce conflict. In the 1990s, Mogadishu was famously divided by a green line separating Habar Gedir and Abgaal-dominated parts of the city. Today, the best-known urban green line is the one dividing the city of Galkayo.

2. Enclave Cities

Most Somali cities are composed of districts or neighbourhoods identified with a dominant clan from the area. Some are the product of clan clustering or localized "ethnic cleansing" during the civil war; many others reflect pre-war settlement patterns. Residents may move across the city to access markets, schools, the airport, and other services, but own property and reside only in the quarter associated with their clan. Enclave cities are mainly driven by the need for security provided by the clan. Beled Weyn, with its east bank/west bank division along clan lines, is an example.

3. Enclave Cities with Cosmopolitan Neighbourhoods

Virtually all Somali cities are now accessible to members of all Somali communities, including those whose clans have no record of historical residence in the city or its surrounding area. Most cities have neighbourhoods that are known to be cosmopolitan or mixed, even though the district may still be politically dominated by a local clan. Typically, members of clans without a power base in the city must forge a protection relationship with a more powerful clan. Mogadishu is an example of this category. The city is dominated by the Hawiye clan family; most districts are closely identified with specific Hawiye clans; and some neighbourhoods such as Medina are known as cosmopolitan hotspots where Somalis of all clans can reside and do business, though with security arrangements that must be negotiated with the dominant local clan.

4. IDP Camps and the Identity Politics of Slums

An important subset of urban inclusion and exclusion is the place of IDP camps in Somali cities. As noted above, many of Somalia's largest cities feature large IDP camps that serve essentially as ethnically-defined slums. Some of the IDPs have been resident in these cities and camps for over 20 years, and have become a pool of cheap unskilled labour with no rights as city residents because they are viewed as IDPs—people with citizenship rights in a distant regional member state. The IDP label risks disenfranchising a quarter of the current population of Mogadishu and an even higher percentage of the Kismayo population.[12]

Conclusion

Cities in Somalia have been the site of both the worst armed conflicts and the most promising examples of re-emerging cosmopolitanism and consolidated peace. Exclusionist practices in some cities—where ethno-hegemony and exclusive claims to rights and resources are established by one clan at the expense of other current or former residents—are a major conflict driver and one of the great unresolved reconciliation issues in post-war Somalia. More hopefully, some Somali cities have been the primary location where constituencies divided by conflict, identity, and politics can and do build shared interests, partnerships, and new, more cosmopolitan identities. Somalia's cities are the most promising engines of identities and interests that transcend subnational identity cleavages and reinforce commitments to peace. Though this observation is self-evident in the Somali case, it has also been invoked as a universal norm and goal, as expressed in the UN Sustainable Development Goals 2030 (SDGs), in which signatories commit to work toward the goal "Make Cities Inclusive, Safe, Resilient, and Just." As a signatory to the SDGs, the SFG has already committed itself to this objective.

Recommendations

The sooner Somalia's major cities become more inclusive, the more durable Somalia's currently fragile political settlement will be. Strategies to support Somali-led efforts to negotiate greater inclusion in their cities should be a top reconciliation and development priority.

Our main recommendation is to support Somali government and civic leaders to develop an urban inclusivity index that would help them measure and monitor changes in degrees of inclusion and exclusion in Somali cities. The index might draw on the list of rights enumerated in this paper, or may come up with other, more appropriate indicators to measure. Once established, the urban inclusion index could be used in periodic public surveys to measure perceived improvements in inclusion over time. The survey and index would have the added value of serving to remind municipal political leaders of their obligation to advance inclusion in their cities, and to reinforce urban inclusion as a core value and norm to challenge *u dhasheey* discourse in Somalia. Finally, the urban inclusivity index could be harnessed as a pilot project in support of an emerging global initiative to measure and monitor urban inclusion, as expressed in UN Habitat Safer Cities Programme and other recent initiatives.[13]

We also recommend that efforts to increase the inclusive nature of Somali cities be carried out in concert with one another, as part of a shared, incremental commitment by municipal and civic leaders across Somalia. Synchronising policies to improve urban inclusion is essential as a confidence-building measure, so that progress in rendering urban areas more cosmopolitan is not seen as providing advantages to only one clan.

NEITHER INEVITABLE NOR ACCIDENTAL

THE IMPACT OF MARGINALIZATION IN SOMALIA

The United Nations Accountability Project—Somalia

Authorship

This paper was collectively authored by UN staff in Somalia who have been working on how to better leverage the UN's role in relation to addressing root causes of exclusion and discrimination.

Summary

The 2016–17 drought has resulted in internal displacement estimated at 761,000 individuals.[1] While the figures illustrate the depth of the crisis, available data do not tell us who the people most affected are, nor explain the political economy of their situation. Given what we have understood from past famines, it is likely that it will be the same communities who were affected in 1991–92 and 2011–12.

The vulnerabilities of these segments of the Somali population can be attributed to a range of factors, most notably a lack of resources, the deprivation of human rights, abusive structures of power, systemic violence, and entrenched discrimination. Consequently, marginalized groups repeatedly suffer from instability, high levels of displacement, and lack of opportunities—and are exposed to life-threatening crises in almost predictable cycles.

This paper argues for the importance of understanding the political economy of protection and its failures. It calls for humanitarian, recovery and stabilization activities to take proper account of forces that marginalize certain groups and action to avoid exacerbating such vulnerabilities. The complexities of grievances in Somalia mean that exclusion must be addressed if genuine peace and reconciliation are to be achieved.

Introduction

In June 2017, the United Nations Office for the Coordination of Humanitarian Affairs (OCHA) called for humanitarian assistance to 6.7 million people severely affected by drought in Somalia and estimated that 739,000 people had been displaced by the crisis and 53,000 infected with cholera since November 2016.[2] These people are vulnerable not only because they lack resources, but also because they have been subjected to serious human rights violations. Analysis shows that the manner in which humanitarian, recovery and reconciliation assistance has been structured in Somalia, while helping to alleviate immediate suffering, has also unwittingly reinforced abusive structures by failing to take into account the political economy of marginalization.[3] A well-known example is the "gatekeeping" system, by which political elites control access to people, information, and resources.[4] Gatekeeping has become a way of life for many vulnerable Somali people, who have been reduced to being owned objects of other citizens. It extends to international actors, whose staff may be affected by gatekeeping networks and power dynamics.[5] In failing to analyse and take steps against gatekeeping, and in neglecting the political economy of humanitarian intervention, international organizations, including parts of the UN, are helping to create the conditions for continued marginalization.

These patterns should be acknowledged, assessed and factored into the design and delivery of justice, services, and peace and reconciliation. Somalia's marginalized groups will only overcome vulnerability if they have full rights of participation and accountability. This would have fundamental consequences for achieving reconciliation, entrenching rights to property and services, and securing adequate political representation.

Marginalization as the Cause of Vulnerability

Marginalized populations in Somalia face the highest risk of famine, as was demonstrated in 1991–92 and 2011–12. Research indicates that over

80 per cent of the victims of the 1991–92 famine were from the Rahanweyn clans and the Bantu Somali community. Similarly, in 2011–12, data indicate disproportionate deaths in this part of the population.[6] In each of these famines approximately 250,000 people died.[7]

The deaths in 1991–92 and 2011–12 were neither accidental nor inevitable, but reflect the way society was structured, the way decisions—including by the international community—were taken and how aid was distributed. With respect to the deaths in 1991–92, a World Bank report found that the main victims "were weak agricultural communities and coastal minority groups caught in the middle of fighting, looted of all their belongings including their riverine lands", noting that "[t]he food aid quickly became part of the war and political economy, a commodity over which militias fought and that warlords diverted to fund wars."[8]

The consequences included a breakdown of the rule of law and blockages to reconciliation efforts. Insecurity provided a permissive environment in which "whole clans found themselves in possession of valuable urban and riverine real estate won by conquest, which they stood to lose in a peace settlement."[9] This situation prevails today, entrenched in large part because many of the same actors in southern and central Somalia still hold strategic social, economic and political positions and the modus operandi of international aid has remained largely unchanged.

A review of the 2011 famine response observed that humanitarian assistance had been "a pillar of the Somali political economy for decades" and noted that diversion of assistance to power holders, conflict over procurement opportunities, use of food as a weapon, and the politicization of humanitarian assistance were endemic problems.[10] These factors disproportionately affect marginalized groups who become the victims of diversion, or, as is being reported in 2017, have their assistance confiscated.[11]

In 2011, 750,000 people were categorized as experiencing famine conditions, of whom 490,000 were classified as rural and poor or very poor. The majority, 81 per cent, were of minority clans; agro-pastoralists from Bay and Bakool, Middle Shabelle and Lower Shabelle.[12] While publicly available information on the links between poverty and marginalization is scarce, a localized 2016 study showed that 20 per cent of households in one community used more than 78 per cent of their income on food, demonstrating their intense vulnerability to food shortages. These people were invariably identified as members of marginalized groups.[13]

The 2016–17 drought has resulted in internal displacement of an estimated 761,000 individuals.[14] In response to the early alarm that Somalia was at risk of another famine, donors have provided US$754 million as of 21 June 2017. The revised Humanitarian Response Plan seeks US$1.5 billion to reach 5.5 million people. While the sums called for and the figures of displaced illustrate the depth of the crisis, available data do not tell us who the people most affected are, nor explain the political economy of their situation.

Given what we know from past famines, it is likely that the communities who are affected by the 2016–17 drought were also affected in 1990–91 and 2011–12. It is regrettable that this information is not available from the various humanitarian needs assessments generated by these crises. Such assessments do not shed light on the structural causes of vulnerability, nor do they address issues of marginalization, exclusion, discrimination and horizontal inequalities.[15]

Marginalization is not identified as grounds for vulnerability, although it is a crucial factor given the disproportionate impact that unequal status has had on particular communities in Somalia. Neither humanitarian assessments nor recovery and stabilization initiatives are asking these questions. Yet, so long as displacement and insecurity continue to affect certain communities, the prospects for peace and reconciliation will be undermined. It is clear that Somalia's long-term challenges cannot be met without recognizing how the political economy shapes the rights and welfare of the most marginalized people, and identifying how this can be addressed.

No Security for the Marginalized

Somalia's fragile security situation is well-documented and it is widely recognized that the state cannot yet guarantee security and protection for all.[16] Clan militias fill the security gap, meaning that weaker, marginalized clans are rendered more vulnerable to insecurity and related consequences. For example, in Lower Shabelle, analysis of the 61 victims of clan-related conflict in 2016 indicates that members of the Biyomaal clan are twice as likely as members of other clans to be victims of such violence, and that minority clans are most affected.

Al-Shabaab's presence, which is closely linked to disaffection and exclusion, affects the ability of humanitarian actors to reach certain populations. For example, in May–June 2017, the Biyomaal community around Marka, which had contributed to the AMISOM effort, suffered systematic attacks by Al-Shabaab and allied militias. Al-Shabaab also imposed a blockade on passage of food and other goods towards Marka/Bufo, where many of the displaced were gathered.

Another example is Northern Gedo, an important hub for accessing humanitarian and resilience programming. Aid resources are systematically captured by Marehan groups, while diminishing availability for other groups such as the Dir, the Gabaweyn and other Rahanweyn sub-clans.[17]

Clan affiliation often determines security. In April 2017 in Balcad, Middle Shabelle, Abgaal-dominated Middle Shabelle security forces' violence against Somali Bantu led most of Balcad's roughly 5,000 residents to flee.[18] Middle Shabelle authorities did not comment on the incidents and no action was taken to investigate. The Bantu community has consistently argued that the administration's Abgaal-dominated leadership, including the Balad District Commissioner, the current governor and former governor (now the vice president of Hirshabelle) are part of the problem as members of their respective sub-clans are believed to be involved in the attacks against Bantu villages.

These cases show how insecurity disproportionally affects marginalized groups and is part of a complex political environment. The physical insecurity such groups experience further exacerbates their material insecurity, rendering them even more vulnerable to displacement or the denial of humanitarian assistance.

Limited Peace and Reconciliation for the Marginalized

The militarization of Somalia has a major impact on the situation of marginalized groups, and affects the degree to which they benefit from efforts to promote peace and reconciliation.

Smaller clans often make short-term arrangements with larger forces to gain temporary power or protection. For instance, the 10 July 2013 Jowhar Ceasefire Agreement between the Walamooy (Bantu Somali) and the Muhammed Musse (Abgaal) sub-clans appeared to lead to a cessation of hostilities.[19] However, the security that was achieved can be largely attributed to the Walamooy's forced departure from their villages to an AMISOM-protected IDP camp. The conflict is still unresolved and the Walamooy are unable to return to their villages. The community regularly raises concerns when it is rumoured that AMISOM will be redeployed, arguing that this presence serves as their primary protection. This shows how, by necessity, outside military forces have also become part of the political economy, demonstrating the need for acute awareness of the forces at play.

The complexities and risks of military alignment are illustrated by the case of the Biyomaal. Until 2016, AMISOM in Lower Shabelle was aligned with

Habar Gidir SNA units and clan militias. Over 2017, however, AMISOM has changed its strategy, training Biyomaal militia to support its operations in Lower Shabelle. This has resulted in the Biyomaal, formerly aligned with Al-Shabaab, being targeted by Al-Shabaab. The Habar Gidir militia are now widely believed to be collaborating with Al-Shabaab. Habar Gidir representatives claim that the Biyomaal are exploiting their new alignment with AMISOM to pursue clan interests.[20] This example illustrates how profound inequalities between groups result in shifting realignments that complicate efforts to achieve stability.

Harmful inequalities are also evident in the design and implementation of peacebuilding initiatives.[21] In 2015 and 2016, a series of peace and reconciliation conferences took place in relation to this conflict. The January 2015 Afgooye Peace and Reconciliation Conference resulted in the Afgooye Agreement between Biyomaal and Habar Gidir clan elders to end the bloodshed.[22] A five-point agreement followed in March 2015 and an implementation plan was developed, including an accountability mechanism for human rights violations. However, this was never put into place and there were further violent clashes between the parties later in 2015. In March 2016, the Lower Shabelle Reconciliation Conference in Afgooye resulted in a 13-point resolution. Yet, the various reconciliation initiatives foundered,[23] and a group of militia leaders and political figures announced in October 2016 the formation of the Lower Shabelle People's Guard, which joined Biyomaal and other smaller militia.[24] Although the Guard claimed to support ISWA, it was never officially recognized and is now moribund.

While political interests and alliances have shifted in Marka, one thing has remained constant: the failure to foster an inclusive peace process that engages all key communities and addresses their grievances. The Somali Bantu, in particular, have been excluded and due to their prolonged marginalization they have become a source of recruitment for Al-Shabaab. The Habar Gidir business community, who finances a clan militia to secure their land interests, has also been excluded.

This case example should be considered against the broader post-1991 landscape. Dozens of internationally and regionally sponsored peace and reconciliation conferences have been held. While individuals from marginalized group always participated, they were never seen as important stakeholders. Unless peace and reconciliation initiatives are genuinely inclusive and move beyond processes that result in narrowly constructed pacts, they will fail to bring lasting stability.

No Voice for the Marginalized

Government authorities and insurgents alike suppress freedom of expression, using harassment and intimidation, including, for example, arbitrary arrest of and heavy judicial sentences for journalists.[25] This intimidation is a primary reason why specific segments of society, most notably internally displaced people, have virtually no voice that counts.[26] Civil society and local NGOs do little to counter this loss of voice. Many local NGOs reflect the clan structure of society and in a number of cases local NGOs themselves are run and owned by family members of those in authority.

Fear of reprisals and intimidation by power brokers, including those who have reached their positions through violence, impedes marginalized people from complaining about injustices that range from violence, land-grabbing, and exclusion from services to loss of access to humanitarian aid. This, coupled with the absence of positive outcomes when complaints are made, explains why many Somalis are reluctant to lodge complaints. Those who want to change the status quo must do so without the support or protection of public institutions. If the international system also fails to support the voice of marginalized people, beyond articulating their victimhood, it threatens to further marginalize them, thereby further undermining the prospects for peace and reconciliation.

Conclusion

Horizontal inequalities, that is, inequalities between groups, are a key feature of Somalia's political and economic landscape, creating complex grievances. Minority and marginalized clans and communities represent a disproportionate number of those suffering the most acute and long-term effects of crises in Somalia. They lack power and protection. Such protection as they are able to find is contingent, involving dependency on more powerful clans and on semi-permanent and often partial international humanitarian support, or shifting alliances with external military forces.

It is vital to understand the decisions that these groups have to make to protect themselves from insecurity, their land and properties from confiscation, and their families from hunger and poverty if national, as well as local, reconciliation is to be successful. Yet there is very little disaggregated data on this issue, which has a major impact on interventions, nor is it a subject of debate. This lack of understanding severely limits opportunities for not only accessing but also increasing levels of accountability to the most vulnerable and politically marginalized.

This paper calls for a greater understanding of the political economy of protection and suggests that this should inform peace and reconciliation initiatives. At the same time, humanitarian, recovery and stabilization activities should identify and avoid exacerbating vulnerabilities arising from marginalization. It is imperative that new approaches are developed and, given the complexities involved, marginalized groups must be involved in their design.

Recommendations

National and international decision-makers should:

- **Require that peace and reconciliation frameworks and humanitarian assessments incorporate a political economy and protection analysis.** This should include analysis of political power, access and control of resources, and minority or majority status and issues, but also an analysis of marginalization, exclusion, horizontal inequalities and group-based abuse. This might, for instance, include looking at how issues such as land access and control have caused many groups to migrate away from their homes to become IDPs.[27]

- **Create a systematic source of in-depth analysis.** Strengthen disaggregated data collection and analysis to understand who the people are behind the statistics and what issues of protection, land and power are at play. This should be used to inform the assistance and protection response, understand root causes and provide political oversight.[28]

- **Desist from the established practice in which humanitarian or recovery action goes ahead without adequate attention to the political economy and protection issues outlined here.** To contribute to long-term reconciliation, rights and prosperity, the UN needs to identify positive ways to act on issues of marginalization and exclusion and translate this into the UN's core activities. This requires different parts of the UN system to work together to bring about coherence in intervention. In this regard, the Global Protection Cluster offers guidance that should be followed.

GOVERNING ENDEMIC CRISES

VIOLENCE AND LEGITIMACY IN THE LIVES OF SOMALIS

Jutta Bakonyi

Author

Dr Jutta Bakonyi is an Associate Professor of Development and Conflict at the School of Government and International Affairs, Durham Global Security Institute, Durham University (UK). Jutta has published on different aspects of war, state-building, and international interventions. Her regional focus is the Horn of Africa.

Summary

The paper builds on interviews with Somali migrants in Kenya. It explores how Somali citizens evaluate attempts to establish political authority in Somalia, and what aspects of these attempts they consider as legitimate. Against the context of "endemic crisis" and normalized insecurity, the ability of a political body to provide physical security was given priority by all citizens.

The enhancement of security was linked to mobility, and the ruling bodies were evaluated primarily with respect to their ability to facilitate "free" movement of people and goods (spatial mobility), to enable the restoration of trade routes and economic infrastructure (economic mobility), and to allow for the establishment of social and political networks across clan and administrative boundaries (social mobility). The experience of restricted mobility and enforced immobility contributed to the de-legitimization of a governing authority. Causes for immobility included the proliferation of roadblocks, the establishment of boundaries between administrative units and clan-based "territories", the intensification of armed fights, and here especially the indiscriminate shelling of residential areas, and the authoritarian leadership style of Al-Shabaab. Enforced immobility infringed on people's ability to actively manage their lives, and promoted passivity and feelings of helplessness.

Beyond physical security, however, the provision of judiciary and other mechanisms to solve conflicts in a fair and equitable manner, and the elimination of clan bias, increased legitimacy of a ruling authority, while disrespect of religious values and patriarchal traditions led to decreasing support. All respondents emphasized their desire for a central government, based on the respect for religious values, but above all based on democratic principles.

Introduction

Research on war and state-building in Somalia is mainly concerned with violent actors and the modalities and forms of authority these actors have been establishing since the collapse of the state in 1991. The paper looks at the efforts to establish political authority from the perspective of those who are governed. It explores how Somali citizens describe their everyday realities in the context of changing forms of local and national authority and rule. Building on theories of legitimacy, the paper examines how authority is experienced in the quotidian and outlines common features of what people consider as legitimate or illegitimate forms of rule.

The paper outlines how interviewees structured their biography through consecutive crises and routinized insecurity. Against this context, attempts to establish authority were foremost evaluated by their effect on security. Security was equated with mobility, and initial support for the Union of Islamic Courts (UIC), and also for Al-Shabaab, was attributed to their facilitation of "free" movement of goods and people. Security was thereby not reduced to physical aspects, but included the provision of unitary rules and thus the provision of order. The established order was, in the case of Al-Shabaab, unsettled by their increasingly authoritarian leadership style, the lack of transparency in the execution of "punishments", and their neglect of traditional patriarchal rules. The paper concludes that legitimacy is not a state that can be reached, but depends on the daily practice of authority, and how citizens are able to explain and justify the forms and modalities of rule.

Legitimation and Everyday Life in the Context of "Endemic Crises"

The concept of legitimacy is closely connected to the operation of social and political orders. Max Weber identified legitimacy as among the crucial explanatory categories for the study of social life.[1] Legitimacy distinguishes power from domination, and the belief in the legitimacy of an existing authority or social order provides social stability. While power refers to the ability to impose one's own will on others, domination is the execution of power with the acceptance and support of the dominated, who "believe" that the actions and commands of the authority are justified.

Peter Berger and Thomas Luckmann expanded Max Weber's notion of legitimacy.[2] They introduced legitimization as the practice of "meaning making" and thus as the way in which humans make sense of power differentials, social relations and institutions that structure their lives. In short, legitimacy tells people why things are what they are, and why certain actions should be performed while others should not.[3] This requires the provision of explanations and justifications, a process which takes place at different societal levels and comprises different degrees of abstraction.[4] On the first level of legitimization, the meaning of social interactions is learned and internalized to the point where actions no longer need explanation or justification. This taken-for-granted knowledge provides the cognitive and normative framework against which individuals evaluate their experiences.

The paper focuses on the everyday practices of meaning making, and explores how Somali citizens are making sense out of their daily experiences with political authority. It differentiates two basic forms of experiences,[5] the first based on continuity with past experiences. New experiences of this type are integrated into the explanatory framework that individuals have already internalized, and shape our expectation that things will fall into the same pattern. This contributes to the feeling of normality, safety, protection, and belonging. The second type of experience, however, is unexpected and unforeseen, and includes the discontinuous and spontaneous moments. These experiences require an expansion and adaptation of our explanatory framework. They can be comprised of significant ruptures or threshold experiences, of which death is perhaps the most terrifying.[6] The second type of experience stimulates reflection, and can lead to the questioning of power and institutional arrangements.

The paper assesses everyday experiences in times of intense and tumultuous political change and crisis. It explores meaning making and thus legitimization in situations where threshold experiences—among them mass violence, flight, death, and destruction—dominate people's lives. The main question is how people in "endemic crises"[7] provide meaning to and make sense of the different attempts to govern.

Government Experiences in Somalia

In order to grasp experiences with political authority in Somalia, 31 biographic interviews (27 men, four women) were conducted with Somali migrants in Nairobi. The views gathered are thus limited to the perspectives of people who eventually decided to flee Somalia. However, 28 of the migrants had arrived only recently in Kenya and have spent most of their lives in Somalia. Their perspectives are therefore unlikely to differ systematically from those who still live in the country.[8] Three have lived longer in Kenya, but have regularly revisited Somalia. Snowball sampling and the help of a facilitator were used to identify interviewees. The aim was to interview people with a broad variety of backgrounds and perspectives. Respondents varied with respect to age (ranging from 21 to 67 years), educational background (madrasa only to university education), clan affiliation, birth place, and main place of residence. In the interviews, people were asked to narrate their biography, focusing however on how change in political authority has affected their daily life. All interviews were anonymized and the names of interviewees changed. The age and birth place of the interviewee are added to the name, to provide the reader with context about the speaker.

Prior to proceeding, a brief explanation should be given of the names that appear in the interview quotes. If respondents refer to leaders of clan-based militias, the characterization "[warlord]" is provided after the name, to delineate the period of clan-based, localized rule (1995–2006). The UIC and Al-Shabaab ended the localized rule of the warlords. When speaking of the different central governments, interviewees usually referred to the names of the respective presidents, in chronological order Abdiqasim Hassan (2000–04); Abdullahi Yusuf (2004–08), Sheikh Sharif (2009–12), and Hassan Sheikh (2012–17).

Living Through Consecutive Emergencies and Crises: Ruptures and Routines

People in southern and central Somalia live on the verge of emergencies. While asked to relate their biographic narrative to political authority, they rather related it to experiences with violence and displacement. Attempts to establish authority were evaluated first and foremost with respects to the effects they had on security. To provide one example:

> The situation was difficult during Abdullahi Yusuf, whereby there was a huge deployment of Ethiopian forces in Mogadishu. /.../ There was firing of artilleries all over. That time /..../ it turned worse because Ethiopians were indiscriminately firing mortars, killing women and children and even destroying buildings. /.../ We fled together. /.../ After returning, and under the government of Sheikh Sharif /.../ the Ugandan troops were firing mortars on civilian houses. That led us to flee again to /.../ the outskirts of Mogadishu. Since that time of Sheikh Sharif and the time of Hassan Sheikh I have regularly visited Mogadishu /.../. But by then Al-Shabaab militants were also there, until I completely left /.../ 2014. (Mustafa, 41, Mogadishu.)[9]

All interviewees described a large spectrum of violent encounters, ranging from localized clan clashes to intense periods of fighting, the shelling of residential areas, suicide attacks and explosions. They remembered the fear, harm, horror and destruction the violence caused, outlined how they "could not sleep because of fear" (Abdul, 25, Mogadishu), had lost their orientation, and felt that they were placed "in a situation whereby you might not know what was going on" (Ismael, 39, Beled Weyne), and where "anything can happen" (Hersi, 51, Kismaayo). People's lives were structured by fear, and they continuously expected to encounter further violence: "You can't take your cup of tea peacefully or you might finish your tea with fear, thinking of when will an explosion occur?" (Hassan, 67, Huddur and Mogadishu).

Many of the violent incidents were described as being without meaning and reason. People died because gunmen "were testing whether a bullet can kill someone" (Mohamed, 28, Mogadishu) and many deaths seemed accidental. People died because a stray bullet hit them, because they lived in a residential area that was shelled, or simply because they were in the wrong place at the wrong time. People in arms—whether members of clan militias, government or intervention forces—were perceived as unpredictable and as being indifferent towards the harm they cause.

As disorienting and shocking as the violent encounters were, most interviewees also referred to their own subsequent adaptation: "I saw several people who have been killed as well as bodies lying all over the streets, even skeletons. It was horrible, but people have adapted to that kind of life" (Mustafa, 41, Mogadishu). In the long-lasting Somali war, periods of intense violence were followed by longer periods of calmness. Violence nonetheless remained a feature of everyday life:

> Later, people were exhausted of fighting among themselves /.../ and the security has improved. Sometimes, it still happened that there was a fight between two militia groups. The civilians would duck and watch the two warring sides exchanging fire /.../. One of the days, when I left my neighbourhood /.../, I encountered fighting between gunmen /.../. By then, all the civilians ducked behind things. But the surprising thing I saw was a goat, which also ducked behind me. The situation trained not only human beings but the animals too. (Mohamed, 28, Mogadishu.)

Violence was expected, and became a normal feature in the everyday. Mohamed, for example, was not surprised that he had accidentally walked into the exchange of gunfire, but that even animals had adapted. The normalization of insecurity was particularly pronounced in younger respondents' experiences. Abdullah (28, Mogadishu), for example, remembered how he used to play football after school, but also how easily a football game could turn violent: "Sometimes clans clashed while we were playing football, and players were injured in the fights. Sometimes it happened that when two teams were playing, the game turned into fights and players went to collect their guns." Ali (25, Baidoa) described the adaptation to the attacks of Al-Shabaab: "Several times deadly explosions occurred which killed several people. /.../ Even when you are in a restaurant it may blow up /.../. People have adapted to the kind of situation. Although there is fear, they don't mind, they just go."

People needed to ignore the possibility of violence in order to re-establish routines. Violence became an expected part of the daily routines, be it a football game turned violent, clan militias clashing while one was passing by, or Al-Shabaab launching an attack on a restaurant. Albeit still perceived as sudden and spectacular, violence lost its exceptionality. It hit in episodes, became recurrent, cyclical and expected. Once violence hit, people (and animals) ducked behind cars and buildings, and were transformed into bystanders and spectators. They may have later tried to help the wounded or bury the dead, but then life continued and people resumed their routines.

*Spatial Aspects of Legitimization: Between Forced Mobility
and Forced Immobility*

Most respondents were internally displaced several times, and had to navigate their way through multiple emergencies and violent attacks. Flight became a routinized response to violence, and all respondents underwent dangerous journeys in the attempt to reach a safer destination. "Enforced immobility", however, can have as dramatic and disruptive effects on people's lives as violent displacement.[10] Interviewees often referred to their loss of mobility to signify "insecurity" and devastation. Their movement was, for example, obstructed by roadblocks, and people tried to limit travel, knowing about the dangers of gunmen extorting money from passing vehicles and people.

Restricted mobility impinged on economic opportunities, as for example pastoralists could not look for pasture (Hassan, 67, Huddur), or traders lost access to markets outside their clan area (Abdul, 55, Bosaso). A large number of interviewees described how they were at times spatially "trapped". Abdul (25) from Mogadishu, for example, remembered how his family was caught between Al-Shabaab and Ethiopian forces: "We were stranded between SOS and Hilwa [in Mogadishu] /.../, we were stuck in the middle due to heavy fighting between the groups." Being deprived of their ability to flee, people were left power- and helpless, and had to endure periods of anxious waiting: "a night when mortar shell hit a neighbour, /.../ we could not do anything but had to wait with people bleeding and dying" (Nur, 45, Mogadishu).

Enforced immobility deprived people of necessary resources and means to actively mould their lives. People minimized outside exposure, avoided the risk of travel, and severely restricted their movements. Whilst violence was experienced as a sudden, abrupt intrusion, life in the midst of crisis was characterized by idleness and boredom: "From home you go to the mosque, you sleep, and you eat since there was nothing you could do" (Mustafa, 41, Mogadishu). People reduced their outside exposure to necessary everyday chores, and as their spatial radius and social relations retracted, life was increasingly experienced as uneventful and idle. Life was "endured" rather than actively shaped. Against this context, the re-establishment of mobility was experienced as government success.

Respondents especially emphasized the success of the UIC and initially also of Al-Shabaab in restoring mobility: "Before you had to beg at roadblocks while travelling. Under the Union of Islamic Courts it was without clan pressure and without fear" (Suleiman, 38, Huddur). Similar comments were made about Al-Shabaab: "Checkpoints were eliminated by Al-Shabaab. [...] As an ordinary civilian, you were safe" (Abas, 43, Wajid); and: "There was freedom of movement. Movement was safe and the time for travelling shortened considerably" (Suleiman, 38, Huddur). Respondents thus evaluated governments with respect to their ability to ensure mobility and to minimize risks. The ability of UIC and initially also of Al-Shabaab to end clan-based harassment at roadblocks and facilitate mobility significantly enhanced their acceptance in Somalia.

Order and Legitimization: From "Law and Order" to Terror

Mobility was often linked to justice, which in turn was attributed to Al-Shabaab's neglect of clan structures. Respondents emphasized that, compared to the warlords, Al-Shabaab did not harass people "because of their clan /.../. They don't bother which clan you belong to" (Abdi, 50, Kismaayo). Al-Shabaab also stopped revenge killings: "You did not have to fear that you would be killed because you belong to a clan" (Suleiman, 38, Huddur). Other factors that enhanced Al-Shabaab's acceptance were their provision of rules for correct conduct, and, more importantly, their ability to punish misconduct and solve disputes, both again without consideration of status or clan: "They will fairly deal with it [disputes], particularly when it comes to land disputes" (Barre, 37, Bardhere); or "They also brought some kind of justice, especially for vulnerable people and for minorities. In the clan system, they were disturbed, their land was taken. Now minorities got their land back" (Suleiman, 38, Huddur).

In contrast to the clan militias, Al-Shabaab was initially perceived as "orderly". They behaved "like normal forces", patrolled the town, were disciplined and neither did they "bother the locals" (Barre), nor interact with them: "They were trained to stay away from people. They were separated and lived in barracks and did not intermingle" (Suleiman).

In short, the initial popularity of Al-Shabaab was closely related to the ability of the Islamist organization to end violence, to provide clear rules, and to establish order. They also implemented their rules in a manner that was perceived as reasonably fair, and that followed the maxims of the Sharia, a body of regulations that is widely respected by Somali citizens. Two factors, however, started to unsettle the support Al-Shabaab could initially muster. The increasingly erratic approach of Al-Shabaab towards their own rules delegitimized their actions, and their defiance of deeply anchored societal traditions—especially the neglect of patriarchal rules—gradually alienated people.

The initial appreciation for the implementation of Sharia was soon replaced by a widespread perception that Al-Shabaab engaged in unjustified punishments, for example when a hand was chopped off for a minor case of stealing (Barre, 37, Bardhere). Also, their general lack of consultation and their failure to contextualize crimes was criticized: "If the UIC arrested you, they consulted and considered context, and released or killed you. Under Al-Shabaab you were arrested and killed without consideration" (Yusuf, 50, Beled Weyne). Most crucially, however, the initial improvement of security was soon superseded by locals' fear of becoming a "target" of Al-Shabaab:

> Security-wise they were good, but to whom? Only to persons who were not targeted. If you were not, you could continue to travel, even in the night time /.../. But, if you were the target, then you were done. And you don't know if you are the target /.../. You didn't know if you are on their list or not. (Hersi, 51, Khasadhere.)

Al-Shabaab increasingly ruled through fear, became unpredictable, and itself posed the main threat to people. Their rule significantly altered the terrain of risk and uncertainty to which people were accustomed. Before, violence was experienced as accidental, unavoidable, and as a quasi-natural force that could break anytime into people's life. Under Al-Shabaab, however, violence became strategic; it looked out for and "targeted" specific people. The organization's rules were no longer understood, and people felt that anybody could be placed on Al-Shabaab's "list". At the same time, doubts increased about the justifiable nature of Al-Shabaab's punishments; many respondents believed that Al-Shabaab harmed "innocent people". As one responded put it: Al-Shabaab "kept the fear alive" (Hersi, 51, Khansadhere), and they did so with methods that horrified and appalled many. Al-Shabaab created a culture of fear that produced "silences" which aligned themselves with "solitude".[11] People under Al-Shabaab's rule were afraid to question its decisions: "What kind of security are they maintaining? You are always in a state of fear, you can't talk and you can't move freely. I don't think that they were good in the security sector" (Farah, 52, Wajid). They also became suspicious of "spies" and started to restrict their social interactions: "Everybody was suspicious and fearing. Even there were no interactions between civilians themselves and the social life was not good. It reached an extent whereby you suspect your partner or friend [of spying for Al-Shabaab]" (Abdi, 50, Kismaayo).

People started to question whether Al-Shabaab's rule reflected Islamic values: "The starting of the group and the way they approached it were very nice. It was only later that they started contradicting the Islamic Sharia" (Abdo, 45,

Mogadishu). Respondents labelled Al-Shabaab as "un-Islamic", or raised doubt about whether they are indeed Muslims (Abdallah, 55, Bosaso). "They kill innocent people and this is not written in our religion. The meaning of Islam is peace, it is not allowed to kill innocent people" (Hussein, 31, Gedo). Arbitrary and unpredictable punishments and the general climate of fear Al-Shabaab created gradually delegitimized their authority.

Legitimization and Traditions

Other authors have already outlined that people in crisis situations tend to cling to traditions which are, however, not just re-vitalized, but renegotiated and adapted to the situation of crisis. Examples in Somalia include the re-vitalization and adaptation of clan relations or of gender relations to the conditions of war, displacement, intervention and state-building.[12] Al-Shabaab introduced a new dynamic with respect to both clan and gender. While the group's neglect of clan relations was appreciated by many respondents, their reinterpretation of patriarchal traditions was not. Many respondents criticized Al-Shabaab's facilitation of marriages without consultation with the involved families, and most notably without the consent of the bride's father: "I never liked their administration because I will not accept a man to marry my daughter without my consent. But they were doing so" (Ahmed, 52, Marka).

Additionally, Al-Shabaab members themselves did not adhere to any rules of marriage. The example of forced marriage was used to explain how Al-Shabaab disempowered and silenced (male) citizens: "They give directives which should be obeyed, /.../ they will decide for you and your family. Maybe your daughter will be married to one of their members and you can't talk with them about it" (Farah, 52, Wajid). Often, Al-Shabaab members put considerable pressure on the girls they fancied. One young woman described her increasing isolation after she refused to be married by Al-Shabaab: "They [Al-Shabaab] came to my house and looked for something /.../. We could not move outside and we could not go to anybody. /.../ We did not have anybody" (Sara, 27, Dinsoor). Respondents also outlined how Al-Shabaab forcefully divorced and remarried women, because their husbands were away for a long period of time (Ahmed, 52, Marka), or because they labelled the husband an apostate. The defiance by Al-Shabaab of traditions, their reinterpretation of patriarchal rules and above all the fact that they forced these rules on people contributed to the organization's declining support. They were increasingly perceived as acting beyond both tradition and religion.

Conclusion

The interviews clearly show that legitimacy needs to be realized in the daily practice of authority, and depends on how citizens are able to explain and justify the forms and modalities of rule. The Somali example shows that horrific and spectacular experiences can be routinized and integrated into the everyday. The experience and expectation of violence then shape the interpretative framework on which people rely to evaluate their lives.

In the context of endemic insecurity, legitimacy is enhanced foremost by providing security in a way that restores mobility of both people and goods, and second by providing equitable access to security independent of clan affiliation. Mobility enables people to actively shape their own life, as it enhances economic opportunities and provides the necessary flexibility to establish and build on necessary social networks. Enforced immobility, in contrast, deprives people of these chances.

Legitimacy thus depends not only on the provision of physical security, but also on people's perception of how conflicts and especially resource-related conflicts are addressed. Legitimacy is reinforced through the provision of rules anchored in religion and/or tradition, the supervision of the "right" conduct of both rulers and ruled, and, if necessary, punishment of rule breaches. However, the examples above also show that people in Somalia expect and prefer to negotiate the rules and modalities of how they are governed.

Although clan relations loom large in most studies on political rule in Somalia, and underpin ongoing state-building attempts, the interviewees expressed ambivalence towards clan as a means of political organization. Politicized clan relations were considered a source of insecurity and described as an obstacle to "good" governance. All respondents demonstrated a desire for the establishment of a state, and many emphasized that this state should be democratic and anchored in Islamic maxims and values.

All respondents—independent of gender, age and clan affiliation—supported the formation of a government, and appreciated the ongoing federalization process. Many, however, also expressed ambivalence towards the clan-based character of authority, emphasizing the potential for clan bias with respect to access to both security and economic chances, but also as an obstacle for democratic forms of government.

Recommendations

The provision of physical security is paramount to increase legitimacy. This requires specialized training, but also the development of a code of conduct for governmental security forces. Such a code of conduct should be speedily implemented and thoroughly monitored, in order to bring an end to the clan-based harassment and indiscriminate violence many respondents had to endure from different violent actors, among them also governmental and intervention forces. An agreement with the Federal Member States on the responsibilities and duties of governmental security forces, the monitoring of conduct and indeed rule-based "punishment" of misbehaviour of security forces would support claims of legitimacy and should become the first priority of the government.

The provision of clear rules and the ability to manage and address conflicts, especially resource-related conflicts (for instance relating to land and housing) were emphasized by many respondents as criteria for successful governance. Therefore, the rapid establishment of local-level dispute resolution and judiciary processes is highly recommended. The government would need to establish unitary guidelines for these processes and communicate and explain these guidelines to the wider public. The government should also ensure that the established mechanisms work in a fair and equitable manner, and eliminate (or at least minimize) clan bias.

However, the responses above also show clearly that people in Somalia are used to, expect and prefer to negotiate the rules and modalities of how they are governed. This should be recognized as a resource for establishing legitimate forms of rules. It suggests the need for a long-term perspective on leadership that allows for participation or at least consultation at every level of government.

Given the ambiguity in the evaluation of clanrelations, it is recommended to move away from the 4.5 principle and to ensure the transition towards a democratic public vote. To conclude by giving voice to one interviewee: "I would like to see a central government which is good for people, and which treats people equally. I would like to see a democratic state which comes with one man, one vote" (Abdul). The new government should therefore indeed embark on the way towards democratic transition.

REMEDYING THE LEGACY OF STATE COLLAPSE

THINKING THROUGH AND BEYOND SOMALI CIVIL WAR VIOLENCE

Lidwien Kapteijns

Author

Dr Lidwien Kapteijns is Professor of African and Middle Eastern History at Wellesley College. Having started as a historian of the Sudan, where she lived and worked for five years, she turned to Somali history in 1986. Her work has focused on gender and popular culture, and on the role of clan as a political technology and popular mindset in Somali history, especially the Somali civil war. Arabic and Somali were part of her university education.

Summary

The complete impunity for the leaders of the clan cleansing campaign that caused state collapse and the break-up of the country in 1991 is the key legacy that undermines political reconstruction and moral repair in Somalia today. It finds concrete expression in the territorial and political divisions on the ground, constitutes the major break-line underlying national/federal politics, and is etched in the minds and bodies of its victims, who have been denied even proper public acknowledgement.

At the heart of the mistrust and mutual rejection in Somalia today lie the actions of former leaders of the United Somali Congress (USC) and Somali National Movement (SNM), who resorted to clan-based killings and expulsions in order to cover up their past complicity with the military regime; spun false clan histories to rebrand themselves as heroic leaders of their clans; and then tried to establish authority over parts of the state and country in the name of clan. Peace and reconciliation require holding these perpetrators accountable and acknowledging the crimes they committed.

Introduction

The centrifugal forces that keep pulling Somalia apart gained most strength from the processes that caused state collapse in 1991. Post-collapse narratives fail to highlight the role played in this divisive process by a particular group of political-military leaders. They first served in Siad Barre's military regime (1969–1991). From 1978, as a result of this regime's dictatorial, divisive, and violent policies, they split into two camps with some joining the regime and others joining armed opposition fronts. Finally, from the second half of the 1980s, when the regime began to totter and then fell, they adopted a policy of mobilizing Somali civilians for violence against other civilians by manipulating clan sentiment.

The Barre regime was the first to unleash large-scale clan-based violence against civilians, deploying the national army against civilians of the clan backgrounds it associated with the armed opposition fronts. This first happened in Mudug, to undermine the Somali Salvation Democratic Front (SSDF); then on a vastly larger and lethal scale in the north-west, to take revenge on SNM, and finally also in other areas whose population the regime associated with opposition fronts that emerged later, especially the USC.[1] The Barre government also played a role in rechannelling people's fury at the regime into clan-based resentment against each other.[2] However, at the very moment the opportunity to establish a better government emerged, it was SNM and USC leaders who disregarded the national political responsibility of the hour and, instead, organized large-scale clan-based violence in the areas they hoped to dominate by mobilizing Somali civilians against other Somali civilians.

This shift is the key legacy that undermines political reconstruction and moral repair in Somalia today. While leveraging communal violence to claim state authority over particular areas—the SNM in the north-west, the USC in south and south-central Somalia—these politico-military leaders re-emerged dressed, so to speak, in clan garb. Adopting new born-again identities as leaders of their clans, they cried crocodile tears about the horrible victimization allegedly *only their clans* had suffered at the hands of a regime they now falsely equated not with themselves but with all civilians of a specific set of clans (including that of Barre himself), irrespective of whether these individuals had been the regime's most abused victims or most cruel henchmen.

It is this legacy, today expressed concretely in the territorial and political divisions on the ground in Somalia and etched into the hearts and bodies of those civilians who were targeted by these men, that must be addressed before social reconstruction and moral repair can succeed. Mogadishu as *goof qabiil* (a clan's home turf) and Hargeisa as self-proclaimed break-away republic; the emergence of the regional states of Puntland and Jubbaland; and the ongoing violence in places such as Gaalkacyo and Laascaanood are all evidence of the clan cleansing policies set into motion by former Barre henchmen at the time of regime collapse. It is a sign of the enormous impunity that characterizes Somalia today that men who committed war crimes as part of the Barre regime and committed atrocities during the clan cleansing campaign and the wars of the militias that followed still seek and hold public office. This is a core challenge for any peace and reconciliation project.

This paper will provide more detail about why the campaign of clan cleansing of 1991–1992[3] was a key shift in the Somali civil war and remains the major break-line underlying Somali national politics today. It will then lay out three principles that might help avoid simply redrawing the lines along which the civil war was fought, and conclude with recommendations for three tangible steps towards peace and reconciliation.

The Campaign of Clan Cleansing 1991–1992[4]

The first stages of what would become a full-fledged campaign of clan cleansing occurred in the north-west, when the SNM—immediately upon its incursion into Somalia—attacked and expelled civilians in nine out of 12 refugee camps located there, as well as targeting non-Isaaq residents in general.[5] The SNM clan project and plans for secession would not have succeeded, however, if Mogadishu had been spared the fratricidal violence that totally destroyed it. The point of no return therefore came in Mogadishu, when USC-Caydiid, after it had expelled the dictator, intensified and expanded the clan cleansing campaign, which eventually brought the whole state down. What made this campaign of clan cleansing such a uniquely important watershed?

Firstly, 1991 marked the first time that politico-military leaders of a particular armed front, the USC, used large-scale clan-based violence against civilians as a political instrument *outside* the institutions of the state.

Secondly, 1991 was the first time that politico-military leaders not only targeted civilians as the intended victims of clan-based violence but also incited and organized civilians to become perpetrators of such violence. Uniquely, 1991 was the moment leaders outside the framework of the state tied their civilian followers to them by causing them to kill civilians of other clans, that is to say, the purposeful incitement and perpetration of communal violence. As the testimony of civilian survivors of the clan cleansing campaign clearly shows, they were hunted down intentionally because of their group identity and even by name by people who knew them well—in fact, precisely by people who knew them well. Meanwhile the top henchmen of the Barre regime whose clan backgrounds fitted the genealogical construct with which the USC associated itself were not just spared but welcomed into the political fold as heroes.

Thirdly, 1991 marked the moment of an unexpected and abrupt reversal of the axis along which civil war violence had occurred until now. Until this moment, the political dividing line had been between military dictatorship and opposition fronts. In 1991, when the USC marched on Mogadishu and drove Barre from the capital, it did not form a new national government that included all those who had opposed the regime at such great cost. Instead, it drew a new line, one based on clan. This meant that the USC included and welcomed with open arms those die-hards of the regime who happened to be of their clan,[6] while targeting for death and expulsion not only regime stalwarts, but also tens of thousands of ordinary people who had themselves been the direct victims of the regime but who were now targeted for terror warfare and expulsion simply because of their Daarood clan backgrounds. The number of those expelled from Mogadishu and south and south-central Somalia as a result of this two-year campaign may be as high as between one and two million people. Meanwhile, individuals of other clan backgrounds, including that associated with the Isaaq-based SNM, were allowed to join the clan cleansers or to go scot-free.

Fourthly, it was the campaign of clan cleansing and the reactions it provoked that caused the collapse of the state and not just the regime.

Fifthly, the architects of the clan cleansing campaign mobilized Somali civilians and militias for clan-based violence against civilians at nearly the highest possible level of the clan template, that of Daroodnimo versus Irirnimo, which encompasses the majority of Somalis.

Sixthly, there has been no proper public acknowledgement of the clan cleansing. The different iterations of Somali political leadership since 1991— many of whom played a role in, stood silently by, or benefited from the clan cleansing—have failed to address it. Moreover, those who associate themselves with the perpetrators, including academics, engage in active ongoing distortion, concealment, and denial of the clan cleansing campaign.[7] Denials have been an integral part of the histories of genocide and ethnic cleansing everywhere. Their existence and persistence in the Somali case are therefore not only a powerful diagnostic but also evidence of how undigested and unreconciled this past continues to be.

The Issue of Intent and the Role of False Clan Histories

The intent to kill and expel—to conduct a campaign of clan cleansing—on the part of USC-Caydiid is a crucial aspect of why this key shift in the civil war continues to be a challenge to political reconstruction and moral repair in Somalia. Intent becomes undeniable for three reasons. First, actions were taken and atrocities committed in a particular order. For example, when the USC at the end of February 1991 attacked, abducted, and executed thousands of civilians in Gaalkacyo, this town had not only already accepted the demands of the new Ali Mahdi administration in Mogadishu, but was also not situated on the road from Mogadishu to Gedo, where the fugitive dictator was then hiding out.[8] Second, the acts of clan cleansing conformed to particular patterns of organization, including how the perpetrators divided up the city quarters among themselves, as well as how, as survivor accounts confirm, local commanders directed the actions of those men who actually rounded up and killed people.[9] Third, the acts of clan cleansing were instigated and justified by particular discourses of incitement that entered the public sphere as normalized speech. I call these speech acts "clan hate-narratives" or "falsified clan histories."[10] In crystallized form they took the form of "code words" that covered up these words' genocidal meaning and thus allowed perpetrators to call for and justify clan cleansing while at the same time keeping deniability in the eyes of outsiders. Such code words included *faqash* ("government scum"), *haraadiga Siyaad* ("leftovers of Siad's regime"), *ha kala reebinina* ("don't leave any of them alive"), and *is raaciya* ("lump them all together").[11]

Clan hate-narratives or falsified clan histories[12] drew on a mix of historical fact and fiction to make people believe that, throughout history, their clan had been uniquely denied equal treatment and opportunity. They emphasized that, if members of the clan did not attack other clans right now, they would never get their rightful share and would be late at the hour of victory. By defining clan identity exclusively in terms of longstanding victimization and exclusion, they allowed the long-term history of group grievances to transcend and overwhelm a sense of everyday life, which Somali neighbours, friends, classmates and, colleagues at work had more or less peacefully shared irrespective of their clan backgrounds.

In 1991, these clan hate-narratives were hitched to the ambitions of politico-military leaders who resorted to clan cleansing both to prevent the establishment of a new national government that might hold them accountable for their crimes as members of the military regime and to assure their ascent to power in at least a part of the country by destroying any alternative to their leadership. These hate-narratives, moreover, became a frame within which people of all kinds could fit all kinds of anger and pain about their plights: private and public, personal and professional, socio-economic and political, and local and regional. These false histories used fact and fiction to portray some clan groups as having always been victims and underdogs, whose opportunity to assert their power had now arrived and must be grasped before it would be too late. At the same time, they falsely portrayed other clan groups as having always been dominant and already scheming to become so again, and thus to be targeted for humiliation, expulsion and elimination. In this way the narratives became a trigger and justification for clan cleansing.

In 1991–1992, the clan hate-narratives had three recurring themes. Firstly, they equated all clans targeted for clan cleansing with the Barre regime irrespective of actual individual or group involvement with the political crimes of the regime.[13] In reality, neither supporters nor opponents could be neatly categorized by clan background; moreover, many of the individuals who were targeted for clan cleansing had been the longest-suffering victims of the Barre regime.

Secondly, the clan hate-narratives presented those targeted for death and expulsion as allochthonous, that is to say as outsiders with no rights to reside any longer in the national capital or other regions of central and south-central Somalia that were not regarded as the "original" homelands of their ancestors.[14] As scholars such as Geschiere and Meyer have pointed out, accusations of allochthony to delegitimize particular groups or individuals have been a common phenomenon in African politics in the last decades and often have less to do with the past than with making claims on the present.[15] In 1991, this claim became a rationale for eliminating and expelling people of particular clan backgrounds from large parts of south and south-central Somalia. That many Somalis supporting USC-Caydiid hailed from the same region as many of those to be expelled as "from elsewhere" did not undermine the power of this hate-narrative at the time.

Thirdly, these falsified clan histories pushed the concept of "100 years of Daarood domination", which represents a particular way of spinning, simplifying, and falsifying Somali history from the era of the establishment of colonial rule, the anti-colonial jihad of Sayyid Maxamed Cabdille Xasan, and the struggle for independence to Barre's military regime.[16] In the context of 1991–1992, these toxic clan "histories" and hate-narratives became the rationales and triggers for clan cleansing; they still permeate mindsets and means of political mobilization today. It must be acknowledged that much of what in the historiography passes for Somali history is the result of purposeful and powerful political spin. What empirical historical realities do concepts such as so-called "MOD (Marehan-Ogaden-Dhulbahante) dominance" during the Barre regime[17] and "100 years of Daarood domination" during the clan cleansing campaign really represent if one refuses to attribute single agency to clans? I am not arguing that hate-narratives and the "spin" from and about the past that feeds into them are without meaning, just that their meanings have not been properly studied. Yet, regarding whole clans as single actors still appears to be accepted practice, and collective punishment in the form of collective blaming not only characterizes popular mindsets but also masquerades as true fact or constitutes a barely concealed agenda in scholarly work. This is a major challenge to any peace and reconciliation process.

*How Might a Peace and Reconciliation Process Approach Clan
and Clan Hate-Narratives?*

Scholars have rightly argued that, when the parties in a conflict sit down at the tables of reconciliation, every party's narrative should matter, as it expresses how that party stands in the present and what ambitions it has for the future.[18] However, it is also true that such narratives, which in the Somali context will inevitably include the falsified clan histories and hate-narratives discussed above, are not all equally legitimate or authoritative about the past. How might a formal peace and reconciliation process approach clan and clan hate-narratives without simply suppressing individual expressions of clan hate-narratives and yet avoid being claimed and overwhelmed by them?

Three principles may be of use. First, we must steer clear of attributing single agency to clans. One cannot discern and establish truths about the past using false categories, for example by speaking as if whole groups of people act and think as one. One cannot overcome violent conflict if one takes for granted or uncritically accepts the categories of group identity in whose names that violence was committed. Clans did not kill, rape, rob, and expel, but people did so in specific circumstances in the name of clan. A category of analysis that cannot distinguish between inciters and organizers, ordinary rank and file perpetrators, beneficiaries, bystanders, and saviours cannot help to bring out the truth but perpetuates the ways of thinking of those who incited and still incite clan violence. Collective clan verdicts must go if we want to speak truth to history. For the UN Initiative, this should mean that, if participants insist on referring to whole clans as single agents, such assertions should be regarded as at the heart of what a peace and reconciliation process must confront and overcome.

The second principle is to take clan identity seriously as a political instrument and popular mindset without accepting it uncritically and overestimating its power and validity. If one avoids attributing single and simple agency to clans, one still must acknowledge and try to explain why, in specific circumstances (such as in 1991–1992), so many individuals flocked to the clan banner and participated in clan-based violence. One must acknowledge that clan identity categories have political meaning and power. Not taking seriously how violence has produced and hardened clan identities, ignoring the investment in such identities by individuals who killed or were seriously harmed in their name, and underestimating how they can be further exploited by politicians of all stripes would be a denial of what constitutes current truths and realities. As has been often said in the context of fighting racism and sexism: we must make race and gender matter and not matter at the same time. One cannot uncritically accept them as valid categories of analysis, for individuals cannot be reduced to them, but we must take seriously the harm they nevertheless can do, and indeed do, to individuals who are often associated with them whether they want to be or not. The same approach is relevant to the categories of clan, caste, and race in the Somali context.

The third principle is to reject the clan hate-narratives as authoritative about the past and to regard them, instead, as obstacles to peace, namely as evidence of hardened "conflict identities,"[19] of the power of purposely "spun" divisive histories, and of the divided historical memory that has resulted. It is easier to keep rehearsing grievances (what "we" suffered at "their" hands) than to publicly reflect on, let alone take responsibility for, the violence committed in one's name. This is a major obstacle to political reconstruction and moral repair.

Recommendations

A formal peace and reconciliation process must consider multiple levels of action.[20]

At the level of individuals, at a minimum those who led, implemented, and benefited from the clan cleansing campaign, and other forms of large-scale clan-based violence against civilians, should be barred from holding public office. Such a policy was in fact adopted during the transition from Transitional Federal Government to Federal Government in 2012 but was not implemented.

At the federal level, peace and reconciliation require meaningful political reform to be preceded by public political acknowledgement of the clan cleansing of 1991–1992. This could only be achieved if Mogadishu ceased to be the capital of Somalia. This is because Mogadishu largely remains a clan-cleansed space. The power concentrated there, continuously bolstered by international political players, shields the perpetrators and beneficiaries of the clan-based expulsions and killings of 1990–1991, as well as those who today still line up with them, from having to take any responsibility for their actions. This allows them to stick to their denials and distortions, enjoy and build on the gains they then made, and boast about their "victory."

Moving the branches of government out of Mogadishu to three different Somali towns would enable and require a nation-wide public discussion that would put public acknowledgement of the clan cleansing of 1991–1992 and its aftermath squarely on the peace and reconciliation agenda. The new seats of government proposed for consideration here have multi-clan populations and face hot conflicts across the deep rift the collapse and break-up of the state in 1991 left behind: Ceerigaabo as legislative capital (which could be the seat of parliament), Gaalkacyo as administrative capital (the seat of the president and the cabinet) and Brava as judicial capital (the seat of the supreme court). Even though there are many practical obstacles to implementing this proposal, putting it on the table for discussion is indispensable to a meaningful peace and reconciliation process.

At the level of society, it is crucial to long-term peace and reconciliation to enable the regions, through state high schools and universities, to undertake relevant educational projects in Somali history, including that of 1991. Such projects should be shared across regions, and there should be cross-regional youth exchanges of many kinds. It is at this level that UN support to reconciliation is most likely to have success.

ENDING IMPUNITY

FOSTERING REDRESS AND ACCOUNTABILITY IN SOMALIA

Tobias Hagmann and *Mohammed Mealin Seid*

Authors

Dr Tobias Hagmann is Associate Professor in International Development at the Department of Social Sciences and Business at Roskilde University, Denmark, and a Fellow with the Rift Valley Institute in London/Nairobi.

Mohammed Mealin Seid is a socio-legal researcher with longstanding practical and research experience in peace and conflict, law, development and humanitarian work in Somalia and the Somali region of Ethiopia.[1]

Summary

Impunity in Somalia has become so deeply entrenched over the years that it has become the norm. Since the Siad Barre period (1969–1991), both local and foreign actors have repeatedly committed war crimes and other serious rights abuses that remain unaddressed to this day. This ongoing impunity and new acts of violence and injustice undermine both state-building and peace-building in Somalia. The absence of accountability for war crimes undermines trust necessary for reconciliation and radicalizes disenfranchised groups. This paper explains why accountability is not only a human rights imperative, but a cornerstone of a more effective political strategy in Somalia. We briefly review main abuses and atrocities of the last 30 years, identify the reasons why perpetrators have literally got away with murder, identify the costs of continued impunity and inaction and propose a number of measures in view of a comprehensive strategy to foster both redress and accountability in Somalia.

Introduction

Dealing with past abuses, human rights violations and atrocities were left out of the agenda of Somali and international peacemakers and state-builders. At any given moment in Somalia's tumultuous modern political history, more immediately pressing issues—state repression, civil war, famine, terrorism—prevented accountability and the redressing of past wrongs. This paper highlights how repeated failures to hold perpetrators accountable and to address egregious injustices gradually institutionalized a culture of impunity.[2] Impunity in Somalia is deeply entrenched, dates back to the Siad Barre period, involves local and foreign actors, and has far-reaching political, economic, social, and moral consequences.[3] Impunity not only creates mistrust between individuals and groups; it nurtures grievances that lead to radicalization and is a constant reminder that perpetrators—in particular powerful actors—literally get away with murder.

More importantly, the absence of accountability effectively undermines peace and reconciliation—the very goals that externally funded state-building pursues. Recent progress in institution-building and the federalization of the country did not halt this trend. On the contrary, abuses of civilians by government, Al-Shabaab and AMISOM troops are ongoing. The same can be said about the continued occupation of properties and land by certain clan militias. Can democratic institutions and peaceful politics take root in Somalia if violence against political competitors and militarily weaker social groups, including internally displaced and women, is left without legal consequences? They cannot. This is why accountability is not only a human rights imperative, but a cornerstone of an effective state-building strategy. This paper reviews past abuses and atrocities of the past 30 years, explains why perpetrators have escaped justice, discusses existing instruments to further accountability, and proposes a way forward to address some of the deeply rooted injustices of the past, but also to deter current perpetrators by means of retributive justice.[4]

Political Abuses and Atrocities

Retrospectively, Siad Barre's banning of the constitution and the restriction of civil and political rights in 1969 were a harbinger for Somalia's four-decades-long human rights crises.[5] Freed from democratic checks and aided by a draconian court system and the National Security Service (NSS), the Barre government executed, repressed, tortured, and mistreated critics and political opponents.[6] The execution of ten religious scholars in 1975 who opposed the controversial family law, and of some 83 military officers in 1977 during the war with Ethiopia, are telling examples of the regime's brutality still lurking in the minds of many Somalis. The emergence of clan-based armed opposition movements led the regime to engage in extra-judicial killings and to kill, torture, and displace individuals and clan groups critical of the regime.[7] In the Mudug region alone, some 2,000 civilians were killed in May and June 1979[8] whereas some 50,000 to 60,000 individuals were killed in (then) north-western Somalia in 1988 as a result of summary executions, aerial bombardment, and artillery shelling by the government.[9]

The ouster of the Siad Barre administration in January 1991 sparked more brutality and impunity. In Mogadishu alone, some 25,000 individuals died in a four-month civil war in 1991/92.[10] UNISOM helicopters fired at crowds on 10 August 1993, killing over 100 Somalis, exemplifying how foreign peacekeepers have also participated in atrocities.[11]

The establishment of the Transitional Federal Government, the ouster of warlords by the Union of Islamic Courts (UIC), the ensuing Ethiopian military intervention and AMISOM deployment in 2006/7 led to new waves of violations.[12] Ethiopian National Defence Forces (ENDF) have been accused of having committed war crimes. For instance, Amnesty International reported 30 extrajudicial executions in October and November 2007. In one incident, Ethiopian soldiers are reported to have slit a young child's throat in front of his mother.[13] According to the UN, ENDF "resorted to using white phosphorous bomb" causing the death of 35 civilians on 13 April 2007.[14] On 21 July 2015, it was reported that AMISOM troops killed 24 civilians in Marka town after opening fire on boys playing on a football ground, entering houses and dragging people out and shooting them.[15] More recently, Human Rights Watch reported that the Ethiopian contingent of AMISOM fired at a prayer gathering and killed 14 elders, clerics and Quran teachers in Wardinle town on 17 July 2016.[16]

Al-Shabaab makes extensive use of suicide attacks in civilian areas, indiscriminate shelling and targeted assassination of politicians, journalists, aid workers, and civil servants.[17] Its members have stormed hotels, restaurants, and entertainment centres, shooting everyone in sight. Among the many Al-Shabaab atrocities are their attacks of a wedding ceremony during which some 20 civilians were killed at Mogadishu's Lido beach on 21 January 2016 and a pizza restaurant that left 17 civilians dead and many more injured on 14 June 2017.[18] The Somali National Army (SNA) is responsible for numerous acts of violence including rape, extra-judicial killing, indiscriminate fire on bystanders after Al-Shabaab attacks, looting of properties, and using security checkpoints to extort bribes.[19]

The conflict involving AMISOM, SNA and Al-Shabaab has claimed many lives. The Elman Peace and Human Rights Centre recorded the death of 1,739 civilians in 2009 and 2,200 deaths in 2010.[20] The World Health Organization (WHO) reported that three hospitals in Mogadishu registered 6,543 "weapon-related injuries" in the first half of 2011 "including 1,482 (23 per cent) children".[21] Similarly, Human Rights Watch highlighted that increased fighting starting late 2010 "has resulted in more than 4,000 civilian casualties, including over 1,000 deaths, and numerous abuses against the civilian population."[22]

Journalists, aid workers, women, marginalized groups, minority clans and internally displaced persons are particularly vulnerable.[23] In 2012, for instance, the UN reported that 1,700 people, of which 30 per cent were under age, were victims of sexual violence in Somalia, mostly by men in government uniform.[24] In 2012, 18 journalists were killed in Somalia, one of them by AMISOM troops.[25] Throughout the civil war and up to this day, minority groups that are held in lower esteem within the Somali clan hierarchy and which often lack military protection have been particularly vulnerable to abuse and violence.

Causes of Continued Impunity

Despite the gravity and longevity of atrocities and war crimes punishment committed by different parties in Somalia, accountability has been elusive. The only exceptions are the punishment of Canadian peacekeepers for abuse of civilians during UNISOM and the two civil cases against Somalia's former Prime Minister, Gen. Mohammed Ali Samantar, and former NSS director of investigation, Col. Abdi Aden Magan, by the Center for Justice and Accountability, a US-based NGO.[26] The two cases were only made possible because the perpetrators lived overseas.

Several factors explain the almost complete absence of accountability for the atrocities outlined above. In Somalia there was no decisive or lasting military victory in the post-1991 period, and therefore no incoming regime to bring perpetrators to justice. Moreover, national governments established after 2000—including the current Federal Government—failed to establish effective executive and judicial institutions capable of stopping ongoing atrocities, let alone addressing past injustices. To make things worse, the international community for a long time enticed faction leaders to form governments of national unity or partnered with them in counter-terrorism operations, deliberately overlooking warlords' record of human rights abuses.[27] To this day, former warlords, Al-Shabaab, UIC and Ras Kambooni brigade commanders are recruited, appointed, or elected to top political and military positions within the Somali Federal Government without proper vetting.

Somali clan institution and loyalties also work against accountability of individual perpetrators. For example, Somali sayings guide clan members to extend protection to one another and to share both bounties and burdens. The saying 'hiil iyo hoo' literally means 'protection and care', reminding clan members to protect each other and to share wealth. The saying 'quud iyo qaaraan' translates to 'consumables and debts', advising relatives to share available resources and to discharge one's social obligations. Both these phrases are commonplace in clan politics.

Loyalty to the family and the absence of state protection led many to participate in the conflict, to shield perpetrators, and to excuse atrocities in the name of "clan".[28] As an interlocutor succinctly put it: "perpetrators are usually heroes of their respective clans."[29] At the same time, warlords and some of the elite consciously mobilized and instrumentalized clan identity for their own gain. The logic of collective political loyalty has subverted efforts to prosecute individuals without offending members of his or her clan. Moreover, the focus of Somalis' famed traditional dispute resolution is on restoring social relations, compensating victims' families, and avoiding further conflict escalation, rather than delivering justice or establishing right and wrong.[30]

For AMISOM perpetrators, article 54 of the mission of status agreement stipulates that AMISOM troops are immune from local jurisdiction. The governments of troop-contributing countries Uganda, Ethiopia, Kenya, Burundi, Djibouti, and Sierra Leone have rarely brought their soldiers to court for abuses during their mission in Somalia.[31]

These different factors, a long tradition of repressive and corrupt regimes and an inhospitable environment for human rights activists explain why even a meaningful discussion about addressing injustice in Somalia has so far remained elusive. In light of these concerns, many observers and interlocutors argue that the prosecution of perpetrators is likely to create more problems and conflict than it resolves. There is indeed ample reason for scepticism with regards to the possibility of implementing a transitional justice mechanism in the current-day Somali territories. This is why a political entity like Somaliland took the decision not to seek revenge against former Siad Barre officials, instead privileging a kind of strategic silence. This allowed former NSS officials to land posts in Somaliland administrations, including Dahir Riyale Kahin, who was appointed president of the breakaway Republic despite his involvement with abuses by the old regime.[32] While attempts at retributive justice in Somalia might backfire, there is no doubt that accountability needs to be strengthened dramatically in order to deter ongoing and future abuses, to individualize guilt, to pursue justice, to fulfil a moral obligation towards victims, and to expose the truth.[33]

Impacts and Costs of Impunity in Somalia

In many parts of Somalia, impunity and the near-certainty that abuses will not provoke legal consequences are part of the way in which political business is conducted.[34] Because impunity has become the norm, its negative impacts on peacebuilding, reconciliation, and state reconstruction are easily forgotten. In reality, the costs of impunity in Somalia are both real and considerable.

First, those who specialize in the use of violence—foreign and national security forces, armed opposition groups and clan militias—have little to fear for their transgressions. In the absence of proper vetting and oversight of national and AMISOM forces, perpetrators have no incentive to change their ruthless tactics *vis-à-vis* their opponents and civilians.[35]

Second, the unwillingness to punish authors of violence undermines state-building itself. As long as formal judicial institutions fail to hold criminals accountable, Al-Shabaab and other non-state groups are able to provide parallel justice.[36] While Al-Shabaab is unable to pacify territory, its courts provide local populations with effective, accessible and swift justice that is perceived to be less susceptible to clan meddling or corruption than state courts. In a situation of lawlessness and a dysfunctional justice system, even a harsh application of Islamic law becomes attractive.[37]

Third, weaker and minority clans' inability to obtain physical, legal and economic protection from the state puts them at the mercy of dominant clan groups. The latter continue to marginalize weaker groups and refuse to return assets stolen during the war or to pay compensation. Impunity thus indirectly radicalizes aggrieved parties that turn to radical groups for protection.

Fourth, physical atrocities and white-collar crime such as widespread corruption and embezzlement of public or donor funds are different in nature, but neither one of them is usually prosecuted.[38] Impunity in Somalia is systemic, ranging from war crimes to petty crime. In the absence of a push for more accountability of serious crimes, it is difficult to imagine how current programmes aiming to improve public finance management, accounting and other types of bureaucratic accountability can succeed.

Fifth, longstanding impunity in Somalia undermines global efforts to uphold justice and the international community's credibility. Since the early 1990s, the UN has repeatedly called for greater attention to and action against human rights violators.[39] However, the UN did not muster the political will to turn its own declarations into actual policy. Nor did it take the lead in lobbying Somali and other governments to halt impunity.

Conclusion

Halting impunity and fostering accountability needs to be a primary, not a secondary, priority for state-builders in Somalia. The continued impunity for political and war crimes undermines trust and reconciliation, radicalizes disenfranchised groups and undermines universal human rights. Rather than a conventional transitional justice effort, a more nuanced and comprehensive approach is necessary in Somalia, combining a mapping, more "backward"- and more "forward"-looking measures.

First, an extensive mapping of past abuses and atrocities as well as more in-depth research—both qualitative and qualitative—on Somali attitudes towards justice for past abuses are required. Second, the long overdue restitution of stolen assets and properties that continue to be illegally held by some groups must be addressed. Restitution should be part of broader inter-community conversations about the past that, ideally, produce apologies, compensation payments and forgiveness for past crimes. Third, in order to disrupt current impunity by Somalis and non-Somalis, the prosecution and punishment of individual perpetrators is an absolute must. This requires a double strategy of winning the support of community leaders, customary authorities and politicians in Somalia as well as influential external powers to endorse retribution for particularly egregious crimes and acts of violence. A politically savvy strategy is required to avoid popular backlash in the name of "clan" when seeking to hold particular individuals accountable. In the longer run, any attempt to foster redress and accountability will have to produce a moral and legal vocabulary and narrative that resonate with Somali conceptions of justice[40] rather than simply reproducing international judicial norms and practices.

Recommendations

The solution to Somalia's protracted human rights crisis will neither be quick nor easy. It requires a comprehensive, balanced and contextualized political and legal strategy that addresses past wrongs and discourages current human rights violators by increasing the costs and risks of their abuses.

Groundwork for Dealing with the Past

Somali government institutions, in particular the Ministry of Interior and Federal Affairs, in collaboration with rights and peace activists, religious leaders, customary authorities, intellectuals and the media to hold public consultations that raise awareness and lead to a strategy to end impunity. This strategy should not only be capable of addressing grievances; it also needs to be sensitive to reasonable fears and take into account the need for trust-building. Donors and local research institutions should undertake a comprehensive mapping of major human rights violations in Somalia in the past 30 years, in other words, from the Barre regime to warlords and Al-Shabaab and from UN peacekeepers to AMISOM. Such a mapping can draw on past UN mapping exercises (OHCHR) in, for example, Afghanistan, DRC, or Sierra Leone.

Legal and Constitutional Reform

The Somali Federal Government should overhaul formal judicial structures, both legal frameworks and actual practices, so that they can effectively respond to impunity and generate public confidence and legitimacy. Parliament should enact enforceable rules that allow tackling impunity. For instance, the ongoing constitutional review should refer to the need of addressing major atrocities and to improve the criminal justice system by enacting evidence-based and realistic rules to tackle impunity and corruption.

Immediate Steps to Halt Impunity

- Legislators should enact laws prohibiting perpetrators of genocide, war crimes or crimes against humanity from holding public office at all levels of the Somali Government.

- Somalia should accede to the Rome Statute to enable the International Criminal Court (ICC) to investigate and prosecute perpetrators that fall under its jurisdiction as per article five of the Statute.
- Foreign states should exercise universal jurisdiction to prosecute individuals in their territories who are suspected of violations of international law.
- The Somali Federal Government, the AU and the UN should pressure AMISOM contributing countries and their donors to implement human rights protocols, stricter oversight, compensation schemes and internal and external investigations.
- Donors should screen beneficiaries of their aid, including contractors, employees and other partners.

UNDERSTANDING LOCAL CONFLICT
AND DEVELOPING EFFECTIVE RESPONSES

ACHIEVING LOCAL RECONCILIATION
IN SOMALIA

Peace and Development Research Center

Authorship

A team of Peace and Development Research Center (PDRC) researchers developed this briefing paper with the assistance of an experienced consultant. Prior to the write-up of the paper, the researchers reviewed the literature, held focus group discussions, and conducted interviews with highly experienced and informed individuals.

Summary

Reducing violence and promoting social reconciliation demand sufficient understanding of the causes and contributors of conflicts. Drawing on its extensive experience in conflict resolution and community reconciliation, and based on more than a dozen consultations, PDRC identified the following widespread causes of conflicts and pillars of social reconciliation in Puntland and across Somalia.

Environmental decline and population growth have exerted pressure on already meagre resources. Access to and control of water sources and grazing lands have caused interminable conflicts among the pastoral population. In rural areas, there have been conflicts following the expansion of encampments over one-time grazing land. In urban areas, land grabbing and over-exploitation of limited economic opportunities have contributed to heightened tensions and the eruption of violent conflicts among communities.

Clan-based political dispositions in post-civil war Somalia have also contributed to political conflicts along clan, sub-clan, and even family lines across the country.

The absence of the rule of law, state enforcement mechanisms, and the abundance of weapons in civilian hands has meant that minor quarrels escalate into violent confrontations among groups, which then draw in their respective communities. Violent conflicts sometimes trigger revenge killings that perpetuate cycles of violence in towns and in the countryside.

In the past, Sharia-based customary laws, *xeer*, provided a dependable conflict prevention and resolution mechanism. Accordingly, traditional leaders and elders were the first to intervene should tensions emerge or conflicts break out. *Xeer's* moral, religious, social, and material enforcement instruments gave way in the face of the modern state (both colonial and post-colonial) mechanisms, although some rural communities continued to uphold *xeer* and the directives of traditional elders.

The collapse of the Somali state brought about a revival in customary laws as the principal mechanisms of conflict prevention and resolution. Nevertheless, the changed environmental, political and socio-economic conditions severely weakened their effectiveness and hampered their enforcement.

Relevant government authorities should seek to end the culture of impunity and take full responsibility for violence reduction, conflict resolution, and reconciliation, with civil society and the international community providing necessary support.

Under a functioning and effective regime of the rule of law, the state should spearhead the fair prosecution of crimes, the pursuit of social justice, and the preservation of the environment in order to ensure the material sustenance of communities and their harmonious coexistence.

Introduction

Devastated by vicious cycles of conflicts and prolonged communal strife, Somalia is now transitioning from "statelessness" to a period of reconciliation and state rebuilding. Nevertheless, the Somali crisis has grown increasingly intractable.

Somalis have generally eked a living out of a harsh physical environment. More than half of the country's current population[1] of 11 million depends on the continuous search for pasture and water. Because these nomadic populations rear goats, sheep, cattle, and camels in the severe weather and climatic conditions, water and pasture become critically important and have been the main sources of communal conflicts. Almost all of the major clan conflicts that took—and continue to take—place stem from disputes over access to and/or ownership of these crucial resources, in other words, water sources and grazing lands.

In the past, Somali nomadic populations depended on open-to-all water sources and grazing lands. The traditional leaders and elders resolved conflicts in accordance with customary laws (*xeer*) that were based on Islamic law, Sharia. While environmental deterioration, an increasing population, and a higher number of livestock led to incremental depletion of these resources, colonial and post-colonial states progressively eroded the supremacy of customary law. Overgrazing and lack of conservationist use of water resources triggered conflicts among the pastoralists themselves and between pastoralists, on the one hand, and small farmers, on the other. Meanwhile, the modern state collapsed allowing for *xeer* to make a forceful comeback, albeit with weakened enforcement mechanisms in the changed times and circumstances.

Although these drivers and dynamics of conflict and pillars of resolution and reconciliation apply throughout Somalia, this paper will focus on the northern parts of the country.

Drivers of Conflict

In order to develop a sufficient understanding of the causes and consequences of Somali conflicts, which is the basis for a successful reconciliation process, PDRC drew on its own extensive experience and research, and conducted new consultations with individuals and groups. We consulted more than a dozen informed members of society across various sectors: religious/traditional leaders, intellectuals, the business community, women, and youth. Many of the participants in this consultation exercise had, in various capacities, played an active part in local social reconciliation processes. PDRC researchers consulted them with the express goal of identifying patterns of conflicts and appropriate methods of violence reduction and local social reconciliation.

Accordingly, we identified conflicts both in the nomadic, rural settings, and in sedentary urban settings. The cause and scale of these conflicts differ, but they most often start as disputes over resources between individuals or small groups and eventually transform into perpetual cycles of contention and clashes among clans. Wherever they erupt, these conflicts have the tendency to traverse vast swathes of territory from rural to urban settings and vice versa.

Rural Conflicts

In rural settings, two main sources of conflict have been identified, especially among nomads: access to resources (water and pasture) and the establishment of new settlements in areas commonly used for grazing livestock. The former exists as one of the long-established, progressively intensifying causes of conflict among the nomadic population during their constant move in search for shrinking pasture and water sources. Competition for such increasingly scarce natural resources combined with a number of sociocultural factors invariably sets them on a collision course with one another.

In the early 1940s rural settlements emerged in the arid, water-scarce areas of the countryside, which had at least two effects. The establishment of rural villages reduced the distance for watering livestock and fetching water for human consumption. Such villages also consolidated the grazing lands or expanded the territorial reach of a traditional hamlet/encampment (usually of an extended family). Both the colonial and post-colonial states played some role either in helping manage such settlements or regulating the attendant disputes. Pre-civil war governments had, for example, decided settlements or villages should be at least 20 kilometres apart.

The rapid urbanization process after the civil war meant that these rural areas acquired greater agronomic and socio-economic importance. In the absence of state-managed regulatory regime, rival farmers and livestock herders haphazardly established new settlements (which is equivalent to land-grabbing in towns) irrespective of the impact on others. Rudimentary dugout water reservoirs, or *haro*, were replaced by more permanent cement-lined *berked*s both for human and livestock use. The consolidation of formerly makeshift encampments and hamlets into large rural settlements and villages negatively affected the environment.

Identified as a major issue of conflict in the rural areas, such settlements are no longer regulated by any authority and some have emerged too close to each other for the available resources to sustain them peaceably. They have affected the concentration and movement of human and livestock populations, disrupted the potential use of resources including watering points (boreholes, shallow wells and water reservoirs), and introduced new trade routes connecting to the main urban centres. The consequent economic opportunities have caused rivalry and competition that escalate to disputes among clans, and sometimes between communities. Countless communal conflicts of this nature have taken place throughout Somalia.

Communal conflicts are not confined to pastoral communities, as they have also occurred in coastal areas over fishing, and in temporary encampments over frankincense harvesting. In the absence of the rule of law, disputes over fishing and the collection of frankincense[2] gums have caused longstanding conflicts among communities, and both involve the systematic exploitation of employees because they are considered low-income occupations. In almost all disputes, generally over resources, disputants recourse to traditional mediation and Sharia rulings to settle them.

The individuals and groups that PDRC consulted in the preparation of this briefing paper identified some of the conflicts that erupted over the establishment of new settlements in northern Somalia, which then led to revenge killings: Ali Jibrail and Ali Saleban (Bari region in 2010–2012); Bahararsame and Omar Mohamoud (Mudug, Nugaal and Sool regions and Zone 5 of Ethiopia—1985–2015); Marehan and Dir (Galmudug in 2010–2013); Ahmed Kheyr and Reer Yoonis (Nugal region in 2010–2011); and the Kalshaale conflict (Habarjeclo and Dhulbahante, 2011–2012).

Conflicts in Towns

In respect to urban areas, the study identified two major sources of conflict: land grabs and politically motivated conflicts. In the past, the control, management, and use of public lands were in the hands of the Somali national government. Following the collapse of the government, rampant land grabbing became a critical source of social tension and conflict in the towns. This is relevant particularly in the main towns where the human population is on the rise due to demographic growth and the ongoing influx of internally displaced persons, paralleled by a continued rise of the cost of urban land.

In the absence of effective conflict resolution mechanisms, violence following disputes over plots of land incites the wider involvement of clans beyond the urban areas and poses threats to general security. The situation is aggravated by two factors: the proliferation of firearms in the hands of civilians, and the weakness or absence of the law enforcement institutions, particularly the police and the courts, in towns as much as in rural areas.

As a religious scholar[3] and dean of the law school at East Africa University pointed out, governments often opt to refer cases of homicide between civil servants or security personnel to religious scholars for resolution. Likewise, if security personnel kill an armed criminal in the line of duty, they are often referred to traditional elders, who then pass the case on to religious leaders for settlement and compensation. When authorities fail to prosecute such crimes and to protect their security personnel, it speaks to the weakness of the rule of law and creates a fertile environment for impunity.

Political Conflicts

Another major issue this study has identified is politically motivated conflicts, which typically start in towns and expand to draw in rural areas too. In post-civil war Somalia, power-sharing, hence access to coveted resources and distributive powers, has become clan-based. In Somalia, nearly all public positions, from local council to state and federal government positions, are allocated proportionally according to clan. Clans and sub-clans therefore either competed with each other or formed alliances to secure powerful positions in public leadership. Political power thus became intricately linked with clan membership or affiliation; consequent rivalries led to the mobilization of grassroots supporters in towns and the countryside.

Interviewees for this study pointed out that, relative to other issues, politically motivated conflicts are comparatively unfamiliar in traditional Somali society and their political history. The appearance of "democratically" elected governments based on clan distribution, under the influence of traditional elders, is a new phenomenon that came with local and international efforts to reconstitute the Somali state. Also, decision-making processes, which used to be conducted in simple ways, usually under trees, have transformed into a complex political arena, with individuals and groups of elders vying with opposing agendas.

Beyond the narrow individual or group levels, politically motivated conflicts have also involved regional states, which are also clan-based. The rivalries between Puntland and Galmudug and between Puntland and Somaliland are some examples. These conflicts tend to drag brotherly and neighbouring communities into fighting on opposite sides, transforming large areas along state borders into conflict zones.

Revenge Killings

In addition to the three major sources of conflicts described above, revenge killing in the Somali context is a major source of clan-based conflicts. It typically starts as a minor incident between two individuals or groups, but quickly escalates to devastating conflict between two communities along family and clan lines. As the participants in the consultation reported, the majority of revenge killings tend to drag on, sometimes for generations. Individual and communal sense of pride inflames the cycle of vengeful violence, creating permanent hostility and fear among communities. In addition, revenge killings often cause cross-border conflicts that involve states or regions.

The study identified revenge killing as a consequence of any one or more of the four indicated conflicts, as well as a cause of perpetuating the cycle of violence. In the past, revenge killings used to be largely limited to remote areas, distant from government control. As the country descended into civil war and the state collapsed, traditional systems prevailed and revenge killings crept back into society at large.

Traditional Conflict Resolution

Somalis have historically resolved conflicts among feuding communities through traditional mechanisms and structures that are coded in *xeer*, the religiously-inspired customary legal system. *Xeer* has been passed from generation to generation, and the majority of the population have used it to settle disputes before and after the arrival of European colonialism in Africa. Unsurprisingly, there are slight variations in the application of *xeer* across regions, largely depending on the elders and traditional leaders whose responsibility it was to interpret and enforce its framework, codes and procedures.

After the collapse of the government system in 1991, *xeer* has practically filled the void left behind by the Somali state and replaced the missing legal system. Thus, during the early years of statelessness, traditional elders and notable religious personalities assumed the role of local authorities. This set-up worked throughout Somalia at different levels and to varying degrees of effectiveness.

In the absence of a government role to deter, contain, and resolve conflicts, clan-delegated elders have come to play a vital role. These traditional elders are the first to intervene when individual and communal tensions rise or when conflicts break out. This is an established tradition, and elders are accepted as "peacemakers", capable of building bridges and managing dialogue to resolve conflicts. Usually, the neighbouring elders of warring communities contact their counterparts to broker a ceasefire, disengage militias and obtain the consent of the parties to mediate the conflict. Ultimately, elders from both sides are brought together to negotiate peace, assess the damages and agree on commensurate compensations. *Diya* (blood money) is usually exchanged in the form of camels, guns, horses and/or *godobtir* (the arranged marriage of a girl into another clan as part of compensation payment or an inter-clan peace settlement). The amount of compensation provided is proportional to the damage involved.

Nevertheless, the rule of customary law in the twenty-first century, in the midst of drastically transformed socio-political and environmental milieus, leaves much to be desired. The people consulted for this study emphasized the inadequate implementation of the agreed terms of ceasefires, settlements, and reconciliation. Failures to fully implement agreements and enforce rulings have resulted in a breakdown of trust, and escalation and persistence of protracted conflict. Among communities without a written tradition this has become a particularly salient problem because agreements are made orally and rulings rendered verbally. This means that it is sometimes unclear whether an agreement has been accidentally or deliberately violated.

All three prevalent legal systems in Somalia today (customary, Sharia and the secular) forbid impunity; but none have effected meaningful remedies. Combatting the culture of impunity is challenging for weak authorities and for traditional elders. To ensure sustainable and consistent violence reduction, relevant government authorities should spearhead and take full responsibility for violence reduction, conflict resolution, and reconciliation, with civil society and the international community providing necessary support. As an elder put it during our consultations, referring to the weakness on the part of the government: "If you see a 70-year old watering his camels, it is because he is lacking a 20-year old."[4]

Conclusion

Almost all communal conflicts in the Somali context arise from competition over and control of meagre natural resources, principally water and pasture. The fast depletion of these resources, expanding population and growing head of cattle have, in different forms, manifested themselves in tensions, rivalries, and conflicts. Hyper-politicization of clan identities, the gaping absence of the rule of law, a return to retrograde concepts and practices, and the militarization of society have all contributed to heightened tensions and inflamed conflicts.

In the past, conflicts that erupted between rural communities rarely affected the urban populations of the same feuding communities. Nowadays, however, violent conflicts quickly spread to urban areas, often with devastating consequences. Tensions spontaneously affect entire urban centres following news of an outbreak of conflict involving relatives in remote areas.

Previously, traditional conflict resolution mechanisms, presided over by elders and religious leaders, were effective in restoring peace. However, changed circumstances have limited the effectiveness of these mechanisms, and in the continued absence of the rule of law, a culture of impunity has flourished.

Reducing violence, averting conflicts, and ensuring post-conflict reconciliation require tackling the root causes of conflicts, combating the contributory factors, and addressing their combined consequences. In light of the limitations of the traditional means of achieving these goals, it is essential that government authorities take the primary responsibilities for these crucial tasks. Under a functioning and effective regime of the rule of law, the state should spearhead the fair prosecution of crimes, the pursuit of social justice, and the preservation of the environment in order to ensure the material sustenance of communities and their harmonious coexistence.

Recommendations

- Somali federal and regional authorities should coordinate with local communities and galvanize international support to address the environmental and material roots of conflicts. The support of governmental, non-governmental and humanitarian organizations would be especially helpful in combating environmental deterioration and its effects, including the shortage of water and pasture. Besides immediate relief to affected communities, assistance should include awareness raising, provisions of technologies and training on environmentally sound practices and resource conservation.
- The establishment and public respect of the rule of law are indispensable for the stabilization of communities and effective functioning of public institutions. Through awareness raising among local actors and the active role of traditional authorities, the new regime of law and order should aim to end the pervasive culture of impunity.
- State authorities should take over responsibility for—and serve as primary vehicles of—timely resolution of new and old conflicts, and champions

of local/social reconciliation. Federal Member States should achieve this through existing formal mechanisms and structures specifically mandated to avert social conflicts and promote reconciliation efforts. Regional states that are being formed—or will be formed in the future—should build such mechanisms into their constitutions and government structures.

- State governments, traditional authorities and civil society should set up joint anti-violence task forces to address conflicts and revenge killings. The scopes and tasks of such inclusive mechanisms can be determined on a case-by-case basis depending on the circumstances of each region.

- Federal Member State governments should allocate substantial annual budgets for continuous awareness raising, conflict resolution and social reconciliation. To ensure the sustainability of this endeavour, the bulk of the needed funds should be raised through regular contributions from the districts to the Federal Member State authorities.

- All armed government security personnel should receive specialized trainings on how best to diffuse tensions, intervene in active conflicts, and enforce ceasefires.

- The development of effective enforcement mechanisms is crucial because timely and diligent implementation of agreements helps reduce violence and promote reconciliation.

- There should be ongoing research into the diverse and evolving conflict dynamics, to identify lessons learned, and compile best practices of social reconciliation.

STATE-BUILDING AMIDST CONFLICT

THE URGENCY OF LOCAL RECONCILIATION

Najum Mushtaq

Authorship

Najum Mushtaq has covered Somalia since 2006 as a journalist, aid worker, and conflict analyst.

This briefing paper was commissioned by the Life & Peace Institute (LPI), an international centre that has supported community-led reconciliation processes across Somalia in partnership with Somali civil society since the early 1990s.

Summary

Rather than promoting grassroots reconciliation between various sets of clans engaged in localized conflicts throughout south-central Somalia, the process of forming Federal Member States has intensified and, in some cases, revived conflicts over regional boundaries, land use and political representation. The urgency to meet the New Deal benchmarks[1] led to what independent observers have considered to be contentious and hasty state-formation.[2] The 2013–17 period was marred by a surge in clan-based violence as discontent grew among those clans that felt they received an unfair deal.

Parallel administrations run by Al-Shabaab, which controls a considerable amount of territory in south-central Somalia,[3] exploited these clan grievances, and undercut reconciliation processes in recovered areas led by the Federal Somali Government (FGS) and AMISOM. The "4.5" clan-based election formula[4] also created new divisions over the question of identifying genuine and legitimate representatives of the various sub-clans within larger groups.

A review of conflict dynamics in South-West State (specifically Lower Shabelle), Galmudug and Hirshabelle highlights the above aspects of Somalia's bid to resurrect a semblance of state, along with its basic structures and institutions. A rise in acts of violence by Al-Shabaab, a defiant posture by other armed groups such as Ahlu Sunna Wal Jama'a (ASWJ),[5] and hostilities between the states of Galmudug and Puntland were also direct consequences of the 2013–17 state-building phase.

Throughout this largely top-down technocratic process, peacebuilding and long-term reconciliation processes to address local clan-based conflicts scattered across the political landscape have been pushed to the margins and do not receive due attention by national and international policy-makers. Ultimately, the lack of local reconciliation led to a flawed and fragile state-building process.

Introduction

The cornerstone of the state-building project in Somalia is stabilization and consolidation of regional states into a federal state, and reconciliation between and within these states. A key lesson from the nation-building experience in Somalia since 1991 is that local peacebuilding and state-building are "potentially contradictory processes—the former requiring the consolidation of governmental authority, the latter its moderation through compromise and consensus."[6] The two tracks are even seen as "separate and in some respects mutually antagonistic enterprises ... because the revival of a state structure is viewed in Somali quarters as a zero-sum game, creating winners and losers."[7] International mediation throughout has been top-down, with representation limited to clan-based elites under the "4.5" formula. As the focus of AMISOM and allied Somali forces is fixed firmly on defeating Al-Shabaab militarily, intra- and inter-clan conflicts—such as disputes between communities divided by civil war grievances, pastoralists in conflict with farmers or among themselves over water and pasture, and clans' territorial domains and boundaries—remain unaddressed or unresolved in the state-building enterprise.

These conflicts persist, and the state-formation phase of the 2013 New Deal's federalism plan encountered similar constraints. This paper presents an analysis of local conflict dynamics in Lower Shabelle in South-West State, Galmudug and Hirshabelle, where state-formation has fuelled old and new clan and territorial conflicts. The merger of regions with diverse clan compositions and opposing armed militias into one federating unit realigned long-standing power dynamics in newly-delineated member states, ignited competition for political positions and representation among clan elites and was further complicated by the role of avowed outsiders like Al-Shabaab, as well as other armed groups.

The paper attempts to describe the correlation between bottom-up local reconciliation and building a legitimate and viable federal state. It identifies key conflict actors in three regional states, and postulates general trends in local conflicts and how to address them. In addition to a review of the United Nations Assistance Mission in Somalia (UNSOM), African Union (AU) and peacebuilding organizations' documents and interviews with Somali peace-building practitioners and activists, the Somali local media and websites were extensively monitored for information. This paper also draws heavily from conflict analysis workshops with LPI and its Somali civil society partners as well as community representatives from these regions at a critical window of opportunity in the post-election period and in the run-up to a drawdown of AMISOM forces.

State-formation amid Festering Conflicts

As Somalia embarks on a decisive phase of state-building under a new leadership and a New Partnership for Somalia,[8] it is instructive to examine the relevance of the process to intra-Somali conflicts. These local divides, in most cases, precede the emergence of Al-Shabaab, and their dynamics will shape this phase of state resurrection as much as the new security architecture to defeat Al-Shabaab.

One of the direct consequences of the civil war is the large-scale continuous internal, and global, displacement of Somali people over the last three decades. This has not only caused human suffering and humanitarian emergencies, but also led to persistent and prolonged disputes and armed conflict over different clans' territorial domains and rights to access and control resources—both political and natural.

Internal migration, often induced by violence, has also made the question of clan representation highly contentious and, in many cases, intractable.

95

Unlike Puntland and Somaliland, the south-central region has a diverse clan composition and faces the prevalence of arms and militia. The problem has been aggravated by a war economy and the dilution and dismantling of the traditional clan structures and mechanisms for dispute-resolution. Despite its procedural utility in making progress towards meeting constitutional benchmarks, the "4.5" clan representation formula used for the elections fortifies clan divisions, despite their de jure unification under a single Somali state. The formula, which by its nature discriminates against minority clans, also undermines citizen-based nation-building.

Whilst it is commendable that the FGS and its international partners were able to put together diverse Federal Member States and navigate diverging clan-based positions in order to establish the beginnings of functional state structures, addressing local conflicts and reconciling mutually suspicious and hostile communities is an imperative for sustaining and building on the gains of the state-formation process.

South-West State and the Case of Lower Shabelle

Merged with Bay and Bakool regions as the South-West State, Lower Shabelle is the breadbasket of Somalia but has been in a state of violent turmoil for decades. The conflict between the Habar Gidir (sub-clan of the Hawiye) and the Biyamal (sub-clan of the Dir) in the Marka district is a representative case of clan feuds lingering on from the anarchic early years of the Somali civil war, when large-scale population movements occurred due to forced displacement and clan militias capturing new territories. The divide between the original resident clans of the land and settlers forms the conflict fault-line and Marka is one of several clan conflict hotspots present in the region.

The present conflict began in 1994, when clan militias loyal to Farah Aidid (Habar Gidir/Sacad, a leading actor in driving out the government of Siad Barre in 1991) captured the region, grabbed land and persecuted the local clans.[9] Since then the region has changed hands many times.[10] In 2012, AMISOM and Somali government forces dislodged Al-Shabaab, who had ruled the region since 2008 and still maintains control of much of the hinterland and strategic coastal towns. The war-time grievances and feuds between the Habar Gidir and Biyamal were thus reignited in 2013 as state-formation began under President Hassan Sheikh Mahamud.[11] Mahamud initially appointed Habar Gidir, especially Ayr, to key regional security and administrative posts. Based on the heterogeneous clan make-up in the area, local clans were unhappy with this arrangement.

Subsequently, fighting erupted between Biyamal and what members of this group referred to as "clans in government uniforms"—as the Habar Gidir militias are heavily represented in the Somali National Army's (SNA) Lower Shabelle units whilst the Biyamal armed factions in Marka are led by the Lower Shabelle People's Guard.[12]

As the 2016 regional and national elections approached, the FGS and AMISOM attempted to resolve clan conflicts in recovered areas of Lower Shabelle without much success. The cycle of violence in the area was temporarily halted when AMISOM and the FGS brokered a peace agreement between the two clan leaders in September 2016, before state and national elections were held in the region.[13] (The mediation efforts were made in the context of the establishment of the Interim South-West State Administration, in order to meet state-formation benchmarks.) The government integrated 150 Biyamal militiamen into the SNA, providing them with administrative positions, including the Commissioner of Marka. Yet, the peace agreement has never been fully fleshed out or popularized within the wider clan communities, nor has it received universal recognition from various factions within the two clans, as the process was regarded as neither inclusive nor representative of the wider communities and, as such, the two sides continue to fight.[14]

The Al-Shabaab Factor

The shadow of Al-Shabaab hangs heavy on Lower Shabelle's political and conflict landscape. The region has been a hub of its activities and the group often co-opts members of clans that maintain grievances against the FGS. Claims of collaboration between clans and Al-Shabaab are used in order to discredit rival groups. For instance, while under assault from members of the Habar Gidir clan, the Biyamal militia fled to coastal areas controlled by Al-Shabaab. This allowed the militia to regroup and regain ground against the Habar Gidir. However, they were accused of holding an alliance with Al-Shabaab. Subsequently, when in the process of setting up the regional state, the relationship between the Biyamal and the FGS improved, local clan dynamics shifted. As Biyamal factions began cooperating with and actively supporting AMISOM troops in anti-Al-Shabaab operations in December 2016, a Habar Gidir sub-clan complained that the rival clan was using AMISOM against them to settle scores.[15] Unsettled and protracted feuds such as this provide space for Al-Shabaab to exploit local disputes to gain political and military mileage in its war with AMISOM and pro-government forces.

Al-Shabaab also targeted and killed several elders from Lower Shabelle who participated in the federal parliamentary election on their return to their areas of origin,[16] which underscores the commitment and courage of those who took part in the political process despite grave threats. Nevertheless, the ability of Al-Shabaab to control territories and run parallel administrations is the biggest hurdle in both achieving local clan reconciliation (as the group downplays clan identities and claims to operate above and beyond clan) and building regional state institutions (as Al-Shabaab does not recognize the legitimacy of the FGS or the state-formation process). This challenge is cyclical, as a lack of meaningful reconciliation creates lingering grievances which are then exploited by Al-Shabaab, allowing them to gain legitimacy, control territory, and establish administrations.

Galmudug: Resurgence of the Galkayo Dispute

Formed through the merger of Galgadud and parts of Mudug, Galmudug is a Hawiye-dominated region and clan conflicts in this region are largely intra-Hawiye with sub-clans fighting over pasture and land.[17] Immediately after its formal inauguration in 2013, Galmudug's conflict with the Mejerteen-ruled Puntland over administration of the city of Galkayo also re-emerged after almost two decades of uneasy but relatively stable peace. The conflict escalated as "[state]-formation amplified the territorial and resource disputes of the city".[18] Puntland rejected the legitimacy of the new administration, believing that its constitution claimed the whole of Mudug region, including northern areas governed by the Puntland administration, which violated previous agreements between Puntland and the FGS, as well as the 1993 Mudug Peace Agreement that had partitioned volatile parts of the region during the civil war.[19] Whilst protests from Puntland and the international community forced Galmudug to withdraw its claim, intense armed conflicts between the two regional forces continued through 2016, resulting in scores of deaths and massive displacement.[20] Mutual suspicion and hostilities reached a high point in September 2016 when a US airstrike hit a Galmudug administration army base mistaken for an Al-Shabaab camp with information allegedly provided by Puntland authorities.

Whilst Galkayo has been the centre of the Galmudug–Puntland conflict, the competition for land extends across the Mudug region. For instance, community members in Puntland argue that clan boundaries in the countryside are known to all communities in the region. Nevertheless, since the creation of Galmudug, Puntland claims there has been a drive by the Sacad clan to grab land in the west of Mudug—land that Puntland argues is known to belong to the Majerteen and Leelkase clans.[21]

Although yet another ceasefire agreement was signed between the two administrations in Abu Dhabi in November 2016, there remains no initiative for genuine localized reconciliation, and dialogue over land and resource sharing, and the status of Mudug in a federal Somalia remains unresolved.

The ASWJ Factor

Galmudug is also the main stronghold of ASWJ, whose claim to political power poses substantial challenges for the region's stabilization. The pro-Ethiopian "moderate" militia, which has fought against Al-Shabaab for many years, notably sought recognition as a political group rather than being broken down into its clan components in the state-formation process, as this disaggregation could decrease its influence. During the Adado process,[22] ASWJ opened an offensive against pro-Somali government forces, which were supporting the presidency bid of Abdikarim Hussein Guled, an ally of then President Hassan Sheikh, and elected its own rival administration at a conference in Dhuusamareeb just days before Galmudug held elections in July 2015.[23] ASWJ refused to recognize the Galmudug administration and was later instrumental in ousting Guled in early 2017. Despite prospects under the Farmaajo administration for ASWJ's integration into the SNA, which in Galmudug at present consists mainly of Habar Gidir militia, ASWJ remains at odds with the regional administration. As an organized force with significant local political leverage and international support from Ethiopia, the group poses a "serious obstacle to creating a coherent administration in central Somalia if the FGS cannot negotiate successfully with the group."[24]

Forgotten Conflicts

The high-profile Galkayo dispute and wrangling for political power and representation among clan elites and militias such as ASWJ, notwithstanding their significance to the state-building process, divert attention from localized clan conflicts in Galmudug. For instance, little attention is paid to a longstanding three-way conflict over water and grazing land between sub-clans of Marehan, Habar Gidir and Dir in Balambale, Guriel and Herale, respectively. The conflict has been compounded by a series of revenge attacks over the years. Initiatives by local and international peacebuilding organizations to establish dialogue forums and bring the communities together for resolution of the conflict were held back during the state-formation process as clan leaders waited for its outcome before re-engaging in reconciliation activities, aware that their relative positions of power may change.

Overall, the formation of the Galmudug state has been deeply problematic from a peacebuilding perspective. The conflict with Puntland, in particular, was a throwback to civil war era clan-militia rivalries. The added element of ASWJ as an armed actor in regional politics means political instability continues to hinder Galmudug's consolidation into a functional Federal Member State. Questions regarding fairness in clan representation and inter-group disagreements, including ongoing accusations of interference in the affairs of the previous federal government, also overshadowed debates on structures for resource sharing and the potential for the establishment of legitimate mechanisms to settle clan conflicts.

Hirshabelle State

The constitutional requirement that two or more regions must merge to become a Federal Member State was particularly problematic for Hiran, as the region wanted to enter the federation on its own. The last of the Federal Member States to be formed in October 2016, Hirshabelle is a merger of Hiran and Middle Shabelle. The process was held back by clan disputes and led to the repeated postponement of the election schedule. Hiran's Hawadle elites were reluctant to join another region, as it is one of eight original constituent administrative units of Somalia and had maintained its territorial integrity throughout the civil war. The Abgal from Middle Shabelle and Galje'el, on the other hand, were in favour of the FGS-led negotiations. Initially, Hiran's Hawadle elders remained withdrawn from the negotiations over the selection of venue for talks, while the FGS, following substantive negotiations, succeeded in persuading a number of them to resume talks in Jowhar—also designated as Hirshabelle's capital. The role of the government in deciding sub-clan representatives and official appointments was also seen by the Hawadle as biased. Although the objections raised by the Hiran elders were not fully resolved by the end of the FGS-led process, a significant number of elders were convinced to return to the Jowhar conference while others remained absent. The perception that the FGS was favouring certain clans (mainly Hawiye-Abgal) from Middle Shabelle in administrative appointments and political decisions undermined and delayed the process.[25]

The lack of full representation was acknowledged by the international community, and after the completion of the process the UN Special Representative encouraged the new administration "to reach out to groups that were not part of the state-formation process and ensure that the interests of all communities are protected ... Reconciliation across Hirshabelle is critical."[26]

The Hawadle and elders from other smaller clans in Hiran accused the FGS of "pursuing the state formation process at the expense of reconciliation. We requested ... the government to support reconciliation among clans in Hiran before state-formation process starts and designate Beledweyne to host the conference. The government ... drove a wedge between the clans and divided them instead of uniting and reconciling them," read a letter written by three dissident elders.[27]

The nascent Hirshabelle government, which currently does not enjoy universal legitimacy, is already grappling with clan violence reigniting in and around Beledweyn. Violence in Hirshabelle—by clan forces such as the Galje'el-dominated Westland Militia and Hawadle-led Ma'awisley—has risen since 2012, with the state-formation period in particular displaying high rates of violence.[28] In this context, minority clans, when needed, have allied themselves periodically with Al-Shabaab, which has taken advantage of the clan grievances emerging during the state-formation process.

Conclusion

State-building without local reconciliation is hollow, and, in some cases, counterproductive. In a context where the central and regional governments and international military partners plan a concerted and decisive onslaught against Al-Shabaab, failing to address the question of historical grievances and disputes among different clans will undermine the overall implementation of the Security Pact. The contentious question of the boundaries of the Federal Member States is also dependent on how, and whether, the different clans in those areas are able to find common ground on addressing political and clan disputes while sharing available land and natural resources.

The process of establishing a credible and effective security sector also suffers in the absence of reconciliation and integration among the clans. Security forces must reflect the diversity of the regions in which they are deployed and not, as appears to be the case during this process, only rely on recruiting and deploying the dominant regional militia—an approach that creates grievances among clans that do not possess an armed militia, or are a minority in the region.

As the acrimonious experience of state-formation attests, local reconciliation must extend beyond putting in place state assemblies and district administrations. In order to be successful, it requires dialogue among people willing to face the past, agree on mechanisms to address their mutual grievances and share common resources, and to have structures in place to mediate and adjudicate in case of disputes. In this sense, local peacebuilding and establishing and strengthening security and judicial institutions should have a symbiotic relationship: neither can be achieved or sustained in isolation from the other.

Recommendations

- *FGS, international stakeholders*: Recognize and commit to long-term community-based dialogues for truth, justice and reconciliation among clans. Equal weight should be placed on trust—between communities, and between communities and security providers—as on the technical capacity of institutions. Accordingly, the allocation of resources for bottom-up peacebuilding should match the international community's latest commitments to top-down building of political and security sector institutions.
- *FGS*: Formulate robust land use and rights policies which provide for mechanisms to monitor, document and address land disputes across south-central Somalia, especially in areas where the Federal or Member State administrations have already established strong control.
- *FGS, FMS*: Create conditions for universal enfranchisement by 2021. If, as in 2016, universal franchise is not practicable, ministries should consider other alternatives to the formula, such as proportional representation for multi-region political parties and broadening the electoral college base beyond clan representatives.
- *Regional stakeholders, African Union-United Nations Mission*: Decisions on the future of AMISOM and an exit strategy should take into account an assessment of its role—constructive or contentious—in influencing local clan conflicts.
- *FGS, international stakeholders*: Align interventions that focus on institutional strengthening with those that explore routes for local-level conflict transformation, by emphasizing, and providing space for, learning, exchange and reflection among government, international non-governmental organizations, and donor stakeholders.
- *International stakeholders*: Support influential actors, such as AMISOM, to understand fault lines within local communities, key stakeholders and con-

flict dynamics, in order to improve their ability to avoid exacerbating tensions, and forge more sustainable local peace. Equally, seek to understand the positions, interests and needs of armed groups with political agendas, including Al-Shabaab and ASWJ, in order to facilitate peaceful participation in a political process. An understanding of longstanding grievances and dynamics are critical to a holistic approach to countering violent extremism.

- *FGS, international partners*: Adopt a consensus-based and conflict-sensitive model for the constitution and organization of local, regional, and national security services, and ensure cross-clan composition of not only the SNA but also regional and district police forces.

SUPPORTING LOCAL RECONCILIATION

LESSONS LEARNED ACROSS THE UN SYSTEM

Adam Day

Author

Adam Day is the Senior Policy Adviser at the Centre for Policy Research in UN University Tokyo. He has a decade of experience within the UN, most recently as the Senior Political Adviser to MONUSCO (DRC), and previously in UNSCOL (Lebanon), UNMIS (Khartoum), UNAMID (Darfur), and in both DPKO and DPA Headquarters. He holds a JD from UC Berkeley and a Masters in Law and Diplomacy from the Fletcher School of Law and Diplomacy, and has authored several publications on international and human rights law.

Summary

This paper offers lessons from a wide variety of UN engagements in local conflict settings, with a view to informing the UN Somalia mission's strategic planning.[1] Based on a comparative review, the paper lays out the essential elements of a successful strategy for local conflict resolution, including analysis; conflict-sensitive design; communications; targeted approaches for enablers and spoilers; capacity development; confidence-building measures; partnerships; and national/local ownership.[2] It recommends that the Somalia team incorporates these elements into the planning, implementation and assessment of its local conflict management strategies, and to embed local conflict resolution into a broader national strategy for Somalia.

Introduction: Local Dynamics, National Implications

Though UN missions are generally tasked to respond to national and regional crises, these are often intimately linked with local conflicts and/or centre-periphery relations between the state and its people. In fact, there is strong evidence showing that local dynamics are both a product of and contributing factor to the national political trajectory of conflict-affected countries.[3] From the top down, national issues manifest themselves locally, whether by national actors stoking inter-communal tensions, state-level decisions impacting groups or communities,[4] or a broader conflict that exacerbates existing societal divisions.[5] From the bottom up, localized violence can cause broader instability and undermine national peace processes,[6] dramatically reducing the prospects for peacebuilding and recovery.[7] In crises from Afghanistan to South Sudan to Libya, it has become clear that engagement with actors at the national level alone is insufficient to resolve local conflicts, and that local dynamics constitute an immediate and longer-term factor in sustainable peace. The following paper examines how the UN has engaged in widely differing forms of local conflict management efforts,[8] draws lessons from past attempts to link national and local processes, and offers specific recommendations for the UN's efforts to support conflict management at the local level in Somalia.

Many Forms of Local Conflict, Many UN Mandates for Reconciliation

Local conflict can take on many forms but broadly falls into three overlapping categories: (1) identity-based conflict (including inter-communal, interethnic, sectarian); (2) resource-driven conflict (including control of trafficking routes, illicit trade, land and natural resources); and (3) politically-driven conflict (mainly over governance structures and institutions).[9] These categories often combine in a particular conflict setting and can be influenced by regional dynamics as well, but there tends to be a dominant driver or root cause which the UN seeks to address through its conflict management efforts.

Some peace operations have been explicitly tasked with addressing local-level conflict as part of their protection of civilians mandates, such as in South

Sudan, Darfur and the Central African Republic (CAR).[10] Others, including the missions in Mali, Côte d'Ivoire and (implicitly) the Democratic Republic of the Congo (DRC), link local conflict resolution to broader political processes.[11] The UN's local conflict management role has variously been tied to extension of state authority,[12] social cohesion,[13] and reform of security and rule of law institutions.[14] Even where no explicit Council mandate exists, UN peace operations,[15] UN agencies,[16] and UN regional political offices[17] have often taken the initiative to engage at the local level as part of their good offices mandate aimed at reducing the risk of violent conflict. While there is no single approach to local conflict resolution in these widely differing situations, recent UN experiences underscore the key elements and capacities necessary for a successful local conflict resolution strategy.

Essential Elements for a Local Conflict Resolution Strategy: Lessons from the Field

This paper identifies the following elements[18] to be considered when developing a strategy: (1) analysis and identification of key actors, root causes and triggers; (2) conflict-sensitive design of reconciliation processes; (3) communications; (4–5) targeted approaches for enablers and spoilers; (6) capacity development; (7) confidence-building measures; (8) partnerships; and (9) local/national ownership. These should be part of a broader strategy that takes into account national political objectives and structural factors related to the local dynamics.

1) Analyse Local Conflict from the Ground Up as a Whole-of-Mission Effort

Despite the growing trend to mandate UN peace operations with local conflict management, it is typically treated as a second-order issue, insufficiently connected to a broader mission mandate. As a result, missions rarely dedicate sufficient resources to understanding local dynamics. A particular shortcoming is the tendency to outsource analysis of local issues to civil affairs in peace operations,[19] without reconnecting such analysis to the mission's strategy. In terms of mapping, this tends to result in an exclusive focus on local conflict drivers in isolation from national-level issues.[20]

However, where missions have developed analytical capabilities based on strong local sources that are linked to broader mission thinking, the result has been positive. MINUSMA's local mapping in Mali includes analysis on links between inter-communal conflicts and non-state armed groups involved in the national-level conflict. MINUSCA's "Flashpoint Index" assesses the extent to which local dynamics in the Central African Republic could pose a risk to civilians, including a useful tasking out to relevant sections for a response. MONUSCO's conflict mapping identifies where local dynamics in eastern DRC could be linked to electoral tensions, and in 2016 this included an analysis of how the electoral timeline could generate "hotspots" at the local level. MONUSCO also developed a community alert network that allows communities in remote areas to transmit protection alerts and incidents to the mission and key partners for response. This local-driven analysis, along with surveys of local perceptions on security and justice, provides a strong sense of how local dynamics interact with national institutions.[21] In several settings, having a dedicated community liaison function has proven invaluable for local reconciliation work, including in Mali, the DRC and Colombia. Across the board, the most salient lesson is that missions need deep, country-based analysis that draws on local knowledge.

Key questions to ask when mapping conflict: What national events could trigger local violence, and vice versa? What actors are capable of instigating violence, and what are their links to local communities? How is the state a potentially positive/negative actor at the local level (for example, absence of state institutions leading to lack of rule of law, predatory state actors fueling conflict to access natural resources)? Incentives of stakeholders?

In addition to the overarching need for country-specific knowledge, dedicated technical expertise is a crucial yet often overlooked aspect of understanding and engaging at the local level. UN peace operations rarely employ experts in natural resources, climate change, livelihoods, land tenure issues,[22] or in micro-economic issues frequently at the heart of local disputes. In some cases, the expertise exists within the UN system (UN Habitat, UNDP,[23] UNEP,[24] and FAO, for example), but these are typically underutilized. Where there are gaps, missions should be flexible in creating positions to fill them, including by relying on outside expertise,[25] and several UN officials pointed to the importance of having dedicated expertise in the realm of political-economic analysis.[26]

2) Conflict-Sensitive Design: A Do-No-Harm Approach to Conflict Resolution

Every intervention has the capacity to cause unintentional consequences, and there are important lessons to be drawn from other UN settings when designing a do-no-harm approach to local conflict resolution.[27] UNICEF has developed a checklist for such an approach, which could be adapted positively to a broad range of local conflict settings.[28] Other UN agencies have also developed "do-no-harm" approaches to conflict resolution, which include steps related to conflict analysis, identifying potential negative externalities associated with an intervention, developing options for addressing the negative impacts, and testing potential intervention alternatives.[29]

In designing a conflict-sensitive engagement, it is crucial to identify factors at three different levels: (1) structural drivers of conflict, such as longstanding interethnic tensions, disputes over geographic boundaries, or natural resources; (2) institutional factors, such as power allocation within municipalities, control of local institutions by particular groups, or monopolies over trade routes; and (3) individual agents, such as local chiefs, political leaders, or armed groups, who can act as spoilers.[30] A well-designed intervention tends to work across these levels. For example, UNAMA's 2013 local reconciliation effort between the Kamdesh and Koshtoz communities in Nuristan province of Afghanistan was principally geared at the longstanding intertribal grievances in the century-old conflict, but also took into account the increasing polarization between the communities as a result of Taliban affiliations in more recent years (thus linking a structural issue with an institutionally-driven one).[31]

Interventions should also take into account the potential negative impacts that UN-supported processes could have on security, political and socio-economic dynamics. MONUSCO's 2016 initiative to address longstanding inter-communal tensions between the Hutu and Nande communities in eastern DRC combined engagement with the respective Hutu and Nande parliamentary caucuses in Kinshasa with support to local reconciliation conferences in Goma, thus bringing together key state-level actors and institutions with local ones. The initiative took place in a context of national political instability, with relatively pro-government Hutu parliamentarians and a strongly anti-government Nande caucus; a range of ongoing development and stabilization projects in both communities; and widespread displacement of Hutu populations in the broader North Kivu area due to insecurity and inter-communal tensions. There was a risk, therefore, that the UN's involvement would be seen as taking political sides, or that development projects might be unevenly distributed amongst the communities. In response, MONUSCO took these political, socio-economic and security considerations into account in its process of identifying participants for local conferences, reconciliation processes and future development projects.[32]

Finally, and in the context of a do-no-harm approach, the UN can play a role in compelling the parties involved in a reconciliation process to adhere to international humanitarian and/or human rights law. For example, a group of tribes in Iraq's Anbar province asked the UN to endorse a locally brokered agreement to facilitate the return of displaced people, but the agreement contained provisions that were likely to be in contravention of international laws governing collective punishment and due process. UNDP convened the key local leadership, the governor of Anbar, the head of Iraq's National Reconciliation Commission,[33] UNHCR and UNAMI, and expressed a unified view that the UN could not endorse the agreement as it stood. While the parties were not able to reopen negotiations, they did reach subsequent agreement on how the terms would be interpreted, bringing it more in line with international law.[34]

3) Communications at the Heart of a Strategy

Communications are frequently considered a second-tier element of the UN's reconciliation work. Instead, messaging and public information should be considered integral to the strategy.[35] Efforts by UN peace operations to support communities and local leaders to play a direct role in disseminating messages and/or outcomes of reconciliation processes have proven effective in many settings. In Mali's Mopti region, MINUSMA supported a conference between farmers and nomadic herders in 2015. The resulting agreement was disseminated by local civil society actors involved in the process (rather than MINUSMA), which appears to have helped allay local fears that the UN might have sided with either the farmers or the pastoralists.

Communications should: (1) frame the conflict in terms that keep the door open to reconciliation; (2) disseminate information about the negative impact of conflict, and the potential gains if reconciliation takes place; (3) identify common objectives among conflicting parties; and (4) credibly push back on biases.

Another important area concerns the vocabulary used to describe a conflict setting. The UN should be careful not to reinforce biases and should instead seek to frame the conflict in terms that lead towards resolution. Examples of bias reinforcement include "the Tuareg rebels" in Mali,[36] conflict between "Africans and Arabs" in Darfur,[37] "ISIS families" in Iraq,[38] and "Islamist Allied Democratic Forces" in eastern DRC.[39] Similarly, the UN should be careful in how it refers to government actors, avoiding terminology that could damage its impartiality.[40]

At the same time, the UN should be cognizant of the need for some local reconciliation processes to remain out of the public eye. A case in point is work undertaken by UNDP in Iraq's Anbar province since 2015. Pursuant to a reconciliation process, UNDP facilitated the return of people displaced by violence. Given the poor relationship between Baghdad and Anbar, and the highly contentious political issues surrounding the participation of some actors in the so-called Islamic State and other armed group activity, UNDP facilitated discreet meetings of a broad range of actors, including the local leadership, the governor of Anbar, and relevant UN agencies, without any engagement with the press.[41]

4) Gendered Conflict, Gender-Sensitive Reconciliation

Local conflict, like armed conflict more generally, has a disproportionate impact on women and girls, who remain far more vulnerable to gender-based and sexual violence. In analysing conflict dynamics and their gendered impacts, three related areas of focus should be considered: (1) the gendered nature of the causes of conflict; (2) the gendered impact of conflict; and (3) the gendered dimensions of peacebuilding (the distinct roles of both women and men in longer-term peace processes).[42] The UN has developed comprehensive guidance for how this can be incorporated into the analysis of conflict settings, which can form a basis for a local reconciliation approach.[43]

Women can play a specific role in both driving and solving local conflict, and are often uniquely placed to facilitate local reconciliation.[44] For example, following a serious escalation of violence in 2014 between the Bafulero and Barundi communities in Uvira, eastern DRC, MONUSCO facilitated a confidence-building workshop with women that contributed to a reduction of violence between the two communities. Similarly, in Darfur, groups of women called *hakamat* ("war singers") were frequently cited as instigators of inter-communal violence in Darfur, mobilizing young men to engage in reprisal attacks against other communities. UNAMID engaged these groups directly as part of its local conflict management strategy by leveraging their influence toward a peaceful resolution of disputes.[45] There are numerous other examples of the crucial role women in particular play in reconciliation from Rwanda[46] to Yemen,[47] with a clear consensus that conflict management and peacebuilding processes should identify the different impacts and roles for women.[48]

5) Targeted Approaches for Youth: Stopping the Mobilization Cycle

Local conflict frequently depends on the new mobilization of fighters, often drawn from disaffected youth populations who are economically and/or politically marginalized.[49] A lesson across a broad spectrum of local conflict settings concerns the need to address youth in a targeted manner, both as potential spoilers but also as important positive actors in local conflict resolution. This often involves non-UN entities that are better attuned to the needs of this population and able to engage youth directly.

Programmes that offer youth a place in society have the dual benefit of cutting off the mobilization cycle and strengthening the communities where they live. One effective approach has been to provide fora for youth to gather and build a sense of community, through sports or organized dialogue. Examples of this include youth clubs for conflict-affected youth in Masisi (eastern DRC),[50] youth "peace camps" dedicated to conflict resolution in Lebanon,[51] a national youth training in Liberia geared at creating "peacebuilding ambassadors", training programmes geared at youth affected by conflict in South Sudan,[52] and a province-wide youth leader forum in Jawzjan, Afghanistan, focused on reducing the ability of insurgent groups to recruit disenfranchised, unemployed youth.[53]

6) Capacity Development: Building Local Conflict Management Skills

Comparative studies of local conflict resolution have demonstrated that a lack of negotiating capacity on the part of those involved is a key factor inhibiting positive outcomes.[54] If a party lacks negotiating capacity, it may be reluctant to enter a reconciliation process. Likewise, talks involving undisciplined parties can fail to produce positive outcomes and can even exacerbate tensions. Building the capacity of local interlocutors, including government actors, to constructively engage in a reconciliation process is often a critical first step.[55] UNAMA had some success in this in 2013 by conducting mediation, negotiation and conflict resolution skills workshops with local leaders. This kind of capacity-building can also spill over into skills needed to consolidate a reconciliation process and show a "peace dividend."

7) Confidence-Building Measures: The Resource Requirement

Beyond facilitating talks, UN support to confidence-building between parties can take a variety of forms, including military separation,[56] joint patrolling,[57] shared financial incentives,[58] and infrastructure investments.[59] An important lesson is for the UN to have sufficient (and sufficiently flexible) financial and logistical resources to provide tangible confidence-building measures in a timely manner. This can be achieved directly in the budgeting for a peace operation, but given the unpredictability of local peace processes it might be necessary to establish externally funded tools to ensure available funds.[60] For example, UNDP supported a skills training programme in Darfur where women from the Massalit tribe trained IDPs in the local camp in food processing skills. The training itself in this case was part of the local reconciliation. Across many different settings, there is a clear lesson: reconciliation should be about more than words—it should result in concrete changes on the ground for the lives of the affected people.[61] Providing sufficient funds and expertise in this area of capacity development is often critical to a reconciliation strategy.

The UN can also play a central role in framing a reconciliation process, often by introducing confidence-building measures as a sort of built-in reward for the participants. In the Misrata-Tawergha conflict in Libya, for example, one of UNSMIL's main contributions was to create a framework for negotiations between the sides that included the basic principles (accountability, reparations, restoration for victims, etc.) but also the provision that initial reparations would go principally to the Misratan side. The purpose of this was to make the return of Tawerghans to Misratan communities more palatable for the Misratan leadership and give the negotiators something tangible to take home to their constituency.[62]

8) Partnerships with State and Other Actors

In every conflict, primary responsibility for its resolution rests with the host government—this also applies to local-level conflicts. Therefore, it is critical that UN-supported processes are able to leave behind sufficient state and local capacity and commitment to sustain the peace. Ideally, this would involve partnership with the government, local leaders and civil society from the outset. However, partnerships can be fraught: local organizations can be seen as biased,[63] governments are often direct or indirect parties to local-level conflict, and even the UN is sometimes seen as a less-than-impartial arbiter.[64] A key consideration in the context of partnerships is to ensure that UN support is not seen as partial, and that the UN finds the best-placed actor to facilitate reconciliation. In some situations where the UN is not best suited to visibly lead, discreet modalities of support to local organizations—including quietly administered trust funds and/or logistical support—may be the best course of action.[65] Provision of logistics support is another method of helping move a process along without being visibly tied to its substance.[66] In Mali, where Fulani radicalized youth were critical to reconciliation processes but difficult for the UN to access, MINUSMA partnered with the Centre for Humanitarian Dialogue to gain access and deepen their understanding of the situation.[67]

In addition to external partnerships, UN actors should align their efforts for managing local-level conflict. This tends to lead to better outcomes, while also reducing the risk of forum shopping by the conflict parties. In the case of Anbar province in Iraq, a UNDP-led process to support tribal reconciliation in 2016 benefited from the inclusion of UNHCR, UNAMI and other UN entities, particularly when it came to establishing a shared understanding of the underlying conflict issues and providing a coherent message to the parties.[68]

9) Linking the Local with the National

Linking local-level conflict resolution to the national level is critical for the sustainability of the outcome. This can be because government funding is necessary for the longer-term implementation of the process,[69] state policies affect the relationship between the parties,[70] or because the government is a direct player in the conflict.[71] Often, structural causes of local-level conflicts require national decision-makers to resolve the issue. In designing a local reconciliation approach, UN actors should identify specific ways in which the national level will be involved, including commitments to projects in conflict-affected areas,[72] identification of government focal points to follow up on local agreements,[73] legislation aligned with local agreements,[74] police and judicial capacity to address past crimes,[75] and/or public statements by state actors in support of locally brokered outcomes.

Local conflicts are also often linked to a lack of national resources dedicated to the periphery, ineffective or predatory governance, or an unequal distribution of goods from the central state.[76] While it is important to link a local process with a national set of institutions, it is equally crucial to design national peace processes in ways that will deliver to the peripheries. Building specific commitments towards decentralization into national peace processes is often critical to sustaining local-level peace beyond the immediate local ceasefire agreement and commitment to peaceful coexistence.[77]

Conclusions

Any national political process for Somalia will need to be supported from below by a locally-driven one; equally, the national peace process for the country should contain specific provisions to sustain locally-brokered agreements and build strong institutions in the periphery. Experience has shown that the UN can play a constructive and central role in local peace efforts, but only when it is able to bring together the above elements into a coherent strategy.

Importantly, local conflict resolution cannot be prepared independently of the other aspects of the UN's involvement in a conflict setting. Placing local conflict within a broader strategy that includes human rights, security, development, and humanitarian and political engagement, is crucial for the success of the UN's approach in the country. Ultimately, local conflict resolution must be driven by a theory of change across a country's society and various communities, one which articulates how the people and institutions will work together to address deeply-rooted patterns of violence.

Recommendations: Towards a Strategy for Somalia

UNSOM should incorporate the above essential elements into the preparation, design and implementation of a cross-cutting local conflict resolution strategy. Steps include:

1. Develop (and fund) sufficient capacity on the ground to produce strong, cross-cutting conflict analysis based on frequent, direct contact with local actors, informing planning and policy;
2. Draw on subject-matter analysts on key issues related to conflict dynamics in Somalia (land tenure, local governance, inter-communal dynamics, decentralization, and so on);
3. Institute a "do-no-harm" checklist to guide development of a conflict-sensitive strategy, with due focus on protection of civilians;[78]

4. Develop a communications strategy integral to the local reconciliation process, and identify actors who will disseminate the outcome;
5. Include specific gender- and youth-based approaches within the strategy;
6. Budget for both capacity development and confidence-building measures to accompany a local reconciliation process;
7. Identify early state, local and international partners who will support the reconciliation process from the outset into follow-through processes, and look for concrete ways to hold them accountable for its implementation;
8. Identify early national-level elements (laws, institutions, actors) that will need to be involved in a local reconciliation effort, include specific steps for engaging them and addressing any of their constraints; and
9. Imbed the local reconciliation strategy in a broader UN-wide approach to conflict in Somalia, with clear roles and responsibilities articulated across the UN family and its partners.

LOCAL RECONCILIATION IN SOMALIA

THE PROSPECTS FOR SUSTAINABLE PEACE

Abukar Sanei and *Mohamed A. Omar*

Authors

Abukar Sanei is the Executive Director of the Centre for Policy Analysis & Research (CfPAR). He has authored several publications on peacebuilding and state-building in Somalia.

Mohamed A. Omar is a Research Associate for CfPAR, whose research focus is the role of civil society in peacebuilding in Somalia.

Summary

The last Somali central government was overthrown in 1991 due to grievances among those who felt they were marginalized from the decision-making process. The same grievances have driven the civil war that started in 1991 and continues to this day. To bring stability to Somalia, genuine reconciliation at the local level is vital. This briefing paper addresses the mechanisms and prospects for local reconciliation.

The briefing paper maps currently active and "silent" conflict areas. Gaalkacyo, Galmudug, and Marka are the active conflict areas; the "silent" conflict area is Benaadir. The Gaalkacyo conflict is about resource sharing as the city is divided between Puntland and Galmudug. The conflict in Galmudug is between the Galmudug administration and Ahlu Sunna Wal Jama'a (ASWJ) and requires negotiations with a view to power sharing. In Marka, the conflict is about resource sharing between the clans in the region. There are grievances in Benaadir, which have never been resolved, and if not addressed, they could trigger violence in Mogadishu at any time.

To identify mechanisms for reconciliation, we carried out a survey in which 114 people participated and conducted three in-depth interviews with current and former officials. To resolve grievances, 59 per cent of survey respondents stated that viable options are: creating a format for power sharing, integrating the security forces, using the media to promote peace, and including women and youth in the reconciliation process. Also, 44 per cent of respondents supported the establishment of a Truth and Reconciliation Commission (TRC), and ending impunity by establishing an effective system of local justice.

The briefing paper proposes some practical policy recommendations on local reconciliation to the Federal Government of Somalia (FGS), Federal Member States, and the partners from the international community.

Introduction

In its basic terms, reconciliation is an attempt to reconstruct the social fabric of fractured societies and rebuild state institutions. The civil war among clan factions in Somalia created enormous grievances among the Somali population. Thousands of Somalis lost their lives due to the civil war, sustained physical injuries, or suffer from post-traumatic stress disorder.

Grievances that led to the overthrow of the last central government of Somalia in 1991, and the subsequent civil war, have continued since then. Reconciling such a divided society, marked by power asymmetries, is extremely complex. Ultimately, Somalia's overall peace and security depends on genuine and inclusive locally-led reconciliation, supported by national and international actors.

This briefing paper begins with a brief look at conceptual frameworks of conflict transformation in war-torn societies. Second, the paper maps where the conflicts are currently taking place, and briefly addresses past efforts at local reconciliation. Third, the report analyses the results of an online survey conducted by CfPAR on the mechanisms that can be established for local reconciliation. We also conducted three interviews in Mogadishu with current and former government officials.

Limitations

This briefing paper is limited to the actors, steps and mechanisms for local reconciliation in Galmudug, Hirshabelle, Jubbaland, Puntland, and South-West, although at present there are no severe conflicts in Hirshabelle and Jubbaland. Two regions are not addressed in this briefing paper: Somaliland, the north-western region of Somalia, and the "disputed area" of Sool, Sanaag and Ceyn.

Benaadir region, which hosts the capital Mogadishu, was not covered in the survey, but was covered in our analysis and interviews. This is because residents of Benaadir come from all regions of Somalia, even though some communities may claim the "ownership" of Benaadir.

Conceptual Framework

This paper takes the view that there are three levels of conflict transformation in war-torn societies. The first category is the top leadership, which includes political leaders. The second category is the mid-range leadership that comprises ethnic, clan, religious, and regional leaders, as well as civil society actors. The third category is the grassroots level, which includes community leaders.[1] Reconciliation, which is an integral part of peacebuilding, can be a top-down undertaking where the political elite leads the process. It can also be a bottom-up process, where the grassroots leaders take the lead. The process can also be inclusive, where all leadership levels play a role.

Mapping Current Local Conflicts and Actors

The continuation of armed conflict in Somalia is due to a combination of external and internal factors including a colonial legacy, military dictatorship, and warlord competition for resources and power. Due to the absence of state institutions that can enforce the rule of law and distribute resources equally, allegiances to clan/tribal interests gain in strength, and competition over resources can be considered as one of the major factors fuelling mistrust.

We identify three major active conflict areas, and one "silent" conflict area in Somalia today. The first area is Gaalkacyo, a city divided between Galmudug and Puntland regional governments. The second area is Galmudug, where the regional administration and Ahlu Sunna Wal Jama'a (ASWJ) compete for power. The third area that is still facing conflict is the city of Marka, which falls within South-West State. The "silent" conflict area is Benaadir. By "silent" we mean that as the clans have not genuinely reconciled yet, violent conflict could erupt in Mogadishu at any time.

The conflict in Galmudug State has its roots in Somalia's colonial legacy when Italy divided Mudug and drew lines between the Daarood and Hawiye clans. This was exacerbated by the division of the city and its key revenue sources—including the airport and main market—between the two main clans in 1993.[2] In recent years, violent conflict has been triggered by the establishment of a federal system, led by the FGS under former President Hassan Sheikh Mohamud. President Hassan Sheikh Mohamud's administration intervened considerably in the Galmudug state formation process, which contributed to violent conflict between Galmudug and Puntland.[3] In addition, during the state formation of Galmudug, the FGS prevented some clans from exercising their political rights.

In Lower Shabelle, there are two main actors in the region's conflicts: the militants of Biyamaal, a sub-clan of Dir, and Ceyr, a sub-clan of Habar-Gidir. Moreover, since 2006, the region has been characterized by unstable power relations; a situation in which different players have fought each other for control of resources and strategically important areas.[4] Clashes between the two rival clans have been reported recently. In early June 2014, local officials reported that "fierce clashes between the two warring militias caused at least 40 people killed and scores injured with another 250 displaced as citizens are fleeing their homes."[5] Far more people were displaced by the violence: "from January 2015 to May 2016, over 40,000 people were internally displaced from Lower Shabelle."[6]

In Mogadishu, people have witnessed a bitter war, especially between the militias of Abgaal and Habar-Gidir clans, two major Hawiye sub-clans. In the early 1990s, the city was divided between the North and South, followers of Ali Mahdi and Mohamed Farah Aidid, respectively. As of today, the two clans are neither at peace nor at war with each other. The conflict between the two groups is in a "silent" mode. Additionally, due to the war between Abgaal and Habar-Gidir militias in 1990s, members of minority clans, who have been living in Mogadishu for centuries, feel that they are victimized, with their properties still in the hands of the militias.

Past Experience of Reconciliation

For almost two decades, the international community has attempted to establish peace and restore a functioning state in Somalia. In the past, a number of peace and reconciliation efforts were undertaken involving the top leadership of the warring parties, and were held mainly outside Somalia. They took a state-centric rather than peacebuilding approach. However, this top-down reconciliation process has not produced any tangible results so far.

Efforts have also been made to bring specific conflicts to an end. For Gaalkacyo, a reconciliation effort with the support of the United Arab Emirates (UAE) was put forward in 2016 but it did not bring an end to the violence.[7]

Efforts to achieve reconciliation between Galmudug and ASWJ are complicated because ASWJ is now split into two groups. However, as reported, "Galmudug's former president stated last year [2016] that the regional government is always ready to negotiate with ASWJ to solve the differences."[8] Furthermore, the FGS is attempting to resolve the conflict. In April 2017, "Galmudug deputy president Mohamed Abdi Hashi along [with] advisors arrived in Mogadishu, and it was reported that the FGS, with the support of the international community, attempted to broker reconciliation deals between Galmudug and ASWJ."[9]

In Marka, the two warring groups came together in 2016 for a reconciliation meeting organized by the South-West Administration and supported by the African Union Mission in Somalia (AMISOM). As ReliefWeb reports, the South-West State Minister for Reconciliation and Constitutional Affairs, Abdulkadir Nur Arale, described the gathering as a major step towards lasting peace in Marka. He also noted that the regional leaders want to strengthen the ceasefire to stabilize the situation until a more reliable peace agreement can be reached.[10] In the end, the two groups agreed that the cessation of hostilities must be observed, and that police forces must be deployed to enforce law and order.

In Benaadir, there has been no genuine reconciliation among the clans. The civil war that ravaged Mogadishu caused profound destruction and created deep mistrust within the community. The population of Mogadishu, the capital city, is constituted of multiple rival clans that compete for the control of land and power. Some clans see themselves as the "natives" of the city and view others as "migrants", whereas others see Mogadishu as the capital city for all. There are grievances that resulted from injustice and aggression perpetrated against minority clans, especially the Benaadiri communities who feel that they are marginalized from power and resource sharing. To overcome grievances, a former official from the Benaadiri community believes that attempts to reconcile people in the Benaadir region should start from the bottom up, rather than follow the past top-down approaches.[11]

Survey Results

For the purpose of identifying effective mechanisms to promote local reconciliation CfPAR carried out an online survey, which involved 114 participants. In addition to the demographics, which covered three questions about gender, age category, and region, the survey elicited respondents' views about steps and mechanisms for achieving local reconciliation. Regrettably, only 16 per cent of the participants were female whereas 84 per cent were male.

35 per cent of participants were aged 26–35, whereas 28 per cent were aged 18–25. Respondents were interviewed at locations in Baay, Hiiraan, Lower Jubba, Lower Shabelle, Middle Shabelle, Mudug, and Nugaal. Participants were asked to indicate the regional state that they come from. 39 per cent of the participants indicated that they were from Puntland; 25 per cent from Hirshabelle; 13 per cent from Galmudug; 11 per cent from Jubbaland and a further 11 per cent from South-West State.

Participants were asked about their awareness of reconciliation activities in their regions. 61 per cent of the respondents indicated that they were aware of the reconciliation activities that had taken place before, whereas 39 per cent stated that they were not aware of any reconciliation efforts in the past.

Mechanisms for Resolving Conflicts and Grievances

Participants were asked what steps could help to resolve conflicts and grievances between the clans, and asked to choose one of five options noted in Figure 1 below.

Almost 59 per cent of the respondents believed that all the measures mentioned should be taken for resolving conflicts and grievances between local clans. The measure which individually received the highest backing, supported by 16 per cent of respondents, was eliminating mistrust through fairness and transparency in service delivery and integrating local security forces, by which we mean creating a professional and inclusive national army. The option that received the second highest level of backing, selected by 13 per cent of respondents, was establishing a clear format for power and resource sharing.

Figure 1

Steps to Resolve Conflicts and Grievances

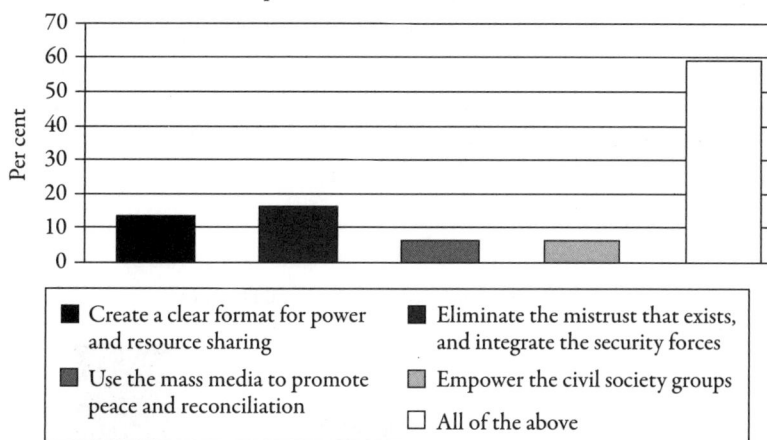

■ Create a clear format for power and resource sharing
■ Eliminate the mistrust that exists, and integrate the security forces
■ Use the mass media to promote peace and reconciliation
■ Empower the civil society groups
☐ All of the above

Techniques to Advance Local Peace and Reconciliations

There has never been a Truth and Reconciliation Commission (TRC) in Somalia. However, as shown in Table 1 below, 32 per cent of the respondents stated that it is important to establish and empower an effective and trustworthy national TRC. Some 18 per cent of the respondents indicated that in order to bring about peace and reconciliation, impunity should be brought to an end through the establishment of a reliable local justice system. Only 5.2 per cent of the respondents indicated that they are in favour of an international tribunal court for Somalia.

Table 1

Techniques and Approaches to Bring About Peace and Reconciliation	Per cent
Establish/empower an effective and trustworthy National TRC	32.4
End of impunity by establishing reliable local justice system	18.4
Establish an international tribunal for clan fights and repetitive human rights abuses	5.2
All of the above	44

Potential Mediators for Local Disputes

Peacebuilding in post-conflict societies requires multiple actors with coordinated objectives. As conflicts are often local, potential mediators who enjoy the trust and respect of the local communities are essential. Survey participants were asked who should mediate for local disputes out of three options: the FGS with the international community; the Federal Member States with the support of the FGS; or civil society groups.

Figure 2

Potential Mediators for Local Disputes

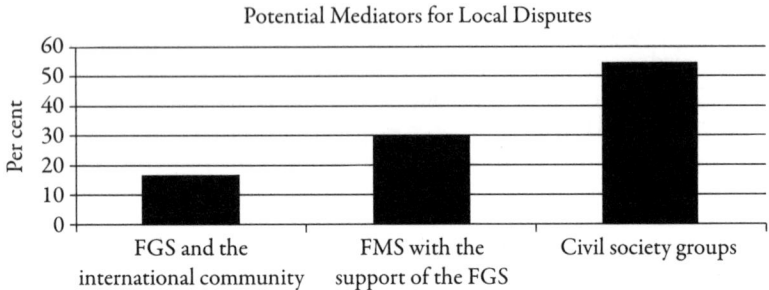

30 per cent of survey respondents said that the Federal Member States (FMS) with the support of the FGS should mediate local disputes. However, in northern Somalia, successful reconciliation and peacebuilding efforts have been led by the traditional elders, especially in Somaliland. As a result, 54 per cent of the participants indicated that the civil society groups, which include local non-governmental organizations, traditional elders, women and youth organizations, should lead the reconciliation process.

Conclusion

Somalia's attempts to achieve local-level reconciliation are complicated due to the many different actors with diverse interests who are involved in the conflicts. Thus, reconciliation efforts require a concrete understanding of local context. This paper briefly covered conflicts in Gaalkacyo, Galmudug, Marka, and Benaadir, but it does not mean that Hirshabelle and Jubbaland communities are immune from clan conflicts. Traditional elders from Hiiraan have complained about the state formation process of Hirshabelle. One survey respondent stated that Hirshabelle State had never had a real reconciliation.[12]

In Jubbaland, it was reported that the Digil Mirifle and Marehan clans had criticized the state formation process, stating that the participants were hand-picked to bring predetermined results that would have been impossible if legitimate representatives were in the room.[13]

Clan conflicts in Gaalkacyo and in Marka, and the political conflict between Galmudug authorities and ASWJ, are alarming. Inclusive and genuine reconciliation processes led by civil society groups are needed to bring about a sustainable and lasting peace in Somalia. Grievances require immediate and effective local reconciliation for all regions, and if these grievances are not addressed properly, they could trigger a new wave of conflicts.

Recommendations

Federal Government of Somalia

1. Within one year, the FGS should establish/empower an independent national Truth and Reconciliation Commission.
2. The FGS should appoint the members of the TRC based on merit and credibility.
3. In consultation with international partners, the FMS, and civil society groups, including women's groups, youth and traditional elders, the FGS should put forward a clearly defined mandate for the TRC.
4. The FGS should enhance state–society relations by being neutral toward the process of local reconciliation.

Federal Member States

1. The FMS should closely work with the TRC, and accommodate all the technical support that the TRC needs at the local level.
2. The FMS should assist the TRC in the establishment of a restorative justice system that will be useful for the TRC's hearing and healing proceedings at the local level.

The FGS in Galmudug

1. The FGS should immediately initiate or continue consultations with local and international experts regarding the resolution of the conflict between Galmudug and ASWJ.

2. In consultation with UNSOM, the FGS should lead a negotiation process between Galmudug and ASWJ.

The International Community

1. The international community, led by UNSOM, should provide all the necessary funds to the TRC, and actively monitor the fulfilment of its mandate.
2. UNSOM, with the support of individual members of the international community, should play a key role in bringing transitional justice experts to work with the TRC.

EXPLOITATION OF NATURAL RESOURCES AS A DRIVER OF CONFLICT

CASE STUDY ON MINING IN BAKI DISTRICT, SOMALILAND

Mohamed Abdi Omer and *Mohamed Farah Hersi*

Authors

Mohamed Abdi Omer is a researcher at the Academy for Peace and Development (APD) with expertise in land-based conflicts, social reconciliation, and governance.

Mohamed Farah Hersi is Director of the Academy for Peace and Development and author of various publications on peacebuilding and democratization in Somalia.

Summary

The briefing paper attempts to capture the volatility of attempted exploitation of non-renewable resources through an in-depth analysis of the Simodi beryllium mining site in Awdal region of Somaliland. The field research was conducted between 7 and 17 May 2017.

The conflict at Simodi has two dimensions. On one hand, the conflict is between the local community, which is sceptical about the scope and impact of the concession granted to the African Resource Corporation (ARC), a Chinese company, and the Somaliland Ministry of Mineral Resources and Energy. On the other hand, the mining at Simodi has reignited an inter-clan conflict between the main Reer Mohamed community and the neighbouring Reer Nour sub-clan community, who are in dispute over who should be the potential primary beneficiaries of the mining.

Different stakeholders have their own specific interests and concerns, while it has emerged that there are cross-cutting issues of concern, such as employment opportunities for local people, protection of the environment, limited government capacity to sanction the activities of the mining company, poor company–community relations, and concerns about corruption, lack of transparency and back door deals. Among these issues, all local stakeholders were emphatic about the importance of protecting the environment given its relevance to the predominant livelihood system in the area—pastoralism.

There is simmering resentment among local communities, which has the potential to evolve into conflict, if their concerns are not carefully analysed and addressed. The propensity of the Somaliland government not to make efforts to establish amicable relations between the host community and the mining company creates an additional risk that local communities will see themselves as being marginalized by their own government.

Local stakeholders agree that there is a strong relationship between natural resource management and stability in Somaliland. By way of recommendations, effective negotiations with local communities can help to ensure conflict-free exploitation of natural resources. In addition:

- Mining concessions should incorporate social services for local communities;
- Laws and policies should be developed by the Somaliland government on resource exploitation that bear the trust of the local communities;
- Opportunities for employment should prioritize local communities;
- Mining companies should be accountable to local government authorities;
- Land ownership should be determined in advance of exploration; and
- Where relevant, mechanisms should be established to ensure an equitable sharing of resources.

Introduction

Resource-based conflicts are a defining characteristic of the post-conflict situation in Somalia. In the face of a weak system of governance, competition among clan groups (or between clan groups and the authorities) over access to and control of resources, leads to conflict and sometimes to violence. Customary laws used to provide a framework for the management of traditional conflicts, but they are not sufficient to resolve increasingly complex natural resource-based conflicts.

In modern-day Somalia, issues of resource sharing and management are contentious, and their non-resolution creates conflict flashpoints. In the self-declared Republic of Somaliland, where relative peace has been sustained for a period of two decades, the government has been seeking new partners to exploit its untapped mineral resources, seen as a means of achieving economic growth. However, not having been internationally recognized as an independent state, Somaliland has found itself in a weaker bargaining position with respect to negotiations over resource exploitation with companies whose records for environmental protection or social responsibility are not fully known. Critics warn that Somaliland's resource wealth may end up being more of a curse than a blessing.

The Field Research

From 7 to 17 May 2017 APD carried out field research at the Simodi mining site in Baki district of the Adwal region of Somaliland. The objectives of APD's research were to:

(a) capture specific stakeholder grievances; and
(b) assess community perceptions of natural resource management.

The following research methods were used:

- *Focus group discussions*—in order to encourage the community to speak frankly with the APD research ream;
- *Semi-structured interviews*—to draw expert viewpoints on issues relating to mining and its potential to cause and contribute to conflict;
- *Observations and informal conversations*—to gather more information on the sensitivity of the mining and especially the perceptions of the community; and
- *Consultative meetings*—one-day meeting to capture collective community perspectives on resource management.

The Context

The Simodi mountain ridge, which is 48 kilometres east of Baki village, has long been the focus of local communities for mining. About 90 per cent of the people who live on the Simodi mountain ridge depend on livestock for their livelihoods; the other 10 per cent or so depend mainly on seasonal farming.[1] However, individuals from both the pastoralist and farming communities practice near-surface open-pit mining. The pits produce columbite-tantalite metallic ore (coltan), among other things for which there is an active market. Foreigners and local business people buy the ores at a low price and usually transport them to other countries in the region. The communities of the area belong to Reer Mohamed, a sub-clan of Gadubursi, while Reer Nour, another sub-clan of Gadubursi, closely neighbours the mining area.

Profile of the Conflict

As explored further below, the conflict at Simodi has two dimensions. On one hand, the conflict is between the local community, which is sceptical about the scope and impact of the concession granted to the Chinese company, ARC, and the Somaliland Ministry of Mineral Resources and Energy (referred to below as "the Ministry"), which is pushing ahead with its agreement with ARC regardless of demands for clarification by the local community. On the other hand, the mining by ARC at Simodi has reignited an inter-clan conflict between the main Reer Mohamed community and neighbouring Reer Nour sub-clan community over the potential primary beneficiaries of the mining.

We understand that in December 2014 the Ministry granted a concession to ARC for mining in the Simodi mountain range. It is reported that the concession relates to the extraction of beryllium, a metal which, being especially light and rigid, is converted into alloys for use in electrical devices, machinery, vehicles, and different types of equipment.[2]

In protest at what was seen as a unilateral decision of the government to grant the mining concession, traditional elders from the area held press conferences articulating their opposition to mining activities taking place without their consent. Other actors then took the opportunity to voice their opposition, especially youth, members of the diaspora, and mining artisans who depended on manual excavation of the minerals for their livelihoods. In what critics say was a heavy-handed approach, the government was reported to have deployed police units and arrested twenty-four elders who were allegedly mobilizing local communities to oppose ARC's mining operations at Simodi. The arrest of the elders enflamed the situation. The sultan of Reer Mohamed demanded the immediate withdrawal of the company and the unconditional release of the elders from detention, stating that their rights had been violated, and that no one could suppress their voices.[3]

To address the situation and appease local communities, the government sent a delegation to the area in January 2015 consisting of officials from the Ministry, as well as from regional and local authorities. This delegation met with traditional elders and listened carefully to their concerns. The elders who had been detained were then released from police custody, while the Vice-Minister laid the foundation stone for a primary school and promised to build a mother and child health facility in the near future.[4]

With regard to the inter-clan conflict, Reer Mohamed, according to the traditional clan territorial claims, believes that it should be the exclusive beneficiary of the mining. The Reer Nour sub-clan that lives adjacent to the Simodi to the south and the east has re-asserted its claim for the benefits of the mining. Those claims have continued to be rebuffed by the Reer Mohamed, who consider themselves the rightful owners of the Simodi mountain and the mineral deposits within it. The government of Somaliland deals with Reer Mohamed as constituting the local communities with respect to the mining. However, the neighbouring Reer Nour sub-clan does not consent to this and believes that it should have equal consideration for the benefits.

Conflict Stakeholders

This section outlines the interest and viewpoints of the stakeholders of the conflict: traditional elders, youth groups, members of the diaspora, pastoralists, and mining artisans.

Traditional Elders

Traditional elders believe that they are entitled to speak on behalf of the affected communities. They stand to defend the collective interest of the communities. The focus group discussions involving community elders revealed grievances about economic issues, such as the lack of employment opportunities for local people. If this is not resolved, it could lead to violent confrontation between local communities and the security forces in the vicinity of the mining. As one traditional sultan put it: "The government ceased petroleum exploration when the local communities stood against that in the eastern regions."[5] Another elder asked: "Why would the government not consider our grievances in the same manner [as those in the east of Somaliland]?"[6]

Youth Groups

Youth groups adamantly oppose the exploitation of the beryllium, given that there is speculation about its toxicity and adverse effects on the local communities and their livestock. (The health risks associated with beryllium are borne out by scientific analysis, including as conducted by the US government.)[7] Participants in the focus group discussions voiced a sense of militancy in reaction to any forcible attempts to restart mining operations. It can also be deduced from our consultations with youth that originally their grievances were inspired by economic factors, especially the limited availability of jobs connected to the mining initiative, but they are currently raising other concerns including around environmental degradation and the health hazards of the mine. Some youth say they are "ready to violently oppose the mining rather than silently die in toxic waste."[8]

Diaspora Community

Members of the Somali diaspora also have a role in the conflict, having elevated the issues of environmental degradation and toxicity. Interviews with members of the diaspora reveal insights into their motives. Some appear to see the dispute as an opportunity to involve themselves in local politics. Others appear to be using the defence of the interests of local communities as a pretext, and their primary interest is in securing local contracts from the mining initiative. Given that members of the diaspora are apparently ready to use resources to drive a wedge between local communities and the government, their involvement in the dispute adds fuel to an already volatile situation. Moreover, as diaspora members are not under the jurisdiction of the Somaliland government, they perhaps have greater potential to stir the local community to violence by remote control.[9]

Pastoralist Community

Based on the widespread speculation of the toxicity of the mining, pastoralists in the area are genuinely concerned about the security of their livelihoods, regardless of the benefits that accrue to local communities. Pastoralists demand that the government carry out an assessment of the ecological impact of the mining. Participants in the focus groups repeatedly criticized the government's attitude and said that it appeared not to be fully aware of the potential damage to the environment on which their survival depends, which could ultimately lead to violent confrontation between the local communities and the government. As one pastoralist said indignantly, "the government seems to [have been] bought off by a foreign company."[10] Some observers say that the government is neither conscious of the potential impact of the mining on the environment, nor it is aware of the concerns of the pastoral communities.

Mining Artisan Community

Local artisans use labour-intensive open-pit mining to extract the metallic ore. Some of the participants in the focus groups described how local artisans had originally been selling coltan to a private Chinese merchant—but that in due course, this individual, acting through ARC, had cut a mining deal with the Ministry.[11] This perhaps contributed to a perception among mining artisans that the Chinese company is acting against the interests of local communities and disregarding their prior commercial activities. The mining artisans suspect that ARC is not only interested in the area covered by the concession but that it is also on the lookout for other valuable minerals in the area, given that their personnel were familiar with the area before the concession was granted.[12]

Local Government Authority

The mining at Simodi mountain falls under the jurisdiction of Baki district authorities. In an interview, the mayor of Baki said that the local authority was not consulted about the concession, which was awarded by the Ministry of Minerals and Energy. "As a local authority we should know the terms of the agreement and the quantity of resources extracted from the mine," the mayor said. "Our position is that the role of the local government should be clear in terms of financial benefits. We need our royalty from the products of the mining."[13] The mayor also said he believed that the company should be accountable to local authorities and that the Ministry should inform local authorities of all mining activities.

The Somaliland Government

It is understood that after a long negotiation the Ministry granted the Chinese company an exclusive exploration licence to assess the quality, quantity, type, and location of deposits. After the company presented its exploration results, the Ministry drafted what is described as an International Standard Agreement.[14] Within the auspices of the agreement, the benefits that accrue to the local communities include a school, health facilities and roads.[15] However, the company has deployed heavy-duty extraction equipment at the mining site, and with all of the issues outlined above, it is unclear how trust can be re-established between local communities and the Ministry.[16]

The Federal Government of Somalia

The Ministry of Petroleum and Minerals of the Federal Government of Somalia (FGS) has firmly stated that mining activities at Simodi by ARC are illegal and a violation of Somalia's territorial integrity and sovereignty. The Foreign Minister of the FGS also met with the Chinese Ambassador to discuss the issue.[17] For their part, Somaliland officials see the FGS as attempting to exaggerate a manageable local dispute in order to justify its interference in Somaliland's internal affairs. This type of conflict has the potential to further complicate the ongoing but sterile negotiations between the two entities.

Cross-cutting Issues

Although different stakeholders have different concerns reflecting their specific interests, all of them have identified the following issues as priorities and key issues to consider in the peaceful exploitation of natural resources.

- *Employment opportunities.* The local communities do not trust the Somaliland authorities and their partners, especially foreign companies, with regard to potential employment opportunities associated with the resource exploitation. Even if the foreign companies are sincere about prioritizing local communities for employment, there are suspicions that some government officials may interfere for their own benefits. In that sense, local communities may feel mistreated and may feel compelled to resort to violence.
- *Environmental degradation.* So far local stakeholders are not convinced that either the Somaliland government or the mining company is seriously concerned about the potential impact of the mining on the local environment. The environmental impact of the mining is the utmost concern for local communities given its relevance to pastoralism as the predominant livelihood system for the local communities. If not addressed, this has the potential to lead to community confrontation with the government and the mining company.

- *Limited government capacity to sanction the activities of the mining company.* Existing local capacities for managing resource-based conflicts are fully strained and overwhelmed by complex new conflict settings, and if activities are not sanctioned at the local level, they could trigger violence. The perceived inability of the government to protect its citizens, environment and economy could contribute to resource-based conflicts. Furthermore, limited government institutional capacities could lead to misunderstandings between the local communities on one side, and the government and foreign companies on the other.

- *Community–company relations.* Local communities feel detached from the mining company, which is carrying out activities that could have an impact on their livelihood systems. At the same time, some observers suspect that traditional elders are not necessarily sincere when they claim to articulate concerns on behalf of local communities but are using perceptions of the common interest as a means of advancing their personal interests.

- *Concerns for corruption.* There is a prevalent perception among local communities that contracts are characterized by a lack of transparency, back-door deals, and a lack of interface between local communities and the foreign companies. This creates a fertile ground for rumour-mongering which negatively influences community attitudes towards the mining initiative.

Conclusion

The government of Somaliland does not have a "monopoly on violence" and as such its authority is limited to ruling over the exploitation and management of natural resources. Moreover, attempts to explore natural resources, let alone extract them, have already disrupted a fragile security situation. It was evident from our consultative meeting with local stakeholders that local communities do not trust the Somaliland government and its foreign partners, and that they are committed to protecting what they see as their rights in the mining of beryllium in their constituency.

As outlined above, the stakeholders from local communities expressed their own particular concerns about the mining initiative, while also sharing several concerns in common. It is essential that these grievances and concerns are taken into account by the relevant authorities. Through consultations, the stakeholders articulated recommendations for future natural resource management that could earn the support of local communities, which are set out below.

Recommendations

- The mining initiative should incorporate social services for local communities (access to education, health and water), the design and development of which should be based on the priorities of community members. This might increase the acceptability of the initiative in the eyes of communities.
- The Somaliland government should formulate laws and policies on resource exploitation that bear the trust of the local communities. Opportunities for employment or contracts related to the initiative should prioritize local communities.
- Those who represent local communities should be individuals who command respect among the local community, which might include well-regarded traditional elders, religious leaders, private sector figures, or social activists.
- The mining company should be accountable to local government authorities that represent the immediate interests of local communities. This should help to avoid the suspicion that the company is using the authority of the Somaliland government against the will of local communities.
- Where deposits lie on or near inter-clan boundaries, the ownership of the area should be settled before the resources are extracted, and a mechanism for equitable resource sharing should be established for the concerned communities.

TRADITIONAL PEACEMAKING
IN SANAAG REGION, SOMALILAND

Abdullahi Odowa

Author

Abdullahi Odowa is General Director of the Somali Observatory of Conflict and Violence Prevention (OCVP), which is a non-governmental and non-political research-oriented organization operating in all Somali regions. He has more than ten years of teaching, international developmental programming, and research experience.

Summary

The civil war that erupted in Somalia in 1990 ignited conflict in the Sanaag region between communities that were affiliated with the government and those which supported the main rebel movement. Resulting hostilities killed, injured and displaced thousands of people and destroyed countless homes and livestock.

To bring hostilities to an end and enable the warring parties to resolve their disputes, local traditional leaders in the Sanaag region established a series of bottom-up peace initiatives in partnership with other key local stakeholders. A number of factors explain why these peace initiatives were successful and sustainable. There was a sincere commitment from all sides to end the fighting and a sense of local ownership in both the plan and resources involved, coupled with limited external intervention. This was reinforced by the capacity and willingness of local actors to forgive and forget past atrocities and focus on the future.

Nevertheless, there remain significant challenges to local peace and stability. Not all matters agreed during peace negotiations have been implemented; not enough has been done to memorialize past peacemaking; and local elites have failed to translate the peace dividend into fruitful and productive regional governance.

Traditional peace initiatives in Sanaag region provide several lessons that could be useful for domestic and international actors engaged in stabilization and communal reconciliation efforts in Somalia. First, it is important to allow hostile communities to initiate their reconciliation at grassroots level and resolve significant collective outstanding issues before moving on to address power-sharing and national-level issues. Second, for the sake of local ownership and peace sustainability, it is important to encourage the mobilization of local resources for facilitating peace talks. Third, since traditional peace meetings are often conducted in an open-ended manner, without restricted deadlines or agendas, and seek eventual consensus, it is important to allow traditional peace initiatives to evolve as a natural process and avoid imposing fixed schedules or predetermined agendas. Finally, it is important to link initial, traditional peace talks to future power-sharing and state formation efforts, so that positive outcomes from the former can contribute to and reinforce the latter.

Introduction

The protracted civil war fought between clan-based militias caused the collapse of the Somali state, which further led to major humanitarian crises and the destruction of public services. The social cost of the conflict in Somalia is massive in scope and devastating to human and material resources, and arguably left deep wounds on the social fabric that once held society together. Therefore, any efforts aimed at resolving the conflict and reconciling warring parties must be informed by a deep understanding of causes and drivers of conflict, and lessons must be drawn from successful peace initiatives in the country.

With this in mind, this policy brief focuses on providing a deep understanding of traditional peacemaking in Sanaag region with a particular emphasis on enabling factors for successful local peace initiatives in the region, as well as some constraints that are associated with the implementation of peace accords. A qualitative research approach was adopted as a research tool for data collection and analysis. Both primary and secondary data sources were employed using in-depth interviews and a desk-based literature review.

From 25 to 26 April 2017, two researchers from OCVP led by the author visited the city of Erigavo, the economic and political capital of Sanaag region, and conducted 11 key informant interviews with purposefully selected individuals who possess special knowledge on the local peace initiatives. Nine male and two female interviewees were selected; they were traditional and religious leaders, business people, and activists with women's organizations. The desk research involved close analysis of relevant books and journals.

Traditional Peacemaking Endeavours in Somaliland

After ousting Siad Barre's regime from Mogadishu and the subsequent collapse of the Somali state in 1991, the Somali National Movement (SNM) took control of most parts of what are formally known as the north-west regions of Somalia.[1] The SNM administration inherited a war-ravaged country, in which major cities were almost destroyed, tens of thousands of people had been killed, and hundreds of thousands had been internally and externally displaced.[2] Further complicating this situation, there were large numbers of loosely-controlled armed clan militias, some of which supported the SNM while others opposed it. The SNM leadership opted for a cessation of hostilities with clans that supported the regime during the civil war (these were non-Isaaq clans, as explained below).[3] Therefore, the immediate task of the new administration in Somaliland and clan elders was to facilitate reconciliation meetings aimed at resolving all major outstanding issues between communities across the country. Hence, a series of "bottom-up" peace initiatives were initiated at both local and national levels by traditional leaders using the unwritten code of conduct/or traditional law called *xeer*.[4]

Soon after the collapse of the central government of Somalia and the subsequent victory of the SNM, there were confrontations within and between the Isaaq clan family and between Isaaq and non-Isaaq clans living in the western and eastern regions of the country. For example, in the western part of Somaliland there was a clash between SNM forces and militia belonging to Gadabursi clan which led to the destruction of the town of Dilla and looting of Borama, the capital city of Awdal region.[5]

In the eastern regions of the country, there were several confrontations between Isaaq clans and Harti clans, in particular the Dhulbahante and

Warsangali sub-clans of Harti in Sool and Sanaag regions.[6] The SNM interim government was unable to disarm the clan militias and establish control of the country. The SNM also experienced internal power struggles between various factions (mainly between the military and political wings of the movement). These conditions enabled traditional authorities to step up and lead the process of local negotiation and reconciliation using traditional values and laws.[7]

For the purpose of this policy brief, the indigenous peace and reconciliation efforts that helped to stabilize and rebuild governance institutions can generally be divided into national and local levels. As explained below, the success of the local peace initiatives at district and regional levels have pioneered the national-level peacebuilding and state-building efforts in Somaliland.

Local Peacemaking Process in Sanaag Region

In order to better understand how local peace was negotiated by different clans in Somaliland, it is worth explaining the clan composition of the population in present-day Somaliland. The majority of the people in this part of the country come from one of the five main clans: the Isaaq family clan, Gadabursi, Essa, Warsangali, and Dhulbahante. The Isaaq family clan which is itself genealogically divided into six main sub-clans—the Habar Yonis, Iidagale, Habar Je'lo, Habar Awal, Arab and Ayuub—is the most populous group in Somaliland and the backbone of the SNM.[8] Geographically, the Isaaq clan settles in the central regions of the country, neighbouring the Gugabirsi clan in the western-most corner, and Dhubatante and Warsangali in the eastern regions of the country.

The districts and regions of the east and west where Isaaq and non-Isaaq clans live together became the conflict hotspots. For instance, at the height of the civil war between the SNM and government forces, in these border districts, the Isaaq became displaced from their settled homelands, which were taken over by non-Isaaq rivals. However, after the collapse of the central government and the victory of SNM, the process was reversed and Isaaq returned to their mixed sedentary areas, displacing non-Isaaq clans who fled from these locations in fear of revenge.[9]

Conflict resolution in the north of Somalia has always been the responsibility of genuine clan elders who have the mandate to represent their clans.[10] However, grassroots peacemaking in Somaliland is regarded as a communal matter. Therefore, while clan elders assume the leadership in peacemaking, they also make effective use of the contribution from other traditional leaders, religious figures, business people, politicians, professionals, the military and, most importantly, poets.[11] Social and criminal matters arising within or between clans or sub-clans are often resolved by these clan elders through a mix of Sharia and customary laws, and if the elders encounter unforeseen incidents with no previous experience, new customary laws are developed to resolve the issue, hence, the traditional conflict resolution mechanism is a dynamic and evolving one.[12]

While there were some 39 peace conferences and meetings that took place in Somaliland between 1990 and 1997,[13] the reconciliation initiatives that took place in Sanaag region were for many reasons the most important and perhaps the most challenging.

First, Sanaag region and its capital city of Erigavo are home to several divergent clans and sub-clans, including the Habar Yoni and Habar Je'lo, an Isaaq clan that supported the SNM during the civil war, and the Warsangali and Dhulbahante, who belong to Harti (Darood) that sided with the regime during the civil war. This makes the region the most heterogeneous in terms of clan composition. The complexity of inter-clan relationships arguably made conflict resolution in this region particularly challenging. For instance, a total of 15 small conferences and one grand conference were organized to restore relations between communities affected by war.[14]

Secondly, the fighting was of high intensity, with massive scope and impact. According to data documented by local elders responsible for agreeing compensation payments between different clans and sub-clans: "Between 1988 and mid-1991, it has been estimated that 3,000 people in the region were killed, 7,000 wounded, 30,000 heads of livestock and 2,000 houses were destroyed."[15] Further complicating the problem is that the fighting was between people who are relatives and knew one another very well, which made the conflict particularly damaging and traumatizing, and its resolution complex. A traditional leader interviewed during the field research of this project has highlighted the close relationship between conflicting parties via inter-marriage: "In my own house, you can find members from all the clans living together in this region, my wife is from one, my sons married women from different clans and my daughters are married to men from different clans."[16]

Enabling Factors for Successful Local Peace Initiatives in Sanaag Region

While recognizing the regional specificity that exists in any given context, several factors can be identified as enabling successful local peace initiatives in the region:

- There was commitment from all sides involved in the conflict to de-escalate the tension and resolve differences through peaceful means. Traditional leaders and politicians from opposing sides have initiated face-to-face meetings in the earlier stages of the conflict. For example, the Dhulbantante's Garaad Abdiqani initiated talks with the representatives of the Habar Je'lo and Habar Yoonis Isaaq clans in February and August 1990 respectively.[17] In the subsequent year the SNM agreed to attend a meeting hosted by Dhulbahante in the town of Oog, during which the SNM delegation was asked to disarm before it entered the town and mingled with the people. This action is believed to have reduced Dhulbahante fears from SNM and enhanced trust between the two parties.[18] In a separate effort, in January 1991, the SNM leadership approached prominent business individuals from Warsangali clan living in Berbera and asked them to convey the message of peace to their community in Lasqorey.[19]

- The regional-level reconciliation efforts were first initiated at the grassroots level and slowly progressed to villages, towns, districts and the region. The peace process in Sanaag started with what is locally known as *go'isutaag*, which could be loosely translated as "wave the flag", in which members of the hostile pastoral communities display a sheet of cloth as a request for a ceasefire. In this one-to-one peacemaking process, men from each warring party raise a piece of cloth and approach each other for peace talks. The process started at a location known as El Qohle and then slowly and spontaneously spread to other locations.[20] These clusters of localized peace initiatives between warring neighbouring clans were critically important in many ways. First, they helped build trust between hostile communities. Second, they led to local ceasefires that allowed the communities to share pasture and water, and finally led to formal peace talks between various clans living the region.

- Unlike other, similar reconciliation conferences in the south, this series of regional reconciliation meetings was locally funded, with the vast bulk of the resources needed for the facilitation of these meetings provided by the members of the local community.[21] Women played a significant role in mobilizing resources, and providing food and moral support for their male counterparts by composing anti-war songs and poems.[22]

- During regional peace talks, government interventions were minimized, while politicians were allowed to participate in the peace conferences as observers with the traditional and religious leaders leading the process.[23] This has arguably allowed the warring parties to discuss outstanding communal disputes before moving on to tackle issues of governance and power-sharing.

- In a spirit of reconciliation, the warring clans have agreed to bury the past and focus on the present and future affairs of restoring peace and stability. Hence, in Erigavo Grand Conference in 1993, delegates adopted a "forgive and forget concept" in which they agreed to annul killings and lootings that took place in the past, and to return fixed assets and livestock.[24]

Constraints for Traditional Peace Initiatives in Sanaag Region

Considering the magnitude and complexity of Sanaag conflicts, local peace initiatives have been successful in many ways, and brought relative peace and stability in the region. However, there are major constraints, set out below, which if not addressed quickly and properly could undermine peace and stability in the region.

- Not all the matters that were formally agreed by the reconciling parties are fully implemented, particularly with regard to the restoration of properties. For example, some people still hold properties—land and houses—that they occupied during the civil war.[25]
- Successful peace initiatives in the region do not lead to a successful governance system. A majority of people interviewed during the field research suggested that the regional administration is dominated by one clan, and that most of the public institutions remain weak and dysfunctional and lack legitimacy.[26]
- There is no memorialization, such as museums, monuments, rituals, and street naming, which is aimed at preserving the memories of peace initiatives and the individuals who supported the process, and who delivered peace dividends to the people of Sanaag region.

Conclusion

Local peacemaking in Sanaag region not only represents organic and classic "bottom-up" peacemaking, but also demonstrates the relevance and effectiveness of indigenous peace processes. Such processes can succeed where they take place in conducive conditions, are led by genuine traditional leaders and where there are little or no adverse internal or external influences. Using local assets and capacity for peacemaking, the people of Sanaag region have initiated a series of grassroots peace efforts that started from two individuals who displayed a sheet of cloth to call for a ceasefire between hostile communities in the region. This slowly progressed to neighbouring pastoral lands and districts, and eventually resulted in a Grand Peace Conference in Erigavo town. These clusters of localized peace initiatives between warring clans in the districts were critically important for an immediate de-escalation of the conflicts, building trust between warring parties, allowing people to share water and pasture, and most importantly, paving the way for more comprehensive peace talks.

Funding those peace talks locally has allowed traditional leaders to take their time in resolving outstanding communal issues one after the other. The process took almost three years (1991–1993) and reached its height at the Erigavo Grand Conference, where 52 delegates from all the major clans living in the region gathered to finalize the regional peace talks and establish a regional administration. More than two decades since peace was negotiated and despite the region being one of the disputed regions between Somaliland and Puntland, the local peace remains strong and stable.

The peace, however, faces several challenges, including lack of implementation of some of the terms of the peace agreement, perceived marginalization among some of the clans, and the absence of effective, legitimate and functioning public institutions in the region.

Recommendations

One of the effects of the collapse of central authority in Somalia was the politicization of clan diversity and subsequently inter- or intra-clan conflicts in different parts of the country. It is therefore important for there to be community-level reconciliation efforts aimed at healing the wounds of the war and restoring the trust between warring clans. The following recommendations are proposed for those who seek to engage in or support community reconciliation, using traditional mechanisms of conflict resolution and peacemaking.

- Peace initiatives and community reconciliation must start from the grassroots up, and allow hostile clans and sub-clans to resolve their immediate disputes and agree the terms of future discussions before moving on to resolving issues of power-sharing and national-level reconciliation.
- Unlike the modern, Western style of peacemaking and negotiations in which there is an agreed agenda and a fixed schedule for peace talks, the traditional peace meetings are conducted in an open-ended matter, without deadlines, until a satisfactory consensus is reached by all parties involved

in the conflict. Therefore, local and international actors involved in local peacemaking in Somalia should allow traditional peace initiatives to evolve in their own way and avoid imposing fixed schedules and importing agendas.

- The unpredictability, slow pace and flaws of traditional peace talks make them delicate and vulnerable to external interventions. It is therefore important to avoid politicizing these initiatives. Politicians from the conflicting clans should avoid leading the peace talks or interfering in the natural process of traditional peacemaking, and instead endorse the peace agreements.
- In order to promote local ownership and enhance the sustainability and effectiveness of peace talks, local people who are affected by the war must be encouraged to fully or partially fund the peace processes.
- From the experience of peace initiatives in Sanaag region, it is obvious that successful peacebuilding does not lead to successful state-building, partly because issues related to power-sharing and governance were not discussed in as much depth as those of community reconciliation and de-escalation of conflict. It is therefore recommended that there is equal investment in and detailed discussions of power-sharing and how to establish effective and functioning public institutions that represent all the people living in the region.
- Memories of peace initiatives and the individuals who supported the process and achieved peace dividends for the people must be properly documented and preserved.

THE SHARIA COURTS OF MOGADISHU

LESSONS FOR PEACE AND RECONCILIATION

Ahmed Sh. Ibrahim

Author

Dr Ahmed Sh. Ibrahim is a Postdoctoral Fellow in Refugee and Migration Studies at Carleton College, Northfield, Minnesota. He has a doctorate in cultural anthropology from the Graduate Centre, City University of New York, and undertook a year and eight months of fieldwork in Mogadishu on the history of the Sharia courts and the Union of Islamic Courts (UIC).

Summary

This briefing considers whether there are lessons to be learned from the experience of the Sharia courts of Mogadishu that are relevant to peace and reconciliation in Somalia. At the outset, I would like to make a distinction, for the purposes of analysis, between community-based Sharia courts and the Union of Islamic Courts (UIC), which came into existence after the courts unified. This distinction is necessary because Sharia courts were communal centres of reconciliation and conflict resolution, whereas the UIC were part of a political formation with complex characteristics.

The Sharia courts succeeded where others failed because they simultaneously built on known cultural and religious norms, authorities, and practices, while at the same time pragmatically responding to the demands of the moment. Two of the most important lessons that the experience of the courts leaves us with are: a) justice in Somalia is inseparable from practices and discourses associated with the Sharia; b) it is hard to establish legitimate political authority if the political space and political leaders are viewed by local people to contradict and counteract the norms of the Sharia.

Based on these two observations, this paper recommends that the Federal Government of Somalia should empower district- and neighbourhood-level religious authorities to establish centres of adjudication and conflict resolution. Such centres would enable the local population to feel that injustice is being addressed, while simultaneously facilitating the government's reach to the local population. This could also win much-needed legitimacy for the government.

Introduction

This briefing paper is based on the conviction that the communal centres of conflict resolution and rehabilitation that began to emerge in Mogadishu after the collapse of the institutions of the central state in 1991 were one of the most important organic reconciliation efforts to have developed in southern Somalia since the eruption of the civil war. These centres became known as Sharia courts because they were based on the discourses, authorities, and institutions of the Sharia. The reconciliation efforts of the Sharia courts worked because their reconciliation processes and mechanisms emerged from and built on known local cultural and religious norms, authorities, and practices. The Sharia institutions, authorities, and discourses that led to the formation of the Sharia courts were indistinguishable from local cultural norms and practices. Consequently, this briefing paper attempts to derive some lessons from the history of the emergence and evolution of the Sharia courts, which may provide guidelines for, or at least shed light on, the shortcomings of internationally-led reconciliation efforts.

Most of those knowledgeable about recent Somali history will concur that when the Sharia courts of Mogadishu unified to create the UIC and proceeded to take complete control of Mogadishu in 2006, it came as a complete shock.[1] By bringing the city under a single power and creating temporary peace and stability, the courts achieved what had seemed until then an impossibility. Though the sudden rise and success of the UIC took many people by surprise, the Sharia courts had been in existence in Mogadishu, in some form or another, since 1992. It seems obvious then that the experience of the Sharia courts has plenty of lessons to offer in terms of peace and reconciliation in Somalia. This briefing is based on the findings from a historical ethnography of the Sharia courts undertaken in Mogadishu for a period of a year and eight months between 2014 and 2015. The methods of the field work were in-depth interviews with key individuals in the Sharia courts and the subsequent UIC, analyses of court records and of historical and biographical texts in Arabic and Somali languages from private libraries, and participant observation of informal Sharia-based mediation and arbitration.

A Brief History of the Courts

After about a decade of armed insurgency, the central state of Somalia completely disintegrated in 1991. In the ensuing power struggle between various armed factions, the country was thrown into a prolonged period of anarchy and lawlessness. The worst affected area was the capital city of Mogadishu, where armed gangs and criminal syndicates transformed the city into fiefdoms of competing warlords and criminal networks terrorizing the local population. Murder, rape, kidnapping, and robbery all became everyday realities of life in Mogadishu.

One of the most important responses to these social upheavals was the formation of community centres in various neighbourhoods throughout the city. The first such centre was established in 1992 in the district of Medina. The centres were established by traditional elders established through lineage and religious authorities, with varying support from business people. The centres functioned as spaces where neighbourhood residents went to have their disputes resolved in accordance with Sharia norms as understood by neighbourhood religious authorities. The centres also served as rehabilitation spaces where delinquent youth were taken by their relatives to be rehabilitated in proper Islamic ethical conduct and social responsibility, again informed by Sharia norms and overseen by neighbourhood sheikhs.

Since Sharia structures of authority and discourse were the bases upon which the centres were established and functioned, the centres became known as Sharia courts. In the majority of cases, a Sharia court represented the wishes and consent of a specific community or extended family (*reer*). Thus a court's jurisdiction was limited to the neighbourhood and community that established it.

By the early 2000s, there were about a dozen of these communal Sharia courts in various neighbourhoods in Mogadishu. Beginning around 2003, the Sharia courts' jurisdictions and power expanded as they garnered more community support, particularly from business people, and began to coordinate their activities. As the communal Sharia courts' power and jurisdiction increased, the courts came into conflict with the city's powerful warlords, who, taking advantage of the opportunity for funding provided by the "war on terror," renamed themselves the Alliance for the Restoration of Peace and Counter-Terrorism (ARPCT) in February 2006.

In the ensuing conflict, the courts succeeded in evicting the warlords from the city and brought the city under a single power for the first time in 15 years. After taking control of the city, the communal Sharia courts and their allies in the conflict with the warlords established the UIC. Until their metamorphosis into the UIC, the Sharia courts were an organic reconciliation effort led by everyday people. The people involved relied on and were motivated by Sharia-derived notions of ethical and social responsibility, and employed traditionally-anchored mechanisms of dispute resolution and conflict settlement. Why then has the experience of the courts been ignored in the literature on peace and reconciliation in Somalia? And why hasn't the experience of the courts featured more prominently in the attempts to find resolution to the conflict in Somalia?

Commentators on the Sharia Courts

The answers to these questions are to be found in the way commentators on Somalia have conceptualized the Sharia courts. Their approach to the courts is a specific example of a more general understanding in academia of Islam and Islamic movements in Sub-Saharan Africa. Academic research into Islam in Africa has often taken place in the shadow of Western desires to distinguish between potential adversaries and allies within Muslim societies. One consequence of that has been the conventional separation of Islam in Africa into two dichotomous entities: "traditional" or "African Islam" and reformist Islam or radical Islam.[2]

"African Islam" is considered to be in a synergetic relationship with African culture, which is itself viewed as distinct from Islam proper. Since some of the practices of Sufi orders (*tariqa*, plural *turuq*) such as saint veneration and tomb visitation are viewed as organically linked to African cultures, Sufism has come to be viewed as the epitome of "traditional" or "African Islam."

Moreover, this so-called "African Islam" is portrayed positively because it is assumed to be tolerant of different practices and less threatening to Western interests, in contrast to reformist Islam.

Reformist Islam, on the other hand, has been associated with pan-Islamic movements. Other commonly used labels for reformist movements are Wahhabi (in reference to interpretations and practices of Islam inspired by the eighteenth-century Arabian reformer Muhammad Abdul-Wahhab) or Salafi (a label which invokes the practices of "the pious ancestors" as a model which today's Muslims should aspire to) or simply "radical." Through such labelling, attempts by African Muslims to change their societies in accordance with what they deem to be the correct teachings of Islam are reduced to emulations of Islam as practiced elsewhere. Movements so labelled are often portrayed as posing a threat and a challenge to traditional "African Islam" and Western interests. This over-simplification of the complex and changing practices of Islam and Islamic reform movements in Africa has influenced how commentators on Somalia understood the Sharia courts of Mogadishu.

In line with the general depiction of Islam in Africa, the Sharia courts have been analysed in terms of where they fit in the categories of "African Islam" and reformist or radical Islam. The courts are usually depicted as an outright radical movement or a vehicle for the spread of radicalism.[3] Since what is referred to as radical or reformist Islam is viewed as foreign to Africa, the Sharia court movement is seen as having roots outside of Somalia. The argument is that the Sharia courts took root and emerged because fundamentalist clerics, informed and influenced by foreign religious networks, took advantage of a vulnerable population to impose a strict, in other words, non-traditional, understanding of the Sharia. These clerics promised that through the strict interpretation of the Sharia, they would resolve the insecurity of Mogadishu. This way of depicting the Sharia courts is popular with many analysts because it is a direct consequence of that old and dichotomous approach to Islam in Africa, which has been rejuvenated by the "war on terror."

It is not that there are no partial truths in this framing of Islam in Africa, but the problem is once this framing is used to explain the efforts of Muslims in Africa to change the conditions of their life, a number of more complex considerations about the history and motivations of such efforts are rendered unnecessary.

To begin with, the courts were not simply a product of the influences of foreign sources. They built on concepts and practices that were deeply entrenched in Somali cultural and religious life. Second, it yields faulty analysis to think of the courts and law of the Sharia courts of Mogadishu in the same way we think of courts or law in the modern sense of these terms. The Sharia courts were not courts in the sense that courts are understood as an arena where "law" is executed by an authority that is distinct and above society.[4] Rather, the Sharia courts were products of their users. The courts, therefore, reflected the Sharia-informed ethical and moral outlook of the community.

Many commentators contend that the absence of the state since its collapse in 1991 created a "vacuum," which allowed the emergence of the Sharia courts and the spread of "radical" Islam in Somalia. On the contrary, I argue that the prolonged absence of the state, and with that its modernizing project of cultural and religious reforms, meant that the attempt to separate Sharia-informed communal ethics and morality from politics came to an end. The Sharia courts movement was an expression of a socio-political formation that was grounded in the ethical norms, discourses, notions of authority, and practices of the community from which it emerged. Any genuine effort at peace and reconciliation in Somalia cannot afford to ignore the experience of the Sharia courts.

Conclusion

My research leads me to conclude that the emergence of the Sharia courts of Mogadishu was an organic reconciliation and conflict resolution process that incorporated Somali custom (*xeer*) and Sharia norms. As such, the courts built on deeply held cultural and religious ideas about justice and legitimate authority. For this reason the search for peace and reconciliation in Somalia cannot afford to ignore the experience of the Sharia courts.

It is interesting to note that the internationally-led state-building project in Somalia often tries to legitimate institution-building efforts by involving traditional elders. This is despite the fact that the office of the traditional elder has, especially in southern Somalia, lost much respect and authority during the civil war. In emphasizing the role of traditional elders, the international community is informed by static notions of tradition and custom.

If, instead, the international community viewed tradition and custom as dynamic and subject to historical transformations, it would have seen that, as a result of the recent troublesome history, religious authorities have either augmented or replaced traditional elders as the locus of authority and governance in society. This is particularly the case for the South.

Historically, Somali custom and Sharia have always had a symbiotic relationship, such that it was always difficult to demarcate where one ended and the other began. Since the onset of the civil war, the distinction between custom and the Sharia, particularly in conflict resolution, has almost disappeared. The most influential traditional elders in terms of conflict resolution were the religious ones. This development was conditioned by the tremendous increase in insecurity and the magnitude of the problems that needed to be resolved. The formation of the Sharia courts was in many ways a manifestation of this fact. The over-emphasis on custom and traditional elders and the complete disregard of the Sharia and religious authorities by the international community is a product of a bias that should be corrected.

Recommendations

The following recommendations could help the government engender the trust of the local population and make them feel that injustice is being addressed. The government should empower district- and neighbourhood-level religious authorities to establish and run conflict resolution and reconciliation centres throughout Mogadishu. It is important that these religious authorities are from the neighbourhoods and districts where they work, and that they enjoy a level of separation and autonomy from the institutions of the state in order for them to have legitimacy in the eyes of the local population.

One way to accomplish this is for the judiciary or Ministry of Justice to either recruit well-known religious scholars (*ulema*) in Mogadishu or ask already existing *ulema* bodies to bring together sheikhs from the different neighbourhoods and districts in Mogadishu. A seminar should then be held for the sheikhs over a short period. The seminar should focus on informing the gathered sheikhs about the basic Sharia texts to be used; processes for resolving conflicts between the sheikhs themselves over the position of the Sharia; how to handle cases; which cases the sheikhs can handle; which they should turn over to other courts; and how to keep records, among other things. At the end of the seminar, all the participating sheikhs should be asked to take an exam. Those who pass the exam should be asked to form conflict resolution and reconciliation centres in the various districts and neighbourhoods of Mogadishu. The gathered *ulema* and sheikhs will know better than any expert the factors to consider in order for the centres to be legitimate in the eyes of those they are meant to serve.

The long-term aim should be to turn these centres into district-level courts and part of the formal court system. The short-term goal is to engender the local population's trust in the state-building project by making them see that injustice is been addressed by authorities and processes that they can understand and relate to. It goes without saying that the steps envisioned in these recommendations are contingent upon establishing a certain level of security in Mogadishu.

DETERMINANTS OF SUCCESS

ANALYSIS OF PEACE INITIATIVES
IN SOUTH-CENTRAL SOMALIA

Galymzhan Kirbassov

Author

Galymzhan Kirbassov is an Information Analyst in the Integrated Analysis Team of the United Nations Assistance Mission in Somalia.

Summary

Analysis of quantitative and qualitative data in this paper suggests that the success rate of local peace initiatives between clans varies significantly. While traditional conflict resolution mechanisms are often the first choice of the parties when dispute erupts, it does not guarantee that the peace agreement will hold for a long period. The findings show that there are several factors that affect the success rates of sustainable peace at local level. First, the intensity of conflict before the peace agreement is signed negatively affects the duration of peace. The higher the rate of fatalities during a conflict, the higher the likelihood that the peace agreement that followed it will fail. Second, military capabilities of the disputing clans determine if the peace agreement will succeed to sustain. Imbalance of military capability reduces the likely duration of peace because the stronger clan may have incentives to renege on the peace accord. In this regard, the success rate of peace initiatives is lower when one or both of the parties are pastoralist clans, which have historically had better access to weapons and been supported by the ruling elites. Third, third-party enforcement of peace accords by a credible and capable actor is found to be a crucial element of sustainable peace. The enforcer monitors the implementation of the peace agreement and can credibly threaten to punish non-compliance. These findings, however, need to be read with some caution. The data and systematic studies on the local peace initiatives in Somalia are very limited. The paper attempted to collect quantitative and qualitative data and build a database of peace initiatives. For more accurate analyses, additional resources need to be invested in data collection and in-depth case studies.

Introduction

Since the collapse of the government in 1991, hundreds of violent clan conflicts have taken place in Somalia, some over political control of cities and regions and some over resources such as livestock, water and land for grazing and agriculture. Somali policy-makers, neighbouring countries, and international partners have engaged in multiple interventions to reconcile the major clans at national and regional levels, with some degree of success.[1] However, less attention has been given to resolving local disputes between sub-clans. These disputes, mostly over land and water resources, in the absence of capable government authorities and law enforcement institutions, have claimed hundreds, if not thousands, of lives. Often, local disputes have been mediated by traditional elders with the application of customary law (*xeer*) in combination with Islamic Sharia. While some of these peace initiatives still hold, others have failed at different times. The fundamental question this paper attempts to answer is what determines the success of local peace initiatives. Understanding these local processes is essential for policy-makers to implement national or regional reconciliation initiatives.

Traditional Mechanisms of Conflict Resolution in Somalia

Legal systems and conflict resolution mechanisms in Somalia have varied throughout history. During the colonial era, for example, south-central Somalia was subject to Italian penal and civil codes while some legal cases in

Somaliland were subject to British Common Law. However, these Western laws were not applied universally and were not the sole bases of the justice system. Rather, a combination of Islamic Sharia and *xeer* along with Italian and British legal regulations was in place to provide justice in Somalia.[2] During Siad Barre's rule, the regime undermined the traditional structures of justice and conflict resolution by supporting certain clans and faction leaders for political gains. This trend continued after the collapse of the state when major sub-clan groups started acquiring weapons and forming alliances with minor sub-clan groups. As discussed below, the militarization of clans led to the diminished significance of *xeer* and undermined the authority of traditional elders in conflict resolution.

Despite its weakened significance, and in the absence of formal mechanisms, *xeer* has been widely applied to resolve local disputes and manage conflicts in agricultural and pastoral communities in the rural areas. A typical local peace process in these communities usually starts with a meeting of traditional elders of both parties, who share information about the dispute and try to contain the escalation. They may agree on several steps during the process including the cessation of hostility (*colaad joojin*), disengagement of forces (*kala rarid/kala fogeyn*) and ceasefire (*xabbad joojin*). After finding common understanding, the elders hold mediation meetings in public and try to reach an agreement, including on the amount of *diya* (blood compensation) to be paid in cases of killing. If the disputing parties cannot find an agreeable solution, a third party, usually elders of a neighbouring clan, offers mediation.[3]

As Islam has been dominant in both everyday life and the public domain in Somalia, Sharia law has been applied to serve justice in combination with customary law *xeer*. For instance, the Sharia is seen by some Somalis as establishing certain punishments for crimes, such as the death penalty in cases of killing. However, Sharia also stresses patience and forgiveness, leaving some room for negotiations in case the parties wish to come to an agreement on compensation and escape the death penalty.[4]

Data Description

The data for this study heavily rely on a few studies on local peace initiatives and academic databases recording clan conflicts. To the author's knowledge, there has not been any systematic data collection specifically on local peace initiatives except for the 2008 report of the Interpeace and Center for Research and Dialogue (CRD).[5] The report records data relating to roughly

70 local peace initiatives in south-central Somalia and establishes a starting point for this paper.

To understand why some local peace initiatives succeed while others fail, the author developed the Somalia Local Peace Initiatives (SLPI) database that included data on the date of peace initiatives, the date peace ended, the duration of peace in months, clans and sub-clans of the actors involved, whether the parties were mainly farmers or pastoralists, the key issue addressed by the initiative and the number of fatalities before the peace process began.

The sample encompasses 65 local peace initiatives which took place in south-central Somalia between 1991 and 2007. It should be noted however that these initiatives are based on the 2008 report by Interpeace and CRD, which does not clarify the coding rules. For example, we do not know if the peace agreements were initiated to resolve armed clashes or non-violent disputes between the parties. Using the Non-State Conflict database of the Uppsala Conflict Data Program (UCDP)[6] and the Armed Conflict Location and Event Data Project (ACLED) database, I identified if the actors involved in the 65 peace initiatives had engaged each other in armed conflict. Only 12 peace initiatives had resolved disputes that involved armed conflict with fatalities and these conflicts caused an average of 69 battle-related deaths.[7]

To identify if the peace initiatives have held successfully (until May 2017) or failed some time ago, I checked the UCDP and ACLED databases and recorded the dates when the disputing parties were engaged in armed conflict after an agreement was reached. I coded the peace as "ended" if these conflicts resulted in at least five battle-related deaths. Only nine of the 65 peace agreements failed to secure a sustainable peace. The average duration of peace in these nine cases was just over five years (61 months).

The number of intra-clan peace initiatives recorded in the SLPI database is 38, compared to 27 inter-clan initiatives.[8] Figure 1 shows the distribution of these initiatives recorded in the database. The following graph (Figure 2) depicts the number of peace initiatives by issue type. Even though observations based on resource and revenge are categorized separately, they are related to each other. Most of the revenge killings start with conflict over resources such as water and land for agriculture and pasture.

Data Analysis: Determinants of Successful Local Peace Initiatives

The SLPI database shows varying duration of peace among the clans. Based on the theories of duration of peace agreements in intra-state conflicts,[9] several

Figure 1: Peace initiatives in south-central Somalia by clan, 1991–2007

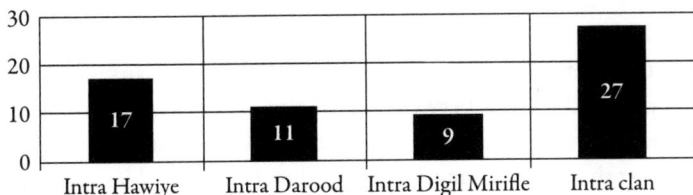

Figure 2: Peace initiatives in south-central Somalia by issue, 1991–2007

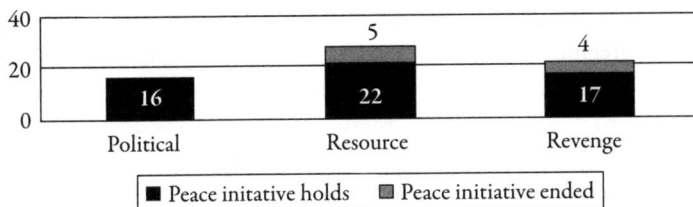

factors were identified which were expected to explain this variation in the data and highlight the patterns of successful peace initiatives.

Xeer, *Traditional Elders and Limitations*

Studies suggest that sustainable peace among clans in conflict can be achieved if a bottom-up approach to peacebuilding is utilized.[10] For example, the Interpeace and CRD 2008 Report explores three cases of local peace initiatives. The first case documents local peace initiatives between Hubeer and Yantaar, two sub-clans of Digil Mirifle in Idale village, located near Baidoa, Bay region. Armed conflict erupted between two sub-clans in 2004 over the use of water catchments for livestock. The conflict claimed about 106 deaths until the traditional elders from both sides decided to meet and resolve it peacefully.

However, at least five peace initiative attempts led by traditional elders failed to resolve the conflict. The sides clashed several times despite the fact that elders of their clans agreed on the cessation of hostilities. Eventually, when the Transitional Federal Government (TFG) relocated to Baidoa in early 2006, the National Reconciliation Commission (NRC) was tasked to step in and exercised its full authority to resolve the conflict. As will be discussed below, capable and credible third-party enforcement, the TFG in this case, is essential to reach a peace agreement and enforce its implementation.

This case shows that traditional conflict resolution methods are necessary but not sufficient to reach and sustain local peace agreements.

The other two cases documented in the same report shed light on local peace initiatives between Galjecel and Jijele (both sub-clans of Hawiye) in Beledweyne in 2005 and between Sacad and Suleiman (both sub-clans of Habar Gidir/Hawiye) in Southern Gaalkacyo and Cadado in 2007. The study suggests that the involvement of traditional and religious elders, private business owners, third-party clans and national and regional politicians in both cases was important in achieving and sustaining the peace initiatives. However, the UCDP and ACLED databases show that neither case succeeded in sustaining those peace agreements. Galjecel and Jijele clans broke the peace agreement in December 2015 and have been involved in violent clashes in Beledweyne since then. The duration of peace between Sacad and Suleiman clans was even shorter. These sub-clans breached the peace agreement in November 2010, killing many members of the opposite clan. Once again, traditional mechanisms and actors were not sufficient for sustaining peace between clans.

Battle-related Fatalities Prior to a Peace Initiative

Some studies of civil wars find empirical evidence for the negative impact of total fatalities on the duration of peace.[11] The higher the fatality rate in conflicts, the lower the likelihood that peace is sustained after an agreement is reached. These findings may also apply in local clan conflicts and peace agreements because of similar forces and dynamics involved. High human cost may produce feelings of insecurity and revenge and reduce the levels of trust and social cohesion between the members of the disputing clans. As a consequence, the likelihood of revenge killings and renewed violence may be high, despite the peace settlement achieved through negotiations.

Although the small sample size in the SLPI database does not allow for regression analysis, it is still useful for conducting correlation analysis and identifying relationships between fatalities and local peace duration. For the analysis, I chose only those peace initiatives where the disputing actors had previously engaged in armed conflict and suffered a significant number of human losses. Out of 12 such initiatives, five failed to secure the peace, and endured for an average duration of three and a half years (42 months) before the agreement was breached. In seven cases peace was sustained. The average duration of peace in these cases is 12.5 years (150 months).[12] While the average fatality count prior

Figure 3: Correlation between fatality and peace duration, r = 0.5

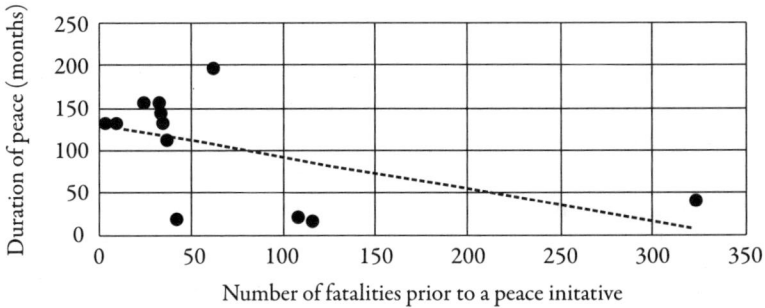

Number of fatalities prior to a peace initative

to the peace initiatives for all 12 cases was 69, the peace initiatives that failed had an average of 125 deaths and the ones that were sustained had an average of 29 fatalities.

The correlation analysis of this data shows a negative relationship between total fatalities and local peace duration (Figure 3). A higher number of deaths occurring before a peace agreement is reached is associated with a reduced duration of peace. To show some examples, Sacad and Suleiman sub-clans often engaged in violent fights over grazing land, livestock loots and subsequent revenge killings in south Mudug and Galgaduud regions. The cumulative fatalities before the peace agreement reached up to 323, a significant number that indicates a high level of hostility. Even though traditional and religious leaders, politicians and private business owners facilitated peace initiatives in 2007 and addressed the issues of conflict, the mistrust between the clans has remained high. The peace was breached in 2010.

Another case of violent conflict between Sacad and Dir clans in Gaalkacyo claimed 108 deaths. Although a peace agreement was reached in 2005 with the mediation of traditional elders, it failed to last longer than 21 months. In contrast, the local peace agreement reached in 2000 between Galjecel and Hawadle (both Hawiye) in Beledweyne and the peace between Afi and Abtisame (both Hawiye) achieved in 2005 in Bulo Burto district in Hiraan still hold. The former clans suffered 62 battle-related deaths before the peace agreement while the latter lost 34 people.

Militarization of Clans and the Balance of Power

Another factor that might affect the duration of peace is the relative military capability of clans. During peace negotiations, stronger clans with superior military capability have greater bargaining power to ensure a more favourable deal. For instance, if a *diya*-paying clan is stronger than the victimized clan, the amount of compensation can significantly be lowered. But clans with greater military capabilities than others may be tempted to exploit this advantage and renege on their commitments under a peace agreement.

Throughout the modern history of Somalia, ruling elites empowered certain clans politically and militarily against others in return for political support. During Siad Barre's rule, the regime heavily supported pastoralist Darood sub-clans and some of the Hawiye sub-clans, and excluded Digil Mirifle and minority clans. For instance, 11 of the 25 members of the Supreme Revolutionary Council[13] were Darood and the rest Hawiye, Dir and Isaaq, with no members from Digil Mirifle. In 1973–74, over 100,000 pastoralists, mostly from Darood and Hawiye clans, were resettled by the government to arable land in the inter-riverine regions, traditionally inhabited by farmer communities of Digil Mirifle clan.[14]

After the state collapse, two Hawiye leaders, Muhammad Farah Aidid of Habar Gidir sub-clan (Hawiye) and Ali Mahdi Muhammad of Abgal (Hawiye), fought a devastating war to control Mogadishu and central Somalia. Two faction leaders heavily armed allied clans. In 1995, Aidid's forces occupied Bay and Bakool regions and captured agricultural lands of unarmed Digil Mirifle clans.[15] Throughout these periods, Digil Mirifle clans were excluded from the ranks of the Somali military and had no access to weapons.[16]

To analyse how militarization and dynamics of clan politics might have affected the peace initiatives, I coded the parties to the peace agreements as pastoralists and farmers, based on the studies on Somali clans. In the absence of reliable data, the categories of pastoralist versus farmers serve as a proxy measure for the military capability of clans involved in conflict and peace initiatives. A number of scholars categorize most of the sub-clans of Hawiye, Darood and Dir as nomads and pastoralists while Digil Mirifle clans are said to be farmers residing between the Shabelle and Jubba rivers.[17] Some clans lived an agro-pastoralist lifestyle and therefore I paid particular attention to the exact location where these clans resided. For example, I coded Hawadle and Abgal sub-clans of Hawiye as farmers as they lived near the Shabelle river basin and primarily made their living from agriculture.[18] Although this categorization is a rough proxy for the military capability of clans, it reflects the politics of the previous Somali ruling elites to support or marginalize certain clans.

The analysis of data reveals that 38 peace initiatives in the SLPI database were concluded between pastoralist clans, 15 between pastoralists and farmers and 12 between the farmers. Importantly, 13 per cent of the peace initiatives between pastoralists and 20 per cent of those between pastoralists and farmers failed to last until the present day. By comparison, only 8 per cent of intra-farmer peace agreements were broken. This finding supports the argument that militarily capable, especially dominant, clans, are less likely to abide by the terms of a peace agreement. When one side in the peace negotiations is a pastoralist clan with stronger military capability, the likelihood of a sustained peace is reduced. For more accurate analyses, however, further studies need to be conducted to measure the military capabilities of the clans in peace negotiations.

Third-party Enforcement of Local Peace Initiatives

Studies find that credible and capable third-party enforcement of peace agreements substantially increases the duration of peace after intra-state conflicts.[19] Third-party monitors and guarantors help to ensure that the provisions of the agreement are implemented and provide security guarantees for the parties. This is an effective solution for the commitment problem, when neither side of the conflict can credibly commit not to renege on the agreement.

Analysis of the local peace initiatives in Somalia suggests that enforcement by a third party is one of the necessary conditions for durable peace. The Interpeace and CRD 2008 Report provides a detailed study of a local peace initiative between Hubeer and Yantaar sub-clans of Digil Mirifle near Baidoa. The peace negotiations led by traditional elders began in 2004 in the neighbouring Xagar village. The communities reached peace agreements several times after this initial one: in Xawaale Barbaar village in January 2005, in Qansaxdhere in April 2005, and in Hagarkaa village in July 2006. All these peace accords were breached by one or the other side, usually by killing a clan member, followed by a fight for revenge.

Another opportunity for peace negotiations came up when the TFG had just settled in Baidoa. The government, through the NRC, exercised full authority to resolve the conflict. The agreement was written in an authoritative manner rather than reconciliatory, identifying penalties for breaches. After the agreement was signed, the government established an inclusive administration and a police station for Idale village. The chairman of the village administration and his deputy were appointed from Yantaar and Hubeer sub-clans respectively. The chief of the police station was from Geeladle, a different Digil Mirifle sub-clan. The analysis of all peace initiatives in Idale village suggests that a third party, the TFG, was essential for securing a durable peace. The government was perceived as credible by both parties, and capable of enforcing the provisions of the agreement.

Although the peace initiatives in Somaliland and Puntland are outside the scope of this paper, some literature suggests that because of the capable enforcement mechanisms in these regions, peace settlements have been sustained for longer than in south-central Somalia. In studying why customary law, *xeer*, worked well in resolving disputes between clans in some regions but not in others, Schlee suggests that some form of government structure was essential to enforce peace agreements.[20] For instance, British rule in Somaliland did not rely solely on *xeer*, but rather reinforced it with formal police. In cases where clans did not pay *diya* compensation, the district commissioner sent police to collect and deliver animals. Similar cases have been observed in Puntland where some structures of capable government and police existed that could enforce local peace initiatives. In the absence of such enforcement institutions in rural south-central Somalia, conflicts mediated and settled by traditional elders through *xeer* often recurred due to the imbalance in the military power of clans.

Mediation and enforcement of agreements by Al-Shabaab have also been reported by different sources. For instance, the militant group seized the administrative control of El Waq, Luuq, Garbaharey and Bardera in Gedo region in 2008. Al-Shabaab mediated clan conflicts and strictly enforced a rule that ensured no clan fought over resources such as water and land. No major clan clash was reported in these locations after the rule was enforced, according to the 2013 report of the Conflict Early Warning Early Response Unit.[21] The long duration of peace was not due to the effectiveness and credibility of Al-Shabaab, but rather to the group's capability to enforce agreements through punishing non-compliance.

Conclusion

Brief quantitative and qualitative analyses of local peace initiatives in this paper suggest that there are several crucial factors that affect the success of local peace initiatives. While the initiation of peace negotiations locally by traditional elders is necessary, it needs to be supported and enforced by a capable third party to endure for a longer period. The intensity of conflict, in terms of fatalities and human cost, has a negative effect on peace duration. The higher the fatality as a result of clan conflict, the lower the likelihood that the peace settlement will be sustained for a long period of time. Additionally, evidence suggests that peace agreements involving militarily dominant clans are more vulnerable to breaches than cases where there is greater parity between the clans.

Recommendations

Local peace initiatives between clans at local levels in Somalia are severely understudied, which limits our understanding of the subject. This paper attempts to explain the factors behind successful local peace agreements, but the findings should be treated with caution due to a shortage of relevant data. The Federal Government of Somalia (FGS) and its international partners should invest in detailed quantitative and qualitative studies on the subject to improve their understanding and draw more nuanced policyguidance. Extension of state authority to districts and rural areas depends on better understanding of successful and failed peace initiatives.

The FGS and the Federal Member States should pay special attention to certain kinds of local peace initiatives that may be more vulnerable to failure than others. These include peace agreements initiated after clan conflicts with very high fatality rates and where there is a militarily dominant clan on one or both sides. Evidence suggests that these peace initiatives may require higher levels of support to succeed.

Measures for the enforcement of agreements are possibly the most important factor in determining the success of local peace initiatives. Although mediation by traditional elders and regional government officials is necessary, it is not a sufficient condition for sustainable peace. Third-party enforcement by a credible and capable authority helps to ensure that neither party reneges on the agreement by raising the costs of non-compliance. Enforcement of this kind also gives time for the conflicting sides to reconcile, improve trust and establish an inclusive mechanism to institutionalize the peace.

During implementation of the Security Pact and Comprehensive Approach to Security, attention must be given not to empower clan militias who were previously involved in disputes with other clans. Training and possibly arming these clan militias can fundamentally alter the existing balance of power between clans and substantially increase the risk of a relapse into conflict despite signed peace agreements. Similarly, steps should be taken to guard against the establishment of police or military units composed of clan militias that have had historic rivalries and disputes with other clans.

AMISOM

CHALLENGES OF INFLUENCE, IMPARTIALITY
AND DISENGAGEMENT

Najum Mushtaq

Authorship

Najum Mushtaq has covered Somalia since 2006 as a journalist, aid worker, and conflict analyst. This briefing paper was commissioned by the Life & Peace Institute (LPI), an international organization that has supported community-led reconciliation processes across Somalia in partnership with Somali civil society since the early 1990s.

Summary

The African Union Mission in Somalia (AMISOM) has faced a number of internal and external challenges since its deployment in 2007. The mission's original mandate, composition and strength, and military strategy have over time been shaped by the political dynamics within Somalia, actions of neighbouring states such as Kenya and Ethiopia and, more significantly, by military considerations on the part of the international community associated with the "war on terror," led by the United States (US) and its Africa command,

AFRICOM. AMISOM has played a critical role in enabling the Federal Government of Somalia (FGS) to meet key state-building targets leading to the 2017 transfer of power. However, AMISOM's core task—to reduce the threat of Al-Shabaab and, in areas recovered from Al-Shabaab, provide security to enable stabilization and peacebuilding—remains incomplete. Modest results on the ground in recent years have been unsustainable, as Al-Shabaab still maintains significant territorial control in the hinterlands of south-central Somalia, as well as the military capability to strike in urban centres, especially Mogadishu.

In terms of local reconciliation and dialogue, AMISOM's ability to create stability to enable intra-Somali dialogue has been undermined by suspicion and mistrust of foreign forces. AMISOM's decentralized command structure, with forces from each participating country carving up zones of operation in alliance with disparate Somali partners,[1] may have deepened the fragmentation of the Somali polity and society. It has also entrenched the culture of proxies in local conflicts as, in addition to Somali government forces, AMISOM also conducts operations with armed forces that are not part of the Somali National and Security Forces (SNSF).[2]

AMISOM's planned exit as envisaged under the May 2017 Security Pact[3] faces the same challenges that the mission has confronted during the last ten years. The benchmarks set in the Security Pact with Somalia suggest a continuation of the militarized approach to addressing peace and security issues. The proposed plan appears to place local reconciliation and peacebuilding within the framework of security sector reform and state-building. This paper suggests that these processes should be founded on a comprehensive peace settlement and a broad-based political response to the threat of Al-Shabaab, as well as to clan conflicts.

Introduction

Even before the advent of AMISOM, persistent and extreme levels of state fragility in Somalia had prompted many UN-sanctioned as well as unilateral foreign military interventions since 1992.[4]

Famine and related humanitarian crises, state-building, and terrorism have been the rationale behind sending national and multinational forces into Somalia's south-central regions. As plans are drawn up for AMISOM's withdrawal after the next Somali elections, the United States has pledged to significantly and indefinitely increase its military presence and scope of operations inside Somalia, symbolizing a full cycle of foreign interventions that had started with the first Bush administration's humanitarian military intervention.[5] None of these efforts have decisively solved the problems of either famine or terrorism, and the state-building process continues to face daunting challenges.[6]

The consequences and results of the foreign presence in Somalia have been extensively documented and analysed, while a number of assessments (both internal and external) of AMISOM's impact have also been produced. Based on these reports and documents, and monitoring of the Somali and international media, this paper presents a brief review of AMISOM's origins, growth and performance, from a Somali peacebuilding and conflict transformation perspective.

The paper aims to draw lessons for future international security cooperation as spelt out in the May 2017 New Partnership with Somalia. The paper employs a comparative contextual analysis approach to take stock of AMISOM's intervention against some key objectives listed in its mandate and seeks to answer the question of how the conflict landscape in south-central Somalia has changed since the deployment of AMISOM. It asks whether AMISOM's multi-pronged strategy of complementing the dominant military approaches with support to the FGS in reconciliation, dialogue and peacebuilding has been successful. The paper also examines AMISOM's military and non-military measures to catalyse progress towards the objective for which this mission was set in motion in 2007.

AMISOM 2007–2017: A Comparative Context Analysis

Analyses of AMISOM's performance differ widely. The African Union (AU) military mission has been lauded for its critical role in successive peaceful transitions of power in Mogadishu in 2012 and 2017, the creation of space for the formation of Federal Member States (FMS) and subsequent elections, eviction of Al-Shabaab forces from most major urban centres in south-central regions and the institution of a rudimentary state security structure.[7] On the other hand, the mission has been developed in the context of disputes over funding issues, weak internal coordination characterized by a sector-based approach, and negative local perceptions—the national agendas of troop-contributing countries having often dictated AMISOM's operations and goals.[8] The mission has also been accused of having a negative impact on local drivers of conflict, as its focus on tackling Al-Shabaab has not been underpinned with a coherent long-term peace strategy.[9] From uncertain and modest beginnings, AMISOM "has morphed into a broader counter-insurgency and stabilization campaign conducted across vast swathes of countryside and many urban settlements."[10]

When AMISOM was first deployed in March 2007, south-central Somalia was in a state of violent turmoil after a brief period of peace in the second half of 2006 under the Union of Islamic Courts (UIC). Ethiopian forces that had dislodged the UIC were under intense assault by Al-Shabaab and Hizbul Islami, the military wings of the Islamic Courts. Authorized by United Nations Security Council (UNSC) Resolution 2124, AMISOM was first deployed in March 2007 with 1,600 Ugandan soldiers to guard selected districts of Mogadishu, to protect the then Transitional Federal Government and as a replacement for Ethiopian forces. Burundian troops joined in December 2007 as Ethiopia prepared to withdraw its troops under an intense assault by Al-Shabaab and its allies, and domestic and international pressure. The withdrawal eventually took place in 2009. However, Ethiopian forces returned in 2011 as Kenya launched Operation Linda Nchi, sending its forces into Jubbaland in October 2011. Neither country had then joined AMISOM. A few months later, Djibouti contributed troops. Even when Kenya (in 2012) and Ethiopia (in 2014) joined the AU force, elements of their troops remained outside the AMISOM fold.

It was during the surge in troops in 2011 and 2012 that AMISOM was able to take control of Mogadishu, Kismayo and other major urban areas from Al-Shabaab. However, as a 2013 Swedish Defence Research Agency (*Totalförsvarets forskningsinstitut* (FOI)) review noted, "an initial defeat of irregular forces does not equate to securing a sustainable peace ... Al-Shabaab still retains the ability to strike within and outside of Somalia. Nevertheless, limiting the organization's control of the capital and other major cities has enabled a new era of state governance in the country."[11] Securing the majority of regional capitals also facilitated the process of state-formation, as stipulated in the 2013 New Deal with Somalia.[12] Initially, AMISOM's core tasks were to support the Somali government's efforts to stabilize Somalia and enable further dialogue and reconciliation. The component of improving the capacity of the Somali National Army (SNA) and police was added to its mandate in January 2014 to enable a safer environment for the political process including reconciliation and elections, as part of AMISOM's exit strategy.

Throughout the AMISOM period, counter-insurgency operations in Somalia led by the United States continued to run parallel to, or in coordination with, AMISOM and local Somali forces.[13] This association with the counter-terrorism operations of the United States, also the main AMISOM donor along with the European Union, further reinforces the AU mission's status as a partner of AFRICOM, rather than a regional peacekeeping force.[14] In 2017 the Pentagon announced its plans to intensify operations in Somalia under relaxed vetting rules for military strikes inside the country, increasing the potential for civilian casualties or striking incorrect military targets, as took place in September 2016 in Galmudug.[15] Stationed in Djibouti, AFRICOM's counter-terrorism task force campaign plan is "to neutralize Al-Shabaab and transition from AMISOM to the Federal Government of Somalia."[16]

This transition framework represents a significant shift, as under the original AMISOM plan, as well as subsequent reviews, transition to a UN peace-keeping force has been the preferred mode of exit. However, the new administration of President Mohamed Abdullahi "Farmaajo" aims for a transition to the SNA and national security forces, also reflected in the new Security Pact with international partners.[17]

AMISOM and Local Clan Conflicts

The sector-based distribution of troops, which divided south-central Somalia into five zones,[18] and the mode of its military operations, which required partnership with local Somali clan forces, undermined AMISOM's effectiveness in creating stability as a prerequisite for dialogue and reconciliation in recovered areas. The formation of sectors has not only resulted in divided command of the forces and lack of coordination between different arms of AMISOM, it has also drawn troops into internecine intra-Somali clan conflicts. For instance, the Kenyan and Ethiopian forces—both in AMISOM hats and under national command—have been deployed in areas along the Somalia border with the implicit purpose of securing their Somali-dominated border regions, thereby creating "buffer zones." The Jubbaland State administration, controlled by the Darood/Ogaden clan, relies on the Kenyan contingent for security and military operations against Al-Shabaab and leverages this alliance in relations with other rival clans, putting AMISOM at risk of becoming a party to local conflicts, and reducing its ability to impartially engage with all stakeholders across clan divides.[19] Ethiopia's AMISOM forces also included Ogadeni clan militia from the Ethiopian Somali region which, analysts have noted, led to clashes with other clans in the border region.[20]

Ethiopia openly supports Ahlu Sunna Wal Jama'a (ASWJ)—the "moderate" Islamic militia—and the Shabelle Valley Alliance, which had helped

AMISOM take back Beledweyn (the capital of Hiran) from Al-Shabaab.[21] In Lower Shabelle, AMISOM has been embroiled in the Habar Gidir-Biyamal conflict, as militias from both clans at different times fought alongside or against AMISOM and being labelled as Al-Shabaab allies when not supporting AMISOM. This phenomenon of Somali clans being seen as proxies to neighbouring countries has damaged the civilian and peacemaking component of AMISOM.

During the process of setting up FMSs, AMISOM was tasked with providing security and facilitating their formation in "liberated" areas. The process was marred by clan conflicts over power-sharing and representation in the new administrations. As the UN Monitoring Group noted in 2015, clan conflicts emerging over the newly-recovered towns, inter-communal clashes and fighting over land and water resources had often intensified after Al-Shabaab withdrew from its strongholds.[22] In fact, the presence of AMISOM forces has provided propaganda tools to Al-Shabaab that "depict[s] a vast global conspiracy against Islam in Somalia while at the same time voicing Somali nationalist outrage over the presence of infidel, Crusader occupying forces on 'our soil.'"[23]

Lack of coordination between AMISOM forces, and unilateral operational decisions, such as Ethiopian troops withdrawing from "liberated" areas, seemingly without coordinating with AMISOM forces or the FGS, has created a security gap, endangering the lives of local communities, particularly elders and youth who have been accused by Al-Shabaab of supporting the "infidel government" when they take over in the power vacuum.[24]

Challenges and Response: The New Security Pact and AMISOM's Future

Immediately after his election, President Farmaajo described defeating Al-Shabaab as his top priority and pledged to work with AMISOM until the SNA has been rebuilt and is adequately prepared to replace AU troops. The FGS envisages a new security architecture in Somalia, and has fast-tracked the process of its approval. In his first meeting with AU leaders and envoys of the troop-contributing countries in Mogadishu, President Farmaajo enunciated his policy with a clear objective and limited timeline, stating that his "vision is to defeat Al-Shabaab in two years."[25] The Special Representative of the African Union Commission for Somalia, Ambassador Francisco Madeira, has also supported the idea: "The President has set up his priorities. He wants Al-Shabaab defeated as quickly as possible. We assured the President that we are with him in that endeavour."[26]

The May 2017 London Security Pact signed by the Somali Federal Government and 42 international partners endorses the "political agreement reached by the FGS and Federal Member States on 16 April 2017 on Somalia's National Security Architecture."[27] The Pact sets milestones and benchmarks over the next four years, towards "achieving sustainable security reform and a transition of primary responsibility of security from AMISOM to Somali security forces."[28]

Within six months, starting on 1 June 2017, the Pact envisaged commissioning a SNA "with a unified Somali doctrine"[29] of at least 18,000 (excluding 5,000 *Danab* or special forces, air force and navy). It also aimed, within the same timeframe, to set up a Somali Police Force of 32,000, divided into federal police and state police, as well as the Somali Coastguard and *Darwish* (reserve) forces at the federal level.[30] The existing regional forces will become part of the SNA or part of the state police.

The Pact also sets the framework for security institutions and decision-making in Somalia. All partners also endorse the New Policing Model,[31] and urge Somalia's leaders to expedite agreement on a federal model for the justice sector. The New Policing Model sets out the framework for how policing will be governed and delivered in Somalia, with a division of responsibilities between the federal level and the states.[32] An amnesty plan has also been announced to encourage Al-Shabaab defectors.

The Somali government has set the bar high, with ambitious goals and tight timeframes, especially given the challenges AMISOM has faced throughout its presence. An assessment of ten years of AMISOM operations by the Mogadishu-based Heritage Institute for Policy Studies identifies the following challenges to AMISOM's presence and successful exit from Somalia:[33]

1. The lack of a political settlement among Somali political and clan elites on the country's future political dispensation and the constitutional review.
2. The persistent threat of Al-Shabaab.
3. Internal AMISOM challenges, especially the lack of adequate military resources, weak centralized command and control, inability to stabilize "liberated" areas and consolidate military gains, and accusations of heavy-handed tactics leading to the death of civilians, sexual offences, and corruption.
4. Problems in building the SNA into a cohesive and organized force composed of individuals from across Somalia rather than being a collection of clan militias.

5. Negative local perceptions of AMISOM, especially due to the presence of troops from bordering states.

Domestic political opposition inside the national parliament, and in the FMS, is also developing against provisions and procedures envisioned in the Pact. For instance, when Somali leaders and international diplomats announced the approval of the newest security architecture, the parliamentary Defence Committee was dismayed at its lack of involvement in the deliberations. It suggested several revisions of its own that included increasing the cap of SNA forces to 22,000,[34] and amending what it considered "unconstitutional" provisions, such as decision-making without parliament's assent.[35]

An additional practical challenge to the plan is the complicated and inefficient procedures for payment of salaries—an issue that also plagued AMISOM and will harm the prospects of building the SNA as well. In March and May of 2017, hundreds of troops staged protests in front of the Defence Ministry in Mogadishu over non-payment of salaries to SNA Forces in Puntland, and the Galmudug region has faced similar problems.[36]

Prominent Somali analysts believe that the "tendency to rely on the NLF [National Leadership Forum—a group of senior national and regional leaders] for execution of major deals risks boxing out parliamentary and independent commissions that are already hampered by low political influence and interference ... Deferring [it] to minor roles may draw complicating reactions, which would not necessarily impact how troops move on the ground but would challenge the public credibility of the security reform process and create new conflicts after AMISOM's withdrawal."[37] The planned AMISOM drawdown will thus need to be calibrated in accordance with the level of the SNA's development, organizational discipline and capacity to fill the vacuum.

Conclusion

The AMISOM experience in Somalia brings into question the primacy of military means in countering terrorism or rebuilding a collapsed state. A decade of military operations by African Union forces in Somalia, with an explicit mandate to achieve security in order to enable reconciliation and dialogue, and to defeat Al-Shabaab, has struggled to achieve either. The flaws and shortcomings of AMISOM have overshadowed achievements in terms of recovering areas from Al-Shabaab. However, the removal of Al-Shabaab has not always translated into stability and consolidation of the Somali government's authority in those areas. As the military operations were not matched or backed by robust and comprehensive diplomatic and political initiatives, a broad-based, Somalia-wide peace and reconciliation process remains a distant goal. The mission was also marked by a lack of unity of purpose and hampered by financial and bureaucratic constraints. Its activities were often dictated by disparate national interests of its constituent forces, and they were seen with suspicion by the several Somali communities and stakeholders.

The AMISOM experience also alludes to the fact that no external military mission can continue indefinitely. Ultimately, the responsibility for securing the country, putting in place state institutions and establishing political order lies with the local political stakeholders, even if international support and partnership remain critical to the success of the Somali state-building process.

Recommendations

The AU and UN should:

- Take into account independent assessments of AMISOM's structural problems, coordination issues and overall performance while recommending an extension of its mandate.
- Urge the FGS and Federal Member State administrations to lead and own local reconciliation and peacebuilding as AMISOM continues to be perceived as an alien and sometimes hostile force in Somalia.
- Prioritize training and integration of a unified SNA as the core task in the next phases of AMISOM's mandate renewal.
- Work with the FGS to initiate processes for a comprehensive, broad-based and inclusive political settlement among all major conflict actors in south-central Somalia before AMISOM's exit.
- Substantially expand the policing component of AMISOM over the next two years to help realize the objectives of the New Policing Model.
- Clarify AMISOM's role vis-à-vis non-AMISOM foreign forces present in Somalia.

AFRICOM/United States and EU should:

- Complement the surge in operations against Al-Shabaab with parallel diplomatic initiatives to find a durable political solution to the Somali conflicts.
- Ensure civilian input into decision-making about military operations in Somalia.

- Prioritize greater transparency in the resourcing, constitution and mandate of AMISOM.

Regional stakeholders should:

- Commit to the withdrawal of both AMISOM and non-AMISOM troops from Somalia within the timeframe stipulated in the new Security Pact.
- Advocate to FMS administrations working in concert with AMISOM to constructively participate in the constitutional review process to reach an agreement on distribution of powers and resources with the FGS.
- Work to reduce the risk of AMISOM becoming embroiled in local proxy conflicts, and leveraged as a tool for local political power contests, by discouraging the delineation of particular zones of Somalia as under the responsibility of particular troop-contributing countries.

The FGS should:

- Work to create political consensus within the Federal Parliament and in consultation with Federal Member States on the new Security Pact.
- Match the effort to meet Security Pact benchmarks with inter-clan dialogues to address lingering grievances and reach enforceable peace agreements at the local level.

PROMOTING NATIONAL PEACE
AND RECONCILIATION

RECONCILIATION IN SOMALIA

REFORM, REPRESENTATION AND RESPONSIBILITY

Aden Abdi and *Alexander Ramsbotham*

Authors

Aden Abdi is Horn of Africa Programme Director at Conciliation Resources. He previously worked on Somalia for the UK's Department for International Development, and development programmes for the Horn of Africa with NGOs CARE International and the International Rescue Committee.

Dr Alexander Ramsbotham is Director of Accord at Conciliation Resources. Previously he was research fellow at the Institute for Public Policy Research in London, a specialist adviser on Africa in the UK House of Lords and head of the Peace and Security Programme at the United Nations Association–UK.

Summary

Reconciliation versus reform: reconciliation needs to be integrated into state reform efforts in Somalia, to ensure that these contribute to the development of a functioning social contract for all Somalis. Currently, reconciliation and state reconstruction are addressed largely separately, with the

179

former receiving much less attention. This follows an enduring pattern from the civil war in the 1990s, and overlooks lessons of more effective state-building experiences from Somaliland.

Restructuring the state: some of the disagreements that have underpinned violent conflict in Somalia are visible today in disputes connected to the federal state restructuring process, for example relating to the distribution and administration of power. This is why reconciliation needs to be built into the process. Three dimensions of tension are discernable: within and among individual Federal Member States; between Federal Member States and the Federal Government in Mogadishu; and across Somalia's national borders.

Representation: representation in Somali political processes remains contentious, but is key to establish trust in the political system and to manage inter-clan relationships. The "transitional" 4.5 clan power-sharing model continues to divide Somalis, but no alternative has emerged. The level and nature of integration of religion and politics is integral to legitimate political transition, and needs to be negotiated inclusively in order to reconcile the interests of different groups.

Responsibility: reconciliation needs to be Somali-owned. Cross-clan support for the newly elected president provides an opportunity for a process with domestic accountability, but to succeed it needs to be inclusive. It also needs to acknowledge and address past violence. Somali customary law (*xeer*) has strong provisions on reconciliation and reparations, and has been widely used by traditional clan elders and religious leaders to peacefully resolve conflicts.

Recommendations

- Reconciliation is an enabler for effective state reform in Somalia and needs to be fully integrated in a comprehensive framework.
- The political function of Islam needs to be negotiated inclusively to reconcile the interests of different groups, including some that remain outside the political system.
- Cross-clan support for the president provides an opportunity for national leadership on a comprehensive framework for reconciliation.
- Progress in state reform needs to find ways to address past violence—acknowledging harm done and establishing accountability for violations of human rights.

- The provisional constitution provides for a truth and reconciliation commission; the commission in Mindanao provides examples of innovative practice to engage local communities.

Reconciliation in Somalia: Reform, Representation and Responsibility

Reconciliation is a priority for progress towards a peaceful polity in Somalia: so politicians can establish working relations, and communities can learn to coexist non-violently.[1] Reconciliation here is understood as "transforming relationships": horizontally, between communities; and vertically, between citizens and state institutions. "Transformation" refers to dismantling antagonistic relationships from the past and supporting efforts to build new relationships for a peaceful and inclusive future.[2]

Efforts to reform state institutions in Somalia are essential to develop a political system that can represent the needs of all Somali communities. But too often state reconstruction has been prioritized over reconciliation, and the essential synergies between the two objectives have been lost. In a society struggling to emerge from protracted and pervasive violent conflict, reconciliation cannot be an appendix or afterthought. It must be integral to state reconstruction, to ensure that such processes go beyond primarily technocratic exercises to build capacity or share power, to become essentially political endeavours to cultivate a functioning social contract based on civic trust.[3]

As Somalia embarks on another transition towards democratic and credible elections in 2020/21, under the new leadership of President Mohamed Abdullahi Mohamed "Farmaajo", this paper looks at the relationship between reconciliation and state restructuring in Somalia, and how one can facilitate the other. It analyses some of the core relational challenges to federal reform, and explores issues of representation and responsibility as key components of a more "reconciliation-sensitive" approach.

Reconciliation Versus Reform

An enduring trend in approaches to peace and reconciliation in Somalia, traceable back to the civil war in the 1990s, has been to prioritize state-building over reconciliation.[4] Perhaps unsurprisingly, therefore, there has been more progress in forming new administrations, creating new Federal Member States and, more recently, the peaceful transfer of power, compared with addressing the underlying causes of the Somali conflict. Failures to address structural drivers of violence, for example regarding challenges of inconsistent representation and exclusion, have contributed to uneven progress in efforts to advance democratization.

Political processes to restructure the Somali state and reform key institutions, in particular as they relate to decentralization, federalism and the constitution, need to accommodate interests of elites, constituencies and communities, and the interplay among these groups. To date, mediating Somali political elites with the aim of establishing governance institutions has been the mainstay of peace and reconciliation efforts in Somalia, focusing almost exclusively on power-sharing arrangements.

State-building in Somaliland is often cited as having been more effective than in other parts of Somalia.[5] In Somaliland, customary institutions, in particular councils of elders (*guurti*), have been integrated with modern state institutions based on elections, including a parliament and president. Traditional actors and customary institutions rooted in clan-based Somali society have been at the heart of the post-war state-building process, which brought a high degree of legitimacy derived from customary clan laws and values (*xeer*), and their capacities to uphold social cohesion and the well-being and security of clan members. Elders also played key roles in cultivating political order through a primarily bottom-up process. The Somaliland parliament comprises an elected House of Representatives and a House of Elders that is selected and appointed by the clans.[6]

One reason for this relative success is that the process in Somaliland in the 1990s started with reconciliation, followed by state formation and state-building: reconciliation was an enabler for state-building, not the other way around. Lengthy indigenous grassroots peacebuilding and reconciliation processes provided a secure foundation on which to establish a government and political institutions, which have combined a hybrid of Somali and Western democratic traditions.[7]

Of course, there are contextual idiosyncrasies that limit the transferability of approaches that have been successful in Somaliland: the clan elders system is comparatively strong; the Isaaq clan is dominant; most of the territory has been controlled by one armed group (the Somali National Movement— SNM); "war-economy" resources have not been significant; and there have been strong incentives to gain international and other recognition as a separate state. Meanwhile, some contestation over the state continues, especially in eastern areas with some Darood clans as well as with Puntland.[8]

Nevertheless, there are important lessons for Somalia today. The relatively successful Somaliland model has been based on an incremental approach—

from peacemaking to state formation in parallel with reconciliation and democratization.[9] Models of extensive and broad-based consultation are well-established in processes of political decision-making in Somali culture. Mechanisms to sustain momentum and assess progress are important, but processes with rigid timeframes have too often led to exclusionary outcomes as parties are forced to move forward without reconciling their differences, resulting in implementation challenges and spoiling actions later on. The rushed 2012 transition roadmap process, for example, produced a flawed provisional constitution, most provisions of which were ignored by the incoming federal administration (of Hassan Sheikh) and emerging Federal Member States. Notably, the reconciliation process in Somaliland avoided arbitrary deadlines and milestones.

Restructuring the State

Dysfunctional political and social relationships have contributed to persistent delays and setbacks to negotiating a more inclusive political settlement in Somalia—one that can accommodate the interests of powerful elites and provide a concrete and convincing basis to engage broader Somali society. The constitutional process and federalization, for example, have struggled to ensure broad legitimacy while also making measurable progress towards agreed benchmarks.

With the exception of Al-Shabaab and Somaliland, contestation over the state in Somalia has shifted to how it should be structured, as opposed to challenging it more fundamentally. Some of the essential disagreements that have underpinned violent conflict in Somalia are manifested in the federal process. This is why the federal process must also incorporate reconciliation efforts, to build trust and broker political agreements among protagonists at key stages of the process.[10] Three dimensions of tension are discernable and are outlined here: within and among individual Federal Member States; between Federal Member States and Mogadishu; and across Somalia's national borders.

First, tensions have been evident within or between individual Federal Member States. The provisional constitution (2012), which itself needs to be finalized and mandated through a popular vote, provides for two or more Somali regions to come together and form a Federal Member State. While the 2012 constitution automatically recognized the two existing administrations of Puntland and Somaliland as Federal Member States, the process of federating the rest of the country was soon mired in dispute.

The Jubbaland administration that emerged after Kenyan defence forces overthrew Al-Shabaab from territories bordering Kenya was recognized as the first Federal Member State. This occurred through a mediation process led by the Ethiopian government under the auspices of the Intergovernmental Authority on Development (IGAD) between the Federal Government and leader of the Ras Kamboni militia, Ahmed Madobe (the current leader of Jubbaland administration). These negotiations were preceded by violent armed confrontation between Ahmed Madobe's forces and opposition militias/clans (allegedly) allied to and armed by the Federal Government. The Addis deal weakened the Federal Government's hand in the federation process and most of the provisions were never implemented. This led then Federal President Hassan Sheikh (2012–17) to form a boundaries and federation commission to guide the formation of Federal Member States, in line with the provisional constitution. Other Federal Member States have since emerged— Galmudug, HirShabelle and the South-West.

There are significant internal reconciliation challenges for new Federal Member States, the majority of which cut across clan divides as most clans span at least two regions. For example, the formation of Galmudug state triggered renewed violence in the disputed city of Galkayo, which had been a site of violent confrontation during the clan wars of the 1990s. Violence in Galkayo reflects wider problems with a federal devolution process driven from the centre without accompanying reconciliation efforts among clans locally, and the fierce clan competition over control of undecided federal borders. The desire for demonstrable progress in restructuring the state has displaced support for bottom-up reconciliation processes, which in Somalia often involve comprehensive and painstaking consultation.[11]

Second, relationships need to be more clearly defined between the centre (Mogadishu) and Federal Member States on issues such as resource sharing (including international aid) and security. The newly created upper house of parliament comprises representatives drawn from the Federal Member States. It needs to develop a framework that governs relationships between the Federal Government and the Federal Member States, as well as between Federal Member States and district/local authorities.

The provisional constitution also stipulates the creation of an inter-state commission to facilitate coordination and dispute resolution between the two levels of government. But no progress has so far been made in establishing this. In its place, a National Leadership Forum comprising the Federal President, Prime Minister, Speaker and Presidents of Federal Member States emerged under Hassan Sheikh's administration. Two important political initiatives were negotiated and agreed through the National Leadership Forum: the 2016 electoral model, which paved the way for the successful election process in 2017; and the 2017 security compact, which governs the structure and role of security between Mogadishu and Federal Member States. Although, as discussed below, the National Leadership Forum has also risked sidestepping due process, this somewhat contradictory development shows both the potential for effective conflict resolution mechanisms to facilitate progress in the federal process, but also the challenges of establishing enduring institutions to support this.

Third, federalism in Somalia also has reconciliation implications outside of the country's borders, regarding relations with neighbouring states with significant Somali populations on issues of security and territorial integrity. External relations apply to sub-national entities as well as nationally, including Somali Federal Member States. For example, in December 2015 three districts of Somalia's Bakool region attempted to form a breakaway administration after claiming communities were being marginalized by the nascent Interim South West Administration (ISWA). Somali media reported that the plan to create Upper Bakool was led largely by a faction of Darood-Ogaden-Aulihan clan members, with strong ties over the border with the Ogaden region of Ethiopia. This dynamic implies complex networks of relationships, between cross-border elites at national and sub-national level, but also among the communities and constituencies they claim to represent.[12]

Representation

Representation in Somali political processes remains contentious, in relation to both clans and the role of religion. It is a key issue for many Somalis to establish trust in the political system and to manage relationships among clans. The 4.5 clan power-sharing model, which was meant to be transitional, continues to divide Somalis, but no other political formula has since emerged to replace it. The transition from the 4.5 system to universal suffrage needs to be managed carefully to avoid reigniting clan clashes.[13]

Political party law has been in place since May 2015 and political parties have contested the last two presidential elections, but these parties have remained essentially "one-person shows" and have been dormant between electoral cycles. Federalism could be an alternative means of representation, but the Federal Member States have been formed and are being controlled along clan and sub-clan lines. The relationship within and between clan elites and the inclusion of marginalized groups such as minority clans, women or displaced populations, are key in ensuring Somalia's reconciliation process contributes to conflict transformation.

The provisional constitution looked to make progress on political representation in Somalia through "one-person-one-vote" elections in 2016. In July 2015, however, the Federal Government and Federal Parliament acknowledged that elections on such a basis would not be possible in the envisioned timeframe, and that a different model was needed to ensure more inclusive representation. The National Leadership Forum agreed on a mechanism in which 135 traditional elders would select 275 Electoral Colleges of 50 members each. These colleges would then respectively elect the 275 members of the lower house of parliament. This proposal was supposed to have been endorsed by the Federal Parliament, but was in fact ratified by presidential decree, which was criticized but was still backed by the international community.[14]

The role of Islam adds another significant dimension to representation and reconciliation in Somalia. The Somali constitution is clear that Islam is the religion of the state and all laws have to be compliant with Sharia. Some Islamic groups are part of the political system and others are not. Al-Shabaab (or some of the transnational elements of the group) is opposed to the current state system and wants to overthrow or radically transform it. The level and nature of integration of religion and politics is integral to legitimate political transition in Somalia, and needs to be negotiated inclusively in order to reconcile the interests of different groups sufficiently to maintain stability and enable transitional progress.

The war against Al-Shabaab needs to balance hard security with much more emphasis on addressing underlying grievances that drive recruitment to the group, in particular the exclusion and marginalization from mainstream politics of youth and minority clans. This issue requires engagement with, and leadership from, Islamic religious leaders drawn from the spectrum of Islamic movements in Somalia.

Responsibility

Somalis should have primary responsibility and accountability for reconciliation through a comprehensive framework led and facilitated by the Federal Government, in a process that also addresses the legacies of past violence. To be effective and sustainable, the process should be increasingly inclusive, in respect of elites and other actors.

Accountability

Accountability is key to effective processes and outcomes that Somali communities can trust. For example, Somali traditional clan elders have a central role to play in establishing legitimate institutions. They derive authority from being chosen to represent their clans and are answerable to them. Their authority empowers them to make and enforce agreements and is integral to Somali clans being able to hold their kinspeople accountable for transgressions.[15] However, it is important to acknowledge clan elders are also subject to manipulation by political elites through corruption and selection of elders who are not legitimate, for instance exemplified in the 2012 and 2017 transitional processes, and are often accused of considering issues from narrow clan perspectives rather than through a national or cross-clan lens.

Successful reconciliation processes in Somalia such as in Somaliland and Puntland, as well as local clan reconciliation initiatives in south-central Somalia, have been Somali-led and Somali-funded with limited external support. External support for national reconciliation today—political, technical and financial—is essential, but should neither dictate Somali agendas, nor disguise Somali mistakes. An inclusive reconciliation process will encourage credibility and acceptance of its outcome. Inclusive processes led by non-political leaders will also ensure continuation and survival of the process in a political system with a very high turnover of governments and elites.

The reconciliation process in Somalia today requires prioritization, leadership, and facilitation from the Federal Government. The cross-clan support for the newly elected president provides an opportunity for such leadership, but the process needs to look to expand inclusivity, to incorporate religious and traditional clan elders and civil society groups. This would be in line with the provisional constitution, which provides for a truth and reconciliation commission with representation drawn from traditional elders, civil society, judges and security personnel, but is yet to be set up. The Farmaajo Government has created a Ministry of Interior, Federalism and Reconciliation and on 13–17 June 2017 convened a Somali national consultation forum on reconciliation, the outcomes of which it is too early to assess.

Addressing the Past

An important component of responsibility as it applies to effective reconciliation is to find appropriate ways to address past violence—acknowledging harm done and grievances on all sides, and establishing accountability for violations of human rights. Somali society is still organized primarily along clan and sub-clan lines, and Somali customary law (*xeer*) and some aspects of Islamic practices govern societal relations. The *xeer* system has strong provisions on reconciliation, acknowledging past wrongs and reparations, and has been largely used by traditional clan elders and religious leaders to peacefully resolve local conflicts.

As mentioned above, application of *xeer* has been integral to peacebuilding and state-building in Somaliland. *Xeer* shapes basic values, laws, and rules of social behaviour. *Xeer* is specific to relations between any two clans or sub-clans, although there are rules that are common to all Somali communities, such as those relating to payment of *diya* compensation. Local peace processes commonly involve the renegotiation or renewal of *xeer* between belligerents, with the peace accord itself representing, in effect, a new *xeer*.[16]

The civil war and the resulting fragmentation of clans and replacement of clan elders by clan warlords have undermined the *xeer* system, but the system can still provide essential ingredients for social reconciliation. The social reconciliation process requires dealing with the past, including brutality and violence committed by the various factions in the Somali conflict—the military regime, armed opposition groups, civil war, clan warlords, and Islamic groups. Social reconciliation also needs to pay special attention to crimes and discrimination against minority clans with no access to protection, solidarity, and arms.

In addition, Somalia–Somaliland relations require acknowledging and righting wrongs and crimes committed against civilians by the military regime as well as the Somali National Movement (SNM) in Somaliland/north-west Somalia in the 1980s and 1990s. This could be undertaken as part of the Somalia–Somaliland talks process (currently stalled) or unilaterally by the Federal Government as an important step towards addressing the question of Somaliland.

Conclusion

Advancing reconciliation in Somalia will not be easy. Some efforts have been made recently, including the Wadajir Framework, a national initiative launched in 2016 which seeks to support reconciliation, civic dialogue, and the establishment of local governance structures. But there is still no agreed comprehensive framework for progress. Commitments remain scattered through different agendas, like the Wadajir Framework, but also the National Development Plan and the Roadmap 2020. And most reconciliation efforts in Somalia tend to prioritize short-term power-sharing between political elites (often those with guns such as warlords, militia leaders, and armed Islamists) over long-term reconciliation and democratization.

There is a need for a comprehensive reconciliation framework in Somalia that takes into consideration political and social reconciliation and spells out structures, accountability, timelines, and funding options. The establishment of a new government and president, who has implied some commitment to reconciliation, provides a good opportunity for progress. Somalia's recent history shows the costs of failing to commit to reconciliation and the transformation of relationships in state restructuring processes, and failing to include people from all elements of society. But experiences of reconciliation and state-building in Somaliland and Puntland, as well as traditional Somali conflict resolution practices and models for legitimate representation, illustrate the significant potential of approaches that are inclusive, effective, and Somali-led.

Somaliland and Al-Shabaab present a different set of reconciliation challenges, as they are fundamentally opposed to the current political system in Somalia. The Federal Government (rightly or wrongly) might not see the Somaliland question as an immediate priority due to the prevailing political and security situation in southern Somalia, but this should not prevent it from pursuing social reconciliation with Somaliland including dealing with the past and people-to-people initiatives. As for Al-Shabaab, Farmaajo's Government, with the support of the international community, needs to invest in combined military and political approaches, including exploring options for movement towards political negotiations.

Recommendations

Reconciliation is an enabler for effective state reform in Somalia and needs to be fully integrated into a comprehensive framework. A "reconciliation first" approach has facilitated state-building initiatives in Somaliland and Puntland, where it has been fundamental to establishing legitimate reform processes that people trust. These have produced appropriate institutions through primarily bottom-up processes that have combined a hybrid of Somali and Western democratic traditions.

The level and nature of integration of religion and politics is integral to legitimate political transition in Somalia. The political function of Islam needs to be negotiated inclusively to reconcile the interests of different groups, including some that remain outside the political system, notably elements of Al-Shabaab. Leaders from the spectrum of Islamic movements in Somalia can help engage youth and minority clans, to address grievances of exclusion that contribute to recruitment to militant groups.

Accountability is key and starts with ownership. Cross-clan support for the newly elected president provides an opportunity for leadership, prioritization, and facilitation of reconciliation initiatives from Mogadishu, but the process needs to be broadly inclusive, incorporating religious and traditional clan elders and civil society groups. Clan elders' authority, which derives from representing and being answerable to clans, empowers them to make and enforce agreements and is integral to clans being able to hold their kinspeople to account.

Progress in state reform needs to find ways to address past violence— acknowledging harm done and establishing accountability for violations of human rights. Application of *xeer* customary law is fundamental to both reconciliation and reform, to shape basic values, laws, and rules of social behaviour.

The provisional constitution provides for a truth and reconciliation commission with representation drawn from traditional elders, civil society, judges, and security personnel. Steps should be taken to establish such a body, which should engage widely across Somali politics and society. An example of innovative practice is the Transitional Justice and Reconciliation Commission (TJRC) in Mindanao in the Philippines, which engaged local communities through an extensive "Listening Process" in order to gather their perspectives and priorities.[17] To be effective in Somalia, the Federal Government would need to overtly back the commission and commit to act on its recommendations.

LAUNCHING RECONCILIATION IN SOMALIA

Joakim Gundel

Author

Joakim Gundel is a political scientist with twenty years' research and analysis experience in Somalia. He is also a former expert member of the UN Monitoring Group for Somalia, and has led monitoring and verification of aid activities in the country. He currently leads KATUNI Consult, which focuses on issues of political economy, justice, women's affairs, and building peace and accountable governance in Somalia.

Summary

A reconciliation process is key to strengthening the Somali state. Political stabilization, state-building and agreeing upon the constitution should all be based on the outcomes of a pertinent reconciliation process. If not, efforts to stabilize Somalia are unlikely to be durable.

Reconciliation has persistently been omitted from past peace processes, and has essentially been replaced by power-sharing arrangements, neglecting the interests and grievances of the Somali population. The continuance of violence in Somalia's regions and within the capital itself shows that there is a serious need for reconciliation. Violence is by no means only a result of the

191

conflict with Al-Shabaab and the manifestation of terrorism. It also reflects grievances and feuds that have a long history and still need to be resolved.

While a solution to the political crisis in Somalia requires changes to the constitution, achieving this cannot be done solely on the basis of technocratic inputs. A new constitution must reflect the outcomes and agreements made through a broad reconciliation process. Without bringing the population firmly behind the national security plan, it will be very difficult to defeat Al-Shabaab as well as to generate sufficient security.

The first step in a reconciliation process would be to bring Somalis together to determine the way in which key issues are addressed, which is likely to involve forgiveness or truth and justice. Beyond this, the agenda of the reconciliation process can be derived from bottom-up, participatory action research (PAR) methodologies in order to identify grievances and the principles for their resolution.

The overall recommendation is that the UN and international community support Somalia in finally launching a truth and reconciliation process. It should be driven by Somalis themselves, preferably through an independent facilitation committee composed of eminent elders, cultural personalities, and academics without vested political interests in the process. This facilitation committee could then be coupled with "The Elders", founded by Nelson Mandela, to provide guidance and international connections. It is recommended that the reconciliation process is established from the ground up, starting at the district level and continuing at the regional level to be finalized at the national level.

The Need for Reconciliation

This briefing paper explains why it is necessary to launch a bottom-up truth and reconciliation process in Somalia.[1] Reconciliation has persistently been omitted from past peace processes. Instead, power-sharing arrangements between elites and state-building efforts have been prioritized, largely neglecting the interests and grievances of the Somali population.[2] There is therefore a need to move beyond power-sharing arrangements between illegitimate and unrepresentative elites. Reconciliation is both long overdue and essential if Somalia is to be stabilized and the Somali state rebuilt.

From a Weak to a Stronger State

Reconciliation is vital if Somalia is to become a stronger state. According to the political scientist Barry Buzan's theory about what constitutes a strong state, there needs to be a strong correspondence between three bases of a state: people and territory, the idea of the state, and the institutional base.[3] Without strong correspondence between these three bases, a state will likely be dysfunctional and weak. The two figures below show how Buzan's theory may be applied to Somalia. The weaknesses of the current Somali state-building process are elaborated in subsequent sections of this paper.

Reconciliation is the most effective way to achieve stronger correspondence between the three bases of the state. This paper considers key issues that only a reconciliation process can address, including the constitution, federalization, security, and the political crisis. These issues are not intended to pre-empt any given reconciliation process, but are examples of issues that could be key points of departure for a reconciliation agenda. The actual issues to be addressed should be determined by Somalis themselves in the course of the process.

Grievances That Remain: Identity, Resource and Land Conflicts

The continuance of violence in Somalia's regions and within the capital itself shows that there is a major need for reconciliation. Such violence is not only a reflection of the conflict with Al-Shabaab and the manifestation of terrorism. It also reflects grievances and feuds that have a long history and still need to be resolved. Al-Shabaab and the armed Islamist insurgencies understand these dynamics very well—and exploit them effectively.

Unfortunately, the dominant discourse in government and international communiqués and official documents focuses on the threat posed by Al-Shabaab, but the conflict in Somalia is far more complex. Furthermore, the idea that a military approach alone is sufficient is not only flawed, but risks creating a durable conflict rather than a durable peace. Grievances from the 1990–1993 civil war remain, and as noted by the UN Monitoring Group report of 2014, the issues often resurface and turn violent.[4]

The ethnic identity of the Somalis (Somalinimo) is in fact disputed, as is the hegemonic identity of pastoralists, which is superimposed on most of the populations of southern Somalia.[5] However, one of the biggest population groups in Somalia—the Digil/Mirifle, in particular the Rahanwein group—is quite distinct from the pastoralist clans of the Darood, Hawiye, Dir and Isaaq.[6]

The so-called "minorities", often referred to as "Bantu",[7] have been victimized and in many cases practically enslaved by the warring pastoralist clans seeking to exploit the agriculturalist Bantu and their fertile land on the banks and deltas of the Jubba and Shabelle rivers.[8] The suppression of these "minori-

Weak and Strong State Theory as Guidance

WEAKNESSES OF SOMALI STATEBUILDING

IDEA OF THE STATE

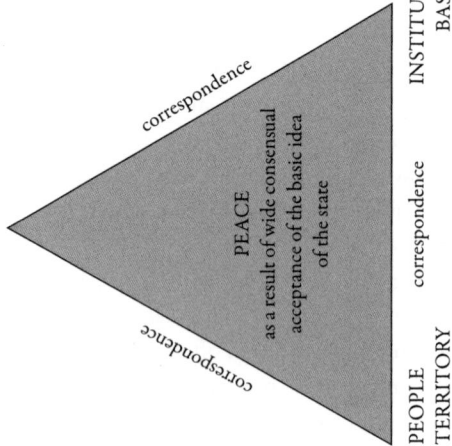

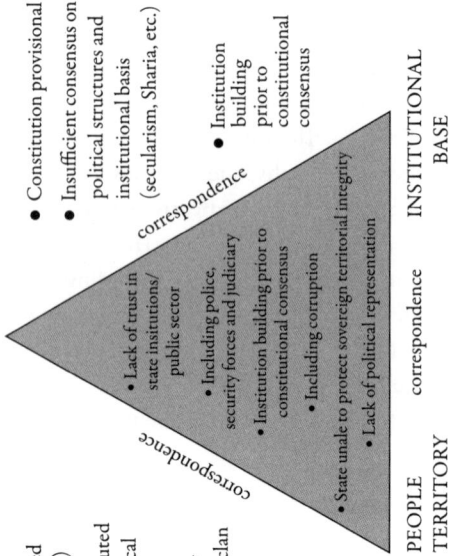

- Constitution provisional
- Insufficient consensus on political structures and institutional basis (secularism, Sharia, etc.)
- Institution building prior to constitutional consensus

correspondence

- Lack of trust in state institutions/public sector
- Including police, security forces and judiciary
- Institution building prior to constitutional consensus
- Including corruption
- State unable to protect sovereign territorial integrity
- Lack of political representation

correspondence

INSTITUTIONAL BASE

correspondence

PEOPLE TERRITORY

- Ethnic identity disputed (pan-Somali nationalis)
- Religious identity disputed (Sufi vs Salafism, political Islam, etc.)
- Social structure weakly reflected in state (incl. clan as socio-political basis)
- People spread across borders
- Lack of political representation

STRONG STATE THEORY (free after Barry Buzan)

IDEA OF THE STATE

PEACE
as a result of wide consensual acceptance of the basic idea of the state

correspondence

INSTITUTIONAL BASE

correspondence

PEOPLE TERRITORY

correspondence

ties" continues today and perpetuates major grievances.[9] Other minority groups have also experienced persecution and suppression. This includes the "Benadiri", "Barawaani" and "Bajuun", who have mixed Arabic descent and heritage, and the so-called "Midgan"—a derogatory term for the people generally identified by their occupations as craftsmen or artisans—who refer to themselves as Gaboye. All these "minorities" have legitimate grievances, and continue to be exploited by Al-Shabaab.

It is therefore crucial to diversify the identity of the "Somalinimo", to include and emphasize the cultural differences and ethnic identities that exist in Somalia. This should be reflected clearly in the Somali constitution, including the existence of more than one Somali language. Reconciliation would be the ideal path to such an understanding, and to recognition of the cultural diversity that exists. In addition to addressing grievances, a major task for reconciliation efforts is to address the persistent lack of trust between the major dominant clans, as well as between their sub-clan groups.[10]

From the early 1990s onwards Somalia became increasingly subject to an unpronounced religious war in which the traditional Somali religious identity—associated with Sufism—became disputed, often violently, by Sunni-Salafi/Wahhabi militant groups such as Al-Ittihad and in recent years by Al-Shabaab.[11] In reaction, to prevent outright extermination, the Sufi armed themselves through the organization of Ahlu Sunnah Wal Jama'a to establish a military resistance against Al-Shabaab. It is crucial to resolve this religious identity crisis, not only to end the conflict, but also to solve the constitutional deficits in terms of the religious identities of the Somali people. This can be achieved through reconciliation by seeking acceptance of and agreement about the religious diversity that exists. It should be reflected in the Somali constitution.

Another major issue, to which reconciliation can provide the principles for a solution, is the vast and complex set of disputes over land ownership and property rights. This issue has a long history, complicated by the civil war, on which The Rift Valley Institute has produced a comprehensive report.[12] A reconciliation process can, and should, involve the Somali people in determining the basic principles for solving land and property disputes.

Ending the Political Governance Crisis

The persistent political governance crisis in Somalia is rooted in the absence of a pertinent reconciliation process, and thus a constitution that does not resonate with the people. A reconciliation process is therefore necessary for achieving the new president's three key priorities: ending the political crisis, combating corruption, and defeating Al-Shabaab.[13]

Ending the Political Crisis

While a solution to the political crisis requires changing the constitution, achieving this cannot be done solely on the basis of technocratic inputs, because the outcome must correspond to the understandings, wishes and identities of the Somali people.[14] A new constitution must reflect the outcomes and agreements made through a broad reconciliation process. In other words, it cannot only be based on brokering deals with the top elite politicians and power-holders in Mogadishu and the Federal Member State capitals. State-building should ideally be based on wide popular consensus about a new national foundation manifested in the constitution.

Combating Corruption

Progress against corruption is necessary to achieve stabilization, because state capture and corruption undermine government institutions. Corruption undermines the legitimacy of elected parliamentarians, and hence also the President and Prime Minister.[15] It underlies the persistent insecurity in Mogadishu because it enables the insurgency to infiltrate the security apparatus. A reconciliation process is a good place to start tackling corruption, because through such a process grievances concerning corruption can be articulated and recognized. A reconciliation process could seek to identify the basic principles for an effective judiciary that builds upon the various Somali justice traditions.[16] The process should also determine the principles of a truth and accountability process, about which there should be broad public agreement.

Security and Al-Shabaab

Insecurity remains a major problem in Somalia despite the progress of pro-government forces in pushing Al-Shabaab back over the past six years.[17] This is primarily because Al-Shabaab maintains an ability to operate in Mogadishu and other major towns in south-central Somalia, and still controls significant territory. Insecurity also remains a problem because "old" conflicts between clans, driven by their elites, and the grievances of suppressed groups, have not been resolved. Therefore the conflict in Somalia is much more than simply a "war against terror", in other words, against Al-Shabaab and groups allied with the so-called Islamic State.

Stabilizing Somalia cannot only be achieved by military means. It takes a broader political solution involving various actors, including reconcilable elements within Al-Shabaab.[18] This is because political stabilization depends as much on the extension, legitimacy and credibility of the state's authority and the re-establishment of the rule of law as on any military operations.

The lack of basic consensus between the clans in southern Somalia is a key reason why there still is not an effective national army and the clans retain their militias.[19] Without bringing the population firmly behind the national security plan, it will be very difficult to defeat Al-Shabaab and generate sufficient security. Indeed, the best way to achieve an effective and truly national army is through a nationwide process of reconciliation.[20]

What a Reconciliation Process Could Look Like

The central proposition of this paper is that only through reconciliation is it possible to overcome the structural problems in Somali politics, move away from power-sharing arrangements and get the horse back in front of the cart in finalizing the constitution. At the same time, the population can be engaged in favour of this process and take part in the securitization and stabilization of the country.

The first step would be for Somalis to accept and support the idea of a reconciliation process and agree on the way in which disputes and grievances should be resolved, which might involve forgiveness or truth and justice.

Since there are formal governments in place, the process should be accepted by the Federal Government and Federal Member States. While these governments should participate in the process, it should not be driven by them to avoid suspicion of political manipulation. Ideally, the process should therefore be established and driven by independent committees that are not set up by or controlled by any government. Due to negative experiences with past peace processes in Somalia, the reconciliation process must not be conflated with determining a power-sharing arrangement or with the often-used term "social reconciliation". Past processes tended to involve a narrow group of actors with no real interest in reconciliation. Any future reconciliation process must not be driven by such groups.

The multiple agendas of the reconciliation process can be established from the bottom up, based on participatory action research (PAR) methodologies that ensure popular involvement. This approach would first identify grievances and then the principles for their resolution.[21]

Principles

This section and the following sub-sections outline the principles and sequencing for the organization and implementation of a reconciliation process in Somalia.

It is vital that the reconciliation process is not organized for the Somalis. On the contrary, the process must be driven by Somalis, organized by them and, to the extent possible, funded by them. If the process is only funded by international aid, the Somali interest in achieving reconciliation would lose credibility.

No government should lead the process or intervene in its direction. This should be left to a reconciliation facilitation committee composed of eminent, recognized elders and other leaders from Somali communities.

To promote genuine commitment, there should be no international remuneration for participation in meetings. International aid should be limited to supporting the work of the facilitation committee.

The process should start at the grassroots level and work upwards to the regional, and then national levels. At each level, participants should determine who will represent them at the subsequent stage of the process.

Preliminary Phase

The most important and difficult challenge in the preliminary phase is the identification of the members of the reconciliation facilitation committee. The ideal option is to establish a national-level facilitation committee, based on eminent elders, cultural personalities and other individuals, who are highly respected by Somalis in general, who can be trusted not to have vested interests in politics, and who have the skills to connect various groups of society.

To reinforce the authority of the facilitation committee and promote its independent role and connections to the international community, it would be useful to link the committee with the globally eminent group of statesmen known as "The Elders".[22]

If it is not possible to establish a committee of eminent elders, the minimum requirement would be to establish a committee independent from the government to oversee the process. In past transitional arrangements, the

Somali parliament nominated members of reconciliation committees. However, the experiences of these committees were not ideal, as they were often too large, inefficient and composed of members who did not have sufficient respect and authority to carry out the task. Hence, neither Parliament nor the Federal Government should nominate members of the committee because this would risk creating mistrust and a suspicion that the process has been manipulated.

A possible way forward could be a combination of the following options for identifying the members of the facilitation committee:

- Parliament sets up a small independent team, which then in a public, open and transparent process seeks to identify nominees and calls for nominations from the public within a given timeframe.
- Apply the customary practice for conflict resolution, in which high-level elders, known as *issim*, of the main clan families and the so-called "minority" groups, are brought together to set criteria for, and nominate, members.
- Bring together a group of respected peace, human rights, and other civic actors, who could put forward nominations.

It may be useful to establish criteria for membership of the facilitation committee first, and then suggest candidates. This could be done in a joint conference, composed of all the above, and supported by "The Elders".

Once the facilitation committee is in place, it will need to establish an organizing entity—which ideally should not be a government agency or a local private company—to organize and facilitate meetings and events. The international community could provide funding for staff and operational costs. The United Nations could do this, for instance, through UNOPS, or such support could be provided through an entirely different organization, preferably one with greater access to the field than the UN due to its restrictive security policies. The organizing entity would be responsible for assisting with the organization of meetings and events, and reporting outcomes to the facilitation committee.

Preparatory Phase

In the preparatory phase, the facilitation committee could establish the points of departure for initiating the process. It could draft the first agendas, explore key issues, explain the process to the public, set timelines for the process, and suggest sequencing of district-level conferences.

During this phase the organising entity could prepare for the PAR process by training qualified facilitators.

The facilitation committee should meet with "The Elders" to discuss the process and issues that may arise. Once the facilitation committee has developed a plan, it should be publicly announced, while the organizing entity prepares for the practicalities of the implementation phase.

Implementation Phase

Due to security and practical considerations, the process cannot be carried out everywhere simultaneously. It can therefore be carried out district by district, where AMISOM is able to provide a sufficient level of security for meetings to take place. Government officials and security forces could contribute to securing key areas, but must not intervene in outcomes, interfere with or manipulate participation, or seek to shape the issues or grievances being discussed.

District by district, the first step would be to carry out an initial PAR process involving communities, to establish core narratives and identify grievances. This could ideally be carried out by the organizing entity, which would present the findings to the facilitation committee.

Thereafter, it may be useful to establish traditional type oath-swearing conferences before initiating district-level conferences.[23] In these conferences, powerful armed actors and government entities, at all levels, should be required to swear that they will recognize whatever outcome and agreements the reconciliation conferences reach.

Local conferences could apply PAR methodologies to identify key conflict issues and grievances. These would then be discussed and addressed on an issue-by-issue basis, drawing on a forgiveness or truth-and-justice approach. Depending on what is agreed, the next step would be to determine the details of the ensuing process.

Determinations should then be recorded in a resolution, which representatives abide by at the next level of the reconciliation process. These resolutions should state whether, with respect to each issue, there is consensus for forgiveness or truth and justice. The resolutions could also record agreed positions regarding other points such as the federal political structure, fiscal issues, resource sharing, and the constitution.

The process must be flexible and iterative. Thus, it must allow for debate, and not be tightly time-constrained. Patience is a requirement. The conferences must not be limited to just one or two "town hall meetings", but allow for several meetings, and break outs, to enable the broadest possible discussions.

Once all the districts have carried out their reconciliation processes, outcomes could be compiled by the organizing entity and presented to the national facilitation committee of eminent elders. They can then present all of the outcomes together in a report and set the agenda for regional-level reconciliation, in other words, at the level of Federal Member States.

Participants at this level can be representatives mandated by the district meetings. The regional-level reconciliation conferences can seek to align the district outcomes, and participants can discuss and agree on how to implement the reconciliation agenda.

These conferences should ideally discuss and confirm the outcomes from the district level, including solutions to the lack of legitimacy of the Federal Member States, as well as the recommendations for changes to the constitution, and any action that is required to reflect the outcomes of the district and ensuing reconciliation processes. As at the district level, the organizing entity can compile and present reports of the outcomes to the facilitation committee.

If the various district conference outcomes are divergent and incompatible, the process could revert to the district level, with recommendations from the facilitation committee to try to obtain agreement on certain issues.

Once the regional conferences, at Federal Member State level, are completed, the national-level reconciliation conference should then be launched. Participants would be mandated by regional conferences, and include members of Parliament and the Federal Government. The outcome reports from the regional level can then be presented by the facilitation committee for discussion and final agreement on how to implement the reconciliation agreements.

Finalization Phase

Based on the final agreements on how to implement the reconciliation outcomes, the finalization phase will involve at least the following elements:

- A session of the Federal Parliament that formally endorses the final agreements, and if agreed upon, the necessary legislation for the implementation of an eventual truth-and-justice process, and the necessary decisions on amendments to the constitution.

- Parliament and government should determine and establish the commissions or courts that might be required to finalize the reconciliation process.

Conclusions

A reconciliation process in Somalia is essential to build a stronger state. In other words, stabilizing Somalia, state-building and agreeing on a permanent constitution should be based on the outcomes of a genuine national reconciliation process. If not, those efforts will remain at a high risk of failure.

The Somali constitution, provision of security, resource sharing and a means of ensuring accountability need to be based on a new consensus—a new social contract among the Somalis, which only can be achieved through a wide reconciliation process. A reconciliation process from the bottom up has the potential of increasing security by involving communities in creating a common foundation for building a new, stronger Somali state.

Recommendations

The UN and international community should support the launch of a reconciliation process in Somalia. It is of vital importance that the process is driven by Somalis, and preferably through an independent facilitation committee. This should be composed of eminent elders and distinguished individuals who do not have vested political interests in the process. The facilitation committee should be coupled with "The Elders", founded by Nelson Mandela, which would advise and support the committee. It is recommended that the reconciliation process works from the bottom up, starting at district levels, continuing at regional levels, to be finalized at the national level.

STATE-BUILDING AND PEACEBUILDING IN SOMALIA

LESSONS FROM OTHER PEACE AND TRANSITION PROCESSES

Thania Paffenholz, Constance Dijkstra and *Andreas Hirblinger*

Authors

Dr Thania Paffenholz is Director of the Inclusive Peace and Transition Initiative (IPTI). She is a leading peacebuilding expert, internationally renowned for her academic and policy expertise on peace and political transition processes, focusing on mediation, process design, and inclusion.[1]

Constance Dijkstra is a policy and research associate at IPTI. Prior to this position, she worked for various international think tanks where she assisted with qualitative research projects and organized high-level policy conferences.[2]

Dr Andreas Hirblinger is a researcher at IPTI. His doctoral research focused on local government reform and decentralization in South Sudan (2003–13). He has extensive experience as an advisor on conflict prevention and peacebuilding in South Sudan and with partners of the African Union.[3]

Summary

This paper provides insights on pertinent issues for Somalia's state-building process by examining how other countries have experienced state-building and peacebuilding, with a particular focus on the inclusion and exclusion of certain actors. It aims to help policy-makers make more informed decisions and avoid mistakes that have been generated in other contexts. This paper focuses on four key themes that are relevant to the context of Somalia: the role of extremist armed groups, the influence of elites, the devolution of power, and the constitution-drafting processes. This paper found that the peacebuilding and state-building processes of Afghanistan, the Democratic Republic of Congo (DRC), Mali, and Yemen are of particular relevance for Somalia.

The first section of this paper examines the role played by armed actors and the consequences of their inclusion and exclusion in the political settlements in the DRC and Afghanistan. It shows that the exclusion of armed actors can be detrimental for the state-building process. However, their inclusion has to be carefully managed as it often poses problems for normative reasons.

Secondly, the paper scrutinizes the consequences of agreements reached between elites in both Yemen and Afghanistan. This analysis shows that such agreements hold the risk of ignoring people's demands and can, depending on the context, lead to increased ethnic rivalry and the reproduction of patronage systems.

The third section examines how decentralization and federalism have been decided and implemented in Mali and Yemen. This comparison shows that such mechanisms can be hijacked by certain actors. In order to contribute to a sustainable peaceful political order, the devolution of power requires political will at all levels and a clear understanding of the institutional framework.

The fourth section looks at the drafting of constitutions in Yemen and Mali. These cases demonstrate the detrimental effects of top-down drafting processes. In order to safeguard against renewed political instability, constitutions need to be drafted through processes that involve popular participation and guarantee that they are anchored in the national political context.

The last section of this paper provides a list of topics that should be examined in collaboration with regional experts in order to come up with relevant policy recommendations.

Introduction

This paper provides insights on pertinent issues for Somalia's state-building process by examining how other countries have experienced state-building and peacebuilding, with a particular focus on the inclusion and exclusion of certain actors and issues. It aims at helping policy-makers to make more informed decisions and avoid mistakes that have been generated in other contexts. To prepare this paper, background research and interviews were conducted with Somalia experts to identify pertinent factors that enable or constrain the current process. We then screened IPTI's dataset for cases that bear similarities with the Somali context. IPTI dataset stems from the "Broadening and Participation" qualitative dataset which includes, so far, 43 cases of peace and political transition negotiations and implementation processes that took place since the beginning of the 1990s. The cases of state-building processes in Mali, Yemen, Afghanistan, and the Democratic Republic of the Congo (DRC) were found to be of particular relevance for Somalia.

In the Somali context, we identified four key topics which are discussed with examples. The first topic focuses on the impact of armed groups, as Al-Shabaab continues to remain an influential actor in Somalia that challenges the state-building process. Yet, the group's persistent use of terror tactics complicates its inclusion in a political settlement. We then examine the role of elites. In fact, whereas some Somali elites have actively worked for the creation of a viable state, others attempt to foster state institutions that will safeguard their vested interests and power. The third theme of this paper focuses on the institutional side of state-building. Somalia has, since 2012, gradually established a federal structure, however with mixed results. We therefore examine the reasons for protracted or failed decentralization processes in other countries. Finally, as Somalia's constitution-drafting process is still ongoing, this paper looks at some constitution-making processes and examines how they have contributed to the success or the failure of peacebuilding and state-building efforts.

Armed Groups and Negotiations: The DRC and Afghanistan

Policy-makers are often divided on whether to include or exclude armed groups during the negotiations and the post-agreement settlement. In some cases, armed actors have been included in peace negotiations. The idea behind this strategy is that by providing armed actors with an opportunity to express their motives and potentially accommodate their grievances, they become less likely to resort to violence in the post-agreement phase and can possibly contribute to the success of the peacebuilding and state-building process. However, accommodating the interests of armed actors has not systematically led to that result. In fact, there is a risk that negotiations primarily focus on the armed groups' self-serving demands instead of leading to arrangements that take into account the underlying causes of conflict. This problem is particularly pertinent if the causes of conflict are partly of an ideological or institutional nature.

This can be illustrated with the case of the Second Congo War (1998–2003) which ended with the Inter-Congolese Political Negotiations. The participants in the negotiations included representatives of the main warring parties, three newly found armed groups, local militias, the unarmed political opposition, and civil society. Armed groups were included in the hope of potentially accommodating their demands and with the aim of reintegrating them in state institutions. However, the Final Act, signed in 2003, was the result of negotiations that were essentially led by warlords and avaricious leaders, and led to the sharing of political power and the distribution of political and military positions between groups who had essentially remained divided.[4] The process thus failed to establish a common vision for the country and did not address the underlying causes of the conflict, such as questions of ethnicity and citizenship. As part of the process, a new national army was created through the unification of all major armed groups, but the various factions associated with the former rebel groups were unable to work together and to agree on the role of the new national army.[5] Major disagreements therefore resurfaced in the post-agreement phase, and were exploited by commanders who soon defected. The most prominent example was Laurent Nkunda, a Tutsi and ex-RCD commander, who formed a new rebel group under the pretext that Tutsis were not adequately protected by the national army.[6] Hence, the inclusion of armed actors did not sustainably end violence as conflict between armed factions restarted in 2004 and hindered the state-building process from moving forward.

In other cases, armed actors have been excluded from the negotiations for normative reasons. In particular, armed groups affiliated with terrorist organizations have often not participated in negotiations, as influential international stakeholders do not wish to legitimize the use of terrorism.[7] However, the exclusion of such armed groups, especially when they control significant parts of a territory and/or represent parts of the population, may lead to the creation of powerful spoilers who can compromise the sustainable resolution of a conflict and the subsequent state-building process.

This was particularly evident in the case of Afghanistan. Following the fall of the Taliban regime in 2001, the Bonn Conference was organized by the

United Nations to agree on a new set of state institutions. Whereas the negotiations did include representatives from various tribal groups, the Afghan diaspora, and actors opposed to the former regime, the Taliban were not included. In fact, because of their affiliation to Al-Qaida, the Taliban were regarded as "non-negotiable" partners. This meant that no efforts were made to demobilize Taliban armed groups and integrate them in a post-war order.[8] Consequently, the situation on the ground deteriorated remarkably and attacks organized by the Taliban increased thereafter.[9] These compelled the Afghan administration and its international allies to focus on counter-insurgency measures rather than on building viable political institutions. This greatly compromised the state-building process. However, the numerous attempts to defeat the Taliban have been fruitless and show that the only viable option is to negotiate with them. Departing from past policies, the current Afghan president, Ashraf Ghani, has tentatively attempted to do so.[10] While a compromise with the Taliban has not yet been reached, the fact that deals have been negotiated with Hezb-i-Islami, a militant group considered a terrorist organization by the United-States, shows that there is room for compromise, and that embattled national governments can reach political settlements with Islamist groups.[11]

Elites and Negotiations: Yemen and Afghanistan

Elites are often defined as a relatively exclusive group of power-holders who enjoy a disproportionate amount of political, social, and economic power compared to the rest of society. In post-conflict settlements, these actors can play a major role and significantly affect the success or the failure of a peace agreement and its subsequent implementation. In fact, peace and stability are often believed to be the result of a compromise between elites in which they agree to a new social contract that facilitates the state-building process. However, an agreement among elites holds the risk of excluding demands of other actors, entrenching ethnic cleavages as well as vertical dependency through neo-patrimonial systems. As a result, negotiations may lead to an illegitimate agreement that is rejected by groups excluded from elite-dominated processes.

This proved to be the case in Yemen. In fact, following protests inspired by the Arab Spring in 2011 that destabilized the country, the Gulf Cooperation Council (GCC) Initiative was signed in November 2011. The GCC Initiative presented a roadmap for the transition of Yemen and called for the resignation of President Saleh, whose regime was characterized by corruption and patronage practices. While providing Saleh with immunity from prosecution, the road map transferred power to Vice-President Hadi, who consequently led the creation of a government of national unity.[12]

It was widely believed, at the time, that the initiative prevented the start of a civil war and would lead to a new social contract that would take into account people's grievances. However, this agreement was essentially a reshuffling of the elites that were in power under President Saleh. These same elites had split during the protests, but came back together under the Initiative when they realized that the prolongation of the protests could threaten their positions. As a result, the country's reform did not represent the aspirations of two groups that had played an essential role during the protests: the Houthis—a militant group that espouses Zaidism, a form of Shia Islam—and Al-Hirak—a coalition of secessionist groups who wish to form a separate republic in the South.[13] The two groups no longer wanted to live under the rule of entrenched elites that exercised power mainly through patronage systems. Yet, under President Hadi, the country remained divided among former elites and failed to carry out the reforms requested by the protesters. Ultimately, therefore, the GCC Initiative failed to avert the resurgence of violence by the Houthis.

In certain contexts, an agreement reached among elites might also provide an unstable political environment that may increase inter-ethnic competition. In fact, such an agreement might encourage elites to influence the state-building process to create social, political and economic structures that serve their interests and contribute to the empowerment and enrichment of their followers while relegating other groups' concerns to the margins.

Again, this proved to be particularly obvious in the case of Afghanistan where, following the Bonn Agreement, President Karzai co-opted different elites by maintaining patron–client relationships.[14] However, this tactic fell short of bringing peace and stability as it resulted in the strengthening of ethnic divisions. The post-Bonn implementation phase was characterized by elite competition over state power and resources mainly between the Pashtuns and the Northern Alliance. This situation was exploited by President Karzai who made use of repressive and coercive policies to exclude certain groups while privileging old factional leaders as well as local and district officials.[15] This resulted in state institutions that lacked legitimacy, as they favoured individuals with whom President Karzai had established a relationship, rather than acting in the interest of all groups present in Afghanistan. The exclusion of certain communities from this patrimonial system favoured inter-ethnic rivalries and partly enabled the Taliban to strengthen their power basis.[16] Overall, this contributed to a precarious basis for the creation of viable state institutions which greatly hampered the state-building process and failed to bring about national unity.

Devolution of Power: Mali and Yemen

A political system that devolves political power to the local level has often been perceived as a way to create state structures that are more representative and responsive to groups' demands. However, when devolution processes have been badly implemented, are hijacked by certain actors and have failed to provide political representation, they have delegitimized state institutions and fuelled instability and armed violence.

This was especially visible in the case of Mali. The National Pact, signed on 11 April 1992, was meant to grant the Tuareg living in Mali greater autonomy through the recognition of the special status of the north of Mali.[17] The Tuareg assumed that decentralization would provide them with political recognition and contribute to economic development. At first, the promise made during the National Pact helped to decrease levels of violence in the north of the country. While at the beginning, the National Pact had been signed by only three Tuareg groups, others later endorsed the agreement and, by 1996, violence in the region ceased to become a national issue. However, over time, the benefits of decentralization failed to materialize. In fact, the newly established decentralization system was mainly used to co-opt some Tuareg, generally from noble families, who acquired significant power within their regions and in national institutions.[18] Yet, on the ground, the responsibilities of the civil service and local administrations remained unchanged, corruption at the local level increased and northern Mali remained marginalized both from an economic and political perspective.[19] Overall, there was significant confusion over the share of responsibilities between the national and the local structures. Further, the Tuareg chosen as representatives seemed to have little interest in ensuring that the decentralization system functioned effectively.[20] The failure of the decentralization system in northern Mali partly explains why violence reoccurred in the region in 2006, which affected the state-building process negatively.

In other cases, the establishment of a system that devolves power has proved to be a point of contention during the negotiations and has contributed to the reoccurrence of violence. This was often the case when groups were unable to reconcile their positions over the nature of the devolution of power pertaining to boundaries and the sharing of responsibilities, related, for example, to revenues and resources. In some cases, a lack of agreement on the devolution of power contributed to the failure of the state-building process, as was the case in Yemen.

In fact, the Yemeni National Dialogue Conference (NDC), held in March 2013, was meant to lead to the creation of a new social contract that mirrored popular grievances and create federal structures that devolved power to key constituencies, including to the Houthis. While the general principles of federalism were agreed during the NDC, there was some disagreement over the establishment of certain federal states, which remained unresolved during the conference. As a result, an unrepresentative 22-member Committee of the Regions decided on the division of subunits, competencies and boundaries of those federal states.[21] This decision resulted in popular discontent among the Houthis as well as Al-Hirak.[22] They felt that this choice ignored the concerns they had raised during the NDC and perceived the division of territory as unfair as it distributed resources unevenly.[23] The decision of the committee partly explains why the Houthis decided to go to war and take over the government in Sana'a in 2014–15, which contributed to the stalling of the state-building process.

Constitution-Making Process: Afghanistan and Mali

In state-building processes, the drafting of a new constitution can be a tedious exercise, mainly because this document codifies the relations between the state and the people. In many state-building processes, it is a necessary step that provides legitimacy to the political transition. In cases where the constitution was imposed from the top and took into account people's grievances superficially, it contributed, partly, to the illegitimacy of the state-building process and acted as a confirmation that the state institutions did not take into account the interests of the people.

In Afghanistan, the Constitutional Loya Jirga (CLJ) attempted to take into account people's needs by including Afghans from various backgrounds, civil society members, as well as women, youth, and minorities. Some provincial power-holders and warlords who had previously been excluded from the talks also participated. However, despite those efforts, the CLJ fell short and the process lacked legitimacy and the backing of the public. This is partly due to the fact that the CLJ resulted in a rather modernist constitution that had been heavily influenced by the United Nations and the United States. This dissatisfied some Pashtuns who remained sceptical about the modernist policy of separating Islam from politics.[24] In addition, the impact of the general public through consultations had been limited, as none of the suggestions emanating from those meetings were taken into account in the CLJ negotiations.[25] Overall, the constitutional drafting process followed a top-down approach where important constitutional changes were agreed by President Karzai behind closed doors.[26] These factors partly contributed to the escalation of violence in Afghanistan and the failure of the state-building process.

In other contexts, however, the constitution-making has not been viewed as a milestone of the state-building process, but rather as a systematic step. Hence, its drafting has been rushed at times and not accorded the requisite importance. This can become problematic for the state-building process in the long-term. In fact, if the design of the constitution is not given enough consideration during its drafting, the mechanisms of decision-making and arrangements by which state institutions relate to one another may not fit the national political context or people's needs.

This can be illustrated with the example of Mali, where, following the fall of President Traoré in 1991, the constitution-drafting process took place in the context of a National Dialogue. The aim of this process was to establish new democratic institutions, enhance national unity and agree on a new electoral code. In a Constitutional Commission, set up in parallel to the National Dialogue, there was a genuine attempt at ensuring that the constitution reflected the needs of Malians as a whole. However, despite the presence of Malians from various backgrounds, the drafting of the constitution seems to have been rushed and followed a top-down approach. In fact, the first draft, which bears strong similarities with the French constitution, was written by a 25-member committee that was also in charge of Mali's overall political transition.[27] The draft was barely amended during the proceeding of the Constitutional Commission, partly because the set-up of the National Dialogue did not provide enough time and opportunities for participants to review the text. As a result, the constitution failed to take into account vital themes related, for example, to peasants' rights and the Tuareg.[28] However, despite those issues, the constitution was approved through a referendum and came into force on 25 February 1992. Over time, though, it became evident that the Malian constitution was ill-fitted for the needs of the country. This proved to be the case in 2012 when Mali entered into a period of insecurity and institutional crisis, which resulted in a military putsch. This crisis was partly the result of a lack of clarity and transparency of certain state structures, particularly with regards to the decentralization mechanisms in the north.[29] This institutional fog and the continuation of corrupt practices by state officials, linked partly to the lack of codifying in the constitution, contributed to the weaknesses and illegitimacy of Malian state structures, and thus hindered the state-building process from progressing.

Conclusion

In this paper, we have examined the state-building and peacebuilding experiences of different countries in order to generate insights for Somalia. Lessons that can be drawn from the comparative analysis are as follows.

The inclusion of armed actors in negotiations should be examined carefully. In the context of Afghanistan, the exclusion of the Taliban from the Bonn Conference was a missed opportunity to take into account their demands and was greatly responsible for the slow progression of the state-building process. Despite the challenges of extremist Islamist groups, the inclusion of armed actors promises to be beneficial only if it is based on a political settlement that addresses the underlying causes of conflict and sets the path for a common political vision.

The accommodation of elites might represent a necessary step to bring about security and stability. However, negotiations that only include elites may lead to the exclusion of demands from other groups, including minorities, which could potentially contribute to the reoccurrence of violence. In certain contexts, the accommodation of elites may contribute to competition along ethnic lines and the reproduction of patronage systems, which hamper the creation of viable state institutions.

Decentralization mechanisms are often an appropriate means for resolving underlying causes of conflict related to the distribution of political power. However, the implementation of devolved governance arrangements has often proved difficult, due to a lack of understanding of the roles and responsibilities of regional and national administrations and a lack of political commitment at both national and state or local levels.

While constitutions are widely seen as an important milestone on the way to peaceful political orders, popular participation in constitution-drafting processes is not always given similar importance. This is partly due to the role of technical support provided by international organizations and the complexity of the drafting process that often involves technical experts and takes place behind closed doors. Yet, insufficient participation risks leading to an ill-fitted constitution that ignores the national political context. While technically adequate, such a constitution is likely to become a meaningless document if the country re-enters a phase of political instability.

Recommendations

The findings of this paper are based on a comparative research approach that examined issues pertinent to Somalia. In order to translate our conclusions into practice, this analysis must further be contextualized, ideally in collaboration with practitioners and regional experts, and should also include additional in-depth comparative research.

We suggest a focus on the following topics:

- The inclusion of Islamist groups into peace processes, with the aim of developing a strategy for a rapprochement between the Federal Government and Al-Shabaab. This could involve a comparison of attempts to accommodate extremist Islamist groups as it happened in Afghanistan and Mali (as failed cases) as well as Sudan (as a relatively successful case).
- The implementation of an inclusive and decentralized governance structure that clearly delineates the role of clan identity in Somalia's federal system and provides non-ambiguous mechanisms to share competences and resources, including through safeguards that reduce the risk of abuse of power and the flourishing of patronage systems. This could involve a comparison of the decentralization attempts in South Sudan and Yemen (as failed cases) and Kenya and Ethiopia (as relatively successful cases).
- The challenges of an inclusive and broad-based constitutional process, in the context of state fragility and ongoing armed violence. This could include an analysis of mechanisms transferring recommendations emanating from broad-based consultations to the constitutional drafting bodies. This research could involve a comparison of South Sudan and Afghanistan (as failed cases) and Uganda (as a relatively successful case).

SOMALI NATIONAL RECONCILIATION

EXPLORING A COMPREHENSIVE APPROACH

Abdurahman Abdullahi "Baadiyow"

Author

Dr Abdurahman Abdullahi "Baadiyow" is a former military officer, electronic engineer, Islamic scholar, and civil society and political activist. He holds a PhD in Islamic History from McGill University in Canada. He is one of the founders of Mogadishu University and the chairman of its Board of Trustees.

Summary

There is a gap in existing knowledge on the topic of Somali reconciliation; and most literature considers the Somali civil war squarely a clan conflict. Moreover, transitional justice, which is an indispensable component of the peacebuilding process, was not included in the Somali case. Since 1979, Somalia has experienced ten periods of excessive human rights violations. Four of these periods occurred during the military regime, while the other six took place after the collapse of the state in 1991. This essay redefines the Somali conflict in refuting Somali exceptionalism and the approach based solely on clan. Instead this briefing argues that the genesis of hostilities is the state–society conflict that, as a consequence, has generated a violent power struggle among the political elite.[1] In turn, this political elite power struggle has provoked political clannism and Islamism: the two indigenous ideologies. These conflicts have been generated sequentially as a result of state–society conflict, and must be addressed as part of a four-part process of reconciliation.

The first phase of reconciliation requires restructuring the state to be in peace with its society in protecting its culture and value system, and adopting a participatory approach. This phase should be realized through constitutional and other reforms. The second phase of reconciliation is among political elites (unarmed Islamist and non-Islamist elites), which can be realized only through dialogue, changing predatory political culture, adhering to Islamic values, and creating consensus, which is part of Somali culture. The third phase is clan reconciliation, which uses traditional conflict resolution mechanisms and elements of transitional justice compliant with Islam. Clan reconciliation should start with a detailed documentation of human rights violations and wide consultation with the clan elders. The fourth element of the process is reconciliation with armed Islamic groups such as Al-Shabaab, which could be initiated in parallel to all other phases. This paper recommends a ten-point programme of reconciliation, which gradually realizes good governance practices and comprehensive elite and clan reconciliation. Further, the essay also proposes a participatory approach and prudent synthesis of modernity and tradition. In implementing such a programme, the international community will be required to provide political, technical and financial support.

Introduction

After the collapse of the state in 1991, Somalia entered a new era in its history. This period has exposed the vulnerability of the postcolonial state and resilience of traditional culture. Under stateless conditions, civil war devastated the country, ushering in fiefdoms controlled by warlords. Since then, talk of reconciliation has come to the fore. However, the definition of the conflict was reduced to "conflict based on kinship" and subsequently clan reconciliation was considered.[2]

The 13 national reconciliation conferences held since 1991 were only elite power-sharing exercises and did not address the core issues of the conflict.[3] It should be noted, however, that in war-torn societies, reconciliation does not stand alone; rather, it forms one of the components of transitional justice.[4] Transitional justice includes a set of judicial and non-judicial measures that provide redress for massive human rights violations, such as criminal trials, truth commissions, reparations programmes, and institutional reforms.

Reconciliation is a non-juridical measure of restorative justice, which aims to restore both the victim and perpetrator of a crime back into harmony with the community. Somali society aspires to a combination of traditional conflict resolution mechanisms and Sharia-based transitional justice.[5]

Despite the mass violations of human rights occurring in Somalia since the 1970s, transitional justice was not included as part of the international programme to support the Somali peacebuilding process. Studies on Somali reconciliation are either scant or simply focus on clan conflict, and the genesis of the conflict has not yet been properly addressed.[6] In general external drivers of the conflict have been under-emphasized, although there is no scope to address them in this brief paper.[7] Rather, the paper seeks to redefine the conflict and propose a comprehensive reconciliation model in Somalia.[8]

Overview of Mass Violence in Somalia

There was no mass violation of human rights in Somalia before the 1970s. However, violations grew considerably during the period of the military regime (1969–1991), which included torture, extra-judicial detentions, executions, and collective punishments. The intensity of these violations increased in the 1980s with the rise of armed conflict between various armed oppositions and the regime.[9] Major human rights violations committed during the military regime period are as follows:

1. In 1975 ten leading Islamic scholars were executed simply because they opposed a secular family law adopted by the military regime. As a result of the subsequent mass repression of Islamic activists and scholars, hundreds were detained and prosecuted. Others fled the country and were exposed to extremist views of Islam. This historical event was the starting point of the radicalization of young Islamic activists, which eventually ushered in the emergence of Al-Shabaab.[10]

2. In 1979 the regime destroyed numerous wells to deny water to the sub-clan of Colonel Abdullahi Yusuf of the Somali Salvation Democratic Front (SSDF). As a result, it was reported that more than 2,000 people perished from mass killings and thirst. Moreover, violations were extended to members of the sub-clan in the form of extra-judicial detentions and executions.[11]

3. In 1988 more than 50,000 civilians were killed as a result of an attack by the Somali National Movement (SNM) on the major northern cities due to government reprisals. Moreover, about 400,000 residents of the urban cities were internally displaced or became refugees in Ethiopia and Djibouti.[12]
4. On 14 July 1989 the security apparatus of the regime opened fire on a peaceful demonstration after Friday prayers in Mogadishu. As a result, 450 persons were killed and about 2,000 were injured.[13] Moreover, 47 persons, mainly from the Isaaq clan, were summarily executed.[14]

Since the collapse of the state in 1991, the conflict between clan-based armed factions and the regime transformed into a war between warlords, each mobilizing his own clan. In particular, the capital city of Mogadishu was engulfed in utter mayhem as the United Somali Congress (USC) militias engaged in the destruction of public and private properties. The same phenomenon, albeit lower in magnitude, was evident in all regions under the control of the warlords. The conflict that began against the oppressive regime was depicted as a conflict between Hawiye and Darood clan-families in southern Somalia. On the other hand, human rights violations in Somaliland occurred most notably during the conflicts of 1994 and 1996. Listed below are the major occurrences of human rights violations in southern Somalia after the collapse of the state.

1. 1991–1992: the outbreak of the civil war and the subsequent internal fighting within USC between the Ali Mahdi and General Aidid camps in Mogadishu, known as the 100 days' war, which caused about 20,000–30,000 deaths.[15] Moreover, the outbreak of famine, in addition to the war between various armed factions in the Bay and Bakool regions, caused 300,000 deaths.[16]
2. 1992–1995: Somalia experienced the presence of intervention forces comprising the Unified Task Force (UNITAF) and the United Nations Operation in Somalia (UNOSOM). This operation led to the death of 24 Pakistanis, 19 US soldiers, and 500–1,000 Somalis at the hands of the Aidid militia and the UNOSOM forces.[17]
3. 1995–2001: low-intensity inter-clan conflicts and marauding militias belonging to various warlords continued to commit human rights violations.
4. 2001–2006: the beginning of the "War on Terrorism" and the emergence of the Union of Islamic Courts (UIC) and its conflict with Mogadishu warlords, which caused human rights violations.

5. 2007–08: Ethiopian military intervention, UIC resistance, and then AMISOM and US counter-terrorism operations and war with Al-Shabaab, which led to numerous human rights violations.
6. From 2009 to the present day: the continuation of the conflict between AMISOM, the Somali military, and Al-Shabaab. Moreover, further sporadic conflicts have occurred between various armed groups in Kismayo, Galkayo, Galmudug, Lower Shabelle, and Hiraan.

Despite these human rights violations in Somalia, the transitional justice component was not included in Somali peacebuilding for a number of reasons, including the lack of prerequisite political conditions.[18] However, victims of the civil war are still waiting for justice to be served to those responsible for the violations noted above. As such, these victims are disappointed with the continuation of impunity. Moreover, it seems that the culture of impunity is tolerated, with perpetrators of violence holding high political positions in the various transitional governments in spite of their records.[19] This essay sets out a comprehensive model for addressing transitional justice, which focuses on reconciliation but does not exclude other mechanisms.

Redefining the Somali Conflict

Discussion of national reconciliation in Somalia has taken place without initial agreement on the definition and the nature of the conflict. The most popular conception does not differentiate between apolitical and political conflicts; thus, the two aspects have been lumped together, giving the appearance of a primordial conflict. In reality, these two conflicts are different in their objectives, scope, means, and type of leadership. For instance, apolitical conflict initially begins as a series of accidental clashes between individuals belonging to different clans. Such clashes are typically about resources, such as pasture, grazing land, firms, watering rights, and so on. This type of conflict is prevalent in the rural communities and is normally managed by the traditional elders who apply traditional conflict resolution methods, well known in Somali culture.

Conversely, political conflict takes the form of an elite tussle for power, prestige, and resources, and clans are mobilized as instruments for purely political objectives. Political conflicts often remain unresolved, since they require different remedies, approaches and mechanisms. The rhetorical peace and reconciliation conferences, which have taken place since 1991, have focused on elite power-sharing based on clan division and cake-cutting exercises.[20] "Clannization" of the conflict is a way of avoiding individual responsibility for the crimes and depicting human rights violations as the collective responsibility of the clans.

The concept of "clannization" of political conflicts was derived from an anthropological interpretation of Somali politics and society, which posits that Somali conflicts are essentially primordial, in accordance with the model of the "state versus clan" (*qaran iyo qabiil*) equation.[21] This relational model accounts for the vertical relations (ancestral or blood relations) and largely excludes all other relations in the societal equation, such as women, minorities, and Islamic scholars.[22] This model emphasizes the role of the clan elder and negates the role of horizontal social relations through mothers, marriages and organizational affiliations.[23] The "state versus clan" model is a distorted representation that places an emphasis on "Somali exceptionalism."[24] For instance, Professor Said Samatar considers the clan factor as a single overriding factor and remarks: "Somali polity is shaped by a single, central principle that overrides all others, namely the phenomenon that social anthropologists call 'the segmentary lineage system.'"[25] This model was criticized as a reductionist approach by many scholars,[26] and this essay presents an alternative model to the "state versus clan" equation, namely a "state versus society" (*qaran iyo bulsho*) conception. This model considers the Somali conflict much like conflicts in other countries and thus disputes Somali exceptionalism. It incorporates all of the components of society and all relational connections and affiliations.

Differentiating clan (*qabiil*) and society (*bulsho*) is the cornerstone of redefining the Somali conflict. Clan is based on vertical relations only connected through ancestry (blood relations). It is founded on the *diya* (compensation) paying unit, amounts for which may swell to high levels during conflicts.[27]

On the other hand, Somali society (*bulsho*) combines vertical and horizontal relations such as collective settlements, matrilineal relatives, intermarriage relations, and organizational affiliations. Thus, the state-society model recognizes that Somali society consists of all Somali citizens irrelevant of their clans, gender, class, and religion. This model presupposes that the Somali equation comprises the dialectical interaction of the postcolonial state and Somali society. This interaction was restructured during the colonial era in such a way that it became conflictual.[28]

The state structure, its legal framework, policies, and political processes were completely alien to traditional Somali society. Therefore, Somali society has confronted this strange system of governance and its oppressive penetration of society, using its available ideological arsenal: clannism and Islamism. In particular, during the military regime which denied political freedom, resentful elites mobilized their clans and established armed factions which brought down the state in 1991. On the other hand, furious Islamists, in reaction to the forced secularization of the military regime, have intensified their ideological opposition and established various Islamic movements.[29] Some of these Islamic movements reverted to militancy and extremism.[30]

Somali elites could be classified into two main categories: traditional and modern. Traditional elites basically consist of clan elders and traditional Islamic scholars. Modern elites do not easily fit into existing structures and comprise non-Islamist and Islamist elites. Non-Islamist elites are not necessarily secular, though they are also not Islamic activists.[31] They are not ideologically driven and simply perpetuate the status quo and the nature of the postcolonial state. Islamists are activists who advocate for the introduction of an Islamic legal system and values to the space of the state.[32] The cosmology of the traditional elites is derived from the synthesis of clan customary law (*xeer*) and Islamic Sharia. The division of labour among the traditional elites is well delineated, and usually, they work in harmony in administering societal affairs. On the contrary, the modern elites (non-Islamists and Islamists) are conflictual in terms of power struggles or the nature of the state, as shown below in Figure 1.[33]

Categorization of the Somali Conflict

There are four types of conflicts in Somalia, each one generating the next. The first is the state–society conflict between the modern state and traditional society. This generates the second conflict, which is a power struggle between non-Islamist elites; while the third is an ideological conflict, shown above, between non-Islamists and Islamists. The fourth conflict is the result of the non-Islamist power struggle, which escalates into civil war. In the civil war,

Figure 1: Somali elites and their relations

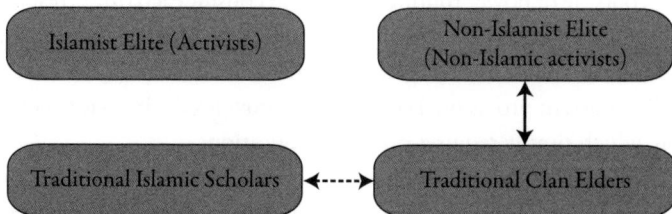

elites use clans as instruments of their struggle and incite clan animosity. The nature of this clan conflict is different from the nature of traditional apolitical conflicts. Thus, these conflicts should be addressed, with each requiring detailed and appropriate mechanisms, while recognizing that a root of all these conflicts is bad governance.

Approaches to Somali Reconciliation

The first step in reconciling state and society requires us to abandon a singular conception of modernity in place of one that incorporates multiple modernities and departs from extreme models of westernization or indigenization of the state. The westernization model was based on moving society towards the state, although this model failed, having been tested in the postcolonial state. The indigenization model was based on moving the state towards society by adopting the "4.5" clan power-sharing formula. The indigenization is completely antithetical to the modern system, which is based on citizenship, individual responsibility, and supremacy of the law. Therefore, reconciling state and society requires moving state and society towards each other to a middle space that is acceptable to both sides. It requires an innovative process which synthesizes modernity and tradition. The reconciliation of state and society can be realized only when the roles of Islam and the clan system are well-demarcated *vis-à-vis* the borders of the state, and when both state and society respect these boundaries. Another component of state-society reconciliation is to address previous grievances through material compensation, recognition and official apologies to the victims of state violations of human rights.[34]

The second stage of reconciliation could be realized through forging an elite consensus, such as adopting a permanent constitution, constructing an acceptable power-sharing model, and promoting a culture of good governance. This stage also extends to promoting national political parties, adopting appropriate electoral laws, and ensuring consultative and inclusive participation in politics. This reconciliation should result in creating a new culture where elites in power and elites outside of power routinely meet and consult each other, respect each other, and listen to each other. In this reconciliation, Islamist and non-Islamist elites should be reconciled by agreeing on the role of Islam in the state and in society. The current provisional constitution provides the basis for such reconciliation, which simply requires prudent applications.

The third stage of reconciliation is clan reconciliation, which is undertaken by reconciled elites. This reconciliation should be approached using a bottom-up approach employing traditional mechanisms for conflict resolution. It may apply shared elements of modern and local transitional justice mechanisms (such as identification of the perpetrators of crimes, payment of reparations, as well as forgiveness and repentance). This step should begin by collecting data and documenting the mass human rights violations, which thereby signals that impunity is not tolerated and that violations will be addressed.

Supplementary Steps for Comprehensive Reconciliation

The primary problems of Somali state-building are organizational deficiency, ideology fluidity and the technical challenges of synthesizing modernity and tradition; however, addressing these issues is beyond the scope of this essay. The greater challenge in Somalia is how to eliminate the anarchy created by statelessness, through reorganizing society. These reorganizations should include (1) reorganizing civil society, including registering modern and traditional Islamic organizations, identifying clan elders, and recording customary laws; (2) revisiting and reorganizing national and federal state institutions; and (3) reorganizing political parties, finalizing party laws, and adopting appropriate electoral laws. This will help to transform elite conflict by unifying political elites so that they operate on the basis of shared legal and cultural frameworks. At the same time, promoting modern civil society organizations helps to bolster social cohesion.

Conclusion

This paper records major human rights violations in Somalia during the military regime and after the collapse of the state, and offers a redefinition of the Somali conflict by departing from the singular "state versus clan" model and adopting a comprehensive "state versus society" model. In the Somali context, there are four types of conflicts: the conflict between modern state and traditional society; non-Islamist elites (over power and resources); ideological conflict between non-Islamist and Islamist elites; and the conflict between clans as the consequence of the civil war.

The first phase of reconciliation is resolving the state-society conflict, which requires abandoning the singular conception of modernity in place of one that incorporates multiple modernities and departs from the two extreme models of westernization or indigenization of the state. The failure of both these models is evident from Somalia's experience during the postcolonial state system and the adoption of the 4.5 clan power-sharing formula.

Reconciling state and society requires moving state and society towards each other to a middle space that is acceptable to both sides. By combining modernity and tradition in an innovative process of synthesis, the reconciliation of state and society can ultimately be realized. Comprehensive reconciliation requires the creation of three separate spaces in Somali society: traditional space (for clans, clan elders and traditional Islamic scholars), civil society space (for professional organizations, Islamic movements, and other non-state institutions and actors), and political space (for political parties and the apparatus of the state). These three spaces must be demarcated so that each of them cannot infringe upon the space of the other.

Recommendations

To the Federal Government:

1. Develop a strategy which mainstreams reconciliation in all state institutions, the education sector and media outlets, and which raises awareness of peace and reconciliation.
2. Enhance and promote national political party formations, in addition to adopting appropriate party laws and an electoral model which weakens clan sensitivities and conflicts.
3. Adopt a proportional representation electoral model where all Somali regions constitute a single constituency to avoid renewed political conflict and clan sensitivities.
4. Adopt a presidential system at the national and Federal Member State levels to prevent fraud in the election of the president through corruptible members of the parliaments, empower citizens, and avoid a power struggle between the president and premier.
5. Consult prominent political figures, political party leaders, prominent academics, and business personalities before adopting major decisions to demonstrate inclusiveness and legitimacy.
6. Enhance and complete the provisional constitution and all other pertinent laws necessary for conducting elections in 2020.
7. Apply provisions of the constitution that promote Islamic ethics within society, and review laws that may contravene the provisions of the provisional constitution.
8. Establish an Independent Reconciliation Commission from credible and highly respected individuals and empower them by providing the resources needed to initiate an effective reconciliation process.

9. Organize national conventions of the traditional elders to consult and debate the best way of conducting clan reconciliation and mobilize them to lead this process.
10. Organize national conventions on Islam in order to unify interpretations of Islam among Islamic scholars and organizations. These conventions will also create a unified voice against extremism and strengthen the legitimacy of the government.

To the international community: provide political, technical, and financial support for the aforementioned ten-point programme for peace and reconciliation.

CHALLENGES AND OPPORTUNITIES

POLITICAL DIALOGUE BETWEEN THE FEDERAL
GOVERNMENT OF SOMALIA AND SOMALILAND

The Centre for Humanitarian Dialogue

Authorship

The Centre for Humanitarian Dialogue (HD) is a Swiss-based private diplomacy organization founded on the principles of humanity, impartiality, and independence. Our mission is to help prevent, mitigate, and resolve armed conflict through dialogue and mediation.

Summary

Reuniting the Somalia Republic is arguably one of the most daunting tasks facing the Federal Government of Somalia (FGS), with the most notable challenge being Somaliland, which declared independence in 1991. While not internationally recognized, Somaliland cemented popular support for its self-declared status in a constitutional referendum in 2000. For decades, Somaliland's political leaders' stance was that political dialogue with Somalia was not feasible, partly due to its unstable political establishment. However, in 2012, through a series of events and quiet dialogue, talks between the two sides started.

While there are many challenges, dialogue nevertheless constitutes the only viable way of resolving the political stalemate. The alternative would be a return to a protracted political conflict and possibly a security crisis. While the two sides have been talking in different forums over the past five years, significant progress is yet to be made in either reuniting the two states or improving the confidence between them for greater cooperation. A new administration in Mogadishu and an upcoming election in Hargeisa herald a timely moment to reflect on the process over the last five years to determine how to help the parties' progress.

The need for a stronger framework of engagement between the two parties has become clear over the last five years of talks. This framework must address the parties' domestic interests and constituencies, offer a combination of confidence-building measures to improve cooperation, and strengthen the dialogue in order to address the core issue of the political status of Somaliland.

This will require dedicated technical and secretarial expertise to support negotiations between the two sides, coupled with political support both domestically and externally to the process to ensure momentum. As ever in mediation processes, informal contacts and backchannels will be important in building confidence between the two sides, achieving consensus and securing the implementation of agreements.

Given the important role international actors have played in the process to date, and in the history of both Somalia and Somaliland, the continued involvement of external players will be key. However, support by the international community needs to be coherent and avoid conflicting or competing approaches. The assistance the international community provides to the FGS in building a federal state should be sensitive to Somaliland's position, and not destabilize the government's engagement with Somaliland.

It is imperative for the parties, along with the international community, to formulate a well-defined mandate for the dialogue process so as to ensure momentum towards a settlement, to build confidence between both parties, and to mitigate challenges that could derail the process.

Introduction

Somalia and Somaliland had parallel colonial experiences under Italian and British rule respectively. In 1960, both gained independence: Somaliland from the United Kingdom on 26 June, and Somalia on 1 July. At the time of Somalia's independence, Somalia and Somaliland entered into a union. In

1969, the civilian government of the Somali Republic in Mogadishu was overthrown in a coup organized by the military, precipitating a brutal civil war. With the collapse of the military government in Mogadishu in 1991, Somaliland declared its independence from the Somali Republic.

The two sides followed quite different trajectories. As the conflict in Somalia continued to escalate, warlords expanded their power and territorial control. International peacekeeping efforts were ill-equipped to address the conflict, and the country developed a reputation for being chaotic and ungovernable.

During this time, Somaliland insulated itself from the worst of the conflict in Somalia, and the complications of international efforts are partly due to Somaliland's relative stability and partly because it lacked international recognition. The dialogue and reconstruction efforts in Somaliland following 1991 were locally led and combined traditional and political leadership. These efforts remain a hallmark of strong local ownership in a post-conflict environment. In 1997, Somaliland adopted what it called an interim constitution, affirming its independence from Somalia, which was endorsed by 97 per cent of voters.

Somalia has slowly begun to emerge from the chaos that characterized the 1990s. With the establishment of the first transitional administration arising from the Machakos peace process, to the Transitional Federal Government elected through the Djibouti peace process, the federal administrations have become increasingly more credible and rooted in the local and national politics of the country. While Somalia continues to face enormous security challenges following the rise of Al-Shabaab after 2006, the present Federal Government of Somalia is seen as being more representative and nationally focused than any Somali government in decades.

Somaliland has had the benefit of several elections and peaceful transitions between political leaders, including from incumbent to opposition. Importantly for the purposes of the Somaliland–Somalia relationship, the election of opposition leader Ahmed Silanyo in 2010 marked the beginning of a shift in Somaliland's attitude towards dialogue. Given the deep-seated feelings about Somaliland's hard-earned stability and independence, this change in thinking did not happen rapidly. Consequently, political leaders in Somaliland do not enter into these talks lightly, but with an increasingly credible administration in Mogadishu, the possibilities for dialogue have been increasing since 2010.

The dialogue between the FGS and Somaliland, which began in 2012, will need to navigate complexities arising from this differing history and forge a way towards reaching a mutually agreed settlement. This paper takes a more detailed look at the recent history of dialogue between the two parties and offers recommendations on how best to establish an effective process.

Developing the Dialogue

From around 2010 onwards, many actors in both Hargeisa and Mogadishu were quietly talking about the need for dialogue. First, however, the issue of international involvement in the process had to be resolved. Somaliland maintained that international engagement was necessary for any talks to take place, while Mogadishu had reservations on this point. A phased approach, beginning in the United Kingdom, helped to overcome this, as did Turkish leadership in later stages.

It is important to recognize the interests that incentivized each party to engage in dialogue. With regard to the Federal Government, as discussions on the constitution advanced and Federal Member States were established, the lack of a settled relationship with Somaliland became more apparent. For Somaliland, the limitations of independence without recognition were beginning to show. While Somaliland had deftly managed its foreign policies, developed good external relations, and benefited from some foreign assistance and investment, it remains constrained by the lack of political status. In order to fully benefit from foreign aid to Somalia and increasing foreign investment, dialogue with Mogadishu became seen as necessary.

The first formal engagement between Somaliland and Somalia took place on the margins of the UK Conference for Somalia in February 2012. Importantly, the conference communiqué made the first formal mention of dialogue: "The Conference recognized the need for the international community to support any dialogue that Somaliland and the TFG or its replacement may agree to establish in order to clarify their future relations."

While the Chevening agreement[1] highlighted the importance of cooperation on key issues such as security and anti-piracy measures, it made no specific mention of the most sensitive, and central, issue: the political status of Somaliland. It was the view of most of those involved in the early stages of the talks that much more work was needed to build the confidence of both sides, to help identify areas of cooperation that could demonstrate the mutual benefit of the relationship, in order to build towards more challenging discussions ahead.

In the lead-up to the UK talks, the government of Somaliland had to manage its own internal legal limitations on dialogue with Somalia. The

Somaliland administration had a longstanding prohibition on talks with Somalia or attending conferences organized on Somalia issues. In order to enter into the talks in 2012, this policy needed to be amended. President Silanyo led consultations to gain support for a policy change, leading to an address to both houses of parliament by the foreign minister to withdraw the provision and enable the delegation to meet.[2] This was approved and gave a strong indication of support for commencement of the dialogue.

The dialogue has continued since 2012, moving from London to Dubai and then to Ankara. The meeting in Ankara on 13 April 2013 saw the talks resume with facilitation provided by the Turkish government, underlining Turkey's influence in Somalia. As summarized by a recent research report: "After the 2010–2012 famine in Somalia, Turkey's involvement intensified, going beyond delivering aid and assistance to famine survivors to hosting international and regional conferences, mediation between regional parties and engagement in capacity-building efforts as well as its involvement in the security and private sectors underscores its efforts to develop its identity as a global peace mediator in Africa."[3]

The meetings held in Turkey were not confidential. This led to a great deal of speculation in advance of each round of talks, and an official communiqué at the conclusion of each set of discussions. Turkey emphasized national ownership of the process and took a light facilitation approach, leaving the parties to largely manage the Ankara discussions themselves.

Some key issues were discussed in Ankara and several important agreements reached. It was in itself an important breakthrough that the two administrations agreed at the highest level that dialogue was required to resolve their outstanding political dispute.

The talks addressed security cooperation—an area of existential importance to both sides. The Al-Shabaab insurgency has remained a core challenge for Mogadishu and has been an increasing concern in Somaliland. Accordingly, security cooperation was given priority in the original Ankara Declaration of 2013—a seven-point agreement signed by the governments of Somalia and Somaliland and witnessed by Somaliland's Ahmed Mahmud Silanyo, Somalia's Hasan Sheikh Mahmud and Turkey's Abdullah Gül. The three presidents underscored that Turkey's contribution to the dialogue between Somalia and Somaliland would continue and they also committed to hold further talks.

The two sides reached agreement on joint airspace management. The importance of this agreement was underscored by the fact that it repatriated airspace management and provided a concrete opportunity for cooperation with clear mutual benefits.[4] The parties also agreed not to politicize access to aid and economic development.

Both parties saw genuine domestic benefit from the talks. The FGS sought to demonstrate that it was making concerted efforts to reinstate the Somali Republic. President Silanyo made numerous pledges in his campaigns that there would be tangible benefits for the people arising out of the dialogue. However, despite important issues being tabled and discussed, little progress was made in terms of practical cooperation between the parties—perhaps in part a reflection of the light facilitation approach taken by Turkey and minimal dialogue between the formal sessions of the process.

While international attention had a positive impact in bringing the parties to the table, this also led to the general perception within the region that the process was externally driven. With a history of peace processes being held outside the country, there were concerns amongst Somalis that the process was not sufficiently connected to the will of the local population. These concerns were reinforced by the lack of public dialogue within Somalia or Somaliland about the dialogue process itself. Such dialogue could have helped to build a wider constituency of support for the process, and the agreements that came out of it.

By 2016 the focus in Mogadishu was squarely on the presidential elections, and there was little political pressure to move forward with the talks. This, and the lack of progress hitherto, contributed to Somaliland's much anticipated announcement in March 2015 that it would not be returning to Ankara for the next round of talks.

However, the election of President Farmaajo in February 2017 has seen a renewed focus on talks with Somaliland and discussions are now underway on how to re-energize the process. The following sections of the paper consider lessons learned from the Ankara process, to help inform future dialogue, covering: process management, implementation challenges, and domestic pressures.

Managing the Process

Over the years the management of the process has changed and there has been no overall vision for future of dialogue. This has led to a lack of commitment to the talks from both external actors and the parties themselves, and other issues have often been given priority. The absence of violence in the political dispute between Somaliland and Somalia is commendable and a tribute to both sides. However, given the existence of other pressing security issues, this contributed to a lack of urgency about the process.

Neither Somaliland nor Somalia was willing to change the status quo, nor were they pressured—or indeed convinced—that it would be in their interest to do so. When the leadership of the process moved to Ankara, external actors other than Turkey took the view that they were not able to play a direct role in the talks. There was therefore little coherent international pressure on the parties to advance the dialogue, or forums for joined-up thinking by the international community on constructive ways to support the process.

Questions were raised in Hargeisa about Ankara's views on the final settlement, with concerns raised that as a facilitator, Ankara was not impartial on the ultimate political issue of Somaliland's status. This further eroded confidence in the process. This issue of perceived partiality could have been addressed and offset by the inclusion of other actors in the process.

The management of the process lacked key elements. For example, negotiation teams, assisted by experts, could have helped to agree on a framework, manage meetings, and specify agenda items in order to secure meaningful discussions and move the process forward in between formal sessions.

Lack of Implementation

As noted above, lack of implementation of many of the issues agreed in the talks weakened confidence in the process, particularly for Somaliland. A secretariat for the dialogue was agreed on but not established, which reduced the capacity of the process to deliver tangible results on the ground, or help sustain relations between the parties in between formal sessions.

In several areas implementation was lacking. For instance, Hargeisa felt that Mogadishu did not honour the commitment to depoliticize economic development, citing the opposition of Mogadishu to the Berbera Port development agreement with Dubai Port World (DPW).

The most striking example of lack of implementation is the issue of airspace management, which had perhaps the greatest adverse impact on confidence in the process. The Communiqué issued on 9 July 2013 by Somaliland and the Federal Government of Somalia stated that the parties "agreed to the return of the air traffic management from the UN and decided to establish a joint control body that is based in Hargeisa." The domestication of airspace management has yet to be achieved and represents an important missed opportunity that could have not only built confidence between the parties, but also generated substantial revenues.

Domestic Pressure

In Somaliland, the government was required to consult widely with the head of the negotiation team tasked with regularly briefing the cabinet and parliament on the outcomes of each session. This had two implications: it raised awareness and increased buy-in to the process across the political spectrum. However, it also raised expectations about what the process needed to deliver for Somalilanders, in order for them to have confidence that it was in their interests. Furthermore, the political leadership had to justify the political capital they were spending on the process.

To ease the domestic pressure, the Somaliland government tended to interpret the agreements made between the parties in a way that pleased the electorate. This was mainly to respond to criticism from those who opposed the talks, but made it difficult to resume the dialogue when results were slow to materialize.

In contrast, the FGS maintained a tight control of the dialogue. Somalia delegates briefed only the president, and there seems to have been considerably less domestic pressure for wider briefings on the issue in Mogadishu. However, this may change as President Farmaajo has publicly affirmed his commitment to the dialogue and stated that he sees it as a priority. In addition, a track-two dialogue process has been initiated since 2016, involving opinion leaders between Somaliland and Somalia, which could serve as a forum for wider discussion on the issue and could support renewed political dialogue.

The tenure of the president of Somaliland ends in November 2017. Regardless of the outcome of the elections, it is anticipated that Somaliland will continue to support talks. Both the ruling party and the main opposition are committed to the advancement of the dialogue and have been involved in the process to date. However, the lack of tangible progress may make the public more sceptical of further dialogue. The Somaliland population seems inclined to oppose a continuation of the present dialogue without reforms to address the challenges we have outlined in this paper. Therefore, the new administration in Somaliland should seek to revitalize the process, clarify what results can be expected in the early stages, and consult with the wider public through track-two processes and other forums.

Public support for the process is particularly important in Somaliland given that the territory's independence is linked to the constitution approved by referendum. The government does not have the mandate to compromise this claim of independence without a wider process of consultation. In other words, Somaliland delegates have limits to what they can agree to in the process and it is therefore especially important that they have the backing of the population.

In Mogadishu, the FGS also faces internal challenges. As the federal authority of Somalia, it has a duty to protect the territorial integrity of the Somali Republic, which is the only entity recognized by the international community. The role of the Federal Member States has increased in the last five years and the FGS is therefore concurrently managing the expectations of these governments. In particular, if an asymmetric arrangement is tabled as a possible solution to the dispute with Somaliland, the FGS will need to initiate parallel dialogues with the Member States in order to have their backing. Such dialogues should take place early in the process, so that the dialogue with Somaliland does not precipitate a political crisis between Mogadishu and the Member States.

Recurrent political and security crises in Mogadishu also negatively affect the dialogue with Somaliland. While the issue of Somaliland is seen as a priority, other urgent issues, especially security crises, pull the focus away from this larger and longer-term issue. Looking ahead, it is critical that the FGS sustains a high-level strategic focus on its relationship with Somaliland and that Somaliland does likewise.

Conclusions and Recommendations

A great deal has been achieved since 2012 in enabling space for Somaliland and the FGS to engage in dialogue. However, the process needs to move to a new phase in order to find a lasting settlement to this political stalemate that is in the parties' mutual interests.

Constructive dialogue between the FGS and Somaliland is a priority for both parties, and is increasingly recognized by the international community as a fundamental pillar for long-term peace and stability. Notwithstanding the challenges, there is presently an opportunity to revitalize dialogue, redesign the process, and clarify the roles of the parties and facilitators.

Learning from the past five years of talks, and from the wide-ranging history of Somali political dialogue, it is important to recognize that efforts to bring about constructive dialogue are more likely to be successful and sustainable when they are driven by Somalis. It is equally important that the delegations on both sides are clearly mandated by their respective political leaders and that so far as possible, they remain in place throughout the process in order to sustain continuity. It is important that the two negotiating teams have authority to represent their principals in the discussions, even if the final decision-making rests with the respective presidents and any final agreement will need the buy-in from other branches of government in Hargeisa and Mogadishu. Both sides should consider identifying teams of similar standing and with the requisite experience in negotiations for the process to progress, and each team should have access to relevant expertise.

The present process has a light footprint. It provides minimal facilitation by a single government convener/facilitator. The process would benefit from an increased capacity for facilitation and support, as long as this capacity is coordinated and supports the leadership of the two parties themselves. Specifically, the process can be more effective if (a) the roles of the facilitator(s) and convener are clear and agreed upon among all participants; (b) adequate technical and material support is available; and (c) the parties provide strong leadership and coordinate all engagements related to the dialogue.

A mechanism could be established to support the dialogue teams in Mogadishu and Hargeisa through: (a) giving advice between formal rounds of talks to help guide the negotiations; (b) facilitating preparatory discussions in advance of formal talks; (c) coordinating technical support to the teams; and (d) supporting the implementation of agreements. Through this mechanism, other informal channels of communication between the parties can also be managed discreetly. This is particularly important as often parties benefit from discreet discussions prior to formal dialogue in order to develop thinking, build confidence and identify mutually beneficial approaches.

Discussions among Somalis should not be limited to the political elites. Both sides will need to widen the constituency of support for the process and build public buy-in for an eventual agreement. The track-two dialogue process already underway should be linked to the track-one dialogue and expanded as a complement to the political process.

Given the increased international attention, there is a risk of pressure on the parties to respond to competing international demands. A "Group of Friends" could be therefore established in order to keep external actors briefed and supportive of the process. This group would provide funding and possibly other technical and political support as requested by the parties or the facilitators.

THE HUMAN DIVERSITY OF CONFLICT

WOMEN, MEN AND YOUTH

BEYOND PRINCIPLES

THE INCLUSION OF SOMALI WOMEN IN PEACEMAKING

Judith Gardner

Authorship

Judith Gardner, contracted by the Life & Peace Institute (LPI) to advise on research on women's roles in the construction of war and peace in Kismayo, has worked in and on Somalia since 1989. This briefing paper was commissioned by LPI, an international organization that has supported community-led reconciliation processes across Somalia in partnership with Somali civil society since the early 1990s.

Summary

This paper presents evidence from recent research with women and men in Kismayo[1] that highlights how the inclusion of Somali women in resolving violent conflict and achieving political settlements is essential for long-term conflict reduction and reconciliation.

Findings suggest a fresh and more critical examination is needed of how the prolonged violent conflict has been constructed and executed. Findings challenge the assumption that men are the only important protagonists in intra-

239

and inter-clan conflict. They indicate that such conflict is constructed through joint effort by men and women, and is part of a continuum of violence in which notions of kinship or clan identity are used to divide and rule. Within this continuum, the parts played by men and women largely conform with the gendered structure and hierarchy of power relations. Accordingly, males are the main combatants but women are instrumental as producers, or co-producers, of violent masculinities and guardians and agents of clannism.

The research study that underpins this paper expands our knowledge of women's roles in conflict and deepens our understanding of how women construct pathways to peace. Their contribution in both areas is evidence, if evidence is required, that women are men's equals in both war and peace. Their systematic exclusion from, or tokenistic inclusion in, peace processes serves to ensure that the continuum of violence is never fully broken. This is an outcome that arguably serves the interests of the male elite.

Introduction

United Nations Security Council (UNSC) Resolution 1325 enjoins member states to ensure the full participation of women in humanitarian conflict resolution, peacebuilding, and post-conflict reconstruction initiatives. Whilst a key milestone in the international recognition of women's rights in policy and law, to date, significantly more policy attention has been paid to women's inclusion in peacebuilding initiatives than has changed in practice. Globally, and across Somalia, peace processes remain elite bargaining scenarios involving mainly male actors. Indeed, some of the organizers of such processes officially deplore women's marginalization, yet unofficially doubt the relevance of women's inclusion, believing that men constitute and lead the warring parties, and therefore have the means to make peace.[2]

This briefing paper shares evidence that suggests there are significant shortcomings in this assumption for the Somali context.[3] It shows women are instrumental in both intra and inter-clan conflict, as financiers, promoters, mobilizers, and fighters. The evidence is drawn from a recent study in Kismayo undertaken by LPI, Somali Women Solidarity Organization (SWSO) and Peace Direct, to deepen understanding about women's and men's perceptions of women's roles in conflict and peace, with the aim of identifying new options for greater inclusion and participation of women in Somali peace and reconciliation processes.

Kismayo has experienced some of Somalia's worst and most prolonged violent clan conflict since 1991. The study joins a small but significant body of literature on gender, conflict and peace in the Somali context.[4] The findings were generated from focus group discussions, interviews and the collection of testimonies from individual women. The study consulted 149 women and 51 men, representative of the range of clan families and traditionallymarginalized groups currently living in Kismayo.

Two important concepts underpin the research. First, the concept that gender is relational rather than synonymous with "women"—that both men and women are gendered beings with socially-constructed gender identities that are developed in relation to each other and are mutually reinforcing.[5] Second, the concept that biological sex is not the only determinant of relative power but intersects with other axes of power such as age, race, clan, religion, and other markers of identity. Some women are more powerful than some men.

This paper explores the roles played by women during violent conflict in Somalia; the ways in which women have contributed to the production of violent conflict; instances of direct engagement in combat by women; the relationship of women to clannism more broadly; and finally, how women can and have worked to foster peace.

Women and the Construction of Clan Conflict

The study confirms that women across all clan and socio-economic groups have experienced traumatic events as a result of the prolonged conflict affecting large areas of southern Somalia since 1991.[6] It also indicates that women who have engaged in conflict, either proactively or reactively, span clan and socio-economic backgrounds.[7]

Women are candid about how they have contributed to the war. In the words of one woman, "the war has impacted us women, but we also took part actively in the fighting ... Everyone participated. No one is clean. Even if you didn't support by holding guns or helped during the fighting, you were supporting in your heart."[8]

Women Financiers, Promoters and Mobilizers

That Somali women have been financiers, promoters and mobilizers for conflict since 1991 is not a new finding, nor is the fact that these are roles expected of women by their clansmen.[9] But the research conducted for this paper reveals the scale and significance of these roles in the violence that followed state collapse.

241

Table 5.1: Summarizes the roles women have played in conflict since 1991 (verified by male respondents)

Type of Actions	Details
Financing	Selling gold, fundraising and mobilizing resources for conflict
Mobilizing men and male youth to fight	Humiliating reluctant male relatives/clansmen into fighting, invoking fury, shame, spreading negative narratives to motivate men to fight
	Motivating clansmen to fight by ululating, singing songs, playing war drums
	Canvassing for conflict to continue or restart
Humanitarian and welfare	Caring for and hiding wounded clansmen
	Protecting clan members from detection by the enemy
Logistical support	Cooking food, providing milk and water for combatants
	Arming the fighters, concealing weapons and ammunition
Intelligence	Acting as messengers and spies
	Counting the dead and wounded
Armed combat	Taking up arms and joining a militia group, or acting as lone combatants
War strategy	Participating in planning large attacks

Both women and men claim women play critical roles in starting and fuelling conflict: "They finance it ... they invest their wealth." Women have personally bought weapons and ammunition for their clan's militia, and when deemed necessary, "they sold their gold to keep the conflict burning", "there were women who sold their houses to fund conflict."

It is notable that there is no mention of coercion. On the contrary, the evidence indicates that women make their own decisions to invest in war and do so as individuals as well as mobilizing among themselves. According to respondents, their motivation is simple: "they want their clan to win and take over the city."

Women and the Production of Clan Conflict

The typical narrative on women and conflict is that women are victims, men are perpetrators. The argument goes that where women are actively engaged, it is because they have been instrumentalized by men: they are used by them and therefore victims nevertheless.[10] Women suffer and they are often used in wars, but as others have argued, to only see them as victims serves to reinforce the prejudice that consigns women to the margins of peace talks and official politics. Moreover, in the Somali context, as the Kismayo study findings show, it masks another side of the truth.

Mobilization of Male Fighters

During the Siad Barre era, both men and women were recruited for the Somali National Defence Force. In the violent conflict that resulted with the collapse of the state, "military duty" is a male responsibility and largely organized along clan lines. Women are crucial to militia-construction as mobilizers, urging men and male youth to fight. As other studies show, Somali manhood is not predicated on violence and not all men are willing combatants.[11] Goading and humiliating reluctant fighters, women sometimes resort to mocking men for being "women". They go to considerable lengths, including "showing their nudity to cause the men to fight," and once fighting, they may need "to beat the drum" to help men keep their nerve.[12]

This "production" of violent masculinity is not taking place within a sociopolitical vacuum. It is part of a continuum of violence, grievance and trauma taking place within a highly gendered social system in which normative male and female roles and responsibilities are clear: men must rise to the defence of their womenfolk,[13] and a woman "sends her son, brother or husband (to fight)."

Women as Participants in Violent Conflict

Women have killed or injured men, other women and wounded men from rival clans in the course of the conflict, as well as killing or violating them by proxy.[14] All the cases mentioned by respondents were apparently motivated by intra- or inter-clan rivalry and revenge. Some women are also said to have held "advisory" and "command" roles in some of Kismayo's conflicts: "Some organize the clan ... they campaign for war." Female and male respondents said the women and girls who have engaged in, and supported, conflict have done so because their clan was involved and "they want their clan/clan militias to win the war."[15] Life stories highlight the extent to which revenge has played its part.

Female Fighters

Apart from Hawa Tako,[16] Somalia's female fighters are a virtually unacknowledged and unrecorded phenomenon. As well as witness and second-hand accounts, the study has heard directly from former women fighters themselves. Together, these findings chart new territory, mapping out how women have targeted, killed or injured men and other women in the course of the conflict, as well as killing or violating them by proxy. This is clear evidence that clan warfare is no longer the sole preserve of males (if it ever was).

Somali society is highly gendered—that is, expectations about roles and responsibilities are dependent on whether you are considered biologically male or female. Yet apparently in war there are few if any roles that a woman cannot undertake. Some had reservations, "they don't fire big guns" and "it doesn't happen that a woman rapes another woman." Women were clear: "We can do everything men do," a view echoed by men, "they don't bury the dead but (they) do all other things."[17] Taking up arms for one's clan appears to be a woman's personal choice.[18] Unlike males, they are not complying with gender expectations—quite the contrary—nor have they been conscripted by their clansmen.[19]

Female fighters fight alongside male counterparts,[20] or they operate independently, as snipers, assassins, or armed guards, among other roles. Findings show no evidence of collective female combatant action,[21] unlike the collective agency women garner to build peace (see below). Apparently pointing to what they saw as a disadvantage for women fighters, male respondents noted that "if there's fighting, women do not have the power to join men with their own (female) militia."

No figures are yet available to indicate the scale of female-to-male combatants. However, according to one former female fighter: "We are not so few women who took the gun ... There is only little understanding or knowledge that there are many females who ... actively fought alongside men ... . They took the guns, went on the technicals,[22]... injured, killed, finished the wounded. Some women used guns, others slashers, or big knives."

Women and Clannism

Women describe a context permeated with clannism, that they consider they are responsible for—a view men also put forward.[23] The findings suggest women have a strong but ambivalent relationship with clannism and through clannism women's political agency in the war is most apparent. Taken with the findings on their roles in building peace, it seems that the same women can be clannism's guardians and agents, and they can become a collective bulwark against it.[24] What position they take at any particular time seems to depend on what is happening: how their clansmen are faring, how much power their clan has attained or ceded, how they are individually being affected by the violence, how safe or under threat their children are, and what is otherwise guiding their actions and motives, such as spiritual belief or ideology.

Women's accounts describe a context in which all actions, including humanitarian gestures, carry political ramifications as they either confirm or cast doubt on one's clan loyalty, with victimization and even death awaiting those who transgress by demonstrating independent thought and behaviour. They testify to clannism's compelling, if destructive, rationale and at the same time the visceral actions and catastrophic scenarios it can inspire. A midwife intentionally performing a lethal post-partum repair on a newly delivered mother because she thought she was from a rival clan, for example; revenge killings triggering further killings; directing militiamen to the doorways of women from rival clans with the purpose of committing revenge rape on them; purposely "creating conflict between a couple so as to start a conflict"; or "finishing off" the wounded from the rival clan.

Women-to-Women Conflict

Given the scale of physical and emotional injury and loss generated by the wars in Kismayo, which involved women, it is hardly surprising that women and men said there had been bad relations between women in the town. Indeed, some male respondents noted, "there used to be a time when women used to carry machetes because there was conflict between them." What seems remarkable, but is evidenced by the study, is how in the past couple of years, women have been prepared to put aside their grievances, at least for the time being, in pursuit of peace.[25] Referring to the internecine nature of the intra-clan conflict that has affected so many people's lives, as one former female fighter put it, "if you look at it, people who were fighting are relatives. Despite the grudges we hold against each other, we are (all) from the same clan."

Women and the Construction of Peace

It has been well documented and even acclaimed that women have been instrumental in ending conflicts at the local as well as regional and national level across south-central Somalia, Puntland and Somaliland since 1991.[26] As well as symbolizing peace, taking actions to bridge warring parties in an effort to end conflict is a traditional role for women. Female agency is widely acknowledged by Somali men in this regard.[27] The Kismayo study enhances existing knowledge, as it also brings to light new dimensions of women's peacebuilding—that of collective activism.

Table 5.2: Summarizes the diverse actions women from Kismayo say they have taken to end conflict and promote peace

Type of actions	Details
Persuade male family members	Beseech, demand, persuade their menfolk at home, for example, by refusing sex, refusing to fulfil their traditional gender roles, threatening divorce
Network, mobilize collectively	Strategize within and across clan lines through women-to-women talks
Fundraise and mobilize resources	Mobilize to fundraise to cover the cost of peace meetings, the demobilization of fighters, or the purchase of civilian clothes
Take direct action	Place themselves physically between the warring parties
Organize demonstrations	Demonstrate through the streets to draw attention/canvass support for peace
	Organize public collective prayer meetings
Advocacy	Lobby their elders and the elders of lineages to which they are related
Peace envoys	Act as peace envoys for the men, taking peace messages to the enemy
Intelligence gatherers	Collect intelligence about the enemy for their own elders to help them prepare
Emotional appeal	Compose and recite or sing poems in front of men
Logistical support for peace meetings	Organize meetings to bring people together, provide the venue for peace meetings: place 'the peace mat' (gogosha)
	Cook, feed, look after the elders attending the peace meeting

Constructing Peace: Building a Collective Women-to-Women Enterprise

According to respondents, "peace starts at home." When women want an end to conflict they start with persuading their closest menfolk to disarm. Men and women believe it is within a woman's power to "build peace by making her husband and son lay down their guns." On this point, male respondents were clear: "women are the centre of peace", "now if my wife tells me 'you will not go to war' to be honest I will stay (home)." Other findings suggest that reality is more complex and the influence a woman has within her marriage or collectively to end conflict will vary depending on the stage of the conflict.

Women believe their agency for peace is greatest when it is collective. They noted that they "don't have a council of elders" and "lack the institutions" available to men, such as *diya* groups.[28] Therefore, they have to construct their peace institutions as they go along. The process involves overcoming internal hostilities, clan divisions and clannism between themselves, including through women-to-women reconciliation, leadership, strategy, delegation, diplomacy, footwork, powers of persuasion and oration, persistence, and mobilization of resources—qualities and skills that are traditionally associated with male leadership.[29]

The process of bringing warring parties to meet and make peace at the local level is conducted with sensitivity and can be as painstaking as any internationally sponsored peace process. Echoing the "do-no-harm" philosophy of international agencies, women speak of needing to "ensure we do not start a conflict." When ready, "women from two rival clans should meet and discuss then each side goes to talk to their men ... if we don't succeed in our talks with our men then we should involve a third party ... [we can] call upon religious leaders ... ." Women "cover the cost of whatever is required to bring peace", but note that their lack of camels is a constraint when it comes to settling the compensation required to make peace, as "men can pay a hundred camels to peace but women cannot."[30] Men made the same point, from the perspective that women mobilize men into conflict but it is men who have to find the resources to settle the peace later on—to pay compensation for rivals killed. That peacemaking comes at a material cost is a point men discussed at some length.

Conclusion

The study has generated findings that Somalis with experience of the war already know—women play an instrumental role in the construction and production of violent clan conflict. They are also vital peacebuilders. At any one time, where a woman stands on the spectrum of conflict promotion to peace promotion depends on context and her individual circumstances. In Somalia, the political is the personal, and women are political actors. Not all women have directly supported conflict but their contribution has been of sufficient magnitude for women to describe themselves and be described by men as "responsible for conflict." What emerges from accounts is how clan conflict is seemingly a joint effort, between men and women. Violence is not a natural male state (or peacefulness a female one). Rather, women have a critical role in the production and re-production of the male violence required for intra-and inter-clan conflict.[31]

Political economy analysis reveals how the clannism that drives much of the conflict in south Somalia, and Kismayo in particular, is rooted in a continuum of violence marked by historical grievances, fuelled by present-day geopolitics, and serving elite, largely male, interests.[32] The study findings shed light on the gendered social structure giving rise to the person-to-person dynamics of clannism. As a result of their position within this structure, women are instrumental to clannism's "success" but at the same time suffer terrible consequences.[33] It seems this female suffering is the social "fuse" that blows, altering the trajectory from one of violence to the pursuit of peace.

The study deepens understanding of how women construct pathways to peace. The risks and painstaking steps involved to produce collective peace actions include building women-to-women reconciliation and consensus within and across clans, as well as the mobilization of resources. The leadership skills and strategic thinking involved are evidence, if evidence should be required, that women are men's equals in both war and peace. As such, delivering on the inclusion of women in peace processes is not just about fulfilling a policy requirement but essential practice to reduce conflict and improve chances of stability and sustainable peace.

Recommendations

Overcoming structural barriers through fresh thinking about building peace

- *Federal Government of Somalia (FGS), Federal Members States (FMS) and other peacebuilding stakeholders:* Invest in women-to-women reconciliation (especially between elites), as a crucial step in social and political reconciliation; be context-sensitive, support intra-women conversations, peace dialogues, and the creation of women's platforms. Ensure women's energy and agency are fully engaged.
- *National and international stakeholders:* Invest in youth, the future generation of peacebuilders with peace education and leadership development opportunities; support youth-to-youth reconciliation.

- *FGS, FMS*: Close the female literacy and education gap, invest in education, including male and female adult literacy; make programmes accessible for marginalized and minority group members.
- *FGS, international stakeholders*: Consult widely with women and men, separately if necessary, to gain a holistic perspective, when designing peace-building and reconciliation policies or strategies, and prioritize inclusion; recognize there may be conflict or competition over resources between women's organizations.

Demobilization, disarmament and reintegration (DDR)

- *FGS, international stakeholders*: Involve relevant women in the planning and roll-out of DDR.
- *FGS, international stakeholders*: Support demobilization of female fighters and females engaged in conflict in non-combat roles.

Peaceful coexistence

- *FGS, FMS*: Promote inclusion and increase tolerance towards families and individuals from outside the dominant clan (this is a role for traditional elders, religious leaders, and women's organizations), and advocate for equal treatment.
- *National stakeholders*: Explore narratives and cultural practices that perpetuate and entrench conflict—for instance war songs—and how these might be shifted to promote and attach value to practicing peace and alternatives to violence.

WOMEN IN AL-SHABAAB

"Khadija" and *Stephen Harley*

Authorship

Lead Researcher: Khadija (real name withheld for personal security reasons) is a Kenyan-born Somali gender expert with over fifteen years' experience working with Somali women, focusing on various issues such as harmful cultural practices, peacebuilding, deradicalization, conflict resolution, and empowerment.

Lead Analyst/Writer: Stephen Harley is a former British Army officer who provides consultancy to: the Federal Government of Somalia (FGS) Office of the President, British Embassy in Mogadishu, King's College London's Department of War Studies, and the NATO Centre of Excellence in Defence Against Terrorism.

Summary

This research was conducted with women who are or were previously married to Al-Shabaab fighters.

The positions of women in Somali society are complex, being at times repressed and sidelined but also in some circumstances influential and in control of significant resources and access. In some ways, the lives of the women

251

interviewed for this paper accord with the broader context of Somali social mores. But, on the whole, their circumstances were considerably better than experienced by most women in Somalia.

Women who are married to Al-Shabaab fighters lead a privileged existence both in terms of the quality of life that is accorded to them by Al-Shabaab's Executive Council, especially in comparison to the civilian population living under Al-Shabaab's control, and also the freedoms they are allowed.

The women interviewed were permitted, and apparently encouraged, to run businesses and in support of that activity they were allowed access to smartphones and could travel relatively freely around Lower and Middle Jubba. The women occasionally participated in Al-Shabaab operations, taking advantage of the lax security that is applied to women to support intelligence gathering and fundraising for the organization.

In addition to these roles, it seems the wives of Al-Shabaab fighters are perceived as fulfilling two important functions by the group. First, they are producing and bringing up the next generation of Al-Shabaab fighters from birth to the age of eight, when they begin instruction in Al-Shabaab madrasas, to the age of 15, when they reach adulthood and become fighters. Second, they offer devotion to Al-Shabaab, inculcate their children with Al-Shabaab thinking, and act as convincing advocates for the group.

Introduction

Between March and May 2017, Khadija travelled to Kismayo on three separate occasions and interviewed in person a group of six women who are or were wives of Al-Shabaab fighters. She met with them both collectively and individually.

All six women answered pre-prepared questions. However, in subsequent interviews, they soon deviated and engaged instead in discussions of their particular circumstances. All six women participated freely and in the knowledge that a report would be produced for a wide audience based on their discussions.

In order to protect the identities of the six women who participated in the research, they will only be referred to as interviewees A to F. The six women and the security elements to which their Al-Shabaab husbands belonged are listed below. Jabha refers to Al-Shabaab's military wing, Amniyat to the group's internal security and intelligence agency, and Hizba to the group's police force.

A. Currently married to a Somali Al-Shabaab fighter (Jabha) who is absent on operations.

B. Currently married to an Al-Shabaab fighter (Amniyat) who is absent on operations.

C. Currently going through a difficult divorce from a Somali Al-Shabaab fighter (Jabha) who is absent on operations.

D. Recently widowed (operational casualty, Jabha).

E. Recently widowed (operational casualty, Amniyat).

F. Recently widowed (husband was Jabha and executed on suspicion of spying for the FGS).

It should be noted that these women say they are held in high regard in their communities for voluntarily marrying Al-Shabaab fighters and for their ability to bear children. Although there have been media reports of forced marriage to Al-Shabaab fighters, this was not the case with the research participants. Their circumstances should not be mistaken for those of normal women living in Al-Shabaab-controlled areas, for whom living conditions are extremely difficult, as they are for men.

Finally, it should be noted that this was a small sample size (six women) and the women were thoroughly indoctrinated. Two were unhappy about specific circumstances that they were experiencing—as noted above, one was going through a divorce and the other's husband had recently been executed—but they remained broadly supportive of Al-Shabaab's objectives. This would appear to support their account of life as a wife of an Al-Shabaab fighter as a good life.

Life as Wife of an Al-Shabaab Fighter

Marriage

According to the women interviewed, the process of marriage allows the woman some degree of choice, usually based on knowledge of the man (familial or physical proximity) and there is sometimes even engagement ("courting") via cellphones. The process still involves the consent of the woman's father and family, and therefore follows the broader Somali tradition. However, if an individual of influence within the security elements of Al-Shabaab (the Jabha, Amniyat or Hizba) requests a wife, it is unlikely that he will be refused.

The women noted that the widow of Faisal, the foreign fighter who was killed at an AMISOM checkpoint in 2010, allegedly at the instigation of the then-leader of Al-Shabaab, is a key figure in recruiting Al-Shabaab wives in Kenya and Tanzania. A Kenyan national, she has also lost a second Al-Shabaab fighter husband but apparently remains at large across the region and continues to recruit.

Children, Education and Ideology

All the female participants had multiple children with their Al-Shabaab fighter husbands, although their daughters were seldom referenced.

At the age of eight, the male children began formal education in an Al-Shabaab madrasa where the standard of education was considered to be very high (although these assessments lack comparison). The madrasas operate residentially, so the children are isolated from their parents for long periods of time. However, none of the women expressed any displeasure about this and, if anything, they were content with the system. At the age of 15, at which point Al-Shabaab considers males to become adults, those children become fighters. This helps to explain the large number of child soldiers that Al-Shabaab deploys. They do not consider them to be children. The women also noted that Somalis tend to look younger than their years.

The women were unanimous in their support for Al-Shabaab's education system and for the jihad, more generally. They tried to recruit Khadija and expressed their intention of participating in the jihad itself if required. They said they would carry out suicide attacks if necessary, in the knowledge that, as women, they routinely encountered lax security when entering FGS–controlled areas.

Interviewee B was the most fanatical in her support for Al-Shabaab, noting that she also operated as an internal security agent within Al-Shabaab-controlled areas. She was occasionally armed with a pistol during security purges, should she need to act immediately against "spies".

Marital Discord and Domestic Violence

According to the women interviewed, domestic violence is uncommon but is viewed with disapproval by Al-Shabaab, especially if the woman has proven herself capable of bearing children.

Divorce is allowed and, in common with the rest of Somali society, it is relatively common. Reasons include the failure to produce children (whether due to the husband or the wife), domestic abuse or degenerate behaviour; or the failure of the husband to provide for the wife.

Interviewee C was particularly disgruntled that her husband, who had been abusive towards her, was trying to gain custody of their children and that the Al-Shabaab adjudication process seemed to be allowing this to happen. However, Al-Shabaab had intervened to halt the physical abuse she was suffering.

All six women stated that female genital mutilation (FGM) is not practised in Al-Shabaab-controlled territory and is viewed as being a barbaric superstition from Somalia's history.

Widows

Given the high maternal mortality rates in Somalia and the recent casualty rates amongst Al-Shabaab fighters, widows are at a premium.

A widow will generally be allowed a three-month mourning period before she will be re-married and the same process of finding a husband is repeated. However, in the case of the former husband being executed or a divorce being granted, then the three-month period can be waived. None of the wives said they resented their treatment and potential commodification.

Daily Life

The women say that while their husbands are absent on operations they are well looked after. The Executive Council of Al-Shabaab has appointed a dedicated "emir" to ensure that fighters' wives are provided with funds on a regular and generous basis and that they are secure. (This means that they are regularly required to move at short notice up and down the Jubba River Valley.)

All the women ran businesses to supplement their already generous allowance from the Executive. The businesses varied from running food stores and selling children's clothes to construction and vehicle maintenance. The women noted that business activity was conducted with the awareness and approval of the Executive. The women were allowed to have smartphones in support of their business interests and travelled extensively, including outside Al-Shabaab-controlled areas—specifically to Kismayo, the nearest major town.

Interviewee E noted that she had performed intelligence-gathering while on business in Kismayo and all indicated that some of the revenue from their businesses went to Al-Shabaab in the form of *zakat*. All the women were well-informed about events in Somalia and the region as a result of their access to communications and their ability to travel. They were all deeply cynical about government as well as private, regional, and international media sources.

Conclusion

Women who are married to Al-Shabaab fighters exercise a great deal of autonomy in their daily lives and are strongly committed to the cause of Al-Shabaab and the jihad. In many ways, the women are pivotal to the future of Al-Shabaab, since they are giving birth to the next generation of Al-Shabaab fighters. However, this could quickly change, as evidenced by their individual grievances and if their circumstances were to alter significantly—for instance, in a security purge, a resource shortage or, in extremis, a more active role for the women.

Recommendations

Policy-makers should:

- Conduct further research focused on women living under Al-Shabaab's control who are not married to Al-Shabaab fighters, and, as an additional sample, women living under FGS control.
- Consider the potential value of engaging with women in Al-Shabaab. They potentially offer significant access and may well be effective influencers in long-term efforts to achieve a negotiated settlement with Al-Shabaab.
- Consider a wider strategic communications campaign that seeks to target women who are married to Al-Shabaab fighters.
- Take steps to make Somali security forces more aware of the role of women in Al-Shabaab in terms of fundraising and intelligence-gathering and consider the recruitment of more female members into Somali security forces.
- With the agreement of the FGS, consider focused development aid on education, specifically in recently recovered areas but also in Somalia more broadly. The proliferation of Salafist ideology in Somali schools that fails to promote critical thinking leaves Somali men and women vulnerable to indoctrination.

FROM THE MARGINS TO THE CENTRE

SOMALI WOMEN IN PEACEBUILDING

Hamdi Mohamed

Author

Dr Hamdi Mohamed is a Partner at Asal Consulting and heads up Asal's research and development work. She leads national monitoring and evaluation projects in Somalia, has university teaching experience in North America and Africa, and has lectured on issues of social policy, international development, gender and politics, and human rights.

Introduction and Summary

Somali women experience exclusion from the political arena, including formal decision-making processes, and any meaningful participation in formal peace negotiations.[1] While women's significant under-representation in formal political spaces accurately reflects the current facts on the ground, it does not tell us the whole story of women's position within society in general and their everyday participation in peacebuilding in particular.

Women's lived experiences in various communities suggest very strongly that throughout Somali history, women have developed individual as well as collective strategies to negotiate space and exercise influence within their communities. Yet, the significant contributions women made, and continue to make, to peacebuilding initiatives in their communities are largely undocumented and are rarely known—contributing to false assumptions on the role of women in the prevention and resolution of conflict and in peacebuilding.

Using data collected from in-depth interviews with 13 Somali women,[2] this paper attempts to address this knowledge gap by re-examining the dominant assumptions about women and peacebuilding. It explores how women's participation in peacebuilding manifests itself in Somali politics, identifies distinctive gender dimensions of peacebuilding, and explores the particular ways women negotiate and influence peace.

The paper makes the case for a new recognition of women's role in peacebuilding and argues that Somali women are already employing successful strategies to negotiate space within the political domain and build peace within their families and communities. As such, the paper goes beyond the false dichotomy of formal/informal peacebuilding activities, and contends that the current narrative, which is based on simplistic explanations of women and politics, fails to take into account the historical context of women's agency and the vastly changing political and community dynamics that impact how women participate in peacebuilding.

Historical Context

Traditionally, Somalis have developed various customary systems (such as *xeer*)[3] and methods to prevent and resolve conflicts. In addition to these established mechanisms of negotiation and mediation to avoid violence, they have established rules of engagement in times of conflict. For example, certain categories of the population, called *biri ma geydo*, are to be protected in case of conflict. *Biri ma geydo* means "those who do not deserve the sword" and includes women, children, old persons, men of knowledge and religion, guests, and all those who are not parties to the conflict.[4]

The *xeer* system also provided a set of moral codes for society and standards by which individuals and groups were judged. *Xeer*, in combination with Islamic principles and values, was used to develop a unique and complex set of norms to govern social and gender relations. While women had little or no access to formal power in the *xeer* system, there are no historical indications that women were strictly confined to the "domestic" sphere. In fact, the very system that excluded women embodied "liberating qualities that enable Somali women to play a crucial role in the affairs of the nation."[5]

Women make important contributions in terms of labour, both productive and reproductive, and to the survival of the community. The contribution of women to the social and economic domain, particularly the household, was indeed recognized and continuously mentioned in Somali oral culture.[6] Women's labour, both in nomadic and agricultural settings, provided the foundation of the household and community economy.

Historical records indicate women had a long tradition of negotiating space and exercising power and influence within their communities.[7] From an early age, young girls were encouraged to be resourceful, industrious and clever. Through exogamous marriages, women were important instruments of peace, building strategic alliances between clans. These strategic marriage alliances were one of the ways the community ensured that peace was sustainable.

In cases of conflicts, women used a practice called "*gambo tuur*" (throwing head scarves off) to signal their discontent. This was an act of shaming men who were perceived as failing their societal role of negotiating a peace settlement and doing whatever they can to avoid transgressions that could lead to conflict. The traditional code of ethics forced men to take women's signal of distress seriously because they wanted to avoid any actions that brought harm to *tan ka dhalatay iyo tan u dhaxday*—their kin relations, including sisters, cousins, and wife.

As a separate social group, women "had their own means of protesting and conscientizing other women through songs and poems as well as through their solidarity networks."[8] They devised creative strategies for change in their everyday and personal lives and developed an autonomous female culture. As Raqiya Haji Dualeh points out, before the women's movement emerged in the form of organizations, "there was a feminist consciousness well under way in the traditional nomadic life of the ordinary women."[9] Therefore, notwithstanding the male-dominated nature of Somalia's political system, the culture expected women to be resourceful and display initiative. These leadership skills will be put to use to negotiate political space in the post-colonial state. Women also participated in struggles against colonialism and fought to be heard at the national level in the post-colonial era. Using many strategies including songs and poetry, they articulated—and continue to articulate—the collective situation of women.

Clannization of Politics

As a socio-political contract that is rigorously structured and codified, *xeer* "consists of an ensemble of values, norms, and laws that form a coherent system within pastoral culture." As described by political anthropologist Ali Moussa Iye, "[It] has its own history, doctrine, literature and jargon. Like any system, it has its own institutions and specialists, its own logic and autonomy vis-à-vis the other pillars of pastoral society."[10] *Xeer* was instrumental in negotiating peace settlements in Somaliland and Puntland.[11] Innovative governance structures were established in Somaliland and, in the absence of state legal and judicial institutions, *xeer* was used to mediate and resolve conflicts, adjudicate legal disputes and for many other functions.[12]

However, the *xeer* system has deeply ingrained practices, which exclude women from actively participating in politics. This tendency "to exclude women from positions of power and authority emanates from and is most evident in the clan system. The *shir*, i.e. the traditional clan parliament, is an all-male institution. Women are completely excluded even when issues directly affecting them are being discussed."[13]

Clan politics has been institutionalized—and distorted[14]—through the "4.5 formula", which legalized new inequality between the sexes and had a major detrimental impact on women. In fact, there is a near consensus among the participants of this research that the clannization of politics has contributed to new ways of disenfranchising women. First, the new and reconstituted clan system does not have the checks and balances of the traditional institution of the *xeer*. Second, the legitimacy of the new "clan elders" is questionable as the traditional code of ethics is either destroyed or circumvented. Third, the traditional system has not had an opportunity to be transformed and evolve as a modern political system.[15]

According to one interviewee, "we traditionally had protection within the kinship and have had citizenship rights within the state. With the politicization of the clan, we lost both." She continued to explain that the traditional kinship system had the ethic of care and responsibility, instead of pursuit of power, at its core. In the traditional system, women's productive and reproductive roles within society were recognized and respected. In the post-colonial state women were expected to assert their citizenship rights by pressuring the government and negotiating political space. They were forced to develop the knowledge and the skills to build strategies to pressure the government, lobby for change in policies, and the mechanisms to have their voices heard.

The new clan politics, therefore, presented challenges for Somali women who were not familiar with the kinship system. These women, most of whom live in urban settings, are part of generations of Somalis who have grown up during the breakdown of kinship ideology and who have constructed national and citizenship identities that transcend kinship. They, as one interviewee explained, "are unfamiliar with the functioning of the tradition system and its many newly reconstructed forms", making it more difficult for them to negotiate for political space.

From the Margins to the Centre

Empirical data show that action to take women's voices and perspectives into serious consideration when developing an agenda for peace is beneficial for the whole society, not only for women.[16] When women are involved in negotiations, the probability of peace agreements lasting over 15 years increases by 35 per cent.[17] Having women at the negotiating table expands conversations so that they cover a wider range of issues, relating not only to women but also to children, minorities and communal welfare. Therefore, "we hear more community issues when women speak, rather than power issues. Humanitarian needs also come up."[18]

Research further indicates women's contributions to peace continue to be undervalued and ignored. This is because much of the analyses on women and conflict have focused on their vulnerabilities, presenting women only as victims. This perception of women solely as victims of war obscures their multiple roles within both conflict and peacebuilding. As one study found, "while women are generally victims during conflict, their condition should not be misconstrued as one of passivity. Because of the extreme circumstances in which they are placed, women often adopted proactive strategies to ensure their survival and to provide for their families."[19]

In Somalia, women initiate and participate in dialogue and reconciliation within their communities, often playing the role of mediator in unofficial peace talks.[20] Yet, they experience new exclusions from the political arena including any meaningful participation in formal peace negotiations and decision-making processes. While some women participated in the Arta and Mbagathi peace conferences,[21] which coincided with the adoption of the UN Security Council Resolution 1325 on Women, Peace and Security, they are significantly under-represented in formal leadership spaces.

Interestingly, women are uniquely positioned to build peace: "women's multiple clan affiliations can give her a structural role as peacebuilder, enabling her to act as a conduit for dialogue between warring parties and exert pressure on them to keep talking".[22] According to many of the women who participated in Asal's research, women take considerable personal risks to broker peace between warring groups.

The clannization of politics presented new challenges and setbacks for women. But this was not passively accepted by women. Instead they fought to change the new political culture that is exclusionary at its core. As a woman in Mogadishu put it, they "faced the new marginalization head on, with courage, perseverance, and creativity". After women realized that none of the five clan delegations at the Arta Peace Conference in 2000 were willing to include women, they established the "sixth clan" which allowed them to secure a formal designation as delegates to participate in the talks and get 25 seats in the 245-member parliament. This is just one example of women coming up with new solutions to negotiate space. It was strategic, effective and a historic achievement by any measure, especially in the challenging new political context.

Women have also taken a leadership role in taking care of the survival of the family and kin when "things fall apart" and minimized their vulnerabilities through courage and ingenuity. As one research participant articulated: women "have the power, knowledge, and the trust to mobilize both sides of their family and kin. They rebuild social capital, amend relations, provide counsel and healing, give to charities and make a huge difference." Women often assume responsibility for providing financial, physical and emotional care—activities that "must be seen as a peacebuilding activity." Instead, such activities are often underestimated, being classified as "informal." This dichotomy of informal/formal peacebuilding activities implies "hierarchical and gendered ordering" of responsibilities, which privileges men's participation and contribution to peace.[23] Separating the "informal" and "formal" peacebuilding also renders women's central role in peacebuilding invisible, depoliticizing their contribution.

There are many cases of women leading civil society organizations that promote peace and reconciliation. At the height of the civil war, women were "among the most visible, articulate, energetic, and respected of the groups working to eliminate barriers."[24] Many of the women interviewed for this research were either leaders or members of women's organizations that are actively advancing peace and reconciliation. They are doing a wide range of political activities, including lobbying and pressuring the government (both national and local) to make political space for women. Three of the organizations interviewed have had formal meetings with the new president and the mayor of Mogadishu to remind them of their constitutional obligations.[25]

Voices from the ground also suggest that the activities women engage in, including the "informal" work of providing support to clan council meetings, are critical to the success of the peace negotiations. One participant shared her research findings that women had the role of mobilizing local communities to bring goats to be slaughtered and prepared for the men at the conference that lasted for months in Borama 1993. These women were also composing poetry to encourage men to go on and find peaceful resolution to the conflict. The way she saw it, "women's role in providing the 'logistical' assistance were indeed political activities. Their 'informal' role was central to the success of the conference. In fact, had it not been for women's participation, there would not have been a conference, nor would there have been a successful negotiation of peace settlement."

Conclusion and Recommendations

This short paper has demonstrated Somali women's lived experiences in developing collective strategies to build peace. Challenging conventional assumptions and rejecting the artificial separation and framing of "formal" and "informal", the paper provides a new lens for understanding the central role women played, and continue to play, in national and local peacebuilding and in the survival of their families, kin, and communities. This approach throws light on the myriad ways women already participate in peacebuilding and opens up the possibilities of reimagining national and local political spaces that are meaningfully inclusive.

Research participants articulated many ways that new political institutions could be more representative and responsive to women. Politicizing the notion of "informal" in peacebuilding is a critical step towards making women's work in the community visible. The ahistorical, essentialist, stereotypical, and monolithic construction of women's identity is problematic. Additional empirical data are necessary to understand women's experiences within specific historical, socio-religious, economic, and political contexts. This new understanding will lead to a much-needed recognition of women's multiple subjectivities and agency.

In recognition of the changing cultural and social attitudes towards women and politics, ongoing public education and engagement campaigns are of paramount importance. It is recommended that the content, messages, and delivery of this public education be developed with a deep appreciation of the Somali context and be informed by a deep knowledge of the ground realities and indigenous culture. The inherently liberating character of Islam should be included in the messages to shift existing attitudes towards women and leadership.

As the late Professor Said Samatar said once, "The peace genre of Somali poetry has a cooling effect, like pouring water over the coals." As such, poetry and other cultural mediums have been highlighted as significantly useful. As one woman, said it, "we must use the most powerful of all tools, the power of words and wisdom."

WOMEN IN PEACEBUILDING IN SOMALIA

Sahro Ahmed Koshin

Author

Sahro Ahmed Koshin is the Programmes Manager of the Somali Institute for Development Studies and Research Analysis (SIDRA), a research think tank based in Garowe but which works throughout Somalia. She is a development expert with over ten years of international work experience.

Summary

This briefing paper is a summary of a research study conducted in Somalia, Galkayo (South and North) and Kismayo and a focus group discussion conducted in Garowe. A public survey was carried out at the three locations involving a total of 152 people. The aim of the study was to explore the level of women's engagement and participation in peacebuilding and conflict prevention and resolution.

The survey cannot be taken as fully representing the population of Somalia; however, the key findings are significant and instructive. A clear majority of respondents (71 per cent) felt that Somali women have an important role in peacebuilding and conflict prevention and resolution.

There are a range of ways, identified by respondents, that women are involved in conflict prevention and resolution, especially preventing conflict in the household (37%), bringing up well-behaved and peace-loving children (22%), mediating among community members (18%), and participating in community peacebuilding committees (13%). Respondents also identified ways in which women are involved in peacebuilding, especially supporting children's education (30%), advocating for peace within the community especially at the household level (24%), and supporting community negotiations (16%).

Respondents identified social and cultural norms as the greatest challenge hindering women's participation in peacebuilding and conflict prevention and resolution. These included: women's involvement in the preparation of the venue and in cooking during peace initiatives (45%); women being seen to be sensitive and emotional (39%); women being seen to be weak physically (32%); and women not being given the opportunity to air their opinions (20%). The biggest challenges to overcoming these hindrances were seen as their low level or lack of education (33%) and their limited finance and lack of funds (24%).

Generally, respondents felt that communities had a negative perception of women's involvement in peacebuilding and conflict prevention and resolution—that women are not valued and included by their clans (39%), or are not capable of building peace (30%). Interestingly, however, over two thirds of the respondents (68%) indicated attitudes of this kind were changing in a positive way.

There are also many opportunities to enhance the involvement of women in peacebuilding and conflict prevention and resolution, including through wider skills development and education, changing attitudes, implementation of certain government policies, awareness-raising activities, and civil society mobilization and lobbying.

Over half of respondents were not aware of UN Security Council Resolution 1325 on women, peace and security and only 11 per cent of the respondents indicated that key partners placed a high priority on women's involvement in peace and security. Policy-makers should recognize that no lasting peace will be achieved in Somalia without adequate involvement of all its citizens.

It is recommended, among other things, that: the Federal Government appoints women as ambassadors and special envoys; Member States increase recruitment, training, retention and advancement of female police; women's organizations coordinate and strengthen local initiatives; and that the UN and NGOs use UNSCR 1325 as a mobilizing force for women's participation in peacebuilding.

Introduction

Somali women's participation in peacebuilding and conflict resolution in Somalia has been very limited, and they have been marginalized in all aspects of decision-making and governance. Compared to men, there are few women in the cabinet, and fewer in parliament. Women are often dismissed or forced to resign and then replaced by men.

Women's political participation is closely linked to peacebuilding and state-building in Somalia, hence the need to undertake a study of various factors which promote or indeed inhibit women's involvement in mainstream peace and reconciliation in Somalia. We therefore believe this study is important, will help contribute to the sparse knowledge in this area and ultimately enhance the level of women's involvement in peace and reconciliation in Somalia.

This paper summarizes broader research conducted in Galkayo (South and North) and Kismayo and a focus group discussion conducted in Garowe. The study addressed four research objectives: (1) levels of women's participation in peacebuilding, (2) factors constraining women's participation, (3) policies, frameworks, rules and regulations encouraging women's participation; and (d) UNSCR 1325 and an agenda to catalyse action and bring about positive change.

Demography

A public survey was carried out at three locations, Kismayo, South Galkayo and North Galkayo. Nearly the same number of respondents were interviewed at each location (48 at Kismayo, 53 at South Galkayo, and 51 at North Galkayo) to make a total of 152 respondents, of which close to three quarters (74.3%) were women. The respondents were young, with 50% below 30 years of age and 79% below 40 years of age. Only 5% of the respondents were above 50 years of age. Slightly over half of the respondents (53%) had a basic education (primary and secondary level) while slightly below one third of the respondents (31%) had a higher education (diploma and degree). 41% of the respondents were married, 37% were single, and 16% were divorced. The remaining 5% indicated their marital status as widow or other.

Women's Participation in Peacebuilding and Conflict Prevention and Resolution

Definitions

To assess community understanding of peacebuilding and conflict prevention and resolution, the respondents of the public survey and the participants of the focus group discussions were asked to give their definition of these terms. Peacebuilding was defined to include living with others in a peaceful way, creating an environment for dialogue and consensus building, addressing conflicts among members of the community when they arise, reconciling community members who have differences and establishing good security systems within the community. Conflict resolution was defined as removing all disputes from the clan and the process of accepting, forgiving and understanding each other as well as the use of *xeer* to reach agreements and payments for compensation.

Importance

From the public surveys, the majority of respondents (71%) felt that Somali women have an important role in peacebuilding and conflict prevention and resolution. Those who did not think so were less than 20%, while 11% were either not sure or did not know. When this question was asked separating conflict prevention and resolution from peacebuilding, 64% of respondents indicated that women took part in conflict prevention and resolution while 78% of respondents indicated that women took part in peacebuilding, indicating less involvement of women in conflict prevention and resolution as compared to peacebuilding.

Means of Involvement

Respondents were asked to identify ways in which women prevented and resolved conflict from a list of options. The key ways identified by the respondents included: preventing conflict in the household (37%), bringing up well-behaved and peace-loving children (22%), mediating among community members (18%), and participating in community peacebuilding committees (13%).

Respondents also identified ways in which women are involved in peacebuilding. These included supporting children's education (30%), advocating for peace within the community especially at the household level (24%), supporting community negotiations (16%), and *godobir* (12%). *Godobir* is the practice of exchanging a young girl as a wife, with or without her consent, often as part of a larger exchange that could include camels, weapons and money, to cement a peace agreement between warring parties.

Evaluation

Respondents of the public survey were asked to evaluate the role of women in peacebuilding and conflict prevention and resolution. 13% gauged it as "excellent" while more than half of the respondents (63%) selected "very good" and "good." Almost a quarter of the respondents (24%) were not positive about the role of women and selected "somewhat good", "bad", or "very bad."

Voices

Concerning the voice of women in peacebuilding and conflict prevention and resolution, more than half of the respondents (54 per cent) of the public survey indicated that women's voices are heard in peacebuilding or during conflicts while a quarter of the respondents (26 per cent) indicated that women's voices were not heard. 18 per cent of the respondents were not sure.

International Support for Women

Respondents identified advantages of international support for women in Somalia to include women's empowerment (29%), improvement in the public perception of women (23%), and increasing appreciation of women's contribution to the community (14%). The risks that may result from such support include increasing conflicts (15%), and increased restriction on women by traditional and religious leaders (15%).

Constraining Factors

Social and Cultural Norms

Respondents of the public survey identified social and cultural norms as the greatest challenge hindering women's participation in peacebuilding and conflict prevention and resolution. These included: women's involvement in the preparation of the venue and in cooking during peace missions (45%); women not being given the opportunity to air their opinions (20%); women being seen to be sensitive and emotional (39%); women being seen to be weak physically (32%); and women not being elected to be members of the community peacebuilding committee (14%).

The challenges that women faced when seeking to overcome these cultural and social norms include: the low level or lack of education among women

(33%); limited financial capacity of women and lack of funds (24%); negative perception of women by the community (18%); early marriages (18%); and traditional and cultural discrimination against women (13%).

The opportunities that exist to address these norms include changing the perception of the community about the role of women (27%); increasing access to education by women (22%); increasing awareness of women on their rights (14%); international support to women's affairs (14%); and the neutral role of women in clan politics and affairs (14%).

Community Perceptions on the Role of Women

Generally, the community has a negative perception on women's role in peace-building and conflict prevention and resolution. Public survey respondents indicated that women are not counted by their clans (39%); are not capable of building peace (30%); and are physically weak (23%). Generally, Somali traditions and customs restrict women to the house to take care of the house-hold, children and cleaning. However, over two thirds of the respondents (68%) indicated that attitudes were changing in a positive way on this issue, indicating a shift in the perceptions of communities towards women.

Informant Interviews and Focus Group

Reinforcing the survey results, the focus group discussion and key informant interviews both identified cultural and traditional barriers as the key constraints for women's participation in peacebuilding and conflict prevention and resolution. These ranged from outright discrimination to family expectation that women should remain at home and take care of family matters. The discussions revealed that Somali culture and tradition favoured men over women and the clan-based political representation system gives all decision-making powers to the traditional elders who would not allow women to represent their clans. In many cases, women are denied the opportunity to participate in community peacebuilding committees, while the conflict resolution process was dominated by men. Women's contributions are generally perceived as not so important or valued. Traditional leaders and elders largely preferred men over women. Women are also told that there are enough men to represent the clan.

Enhancing Women's Participation

Existing Mechanisms and Policy Options

A large number of the respondents (66%) did not know of any mechanism in place in Somalia to build peace or prevent and resolve conflicts. Of the other respondents, 18% indicated awareness of formal mechanisms, while 13% reported awareness of informal mechanisms. Regarding policy options for enhancing women's participation in peacebuilding and conflict prevention and resolution, nearly half of the public survey respondents (46%) indicated that there were no such policy options, less than a quarter of the respondents (22%) indicated being aware of such policies while more than a quarter of the respondents (26%) had no opinion on whether or not such policy existed. Over half of the respondents (58%) indicated that policy options for enhancing women's participation had not been tried compared to slightly over one quarter of the respondents (28%) who indicated that these policy options had been tried. For the respondents reporting application of policy options, 40% reported success, 31% reported failure, and 25% did not know the outcome.

Opportunities

Focus group discussions identified a wide range of opportunities to encourage women to participate in peacebuilding and conflict prevention and resolution. In peacebuilding, opportunities include: improving skills that have allowed women to take important roles in development, including in the sectors that were previously reserved for men; changing community attitudes towards women and recognition of the role of women in development; an increasing level of education among women; support for women by development partners; unity among women themselves; and, in some cases, the preference for women in mediation due to their peacebuilding skills and clan neutrality.

Policies and Strategies

Key informant interviews explored existing government and organizational policies, strategies and laws to ensure and promote women's participation in peacebuilding and conflict prevention and resolution. Strategies that ensured women's participation included: government policies to unify women (for example in Galmudug state); enforcement of the 30 per cent quota for women in parliament and government jobs; and continuous awareness raising about women's rights through campaigns, public forums and media. The informants observed that policies, strategies and plans were only operating at the state and regional levels but not at the district level.

Strategies that promoted women's participation included: policies promoted through women's ministries (for example the Ministry of Women, Family Affairs and Human Rights in Jubbaland); the use of numerous women's development principles and agreements; and lobbying by civil society organizations and women's associations. One informant indicated that women still continued to face discrimination and that there was still a lot of work that needs to be done. For example, in a recent government recruitment of 21 directors, only one woman was included.

UNSCR 1325

Over half of the public survey respondents (57%) were not aware of the UN Security Council Resolution (UNSCR) 1325 on Women, Peace and Security and only 18% of the respondents were aware of it. This being the case, only a quarter of the respondents (26%) thought that this resolution was useful for catalysing action to bring about positive change in Somalia. Over half of the respondents (53%) indicated that the resolution was either somewhat useful or not useful.

More than half of the respondents (57%) indicated that key national partners placed a medium level of priority on women, peace and security while 11% of the respondents indicated that key national and international partners placed a high priority on women, peace and security. A substantial number of respondents (30%) indicated that Somali key partners did not place any priority on women, peace and security. 42% of the respondents were of the opinion that there were no specific mechanisms in Somalia where topics on women, peace, and security could be discussed regularly, compared to just 20% who thought that such platforms did exist.

Conclusions

The aim of this study was to explore women's engagement and participation in peacebuilding and conflict prevention and resolution in Somalia. A number of conclusions can be drawn from our research.

• Somali women play an important role in conflict prevention, resolution and peacebuilding. This role was seen by most respondents as being either excellent, very good, or good.

- Women advocate for peace at the household level, bringing up well-behaved and peace-loving children and supporting community peace initiatives.
- The community had a wide range of interpretation on the meaning of peacebuilding and conflict prevention and resolution.
- Factors that have helped successful women to actively participate in peacebuilding and conflict prevention and resolution included higher level of education; confidence and motivation; awareness of women rights; networking; and support by family, government and development agencies.
- Most community members are not aware of UNSCR 1325 on Women, Peace and Security and its potential for catalysing action to bring about positive change for women in Somalia.

Recommendations

Recommendations to the Federal Government of Somalia:

- Ensure effective participation and representation of women in peace and security sectors as specified in UNSCR 1325 by, among other things, appointing women as special envoys such as ambassadors in the UN, foreign countries and the African Union.

Recommendations to Federal Member States:

- Encourage women to participate and be adequately represented in the peace and security sector in line with UNSCR 1325 and increase recruitment, training, retention and advancement of female police at state level and promote female police officers to higher ranks such as Captain, Colonel, and General.

Recommendations to women activists and women's organizations:

- Coordinate and strengthen local initiatives that promote women's participation in peacebuilding and conflict resolution and prevention.
- Improve communications and arrangements between Member States and the Federal Government to allow development and advancement of women's participation in peacebuilding and conflict resolution.

Recommendation to UN organizations and local and international NGOs:

- Use UNSCR 1325 as a mobilizing force for women's participation. Findings suggest that UNSCR 1325 acted as an important starting point for the mobilization of women outside formal peace processes. Peace processes in other parts of the world reflect how UNSCR 1325 can be used as a mobilization tool both outside and inside formal processes.

BETWEEN A ROCK AND A HARD PLACE

YOUNG SOMALI MEN TODAY

Judy El-Bushra, Judith Gardner and *Adan Abokor*

Authors

Judy El-Bushra and Judith Gardner each worked as consultant researchers for the Rift Valley Institute (RVI). Their previous collaborations include *Somalia—the Untold Story: The War Through the Eyes of Somali Women.*[1]

Dr Adan Abokor is RVI's Representative in Somaliland.

All three were responsible for the inception study on which this paper is based, "The Impact of War on Somali Men."[2]

Summary

Male Somali youth horizons and choices are currently limited by delayed adulthood, militarization, political marginalization, and low status within traditional clan-based forms of government. Young men's needs and aspirations are routinely overlooked by state-and clan-based authority because they are low status, yet they are also seen as a potential source of opposition and resistance. Male youth struggle to fulfil the exacting cultural norms expected of Somali men. Though most are against taking up arms, young men remain both the primary perpetrators and victims of violence. Al-Shabaab, warlords and corrupt clansmen exploit male youths' energy, desperation and low status for their own ends.

Addressing the needs of young Somali men, and fostering their greater inclusion—including in the search for peace and reconciliation between Somalis—needs a greater understanding of their lived experience, instead of relying on preconceived and dated notions. In Somali society male youth are traditionally characterized as "troublesome", "unwise", and "impulsive".[3] Such descriptions are used to justify their exclusion from collective decision-making until they mature or reach elder status. Modern policy-makers also view male youth through a similarly negative lens, most recently security- and counter-terrorism-focused.

This study's findings contradict these mainstream normative views, revealing that male youth weigh risks carefully, value moral and legal structures, and seek security and stability in order to access education and opportunity. Domestic policy-makers, supported by foreign actors, should invest in a more positive narrative about young people and must find ways of offering choice and opportunity to young men, instead of allowing untapped potential to be channelled by negative interests.

Recommendations to the Federal Government include:

- Strengthening legislation and its implementation to end culturally-sanctioned male-on-male violence such as clan revenge killings and forcible recruitment;
- Limiting clan interference in formal justice proceedings; and
- Achieving more equity in employment and appointments.

Recommendations to Federal Member States include:

- Including youth in building Federal Member States' local administrative and consultative structures; and
- Working with religious and cultural institutions to promote inclusion and peaceful coexistence, across generations and between clans and other identities.

To all levels, the paper recommends expansion of non-militaristic livelihood and development opportunities for young men.

Introduction

Throughout Somalia's recent history—civil war, state disintegration, external interventions, local attempts to rebuild government, and latterly, religiously-inspired extremism—scant attention had been paid to the lived male experiences of these processes. This briefing paper, based on findings of RVI's long-term study "The Impact of War on Somali Men", seeks to understand what it is like to be a young male in Somali society today, and the social factors that shape males' lives and opportunities. It exposes the challenges that men and male youth face in trying to uphold traditional male gender roles and responsibilities in a radically changed context. It also assesses the relationship between these male experiences, the social expectations placed on men, the dynamics of conflict and the potential of young men to contribute to peace and reconciliation in future.

A quarter of a century after Somalia's formal state collapse in 1991, its impact continues to be felt. Among its consequences, the reassertion—and in some cases the reinvention—of clan or kinship relations as a central organizing force is the most significant.

The recourse to a largely rural clan tradition had particular implications for the male ideal, since it was men who, by tradition, embodied clan honour. This male personification of the clan ideal obscured the varying forms of masculinities—different ways of being a man—which had emerged during the modern state era, especially in urban areas. Now traditional ideals appear to circumscribe the possible roles for a man even though they are extremely difficult to fulfil, living in an urban, conflict-affected context. Fulfilling these ideals of manhood even fuels conflict and perpetuates insecurity, a dynamic which other men can manage and manipulate to secure wealth and power.

The RVI study was conducted in nine locations across Somalia: southern and central areas, Puntland, Somaliland—and in the diaspora centres of Kenya Dadaab and Eastleigh. The project consulted with over 400 men and 90 women, and collected 44 men's life stories. Half of all men consulted were young men aged 18–35 years old. Unless otherwise noted, all quoted speech is from the study's interviews. This paper presents and analyses the key findings in relation to the current situation and future outlook for young Somali men.

Somali Norms of Masculinity

Men in Somalia are "responsible for everything after Allah," with the well-being of one's family being the foremost male responsibility. Contrary to some external assumptions, Somali manhood is not predicated on violence and the oppression of women. The Somali ideal of masculinity imposes extremely high moral standards of behaviour, most of which are unrealistic for the majority of men in the present context. These values are rooted in a rural, pastoral and agro-pastoral past, a context which no longer applies to the majority of men. This core set of exacting ideals is common to all age groups and regions. Among the many expectations of a man, he must demonstrate self-discipline, courage, humanity, and generosity. He must be prepared to do whatever is required for the survival of his family and his kinship group or clan. These ideals continue to be the essential criteria against which males across the country are measured, and measure themselves. It is only by meeting these standards of behaviour that men may attain *raganimo*, meaning manhood or the masculine ideal.

Defined stages in a man's life include boyhood, youth, adulthood, and elderhood. Expected gender roles and responsibilities vary from stage to stage. The role of male youth between the ages of 14 and 25, though it can be prolonged until 35, is, in the words of one interviewee, to be:

> useful and reliable, and a model for younger siblings. They should be capable of filling their father's position in the family as provider, protector, and resource manager. He should know and respect cultural norms and practices, be well-mannered and exhibit good behaviour. He should repay the investment his parents made in him, and train and be ready to fight for his kinsmen and clan.

Clanship, Clannism and Nepotism

Siad Barre's policy to ban tribalism spectacularly failed, yet did succeed in influencing discourse on clan for a limited period, especially in urban environments. Many people born in Mogadishu in the late 1970s and '80s were brought up unaware of their genealogy because it was not relevant to their urban lives—that is until the city was engulfed by war and clan identity became a matter of life or death.[4] In the context of current clan-based politics and ongoing insecurity, resources and employment opportunities are almost always only accessible through kinship connections.

Young men are acutely aware that how they fare depends on clanship and how well their clan is faring, for example, in terms of obtaining its share of and control over resources. The study heard that a youth should "shine for the clan," meaning he should grow the wealth and honour of the clan. As a male, you must "wear your clan like your shoes," meaning never forget it, "do not go out without it" and "stay close" to other clansmen. Young men who fail to comply will find that employment and access to resources are limited, and personal security may be diminished.[5] As one noted, "it is not easy if you are not from a strong family ... You need both clan support and education to get employment and status."

Youth's Double Bind

Many young men explain that they feel under constant pressure to conform, compromising their inner moral values. The exacting values attached to manhood require them to obey older kinsmen. This often pushes them into unacceptable activities, but alternatives either do not exist or are beyond reach. They believe success comes more easily to those who dispense with moral baggage. Educated youth in Hargeisa said, "the clan members want the ones who blindly support the clan [whether what they are doing is] wrong or right." A former militiaman in Mogadishu observed, "a man can be useful for his clan if you are a warrior warlord who can get land and property for the clan. This is what the bad people in the clan value."

In all the study sites, young men were insightful about the power dynamics of the worlds they inhabit and what it takes to succeed as a male in this state of male power, insecurity, and inequality.[6] They have no experience of a different life, under a central, functioning state, yet they draw a contrast between the past and the present. According to educated youth in Hargeisa, "in the past, men were expected to support the country or society, now they are just expected to support their family and their sub-clan—these are the priorities now, not the country." Expressing a similar sentiment, a group of largely illiterate former young combatants in Mogadishu noted, "many men are treacherous. They have no feeling and moral responsibility. They take bribes. They don't care about the country."

The same young men noted, "but the good ones in the clan value the doctor, the sheikh and the educated". The fact that "good men" can be identified and are esteemed among young males seems a potential entry point for building a fairer, more peaceful, and gender equitable society.[7]

Violence and Insecurity

Traditionally, young men are designated as their kinship group's warriors (*waranle*) and are expected to fight to defend collective interests when required by elders. The civil war revived this tradition, and young men's compliance with the call to arms has helped sustain the inter- and intra-clan conflicts that persist, with armed groups increasingly recruiting young boys. So much so that according to a recent report possibly half of all Al-Shabaab's forces are males under the age of 18.[8] Just how willing most young men are to fight or to continue fighting is moot. Many young men have migrated from the rural areas, or have been brought to the towns, expressly to take part in war. Women's role in the mobilization of militiamen is also under-reported. They often deploy songs and poetry, and techniques of humiliation and emasculation, to goad young men into fighting or to holding their nerve.[9]

One former young militiaman in Mogadishu explained why compliance and joining the fight is in a young man's interests: "During inter-clan conflict, each sub-clan is expected to bring militias. If you refuse [to join] and something then happens to you, the larger clan will not support you. It is in your own interest therefore to carry a gun and defend the clan." The attractions of status and job security that can come with joining a clan militia were highlighted by youth in Baidoa: "For the youth, joining the clan warlord's militia is a very good employment option ... It is [a job] respected by the clan. He feels safe in that net."

Insecurity and Gender-based Violence

Combat roles aside, physical insecurity is a daily reality for many young men consulted, one of whom noted: "Youth in Somalia live in fear and have an unhappy life. Even those who make money are not happy. They fear the uncertain future and the possibility of losing everything." The potential for violent conflict is a source of fear and anxiety. In Las Caanood at the time of the research team's visit, most male youth were staying in the rural area, partly for safety. An NGO worker from the region explained:

> Most of the youth in Las Caanood did not experience war directly, unlike the Mogadishu and Hargeisa youth. But nevertheless they live with the fear that conflict will happen at any time. This fear drives many to leave for Dadaab refugee camp in Kenya, believing that it is better to go before the fighting begins. For the youth who stay, there are few livelihood options, as the economy is livestock dependent.

Young men in all regions try hard to avoid direct engagement in high-risk activities. Yet in many places, including Dadaab in Kenya, they still face danger and experience physical insecurity, including from three sources that can be classified as male-on-male gender-based violence: revenge killings; abduction and other forms of forced recruitment by armed groups; and assassination by

Al-Shabaab. Physical insecurity, particularly brought about by revenge killings, significantly limits male freedom of movement and hence male livelihood opportunities.

Family Pressures

The high cultural value placed on a male child comes with a weight of family expectations, which young men claim "is more so than of girls, and they expect to get a return on their investment, whereas little is expected of girls except a dowry, as they will marry and be given to another family [in other words, clan]." Young men try hard to repay their families' investment by securing income. Evidence indicates most try to find income without recourse to illegal or violent means. It shows young men (and young women) sometimes risk extreme suffering in an attempt to find a more secure and better future, for example by attempting illegal migration (*tahriib*) at the hands of human smugglers. *Tahriib*'s impact on families, emotionally and financially, is considerable, yet many parents encourage their children to undertake the journey, oblivious to the deadly risks they will face.[10]

Prevailing poverty, and the need for increased family income, drive parental pressure on urban boys and male youth to find work or other sources of income. Many young men are growing up in broken families, with absent or unemployed fathers, and in households where the mother is the main income provider. Respondents pointed out that "the expectation from families and the desire to earn a living are pushing youth into many evils, including joining Al-Shabaab," where, although their life expectancy may be shortened, they will earn a monthly salary.

Periods of depression and hopelessness, even despair, punctuate every life story collected from male youth, seemingly brought on by prolonged frustration, disappointment, and powerlessness.[11] Early marriage, under the age of 18, is said to be one way male and female youth are responding to their frustrations, often with the encouragement of desperate parents.[12]

Regional, Class and Ethnic Differences

Although cultural expectations placed on young men are common across Somali-speaking regions, there are regional differences in the experiences of youth. Male youth life stories gathered from south-central Somalia feature instances of direct involvement in armed violence, which are absent from accounts from other regions. Male youth in Eastleigh, Kenya, who had fled south-central Somalia to escape recruitment by extremist groups, described how on one side the government and clan are pushing them to take up arms, while on the other they are targeted by Al-Shabaab, whose leaders and recruitment agents are also clan members and able to exert clan-based pressure.

Other regional variations show that Puntland's young males tend to be more exposed to military recruitment, while young, educated Somaliland men focus on how kinship and clan preferment can thwart ambitions. In Las Canood, in the disputed Sool region between Somaliland and Puntland, families send their boys to live in the rural area for safety and cultural education. Male youth in Kenya's Dadaab refugee camp articulate some of the bleakest perspectives, describing themselves as "particularly lost, disoriented, uneducated and feeling hopeless in this prison."

Class and ethnic identities also impact male youth vulnerability. Members of traditionally marginalized groups (often misleadingly termed "minorities"), who cannot access the same level of clan protection as members of large clans (also misleading described as "majority" groups), are vulnerable to physical and verbal abuse, physical violation, intimidation, and humiliation. Males in certain occupational castes have lost their livelihoods or seen them reduced, as non-caste group males enter the same supply system in search of income. Youth from traditionally marginalized and numerically smaller groups are particularly vulnerable to exploitation and militarization: "Warlords used the youth from the poor families and ruined their future for their individualistic greed. But they sent theirs [in other words, their young people] abroad to study and later return and take on important government positions because they are educated and rule us."

Conclusions

The normative view of male youth is that they are "troublesome", "unwise", and "impulsive"—all reasons given to justify their exclusion from politics and other forms of collective decision-making until they reach "adulthood." Youth as a group are culturally and structurally disempowered, marginalized by older, more powerful men, who often use younger men for their own ends. Abuse of power and status by elders is not held to account because of the persistence of clan-based politics and the lack of impartial protective mechanisms and legal structures.

Research findings suggest that while their circumstances may leave young men with few safe or desirable choices, they tend to be risk-aware. Broadly speaking, they emerge from the study as an important and valuable resource for good. Their visions and interests transcend violence and corruption; they seek a better, safer world in which they can fulfil their family responsibilities through honest means. They demonstrate attitudes compatible with the promotion of peace, reconciliation and state-building. They also want to be good husbands, fathers and sons. These ambitions appear to sustain them through adversity, and drive their optimism about the future.

But in this struggle, few young men seem to have good male role models. On the contrary, many consulted are sons of families broken by the war, with fathers who are idle, absent, or traumatized ex-combatants. Yet, even this experience can sometimes inspire positive aspirations. Speaking about his absent father, a young man in Las Canood expressed sentiments shared by many respondents: "He is my parent, he was supposed to remember me as his child. There is no one who can exist without parents. He should have thought about me. However, he did not. But I hope I will not be like him. I will take care of my children. I will work day and night and every hour to take care of them."

Recommendations

Above all, the prevailing negative narrative about male youth in Somalia should be replaced with a positive vision of youth, male and female, as the future of Somalia and the country's peacemakers. This should be a core feature of stabilization strategies, and, if effective, could deny Al-Shabaab an entry-point for recruitment.

Other recommendations for policy-makers, for initial efforts, are as follows:

1. Improve physical security

• End tolerance of violence against men, youth and boys (in the form of revenge killings, forced recruitment, and assassinations) as well as violence against women and girls.
• Strengthen legislation and its implementation to end culturally-sanctioned male-on-male violence such as clan revenge killings and forcible recruitment. (Relevant to Federal Government.)
• Gather data and audit violence—against men, youth and boys as well as against women and girls—to inform policy-making. (Relevant to Federal Member States.)

- End tolerance of clan-interference in the prosecution of cases of criminal acts—if a person is found guilty their custodial sentence should be enforced. (Relevant to federal legal and custodial services.)

2. Develop more equitable male employment opportunities

- End tolerance of nepotism and clannism within the civil service/public sector. Institute and enforce equitable employment practices and codes of conduct.

3. Support personal and youth leadership development opportunities

- Encourage the creation of new developmental opportunities for male youth that are not based on militarization. (Relevant to Federal Government, civil society youth movements, and international donors and policy-makers.)
- Establish a programme to support male and female youth leadership development: offering exposure to employment opportunities including exchange programmes with other youth in Africa. (Relevant to international policy-makers.)
- Invest resources in improving educational services and making education available to all, including male and female adult literacy; and involve educated youth as literacy promoters.
- Promote greater tolerance of young people participating in sports, arts, and other activities that stretch the boundaries of their existence.

4. Promote peaceful coexistence

- Promote inclusion of and increase tolerance towards families from outside the dominant clans (Relevant to traditional elders, religious leaders, and women's organizations.)
- Demonstrate and promote positive normative leadership qualities and values of manhood: generosity, humanity, wisdom, mediation. (Relevant to politicians, lineage leaders, and traditional elders.)

ADDRESSING THE GAP

PROMOTING YOUTH INCLUSION IN SOMALI PEACE AND RECONCILIATION

Sagal Aziz Deria, Erin Gillette, Katherine Henshaw, and *Savannah Simons*

Authorship

This report was a collaborative effort by Transparency Solutions' team of researchers and practitioners. Authors are Sagal Aziz, Erin Gillette, Katherine Henshaw, and Savannah Simons. Key contributors were Amel Saeed, Abdirahman Mustaf Mohamed, and Khayre Ali Isak from Hargeisa, Kismayo, and Baidoa respectively. Transparency Solutions' expertise lies in research, project management, training, and strategy through a locally-led approach.

Summary

Youth in Somalia have great potential to positively contribute to peace and reconciliation and a desire to be involved in processes that will bring stability and prosperity to their country. However, there is currently a gap between rhetoric and practice concerning youth's involvement in peace and reconciliation. Young people in Somalia are looking for ways to meaningfully contrib-

285

ute to society, but feel disappointed and disenfranchised in light of the lack of opportunities available to them. Even when opportunities are available, barriers that prevent or minimize their ability to engage obstruct youth involvement. In this context, some youth turn to other paths available to them such as joining militias and/or extremist groups like Al-Shabaab.

There is much room for growth in engaging Somali youth. Two opportunities for involving youth in Somalia are sport and social media, both of which have the potential to bridge the gap between rhetoric and practice. By taking a holistic, integrated approach to youth participation in peace and reconciliation, young people would be able to attain their full potential as agents of change. Young people's engagement in peace and reconciliation processes would not only benefit them, but also has the potential to benefit Somali society as a whole.

Summary of Recommendations

- Promote intersectional "youth champions" from across Somali society as agents of change in championing youth participation and inclusion.
- Exploit the reach of social media among Somali youth, using popular online platforms like Wakiil to counter violent extremism and to promote peace, reconciliation and democratic principles.
- Create more opportunities for youth involvement in civil society and invest in job creation schemes and skills development through increased support for youth-focused and Somali-led initiatives.
- Ensure that youth are included in formal and informal peace and reconciliation initiatives and that they are not sidelined by more powerful actors. Create a forum for intergenerational dialogue which would encourage youth and elders to communicate and dispel harmful misconceptions.
- Invest in activities such as sport, which are an effective, popular tool for peace and reconciliation among youth. Donors must not only increase funds for this, but take practical steps to ensure that everyone can participate.

Introduction

Since 1991, Somalia has experienced ongoing multi-dimensional conflict creating an environment of insecurity and governmental fragility. The rationale for this paper is to bridge the gap between rhetoric and practice concerning the role and agency of youth. This paper seeks to gain an understanding of the reality and complexities of youth involvement in peace and reconciliation. By listening to the voices of Somalia's youth at a granular level, Transparency Solutions aims to shed light on ways to bridge this gap and to employ a holistic, integrated approach to youth involvement in peace and reconciliation.

This report is based on desk research and 43 semi-structured interviews with youth between the ages of 18 and 30. The interviews were conducted face-to-face, in the Somali language, in three locations: Baidoa, Kismayo, and Hargeisa. Respondents were anonymized and the legend is as follows: the 15 interviews conducted in Baidoa and Kismayo are numbered 1–15B and 1–15K respectively and the 13 interviews in Hargeisa are numbered 1–13H.

The sampling method, while not claiming to be representative of all Somali youth, aimed to draw a diverse number of respondents in order to encompass a wide variety of perspectives. The respondents comprised a range of socioeconomic groups, professions, education levels, and life experience. The employment sectors of the respondents are shown in Figure 1.

Differences in context between south-central Somalia (Baidoa and Kismayo) and Somaliland (Hargeisa) were taken into account by adjusting some of the interview questions. Processes of peace and reconciliation developed differently between the two regions. Somaliland underwent an organic process driven by internal actors via clan-to-clan resolution and national-level proceedings whereas south-central Somalia has been largely shaped by external actors, without the same degree of local ownership. The trajectory of the interviews reflected these differences.

Figure 1

Employment Sector of Respondents

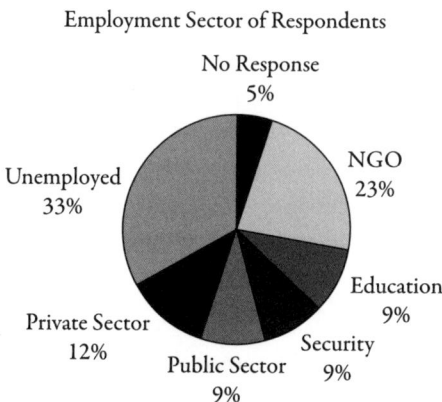

This paper begins by presenting the views of the respondents concerning peace and reconciliation before moving on to an analysis of the existing barriers and motivations of youth engagement. It will next consider the extent to which militias and extremist groups, especially Al-Shabaab, obstruct the inclusivity of youth in peace and reconciliation. Finally, it will conclude with a summation of the themes that have emerged and the resulting policy recommendations.

Perceptions of Peace and Reconciliation

The youth population in Somalia is one of the highest in the world. According to the Ministry of Planning and International Cooperation (MOPIC), youth in Somalia comprise an estimated 70 per cent of the population.[1] Furthermore, youth have grown up knowing nothing but war and its aftermath, which has shaped their perceptions of peace and reconciliation. To 37 per cent of the respondents, peace was defined as the absence of war and fear, expressing a negative premise for defining peace.[2] International post-conflict research supports the importance of encouraging cooperation across societal divides, a view echoed by 34 per cent of Somali respondents who emphasized the importance of cross-clan dialogue.[3] Respondent 8K described peace and reconciliation as the creation of "a place where all citizens can live in harmony."[4] In a Somali context, this necessitates addressing longstanding grievances, especially those concerning clan, which is the primary ordering mechanism of society. One example of a lingering resentment to be addressed is the systematic exclusion of minority clans from political power and resources due to the 4.5 power-sharing system in south-central Somalia.[5] If peace and reconciliation in Somalia are to be effective, the process must be more inclusive.

"Reconciliation is bringing together clans who are still living in hostile environments." Respondent 15K	*"Peace and reconciliation means life to me. If there is no peace, there is no life."* Respondent 2K

Somali Youth and Peace and Reconciliation

50 per cent of respondents fully agreed that youth are actively involved in peacemaking, yet significantly, when asked, only 27 per cent of respondents

could provide an example of such a young person, or an opportunity to be involved in. Rather, a common theme within the interviews was the lack of space for youth involvement and opportunities for young people to provide meaningful contributions to society.

Youth unemployment levels in Somalia and Somaliland are amongst the highest in the world. In 2012, the United Nations Development Programme (UNDP) estimated that the unemployment rate for youth aged 14–29 was around 67 per cent, however, in 2016 the International Organization for Migration (IOM) estimated that the rate may now be closer to 80 or 90 per cent.[6] A combination of weak governance, lack of civil society, and poor economic development all contribute to little community engagement and few recreational activities. Furthermore, the prevailing culture, particularly in Al-Shabaab-occupied or recently liberated areas, limits opportunities for safe self-expression. These realities combine to create a void, leaving many youth feeling bored, undervalued, and powerless. The absence of opportunities that could provide Somali youth with a sense of purpose and empowerment leaves them vulnerable to less positive life paths.

The Role of Sport

Sport in Somalia is a key example that demonstrates the gap between youth opportunities and involvement. 56 per cent of respondents from Kismayo and Baidoa cited sports tournaments as an effective method for engaging youth in positive activities, which reduce the likelihood of their joining violent groups due to boredom or lack of opportunities. The respondents, however, were unable to provide examples, nor did desk research produce compelling evidence of local sports programmes. What can be evidenced, however, is that sport has become firmly embedded into the rhetoric of youth and peace and reconciliation. One possible reason for this discrepancy is the universality of sport as well as its high visibility in societies.[7] Second, sport is seen as having "a unique power to attract, mobilize and inspire", thus being a powerful tool through which to engage youth.[8] Former UN Secretary-General Kofi Annan stated that sport has an "almost unmatched role ... in promoting understanding, healing wounds, mobilising support for social causes, and breaking down barriers."[9]

While these examples support sporting activities as an ideal method of youth participation, the discourse frequently overlooks practical problems. In Somalia, for example, sports facilities are few and far between, making access for youth programs difficult. Additionally, facilities that are available are not always conducive to women's participation due to the social and cultural constraints such as the need to have an enclosed exercise area so that men cannot see. In theory, sport is a straightforward and attractive way to facilitate youth involvement. However, this example demonstrates the gap between youth perceptions and the realities of their involvement through sport.

Social Media as an Emerging Platform

Somalia has traditionally been an oral society, however, the news and information landscape is becoming increasingly globalized, interconnected, and internet-based. A 2013 Broadcasting Board of Governors (BBG) report found that the home internet access rate is 18.7 per cent countrywide and 26.7 per cent in urban areas.[10] With the increase of internet access in Somalia, social media usage has grown exponentially and is increasingly a significant platform for Somali youth.[11] Our data corroborate the importance and reach of social media; 60 per cent of respondents say they use social media daily, as shown in Figure 2 below.

Al-Shabaab has been especially adept at targeting youth through social media, using it both as a communication platform and recruitment tool. Al-Shabaab has also recognized it is "as much as a threat as a tool" as it has the potential to expose Al-Shabaab members and controlled populations to opposing perspectives.[12] Social media, as demonstrated by Al-Shabaab, is an effective platform through which to engage Somali young people. In 2015, the UN Global Forum on Youth, Peace and Security recommended social media as a means to promote youth inclusion.[13] A positive example of the application

Figure 2

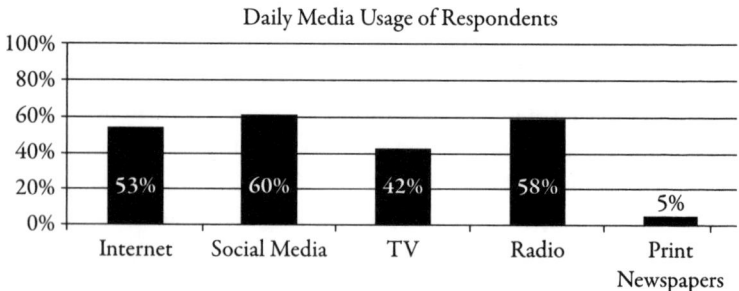

Daily Media Usage of Respondents

Internet 53%	Social Media 60%	TV 42%	Radio 58%	Print Newspapers 5%

of social media in engaging citizen participation in Somalia is Wakiil, which promotes Somali democracy and accountability.[14] Respondents cited social media as a promising platform for engaging youth.[15] Specifically, they viewed it as a way to facilitate open dialogue as well as a forum for "youth to openly voice their opinions and concerns."[16] Social media enables youth to be exposed to and learn from other peace and reconciliation processes and be exposed to youth participation worldwide.[17]

Barriers to Youth Involvement

While sport and social media are two promising activities, there remains a lack of opportunities for youth in Somalia. This lack of space is further exacerbated by factors that obstruct youth inclusion in the peace and reconciliation process. The interviews highlighted several barriers that included: perceived mindset differences between generations, lack of community and government support; and security concerns.

The majority of respondents believe that the attitude of the older generations is a primary barrier to more youth involvement in the peace and reconciliation process. Respondents expressed the opinion that older generations are unwilling to involve youth for various reasons.[18] One common response was that elders see them as a threat or a destabilizing force; for example, "the passion of youth" could inspire aggressive reactions from older generations.[19] Amongst elders there is a belief that youth are "unwilling to work within the current status quo" and that they have the potential to disrupt traditional existing structures.[20] Here too, there is a gap in the rhetoric if not necessarily the practice, as these "traditional existing structures" were variably defined by respondents as being based on clannism, nepotism, or corruption. Whether intentionally or otherwise, elders are discouraging youth who want to engage in peace processes and who are eager for recognition and approval from older generations.[21] Voicing support for youth and encouraging receptivity amongst older generations would add significant leverage to bridging the gap between rhetoric and practice concerning youth inclusion.

> *"Elders always discourage young people by telling them that they do not know what is going on in the process of peace and reconciliation."*
>
> Respondent 5K

Another significant barrier to youth participation in peace and reconciliation activities is a lack of capacity to support their involvement. One critical way this manifests itself is through inadequate funding and encouragement of youth initiatives.[22] A noticeable effect of failing to provide the appropriate support is that it signifies to youth that their inclusion is not a priority. Creating opportunities, however, is not enough. Rather care must be taken that traditionally under-represented groups, such as women or clan minorities, are not overshadowed or silenced, but that all voices are heard and taken seriously. A number of respondents pointed to the lack of positive role models, believing that individuals involved in youth peace and reconciliation activities should be promoted and "rewarded for doing good."[23] Positive encouragement and reinforcement that youth empowerment is a priority, articulated by credible, relatable actors, is an effective and low-cost option.

> *"Lack of financial support for their activities against radicalism and tribalism."*
>
> Respondent 2K, ex-Al-Shabaab member

A third barrier to youth participation is security concerns. The issue of security is the area where respondents displayed the greatest differences between the geographic regions. 75 per cent of respondents in Kismayo and Baidoa cited hostility of environment and fear of being targeted by militias and extremist groups as the primary obstacle to youth involvement. Furthermore, 14 out of 15 respondents in Baidoa stated that fear of injury or death was a risk of becoming involved in peace and reconciliation. While respondents in Kismayo saw violence as a barrier, they did not perceive it as a risk to the same degree as those in Baidoa. This geographic variation can perhaps be explained by greater political unrest and instability in Baidoa.[24] Respondents from Hargeisa did not raise security concerns, reflecting the relative stability of Somaliland. As the interviews in Baidoa and Kismayo reflect, there are important security concerns to be considered when encouraging youth participation.

These barriers, while hindering youth's involvement in peace and reconciliation, also place them at greater risk of joining violent and/or extremist groups. The interviews revealed several examples of young people who turned to militias and extremist groups such as Al-Shabaab. The following section will examine three key factors that motivate youth to join militias and extremist groups: economic concerns, ideological reasons, and socio-political factors.

> *"If I became involved in peace and reconciliation activities I would fear for my life."*
>
> Respondent 6B
>
> *"Youth are deterred from engaging in peace and reconciliation due to fear of being targeted by extremist groups."*
>
> Respondent 2K, an ex-Al-Shabaab member

Youth Attraction to Militias and Extremist Groups

The primary reason for youth joining militias and extremist groups, cited by 40 per cent of respondents, is the high rate of unemployment in Somalia. A related contributory factor is the high rate of poverty in Somalia, which the UN estimates at around 73 per cent.[25] Notably, there were significant geographic correlations between the relative importance of poverty and the "need for money to sustain daily life" as a motivation to join militias and extremist groups.[26] Baidoa had the most respondents citing poverty as a primary motivation followed by Kismayo and then Hargeisa, reflecting the overall economic situation of each area. In a 2003 UNDP and World Bank survey, the estimated annual income per capita of the three interviewed regions was: Baidoa US$100–150, Kismayo $201–250, and Hargeisa $301–350.[27] The effects of these economic realities were made clear by respondents from Baidoa and Kismayo.[28] Poverty and lack of employment are seen as powerful drivers in young people joining militias or extremist groups.[29]

Religious or ideological reasons are another driver for young people to join extremist groups. According to Diab M. al-Badayneh, extremist groups exploit the vulnerabilities of youth, taking advantage of their religious beliefs and devotion.[30] 56 per cent of respondents from Kismayo and Baidoa believed that extremists utilize this devotion by manipulating religion to "brainwash and mislead young people toward a specific religious understanding."[31] Al-Shabaab "entices young people to fight to seek God."[32] Youth who become involved in extremist groups are frequently fed the idea that their participation is leading them down the "right path".[33]

Youth recruitment to extremist groups is further facilitated by a lack of education and, as one respondent put it, "youth's innocence and ignorance".[34] Some choose to leave and pursue other life paths, particularly after experiencing first-hand the harsh reality of being part of an extremist group. Former Al-Shabaab members interviewed cited the realization that their ideology was a distortion of Islam that included torturing and killing innocent people as a significant factor in their decision to leave.[35] One respondent gave additional details, saying "former extremist members left due to the fear of death and the fear of killing others as well as injustice within the group and the presence of sexual and physical violence."[36] Ideological factors therefore not only attract young people to join extremist groups but these same factors, viewed through a different experiential lens. also contribute to the decision to leave.

> *"They promote a wrong idea and they translate the religion as wrong."*
>
> Respondent 7B

The third significant factor highlighted for joining militias and extremist groups and linked to lack of opportunity elsewhere is a desire to have status in society. Being part of an organized militia or a known extremist organization provides a sense of belonging and self-worth. This is especially relevant in the case of Al-Shabaab, which provides opportunities to youth regardless of clan, education, and socio-economic status. This transgression from socially constructed tribal, economic, and socio-political lines is a testament to Al-Shabaab's ability to recruit from all subsections of society which has both earned them the respect, however misguided, of many Somali communities and is part of their appeal. This is especially true of youth who, as discussed earlier, are much more likely to perceive clannism as an outdated concept, held onto by the elders.

Additionally, militias and extremist groups exploit youth's sense of being neglected by their government and society. Such groups are able to tempt young people into joining by the promise of addressing long-held grievances and fears, gaining empowerment and self-worth, providing responsibility, and increasing their socio-political position. These promises are further perpetuated through peer and social pressures where they exist, such as current combatants, or sympathetic family members, imams, and clan elders.

There is a direct correlation between the gap created by the rhetoric of youth inclusivity and the lack of opportunity. The barriers to youth participation and the motivation to join militias and extremist groups are interconnected. Increasing opportunities for youth engagement as well as addressing the barriers that hinder their involvement would bridge the gap between rhetoric and practice as well as enable youth to attain their full potential within processes of peace and reconciliation.

Conclusion

Youth in Somalia have great potential to positively contribute to peace and reconciliation matched with a strong desire to be involved in the process of bringing stability and prosperity to their country. What was striking is the power of the rhetoric of youth participation despite compelling evidence that the reality of their involvement is far less than is assumed. There is a mismatch between perception and experience. The implications of the misleading premise of youth participation are of concern since false assumptions lead to false conclusions, which ultimately lead to negative results and poor outcomes.

In reality, the vast majority of Somali youth lack the opportunities, space, and support they need to become actively involved in processes of peace and reconciliation, and when they are involved, invariably their voices are marginalized or drowned out by older and more powerful actors. The combination of these factors contributes to a feeling among Somali youth that they are disenfranchised and under-represented, further deepening the void between rhetoric and practice. If this gap is to be addressed, the barriers to youth participation need to be decreased and the drivers for change must be promoted. Interestingly, even though youth in Somalia and Somaliland have had different experiences of peace and reconciliation at a national level, the only significant difference in terms of individual experience is the appeal of militias and extremist groups. Youth throughout Somalia and Somaliland would greatly benefit from the creation of opportunities and their increased ability to contribute to peace and reconciliation in meaningful, visible ways. The involvement of youth through more holistic, inclusive peace and reconciliation processes will further enable them to become agents of positive change in Somalia.

Recommendations

1. Promote "youth champions"

Stakeholders must promote credible and diverse youth champions and older individuals from across Somali society, championing youth inclusion. For the first time in Somalia's history, a quarter (24 per cent) of MPs are aged 40 or under and young activists such as Ilwad Elman are gaining greater prominence.[37] There is a unique opportunity for them to be supported as agents of change in achieving greater youth participation and inclusion. This could take the form of a media campaign, making use of TV, radio, and online media.

2. Exploit the reach of social media

Social media has a strong, ever-increasing penetration amongst youth in Somalia. Government, civil society and practitioners must utilize it to counter extremist views and promote peace, reconciliation, and democratic principles. This can be achieved through campaigns on popular media outlets from Facebook to Twitter, and/or by replicating successful platforms such as Wakiil.[38]

3. Create more opportunities for greater youth involvement in civil society

The international community, government and NGOs must increase funding and support of formal peace and reconciliation initiatives which are youth-focused and Somali-led. There is an urgent need to enhance youth skills, invest in job creation schemes, and to increase opportunities for active participation in grassroots and community-based organizations such as youth groups.

4. Ensure all youth voices are heard in peace and reconciliation processes

All formal and informal initiatives in peace and reconciliation must include mechanisms to ensure that youth are not sidelined within these processes or overshadowed by more powerful actors. This should be coordinated by the Federal Government of Somalia and disseminated to ensure a consistent approach. Creating a forum for intergenerational dialogue would help youth and elders to communicate and dispel harmful misconceptions that lead to exclusion.

5. Invest in activities such as sport

Sports work for peace and reconciliation in Somalia. Donors must fund more of the same but additional practical considerations must be made to ensure accessibility to all groups, notably women. The full report contains additional findings to inform ways in which this should be done.

UNDERSTANDING AND RESPONDING
TO AL-SHABAAB

SOMALIA'S SOUTHERN WAR

THE FIGHT OVER LAND AND LABOUR

Catherine Besteman and *Daniel Van Lehman*

Authors

Dr Catherine Besteman, Professor of Anthropology at Colby College, published three books and over 30 articles and reports on Somalia and the Somali diaspora. Her ethnographic fieldwork in the Jubba Valley in the 1980s focused on racialized identity politics and land tenure.

Daniel Van Lehman, faculty member at Portland State University, wrote his master's thesis and published articles on Somali Bantu demographics and human rights. Van Lehman worked for the UNHCR in Dadaab, Kenya and Mozambique.

Summary

Progress against Al-Shabaab in the Jubba River Valley has suffered from a lack of knowledge not only of the group, but also of its primary victims. Our research shows that Somali groups from outside the Valley are using their networks and superior access to finance and weaponry to launch a takeover of the Valley that will endanger and displace the resident farmers. Al-Shabaab's primary focus in Somalia is not the expansion of an extremist version of Islam but rather the continued extortion of defenceless minority groups such as the farming communities of the fertile Jubba River Valley, here called Somali Bantus. Recent survey results from displaced Somalis who recently lived under Al-Shabaab or have family still under its rule support a 25-year trend of militias from outside the Valley vying to exert control over the Valley in order to profit from the extortion of land and labour from the minority riverine farmers.

Our research shows that Al-Shabaab differentiates in its application and enforcement of religious, governance and economic rules between Somali Bantus and Somalis from the major clans by extorting a greater percentage of harvests, remittances and "religious-adherence" fines from Somali Bantus than from other Somalis. Al-Shabaab's penalties for non-compliance with forced conscription of boys, forced marriage of girls and restrictions on movement in and out of the Valley are likewise more severe for Somali Bantus. Somali Bantus who cannot pay the required extortion fees may be forcibly evicted from their ancestral farmland that is then sold by Al-Shabaab to Somalis from major clans.

Like the cross-clan militia cooperation of the Jubba Valley Alliance in the 1990s, Al-Shabaab's economic survival now appears to depend on its business relationship with the major clans from areas adjacent to the Jubba River Valley. Based on 25 years of fighting to occupy the Jubba River Valley, we can predict that if Somali Bantus are not empowered to govern themselves in the Jubba River Valley, then major clans and other militias will continue to violently compete against each other for control of the Valley.

Introduction

This briefing paper explains the ongoing violence in the Jubba Valley as based in economic exploitation by Somali militias against the subsistence farmers (called Somali Bantus in the diaspora and Jareer Weyn in Somalia) in the Jubba River Valley. To avoid confusion with nomenclature, we utilize "Somali Bantus" rather than "Jareer Weyn," to refer to riverine minority farmers in the Jubba Valley but with the understanding that the term used in the diaspora is not necessarily used by minorities living in the Valley. The briefing paper will investigate the extent to which Al-Shabaab, like earlier militias in the Lower and Middle Jubba regions, is extorting the farmers' land and labour. Our findings shift the perspective of Al-Shabaab as a group intent on spreading radical Islam throughout Somalia to one that misuses Islam to dominate and exploit for economic gain the unarmed ethnic minorities in southern Somalia. While the groups exploited by Al-Shabaab are also Muslim, responses to our interview questions suggest they do not support the form of Islam practiced by Al-Shabaab.

The briefing paper is concerned with the question of how to ensure regional security and stability that will enable Somali Bantu IDPs and refugees from the Valley to return as self-sustaining farmers with symbiotic food-security arrangements with neighbouring pastoralist communities and contribute to national food security and the livestock and crop agriculture export industries.

Field research was conducted with displaced Somalis whose relatives currently live, or who themselves recently lived, under Al-Shabaab's rule in the Jubba River Valley. A small survey was conducted face-to-face by two respected interviewers who have experience with census and survey research. 41 respondents participated in the survey, which took 20 to 30 minutes per interview to complete and had a response rate of 28.1 per cent (AAPOR Response Rate 1).

Somali Bantu Demography and Media Reports

Demographics

Most of the Somali Bantus in the Jubba River Valley descend from autochthons from the upper Shabelle River Valley and the estimated 50,000 slaves from south-east Africa who were brought to southern Somalia in the nineteenth century primarily to work on Somali-run agricultural plantations.[1] Toward the end of the nineteenth century, many Somali Bantu slaves escaped to the sparsely populated Jubba River Valley and were later followed by manumitted slaves. Although no accurate population figures exist on the number of Somali Bantu in the Lower and Middle Jubba River, 2014 estimates extrapolated from the historical record put their population at approximately 1,500,000 or about 12 per cent to 15 per cent of the national population.[2]

Somali Bantu farming communities also reside in the Shabelle River Valley and have a similar, if not greater, population than those in the Jubba River Valley. The Somali Bantu population, along with the other "minority" clans in Somalia, likely constitute a demographic that is as large as or larger than any of the four "major" clans, namely the Darood, Hawiye, Isaaq/Dir, and Digil Mirifle or Rahanweyn. The Somali constitution, however, only allocates 50 per cent representation to the minority groups while allocating full or

100 per cent representation to each of the four major clans in an arrangement known as the 4.5 system. The current 4.5 system of political representation thus reflects demographic and political discrimination against Somali minorities.[3]

Homogeneity Myth

A failure to acknowledge the particular forms of violence perpetrated against Somalia's minority groups enables a perpetuation of Somalia's "myth of homogeneity." This national narrative has helped obscure the systematic victimisation of Somalia's minority groups over the past 25 years.

Somali Bantus as Al-Shabaab Supporters

Published reports have indicated that the Somali Bantus support Al-Shabaab and even see their occupation by the terrorist group as an opportunity.[4] Survey results, however, contradict this; respondents say that once Al-Shabaab is eliminated from the Jubba Valley, they will cease following Al-Shabaab's restrictive religious and governance rules. Additional evidence against Somali Bantus' support of Al-Shabaab are the estimated 50,000 Somali Bantu refugees in Kenya, the 1,100,000 IDPs—many of whom are Somali Bantu—in miserable camps,[5] and those Somali Bantus who risk execution attempting to escape from Al-Shabaab's control.

History of Extortion Against Somali Bantus in the Jubba Valley

Pre-War Years

The riverine farmland of the Jubba Valley offered a refuge to former slaves, but was also targeted by Italian colonial authorities for large-scale plantations on land expropriated from local farmers, who were forcibly conscripted to work for the colonial authorities. After independence, Siad Barre introduced a land registration campaign, which enabled urban-based political and business elites to claim titles to Jubba Valley land that they did not actually own.[6] Riverine land gained value because of the promise of a World Bank-financed dam along with plans for irrigation and roads in the valley funded by foreign aid.

1991–95 War Years

Shortly after the fall of the Siad Barre regime in 1991, Darood and Hawiye militias fought amongst themselves to control the areas in southern Somalia inhabited by Somali Bantu minority farmers. Local farming communities were subjected to a pattern of looting, murder, rape, and extortion by these militias. Historian Lee Cassanelli described these patterns in 1995:

> The "war" is now concentrated in key resource areas of the south, which are largely, although not exclusively, inhabited by minorities. While planting and harvesting has resumed in many districts of the south, the larger economy is one based on extortion of surpluses from the unarmed to the armed. Even if the dominant groups do not aim to forcibly displace these minorities, they [warlords] do effectively dictate to the local residents, who must turn over their surplus harvests to the young militiamen, serve as magnets to attract NGO aid, which can then be skimmed off by the powerful, offer public support and legitimation to the leaders of the occupying forces when the latter claim representation on emerging local and district councils. Because no social contract based on clan affiliation exists between the occupying forces and the villagers, there is no assurance that the benefits in the form of relief aid or services will reach the villagers themselves.[7]

A version of this system is currently employed by Al-Shabaab against the remaining Somali Bantus in the Jubba River Valley.

1996–2017 Militia Control

Infighting among the primarily Darood and Hawiye militias that continued into the late 1990s resulted in a power-sharing agreement whereby sections of the Jubba River Valley were divided among the Darood Clan's Marehan and Ogaden sub-clans and the Hawiye's Habar Gedir sub-clan. This arrangement, known as the Jubba Valley Alliance, allowed these militias to carry out extortion of Somali Bantus without fear of defending their "turf" from competing militias.

In the mid-2000s, the Union of Islamic Courts (UIC), with the current Jubbaland State president, Ahmed Mohamed Islam "Madobe," as its mayor of Kismayu, defeated the JVA to control the Jubba River Valley. After the Ethiopian Army ousted the UIC in the 2000s, hard-line remnants of the organization formed Al-Shabaab. Al-Shabaab's control brought a more severe variant of persecution and extortion that resulted in the deaths of hundreds of thousands of minorities and an exodus to IDP and refugee camps for many more.[8]

Survey Results

The survey results show how Al-Shabaab targets Somali Bantus with higher extortion, taxes, *zakat*, and penalties than are levied against other Somalis.

Likewise, forced conscription of male children as well as rape and forced marriage of girls predominantly affect Somali Bantus. Somali Bantus who are employed or conscripted as labourers and soldiers by Al-Shabaab are paid at lower rates than labourers and soldiers with other backgrounds—and are sometimes not paid at all. In southern Somalia Al-Shabaab is capable of exploiting only those groups who lack militia defences of their own, namely Somali Bantus and certain coastal minority communities.

Harvests

97.5% of respondents reported that, in their village, Al-Shabaab confiscates "about 50%" or more of harvests from Somali Bantu farmers in "every year" or in "most years" while 2.5% of respondents reported that Al-Shabaab confiscates "less than 50%" or "none (0%)" from Somali Bantu farmers in "every year" or in "most years."

9% of respondents reported that, in their village, Al-Shabaab confiscates "about 50%" or more of harvests from non-minority Somali farm owners in "every year" or in "most years" while 91% of respondents reported that Al-Shabaab confiscates "about 45%" or "none (0%)" of harvests from pastoralist clan Somali farm owners in "every year" or in "most years."

House Tax

Respondents reported the range of Al-Shabaab's "house tax" on every Somali Bantu household each month ranges from US$20 to US$100 with a mean amount of US$66.40. Respondents reported the range of Al-Shabaab's "house tax" on every non-minority Somali household each month ranges from US$0 to US$50 with a mean amount of US$21.20.

Remittances

44% of respondents reported that, in their village, Al-Shabaab confiscates "about 25%" to "about 33%" of all Somali Bantu remittances while 56% of respondents reported that Al-Shabaab confiscates "about 20%" to "about 15%" of all Somali Bantu remittances. No respondents reported that, in their village, Al-Shabaab confiscates "about 25%" to "about 33%" of all non-minority Somali remittances while 100% of respondents reported that Al-Shabaab confiscates "about 20%" to "none (0%)" of all non-minority Somali remittances.

Military Conscription of Somali Bantu Boys

97.5% of respondents reported that, in their village, Al-Shabaab forcibly conscripts Somali Bantu boys. The age of conscripted Somali Bantu boys ranges from 10 to 17 years old with a mean age of 14 years. 83% of the respondents reported that the consequence for a family not allowing their child to be forcibly conscripted is "violence or punishment against the family member," 7% stated the penalty is "execution of the son or other family member," while 10% reported the family could pay a fine of between US$600 and US$1,000 to free their son. 85% of respondents reported that, in their village, Al-Shabaab does not forcibly conscript non-minority Somali boys. 15% of respondents reported they did not know if Somali boys are forcibly conscripted.

Rape and Forced Marriage of Somali Bantu Girls

97.5% of respondents reported that, in their village, Al-Shabaab members commit rape through the forced "marriage" of Somali Bantu girls. The average age at which girls are "eligible" for rape through forced marriage ranges from 9 to 17 years old, with a mean age of 13 years.

68% of the respondents reported that the consequence for a family not allowing their child to be raped and her labour exploited through forced marriage is "violence or punishment against the family member." 10% stated that the penalty is "execution of the daughter or other family member," while 22% reported the family could pay a fine of between US$200 and US$1,000 to free their daughter.

80% of respondents reported that, in their village, Al-Shabaab does not rape (through forced marriage) non-minority Somali girls. 20% of respondents reported that non-minority Somali girls were raped through forced marriage, but at a lower rate "than Somali Bantu girls."

Zakat

Al-Shabaab forces households to pay *zakat*, an Islamic charitable contribution. Respondents reported that the amount of *zakat* Somali Bantu households were forced to pay each year ranges from US$100 to US$1,000 with a mean amount of US$574. Respondents reported the *zakat* confiscated by Al-Shabaab from every non-minority Somali household each year ranges from US$0 to US$500, with a mean amount of US$231.

Restrictions on Movement

100% of respondents reported that Somali Bantus in their villages cannot "move freely between Al-Shabaab-held areas and government-controlled areas," while 90% reported that Somali Bantus in their villages "would like to leave the Jubba Valley but are too afraid to do so." 97.5% of the respondents reported that Somali Bantus caught trying to flee Al-Shabaab-controlled areas "will be imprisoned for ransom" with the amount of the ransoms ranging from US$0 to US$1,200 with a mean amount of US$594.

100% of respondents reported severe consequences should a Somali Bantu "go back to Al-Shabaab-controlled areas after being in Kismayu or outside of Somalia." 39% of respondents reported that Somali Bantus caught returning to Al-Shabaab-controlled areas face "execution," 41% face "imprisonment and interrogation," and 20% are "taken to an unknown area" or "will be taken to fighting place [front lines]."

97.5% of respondents reported that, in their villages, non-minority Somalis can "move freely between Al-Shabaab-controlled areas and government-controlled areas." 100% of respondents reported that Al-Shabaab allows freedom of movement in and out of areas under its control for Somali traders from Kismayu to do business in the Valley.

Failure to Pay Extortion

97.5% of respondents reported severe consequences for Somali Bantus who do not or cannot pay Al-Shabaab extortion, taxes or fines while 2.5% said they "do not know what the consequences would be for non-payment of extortion to Al-Shabaab." 17% of respondents reported that Somali Bantus unwilling or unable to pay Al-Shabaab face "execution" while 80% face "violence or punishment against a family member." 27% of respondents reported severe consequences for a non-minority Somali who does not or cannot pay Al-Shabaab extortion, taxes, or fines, 66% reported "nothing," 2% "paid a fine," and 5% said they "don't know."

Expropriation

Follow-up interviewer questioning revealed that Somali Bantu farmers who cannot pay the extortion and fines have their farms confiscated by Al-Shabaab, which then sells them to neighbouring non-minority Somali newcomers. This land expropriation campaign, along with the other atrocities committed by Al-Shabaab, is accelerating the displacement of Somali Bantus from their homelands. This latest trend of Al-Shabaab land expropriation matches that under the Siad Barre government in the 1980s. Somali Bantus state there has been a decades-long campaign to expropriate their land. Repopulating the fertile areas of the Jubba River Valley with Somalis from major clans will help their leaders justify claims that ancestral Somali Bantu farmland now belongs to newcomers from major Somali clans.

Conclusion

Warfare in Somalia is now in its twenty-fifth year. The fighting has been concentrated in the nation's southern regions and has disproportionately impacted Somali Bantus and other ethnic minorities. The peacemaking equation in Somalia, however, has failed to factor in the plight and potential of Somali Bantus, who currently dominate IDP camps in Somalia. In order to break the cycle of violence and famine in southern Somalia, stakeholders must acknowledge and include the Jubba Valley's farming communities in diplomatic, security, and development decision-making processes.

Al-Shabaab is often described as a group intent on using military means to expand its extremist interpretation of Islam. However, our research indicates that, in the Jubba Valley at least, Al-Shabaab is a militant group misusing Islam to profit from its extortion against defenceless minority groups. In many ways, Al-Shabaab is only the latest in a long line of outside militias occupying the Jubba River Valley. Strategies to defeat Al-Shabaab may find success combating its economic extortion activities.

If the current trend of Somali Bantu land expropriation is allowed to stand in a post-Al-Shabaab government, then Somali Bantus will be reduced to sharecropping on their land, an outcome that will diminish Somalia's ability to achieve food security. Furthermore, any outside militia that controls the Jubba River Valley will be the object of competing militia resentment that could likely, as history has shown, erupt into new iterations of clan warfare.

With the devastation of southern Somalia's economic, social, and security infrastructure, stakeholders have an opportunity to create a reconstruction plan for the South that includes Somali Bantus. A just and sustainable peace in the South is the necessary foundation upon which a successful plan can be built. That foundation requires the input of the millions of displaced minorities as well as those struggling to survive in their home regions.

Recommendations

Policy-makers should:

- Close the "Gatekeeper" IDP camps in Somalia and establish one for and run by Somali Bantus in the Jubba River Valley that is protected by a non-regional international military force.
- Nullify illegal land expropriation deals conducted by Al-Shabaab, previous warlord administrations, and the Siad Barre regime.
- Request the United Nations Population Fund to expand its "Population Estimation Survey for Somalia" conducted in 2014 to include an estimation of Somali Bantu people in Somalia and in neighbouring country refugee camps.
- Desist from supporting the 4.5 system and insist minorities fully participate in civil society, particularly in political representation and security matters.
- Reconsider acknowledgement by UNSOM that the Jubbaland State is the legitimate government entity in Kismayu and the Jubba River Valley.
- Investigate collaboration between Al-Shabaab and the Jubbaland State in regard to the systematic extortion of Somali Bantus and other minorities and the expropriation of their land.
- Notify UNHCR that it is not safe for Somali Bantus and other minority refugees to repatriate and that they should be granted heightened protection status in locations outside of Somalia, including Kenya.
- Request that the United Nations investigate whether genocide has been committed against Somali Bantus.

MOTIVATIONS AND DRIVERS OF AL-SHABAAB

Roland Marchal

Author

Dr Roland Marchal is Senior Research Fellow at the National Centre for Scientific Research (CNRS), based at the Centre for International Researches, Sciences-Po, Paris. He is a specialist in conflicts and politics in the Horn of Africa and Central Africa.

Summary

Al-Shabaab has built itself on a clear agenda: ridding Somalia of foreign forces, portrayed as Christians, and implementing the Sharia. These goals implied the need for reform and discipline of Somali society using all means: *dawa* (preaching) as well as violence. While the goals fit well with Somali nationalistic and Salafi agendas, more fluidity or even flexibility is shown by Al-Shabaab in a situation of weakness. However, there is no doubt that Al-Shabaab eventually intends to monopolize the religious arena and curb the political and social influence of any contenders. Among the rank and file of Al-Shabaab, drivers of membership include a strong desire for revenge and a will to build a "better" community where youth would be fully included. Al-Shabaab offers a way to reform the private sphere and reframe the public sphere, which responds to many grievances of its membership. The key question is why the Somali government is unable or unwilling to make its own alternative offer.

Introduction

Over its nearly 15 years of existence *Harakada Mujaahidiinta Al-Shabaab* (hereafter Al-Shabaab) went through very different periods of organizational growth. It developed from a small group of militants to the strongest military component of an alliance that rid Mogadishu of clan-based factions. It faced annihilation and two years later was in control of nearly all south-central Somalia. It was able to survive an important internal leadership crisis at a time of military downturn. It also went from a focus on the capital city to developing the ability to strike even beyond national borders.

Motivations of an armed movement could be changing and are certainly not identical if one tries to compare the recruits' views with the leadership's motivations. While hard data are missing, consideration of motivations is nonetheless a useful exercise in the sense that it shows that Al-Shabaab is a political organization, not merely the terrorist organization eager to kill a population as mentioned in media headlines. The exercise also reveals that many of the members' motivations are shared by segments of the Somali population, albeit not with the same intensity and with no will to defend them by using weapons and terror methods.

The first part of this paper looks at the leadership motivations and the second, though based on several assumptions that could be nuanced, tries to shed light on Al-Shabaab's grassroots level motivations at different periods of the current crisis. The conclusion is that a space for discussion has existed at different moments over the years. These opportunities were missed, as external actors were wrongly convinced they could win a war of attrition against Al-Shabaab. Today, the prospects to open such a channel of discussion are significantly hindered by the challenges created by the so-called Islamic State's (IS) emergence in northern Somalia and a sense of invulnerability rooted in the survival of the organization against all odds.

Framing Nationalism and Monopolizing the Politico-Religious Arena

Al-Shabaab's motivations or drivers may have changed over time but one should consider that two goals have been recurrently reasserted, whatever changes were witnessed. The first one is the refusal to have any foreign "Christian" troops inside Somalia. The second is at the core of Salafi ideology and refers to the implementation of the Sharia. These claims have taken different forms according to Al-Shabaab's ability to control populations and the balance of forces with hostile Somali and foreign forces.

The presence of foreign troops in Somalia was a key recruiting argument for Al-Shabaab (and others). For Al-Shabaab's leadership, it encompassed different motivations. Many of its leaders were indeed targeted before 2006 by Ethiopian (and/or) foreign secret services or special forces, some being killed or kidnapped and taken to Ethiopia. When the Transitional Federal Government (TFG) was set up in Kenya in October 2004, there was a strong sense that it only existed because of regional and Western support. This view was reinforced when Ethiopian troops went to Baydhabo in August 2006 to protect the TFG leaders after an attempted killing of the country's president, Abdullaahi Yuusuf Ahmed, allegedly (but likely) perpetrated by Al-Shabaab.

The massive Ethiopian intervention in December 2006 was a blessing for Al-Shabaab, though at first it nearly destroyed the whole organization. For two years, Al-Shabaab propaganda could make the opposition to the presence of Ethiopian troops resonate with the secular nationalism that was a pillar of the Mahamed Siad Barre regime. The strength of that argument weakened when AMISOM troops took the lead against Al-Shabaab at a time when the new TFG president, Sheekh Shariif Sheekh Ahmed, came to power. By that time, the frontline ran through Mogadishu and Al-Shabaab believed that it could even win a conventional war against AMISOM.

The claim to rid Somalia of foreign troops not only reflected the situation on the ground but also constituted a strong analogy with the position taken by Usama bin Laden when the Saudi king authorized the presence of US (and international) soldiers on Saudi soil. The notion of a Western re-colonization of Muslim (and here African) land had a strong appeal beyond Salafi and extremist trends. Al-Shabaab took little risk in adopting a radical stance, as it was clear that sooner or later most Somalis (but not all) would support that view.

An interesting question is what territory Al-Shabaab is referring to when it speaks of Somalia. Again, Al-Shabaab's views have been largely shared among the Somali population beyond Islamists. Somalia refers to the Somali territory, with little concern for the real demographic reality and whether Oromo or other ethnic groups also have rights in these territories. It is true that Islamist leaders, when engaged on this topic, show a greater sense of geopolitical realism and do not resort to any irredentist agenda. But they emphasize that Somalis should be better treated in both Kenya and Ethiopia. The Somali population at large agrees, but few are ready to wage war for only that reason.

In the years 2007–10, Al-Shabaab was not the only organization to claim a nationalistic agenda, but was smart enough to promote its military effectiveness (even if not always well-founded) against the clan divisions that were weakening the other groups at a time the situation required them to be unified against a common enemy. The Eritrea-based Alliance for the Re-liberation of Somalia and Hisbuul Islaam were indeed affected by complex internal rivalries.

Furthermore, one should not forget the second pillar of Al-Shabaab's agenda: the implementation of the Sharia. This has been the aim of all Somali Salafi organizations from their early days of existence and Al-Shabaab was never shy about its intention. It is interesting to notice that this took different forms according to the situation and the strength of the organization. For instance, in 2006, Al-Shabaab did not feel powerful enough to directly antagonize Sufi orders, which it did in 2008 and 2009. After 2012, this policy faced ups and downs according to the balance of forces in the region. Sometimes, local Al-Shabaab commanders were willing to take steps to regain popular support; sometimes they wanted to make a demonstration of force.

This aim of implementing the Sharia is very ambitious in many regards. For Al-Shabaab, first and foremost, it was a symbolic weapon that was used against a foreign occupation force and what it described as a surrogate Somali government. Al-Shabaab, like most jihadi movements, was lacking in religious expertise and its understanding of the Sharia was highly debatable even among Salafi circles. But it meant two important things: first, Al-Shabaab would be uncompromising and second, the group was ready to enforce all punishments, especially *huduud*. This is an Islamic term referring to punishments that are seen as mandated and determined by God, ranging from public lashing, to publicly stoning to death, to the amputation of hands. Al-Shabaab declared that nobody could escape God's law: rulers, wealthy people, and force commanders had to comply or be punished as with anybody else. Having said that, over time and space Al-Shabaab proved more flexible, especially in cases of its own members infringing the Sharia: instead of facing a harsh punishment, they were relocated.

Variations in implementing the Sharia were also connected to the people in charge of Al-Shabaab and the situation on the ground. Once Al-Shabaab was clearly in control, it could show greater tolerance. After 2014, it became clear that the frontline could evolve quickly and it was thought necessary to retain as much popular support as possible. Some *wilayat* (provincial) governors, because of their seniority in the organization and their political capital, could be more reasonable than others.

Western observers too often reduce Sharia implementation to *huduud*. While there is an important debate within classical Islam on what the Sharia actually says and does not say, one should be aware that Al-Shabaab courts addressed many problems of the population it controlled (such as inheritance, divorce, and land title disputes) and provided solutions it was able to enforce. For the population at large, regardless of its sympathy for the group, decisions based on the Sharia were legitimate and helped solve practical problems. Moreover, one should admit (which many are reluctant to do) that Al-Shabaab expended resources to put this judicial system in place and that the various Somali governments supported by the international community have shown little resolve to do likewise, nor with the same genuine commitment exhibited by Al-Shabaab.

The call for the Sharia has had other consequences. The first is that Al-Shabaab can claim a monopoly on the religious arena: the only correct way to understand and practice religion is Al-Shabaab's way; whoever dissents is not a good Muslim. This allowed the group to theologically justify the marginalization of its ally, Raas Kambooni, in 2009, and to force Hisbuul Islaam to merge with Al-Shabaab in December 2010. It is based on a Salafi core principle that Salafis must vigorously oppose the classical Islamic principle of *al-ikhtilaf*, the differing of religious opinion in which several solutions may be valid.

The second consequence, which is rooted in many Islamist ideologies, is that the Islamic vanguard first has to discipline society and that excesses are justified by this overall aim. There is no belief in the ability of people to learn without coercion: if not trust, at least obedience. This is reinforced by the religious weakness of the armed groups. Commanders who often have only basic religious education plus a simplistic understanding of Salafi principles do not want to get involved in theological discussions: the simpler, the better.

To change society and to have a chance of succeeding, Al-Shabaab had to become a true social reformer. Its policy toward clan is very complex but aims to weaken any alternative social authority to Al-Shabaab appointees. This hostility to clan-based appeals resonates strongly among the youth, who can see how older people have monopolised positions of power and accumulated resources. Young people may also be bitter against clan customary chiefs who have been unable to bring the country out of a civil war into an Islamic or Somali modernity. Al-Shabaab is therefore modern in many regards: in sociological jargon, it helps to build individuation and breaks holistic rules imposed on the youth; it makes access to a spouse and social authority much easier.

Al-Shabaab, willingly or unwillingly, has made an assessment of the costs of civil war. To obtain their support, it targets clans and segments of the population that have suffered much from the armed confrontation of the major clans over the last two decades and demonstrates that it can show them respect and give an equal chance to all. Bantus, Gibil 'Ad, and minorities have better chances to be promoted among Al-Shabaab than among any government structures.

The TFG and the Federal Government of Somalia (FGS) have showed no interest in going beyond lip service to acknowledge the damage caused by the civil war, the responsibilities of the major clans they often belong to in victimizing the population, and the need for apologies and reparations. Al-Shabaab clearly offers an alternative that has its defects but is not purely rhetorical.

This policy towards clan also sheds light on Al-Shabaab's recruitment strategy. The group recruits more easily in multi-clan locations because conflicts there are likely. Its strategy has often been to trigger (or exacerbate) a conflict to get rid of influential people who would oppose the group's presence, and then solve the conflict as a way of proving how ineffective clan elders are compared to the good Muslims of Al-Shabaab. While this strategy is very well known among Somalis, neither the TFG nor the FGS have been eager to address reconciliation in a strategic manner. Instead, it was mostly a way to buy one clan over another or to grab money that was eventually shared between ministers, MPs, and local elders.

Al-Shabaab's Motivations and Drivers: Views from Below

A perspective from below is not radically different from what has just been described. But there are several further points that can be made: the importance of revenge; the call to follow friends; and economic grievances.

Western observers are often reluctant to discuss the cost of policies implemented by their state in any crisis. Today, most Western politicians would acknowledge that the Ethiopian military intervention was a "mistake" but none would quote any figures of the people killed or the harm done to Somalis. Many Somalis joined Al-Shabaab to exercise their rights to take revenge against foreigners and Somalis who destroyed their family or properties, even if that meant doing exactly the same.

This sense of a bitter past and the necessity of revenge is structural in the recruitment strategies of Al-Shabaab and one should ask why so little has been done to address those feelings and offer some non-violent alternatives. As in many armed movements, either secular or religious, there is a cult of violence among Al-Shabaab's rank and file, but analysis should move beyond that recognition.

The decision to join Al-Shabaab is rarely an individual decision and even less an ideological move. Over the years, Al-Shabaab has tended to be able to control a place and ask local elders to provide young recruits in the same way as "warlords" did in the early 1990s, or the Eritrean People's Liberation Front (EPLF) or the Tigray People's Liberation Front (TPLF) did in their own— very secular—wars. This has often been based on a transaction: Al-Shabaab brings stability to an area and requests recruits who are then socialized within its rank and file, and can go back to their villages to convince others to join.

In 2006 and 2007, Quranic schools became places of potential recruitment as the teachers had authority over their students and could order them to join Al-Shabaab to fight the Christian occupation. Most became cannon fodder, especially in December 2006. This pushed parents to seek more control over what the Quranic schools were teaching and who the teachers were.

After Sheekh Shariif Sheekh Ahmed was elected president in January 2009 and, as a consequence, Al-Shabaab lost its religious appeal, recruitments became more individualistic and many people joined because their friends were already in the group. Motivations also changed because the sense of fighting against the Western world was more evanescent.

At first, propaganda put an emphasis on the economic rewards of belonging to Al-Shabaab: salaries were good and were regularly paid while the Somali government was recurrently failing to do the same. It is clear that some—especially among the youth—pay attention to that factor but it would be unwise to consider money a main driver except for some surrogates (such as kids spying in the streets). Bringing Al-Shabaab fighters over to the government side is indeed difficult and dangerous, and nearly impossible at this stage, despite a fair number of defectors: there is insufficient stability and the FGS still has difficulty paying regular salaries.

In contrast, one should notice how Al-Shabaab has been able to recruit among the middle and upper middle classes, in the diaspora and in areas where foreign troops have had little presence, such as Puntland and Somaliland. Almost all major Somaliland politicians have lost a son who died while fighting for Al-Shabaab; this remains so up to the present day. This certainly demonstrates that Al-Shabaab is a national phenomenon, not some form of cancer affecting only south-central Somalia.

One should highlight a final aspect: many of those joining Al-Shabaab share two important beliefs. One is that they are not alone, but part of a global Islamic revolt against injustice and the West. It does not mean that they are global jihadists, but their often-local concerns are also connected to a more transnational perspective thanks to Western discourses and propaganda from all sides. This also means that the longer the war, the stronger the ideological links with other crises in terms of jihad.

Another trend is that they want to achieve something tangible. Being in a militia is a very tough life and the salary may not be that meaningful after the member has lost friends or relatives killed in action (regardless of the usual claims about martyrdom). So long as the war lasts, people want to defeat the enemy but also build something that may survive them. The call for establishing an Islamic State came at different moments in Al-Shabaab's life and one might argue that rather than a product of hubris it is a response to the frustrations of their rank and file, eager to prove that they are building a better world, not only destroying an unfair one.

The interest among members in observing the so-called Islamic State (IS) in Somalia is linked to several factors. Some factors are purely an effect of the IS propaganda machine, and the West's evident fear of that movement. Some are rooted in the prospect that building some form of an Islamic state was achievable and legitimate. Against Al-Qaida's eschatological call to rid the world of non-believers, IS has been offering a more concrete and immediate purpose: thinking globally and acting locally.

It would be wrong to assume that recruitments are failing because Al-Shabaab's popularity is "collapsing." The drivers noted above show how Al-Shabaab can reinvent itself after any major defeats because the FGS and its international partners are unable to defuse social mechanisms that dissuade people from joining an organization that is unable to rule their country.

Like many "totalitarian" armed movements, such as EPLF and TPLF, Al-Shabaab reshapes the private lives of its members and offers symbolic and material rewards in the public sphere in order to promote its policies and prove to the population that the movement is pursuing the right path.

Conclusion

Until today, the Somali government and its foreign allies have only responded in the same field they want Al-Shabaab to be identified with: violence, war, and coercion. Assessing Al-Shabaab's motivations and drivers is actually the best way to look at what went wrong with the various Somali governments, established with the full support of the international community.

A contentious point, which has not been discussed here, is how Al-Shabaab—despite its ideology and world vision—is still very much a Somali organization. One can doubt this, when reading the group's statements, but the veracity of the claim is substantiated through analysis of the way the group behaves with the population in the countryside and acquires an understanding of the weaknesses of its enemies.

In contrast to the common view that Al-Shabaab is a terrorist organization, one should more cautiously admit that Al-Shabaab is a politico-military organization that effectively combines politics and terror. Its vision and aims are not static, except if one considers them in the abstract. Ground analysis often proves how flexible the organization can be if its own survival or popularity is at stake.

Of course, one can add nuance to the description provided here but it would be wrong to dismiss the know-how Al-Shabaab has acquired over the years beyond the coercion and terror that all analyses mention. The political dilemma is how to reconcile the various Somali viewpoints that are not always antagonistic to Al-Shabaab's and to make the war not only unwinnable for Al-Shabaab, but also unnecessary.

Recommendations

1. In light of Al-Shabaab's motivations, the Somali government and its international partners should question why no post-conflict reconciliation policies were defined and implemented in Somalia.
2. While Al-Shabaab articulates a Salafi ideology, it is important for policymakers not to be prisoners to that thinking. Al-Shabaab has proven more flexible than its critics. Research should be carried out to throw light on how the situation on the ground differs in Al-Shabaab-controlled territories.
3. Recruitment patterns have evolved over time and drivers as well. It is important to deconstruct the motivations of the recruits and understand what they say about local social stability and security. The danger for observers is to consider Al-Shabaab either as a fully decentralized armed group or as an over-centralized movement led by its security division, the Amniyat.
4. Al-Shabaab is a political organization. Decision-makers may resolutely oppose it, but one should not ignore its political message, even at a time when the group uses terror as a means to survive—and potentially expand.

WHY THEY FIGHT AND WHY THEY QUIT

AN ANALYSIS OF INTERVIEWS WITH CURRENT
AND FORMER AL-SHABAAB FIGHTERS

Richard Barrett

Author

This paper is the work of The Global Strategy Network (TGSN). Richard Barrett, its director, is currently engaged in several projects in Somalia concerning the threat from Al-Shabaab and the Federal Government's response. The main Somali contributor was Mohammed Mubarak, an associate of TGSN, who conducted the TGSN survey. He is Director of Marqaati, a Somali NGO based in Mogadishu.

Summary

Interviews with over 100 individuals currently or previously associated with Al-Shabaab demonstrate a fairly predictable range of reasons for joining the movement, both over time and across age groups. The majority seek a sense of belonging and purpose, strongly influenced by Al-Shabaab's claim to be acting in defence of Islam. For many younger recruits, Al-Shabaab offers opportunity and adventure where both are in short supply, as well as economic security. As with other insurgent or violent extremist groups, individuals often join because friends are planning to do so or are already members of the movement.

The reasons for defection are often the converse of the reasons for joining. Life in Al-Shabaab is harsher than expected; but more importantly, so too is Al-Shabaab's treatment of its members and the people who live under its control. Its failure to act in accordance with Islamic principles, particularly through arbitrary imprisonment and unjustified brutality, undermines the religious legitimacy that might otherwise have preserved the loyalty of its recruits. Al-Shabaab is pervaded by an atmosphere of fear and suspicion, especially in the higher ranks outside the small leadership circle.

Family members outside the movement have frequently persuaded people to leave, but the practical difficulties of defection, and the dangers associated with it, have often led people to stay far longer than they would have liked. Al-Shabaab keeps a tight watch on its members and almost all defectors interviewed by TGSN have stories of long and complicated journeys and of narrow escapes. It is likely therefore that significant numbers in Al-Shabaab would also like to leave, and that many of the men who fight for Al-Shabaab do so reluctantly. Several who took part in the survey said that they now see the battle as one between political groups rather than one driven by conviction or ideology.

Introduction

This study is based principally on the results of three surveys: one involving 30 face-to-face and telephone interviews with 25 previous and five current members of Al-Shabaab at all levels, including the most senior,[1] conducted by TGSN in Mogadishu, Kismayo and Lower Shabelle during May 2017;[2] another with 27 low-risk defectors carried out by the Rehabilitation Support Team (RST) at the Serendi rehabilitation centre in Mogadishu in November 2015,[3] and a third with 88 defectors carried out by the Institute for Strategic Studies (ISS) in April 2014.[4] The paper also draws on other research and the impressions of experts, both in Somalia and outside.

The study is designed to help the Federal Government of Somalia (FGS) understand why people are fighting rather than just navigating the conflict on the battlefield. Al-Shabaab has a hard core of committed and experienced fighters, but also relies on recruits whose reasons for joining do not automatically put them in opposition to the FGS.

Why People Join and Leave Al-Shabaab

Leaders

The TGSN survey interviewed six mid- to high-level Al-Shabaab leaders, most of whom had left the movement and none of whom continued to support its aims. Most had joined Al-Shabaab between 2009 and 2011, usually via membership of another group, such as Hizbul Islam, that had merged with it. One had joined as a senior clan member in a liaison capacity. These six senior leaders had achieved their position through ability or expertise, whether as a technical expert or, for example, as a Sharia scholar. One skilled worker, a medic, reported having been pressured to join because of the need for people with his training.

This does not mean that even the reluctant recruits were initially unsympathetic to Al-Shabaab's stated aims. They supported efficient government, and believed it should be run according to Islamic principles, and they opposed the influence and presence of foreign forces. In most cases these senior members had joined because they sought opportunity and Al-Shabaab offered the best prospects; typically, many of their friends and acquaintances joined the group at the same time. It was only after some years living within Al-Shabaab that disillusionment set in. All said that the top leadership imposed control in an inappropriately authoritarian and unjust manner. A further factor in almost all cases of defection was concern for personal safety. These senior defectors reported on the widespread air of mistrust and suspicion within the leadership, with even mid-level or senior Amniyat (intelligence and security) and Jabha (army) officials fearful of death or imprisonment if they fell foul of more senior officials.

Disaffection with the leadership usually resulted from disagreement on the treatment of other Al-Shabaab members or of civilians living in areas under Al-Shabaab control. Some complained that Al-Shabaab disregarded the advice of religious leaders, sometimes ignoring Sharia court judgements if they failed to accord with what the leadership wanted to hear. All said that Al-Shabaab had diverged from its original objectives of ruling the country according to Islamic principles and correcting injustices. However, ideological disappointment was not at the heart of most of this group's decision to leave.

The most common reason for senior and mid-level members of Al-Shabaab to abandon the movement was a change in leadership or other developments that caused them to lose their position, lose influence, or fear for their lives. Where people could escape, they did, even if at considerable personal risk.

Where senior leaders had become disillusioned or disappointed but could not try to escape for fear of discovery or the lack of a viable post-defection option, they carried on as members of Al-Shabaab but without any commitment to its leadership.

Given the risks these people ran in talking to the interviewers, it is reasonable to suppose that there may be many others who are also disaffected with the direction that Al-Shabaab has taken and believe it is time to seek another way to contribute to the future of Somalia. The TGSN survey showed a growing sense that the insurgency was at a stalemate. It also showed that leaders increasingly saw Al-Shabaab fighting a local, political battle rather than an ideological one. While there was little appetite or interest in the global agenda of Al-Shabaab, or its affiliation with Al-Qaida, the religious aspect of its messaging was still important, and this made its departure from Islamic norms still less acceptable.

Foot Soldiers—Why They Join

The three surveys on which this study is based are inevitably more informative about foot soldiers than about leaders. Most respondents were young, generally in their late teens or early twenties. Two in the TGSN group were 15. Both had "joined" in 2015; one had been taken forcibly from a madrasa with five classmates to an Al-Shabaab training camp, and the other had joined on the promise of receiving an education. Only 9 per cent of the ISS survey and just under 15 per cent of the TGSN survey had joined in their thirties. The oldest in the TGSN survey was 40 when he joined in 2008. He said that he did so because Al-Shabaab was fighting to protect Islam.

The Islamic credentials claimed by Al-Shabaab appear to act as an important recruitment tool. Around half of both the ISS survey and the TGSN survey gave some form of religious motivation as their reason for joining.[5] These varied from a belief that Al-Shabaab was doing God's work; a desire to defend Islam as an act of jihad that would earn rewards in paradise; to a less well-expressed desire for Islamic brotherhood. Two from the TGSN sample joined specifically to fight against the occupation of Somalia by foreign (non-Muslim) troops. This religious element however was far less apparent in the RST sample, possibly because the people at Serendi had been less committed to Al-Shabaab than was true for the other two groups.[6] Conversely, the people at Serendi may have been afraid to cite religious reasons for fear of being labelled as extremists.

Al-Shabaab still purports to promote an Islamic identity over a national or ethnic identity, even though, by 2017, it would be surprising to find any new non-ethnic Somalis in its ranks, and very few from outside the region. The attraction of religion as preached by Al-Shabaab seems to be particularly strong for young men who seek both a sense of belonging and of purpose. Particularly since Al-Shabaab retreated from urban areas, its recruits have been more likely to be uneducated (30 per cent of the TGSN survey; 40 per cent of the ISS survey), or if educated at all, only in religious schools (30 per cent of the TGSN survey; 43 per cent of the ISS survey). The religious instruction that these recruits received, whether from madrasas in Al-Shabaab-held areas before joining or in Al-Shabaab training camps subsequently, offered a more severe, binary view of a world of "them" and "us" than typical in the traditions of Somalia. A resultant sense of inclusion may have increased the appeal of Al-Shabaab to young people as it contrasts with Somali tribal traditions that largely ignore the views of the young.

The appeal of a sense of belonging and comradeship among young recruits is also evident from the number that joined the movement with friends or because friends were already members. In both the TGSN sample and the ISS sample, 30 per cent said that a friend had persuaded them to join. In addition, 64 per cent of the ISS sample said that they had joined with friends. Family members had also played a part in recruitment in one or two cases, but in the TGSN sample, this had been at the initiative of the recruit wanting to make contact with a recruiter rather than a proactive effort by the family member to bring more people into the movement.

In the RST sample, 50 per cent claimed that they had joined Al-Shabaab out of a sense of adventure, while only one recruit offered this as a reason in the TGSN sample, though another offered curiosity; and none was recorded as doing so in the ISS sample. This may say more about the people interviewed by RST than the changing appeal of Al-Shabaab, but it is likely that many of the younger recruits were attracted by the propaganda of Al-Shabaab as a strong and militarily capable movement engaged in daring and exciting work. The projection of power by Al-Shabaab was certainly effective in keeping people in the movement, with 99 per cent of the ISS sample saying that they enjoyed the respect they felt as a member of Al-Shabaab. Indeed, the search for power and respect was mentioned specifically as a reason for joining by 10 per cent of the TGSN sample, and 45 per cent of the RST sample.

Another major driver of Al-Shabaab's recruitment was economic hardship. The need for a job and an income was given as the main reason for joining by

20 per cent of the TGSN sample, 27 per cent of the ISS sample (though this climbed to 52 per cent when combined with religion as a motivator), and 50 per cent of the RST sample. Though many people facing the same economic circumstances have not joined Al-Shabaab, the promise of an income even of US$50 per month would be an attractive incentive for men who had no other obvious opportunity to provide for themselves or their families. As Al-Shabaab has become less able to pay salaries, and word of this has spread, economic benefit may have become less of a factor in recruitment.

In areas where Al-Shabaab is dominant, people may judge whether or not it offers good government and opportunity. Low numbers in all samples said that they were attracted to join Al-Shabaab because they believed in its ability to govern well and wanted to help. Only one person in both the TGSN sample and the RST sample offered this as a motivation, though 20 per cent of the ISS sample had a positive opinion of Al-Shabaab's governance. This no doubt reflects a general decline since 2014 both in Al-Shabaab's interest in providing good governance and in its capacity to do so.

In places controlled by Al-Shabaab there are anecdotal stories of people being forced to join the group, or families being forced to provide either a recruit or a monthly payment to the movement, but the numbers who claimed this had happened to them were just 10 per cent in the TGSN survey, 30 per cent in the RST survey, and 13 per cent in the ISS survey,[7] despite this being an obvious story for a defector. One person in each of these surveys said that they had joined because they believed Al-Shabaab would protect them from unspecified threats from within their own community.

Foot Soldiers—Why They Leave

While the process of joining Al-Shabaab is typically rather fast—the ISS survey reported that 48 per cent of respondents had done so within 30 days of their initial contact with the movement—the process of leaving is often drawn out, both in terms of making the final decision to leave and in finding the opportunity and summoning the courage to do so. Comradeship, routine, fear, and uncertainty about the future appear to be the main inhibitors, along with a sense that despite the actions of some leaders, Al-Shabaab is providing services and acting in a religiously appropriate way.

It follows then that the irreligious behaviour of Al-Shabaab has proved to be one of the main reasons that people have given for deciding to leave. The most common example of this, mixed no doubt with a sense of fear and horror, was the unnecessary killing of other Muslims, whether members of

Al-Shabaab or not, on the basis of false accusations or for no apparent reason at all. Such killings were given as the reason for leaving by 40 per cent of the TGSN sample, and in a 2016 follow-up to the RST survey, it was more common than any other factor.

Other reasons for disgust at Al-Shabaab's treatment of people included the use of secret prisons, the torture of prisoners, and the way that Al-Shabaab members were forced to rob, beat, or kill people for the sake of the movement or as a test of loyalty, leading to a sense of guilt and trauma. A broader betrayal of Islamic principles was also given as a reason for leaving, generally being described as Al-Shabaab's lies about how it governed and what it stood for. This reason was given by 25 per cent of the TGSN survey. An associated complaint concerning corruption, abuse of power, favouritism and other injustices, accounted for a further 10 per cent, with slightly more saying that they were concerned that they might find themselves on the receiving end of such mistreatment.[8]

Beyond the behaviour of Al-Shabaab, the harsh living conditions under which its members had to live were also frequently mentioned as a reason to leave, accounting for about 20 per cent of the RST survey though less than 10 per cent of the TGSN survey. Hunger, thirst, the lack of medical care, and tiredness from walking long distances—sometimes without shoes, all took their toll on morale, particularly when members were removed from their friends or posted outside areas they were familiar with. In these cases, motivations for joining such as purpose and belonging gave way to feelings of loneliness and fear.

Another common reason for desertion was war-weariness. Al-Shabaab members wonder when and how the fighting will end. Many of them, especially those under 40, have known nothing throughout their lives except political chaos and uncertainty. They say that they want a normal life, socializing with their friends and families and being able to choose where to go, what book to read or what radio station to listen to. They see Al-Shabaab's motivation being increasingly political rather than ideological (12 per cent of the TGSN survey), and therefore less compelling. Interestingly, the ISS survey found that 82 per cent trusted clan leaders, whereas trust in the Al-Shabaab leadership had declined.

Conclusion

The responses to the TGSN survey and other, earlier work, suggest that the main reason Somalis throw in their lot with Al-Shabaab is their lack of confidence in the ability of the FGS to provide good governance according to Islamic principles, reliable security, steady employment and useful education. Criticisms of Al-Shabaab however run along similar lines, and in this respect the competitive messaging put out by both sides is important. People joining and leaving Al-Shabaab identify strongly as Muslims, and confidence in its religious credentials and legitimacy is a critical issue for its members. The fact that Al-Shabaab often falls short of the standards of behaviour it claims to have is already evident to the group's members. However, the FGS can take steps to demonstrate that Al-Shabaab is wrong in its wholly negative description of the government.

Although Al-Shabaab members want to see the imposition of Sharia as the legal system of the country, this is more a reflection of the desire for predictable and impartial justice than a desire for a state that runs on purely religious lines. While all respondents regarded religion as an important element of their lives, they were as likely to identify as Somalis or as members of a clan as they were to identify as Muslims. Clan elders are therefore important influencers, while family members often prove decisive in persuading a member to leave Al-Shabaab. A combined effort to weaken the movement could therefore be effective, particularly as its members increasingly see it as a political group rather than a religious one.

The surveys suggest that by understanding why people join and leave the movement, the FGS will be better placed to identify the services that people want and the main deficiencies in Al-Shabaab's governance that the FGS should aim to fill.

Recommendations

The FGS should:

1. Learn as much as it can, from all sources, including defectors, about the internal dynamics of Al-Shabaab. It should identify both the strengths and weaknesses of the movement, opposing views within the leadership, and the main pillars of its local support.
2. Aim to undermine any religious credibility that Al-Shabaab retains.
3. Adopt a clear amnesty policy and broadcast it widely through communication channels that are most likely to reach Al-Shabaab members. The amnesty policy should be enshrined in law and be acceptable to the Somali people.

4. With international support, ensure that there is an effective, Somali-led programme for the training and future employment of defectors.
5. Seek indirect ways to engage in dialogue with Al-Shabaab, even while continuing to degrade it militarily.
6. Enlist the help of clans in discouraging their members from joining Al-Shabaab and in helping those who have joined to leave.
7. Design rural development programmes for ready deployment in areas recovered from Al-Shabaab.
8. Develop the capacity to provide education that ensures religious literacy and the basic tools of critical thinking.
9. Work with AMISOM partners to draw up a timetable for their withdrawal, depending on the achievement of agreed benchmarks in the de-escalation of violence.

Further Recommendation

The more the FGS knows about the reasons people give for joining Al-Shabaab, and for leaving it, the better it will be able to undermine Al-Shabaab's appeal. This will not just be through a communications strategy led by the Ministry of Information, but also by a legislative programme that establishes the criteria for amnesty, and by overall provision of governance that reveals Al-Shabaab messaging about the FGS to be false. The importance of friends in the decision to join Al-Shabaab suggests that many defectors may still be in touch with comrades who have decided—for whatever reason—to stay. This means the treatment of defectors is especially important. The FGS should cater to the reasons people gave for joining in crafting programmes for those who leave. These should focus on education and employment, hence the need for more international investment and support in addition to military support. Mistrust of the FGS is high, even among those that oppose Al-Shabaab; this places the burden on the FGS to demonstrate growth in national capacity to provide security, opportunity, and justice.

YOUTH RADICALIZATION

CAUSES, CONSEQUENCES AND POTENTIAL SOLUTIONS

Hussein Yusuf Ali

Author

Hussein Yusuf Ali is a Somalia researcher who has previously undertaken research for the Heritage Institute for Policy Studies, Mogadishu. He has degrees from Haaga-Helia University of Applied Science, Finland, and London Metropolitan University.

Summary

Radicalization is undermining Somalia's peace, stability and development prospects. Religious extremism in Somalia has also become a pertinent security concern for the region and for the world. Young, uneducated Somalis who never left the country and their well-educated diaspora peers—who grew up in an affluent life in the West—have become foot soldiers and suicide bombers for Somalia's extremist insurgency, Al-Shabaab. An intertwined array of internal and external factors has rendered Somali youth susceptible to Al-Shabaab's seductive ideologies and contributed to the rise of one of the world's most lethal insurgencies.

The emergence and evolution of Al-Shabaab has primarily been facilitated by the fracturing and dissolution of the Somali state and external interference. The group's resilience is reinforced by widespread injustices and political malfeasances perpetrated by national political leaders and local power brokers. Failure by mainstream Islamists to counter the Al-Shabaab narrative, widespread unemployment, external actors' destructive policies, the presence and ineffectiveness of African Union (AU) forces in Somalia, as well as complacency and tacit collaboration with the insurgency by critical segments of society—namely the business community—have all made Al-Shabaab a potent and powerful destabilizing force in Somalia.

This paper evaluates causes, drivers, and contributing factors of radicalization in Somalia. The study also assesses the strategies adopted thus far to deal with Al-Shabaab as well as other feasible options to address the issue of radicalization in Somalia. At present, over 20,000 UN mandated forces with the AU Mission in Somalia (AMISOM) forces are in the country battling with Al-Shabaab, and US military forces are also engaged in aerial attacks and at times special forces raids. Despite such combined efforts, Al-Shabaab endures as a strong force, unleashes devastating terror acts, and is poised to remain potent unless effective strategies are adopted.

The introduction of a national countering violent extremism (CVE) strategy represents a positive start, but further empirical research and analysis are required to establish how effective it can be over the short term. The Federal Government, working in conjunction with the regions, must implement the policies and practices outlined in the CVE strategy with immediate effect, starting with reform of its rehabilitation centres and prisons. Proposed counter-terrorism strategies must be Somali-led and implemented in line with internationally accepted norms. The predominance of strategies developed by foreign entities or establishment of parallel counter-terrorism mechanisms will compromise national sovereignty. To succeed, the Federal Government must strive to fulfil core state functions by replenishing mechanisms of governance throughout the country, while also addressing deep-rooted grievances caused by political, socio-economic and legal injustices. In addition, the AMISOM exit strategy must be clearly set, and contingency plans must be put in place for a post-AMISOM era in Somalia.

Methodology

This paper is informed by qualitative research, in the form of interviews with key informants, especially former members of Al-Shabaab. In addition, desk research was conducted to complement the primary sources. In each of the seven Somali cities ten key informant interviews and a single focus group discussion were conducted, producing a total data set comprising 70 individual interviews and seven focus group discussions. All respondents were asked to discuss the root causes of youth radicalization in Somalia and suggest potential solutions.

Introduction

For over a quarter of a century, Somalia has been at the epicentre of violent conflicts. Tribal conflicts, resource-related contests, wars waged by neighbouring states, failed international interventions, and factional fighting have created a population tired of exploitation and ripe for radicalization. In 2006, the majority of Somalis had never heard of Al-Shabaab, which operated in secret as a tiny wing within the Union of Islamic Courts, responsible for removing warlords from Mogadishu. However, by 2009, Al-Shabaab was a fully-fledged and functional insurgency controlling huge swathes of territory in south-central Somalia, collecting hundreds of millions of dollars in taxes.[1] In the decade since its emergence, Al-Shabaab has become one of the most violent and militarized extremist organizations in Africa. Over 20,000 UN-mandated AMISOM forces are currently in Somalia battling with Al-Shabaab. International military assets have also been deployed to the country, including active US military forces, mostly engaged in drone attacks and raids which have killed Al-Shabaab leaders, including the former *emir* [leader], Ahmed Godane.

Sustained AMISOM operations have removed the overt influence of Al-Shabaab from major urban centres, and US drone and commando attacks have deprived the group of its leaders and its access to ports, reducing its ability to carry out surprise assaults. Nonetheless, the group (whose name means "The Youth" in Arabic) is becoming ever more voracious. Every couple of months, half a dozen or a dozen Al-Shabaab fighters engage in suicide missions, staging complex attacks on important facilities such as hotels, government compounds or AMISOM garrisons. Al-Shabaab's propaganda and terrorism have penetrated the entire Horn of Africa, as the group has staged deadly attacks in Kampala and Djibouti, and repeatedly stormed multiple locations in Kenya. Many Western countries with significant Somali diaspora populations, such as Britain, Canada, and the United States, have classified Al-Shabaab as a serious national security threat. Radicalized Somali and non-Somali youths in these countries have joined Al-Shabaab and, more lately, the so-called Islamic State, to participate in their campaigns of violence and some have repeatedly threatened Western countries and their interests.

Even though some commentators believe Al-Shabaab has become "the hunted" instead of "the hunter", there is no question that the group's operational capacity is relatively intact and that it retains a significant number of dedicated followers among Somalis, particularly the youth. The majority of Al-Shabaab fighters and suicide bombers, and of course its leaders, are Somalis; however, the group has access to a significant international network of financiers, sympathizers and affiliates. Al-Shabaab's message of jihad against Somalis and external actors in Somalia has apparently struck a chord with a significant proportion of the country's youth population. Given that 70 per cent of Somalis are under 30 and half of the population is under 15, Al-Shabaab has a vast reservoir for potential recruiting. Interference by Somalia's neighbours, widespread corruption by politicians, high unemployment, fractured and flawed statebuilding, and external exploitation have rendered once-promising Somalia a failed state and enabled the emergence of Al-Shabaab.

State failure alone cannot explain the root causes of radicalization and violent extremism in Somalia. Both the internal and external factors that contributed to the rise and resilience of Al-Shabaab must be examined. Particular attention should be paid to the nature as well as the effect of Al-Shabaab's ideology, and its communication techniques. Similarly, the absence or ineffectiveness of strategies deployed by religious actors to provide a counternarrative, gaps in governance in Somalia, and the impact of external actors, should all be closely scrutinized.

Scope and Limitations of the Study

Research was conducted in seven geographically relevant and diverse Somali cities: Baidoa, Beledweyne, Bosaso, Burco, Galkacyo, Kismayo, and Mogadishu. Due to the nature of the youth radicalization being studied, local communities across the seven locations were very sensitive about the research. Some potential respondents stated that they feared reprisal from Al-Shabaab, whereas others suspected the researchers were engaged in intelligence gathering. Some of the interviewees consulted also expressed frustration regarding the multiple and repeated surveys conducted by different organizations who then never return to address the issues faced by communities. In order to overcome the reluctance encountered, the research team relied on the assistance of local partners to invite influential and credible spokespersons to communities to support the research activities. Prior to conducting the research, the team assured local authorities and target groups that the research is being carried out by an independent researcher. In some locations, it was difficult to contact representatives of local authorities, as there were no functioning systems in place.

Findings on the Root Causes of Radicalization

This paper considers the root causes of radicalization as falling into the following broad, interrelated categories, which are considered below: weak governance and state fragility; political injustice; socio-economic injustice; injustices perpetrated though the courts; and the presence of foreign troops.

Weak Governance and State Fragility

Weak governance and state fragility in Somalia are the primary causes of youth radicalization. According to respondents, radicalization is a direct consequence of the prolonged leadership gap in the country, particularly in regard to security, governance and the provision of justice. In contrast, Al-Shabaab's success is seen as a result of its ability to establish effective security and justice systems in the territories it controls, and to put in place mediation and conflict resolution mechanisms among warring clans, resulting in a drastic reduction of clan-based armed conflicts.[2] Al-Shabaab has also exported mobile courts to areas adjacent to government-controlled cities and towns for arbitration of commercial and land disputes. Rather than this being the benevolent provision of services on the part of Al-Shabaab, getting closer to where the bulk of citizenry lives enables Al-Shabaab to generate revenue.

Political Injustice

The prevalence of injustices dominated the focus group discussions. Respondents listed forms of injustice most prevalent in the country. They started with the political marginalization of certain clans, describing the 4.5 formula as a humiliating form of power sharing in the country, one that leaves out a whole set of clans, offering preferential treatment to others. Under-representation is an issue that fuels the sense of injustice. Some Islamic movements also feel under-represented or entirely unrepresented in power-sharing arrangements, because the political framework in Somalia is dominated by

Western ideals of liberal democracy, which leaves minimal political space available to the political Islamists.

Respondents articulated that many young people feel politically excluded, with the majority of government officials being from the older generation, while over 70 per cent of the total population is under 30 years of age. In contrast, Al-Shabaab provides leadership opportunities for youth. Al-Shabaab's operations are led by young people, and they have key roles, such as undertaking daring raids against AMISOM garrisons or storming government facilities or public spaces frequented by government personnel. The respondents stated that foreigners provide coaching and training of a military and ideological nature to younger members of Al-Shabaab so they can be more effective in their operations and propaganda. This trend has begun to dwindle due to the division between the local and international fighters within Al-Shabaab and the subsequent suppression of the latter.[3]

Socio-economic Injustice

Respondents put forward many potential socio-economic reasons for radicalization. For example, for successive transitional and non-transitional governments (and even in local governments), the looting of public resources is regarded as an open secret. Certain wealthy business people, with the endorsement of corrupt politicians, are controlling many productive sectors of the economy, and public lands have been distributed for private use. Respondents complained about major improprieties involving top government officials in league with foreign firms engaging in transactions that are secretive, lopsided and exploitative and that compromise national sovereignty, often in critical sectors such as infrastructure and natural resources. This actual and perceived pillaging has induced resentment among the public and, in particular, the younger generation, many of whom remain jobless despite witnessing the rapid emergence of many wealthy people. The result is a relatively aggressive and violent attitude toward foreigners and public officials. The respondents further mentioned that many youths are convinced politicians work to secure contracts solely to benefit themselves, their families, clans, and political allies, and do not care about the youth population, many of whom are deprived of the most basic necessities of life.

Some Somalis also believe that foreign business interests are facilitated without any direct benefit for the general population. It is asserted that people in power typically secure financial rewards or political backing. Many minority clans feel exploited and marginalized, as they are treated as second-class citizens and are often relegated to menial jobs. For instance, some of these clans face deep-rooted discrimination preventing them from intermarrying with other clans. Others do not have a say about how economic opportunities and political power in their localities are dispensed. These socio-economic inequalities have intensified Al-Shabaab's success in terms of recruitment among marginalized clans and communities, especially those found in south-central Somalia. The group has been able to recruit not only among clans that have long been subjugated, but also in marginalized communities within the mainstream clans.

While empowerment is therefore a key motivation for youth to join Al-Shabaab in many communities, particularly in south-central Somalia, political and ideological motivations may be a more significant factor for those who come from relatively stable places such as Somaliland and Puntland.

Injustice in the Courts

Many respondents believe that injustices are inherent to the Somali court system. The system is supposed to be run by legal professionals. However, unfortunately, in many jurisdictions, judges and prosecutors are not selected on the basis of merit. Respondents complained about the bribes demanded by top judges and prosecutors in return for justice. It was suggested throughout the discussions that some suspects and guilty individuals are routinely released because they belong to an armed clan or have paid money, while others are detained without due process and their release becomes conditional on paying a bribe.

A further example of corruption affects land disputes, which are seen as commonly settled on the basis of who pays the most during legal proceedings. Al-Shabaab has taken advantage of the anger arising from the judicial vacuum and pervasive injustices. The group has managed to respond to the community's need for justice, specifically in the areas of land and property disputes, commercial disagreements, and access to natural resources (particularly pasture and water), discrimination against unarmed clans, unlawful arrests, detention, extortion, and killings among the civilian population. At one point during the data collection process, a respondent mentioned that a judge in Mogadishu had advised him to seek justice for his case in Al-Shabaab courts.[4]

Respondents observed that there is no justice available in the regional court, or even the federal high court, but that it is a "market place" where justice is for sale and the highest bidder obtains "justice". Thus, if the person pushing for a case is poor, they receive little attention, being subjected to repeated postponements of hearings, until the victim is forced to forfeit his or her pursuit of justice. Overall, grievances generated by this flawed court system may have compelled many people to join Al-Shabaab.

The Presence of Foreign Troops

The notion that the country is in some way under occupation resonated with respondents in all seven cities. Experience from other settings supports the argument that there is a direct correlation between external intervention and intense radicalization. The author Robert Pape explains that there were no insurgents using suicide terrorism in Afghanistan, Iraq, and Somalia before the intervention of foreign troops in 2001, 2003, and 2006, respectively.[5] Many respondents pointed to the intervention of neighbouring countries like Ethiopia and Kenya, and expressed the view that Ethiopian troops as part of AMISOM may have augmented the insurgency. They also cite the notable salary disparity between the rates paid to soldiers serving with AMISOM and the Somali National Army: US$900 per month for the former and as little as US$100 for the latter, which is sometimes not paid for months. Consequently, Somali armed forces have lost morale and begun to prey on the citizens they were recruited to protect. The Somali police force, which operates closer to citizens, is ranked as the seventh most corrupt police force in the world, at a time when Somalia is in dire need of reliable law enforcement.[6] Respondents also underlined the issue of mistreatment of ordinary civilians by AMISOM troops; for example, indiscriminate shootings, armoured vehicles running over roadside traders and pedestrians, and the alleged illegal selling of weapons to private individuals.

Conclusions and Recommendations

- The Somali Federal Government should reform current executive institutions to make them inclusive, accountable, and transparent, so as to perform the core functions of the state while focusing on public service delivery and addressing the deep-rooted collective and individual grievances against government policies and practices, which are mainly attributable to prevailing political, social, economic, and legal injustices across the country. Such reforms would enable and encourage citizens to develop grassroots initiatives to promote peace, security, and development.

- While AMISOM and its international partners have sacrificed human and financial resources to restore peace and security in Somalia, which is appreciated by the majority of Somalis, it has become obvious that AMISOM can never be a substitute for Somalia's defence forces. Therefore, there should be a clear and well-thought-out timeline for AMISOM's eventual exit strategy. In the meantime, AMISOM must respond to the allegations made against its soldiers by Somali citizens, as AMISOM abuses could easily serve to strengthen Al-Shabaab's argument that the mission is in Somalia to harm rather than help Somalis.

- The fact that Somalia has developed a national CVE strategy is remarkable. For the time being it can serve as a useful guide for policy-making, but in-depth research and analysis are required on what measures will be effective in Somalia's context. It is extremely important that Somalia's Federal Government, in cooperation with Federal Member States, rapidly develops a national de-radicalization curriculum. The curriculum should be based on universal values of tolerance and peace, demonstrate acceptance of disengaged combatants and vulnerable youth in Somalia, and emphasize the role of women in peace and security.

- Ten years have elapsed since the war against Al-Shabaab first began, and although some significant gains have been achieved, ruling out the possibility of the organization presenting an existential threat to the country, the reality is that Al-Shabaab remains a force to be reckoned with. Therefore, recognizing that it may not be possible to comprehensively defeat Al-Shabaab, it would be advisable to explore the potential of genuine negotiations to end the conflict.

- Since one of the principal contributors to youth radicalization is unemployment, there must be a robust campaign to develop youth-focused programming, starting with the establishment of vocational schools to provide technical training for youths who need skills to empower them to earn income and become an internal resource for the reconstruction and development of Somalia. This is also vital because the country urgently needs a skilled workforce, having suffered a protracted brain drain and generated few skilled workers over the past 27 years.

- Somalia's counter-terrorism strategy must be revisited to balance the protection of citizens with the preservation of human rights. Parallel counterterrorism strategies, implemented by foreign agencies in Somalia, may compromise national sovereignty, and, given cases of torture, execution, and indefinite detention without due process, potentially breach international law governing armed conflict.

- Various national actors and international stakeholders have joined hands to defeat Al-Shabaab. They have mitigated the threat the group poses by killing senior leaders and recapturing strategic strongholds, making it hard for the group to radicalize as many youths as it did several years ago. However, the reality is that Al-Shabaab remains a powerful force, and as long as it controls territory in Somalia the group will be able to radicalize and recruit young Somalis. In the absence of root-and-branch reform, the Somali Federal Government, along with its international partners, faces a clear choice: either wage all-out war against Al-Shabaab to recapture the remaining territories it controls, as the Sri Lankan government did with the Tamil Tigers, or explore genuine negotiations with Al-Shabaab, as the United Kingdom did with the Irish Republican Army, to end the longstanding conflict there. This author favours the latter proposition.

AL-SHABAAB'S YOUTH RECRUITMENT PROJECT

Mohamed Haji Abdullahi "Ingiriis"

Author

Mohamed Haji Abdullahi "Ingiriis" is a PhD Candidate in the Faculty of History, University of Oxford. He is also a Research Associate in the African Leadership Centre, King's College London.

Summary

Although Al-Shabaab recruits both Somalis inside of Somalia and in the diaspora, the militant movement has increasingly recruited more local Somali youths than diaspora Somalis or non-Somalis. This is quite unlike other militant movements in Africa and Asia. Why is this? The recruitment methods of Al-Shabaab are both unique and universal. They are unique because the group solicits support from diverse youth who, due to a confluence of factors, join the insurgency movement in various ways. The group's methods are universal because it recruits not only Somalis in Somalia or in the diaspora but also Muslims and Muslim converts around the world.

This pattern appears unmatched by its nemesis, the Federal Government of Somalia in Mogadishu. The Federal Government should come up with new innovative approaches to challenge the trends and trajectories allowing

Al-Shabaab not only to successfully recruit but to sustain itself. The Federal Government should present a concrete and comprehensive economic and political plan to engage with Al-Shabaab rather than sticking to the rhetoric of "flushing it out" militarily. This has been unsuccessful since 2007, when the movement came across as a liberating force against the Ethiopian military presence in Mogadishu and other parts of southern Somalia.

Introduction

Many excellent studies have sought to investigate *Harakaat Al-Shabaab Al-Mujaahiduun* (henceforth Al-Shabaab), yet there is little in-depth study specifically examining the youth recruitment project of the insurgent movement. The literature on Al-Shabaab tends to emphasize the number of non-Somali recruits due to global security concerns, lest they return to their home countries and use the military experience gained from the Al-Shabaab training centres.[1] However, critical aspects of their local recruitment are overlooked, as the literature continues to concentrate on the external recruitment of Al-Shabaab, notably in Canada and Kenya, and identifies different methodologies of recruitment in specific contexts.[2] Somali youths are presented in the existing literature as having no alternative other than joining various armed groups (like Al-Shabaab) competing for economic resources. They are motivated by the spoils found through looting, banditry and robbery in war-torn societies, what David Keen calls "economics by other means".[3] The fact, however, is that the most salient and significant factors that explain recruitment—political marginalization and economic exclusion—are less explored.

This briefing paper examines the extent to which the push and pull factors of youth recruitment in Al-Shabaab have reinforced radicalization in Somalia. Whereas the push factors are facilitated by negative dynamics, such as the hostile environment and indoctrination, the pull factors are reinforced by issues of identity, ideology and economic exclusion. Methodologically, the briefing paper is based on intensive one-on-one and group interviews with former Al-Shabaab defectors.[4] In addition to various Somali sources, the article was also informed by field-based qualitative ethnographic research carried out between May 2015 and August 2016, except with brief intervals.

Scholars examining Al-Shabaab often approach and interview current and former major figures of the movement over the phone, but they tend to overlook the voices of young defectors of Al-Shabaab.[5] New ways of gathering empirically-grounded oral data are indeed necessary to understanding how youth join Al-Shabaab and how they are attracted to the movement.

Understanding Al-Shabaab from various angles through an empirically-grounded analysis is crucial for two reasons. First, it will help the Somali government to find ways of tackling the threats posed by ongoing insurgency activities. Second, it will contribute to the efforts of creating peace and stability in southern Somalia. In the following sections, the main reasons why many young Somalis join Al-Shabaab are identified by analysing four clusters: (1) economic vulnerability, (2) social injustice, (3) environment and demography, and (4) political exclusion.

Perspectives of Youth Recruitment

Why do many youths decide to join Al-Shabaab? Where do they mostly go to join? And how and when do they join? And why are young men more prone to radicalization in southern Somalia than in other areas? The main question is not how they joined but why. According to recent literature, young Somalis are vulnerable to being recruited because of the desperate impoverished situation in southern Somalia.[6] It is sometimes assumed that recruits are poor unemployed orphaned youths acting as "fortune-seekers" in opportunistic banditry, recruited from marginalized communities by armed groups.[7] But this is not a sufficient explanation of why many youths involve themselves in violent conflict and insurgency.

A prominent case in point was the late powerful leader of Al-Shabaab, Abdi Ahmed Godane, known as Abu Zubeyr, himself a young man in his mid-thirties, who hailed from north-western Somalia (present-day Somaliland). The level of youth emigration to Europe has recently been higher in Somaliland than in southern Somalia.[8] Despite unemployment and impoverishment, unemployed youths in Isha Boorame, one of the poorest neighbourhoods in Hargeisa, Somaliland in north-west Somalia, where many youths live in poorer conditions but in a more peaceful environment than in southern Somalia, would not dare to travel to southern Somalia to join Al-Shabaab.[9] Thus, this is an indication of other salient factors except impoverishment that push youths to join the insurgency.

It is worthy of note, however, that Al-Shabaab has attempted to recruit from Somaliland youth on several occasions in the last ten years and recently sent a whole armed brigade, mostly comprising young men and children, to Puntland in 2015. It must also be recognized that many in the rank and file of Al-Shabaab were unemployed impoverished youths—or, much worse, orphans lacking families or relatives able to take care of them—who found good opportunities within the movement to improve their lives.

Indeed, the dominant argument in the existing literature is that unemployment pushes Somali youths to join Al-Shabaab. From this perspective, many youths can find no alternative other than joining various armed groups competing for economic resources. At the height of the Somali civil war in the 1990s, when security was generally privatized, many private businessmen hired armed youths to provide protection to foreign international aid agencies and generate money from them. This resonates with the deadly case of the "banana wars" between the American-owned Dole-Sombana banana company versus the Italian-owned Somali Fruit company in southern Somalia in 1995. The two companies blamed each other for arming formidable militias to wreak the profitable banana business out of statelessness.[10] In addition to the deadly competition between the foreign companies, local Somali factional armed groups and businessmen profiting from the war economy also used youth militias in the 2000s to fight each other.

Roland Marchal, who did some of the first field-based research in southern Somalia during the early 1990s, has published extensive reports in which he described the emergence of freelance armed youth being drawn into the war economy by politico-war entrepreneurs monopolising the informal economy—basically the only available resources of the country.[11] Other scholars have summarized the main reasons for joining armed resistance in Somalia as being protest, revenge, and material interests.[12] Stig Jarle Hansen and other scholars have noted Al-Shabaab's success in recruitment but have not fully explained how and why.[13]

Beyond Economics and Interest

Al-Shabaab's recruitment strategies are difficult to decipher as the reasons for joining the movement vary from one recruit to another. Recruiting youth into Al-Shabaab is flexible, depending as it does on the desires and determinations of those who join the insurgency movement. Local—rather than external—recruitment is less costly for Al-Shabaab and can take the form of forced recruitment, though this happens rarely.

Forced recruitment is conducted when Al-Shabaab's leadership feels increasingly threatened by external forces, such as the 2011 retreat from Mogadishu.[14] In March 2016, the case of Al-Shabaab's attack in Puntland in north-east Somalia, where the militant movement dispatched militias consisting of children, was a prominent case in point in terms of the uses or abuses of indoctrination and forceful recruitment to boast more fighters. Young and elderly fighters who were captured on the battlefront asserted on Somali television screens that they were either indoctrinated by their friends or conscripted by force by Al-Shabaab.[15] Aside from these statements, there are other various reasons, such as the prospects of paradise after martyrdom in the jihad. Indeed, the fact that youth radicalization also plays a decisive role cannot be underestimated. There is strong evidence that youth radicalization helps Al-Shabaab recruitment strategies—and theory identifies several ways in which youth can be radicalized which revolve around deprivation and poverty.[16]

In addition to the indoctrination process, most young men join Al-Shabaab for their own reasons and according to their desires, whether they feel grievances, seek power or look for personal gain. Al-Shabaab's strategy for youth recruitment, as one Somali from the diaspora would say, is like "when chickens come home to roost."

Drawing from a political economy perspective, Marchal maintains that joining Al-Shabaab "was a matter of necessity, not ideology".[17] However, the power of ideology in explaining recruitment should not be underestimated because there is a strong correlation between grievance, religion, clan and profits.[18] Recruits driven by extremist ideology or motivated by grievances are often not distinguished from those who are looking for power and profit.

There are reasons why some youths, feeling dispossessed, join Al-Shabaab, the most powerful of which are grievance-based motivations. Al-Shabaab exploits the growing grievances against "the government's lack of ability" to distribute power and resources equally among the Somali clans.[19] Young people joining the movement see the Mogadishu government and other mini-states in the country as ultra-predatory, based on patrimonial political machines, echoing the political metaphor of living off the public assets, which means watching others siphoning off public resources through economizing collapsed state institutions to serve personal interests.[20]

Many young men in Mogadishu complain about their perceived powerlessness and talk about the possibility of changing the status quo through violence. This resentment discourse is very strong among Al-Shabaab's fighting force.[21] No secular, nationalist narrative, in the Somali setting, can work against Al-Shabaab, such as the counter-ideological religious messages broadcasted regularly on government radio. Al-Shabaab employs powerful religious discourse to dominate the religious sphere. To counter the predominant Al-Shabaab religious narrative, the Federal Government enlisted higher *ulema* (religious scholars) but it could not chart a common and convincing, let alone alternative and authentic, narrative that could successfully overcome Al-Shabaab's compelling call for jihad against the West and its Somali partners.

Many Somalis continue to support Al-Shabaab purely for nationalist purposes. In Do'oleey, central Somalia, dozens of old men cheered in the presence of this author when they heard on the radio on that morning that Al-Shabaab had ambushed a convoy of Ethiopian forces, killing 19 of them at Leego, southern Somalia.[22] The attraction of Al-Shabaab to average elderly Somalis is illustrative of the significance of the nationalist cause and grievances against the neighbouring countries. Against this background, it is scarcely surprising that Ugandan leader Yoweri Museveni berated the Federal Government for the lack of a clear ideology to counter Al-Shabaab.[23]

Many Somali youths in Europe and America believe external powers have caused and continue to perpetuate the condition of Somalia as the most failed state on earth, captured by leaders who think for themselves rather than for their people. Paradoxically, some young men are thus joining Al-Shabaab for the sake of doing something to change the situation in south-central Somalia by punishing those Somalis and non-Somalis they deem to be perpetuating the protracted armed conflict. Somali youths often stand in front of the camera and talk about how they could change such an unnerving image of a failed state, which wounds their personal pride and national belonging.[24]

Indeed, in a recent speech, the former president of the Somali Central Bank Yusur Abraar powerfully highlighted the negative impact of maladministration and corruption.[25] Her reflections conform with the most recent conclusion by The Fund for Peace's Fragile States Index 2016, which has repeated for the eighth year in a row that Somalia remains the most failed and fragile state in the world.[26]

The desire of some young men to lead an adventurous life also plays a role in Al-Shabaab's recruitment success. Viewed from this perspective, Al-Shabaab appears to be the "anti-politics machine"[27] where teenage males could present their manhood. There are two types of such recruits within Al-Shabaab: the *qurbajoog* (diaspora) youth, who while they mostly lived in poor conditions in the West, are considered "privileged", and the *qorraxjoog* youth, literally meaning those Somali people who live under the sun, who are regarded as "poor" because of their local background.

The two youth groups differ in their aims and objectives for joining Al-Shabaab, yet their motivations have often been misunderstood. The youths from poor backgrounds have long been perceived as easy prey for recruiters from Al-Shabaab, whereas the youths from the diaspora background are labelled as innocent "brainwashed" youths remote from their "unbroken" families. Quite the contrary: evidence gathered from local former Al-Shabaab defectors suggest that the *qorraxjoog* boys are no less susceptible to being brainwashed and recruited into the movement than the *qurbajoog* boys, despite the supposed privileged background in the diaspora.[28]

There are other types of Al-Shabaab recruits, as explained by one local resident living in Afgooye town, just under 30 km away from Mogadishu:

> There are no educated men among these youths in the middle of Al-Shabaab. You find a child whose parents could not afford to pay their education; who came to the town from the rural areas; they are from rural areas, they are eager to have a name; urbanites are small in number and very few are educated. There are also others who want revenge because they have been displaced from their land, so a difficult life forced them to join [Al-Shabaab]. There are also others who want power and to become famous; others also who want money; you would see someone [from Al-Shabaab] say to you 'I was given US$200 dollars to carry out controlled bomb explosions'.[29]

This observation was also echoed by a senior Somali member of a "moderate" Islamist group opposing Al-Shabaab, who argued that there is no well-known Al-Shabaab member who had been a "well-attending religious person" before the emergence of Al-Shabaab.[30]

Conclusions

Previous studies have revealed the importance of ideology and individualism within Al-Shabaab,[31] but the group's recruitment remains diffuse and difficult to track. This briefing paper has discussed the various ways in which Al-Shabaab recruits fighters from Somali communities inhabiting the areas of war-torn southern Somalia that are broadly under its control. The paper looked at motivations and drivers of Al-Shabaab to inform policy discussions on youth recruitment.

A key question is: what prevents youths recruited by Al-Shabaab defecting to the government? According to one former Al-Shabaab defector, many recruits are wary of defecting to the government for fear of reprisals for the crimes they committed while fighting for Al-Shabaab.[32] As a result, they have no choice other than taking two routes: to stay in Al-Shabaab and wait for their final fate, or to flee and migrate to Asia (mainly Saudi Arabia and Yemen) or Europe by criss-crossing Sudan or Turkey.

Conversely, a small number of individuals with the Mogadishu government join Al-Shabaab because they have been involved in criminal activities within the army or security apparatus. Yet, this pattern was not as large as it was between 2009 and 2012, when many officers trained in Djibouti or Uganda by American, French, German and other trainers joined Al-Shabaab in senior positions after being found involved in criminal activities like selling army equipment to Al-Shabaab.[33]

Taking advantage of clan marginalization to advance its insurgency activities, Al-Shabaab encourages government defectors to resist political marginalization by using its call for jihad against aggressors and oppressors. Most recently, two government officers, with their military vehicles, defected to Al-Shabaab from their army stations in Afgooye.[34] This alternative defection between the government and Al-Shabaab warrants further investigation.

The briefing paper has examined the ways in which Al-Shabaab succeeds in its recruitment project. The evidence presented in this paper suggests that it is not necessarily unemployment or impoverishment, but other enduring underlying factors which are more prominent in southern Somalia than in other areas of the country. While the youths who joined and fought for Al-Shabaab as a militia have been driven by various factors, the most important factors in southern Somalia are political marginalization, economic exclusion and indoctrination, which all contribute to personal or communal grievances, which lead recruitment. The situation is exacerbated by clan favouritism, resulting in inclusion or exclusion. The existence of unequal political power and socio-economic balance has made young local Somali men prone to extremist ideologies of empowering marginalized clans and communities while punishing those who accumulated wealth through the government's patronage system.[35] Ultimately, political and socio-economic factors are used in Al-Shabaab's strategy or approach to attract recruits—and the issue undoubtedly deserves further empirical research.

Recommendations

- The Federal Government should consider creating a viable institution led by competent and credible technocrats to counter Al-Shabaab's recruitment efforts. There is a need to create a special branch within the police or a sub-agency that should deal specifically with Al-Shabaab defectors. Apart from the rehabilitation programme, there should be a whole package for creating jobs to support the defectors' reintegration into society.
- Government authorities should strive for strategies aimed at winning the minds and hearts of young men who joined or are joining Al-Shabaab. The

derogatory government terms like *"kuwa maskaxda laga xaday"* (those whose brain was stolen), *"kuwa nabad-diidka ah"* (those who reject peace), should be abandoned and replaced with carefully chosen reconciliatory words that attract and accommodate youth.

- Al-Shabaab can hardly be countered when the Federal Government is deeply implicated in economic inequality, social stratification, political marginalization, and power disproportionalities, of which certain clans and communities feel they are the victims. Federal Government authorities must reconsider and rethink ways in which they can resolve those grievances.

- This means that the symptoms of the Al-Shabaab syndrome should not be the principal consideration; rather, the focus should be the root causes of the syndrome. More than mere amnesty, offers are required to reduce the growing number of young men joining Al-Shabaab.

- It should be recognized that the best way to inform policy that seeks to counter Al-Shabaab's recruitment is to consult former members of the insurgency movement.

- Al-Shabaab defectors should be involved in a process of direct negotiation with the militant movement to help persuade their former colleagues that defecting to the government would mean better opportunities and more prospects for daily lives.

RIVALS IN GOVERNANCE

CIVIL ACTIVITIES OF AL-SHABAAB

Roland Marchal

Author

Dr Roland Marchal is Senior Research Fellow at the National Centre for Scientific Research (CNRS), based at the Centre for International Researches, Sciences-Po, Paris. He is a specialist in conflicts and politics in the Horn of Africa and Central Africa.

Summary

Al-Shabaab's ambition to rule Somalis means that it has to dedicate people and resources to govern large areas of the country and address governance issues. Since its membership is limited compared to the territory it rules, it uses different models of governance, some relying on fear and others on devolution of limited powers to some segments of the population. Contrary to common belief, Al-Shabaab not only secures the areas it controls, it also provides important public goods by managing public infrastructure, helping the destitute, and addressing important issues for the population such as disputes over family issues, inheritance, and property titles.

Introduction

Testimonies of the early days of Al-Shabaab in 2004 reveal an important internal debate. Some led by Aadan Haashi Faarah 'Ayroow had a militaristic understanding of what Al-Shabaab should be built for: killing spies and all opponents allied with Ethiopia and Western countries. This trend had the support of some Al-Qaida members such as Abu Talha al-Sudani, killed in early 2007.[1] This option spoke to the dangerous environment they had been living in for months or even years.

There was a second trend in the group that was more political and viewed its role as a political vanguard that would educate and lead society rather than just destroy their enemies and any dissenters. The death of 'Ayroow in May 2008 and the dramatic increase of territories and their inhabitants controlled by Al-Shabaab in the following months meant that Al-Shabaab could not escape its responsibilities and had to rule over large populations.

While emphasis has been put on Al-Shabaab's "coercive security", in other words, its capacity to maintain order by terrorizing people and exacting harsh punishments over the breach of basic regulations, little attention has been paid to less strategic policies that were not always instruments of control but were conceived as a step towards the kind of society Al-Shabaab wanted to see.[2]

In many regards, what follows could be a rough description of what the so-called Islamic State (IS) did in the areas of Somalia that it controlled after 2014. Broadly speaking, it corresponds to a certain vision of how society is managed in Saudi Arabia, though without the many tensions and compromises made in that society which create some space for virtual dissidence.[3]

What follows describes Al-Shabaab's intentions as they correspond to the reality on the ground, and illustrates a great variety of social responses to Al-Shabaab's stimuli. In certain areas, people played into Al-Shabaab's hands and civil activities flourished. In others, the distrust was such that Al-Shabaab could only do the minimum to stay in control.

Three main sectors have been selected here: preaching and education, organizing civil society, and justice. It would be wrong to assume that these activities took place in an amicable atmosphere, but it would be equally wrong to believe that the population remained uniformly opposed to all of Al-Shabaab's attempts to enforce its domination. Al-Shabaab offered paths to social promotion as does any authority for those who accept it and become its clients.

Dawa *and Religious Education*

Al-Shabaab does not have a utilitarian understanding of Islam—it believes what it says about religion. This means that *dawa* (preaching) is an important part of the duties that have to be carried out by the movement whenever they take over a village or a city.

It also points to a common misunderstanding: Westerners tend to overlook how Islamic Al-Shabaab can be. Al-Shabaab continues to use its Islamic credentials to legitimatize itself in the eyes of the population. Fear is used under conditions that make sense for believers, even if they disagree with such an understanding of Islam. As a consequence, whenever Al-Shabaab faces hostility from a population, it may call one of its religious authorities to discuss the issue with the people and ease tensions. This suggests that Al-Shabaab's religious figures are important, often more so than military commanders who can be easily replaced.

Dawa has an important role for Al-Shabaab, and requires a considerable amount of time in the mosque. Consequently, disapproval of Al-Shabaab may take the form of empty mosques to make the group feel a lack of popular sympathy. *Dawa* not only focuses on the latest military achievements of Al-Shabaab; it also provides a vision of what is happening elsewhere and reminds the public audience that mistakes should not be tolerated, but corrected. Though jihad is often mentioned, other Muslim duties are also highlighted, according to the calendar and the local situation. Paying taxes (to Al-Shabaab) and helping poor people are regularly brought up.

Al-Shabaab has also tried to invest in the religious education of children. The group considers sending children to a Quranic school a basic duty of any family. But Quranic teachers need to earn a living and many parents are unwilling to spend a lot on such schooling, reasoning that faith can manifest itself in other ways than reading the Holy Quran. Al-Shabaab has therefore been anxious to improve access to religious education and to improve the quality of teaching.

According to some testimonies, Al-Shabaab has tried to limit the number of students in Quranic classes to a maximum of 50 children. If parents are not able to pay the teacher enough money, Al-Shabaab will pay a supplement to allow the teaching to continue. Moreover, it organizes special sessions for the teachers, including refreshment courses and pedagogy. Al-Shabaab may emphasize jihad as a pillar of Islam, but are careful to reiterate that it is not the only activity which renders one a good Muslim. The teaching uses the Saudi curriculum, which also explains why parents have difficulty vocally opposing it.[4]

Until the emergence of IS and Boko Haram, Al-Shabaab had little interest in the normal school curriculum, which are often managed by pious Muslims or even Islamists. Recently, Al-Shabaab hardened its discourse on these schools and required them to give up the UNICEF curriculum (basically, the pre-war curriculum) and adopt another that was close to those followed in the Gulf states. Efforts should be made to verify the degree to which this decision has been enforced. Threats were publicly made against schools that did not accept this decision. However, it should be determined whether this was a general policy or a decision taken only by some *wilayat* (provincial) governors.

In many classes where the lectures are delivered in Arabic, the fluency of the teachers is so limited that after 30 minutes in Arabic, the teacher will fall back on Somali to sum up and explain what he is supposed to have taught. Al-Shabaab has no alternative to that situation: learning Arabic is a significant investment that few adults can afford due to their low salary and the lack of good Arabic teachers. Of course, teaching the Saudi curriculum does not make Al-Shabaab extremists.

We should be more concerned by some attitudes exalted by Al-Shabaab that are quickly adopted by the youth: the intolerance of dissenters; a dogmatic view on religious issues and a refusal to admit that others may have the right to differ on some specific religious viewpoints; and the idea that those in power know religion better than all others.

These attitudes may be altered: the same intolerant teenager could fall in love with Facebook and his smartphone. Youth may shift their views with the same speed that they accepted them. However, the overall impact may be significant. Tolerance and open-mindedness are the first two casualties in this ongoing cultural war.

Organizing Society and Keeping Elders at Bay

As analysed elsewhere, Al-Shabaab works to undermine any alternative source of moral and social authority in Somalia. Therefore, its policy towards clan elders is complex because it cannot afford to antagonize the whole of local society, but wants to make clear that people are ruled by the Sharia and not by *xeer* (customary law).[5]

Whenever a village is taken over, Al-Shabaab will gather the elders in front of the population, make some requests in terms of recruits, weapons, and sometimes taxes and then reminds all that Al-Shabaab will establish its rule according to Islamic law and that elders should not try to interfere, their reign being over. Elders will have to pledge *bayah* (allegiance) to Al-Shabaab, which is supposed to be their last public act as customary chiefs. Of course, the balance of force is not always in Al-Shabaab's favour, but the empowerment of elders is very rare and always a short-term policy to regain the support of a segment of the population or solve an immediate problem. Al-Shabaab's policy of ruling through Islamic law (not customary law) also prevents the elders of any given village from running their community; in some cases they are relocated in order to avoid the emergence of clan issues.

While elders are kept at bay, the fate of the local intellectuals is not much better. Al-Shabaab is often hostile to educated people who could seek to play an alternative role to the elders and lead the population. Those who want to be accepted will have to prove their readiness to endorse Al-Shabaab and keep quiet. Many prefer to leave and settle in Mogadishu or any big cities under AMISOM control.

If Al-Shabaab threatens certain social groups, it also promotes others, intending to organize women, teenagers, and traders in addition to other economic operators. The group also encourages marriages between its fighters and local girls. While such relations are usually forced, it appears to be an effective method of entering local society, knowing who is who and building a local leadership under Al-Shabaab's influence.[6] Obviously, such marriages may entail misery for the women concerned. However, they can also provide a social advantage because the wife may become a member, or even the chair, of the local women's committee, tasked with gathering women for religious meetings or collecting money to be distributed to the poorest families. For her relatives, the wedding means a higher level of protection in the case that Al-Shabaab members are investigating them.

A similar kind of committee is often set up to manage the market place. This committee is often deliberately comprised of relative unknowns, so as to include people who are useful to ensure honest trading, but are seen as irrelevant by the main economic operators. Members of the committee are not selected democratically. Rather, selection is in defiance of traditional practice, which would give the upper hand to men who belong to locally important clans. This means that the committee is scrutinized by Al-Shabaab and cannot act without its agreement. Its duties are to manage the market, ensure it functions cleanly, and make people aware of the taxation collected by Al-Shabaab. If need be, the committee also gathers money for rehabilitating community infrastructure or helping poor families or widows.

These committees serve as a powerful network to collect data on certain individuals and to police the area. They function as a panopticon that makes it hard for any opposition to gather and organize against Al-Shabaab.

Teenagers are also a strategic target for Al-Shabaab and resources are spent on spreading the idea that, sooner or later, they will have to support the group, whether by spying on their own community or joining local militias or even the core fighting force. However, the group, except in exceptional cases, is careful not to kidnap these young people because the population may not tolerate this. Forced conscription does happen but never in a systematic way.

Justice and Police

Al-Shabaab offers people something that has been long missing during the civil war: predictability. People know what Al-Shabaab expects from them. They learn the hard way to respect the prohibitions of this rudimentary Salafi legal system: no football, no movies, no music, and no dating. If they respect these prohibitions, they, in theory, have nothing to fear from Al-Shabaab. People may not be happy with the system, but they can survive.

Whenever Al-Shabaab takes over a city or a village, it first sets out to prove that its implementation of Sharia is uncompromising and inescapable. Usually, several *huduud*[7] are meted out in the first months in front of the local population that is obliged to gather to witness the execution or the amputation of limbs. Fear is an essential component of Al-Shabaab's governance.

But it would be wrong to assume that this is the only function of Al-Shabaab's courts. As in any human community, many problems arise and require settlement. Most often, the courts are busy with issues related to divorce, reimbursement of dowry, debt, business contracts, inheritance, and conflict over land.

People rely on Al-Shabaab for three main reasons. Firstly, Islamic law is widely seen as being incontestable, which is less the case regarding customary law or the law of the state. Secondly, Al-Shabaab magistrates are much less corrupt than state magistrates or the elders. Thirdly, which makes the real difference, Al-Shabaab enforces the judgements of its courts, while the elders have no power of that kind and the state courts often work independently from the police.

Al-Shabaab also acts when lay people make allegations of corruption. Al-Shabaab's Internal Security division, known as Amniyat, may investigate the case and decisions can be made to reverse a previous judgement and even to punish a judge. It is far from an ideal judicial system but, for most, compares favourably to the other available options.

Al-Shabaab courts also demonstrate seriousness in the way they investigate a case. They ask for testimonies and documents. They cross-check what parties declare at court. They even try to obtain official documents from the Siad Barre era to corroborate viewpoints. In short, they do what is required despite the obvious shortcomings created by war conditions. This transparency in the administration of justice does not go unnoticed by people.

This explains why in Lower Shabelle, farmers are ready to walk 30 km to attend the court and make their case. They do not go to Afgooye or Merka because they have no faith in a positive outcome. They also fear punishment for having interacted with the Somali government. Even people in Mogadishu go to Al-Shabaab courts in Lower Shabelle (particularly Torotoroow court) to open a case (often a land issue, debt, or business matter). If the defendant refuses to accept the court's involvement, Al-Shabaab sends messages and eventually an Amniyat cell may kidnap a member of his/her family to make clear that everyone has to comply with their court. The main advantage is that the court's decision is respected by all those involved in the case, because of the fear of reprisal.

This description begs a question: why does the government not act in the same way? Al-Shabaab's methods are basic, based on common sense more than judicial expertise, and understood by everyone. Why should the government not do the same, which would not require huge foreign funding and international legal experts? In 13 years of existence, the Somali government has been able to sell land to the rulers of the UAE, but has done little for the local population. The usual claim is that no one was living on the land that was sold to foreigners, but reports suggest that local communities were not consulted.

Yet, we should also not be too naïve. State laws have many advantages for people, especially women. Al-Shabaab makes judgements but no one knows for sure that the entire legal process might have been confirmed by a state court. Al-Shabaab's role in justice weakens the system as a whole and reminds people that they cannot escape war, even if fighting does not take place in their neighbourhood.

Conclusion

Al-Shabaab, as a politico-military organization, has to fulfil a number of duties that are rooted in the governance of the population it controls. It corresponds to priorities that one can identify in other Salafi movements such as IS.

Dawa is prominent among these and allows the movement to explain its actions and counter the Federal Government of Somalia's (FGS) propaganda while enhancing its own. This Salafi importance given to *dawa* also explains why Al-Shabaab commanders have been eager to improve the quality of the Quranic schools and the pedagogy of their teachers. Resources are poured into that sector because they represent an investment in the next generation, and policy-makers should be vigilant as to its long-term impact on youth.

Al-Shabaab claims a monopoly within the religious arena and does not accept any alternative source of authority. The Sharia, as understood by Al-Shabaab, prevails over any other legal system, either the customary law (*xeer*) or the state laws.

Elders have been edged out as Al-Shabaab appoints committees to deal with social functions and women's issues. Their objectives are twofold. These serve as a way to rule the population and avoid being seen as outsiders, and function as a network of people to eventually collect intelligence on their fellow citizens.

After 27 years of civil war, Al-Shabaab undoubtedly provides some kind of rule of law that allows people to get important day-to-day problems solved in a non-contentious way: especially divorce and disputes relating to inheritance, property titles, business issues, and debt.

Al-Shabaab may inspire fear and terror but it also delivers public goods. There is no way it can be defeated without responding to this challenge.

Recommendations

1. The challenges facing Al-Shabaab go beyond the military or security realm. Al-Shabaab's civic achievements do not explain why people support or do not support the group. However, the FGS should be aware that it is not the only actor engaged in a state-building project in Somalia and that Al-Shabaab may win a degree of legitimacy through achievements that the FGS is unable to realize.

2. Al-Shabaab's governance needs to be better assessed since it offers a counter-model to what the FGS claims to have achieved, with scant results so far. In particular, policy-makers should pay attention to the way Al-Shabaab devolves powers at the local level and allows some kind of local governance, which should be a goal of the current Somali government.

3. Al-Shabaab's judicial system should be analysed carefully because many of its decisions affect the day-to day life of the lay population and are well

received. Consideration should be given to updating Somali laws and making them more realistic for a population that has suffered much from the arbitrariness of the civil war.

4. Al-Shabaab is instrumental in reforming the social fabric of Somalia. One may disagree with its means and its priorities, but its relative successes show that the status quo is no longer acceptable. The question is: does the FGS have sufficient ambition and imagination to rise to this challenge?

CAN AL-SHABAAB DELIVER?

REALITY AND RHETORIC IN THE STRUGGLE FOR POWER

Richard Barrett

Author

Richard Barrett, Director of The Global Strategy Network, was the Coordinator of the United Nations Al-Qaida/Taliban Monitoring Team from 2004 to 2013. Subsequently he has been working on a UK-funded project that takes him on a regular basis to Somalia where he interacts with government officials, civil society organizations, and international officials based there.

Summary

Despite its globalist agenda, reinforced by its allegiance to Al-Qaida, Al-Shabaab is at its core an ethnic movement with its focus on Somalia. As such, it can only survive, let alone expand, by offering better security, better prospects, and better governance than the structures established by the Federal Government of Somalia (FGS). Initially, it may have done so, but having lost territory and resources as the federal authorities take firmer root, Al-Shabaab has had to find ways to stem its decline. It has done so by appealing to Somalis as Muslims to support its role in the global campaign against "Western aggression", while mounting attacks inside the country to undermine any appearance of growing stability, and attacking outside the country to dissuade Somalia's regional allies from continuing their support.

Al-Shabaab's goals are expressed in terms of religion. It appeals to a common, transnational Islamic identity rather than to any particular ethnicity. But as with any other group vying for power in Somalia, it has to operate within the environment it finds itself, and Somalis are more concerned about local issues. Currently the FGS is dominant and Al-Shabaab does not look like a viable alternative. Given the growing gap between what Al-Shabaab claims to stand for, and its ability to deliver, it is an opportune time to exploit the inherent divisions within the movement and reduce its influence still further. This may best be done by the FGS negotiating agreements with clans and key individuals currently supporting Al-Shabaab, while at the same time increasing its own capacity to provide security and deliver good governance. In doing so, the FGS will need to strengthen its concord with the regions. Although it will take military effort to defeat Al-Shabaab, the route to victory lies in a successful political strategy.

Introduction

This paper draws on interviews with Somali and non-Somali experts and desk-based research.[1] It starts from the premise that whatever Al-Shabaab claims are its inspiration and goals, it can only survive and prosper by attracting local support. This requires it to diverge from its central message of international "jihad". By understanding the origins of Al-Shabaab and the gap between its rhetoric and practice, the FGS and its allies can identify its non-military strengths and vulnerabilities. This knowledge will help any effort to bring Al-Shabaab into a political process or to reduce its influence to the point of irrelevance. Interviews and research behind this paper have attempted therefore to collect impressions of the internal tensions of Al-Shabaab and the apparent contradictions in its messaging. Given the opacity of the subject, the adaptability of Al-Shabaab, and the lack of first-hand accounts, the study can only represent one interpretation among many.

What Al-Shabaab Offers

Al-Shabaab had the dubious distinction in 2016 of being the most deadly terrorist group in Africa, killing even more people than Boko Haram on the other side of the continent.[2] Indeed, with Al-Shabaab behind the deaths of approximately 4,000 people, including its own members, 2016 marked its most lethal year ever. But its accelerated campaign of killing was born as much from its stagnation as a movement as from any increased ability to mount attacks. The main problem facing Al-Shabaab is that it is caught between the limited local appeal of its global agenda, and its inability to offer a coherent political programme for Somalia that is clearly more appealing than that offered by the FGS. Its fortunes vary more in relation to the progress and setbacks of the FGS, than as a result of its own campaign for support.

At the end of May 2017 Al-Shabaab released an hour-long video that stressed its role as part of the Al-Qaida-led resistance to what it claims to be a global attack on Islam led by the United States.[3] Like Al-Qaida, it argues that it is the obligatory duty of every Muslim to fight in defence of Muslim lands and recover the wealth and territory that have been lost. Although the United States is cast as the main enemy, the video also says that AMISOM troop-contributing countries are no different. It describes the fight in Somalia as merely one part of the worldwide campaign.

Somali contact with Al-Qaida dates back to the 1980s when a handful of Somalis joined the fight against the Soviet occupation of Afghanistan. Others with similar views established Al-Ittihad Al-Islami (AIAI), which received support in due course from Al-Qaida in East Africa. After the collapse of AIAI in the late 1990s, the Union of Islamic Courts (UIC) attracted many of its followers, but a second wave of militants, including several future leaders of Al-Shabaab, went briefly to Afghanistan in 2001 and 2002.

In 2005, a group of Afghan veterans, ex-AIAI members and East African Al-Qaida supporters set up a militia to support the UIC and in 2006 adopted the name Al-Shabaab. Following the defeat of the UIC in December 2006 by the Transitional Federal Government (TFG), with considerable help from Ethiopia, Al-Shabaab grew to become the principal expression of opposition, both to the presence of Ethiopian troops and to the corrupt and predatory practices of the TFG. In these circumstances, the Al-Qaida-esque narrative of protecting Muslim identity and ensuring Islamic practice appealed to some Somalis, even if they regarded their tribal or ethnic identity as more important than their religious one.

Al-Shabaab first announced its support for Al-Qaida in September 2009.[4] Usama bin Laden decided however that the relationship should remain informal and unadvertised and it was not until February 2012, soon after bin Laden's death, that Al-Shabaab became an Al-Qaida affiliate. In practice, despite supporting Al-Qaida's global campaign, Ahmed Abdi Godane (aka Mukhtar Abu al-Zubayr) the then-leader of Al-Shabaab, focused his external activities on neighbours, particularly those who had sent troops to support the government. Significantly, while Al-Shabaab's close relationship with Al-Qaida in the Arabian Peninsula has provided logistical support and a potential safe haven, it has not led to joint operations.

The withdrawal of Ethiopian troops in early 2009 did little to lessen support for Al-Shabaab, even though it removed one pillar of its appeal. But internal disputes over ideological objectives, strategy and tactics increased, in particular the argument over whether Al-Shabaab was a national insurgency or part of a global movement. As a result, while Al-Shabaab continued to develop its capacity to communicate, its message became confused and began to lose impact; and it did not help that supporters in the diaspora also divided along similar lines. Nonetheless, Al-Shabaab took control of more territory and operated as a successful alternative government by providing security and justice, and by resolving clan disputes.

In 2010, Al-Shabaab merged with the more outwardly nationalist opposition group Hizbul Islam, led by Hassan Dahir Aweys, formerly head of AIAI. The merger was more a surrender than a partnership, and disputes over leadership, direction and the role of foreigners led to Aweys seeking refuge with the Federal Government in 2013. This further eroded Al-Shabaab's popular support.

Attacks such as in Kampala in 2010 and Nairobi in 2013 did not signal a fundamental change in Al-Shabaab's policy.[5] Al-Shabaab remained a local movement, even after Godane reorganized his forces to promote external attacks in late 2013, and then called for jihad against Ethiopia in March 2014.[6] This parochialism continued to cause friction between the Somali leadership and the more committed Al-Qaida supporters, such as Fazul Abdullah Mohammed, a hard-core Al-Qaida leader from the Comoros who was killed in 2011, and foreign fighters such as Omar Hammami, an American killed by Al-Shabaab in 2013.

What Al-Shabaab Delivers

Al-Shabaab's call for an Islamic state that would stretch beyond Somalia has turned out to be more of an aspiration than a core objective. Some of the original Afghan veterans who might have pushed for a more global orientation, such as Adan Hashi Ayro, have died in combat; Godane eliminated others, such as Ibrahim al-Afghani, whom he saw as rivals; while members of smaller groups, such as Mukhtar Robow, a one-time deputy leader of Al-Shabaab, remained in an uneasy relationship with the organization and its leadership. Somalis who support a broader battle now join other affiliates of Al-Qaida, or the so-called Islamic State.[7]

Outside Somalia, Al-Shabaab has found most support from ethnic Somalis in the region, especially in Kenya, where it has managed to tap into the deep racial and religious fissures in the country.[8] But although Al-Shabaab has recruited disaffected Kenyans, especially vulnerable young men in prisons, with the prospect of regaining control over what it describes as "occupied Muslim lands," its objective is also to boost Al-Shabaab's manpower in Somalia. Attacks in Kenya aim to encourage Kenya to withdraw its troops from AMISOM, rather than create a greater Somalia.

Al-Shabaab leaders have recognized that Somalis in Somalia, like people everywhere, are more interested in their own immediate circumstances than in supporting more remote objectives that provide no obvious or immediate benefit. Following the Ethiopian military intervention at the end of 2006, Al-Shabaab offered an appealing package of organization at a time of chaos; the resolution of basic disputes over land and water at a time when force too often determined ownership; religious principles as a way to guide decision-making at a time when cronyism and corruption were rampant; and national interest over the interests of clans or foreigners.

To an extent Al-Shabaab still serves these functions, but far less convincingly. The reality of Somalia and the gradual increase in the reach and effectiveness of the Federal Government have challenged the group's relevance. Ahmed Omar Diiriye (Abu Ubaydah), the group's leader since the death of Godane in September 2014, has had to pull together a movement that tends towards division.[9] Al-Shabaab was born of conflict and disorder; its advantage over its rivals was an ability to provide a degree of stability based on principles that all Somalis could support—to some extent. The identity it offered was inclusive, putting ethnic Somali origin over clan membership, and adherence to Islam over nationality. Al-Shabaab has been able to rise above clan politics more than other organizations and has managed to place people in authority in areas where their clan does not have a significant presence; but ultimately it does not have the capacity to control vast areas of rural Somalia without seeking the support of local elders.

The clan divisions in the country are a deeply embedded reality and offer a more immediate and familiar structure than an Islamic system that demands adherence to a narrow set of rules and acceptance of a way of life that has more cultural affinity with the Arabian Gulf than the Horn of Africa. Godane and now Diiriye have not been able to fashion a manifesto with widespread support. They have had to surround themselves with a tight-knit group of close supporters, none of whom can be sure of their future. Anyone who appears to be creating a power base is likely to be moved or struck down; orders must be obeyed, and loyalty to the leadership must be unquestioning. The glue that holds Al-Shabaab together is as much fear as it is ideology.

Uncertainty and frustration within the movement have also allowed the so-called Islamic State (IS) to challenge it for members. A video released by the Islamic State in March 2015 argued that as both groups faced the same enemy, Al-Shabaab should swear allegiance to Abu Bakr al-Baghdadi, the IS "caliph". The subsequent defection of a small group of Al-Shabaab members led by Sheikh Abdi Qadir Mumin in October 2015 created an alternative destination both for possible Al-Shabaab recruits and for members who wished to leave but would not defect to the government. The creation and survival of an IS offshoot has again highlighted the weakness of Al-Shabaab's ideological cohesion,[10] and challenged its transnational agenda.

Al-Shabaab delivers a form of governance inside the predominantly rural areas it controls, while it attempts to sustain political relevance by attacking rival militias, AMISOM and FGS forces beyond them. The election of President Farmaajo in February 2017, with cross-clan support, challenged Al-Shabaab's narrative that it alone can rise above mutually exclusive clan interests. In reaction, Al-Shabaab significantly increased the tempo of its attacks, directing them against tribal elders who participated in the election, as well as traditional political, intelligence, police and armed forces targets. Even though bombings and killings help Al-Shabaab promote the idea that the FGS is unable to offer security, even in the capital, and the assassination of elders undermines traditional systems of power-broking, they do not pose an existential threat to the FGS. Al-Shabaab is no doubt hoping that war-weariness, public anxiety and uncertainty about the future will allow it over time to regain the prominence it enjoyed in 2009, but at present this is a very distant prospect, and it cannot do so through insurgent and terrorist tactics alone. It must gain wider public acceptability.

The distinction between FGS supporters and Al-Shabaab supporters is not easily drawn. Some politicians,[11] businessmen and clan elders will have a foot in both camps, and even members of the security forces may spend part of their time with one side and part with the other. Clans have sought to infiltrate the movement with their members.[12] At the same time, clans secure senior positions on the Federal Government side to ensure that they can gain advantage whoever comes out on top. The challenge for both Al-Shabaab and the FGS is to persuade people that they offer a better future for the country than their rival. In a more mature political system, the two sides might compete to demonstrate their ability to deliver state services, but instead the emphasis has been on ensuring that the other side is unable to do so.

Where Al-Shabaab is in control, it offers justice through Sharia courts, though not always in strict accordance with Sharia law; it raises taxes and levies, though not always according to the rules it espouses; it delivers aid, though not always without favouritism; it provides education, though not always imparting the skills that are most needed; it mediates between clans, though not always impartially; and it does not deliver these services evenly across all areas under its control. This is hardly surprising as Al-Shabaab faces the same problems as the FGS, and since losing control of the cities has fewer educated members to draw on to run its bureaucracy. In order to claim more legitimacy than the government, it argues that it operates in accordance with the teachings of Islam, whereas the FGS is under the influence of non-Muslim foreigners, but this claim weakens over time, with many Somalis seeing Al-Shabaab as even more subject to foreign influence. For example, Al-Shabaab made a point in April 2017 of appealing to Somali conservatism by claiming that unlike in government-held areas, where education is in any case severely underfunded, the curriculum in its schools would focus on Islamic education and be taught solely in Arabic.[13] But for people in a country facing all sorts of problems, including at the time a severe drought, piety and Salafist asceticism were not the first priorities.

Conclusions

Al-Shabaab's emphasis on its religious credentials is less persuasive in 2017 than it was ten years earlier when the presence of non-Muslim troops and foreign influence were more significant issues. Furthermore, Al-Shabaab's puritanical and literalist approach to religion is still at odds with the majority of Somali elders who have grown up in a more mystical, Sufi tradition. So too is its support for Al-Qaida, which to most Somalis appears irrelevant to their everyday needs and an unnecessary complication for an already fractured state.

To grow, Al-Shabaab would need to demonstrate the practical advantages of its rule and increase its popularity through a communications strategy that stresses its ability to deliver social benefits and good governance. At present it diverges from this objective by focusing on military victories that offer people little if any advantage and no promise of an eventual peace. The FGS has an advantage here, especially insofar as it can blame its lack of capacity to deliver governance on its need to devote resources to defeating Al-Shabaab.

Recommendations

The FGS should:

1. Deepen its knowledge and analysis of Al-Shabaab to understand and exploit the causes of friction within the movement;
2. Emphasize the irrelevance of Al-Shabaab's global agenda to the needs of Somalis;
3. Devote the maximum possible resources to education, and ensure that it reinforces local traditions and outlooks;
4. Ensure that its justice system is transparent and efficient, and comparable to or better than that offered by Al-Shabaab;
5. Improve the coherence of its security architecture and ensure cooperation and coordination between agencies based on clearly defined responsibilities enshrined in law;
6. Identify influential members of Al-Shabaab who may be interested in dialogue;
7. Avoid military campaigns that, if successful, cannot be sustained; and
8. Reassure regional powers that Somali nationalism is not a threat.

The international community should:

1. Ensure that capacity-building is consistent across programmes and focuses on governance;
2. Avoid drawing Somalia into regional disputes; and
3. Place more emphasis on the need for a political solution to Somalia's insurgency, rather than a purely military one.

Further Recommendation

Without a better understanding of Al-Shabaab, its strengths and weaknesses, the FGS will be unable to defeat it. Knowledge gained from defectors and other means is wasted unless properly stored and analysed. The National Security Office (NSO) should ensure this happens as part of its coordination role. It should also ensure that the right people get the right information at the right time. The NSO should also provide assessments that can inform strategic thinking, and should act as a knowledge base on Al-Shabaab. It should liaise with national and international partners to share information and demonstrate Somali excellence in this area of Somali national security.

The Ministry of Information could do more messaging to draw attention to Al-Shabaab's affiliation with Al-Qaida as a foreign group that promotes a foreign agenda. The FGS should invest in education, promoting a Somali identity and a traditional, non-Salafist interpretation of Islam. It should regulate madrasas to ensure they teach the national curriculum. UNICEF and other international organizations can provide expertise and assistance.

While maintaining military pressure on Al-Shabaab, the FGS should persuade its people and its allies that a Somali-led political process is the only way to achieve peace. The FGS should actively seek ways to weaken Al-Shabaab politically and economically, and avoid tolerating an "acceptable" level of violence. In order to widen its support—and weaken support for Al-Shabaab—the FGS should focus on enforcing the rule of law. Insofar as the FGS and Al-Shabaab are in competition, there should be no doubt as to which provides better governance.

IS ANYBODY LISTENING?

AL-SHABAAB'S COMMUNICATIONS

Mary Harper

Author

Mary Harper is the BBC's Africa Editor and a specialist on Somalia. She is the author of *Getting Somalia Wrong? Faith, War and Hope in a Shattered State* and is currently writing a book about Al-Shabaab. She is an advisor, research consultant, and expert witness on Somali-related issues.

Summary

Since Al-Shabaab's inception more than a decade ago, communications have played a central, indeed exaggerated, role in its strategy. The group has stated that the "media battle" is one of the most important elements of its campaign.[1] Al-Shabaab recognizes the media-savvy nature of Somalis for whom rapid information flows have always been crucial to their existence.

Those involved in counter-messaging have struggled to keep up with the group, which often grasps the initiative and is versatile and resilient. Some Somalis are astute and critical recipients of the multiple messages they receive, constantly shifting, evaluating, and prioritizing information. But many, especially the uneducated and those who have been through madrasas and similar institutions, are more impressionable.

Introduction

Given the author's 25 years of journalistic reporting on Somalia, and her wide range of media and other relevant contacts, including members of Al-Shabaab's public relations department, the focus of this paper is on communications. It examines the communications strategies and techniques of Al-Shabaab and other parties, and analyses how this information is received and what kind of impact it makes, if any.

The methodology combined desk research, the author's knowledge—built up over many years of reporting on Somalia—and fieldwork in south-central Somalia (Mogadishu and Baidoa), Somaliland (Hargeisa, Berbera, Bur'ao, Gebiley, Borama, Tog Wajaale, and rural areas), Ethiopia (Addis Ababa, Dire Dawa, Jigjiga, and rural areas), Kenya (Nairobi, Garissa, and Dadaab), and the United Kingdom (London, Birmingham, Sheffield, Bristol, Cardiff, and elsewhere). The research in Kenya was conducted in 2016 for a different project but is relevant to this paper.

A broad range of individuals was interviewed, mostly face-to-face. Some, including Al-Shabaab and interviewees in Gulf states, other parts of Somalia, Europe (outside the United Kingdom), and the United States, were communicated with by phone, Skype, WhatsApp, Imo, Telegram, Viber, Facebook, Twitter, Instagram, and Snapchat.

Interviewees comprised members of the Somali federal and regional governments (including three presidents); the security services (Somali and non-Somali); the United Nations; the diplomatic, civil society, aid, and business communities; religious groups, including Al-Shabaab itself; street-traders; taxi drivers; housewives; academics; musicians; writers; students; IDPs, refugees and asylum seekers; beggars, and others. Somali interviewees included members of majority and minority clans.

Many people asked to remain anonymous, as they feared recrimination from Al-Shabaab, the Somali authorities, and others. In order to protect those who contributed to this paper, all interviewees have been anonymized.

The Battle to be Heard

The Winners, the Losers and the Opportunists

"Al-Shabaab has won the propaganda war. It has been ahead of us right from the start."[2]

"I have received tens of thousands of dollars from international donors for counter-messaging projects which I know are almost entirely ineffective."[3]

"Information campaigns are pointless because hardly anybody pays any attention to them."[4]

These are just three of the many comments obtained from interviewees on the effectiveness of Al-Shabaab's communications machine compared with efforts to counter it. While the multiple parties involved in Somalia have expended significant funds, time, and manpower on information campaigns, many of those interviewed for this paper believe Al-Shabaab's communication strategy is significantly more successful than those of its competitors.

Despite, and perhaps because of, its military setbacks, Al-Shabaab continues to run a relatively slick, efficient and nimble information department. Its communications are often more compelling and relevant to its multiple audiences than those of its opponents. Counter-messaging may be a fairly cheap and easy part of the Countering Violent Extremism (CVE) effort, but there was a consensus amongst several interviewees that it is not working, and might never work.

According to a Western senior military official, some counter-messaging is entirely counter-productive, indeed dangerous, as it can draw recipients' attention to the existence and philosophy of violent Islamist extremism. He remarked how it can also highlight the failure of Al-Shabaab's competitors to provide adequate security, health services, employment, education, and entertainment, the lack of which can be factors in driving people towards the group.[5]

Interviewees were generally adept at recognizing counter-narrative messages funded or created by non-Somalis. In general, they reacted to them with hostility, sarcasm, amusement, or scathing cynicism. Some felt the messages are part of a neo-colonial project; others that they are pointless, and simply serve as a money-making industry for those involved.

Some Somali and non-Somali individuals involved in counter-messaging activities appear to believe in what they are doing, and to work hard and thoughtfully.[6] Others are more sceptical: "We distribute US-funded comic books and put up billboards promoting tolerance. Their impact is minimal. Nobody changes their minds about Al-Shabaab because of our billboards in Kismayo."[7] Some are cynical and say they are in it for personal profit. Some non-Somalis, especially those based in Somalia, say they enjoy the extra "danger money" and frisson of working in a conflict zone.[8] A number of Somalis involved in internationally funded information campaigns boasted about how effective they are at extracting money from donors: "I know which button to press. I have pressed the buttons of FGM, HIV, gender awareness and CVE. Now the most lucrative button is migration, where foreign funders have more money than they know what to do with."[9]

Media Operations

Much has been made of the slick, seductive media operations of violent Islamist movements, including Al-Shabaab, which was in some ways a pioneer amongst such groups in the use of social media, especially Twitter.[10] Less has been said, at least publicly, about the depth, reach and impact of Al-Shabaab's public relations arm.

In some respects, the group's communications department operates like a modern, international media body. The advent of the smart-phone, which serves as a one-stop-shop camera (stills and moving images), voice recorder, editing facility, transmitter and distributor, has enabled even the poorly resourced to produce and distribute relatively high-quality media on multiple platforms. It means Al-Shabaab can project an exaggerated, glossy image of itself and its activities, leading some people to believe it is more powerful than it really is. And if people believe Al-Shabaab is strong, it becomes so in reality, at least to a degree.

Al-Shabaab delivers specially tailored, multilingual information for its international, regional, national and local audiences, including funders and possible future recruits. It has cultivated "media stars" such as the now deceased Abu Mansoor al-Amriki, an American citizen who achieved cult status amongst would-be jihadists. Its videos, online magazines and other material currently feature Kenyans of Somali and non-Somali ethnicity, reflecting and perhaps exaggerating its presence in the country and its ability to recruit Kenyan nationals.

Al-Shabaab's media operations are highly agile. Its websites, films, and radio station, Al-Andalus, pop up in other locations, physical and virtual, almost as soon as they are shut down, as do those of its affiliates and sympathizers. In some ways, this is part of the group's appeal. Its audience derives excitement from playing cat-and-mouse games for the forbidden fruit of a graphic Al-Shabaab video, complete with rousing music, animation, blood, gore, and martyrs' testimonies.[11] The availability of cheap, reliable internet services in Somalia means Al-Shabaab material can "go viral in Baidoa"[12] and elsewhere, providing entertainment for bored youth who say they have nothing better to do: "The frequent explosions and lack of social activities here in Mogadishu mean I don't go out very often. I just sit in my room and watch YouTube videos."[13]

Al-Shabaab offers bespoke communication packages for individuals it wants to recruit, which often contain threats. People who have recently fled the group described its indoctrination and recruitment techniques, which range from long lectures in mosques, to films projected on large outdoor screens, to false promises of laptops, white Land Cruisers, and driving lessons.[14]

The group has a highly effective public relations department which targets specific well-placed journalists in the local, regional, and international media, including this author. No other group or individual connected with Somalia engages with the author as directly, reliably, and efficiently as Al-Shabaab. As far as the author is aware, the group does not claim attacks for which it is not responsible, although it has been known to exaggerate the numbers of dead and wounded, and the quantities of vehicles, arms, and ammunition seized.

Members of its communications team will call relentlessly, and text or email press releases written in good English, which are largely accurate and have correct datelines, catchy titles, and numbered paragraphs. If the press officer does not know the answer to a journalist's questions, he will say so, do his best to find out the information required, and call back once he has an answer. Al-Shabaab monitors media output and contacts journalists if they make mistakes in their reporting.[15]

This contrasts with the more hands-off approach of the Somali Government, AMISOM, the UN, and others involved with Somalia, who tend to send generic press releases which are often deleted unread from journalists' overcrowded inboxes.[16] Some communications specialists offer sophisticated training and advice to Al-Shabaab's many opponents, but in the author's experience, this has not been heeded effectively.[17]

Al-Shabaab threatens Somali journalists working in Somalia, the East and Horn of Africa, and further afield.[18] This can be face-to-face, by email, text message, or phone call from a withheld number. This Mogadishu-based journalist explained how he was threatened by a member of Al-Shabaab:

> A man approached me in a tea shop near the radio station where I worked. He asked why I had not broadcast as breaking news the full recording Al-Shabaab had released the previous night of its leader Ahmed Godane. It was 40 minutes long but I only played it for five or six minutes, and not as breaking news. The man threatened me and said next time I must play the entire recording. Otherwise I would pay the ultimate price.[19]

Another journalist explained how, after he broadcast a report on a failed Al-Shabaab attack, the militants abducted him and cut his chest open with a knife.[20] On at least one occasion, the group has infiltrated Somali media.[21] It also appears to have sympathizers working in international media houses.[22]

Although Al-Shabaab has benefited from modern communications technology, the internet has also served as a forum for people to criticize the group and provide alternative world views. There are frequent Twitter and Facebook "battles" between sympathizers and opponents of Al-Shabaab.[23]

Parallel Universes

Somalis are arguably one of the most media literate populations in Africa, having an enduring oral culture, a profound and active relationship with broadcasters, including the BBC, whose Somali service was 60 years old in 2017, and a "life or death" necessity of knowing what is happening around them. They have enthusiastically embraced digital media, with the number of Somali news websites exploding from 20 in 1998, to 527 in 2006, to 748 in 2014.[24] Many of these emanate from the diaspora.[25]

However, Somali "journalists", including those working for Al-Shabaab and its affiliates, are highly experienced creators of "fake news". Al-Shabaab presents distorted stories for all of its audiences. These include war movie/video-game genre films of its claimed military achievements,[26] largely aimed at international viewers and would-be recruits, funders, and sympathizers. For local consumption, it distributes glowing reports of its humanitarian work during times of drought, and rustic films of rural idylls, showing irrigation and bridge-building projects, Eid games, and happy farmers.[27]

Equally unrealistic are the sanitized, airbrushed images created for counter-narrative projects supported by Western states, including the #SomaliaRising and #MogadishuRising initiatives. "These are even more evil and unfair than Al-Shabaab's propaganda. They make Somalia look like a place where everybody spends their time on the beach, playing football and eating ice cream and lobster."[28] "I came back to Somalia because of these messages, after living abroad for nearly 20 years. The reality is completely different. I have had three near-misses from explosions, and part of my home was blown up in an Al-Shabaab attack."[29]

Much of Somali broadcast, print and digital media is also unreliable and untrustworthy. Members of the diaspora and local outlets often serve the interests of a particular region, clan, religious, or political group.[30] Many Somali media houses are corrupt, serving as little more than a money-making opportunity for the editors and journalists involved.[31] Media workers based overseas operate in relative safety and with near complete impunity.[32] The international media is also problematic as it tends to lack nuance, slipping into overly positive or negative stereotypes, and sometimes giving undue prominence to Al-Shabaab's activities.[33]

Many Somalis have a healthily sceptical attitude toward the media, and do not believe everything they are told.[34] But some, including some women and rural populations, are more impressionable.[35]

The New Cold War

A number of Somali interviewees expressed concern about the current state of education in the Somali territories. They said Gulf states have too much influence and are funding schools and universities which are "breeding the next generation of Taliban, they are doing the jihadis' job for them, whether they are Al-Shabaab, so-called Islamic State or Al-Qaida."[36] A high school student in Hargeisa explained how much happier she is now that she has moved permanently to Somaliland from London, where she was born and raised for the first 16 years of her life: "I came here less than a year ago and it is so beautiful. This is due to the religion. I no longer read Western books as they are against Islam. Now I wear the full niqab and follow my religion as closely as I can."[37]

There are some spaces, such as book fairs, cafes and music venues, which offer an opportunity for more marginalized Somalis, including women and youth, to be heard, although the author is not aware of many members of minority clans frequenting such places. They also provide a place for a broader range of ideas to be explored and for dominant, rigid norms to be challenged. However, these are under increased threat from religious conservatives, including in Somaliland.[38]

There are individuals who have formed their own opinions about Al-Shabaab, without being spoon-fed carefully crafted counter-narratives. For example, a man who recently left Al-Shabaab after six years as a foot-soldier explained how he came to realize the group was not fighting in the name of religion when he was ordered to kill an old man who could not walk, see, or hear.[39]

Conclusions

Although Al-Shabaab has suffered military setbacks, losing crucial territory and access to resources, its propaganda machine continues to thrive. Despite the significant resources poured into counter-messaging, Al-Shabaab remains ahead of the game in the communications war. It is possible that, the weaker it gets, the more committed the group will become to investing time and resources in its media operations. In this way, it is able to project an image of power and success. Even though this is only in the virtual world, many inside and outside Somalia are likely to perceive the group as bigger and stronger than it really is, and therefore to respond to it as such.

Some of the intended audiences of counter-messaging appear fully aware of who is behind these operations and who is profiting from them. In their present form, many of these messages do not appear to be making much of an impact, and may backfire at times.

Recommendations

These recommendations are drawn from the information and analysis in this paper but are not attributable to the author.

- The UN, AMISOM and other foreign parties should adopt a more hands-off approach to counter-messaging, especially the dishonest, glossy narratives around initiatives such as #SomaliaRising. Somalis are all too aware of who is behind such messaging, even if it is presented as "Somali-owned". In all likelihood, Al-Shabaab has insider knowledge of how these operations work.
- Allow genuinely home-grown alternatives to develop, even if they are rough around the edges and do not contain exactly the kind of messages desired by communications specialists. International actors should distance themselves in terms of funding, offering advice, and other forms of support.
- Focus on young male role models, preferably not from the diaspora. The popular singer, BK, is a case in point, as are young businessmen, students, activists and writers—as long as they are not sponsored, created, or highlighted by international actors.
- Learn to live with Al-Shabaab propaganda and to challenge it more effectively. The more effort is put into closing it down, the more it pops up and the more people become excited about trying to find the "forbidden fruit". Let the propaganda emerge, even interview members of Al-Shabaab in a robust, intelligent manner, as it is likely this will expose their weaknesses and inconsistencies.[40]
- More enthusiastic, focused and honest media briefings from Al-Shabaab's competitors, who could also come up with more interesting and varied stories to "sell to" national, regional and international media.

- More investment in education which promotes critical thinking and challenges the spoon-fed, rote-learning approach of many madrasas, some of which also serve as "holding pens" for children while their parents go out to work or to seek employment or livelihood assistance.[41] According to a recent survey, education is the second most important priority for Somalis, after security, with two-thirds of children out of school.[42]
- Educate Somalis how to be sceptical about all media. The global preoccupation with "fake news" provides a golden opportunity for this approach. Do not single out Al-Shabaab messaging, but simply include it amongst others. Otherwise Somalis are likely to pigeon-hole such an initiative as a Western-led counter-terror project.
- Improve the Somali media—a giant task. There have been countless workshops and other training projects for Somali journalists which appear to have had limited impact. One approach could be to embed talented, ethical, experienced Somali journalists on the shop floors of Somali media outlets, so people could learn from them on the job. Respected media organizations such as the BBC, VOA, and Al Jazeera could be encouraged to offer paid internships for Somali journalists.
- Increase practical, potentially life-saving messaging, such as noticing, avoiding, and reporting people who act suspiciously; how to respond if caught up in an attack; or what to do if you encounter a suspicious vehicle, bag, or other device. Such information might help alert people to the life-threatening activities of Al-Shabaab and therefore change perceptions. This is only likely to work if the authorities, especially the security forces (Somali and non-Somali) are perceived as more trustworthy, reliable, and effective than Al-Shabaab.
- Recognize that many people, especially those in areas directly affected by Al-Shabaab violence, do not join the group because of its propaganda, but because they lack alternative sources of income, protection activity, employment, and spiritual fulfilment.

ANATOMY OF COUNTER-JIHAD

COMMUNITY PERSPECTIVES ON REHABILITATION AND RECONCILIATION

Stig Jarle Hansen, Linnéa Gelot and *members of the ISHA human rights group*

Authors

Professor Stig Jarle Hansen is a Professor at the Department of International Environment and Development Studies, Norwegian University of Life Sciences. He is a specialist in jihadist war economies and Al-Shabaab.

Dr Linnéa Gelot is Associate Professor of Peace and Development Studies and a Senior Researcher at the Folke Bernadotte Academy, Sweden. She is a specialist in African conflict management.

Alin Hilowle is the Founder, Executive Director and Chairperson of the ISHA human rights group based in the Bay and Bakool area of Somalia.

Summary

According to a majority of respondents, communities in Bay and Bakool are prepared to speak out against Al-Shabaab and resist the group. However, respondents refrain from blaming people in the community for their various supporting roles concerning Al-Shabaab. Almost all respondents knew one or several persons from their own immediate families, clans, and communities who used to be or were still involved in some way with Al-Shabaab. Respondents expressed strong motivation to participate in inclusive reconciliation processes, and to work towards improved community cohesion, shared norms, social trust and the prevention of radicalization. Contextually appropriate reconciliation programmes can play an important role in repairing a history of communal violence and active and passive support for Al-Shabaab.[1]

Al-Shabaab enjoys semi-territorial control in the Bay and Bakool region. The involvement of sheikhs and clan elders is therefore all the more important as they wield considerable influence in communities and can strengthen countering violent extremism (CVE) efforts. Local sheikhs hold the key to counter religious indoctrination, but they must be drawn upon wisely. We recommend that a wide, inclusive approach is used, drawing upon a combination of different types of religious leaders, in which Sufi, Shafi'i, and Quietist/non-political Wahhabism are represented. The role of elders is also key; they are currently the best functioning early-warning network, as they often were the first to be warned about individuals becoming radicalized.

- We recommend initiating a reference group or advisory board on CVE consisting of local elders representing all clans in the area, and religious leaders for all denominations.
- A religious leader forum should be initiated to ensure appropriate teachings in schools and more broadly in local society.
- Rural security should be a major priority for the Special Representative of the UN Secretary-General (SRSG), the Federal Government of Somalia (FGS), and for the broader set of international donors and allies.

Introduction

This study of Bay/Bakool supports Stig Jarle Hansen's previous finding that CVE interventions must be cognizant of and tailored to regional/local conditions and that a people- or community-focused approach to CVE has a higher likelihood of success.[2]

We discuss three main issues:

1. Social mediation and rehabilitation resources and strategies in the Bay/ Bakool area.
2. Local perspectives on how to resist and overcome Al-Shabaab.

3. Perspectives on international, regional, and national requirements for security provision.

We base the study on qualitative data, gathering tools including focus-group discussions (FGD), semi-structured interviews, and meetings with key respondents. Collective views and general patterns referred to in this study rely on multiple sources, that is, all findings and recommendations have been rigorously triangulated. Gelot conducted two field missions, one in November–December 2016 and one in April 2017. She conducted FGDs and semi-structured interviews in Mogadishu and Baidoa with key think tank actors, CVE/PVE actors, intellectuals, youth leaders, women leaders, and traditional elders, and conducted follow-up interviews with senior UNSOM and IOM officials, ISWA politicians and ministers, select CVE/PVE partners, and donors. She interviewed one former member of Al-Shabaab in Baidoa prison (in total 54 respondents). ISHA conducted seven FGDs with traditional elders, religious leaders, women leaders, youth leaders, MPs, police, and the business community, as well as follow-up individual interviews with one representative from each category (55 respondents in total). The CVE actors we interviewed are involved in micro-level initiatives, such as grassroots nation-building, reconciliation and trauma-healing, and local governance efforts, but also vocational training for ex-members and disengaged fighters. Unsurprisingly, they do not share one definition of extremism nor one view of what makes their work CVE-relevant.

For this study, close collaboration with district-level authorities and community-level actors has been necessary. We express heartfelt thanks to Baidoa district commissioner, and all the respondents from Bay/Bakool area.

A Sense of Insecurity

Somalia is on the verge of establishing a federal state structure consisting of a central level and regional states, where substantial police forces will be established in the regional states. Alternative governance structures exist parallel to these structures in the form of clan leaders and leading segments of the patrilineal clan structure. These make up the only functioning justice system in the Somali countryside, where clan groupings settle crimes between them based on the tribal law, *xeer*. Insecurity is ripe, as police forces often go unpaid and sometimes predate on the local population. Al-Shabaab is seen by many as a more stable provider of justice than regional state and central justice institutions. "90 per cent of people here trust Al-Shabaab more than the regional

381

state to deliver justice," said an active CVE community respondent. Police often do not exist in the countryside, and the *xeer* is partly based around "balance of power" thinking, where strong clans can discriminate against weak minority clans.

Respondents highlighted a general feeling of insecurity. Firstly, Al-Shabaab remains successful in communicating its potential for violence. According to a respondent, Al-Shabaab is a psychological actor: "there is propaganda [about] spectacular acts of violence, but no real force." Defections from the regional state and central government contribute to the insecurity. As claimed by one respondent, "one day a special police officer and the next an Al-Shabaab operative, then back to being a beneficiary of a vocational programme, but when facing unemployment carr[ying] out a small job for Al-Shabaab." Several community actors also believe that Al-Shabaab gets information from Hormuud. Al-Shabaab is known for tracking down people and getting their mobile numbers from somewhere. Routinely, people receive anonymous calls whereby someone passes along a message on behalf of Al-Shabaab. The calls fulfil various functions: applying pressure to enforce a marriage proposal, demands for information/intelligence, extortion, death threats, and requests for specific services.

The nature of community recruitment by Al-Shabaab has also created additional layers of divisions and social challenges such as broken families (single-headed households) at the local level. As one respondent put it, Al-Shabaab has "killed our social institutions." Another spoke of the importance of community reconciliation, "We need to come together and forgive each other." In the place of local government, these actors have directed their efforts at families and community. One respondent said, "Al-Shabaab is everywhere, so we have to begin with families." One CVE actor concluded that even if the group's ideology is being defeated, the fear among ordinary people and the collusion of business circles and politicians remain daunting as well as the urgent need for education and employment.

Somalia's religious traditions have been uprooted over the last 40 years. During Siad Barre's dictatorship, religious leaders and traditional sheikhs were captured and killed on charges of radicalism. When the Somali government collapsed in 1991, Islamism from the Gulf countries was able to extend its influence in many parts of Somalia and respondents give rich illustrations of this gradual process in Bay/Bakool that accelerated mid-2000s, through the establishment of madrasas, orphanages, humanitarian relief organizations and charities, and the provisions of microcredits for businesses. People were taught that cultural practices such as making animal sacrifices or honouring sheikhs were un-Islamic, and that women had to change their dress code. These trends were also seen by many to have contributed to Al-Shabaab recruitment.

Al-Shabaab possesses an efficient propaganda apparatus. For a long time the group effectively claimed to wield the "correct" version of Islam. In trainings for minors, jihad videos and propaganda materials for example show that children bearing arms can protect and defend communities and become "heroes". Al-Shabaab also offers to promote reconciliation between warring clans.

The Dynamics of Semi-Territoriality

As highlighted by our respondents, Al-Shabaab's rise has been induced by major structural factors affecting Somali society, namely lack of security, lack of opportunity, clan conflicts, and lack of justice. One respondent summed this up, "Radicalism *is* lack of education, employment, and justice!" A strong pattern is that respondents refrain from blaming people in the community for their various supporting roles concerning Al-Shabaab. As mentioned earlier, almost all respondents knew at least one person from their own immediate families, clans and communities who used to be or were still involved in some way with Al-Shabaab. Involvement or support for the group covers a wide range of activities and includes lower-level and non-radical acts such as paying or collecting *zakat*, collecting supplies, living as an infiltrator in the community, or accepting services provided by Al-Shabaab such as justice provision or financial aid to run a market stand that doubles as a tax collection point. Respondents explain that these passive supporting acts are carried out because people fear for their lives and property. Hansen's concept of semi-territoriality is useful to explain the situation in Bay/Bakool.[3]

The concept describes a state where the jihadist organization wields large control over areas despite facing a superior military force, since the latter fails to provide full security, staying in the base areas sending out a limited number of patrols. In this situation, locals know that their primary interactions will be with Al-Shabaab. Overall, AMISOM and SNA joint operations can capture and hold a town, but they do not in normal circumstances pursue Al-Shabaab or protect the surrounding civilian settlements. SNA/special police with AMISOM and the Ethiopian army typically fail to permanently secure the local population. Al-Shabaab will reliably return after the government forces and its allies leave, thereby ensuring a form of loyalty as the local people fear reprisals. The Al-Shabaab presence and ability to tax are permanent enough to secure stable incomes for recruits—making opportunism and the desire for income more important for recruits, as well as the need for safety.[4]

Currently, ISWA has been "taken hostage" according to many respondents. The mobility of government representatives and traditional elders depends on the protection of AMISOM forces and Ethiopian National Defence Forces (ENDF). The authority of the elders has been damaged by their supportive role in the state formation process as they remain fully reliant on security escorts by AMISOM, combined with the Ethiopian political leverage in the region. Since a drawdown of AMISOM troop levels is being discussed, people are frustrated that federal and national security forces are unable to provide security.

The Somali government oversees approximately 3,000 special police forces known as *Darwish*, which are locally recruited. Some respondents were strongly supportive of *Darwish*, believing that their local connections make them highly motivated to pursue and defeat Al-Shabaab militants. However, it was also clear from interviews that the conduct and impact of *Darwish* have been uneven.

Communities need to see examples of professional conduct by the national security forces. The former Al-Shabaab member/prisoner explained how he hesitated to surrender for a long period because he feared that he would be tortured or shot depending on who, at what point in time, got a hold of him. This fear is well founded. The SNA in Bay/Bakool/Geddo is making progress but there have been repeated practices of shooting ("finishing off") those who surrender and torturing captives before they are handed over to the National Intelligence and Security Agency (NISA). The former member also feared the Ethiopian troops—there are community members who never find out what happened to family members who were detained by ENDF. He had also feared that if handed over to NISA, anything could happen. Notably, in prison the young man felt "freer than ever before" because as Al-Shabaab you are vigilant, "there is no life." Improving security forces' conduct, discipline and community relations is, according to respondents, the most efficient way to encourage higher levels of Al-Shabaab disengagement.

According to an SNA commander, the primary frustration was the need to militarily match the enemy, "We are ready to defeat them to protect our community!" However, partners are well aware of the corruption in the SNA (such as illegal checkpoints and protection rackets). Ammunition and supplies end up on local markets, and it is hard to substantiate if these are instances of opportunism by individual soldiers, or at company- or command-level. Al-Shabaab also probably uses bribes in the course of attacks, as repeatedly vehicles are cleared past AMISOM checkpoints and detonate shortly after. On this point, ENDF are perceived by the majority of respondents as a conflict actor (for some, an oppressor) in Bay/Bakool. Community leaders give detailed accounts of instances whereby ENDF and Al-Shabaab collude through, for instance, temporary and localized security "pacts".

In such a situation, where Al-Shabaab has semi-territorial control, it has been necessary to keep the group happy in order to stay alive. In some areas, Al-Shabaab has been the sole provider of regular incomes. It should be noted that Baidoa is influenced by such mechanisms. While the city is under the control of the regional state, the regions around it are not, and many Baidoa residents have relatives in these areas. They described how this affects the risk calculus at the personal level. Al-Shabaab's recruitment efforts were said to mainly target youth under 18 and minority clans. Most of the recruited youth in the region are from rural areas, goat or camel herders, and largely uneducated. They are vulnerable to the idea that you can transcend the difficulties of earthly life and "go to *Janna* [heaven] with your family." Marginalized clans are attracted by the alleged equality that global jihad brings, and Al-Shabaab thus becomes a solution to clan discrimination.[5]

One strongly held view among respondents was that a terrorist lens is one among other possible lenses, and should not overshadow the underlying fact that the reasons people join Al-Shabaab can be both related to economics and to the need for security.

What is Needed?

According to a majority of respondents, the community in Bay/Bakool is prepared to speak out against Al-Shabaab and resist them. A traditional elder said, "We have revealed to people who Al-Shabaab really are." The tipping point in people's willingness to resist—the "real extremism"—has been the arbitrary and indiscriminate violence inflicted by the insurgents on civilians. However, CVE and PVE should not be rebranded development work. CVE/PVE enables consideration of activities and measures that target enabling factors beyond structural vulnerabilities. Furthermore, CVE and PVE is no exact science and the quality and success of such programmes will depend on the ability to work with and for communities.

Respondents who self-identified as relevant and active CVE/PVE actors spoke at length about their developmental activities, education or vocational programs, and community engagement (inter-faith, inter-clan and female empowerment). One respondent explained that the work they do is "positive", since it aims at rebuilding a cohesive community. Others shared examples of how communities do not need specific interventions to "deradicalize" certain groups. The concern was that the CVE lens frames the community in terms of good and bad (passive and active) members, and that through such inclusive and exclusive logics it could complicate the rehabilitation of former Al-Shabaab members.

Acceptance levels of former Al-Shabaab members is also important. A former Al-Shabaab member for example claimed, "if family accepts me, maybe others can." Many of the actors had in their own assessments and mappings found that the defectors and disengaged return, principally, to parents and in some cases wives or husbands, and if these are missing, the next available kinship relation is activated. Reconciliation therefore starts from the household level.

Respondents recommended highlighting radicalization amongst females and having separate programmes for females. Importantly, women are not only subjects but have active roles within Al-Shabaab. Typically, they are shop-keepers, tax collectors, informants, check point guards, teachers in schools, or wives; they are also involved in fetching supplies. Empowerment initiatives for single mothers and female defectors can provide incentives for them not to be involved in the informal/shadow support roles of radical networks. These initiatives can also create trust and improve societal relations. For example, one female CVE respondent explained how social workers, health workers and legal aid projects visit families and gain the confidence of women and children. Such work might also draw mothers into wider CVE work. As the state formation process advances, this is a foundation for more gender equal state–society relations.

Several other issues were highlighted by the respondents, including the need for sheikhs to be involved in CVE programs. Al-Shabaab was reported to be using *doweriyat* [seminars] in the areas under semi-territorial control as a form of religious indoctrination. Sheikhs could here function as an antidote. Local sheikhs hold the key to counter this type of argumentation, and have to be integrated into anti-Al-Shabaab efforts. They can, for example, highlight that clans are equal in Islam.

That said, some sheikhs are perceived as corrupted/politicized, and some have succumbed to pressure from Al-Shabaab and recruit young boys in their communities. However, a wider advisory council with members from different

Islamic denominations is a useful way of obtaining information on these issues. A wide approach, drawing on a combination of different types of religious leaders, where Sufi, Shafi'i, and quietist/non-political Wahhabism are represented, could be useful. Many respondents shared the view that moderate religious leaders should become more visible in society, and work together to engage in awareness-raising and mobilization around tolerant interpretations of Islam.

The role of elders featured strongly in our interviews, and they should be included in any such advisory councils. Elders were said to have an important role in persuading recruits from their own clans to leave Al-Shabaab. Their role in social mobilization was also highlighted. They constitute what is currently the most effective early-warning network, as they are often the first to be warned about individuals becoming recruited or radicalized.

Conclusions

The context of CVE efforts is important. In Bay/Bakool, semi-territoriality makes it important for rural villagers to appease Al-Shabaab. At the same time, there is a multitude of regional state, central state, and AMISOM security providers, including regional police, federal police, *Darwish*, the Somali Army, and Ethiopian forces. In reality, additional security providers also include clan militias—and the lines between army, police, special police, and clan militia are frequently blurred.

In this context, sheikhs and clan elders can have positive influence on CVE efforts, and their involvement must be considered. At the same time, some sheikhs have been advocating radical messages and some elders and clans have at times appeased Al-Shabaab due to the dynamics of semi-territoriality.

Security provision, coordination and scrutiny are important for trust-building and efficiency in CVE work. One useful tool is to avoid gatekeepers and facilitate a wide dialogue. Dialogue has its challenges: a deep dialogue will mean that all relevant clan elders in an area are consulted as well as all major sheikhs. Dialogue partners in individual meetings as well as group meetings have to consider which actors have a positive and negative role in CVE. From these meetings an advisory group for CVE can be selected. One way of doing this is to create "expert" boards for CVE programmes, with representation from all of these institutions. Such a board could promote the role of religious authorities in overseeing madrasas and how the Quran is taught, as a complement to national oversight. Such boards could help to promote trust in the programme by involving wider civil society, including traditional and religious leaders. They might also be used to build confidence between various security actors, including Ethiopian forces, and local sheikhs and elders.

CVE should be tailored either to conditions of semi-territoriality, or to urban environments more controlled by regional forces and AMISOM. For its success, it requires sustainable security forces which must be paid and function under local ownership. These three factors will ensure that a locally funded *Darwish* and the regional state police can play constructive roles, act in a complementary way, or sometimes even achieve greater operational effectiveness than the SNA.

Recommendations

- There is a multitude of potential allies in CVE work. Different actors relevant for CVE can be drawn together, including elders and sheikhs. Interaction can be systematized between AMISOM and local religious and clan leaders in relation to CVE.
- The national strategy and action plan for preventing and countering violent extremism should be operationalized and implemented at state level.
- CVE efforts should be anchored by a reference group or advisory board consisting of local elders representing all clans in the area, and religious leaders of all denominations.
- A religious leader forum should be initiated to ensure appropriate teaching in schools.
- The entry point for successful CVE work is at the local level. Local institutions such as the clan system and religious institutions should be drawn upon, not only diaspora-based organizations.
- Separate CVE efforts should be considered for females and their passive to active roles in Al-Shabaab need to be better understood.
- Rural security should be a major priority for the SRSG, FGS and international partners/donors. Rampant insecurity in rural central Somalia and violent repercussions of semi-territorial rule should not be tolerated.
- In conducting CVE initiatives, careful consideration should be given to the safety of all participants, especially those who have travelled from and will return to rural areas.

INTERNATIONAL ASPECTS OF AL-SHABAAB

AL-QAIDA AND AL-SHABAAB

A RESILIENT ALLIANCE

Tricia Bacon and *Daisy Muibu*

Authors

Dr Tricia Bacon is an Assistant Professor at American University's School of Public Affairs. Prior to joining the faculty at American University in 2013, she was a counter-terrorism analyst at the US Department of State for over ten years.

Daisy Muibu is a PhD student at American University's School of Public Affairs. She previously worked for the United Nations Office on Drugs and Crime's Justice Sub-Programme in Nairobi, focused on Somalia and Somaliland.

Summary

The alliance between Al-Shabaab and Al-Qaida is the product of connections and cooperation that date back over three decades. Though the relationship has not been free of friction, it has withstood personnel losses, periods during which the groups were weakened, and the Islamic State's efforts to persuade Al-Shabaab to defect. The alliance's resilience lies in the interaction of several factors, including Al-Shabaab's close ties with Al-Qaida's affiliate in Yemen, Al-Qaida's ability to help Al-Shabaab accrue resources, the religiously binding oath between the two groups, ideological affinity among key members, and both leaders' commitment to the relationship. In addition, Al-Shabaab and Al-Qaida have developed trust, which most terrorist groups struggle to forge. Once forged, trust encourages groups to return to each other for assistance. Overall, both groups will be reluctant to relinquish their alliance, which offers a "rainy day" resource to which they can turn, when needed. In the face of counterterrorism pressure and the challenge from the Islamic State, Al-Qaida relies on its affiliates to project strength and rebuild. In return, Al-Shabaab gains jihadist prestige from Al-Qaida, while still enjoying its coveted autonomy.

Policies that focus on countering Al-Shabaab as an Al-Qaida affiliate risk overlooking the domestic sources of the Somali group's resilience and strength, specifically its ability to provide security and dispute resolution and to exploit the grievances of disenfranchised clans. Yet, as long as Al-Shabaab remains an Al-Qaida affiliate, it will be difficult to gain international backing for negotiations and reconciliation. No policy interventions can sever the relationship, but efforts can be undertaken to weaken the pillars upon which it rests, particularly disrupting cooperation between Al-Shabaab and Al-Qaida in the Arabian Peninsula, targeting key leaders committed to the relationship, developing a face-saving way for Al-Shabaab to relinquish its religious oath to Al-Qaida, and publicly highlighting their differences.

Introduction

Why has the alliance between Al-Qaida and Al-Shabaab persisted? What are its future prospects? The alliance has survived the loss of leaders and key personnel as well as the Islamic State's campaign to lure Al-Shabaab from Al-Qaida's affiliate network. Their ability to weather these challenges suggests that their alliance has staying power. This is important because terrorist groups with allies tend to survive longer, inflict more fatalities, demonstrate greater resilience, and are more prone to seek weapons of mass destruction.[1] It remains unclear why some terrorist group alliances persevere while others fail. To help address this gap, this paper examines the origins of Al-Shabaab and Al-Qaida's alliance, why it persists and its future prospects, and seeks to identify factors that could disrupt or weaken the relationship.

For the purposes of this paper, an alliance refers to a relationship involving cooperation and mutual expectations of some degree of coordination or consultation in the future.[2] In the case of Al-Qaida, a subset of its alliances are relationships known as affiliates, specifically those groups whose leaders have sworn an oath of loyalty to Al-Qaida's deceased leader, Usama bin Laden, and its current leader, Ayman al-Zawahiri, and have had their oath officially accepted by them.[3] The Islamic State has a similar alliance arrangement, but usually identifies those who swear an oath and have it accepted by the group as provinces (or *wilayat*).[4]

The paper's findings are based on secondary source research, primary source information, and over thirty extensive interviews with current and former government and UN officials, intelligence analysts, private security contractors, elements of AMISOM, think tank analysts, journalists, civil society activists, and NGO workers conducted between December 2016 and May 2017 in Nairobi, Mombasa, Mogadishu, Washington, DC, and over Skype with individuals elsewhere.[5]

The Origins of Al-Qaida and Al-Shabaab's Relationship

While Al-Qaida leader Dr Ayman al-Zawahiri publicly announced the alliance with Al-Shabaab in February 2012, the relationship between Al-Qaida and its Somali jihadist counterparts dates back decades. To briefly summarize, the connections formed when Somalis who went on to create Al-Shabaab's predecessor, Al-Ittihad Al-Islami (AIAI), travelled to Afghanistan to fight the Soviet Union during the 1980s.[6] There they cooperated with the still nascent Al-Qaida, which sought to harness foreign fighters' efforts into an "Islamic Army." After the Soviet withdrawal from Afghanistan, Usama bin Laden used Somalia in his efforts against the Communists in South Yemen.[7] Al-Qaida saw the potential for Somalia to be a base in East Africa.[8] It offered training for AIAI during the 1990s, though it struggled to get AIAI to wholly embrace its jihadist agenda and to navigate the clan complexities of the failed state.[9] Al-Qaida became more engaged in Somalia when U.S. forces arrived in the early 1990s, which it saw as a bid to control the region, but largely disengaged when the group shifted back to Afghanistan.[10] Furthermore, some elements of AIAI assisted Al-Qaida with the 1998 embassy attacks, particularly by providing the perpetrators a haven in the aftermath of the attack.[11] Somalis—many of whom were previously members of AIAI and who would become leaders of Al-Shabaab—also went to Afghanistan in the late 1990s and immediately after 9/11 to train and fight alongside the Taliban and Al-Qaida.[12]

After 9/11, the main connection between Somali jihadists and Al-Qaida ran through Al-Qaida's East Africa cell. Comprised of veteran Al-Qaida operatives from the region, this cell was responsible for the bombing of the Paradise Hotel and an attempt to shoot down an Arkia airliner in Mombasa in 2002.[13] These operatives received protection in Somalia from Al-Shabaab's future leaders when they sought a reprieve from the resultant counter-terrorism pressure.[14] Consequently, they were already closely connected to Al-Shabaab when the group emerged from the Union of Islamic Courts.[15] The East African Al-Qaida operatives enjoyed substantial influence in the group, though some had reservations about Al-Shabaab's conduct, particularly its undermining of the Islamic Courts.[16] Their involvement also increased the counter-terrorism pressure on Al-Shabaab, and the last remaining East African Al-Qaida operative from the cell was killed in 2011.[17]

For its part, Al-Qaida Core in Afghanistan and Pakistan made periodic statements in support of the cause in Somalia after the Ethiopian intervention in 2006, but refrained from specifically endorsing Al-Shabaab.[18] Despite Al-Qaida's omission, Al-Shabaab publicly declared its allegiance to Al-Qaida and sought to portray itself as an Al-Qaida ally.[19] Though unwilling to publicly recognize Al-Shabaab, as early as 2007 Al-Qaida leaders included Somalia as among the primary "hotspots," where its senior religious figure was responsible for "provoking jihad" and "supporting mujahidin."[20] It was not until 2010 that bin Laden agreed to forge a formal alliance with Al-Shabaab. However, in a departure from Al-Qaida's previous affiliates, bin Laden instructed Al-Shabaab that the relationship would not be publicly declared.[21] Nonetheless, Al-Qaida took the need to support Al-Shabaab seriously, providing guidance and input on how it should govern, attacks and targets, economic opportunities, and religious counsel.[22] It also sent messages to encourage the Somali group.[23]

Zawahiri objected to bin Laden's decision to withhold a public announcement of the alliance;[24] however, bin Laden's view prevailed until his death in 2011. Following bin Laden's death, Al-Shabaab quickly pledged allegiance to Zawahiri publicly.[25] Then, in February 2012, Zawahiri reciprocated, publicly acknowledging Al-Shabaab as an Al-Qaida affiliate, which doubled as an opportunity for him to show that Al-Qaida was growing, despite its founding leader's death. However, unlike prior affiliates, Al-Shabaab did not adopt Al-Qaida's name. Despite the lack of an Al-Qaida moniker, Al-Qaida charged Al-Shabaab with responsibility for operations in the Horn of Africa.[26] It also offered Al-Shabaab guidance and treated Al-Shabaab like the other affiliates, including the Somali group in messages and policies sent to the affiliates.[27]

The decision to ally with Al-Qaida exacerbated the internal fissures within Al-Shabaab and contributed to a purge by now deceased Al-Shabaab leader, Ahmed Abdi Godane, that occurred between 2011 and 2013.[28] Some opposed Godane's desire to ally with Al-Qaida, while others were more concerned that the alliance was part of his campaign to further consolidate his position.[29] Indeed, Godane was determined to control the relationship with Al-Qaida.[30] Either way, Godane responded by eliminating opponents and emerged more powerful.[31] When he died in 2014, he was succeeded by one of his loyalists, Ahmed Diiriye Abu Ubaidah, who quickly re-affirmed Al-Shabaab's continued allegiance to Al-Qaida.[32]

Why the Al-Shabaab and Al-Qaida Alliance Persists

Though the alliance took time to become formalized, it has proven resilient. The alliance has survived senior East African Al-Qaida operative Harun Fazul's criticisms of Al-Shabaab and his suspicious death in 2011, bin Laden's refusal to publicly acknowledge Al-Shabaab as an affiliate, the death of the leaders of both groups, and the Islamic State's efforts to court Al-Shabaab, with all the resources, prestige, and appeal that the Islamic State enjoyed in the 2014–15 timeframe. Al-Shabaab's rebuffing of the Islamic State's overtures was particularly telling, because the Islamic State could have offered Al-Shabaab more resources, recruitment power, and cachet than Al-Qaida at that juncture. Al-Qaida and Al-Shabaab's cooperation is probably neither constant nor regular and they do not need one another to survive; however, the relationship has become embedded in both groups. Their relationship's resiliency does not rely on one linchpin. Instead, multiple, inter-related factors operate to reinforce the ties between the two groups, and the importance of any one factor may ebb and flow over time. Combined, they offer a stable foundation for the alliance to sustain, despite some differences and only sporadic cooperation.[33]

First, and perhaps most importantly, a critical mainstay of Al-Shabaab's alliance with Al-Qaida is Al-Shabaab's ties to Al-Qaida's Yemeni affiliate, Al-Qaida in the Arabian Peninsula (AQAP).[34] The alliance with Al-Qaida also offers Al-Shabaab access to support, at least publicly, from the other affiliates—a valuable perk.[35] At this juncture, Al-Shabaab's connections to Al-Qaida are likely rooted as much or more in its relations with AQAP than with Al-Qaida Core in South Asia.[36] Al-Shabaab and AQAP have more ready access to one another through their geographic proximity and the corresponding deeply rooted cultural and commercial ties between the two countries.[37] Al-Shabaab forged close ties with AQAP from its inception, with Yemenis connected to AQAP deploying to Somalia as early as 2005–06.[38] Al-Qaida leaders recognized the importance of these ties; therefore, they charged AQAP with taking "care of the brothers in Somalia" and urged AQAP to "[k]eep in mind that communicating with the brothers in Somalia is very important."[39]

During periods in which Al-Qaida has been on the defensive, AQAP has been able to act as Al-Qaida's "flag bearer," facilitating cooperation with affiliates and producing propaganda in support of them.[40] Al-Shabaab's ties to AQAP and AQAP's strength offered a critical counterbalance during the period when the Islamic State sought Al-Shabaab's allegiance.[41] AQAP also offers Al-Shabaab the ability to improve its operational capability and acquire materiel.[42] In particular, AQAP is strongly suspected of being a key source of Al-Shabaab's more sophisticated explosives capability.[43] For its part, Al-Shabaab has reportedly provided AQAP with fighters and manpower at various points.[44]

Second, the alliance with Al-Qaida offers Al-Shabaab access to some resources.[45] Admittedly, resources alone cannot explain the persistence of the alliance, given Al-Qaida's diminished coffers. Moreover, Al-Shabaab does not depend on funds from Al-Qaida and can generate funds through its internal activities, particularly taxation.[46] Though Al-Qaida does not have the robust coffers that it once did, it can probably still acquire resources to share with Al-Shabaab when needed. As an affiliate, Al-Shabaab also benefits from access to Al-Qaida's donor base.[47] In addition, Al-Qaida leaders have publicly encouraged supporters to contribute to Al-Shabaab.[48]

Third, the alliance with Al-Qaida offers Al-Shabaab the ideal combination of conferring benefits while allowing Al-Shabaab to retain a high degree of independence, especially compared to an alliance with the Islamic State.[49] On the whole, Al-Shabaab operates autonomously and focuses on its local agenda,[50] while paying occasional lip service to broader global jihadist causes.[51] Its investment in issues of governance in Somalia, such as dispute resolution and security, limits its emphasis on global jihadism, and Al-Qaida does not demand that it do otherwise.[52] While the alliance is not consequential to Al-Shabaab's day-to-day operations, affiliation with Al-Qaida offers Al-Shabaab greater jihadist prestige that it can draw upon, especially when it needs an alternative to clannism or nationalism.[53] As needed, Al-Shabaab can also turn to Al-Qaida for assistance, consultation, or public recognition of its agenda.[54] Unlike the Islamic State, in exchange, Al-Qaida does not demand that

Al-Shabaab give up its independence or its local focus. Because the Islamic State has proclaimed the return of the caliphate and caliph, it demands complete obedience and thereby forces its "provinces" to relinquish much of their autonomy.[55] In sum, the balance of autonomy and the ability to collaborate and assist is a strength that helps sustain Al-Qaida and Al-Shabaab's relationship.

Fourth, Al-Shabaab's *bayah* to Al-Qaida reinforces its sense of obligation towards Al-Qaida.[56] *Bayah* is a religiously binding oath of allegiance. The origin of this practice is tied to reports that Islam's early believers pledged *bayah* to the Prophet Muhammad.[57] For Al-Qaida affiliate purposes, *bayah* has to be offered by the leader of a group and then accepted by Al-Qaida's emir.[58] Al-Shabaab has had two major opportunities to discontinue its *bayah* to Al-Qaida: 1) when bin Laden died and Zawahiri took over in 2011; and 2) when Godane died and Diiriye became emir of Al-Shabaab in 2014. Any leadership change creates an opening to end the *bayah*, while breaking *bayah* under other circumstances can incur significant reputational damage.[59] Moreover, Sunni jihadist leaders rely on *bayah* from their followers as a means to secure loyalty. Thus, by breaking *bayah*, leaders can create vulnerabilities and disunity within their own organization, something Al-Shabaab in particular seeks to avoid.[60]

Fifth, ideological commitment and longstanding personal ties between members of Al-Qaida and Al-Shabaab reinforce the alliance.[61] Though not the majority, within Al-Shabaab there is a hard core of "true believers" who are ideologically committed to Al-Qaida.[62] Under Zawahiri, their ideological compatibility may have even improved, given Zawahiri's origins as a jihadi nationalist and support for efforts to control territory.[63] Importantly, the groups have been able to replenish personal ties between members who are ideologically committed, probably in significant part through AQAP, when key interlocutors have been killed or detained. These bonds have led analysts to draw analogies such as a "family" relationship and refer to the groups as "growing up together."[64] Cooperation need not be regular or consistent, but the core ties between the groups remain strong.[65]

Sixth, Al-Shabaab's leaders and those with decision-making authority have remained committed to the alliance,[66] in part to reinforce their power and control of the group. In so doing, they made opposition to the alliance with Al-Qaida synonymous with challenging Al-Shabaab's leaders and fostering disunity, something they have responded to violently.[67] Between 2011 and 2013, Godane purged key rivals, including those who doubted the wisdom of an alliance with Al-Qaida, which not only eliminated opponents to the relationship, but also discouraged others from questioning the alliance.[68] Because Al-Shabaab's current and previous emir hailed from Somaliland and lacked a clan base of power in southern Somalia, the alliance with Al-Qaida offers a source of prestige and bolsters the group's claims to have transcended clannism.[69] Having invested in the alliance and purged opponents of it, leaders are not only committed to the alliance but may also fear that a break from Al-Qaida or shift of allegiance to the Islamic State could damage Al-Shabaab's precious unity.

Moreover, though the Islamic State's emergence and efforts to woo Al-Shabaab fostered divisions within the Somali group, the challenge from the Islamic State also inadvertently reinforced Al-Shabaab's alliance with Al-Qaida.[70] Al-Shabaab leaders turned violently against those who advocated defecting to the Islamic State, seeing it as a challenge to their leadership.[71] In addition, a splinter faction in Puntland claims allegiance to the Islamic State, thereby provoking a rivalry that solidified Al-Shabaab as part of Al-Qaida's camp in the competition between the Islamic State and Al-Qaida within the Sunni jihadist milieu.

Lastly, because of the hurdles to forming alliance and the problems building trust, terrorist groups tend to return to their existing partners for help once they have established an alliance and trust.[72] Trust leads to expectations that the terms of the collaboration will be honoured,[73] which mitigates the uncertainty and risk inherent in alliances. Trust is perhaps even more essential for terrorist groups' relationships because of the lack of an outside guarantor or other enforcement mechanisms.[74] Al-Shabaab and Al-Qaida have cleared this difficult hurdle and thus will be reluctant to sever ties because the alliance offers a reliable resource to address future needs.[75]

Conclusion

The Al-Shabaab and Al-Qaida alliance presents a paradox. It does not influence Al-Shabaab's day-to-day functioning or its focus on the local situation in Somalia. Cooperation between the two groups is probably neither regular nor frequent. Yet, the alliance derives strength from some of these same factors. Al-Qaida is satisfied with allowing Al-Shabaab a high degree of autonomy; indeed, with its security limitations, Al-Qaida cannot be in regular contact with Al-Shabaab. Nonetheless, Al-Qaida offers tangible and intangible resources that Al-Shabaab can draw upon, as needed, not least of which is access to the other affiliates. The two groups have succeeded in building sufficient trust such that they are apt to return to one another when they need assistance. Ties between personnel in the two groups date back decades, and they have regenerated connections in the face of losses. Perhaps most important, the alliance enjoys the support of the leadership of both groups and is reinforced by ties between Al-Shabaab and AQAP, which have more ready access to one another. Thus, the alliance will remain resilient, though it will not determine or alter Al-Shabaab's strategy or agenda in Somalia.

Recommendations

It is important to note that policies focused on countering Al-Shabaab as an Al-Qaida affiliate overlook the group's sources of strength. Al-Shabaab has garnered influence in southern Somalia not because of its ties to Al-Qaida, but because of its ability to provide a modicum of security and justice and to exploit the grievances of marginalized and disenfranchised clans. Thus, recommendations on how to disrupt Al-Shabaab's alliance with Al-Qaida should support policies to diminish Al-Shabaab's ability to function as a shadow government.

Because there is not a linchpin holding the relationship together, there is no silver bullet to disrupt it. Instead, efforts can be undertaken to weaken elements that underpin their relationship. However, two cautionary notes are warranted. First, efforts to sever the alliance risk encouraging Al-Shabaab or factions of it to ally with the Islamic State—an equally bad scenario for reconciliation. Second, reconciliation efforts may persuade some to relinquish the fight, but leave behind a hardened core deeply committed to Al-Qaida and violent jihad.

Since the alliance relies on Al-Shabaab's relationship with AQAP, inhibiting their cooperation could help weaken ties. While targeted strikes have become more common than capture operations in both Yemen and Somalia, capture operations may offer a critical opportunity to garner intelligence about the relationship and to stymie their cooperation. Intercepting emissaries or materiel between the two groups would impede their ability to assist one another, as would efforts to hinder their communications. Improvements in border and maritime security, even simply increasing patrols or searches, may constrain their cooperation, thereby weakening their relationship over time.

Admittedly, it may be difficult for Al-Shabaab to renounce its *bayah* to Al-Qaida, even if it wanted to. Thus, Al-Shabaab would need a face-saving way to relinquish the oath, perhaps through a *fatwa* from a respected religious authority.

Because the alliance with Al-Qaida relies on Al-Shabaab leaders' commitment, targeting these individuals may weaken the relationship. However, there is some support for the Islamic State, particularly among Al-Shabaab's younger generation, which means that leadership losses may provide an opening for the Islamic State. Alternatively, the death of either leader offers a window to prevent a renewed *bayah*.

Lastly, public diplomacy efforts or credible voices can emphasize differences between the two groups in order to undermine trust between them, such as highlighting admonishments from Al-Qaida that Al-Shabaab should refrain from harming Muslim civilians and be more selective in its targets.[76]

AL-SHABAAB AS A TRANSNATIONAL
SECURITY THREAT

Sahan Africa

Authorship

Sahan Africa is a think tank and research organization with offices in Somalia, Kenya, and the United Kingdom. Its team has expertise in political affairs, security dynamics, and governance, and focuses on the Horn of Africa, East Africa, and the Middle East.

Summary

Harakaat Al-Shabaab Al-Mujahidin, Al-Qaida's affiliate in the Horn of Africa, has long been perceived as a Somali organization—albeit one that represents a security threat to the wider region. But since 2010, Al-Shabaab has aspired to become a truly regional organization, with membership and horizons that transcend national borders.[1] Since then, it has become active in six countries of the region, striking five of them with terrorist attacks.[2] Al-Shabaab is clearly no longer an exclusively Somali problem, and requires a concerted international response.

This expansion of Al-Shabaab's operational reach is in large part the result of the strategic direction adopted by its former leader, Ahmed Abdi Godane.

In 2013, Godane reorganized Al-Shabaab's military wing to include two transnational units—one dedicated to operations against Kenya, Tanzania, and Uganda, and another against Ethiopia—and gave instructions for Al-Shabaab's special operations wing, the Amniyat, to step up attacks against neighbouring countries.

Al-Shabaab-affiliated networks and sympathizers in Kenya also continued to plan terror attacks during this period. Although Al-Hijra, Al-Shabaab's Kenyan affiliate, experienced growing pressure from the security services and withdrew from major hubs of activity, its radicalization and recruitment efforts subsequently targeted the prison system, while operatives and recruits—including a growing proportion of women—continued to travel to Somalia for training and instructions.

The report concludes with the following recommendations for further action:

- Enhanced security cooperation in countering Al-Shabaab, including a joint review to identify gaps, challenges, and opportunities in strengthening collaboration; more joint activities, including inviting Tanzania to participate in relevant IGAD activities.
- Better understanding of the Improvised Explosive Device (IED) threat and possible counter-measures, including appropriate Counter-IED (C-IED) strategies, enhanced technical capabilities for post-blast investigation and analysis, and improved information sharing.
- Adaptation to evolving patterns of radicalization and recruitment, such as the shifting of extremist activities to new geographic areas; sensitization and training of public officials; enhancing surveillance of terrorist networks inside the prison system; and undertaking additional research into current trends of radicalization and recruitment among young women.

Introduction

The Horn of Africa has long been confronted by numerous complex and fast-evolving transnational security threats. Intra-state warfare, boundary disputes, resource conflicts, and the proliferation of small arms are longstanding and persistent challenges. But in recent decades the region has been confronted with new threats, such as terrorism, organized crime, piracy, cybercrime, and trafficking in drugs, humans, and weapons. The expansion of internet access, ease of travel, and the growing sophistication of extremist and criminal groups render these threats increasingly transnational, thus requiring a collaborative response.

In 2015, the IGAD Security Sector Program (ISSP) launched a new Transnational Security Threats (TST) Initiative to promote security cooperation between Member States. Under the TST Initiative, the governments of the Federal Democratic Republic of Ethiopia and the Republic of Kenya requested that ISSP assist them in preparing a submission to the Sanctions Committee that responds to successive United Nations Security Council (UNSC) resolutions calling on Member States to take specific actions against Al-Shabaab.[3] These developments led to research by Sahan which forms the basis of this paper, focusing on Al-Shabaab's presence and activities in each country, as well as the opportunities for enhanced cooperation in countering this threat.

Between April 2015 and June 2016, a Sahan team operating under the auspices of ISSP conducted primary and secondary research on the presence of Al-Shabaab in Ethiopia and Kenya, with special emphasis on cross-border networks and operations. Sahan personnel, working in close consultation with the Member States, interviewed members and former members of Al-Shabaab and its Kenyan affiliate, Al-Hijra, as well as close associates, and received regular briefings from government officials, access to relevant documentation and evidence, and the opportunity to observe operations against Al-Shabaab. The Sahan team adhered strictly to the standards of evidence required of UN Expert Groups and other research bodies. The team based its findings on a "reasonable grounds to believe" standard of proof. Minimum standards included reliance on at least two credible, independent, and mutually corroborating sources or a single credible source supported by independently verified physical, documentary, audio-visual, or electronic evidence.

The second phase of this initiative commenced in August 2016 and concluded in May 2017 with the submission of a report to the UN Security Council Committees on Somalia/Eritrea and the so-called Islamic State (IS)/Al-Qaida. This summary covers only Phase 1 of the Initiative, but some information has been updated in light of the findings of Phase 2.

Harakaat Al-Shabaab Al-Mujahidin

Al-Shabaab continues to pose a threat to peace and security in Somalia, conducting an insurgency against federal and regional Somali forces as well as troops contributing to the African Union Mission in Somalia (AMISOM).

Figure 1: The leadership of Al-Shabaab in 2016

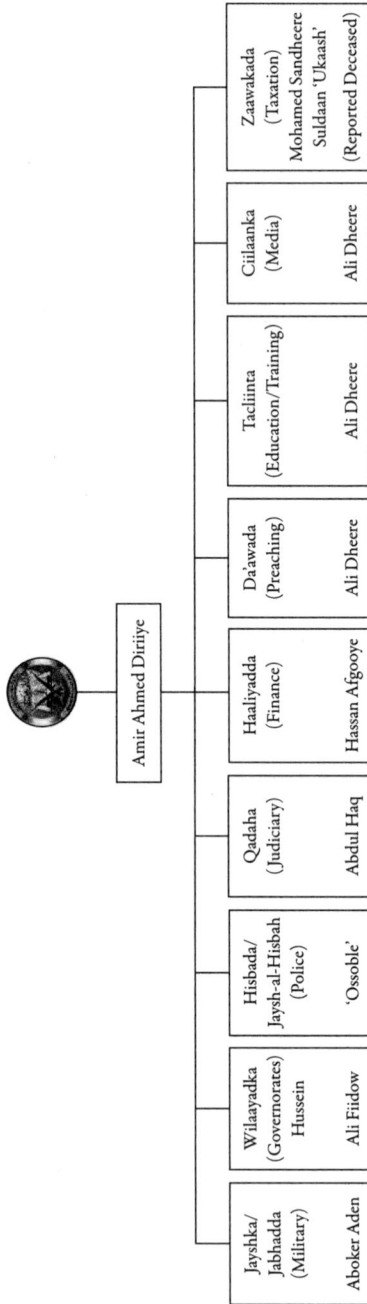

Amir Ahmed Diriiye								
Jayshka/ Jabhadda (Military)	Wilaayadka (Governorates) Hussein	Hisbada/ Jaysh-al-Hisbah (Police)	Qadaha (Judiciary)	Haaliyadda (Finance)	Da'awada (Preaching)	Tacliinta (Education/Training)	Ciilaanka (Media)	Zaawakada (Taxation) Mohamed Sandheere Suldaan 'Ukaash' (Reported Deceased)
Aboker Aden	Ali Fiidow	'Ossoble'	Abdul Haq	Hassan Afgooye	Ali Dheere	Ali Dheere	Ali Dheere	

Al-Shabaab's zone of control has remained relatively stable as the organization continues to engage in asymmetrical warfare, waging steady attacks on political, military, and civilian targets, collecting taxes, extorting rents from businesses, and running effective, parallel justice and educational systems—even in government-controlled areas.

The jihadists' tactics, techniques, and procedures (TTPs) have also remained consistent, although the reporting period featured an increase in the number of complex attacks against hotels in Mogadishu and AMISOM/Somali National Army forward operating bases. The proliferation of attacks inside Mogadishu demonstrates that Al-Shabaab maintains considerable freedom of movement and operational capacity inside the capital.

Leadership

Al-Shabaab's overall leadership structure throughout remained largely unchanged in 2016, with changes made to the positions held by certain individuals during 2017. Despite persistent rumours of his ill health, the new "Amir" Ahmed Diiriye continues to hold power without any overt challenges to his position. The group has endured some second-tier leadership losses, including the reported killing of a top tier Amniyat officer. As with previous leadership attrition, however, these deaths do not appear to have significantly altered the operational capacity of the organization.

The most notable alteration in Al-Shabaab's leadership has been the establishment of a new "Council of Clan Leaders", which held its first congress in October 2016. The event was hosted by the group's "governor" for Bay and Bakool regions, Abdullahi Ma'allim Geeddow (aka "Abu Farhiya"). Following the conference, the then head of Al-Shabaab's "Office for Governorates", Hussein Ali Fiidow, announced the reorganization of the group's governance structure from seven governorates (or *wilayat*) into 11 across Somalia. The Council, which currently comprises four elders from each *wilaya*, signals Al-Shabaab's most overt attempt to co-opt traditional clan elders into the group's governance structure.

Modus Operandi

Composite Insurgency

Although Al-Shabaab's rank and file are from all Somali clans, as well as other countries, the movement skilfully appropriates local grievances, aligning itself with disaffected groups. Al-Shabaab typically targets communities that harbour grievances against government authorities; feel historical resentment against more dominant clans; belong to minority groups that have long been marginalized; or have lost influence during the civil war. The result is a "composite insurgency" in which a patchwork of different groups support, tolerate, or collude with Al-Shabaab to varying degrees, albeit for largely parochial reasons.

During 2016, Al-Shabaab made significant efforts to influence the behaviour of specific clans, employing alternating cycles of violence and negotiation to steer them into the jihadist camp. Key examples included the Gaalje'el and Awrmale in Lower Jubba, elements of the Dir in Lower Shabelle, of the Abgaal in Galgaduud, and a sub-group of the Habar Gedir in Mudug. In several cases, Al-Shabaab applied "collective punishment" against the clan concerned, killing community members, confiscating livestock, and threatening forced displacement unless they came to the bargaining table.

Similarly, Al-Shabaab has at times intervened to influence the choice of clan leadership. While engaging in a negotiation with a sub-clan in Lower Jubba in December 2016 for example, Al-Shabaab leaders demanded that the community appoint a new *Ugaas*[4] who met with the jihadists' approval.

Protection, Taxation, and Justice

In areas under its direct control, Al-Shabaab provides security through its rudimentary justice system based on the group's interpretation of Sharia law, and imposes a structured form of taxation. In some areas, the group also places rules and restrictions on the movements of people and goods, violation of which can result in imprisonment, fines, or even accusations of spying.

Al-Shabaab extends some of these measures to areas beyond its control with varying degrees of success. Al-Shabaab courts are widely considered to be more effective and less corrupt than the alternatives, especially with respect to disputes over land and property. Residents of Mogadishu routinely travel to an Al-Shabaab court near Afgooye to lodge complaints, while disputes in Kismayo may be heard by Al-Shabaab courts in Behane or Jilib. Yet the group's attempts to expand *zakat*[5] have encountered mixed results. In towns under government control, businesses routinely pay "taxes" to Al-Shabaab in exchange for peace and security: essentially a protection racket. But in rural areas, Al-Shabaab has encountered resistance from communities that perceive the group's demands as unwelcome or excessive.[6]

Improvised Explosive Devices (IEDs)

Somalia experienced a significant increase in the number of IED attacks conducted by Al-Shabaab in 2016, with 395 IED incidents recorded in comparison with 265 the previous year. Although targeting has largely remained the same—focused on members of AMISOM and Somali security forces—the number of reported casualties from such attacks has risen alarmingly, the majority of them civilians:[7] an estimated 1,839 IED-related casualties were recorded in Somalia in 2016, with 1,116 individuals wounded and 737 killed—an increase of more than 800 victims over 2015.[8]

The rise in deaths and injuries can be at least partially attributed to an upswing in the number of complex attacks, notably against hotels in Mogadishu[9] and AMISOM forward operating bases. Such attacks generally involve various types of IEDs, including Person-Borne IEDs (PBIEDs), Vehicle-Borne IEDs (VBIEDs), Suicide-Vehicle-Borne IEDs (SVBIEDs), and suicide infantry.

Indeed, Al-Shabaab has augmented IED usage during the course of the reporting period, notably through an increase in both the number and size of S/VBIEDs and Directional Fragmentation Charges (DFCs).[10] Instead of using cars or minivans to deliver VBIED attacks, the group has more recently shifted towards the use of SVBIEDs carried inside much larger trucks, allowing an augmentation of the quantity of explosives.[11] Al-Shabaab conducted only one such attack in 2015, but carried out five in 2016[12] and two more in the first quarter of 2017.

Other TTPs include the increasing use of secondary IEDs to target primary responders in Mogadishu or AMISOM/SNA convoys in remote rural areas;[13] of area saturation (the placement of multiple IEDs within a target area) as a defensive measure; and of command-wire IEDs (CWIEDs) instead of the common radio-controlled IEDs (RCIEDs) in order to circumvent electronic counter-measures used by AMISOM and the SNA.

Traditionally, Al-Shabaab has built IEDs using military-grade explosives scavenged from locally acquired munitions and supplemented with aluminium. But the difficulty in acquiring high quantities of such explosives in some parts of Somalia has led the group to produce fertilizer-based home-made explosives (HME).[14] Fertilizer is imported legally into Somalia for agricultural use and is easily procured in local markets.[15]

Finally, throughout 2016 and into early 2017, IEDs in at least three distinct locations across southern Somalia have been manufactured with identical components, and in certain cases likely from the same munitions supply. The same types of large pipes that hold explosives charges in SVBIEDs and VBIEDs were found in the production of RCIEDs and DFCs. These observations suggest that Al-Shabaab is currently using a centralized logistical chain for the production of IED components, which are then delivered to smaller hubs across the country where they are assembled for targeting.

Al-Shabaab as a Transnational Threat

Overview of the Regional Threat

Although Somalia remains Al-Shabaab's geographic centre of gravity, the group has long demonstrated a determination to operate beyond Somalia's borders and maintains a significant presence in at least six countries of the region. As early as 2010, Godane harboured aspirations for Al-Shabaab to acquire a regional character.[16] He established two new units dedicated to external operations, one targeting Kenya, Tanzania, and Uganda, and the other Ethiopia, while also tasking Al-Shabaab's special operations and intelligence branch, the Amniyat, with targeting Somalia's neighbours.

Al-Shabaab has also inspired and encouraged the emergence of affiliated groups and autonomous networks of jihadists across the region. Although they differ considerably with respect to operational capability and the nature of their relationship with Al-Shabaab, all of these groups aspire and actively plan to engage in acts of terrorism.

Kenya

Jaysh Ayman

In 2014, Al-Shabaab launched a new offensive in Kenya, with the creation of a new unit dedicated to staging operations in Kenya, Tanzania, and Uganda: Jaysh Ayman (a.k.a. Jeshi la Ayman). Despite its profile as an East African force,[17] the group has limited its activities to northern Kenya, particularly in Lamu county, and southwards along the Kenyan coast. Attacks typically originate within Somalia, with groups of militants crossing over into Kenya to conduct operations and then retreating across the border.

Jaysh Ayman proved capable of carrying out a sustained campaign against Kenyan government and civilian targets, causing mass casualties and characterized by extreme brutality. From June 2015 however, it suffered significant losses at the hands of the Kenyan security forces, and today the threat in Lamu county[18] and at the coast[19] appears to be contained. The militants' operational tempo in Garissa County also seems to have declined since the death in May 2016 of Mohamad Kunow, Al-Shabaab's military commander in Lower and Middle Jubba.[20]

Since mid-2016, new trends in cross-border attacks include the targeting and looting of Kenyan police camps[21] and vehicles,[22] the reported use of IEDs to target first responders,[23] and the destruction of communications masts near the border.[24]

Al-Hijra

Despite its operational limitations, Al-Hijra (formerly known as the Muslim Youth Centre, or MYC) remains Al-Shabaab's most important and active affiliate in the region. Faced with enhanced scrutiny from security services and the attrition of its leadership,[25] Al-Hijra has shifted its activities and radicalization and recruitment efforts away from Nairobi and Mombasa, the traditional hubs for jihadist activity in Kenya. Not only has the group invested in safe houses and networks throughout the country,[26] it continues to operate from within Kenya's prison system.[27] Imprisoned Al-Hijra members still direct plots against targets in Kenya using a variety of cells and networks, and routinely assist in the facilitation of individuals looking to join Al-Shabaab or IS. Al-Hijra is also placing a growing emphasis on the recruitment of girls and young women.

Sympathizers and Affiliates

Since 2006, the conflict in Somalia has left its mark on a generation of young East Africans, propelling growing numbers toward extremism. Some of these sympathizers have organized themselves into cells along the coast, using social media and mobile phone applications to share information and attempt to organize attacks, and hundreds (possibly thousands) have used Al-Shabaab and Al-Hijra networks to travel to Somalia, and even Syria.[28]

In Tanzania,[29] an emerging network has operational ties to Al-Hijra, and unconfirmed connections to Mombasa-based cells.[30] The group's motivation remains unclear but an initial assessment suggests a financial rather than an ideological inclination.[31]

Ethiopia

Al-Shabaab has long sought to strike Ethiopia—so far without success. It came closest to its goal in 2013, when a team of suicide bombers succeeding in deploying to Addis Ababa, but accidentally blew themselves up following an abortive attempt to bomb a World Cup qualifying match at a major stadium. In March 2014, months before his death, Godane renewed his call for "jihad" against Ethiopia.[32]

Jaysh al-Usra's Ethiopian Wing

In parallel with the establishment of Jaysh Ayman, Godane took steps towards the establishment of an Ethiopian Al-Shabaab military unit, initially headed by a veteran jihadist commander named Ali "Diyaar" (a.k.a. "Warsame").[33] The new Jaysh unit was based at Diinsoor and by late 2014 had approximately 500 fighters: mainly Ethiopian Somalis, but also a significant Oromo contingent as well as smaller numbers from other Ethiopian ethnic groups. The unit has yet to stage any significant military operation inside Ethiopia.

The Amniyat

In late 2013, Godane also tasked key figures in Al-Shabaab's special operations and intelligence branch, known as the Amniyat, to begin planning and preparing operations against Somalia's neighbours. The Amniyat network[34] has been implicated in the 2013 Westgate Mall attack in Nairobi, the 2014 suicide bombing of La Chaumière restaurant in Djibouti, and the massacre of over 60 Kenyan civilians near Mandera in two separate attacks in late 2014. Since May 2014, it actively began planning suicide attacks against the Ethiopian capital, Addis Ababa, recruiting and deploying members of attack cells, mobilizing networks of activists and sympathizers, and collecting information on possible targets. Its largest operation in Ethiopia to date is the "Bole Wedding plot", which involved the attempted bombing of a shopping mall in Addis Ababa. Although the plan initially involved deploying three teams[35] totalling some 20 operatives, it ultimately failed.

Conclusions

IGAD Member States have already taken measures to counter the expanding threat from Al-Shabaab, whether within their own borders, through their support to Somali authorities, or through regional and continental security cooperation mechanisms. Indeed, IGAD Member States participate in the African Union Mission in Somalia (AMISOM) combating Al-Shabaab, and are engaged in diplomatic efforts to bring political stability to Somalia. Ethiopian National Defence Forces (ENDF) have been committed to AMISOM since January 2014, playing a leading role in the ground offensive of Operation Jubba Corridor in south-western Somalia,[36] and helping their Somali counterparts by opening roads, providing technical expertise,[37] and monitoring Al-Shabaab activities.

The Kenya Defence Forces (KDF) entered Somalia unilaterally in October 2011 in response to the Al-Shabaab threat in the border area[38] then joined AMISOM in 2012.[39] They played a key role in liberating Kismayo in October 2012, and have since been operationally active with their Somali counterparts, engaging in joint operations, capacity-building, community engagement, and intelligence sharing.[40] Kenyan security forces have also expanded their footprint in northern Kenya, increasing their presence and monitoring of the border area, and launching several operations targeting Al-Shabaab in Garissa[41] and Lamu counties,[42] as well as stepping up efforts to identify Al-Shabaab networks and disrupt their activities across the entire country.[43]

Yet the importance of further emphasis on cooperation and coordination cannot be overemphasized. As extremists linked to Al-Shabaab exploit weaknesses to operate across the region's borders, states must be capable of working together to ensure that security services throughout the region share a holistic view of the threats that they face. Member States should therefore consider working towards a more robust regional framework for security cooperation, intelligence sharing, and mutual legal assistance.

Recommendations

Specific, immediate measures to enhance cooperation in countering Al-Shabaab

Member States should consider convening a joint review to identify gaps, challenges, and opportunities in strengthening cooperation. The objectives of such a review might include:

- Establishing a clear understanding of the types of information all parties can share and the processes for doing so, including necessary levels of authorization, points of contact, and protocols for handling sensitive information (for example, call data and financial records).

- Engaging systematically in more joint activities, such as:
  - Joint analytical teams or expert committees;
  - Joint units to investigate specific threats;
  - Establishment of enhanced liaison or "secondment" positions to allow familiarization across countries.

IEDs and Counter-Measures

Al-Shabaab's use of IEDs has evolved at an alarming pace. Although Somalia is the epicentre of the regional IED threat, the TTPs tested in that country are routinely exported to neighbouring countries.

IGAD Member States vary widely in their capacity to prevent such attacks, and to conduct investigations after the fact. Most lack a comprehensive counter-IED (C-IED) strategy. It is therefore proposed that they seek ISSP's support in enhancing their collective understanding of the IED threat, develop appropriate C-IED strategies, strengthen their technical capabilities for post-blast investigation and analysis, and improve information sharing within the region.

Adaptation to evolving patterns of radicalization and recruitment

As Al-Shabaab's radicalization and recruitment efforts adapt to the investigative measures employed against them, authorities should maintain a proactive and flexible approach to monitoring these activities. Short-term operational responses might include:

- Sensitization of security officials in areas previously unaffected by extremism in order to identify and react appropriately to potential threats;
- Anticipating the swift reallocation of dedicated resources to areas with newly emerging threats to disrupt networks as quickly as possible;
- Enhancing surveillance of terrorism suspects and convicts inside prisons to identify individuals attempting to radicalize their peers or remain operationally engaged. Additional measures include:
  - Tighter controls to prevent contraband, especially mobile phones;
  - Closer vetting of and enactment of stiffer penalties for prison staff; and
  - Development of disengagement programmes for extremists in the prison system.
- Undertaking additional research into the radicalization of young women.

FOREIGN FIGHTER INFLUENCE IN AL-SHABAAB

LIMITATIONS AND FUTURE PROSPECTS

Tricia Bacon and *Daisy Muibu*

Authors

Dr Tricia Bacon is an Assistant Professor at American University's School of Public Affairs. Prior to joining the faculty at American University in 2013, she was a counter-terrorism analyst at the US Department of State for over ten years.

Daisy Muibu is a PhD student at American University's School of Public Affairs. She previously worked for the United Nations Office on Drugs and Crime's Justice Sub-Programme in Kenya, focused on Somalia and Somaliland.

Summary

In recent years, foreign fighters in Al-Shabaab have largely come from East Africa—primarily Kenya, followed by Tanzania and Uganda—and have generally not accrued significant influence within Al-Shabaab in Somalia. Rather, they have mainly occupied rank and file roles in the group's military wing. However, they have expanded the group's Swahili propaganda and its ability to operate and recruit in the region, especially when coupled with localized networks that exploit local grievances. Most significantly, foreign fighters, probably from Yemen, have contributed to Al-Shabaab's explosives capability. However, foreign fighters from other parts of the world declined significantly after Al-Shabaab's well-publicized purge of some high-profile foreign fighters between 2011 and 2013 and after Syria emerged as the primary destination for foreign fighters.[1] Moreover, Somalia has become a less desirable location for foreign fighters outside the region, as the conflict has become more localized and clan-based.

Somalia is unlikely to see the return of a significant number of foreign fighters from outside the East Africa region, unless it becomes a destination for foreign fighters who fought in Syria and wish to continue their involvement in jihadist causes, but find they cannot return home. In addition, while most East African foreign fighters do not exert strategic influence over Al-Shabaab or the conflict in Somalia, they may pose a future threat at home. Three main recommendations flow from these findings. First, reconciliation efforts should involve a carrot-and-stick approach aimed at discouraging locals and Al-Shabaab from hosting foreign fighters. Second, the governments of neighbouring states should implement policies focused on hindering foreign fighter recruitment and dealing with returnees. Lastly, effort must be made to hinder the exchange and cooperation between jihadists in Yemen and Somalia—admittedly a difficult task.

Introduction

What influence do foreign fighters have in Al-Shabaab? Moreover, what are the prospects that foreign fighters will exert significant influence in the future? Significant attention has been paid to why individuals become foreign fighters, especially from the West, and to the potential threat they could pose upon returning home.[2] Less work examines how foreign fighters influence the organizations they join. In Al-Shabaab, the role and influence of foreign fighters have varied over time. In Al-Shabaab's early years, there were numerous reports highlighting the importance of foreign fighters;[3] however, in recent years, their influence has been limited. This briefing paper examines foreign fighter influence in Somalia, focusing on their current roles and future prospects.

Arguably, in no other conflict is the question of who should be considered a foreign fighter more complex. Somalia's prolonged state failure and humanitarian and security crises have dispersed Somalia's population, creating a global community with varying levels of connection and identification with Somalia.[4] Therefore, identifying when a member of the diaspora becomes "foreign" is problematic. To manage this ambiguity, we utilize Thomas Hegghammer's widely used definition of foreign fighters as those who (1) have joined and operate within the confines of an insurgency, (2) lack citizenship of the conflict state or kinship links to its warring factions, and (3) lack affiliation to an official military organization.[5] By excluding those with citizenship or kinship ties, we thereby exclude Somali diaspora from our definition.[6] This approach has drawbacks, because ethnic ties have predictive power in terms of where individuals volunteer to fight.[7] In addition, members of the diaspora have reportedly been disproportionately involved in suicide attacks and other activities in Somalia.[8] However, including diaspora with other foreign fighters risks conflating different phenomena, so we have opted for a narrower interpretation.

The paper's findings are based on secondary source research, primary source information, and over 30 extensive interviews with current and former government and UN officials, intelligence analysts, private security contractors, elements of AMISOM, think tank analysts, journalists, civil society activists, and NGO workers, conducted between December 2016 and May 2017 in Nairobi, Mombasa, Mogadishu, Washington, DC, and over Skype.[9]

Foreign Fighters in Al-Shabaab

Just after the Islamic Courts defeated the warlords in June 2006, its forces met at the Ramadan Hotel in Mogadishu. Al-Shabaab did not attend but among the requests that it sent was that the Islamic Courts welcome foreign fighters without any conditions.[10] Al-Shabaab has subsequently sought to propagate the notion that fellow Muslims are not foreign and therefore are welcome.[11] Moreover, it has used foreign fighters to try to demonstrate that it is an organization that transcends clannism and nationalism.[12] In practice, Al-Shabaab has viewed and treated foreign fighters differently, thereby affecting their roles in the group, which have changed over time.

Foreign fighters have varying utility to the groups they join. Al-Shabaab, like other groups, recruited foreigners by framing the conflict as one that "necessitated a defensive mobilisation," against infidel invaders.[13] Among those who have responded to the call are "jihadi tourists"—foreign fighters with limited skills in search of adventure. These foreign fighters have little value and are actually a drain upon Al-Shabaab's resources, because they have to be housed and trained and they attract counter-terrorism attention, but offer little in return.[14] In contrast, higher-calibre foreign fighters can bring resources, tactical innovations, or promulgate alternative narratives that influence the movements they join.[15]

Because Al-Shabaab dominates the jihadist opposition in Somalia, it has largely been able to manage foreign fighters' influence. Al-Shabaab has limited competition with other groups in Somalia for foreign fighters, though greater competition could create pressure for the group to give foreign fighters more sway or result in a loss of foreign fighters. Since late 2015, the Islamic State-aligned group in Puntland has garnered some appeal amongst foreign fighters in the region, which would probably increase if the Islamic State officially recognizes the group.[16] To date, it has channelled some foreign fighters away from Al-Shabaab, and Al-Shabaab has killed foreign fighters who attempted to defect.[17] However, it does not pose a significant challenge to Al-Shabaab, particularly because its composition is largely limited to one sub-clan.

Despite some inroads by the Islamic State, Al-Shabaab maintains well established recruitment networks in the region, and the vast majority of its foreign fighters now come from Kenya, followed by Tanzania and Uganda.[18] However, the number of foreign fighters joining Al-Shabaab who come from the Arab world and the West has decreased substantially.[19] One exception is the flow of people, goods, and materiel between Yemen and Somalia, rooted in the longstanding connections between the two countries.[20] In addition, there are reports of some foreign fighters hailing from Sudan and South Africa.[21]

In recent years, Al-Shabaab has constrained foreign fighters' influence. Though a former Al-Shabaab leader publicly professed a need for "Somalia's Zarqawi,"[22] the group's attitude towards foreign fighters is that it welcomes their contribution as long as they advance and adhere to Al-Shabaab's agenda, rather than trying to change it.[23] Leadership positions are overwhelmingly, if not exclusively, held by Somalis.[24] The group balks when foreign fighters seek too much attention or influence.[25]

There are exceptions to these limitations on foreign fighters, based on individuals' abilities, achievements, and circumstances. Overall, in the period between 2006 and 2011, foreign fighters' influence peaked.[26] During these years, some of the East African Al-Qaida operatives in particular garnered significant influence through their jihadist credentials, experience, ideological authority, and longstanding ties to Somalia and Al-Shabaab leaders—a combination difficult to replicate.[27] They were later joined by foreign fighters with connections to Al-Qaida in the Arabian Peninsula (AQAP), who also brought considerable experience and prestige, but who were not integrated into Al-Shabaab's leadership structure.[28]

Since then, the influence of foreign fighters has decreased because of counter-terrorism pressure[29] and the concerns about spies it stokes, as well as the decision by the now deceased Al-Shabaab emir, Ahmed Mukhtar Abu al-Zubayr Godane (Godane) to purge challengers, which included killing some foreign fighters and caused others to flee.[30] Today, some foreign fighters, particularly those from Kenya, have accrued some responsibility for foreign fighter units or for activities such as fundraising in the region outside of Somalia. Some have reportedly risen to mid-level commander positions in Somalia.[31]

Nevertheless, there is a ceiling to their promotion potential, and their influence is limited to operational and tactical matters, rather than strategic direction.[32] Furthermore, in order for a foreign fighter to accrue significant influence in Somalia, he must acquire the protection of a Somali national; in return, he must behave in accordance with Somali traditions.[33] Only a few, such as the American foreign fighter Jehad Mustafa, reportedly a senior advisor to Al-Shabaab's current emir, have managed to secure this arrangement.[34]

The Roles of Foreign Fighters

It can be difficult to assess the role of foreign fighters in Al-Shabaab because there is a tendency to attribute aspects of Al-Shabaab to foreign fighters when no other clear explanation exists or to see a foreign hand behind unexpected developments. Moreover, it is hard to determine whether instances in which foreign fighters are observed—or not observed—in specific contexts are representative of their involvement, especially because Al-Shabaab is decentralized. Observers have attributed Al-Shabaab's administrative organization, tactics, ability to indoctrinate suicide bombers, and other aspects of the group to foreign fighter influence.[35] However, a number of Al-Shabaab operatives have lived abroad and even been foreign fighters in other conflicts; thus, they may have imported knowledge and skills.[36] Alternatively, the group may imitate successful approaches used elsewhere.

The available evidence suggests that foreign fighters appear to exert the most influence in offering tactical innovations, particularly as they relate to Al-Shabaab's expertise in explosives, and producing propaganda to reach audiences beyond Somalis.

Explosives Capability

The most consequential role that foreign fighters play is in bolstering Al-Shabaab's explosives capability. Some even speculate that Al-Shabaab's primary bomb maker is a Yemeni or foreign fighter.[37] However, this issue is also shrouded in secrecy, conjecture, and disagreement. What is clear is that AQAP possesses sophisticated explosives capability and seeks to bolster its allies' capacities in this area, even offering instructions in its publications.[38] AQAP probably prefers to cooperate with Al-Shabaab because the environment in Somalia also offers a place for AQAP to experiment with innovations.[39] Al-Shabaab has likely received episodic explosive fabrication training and materiel from AQAP, such as triggers and pressure sensors.[40] In particular, the sophistication of the laptop explosive device used in the attack on Daallo Airlines last February and the size of some of Al-Shabaab's vehicle explosive devices point to external infusions of capability, possibly from its Yemeni ally.[41] The frequency and nature of such exchanges is unknown, but they appear to be irregular.

On the other hand, it is possible to overemphasize the role of AQAP or outside assistance to Al-Shabaab. Al-Shabaab has proven to be sufficiently capable, innovative, and adaptive that it need not rely on outside assistance to execute many of its attacks.[42] Furthermore, once Al-Shabaab operatives have been trained in tactics and skills, they can adapt and apply them without regular assistance.[43]

Propaganda

In addition to bolstering Al-Shabaab's explosives capability, foreign fighters have long played a role in the group's propaganda, primarily in its efforts to reach out to non-Somali speakers.[44] While this is an important facet of the recruitment of foreign fighters, the visibility of this role may give the impression that the propagandists are more influential in Al-Shabaab than they actually are.[45] Swahili is now the second most common language in its publications, a product of the group's East African foreign fighter cadre.[46] Since 2013, Al-Shabaab has produced propaganda in Swahili directed towards Muslim populations in the region, primarily Kenya and to a lesser extent Tanzania and Uganda.[47] One particularly visible spokesman is Ahmad Iman Ali, a Kenyan engineer who now leads Al-Shabaab's Kenya wing.[48] The propaganda seeks to exploit grievances against the Kenyan government, particularly its counter-terrorism efforts.[49] The group produces Swahili-language material that analysts have likened to a Swahili version of *Inspire*, AQAP's notorious English language magazine.[50] In addition, foreign fighters have propaganda value beyond their outputs, as Al-Shabaab points to foreign fighters as evidence that it has transcended clannism and embodies the *umma*.[51]

Foreign fighters from the West who arrived in the early years of the conflict were instrumental in producing English language propaganda. However, this effort ultimately failed when Al-Shabaab's deceased emir Godane had the group's highest profile American foreign fighter, Omar Hammami, killed in a purge that also removed some of the challengers to his leadership.[52] Even during this period, foreign fighters who were quite visible on the propaganda front were often not assimilated into Al-Shabaab's command structure, and thus they exerted less influence over the group than it appeared.[53] Their propaganda served more to expand recruitment, radicalize supporters in the West, and shape outside perceptions of Al-Shabaab, than to influence the group.

Training

Apart from bolstering Al-Shabaab's explosives capability, foreign fighters have occupied roles as trainers. Their influence as trainers was at its apex shortly before and after the Ethiopian military intervention in 2006 and lasted through 2011, when reports abounded about foreign fighters operating as military advisors and conducting training for Al-Shabaab.[54] However, this role has diminished in recent years, though there are still sporadic reports of foreign trainers.[55]

Foot Soldiers

Many foreign fighters, including East Africans, are foot soldiers for Al-Shabaab and populate the lower ranks of Al-Shabaab's military wing, Jaysh al-Usra.[56] Within Somalia, the East African rank-and-file fighters are reportedly treated as expendable and exert minimal influence, though accounts of this rely disproportionately on defectors who have a motive to minimize their role.[57] Some foreign fighters, particularly Kenyans, have accrued some responsibility for activities concentrated outside of Somalia, most notably Al-Shabaab's externally focused wing, Jaysh Ayman, which seeks to conduct attacks in the region, particularly across the border in Kenya.[58] In a May graduation ceremony for primarily Kenyan recruits, Al-Shabaab's spokesman urged them to become an "army that will conquer Kenya."[59] In addition, female foreign fighters from the region are increasingly involved in combat roles, rather than solely fulfilling traditional gender roles.[60] While some foreign fighters have become suicide operatives,[61] Al-Shabaab does not depend on them for suicide operations and they may have limited utility in Somalia because they attract attention.[62]

Variation and Limitations on Foreign Fighter Influence

With a few exceptions, foreign fighters exert limited influence over Al-Shabaab. They exerted more influence in the early years of the conflict, when Al-Shabaab was a young organization and the foreign fighters included experienced and respected operatives. Overall, though the group will continue to exploit local grievances to recruit in the region, seven inter-related conditions inhibit foreign fighters' influence within Al-Shabaab.

1. Many of Al-Shabaab's activities are intensely local.[63] Its administration, such as taxation, dispute resolution efforts, as well as its intelligence collection, require an in-depth understanding of Somali clans and culture that foreigners are unlikely to possess. In essence, Al-Shabaab's composition reflects its priorities, and its priority is Somalia.[64]

2. Despite Al-Shabaab's claims to transcend clannism, its power is derived in large part from its ability to manage and exploit clan politics, particularly the grievances of marginalized and disenfranchised clans.[65] Foreign fighters rarely contribute to these activities, because they struggle to grasp the intricacies of Somali clan politics and because locals resist such foreign interference.[66]

3. The foreign fighters best positioned to garner influence in Al-Shabaab are less interested in what has become largely a clan-based conflict, especially in a location outside of the Middle East. Even recruitment networks in the West that once channelled fighters, including diaspora members, to Somalia have largely shifted to sending foreign fighters to Syria.[67]

4. Al-Shabaab's need to recruit foreign fighters to bolster its jihadist credentials diminished when it became an Al-Qaida affiliate, especially after being publicly recognized by Al-Qaida in 2012.

5. Cultural dynamics militate against East African fighters gaining strategic influence in Al-Shabaab. Although Al-Shabaab has sought to shed xenophobia, it tends to look down upon its East African counterparts.[68]

6. Mistrust, particularly fears that foreign fighters are spies, often bedevil foreign fighters' ability to garner influence, a problem exacerbated by their tendency to attract counter-terrorism pressure.[69] While Al-Shabaab also punishes locals for spying, foreigners have come under scrutiny for spying and lack clan protections, making them particularly vulnerable to accusations of being spies.[70]

7. Lastly, regional foreign fighters are recruited for largely practical reasons—to build up Al-Shabaab's numbers and to draw in Swahili speakers for propaganda and media operations—rather than for roles that would involve leadership and decision-making.[71]

These factors explain foreign fighters' limited influence in Al-Shabaab. However, for two reasons, policy-makers should not be complacent about the threat they pose. First, there has been a decline in foreign fighter flows to Syria. By September 2016, reports suggested that the number of foreign fighters crossing the Turkish-Syrian border dropped from a peak of 2,000 per month, to a low of 50.[72] In the wake of the Islamic State's territorial losses, some foreign fighters have even sought to leave Syria.[73] Should the Islamic State's fortunes continue to decline, there may be a larger exodus of foreign fighters, most of whom cannot return home. They may seek to join jihadist conflicts in places ill-equipped to keep them out, such as Yemen, Libya, and Somalia. At least 70 Somalis have gone to Syria,[74] in addition to an unknown number of Somali diaspora members. It would not take many capable foreign fighters coming from Syria to bolster Al-Shabaab's capability, particularly if they possess jihadist credentials, combat experience, and operational skills.

Second, despite the limitations of foreign fighter influence on Al-Shabaab, the foreign fighters who have joined Al-Shabaab from the region may pose a threat to their home countries. They may return home with greater ideological commitment, jihadist credibility among locals, and some experience. While a minority of foreign fighters who return home engage in terrorism in their home countries, those who do are particularly lethal and effective.[75] Thus, the East Africans who have joined Al-Shabaab are likely to form the basis of the future terrorist threat in the region.[76]

Conclusion

Overall, foreign fighters will not determine Al-Shabaab's future trajectory. Instead, they will provide manpower, help to expand the group's recruitment beyond its Somali base, and offer sporadic improvements to its operational capability. They can help implement and operationalize aspects of the group's strategy, but play only a limited role, if any, in determining it. Few foreign fighters will reach the senior echelons of the group, though the more capable may become commanders in Al-Shabaab's military wing or be responsible for activities in East Africa outside of Somalia. Given Al-Shabaab's degree of decentralization, foreign fighters' level of involvement at the local level will vary significantly, but they will not be able to take lead roles in governance activities—a pillar of the group's strength. Foreign fighters will be particularly vulnerable to mistrust and accusations of spying during periods of heightened counter-terrorism pressure.

Consequently, foreign fighters will have limited input into Al-Shabaab's reconciliation posture. However, they are more likely to have global jihadist aspirations and thus be among those opposed to reconciliation.[77] Moreover, the hardliners in Al-Shabaab most opposed to reconciliation are probably also those closest to Al-Qaida and AQAP. By extension, hardliners will be the beneficiaries of foreign fighter assistance and thus have the potential to act as spoilers, particularly by employing the explosives capability imparted by their Yemeni ally.

Foreign fighters are likely to resist reconciliation efforts that do not offer them a viable exit option. Moreover, without an exit option, foreign fighters may return to their home countries disenfranchised, radicalized, and with combat experience. Those who continue involvement in violence could damage regional political will and support for reconciliation efforts in Somalia.[78]

Recommendations

Given foreign fighters' limitations in Al-Shabaab, there are exploitable fissures and opportunities for Somalia, East African nations, and partnering nations to mitigate this problem. In Somalia, policy-makers should seek to discourage Somalis and Al-Shabaab from hosting foreign fighters. In particular, they should offer carrots and sticks to clans to discourage them from offering protection to foreign fighters and to encourage them to expel resident foreign fighters. Policy-makers in Somalia should consider placing pressure on clans in areas in which foreign fighters operate in order to increase the costs associated with hosting foreign fighters.

These efforts should be coupled with policies in the countries from which foreign fighters hail, particularly Kenya, Tanzania, and Uganda. In particular, policies should focus on hindering foreign fighter recruitment and dealing with foreign fighter returnees. To dampen recruitment, countries in the region should bolster counter-narrative efforts against Al-Shabaab, particularly using defector accounts to expose how Al-Shabaab has treated foreign fighters, their limited influence, and the disillusionment that some experience. Counter-narrative efforts could also portray the cause in Somalia as a local, clan-based conflict, which may have less appeal among foreign fighters. Moreover, improved community–police relations would enable members of the community to report to authorities when they have concerns about individuals being radicalized or recruited. These countries also need to implement policies to encourage and manage foreign fighter returnees. Policies should include programmes to deradicalize and reintegrate foreign fighters back into their community. As appropriate, countries in the region could consider amnesty programmes to encourage defections.

One of the most difficult challenges is addressing the exchange and cooperation between Yemen and Somalia. The cultural and commercial connections between the two countries expand well beyond the Al-Shabaab–AQAP relationship. However, even limited improvements in border and maritime security could hinder AQAP and Al-Shabaab's ability to cooperate. Interceptions of emissaries between the two groups, as occurred in 2011, could significantly hinder cooperation.

TRAVELLING FOR AN IDEA

THE APPEAL OF AL-SHABAAB TO DIASPORA IN THE WEST

Joshua Meservey

Author

Joshua Meservey is the Senior Policy Analyst for Africa and the Middle East at the Heritage Foundation in Washington, DC. He lived in Zambia and Kenya, and worked at the United States Army Special Operations Command and the Atlantic Council's Africa Center. Meservey holds an MA from the Fletcher School at Tufts University and a BA from the Templeton Honors College at Eastern University.

Summary

Members of the Somali diaspora in the West (hereafter referred to as the "diaspora") were the major source of Al-Shabaab's Western foreign fighters. Previously, a considerable number of members of the diaspora joined or attempted to join Al-Shabaab (referred to below as "travellers"), and while the group's attractiveness for potential travellers has waned, the risk remains that it could revive.

Understanding who the travellers were and what motivated them is the first step to ensuring they do not again become a significant danger and disrupt efforts to achieve peace and reconciliation in Somalia. The lack of information on travellers makes doing so difficult, but the data we do have reveal several important trends. The majority of travellers for whom there is information were young, male, of the "1.5 generation" (those who were born to first-generation parents or who immigrated to a host country at a young age), relatively well educated, and radicalized in their country of birth or host country.

Alienation is a risk factor for radicalization, and many factors converge to isolate diaspora from the mainstream society of their host countries. The fact that so many travellers were from the 1.5 generation, members of which may feel uniquely estranged from their parents' country and their host country, suggests that disaffection and marginalization were important to travellers' radicalization.

Paradoxically, however, travellers are usually among the least alienated people within their communities. They are often comparatively well-educated and have better local language skills, and acquaintances frequently describe them as normal and happy people prior to their radicalization. This suggests it is the pull of the ideology of Al-Shabaab, rather than the push of negative environmental factors, that best explains travellers' attraction to Al-Shabaab.

The thesis of this chapter is that alienation plays a role in radicalization, in so much as travellers' acceptance of Al-Shabaab's violently anti-Western rhetoric demonstrates they were not deeply assimilated into the mainstream values of their host countries. It was Al-Shabaab's ideology that primarily attracted travellers, however. Governments must try to delegitimize Al-Shabaab's worldview while promoting the attractions of their own ways of life if they wish to ensure travellers will not again seek out Al-Shabaab in large numbers.

Introduction

Travellers have participated in Al-Shabaab throughout its existence, which should be of concern to all countries affected by terrorism. Travellers are a propaganda victory for Al-Shabaab, buttressing its claims that the sinful West is inhospitable to and unworthy of true Muslims. Recruiting one person from the West often enables recruitment of others as well, given the potency of peer-to-peer recruitment.

Travellers also give Al-Shabaab far more flexibility for attacking targets outside of Somalia. They blend in easily in their home countries with their fluency in Western languages and cultural knowledge, and carry passports that grant them easy access to most countries. Tracking them requires excellent intelligence services, and some are still likely to return back home undetected. Even known returnees are a challenge—discreetly monitoring one person requires as many as 25 trained personnel.[1]

Travellers also strengthen Al-Shabaab by providing manpower and in some cases advanced skills, such as facility with computers, social media, or technical knowledge it would be otherwise difficult for the group to obtain. Many are also unusually committed to the cause. At least 12 travellers—from the United Kingdom, Canada, Denmark, Germany, Norway, the Netherlands, and the United States—launched suicide attacks inside Somalia. A Somalia-born Norwegian citizen, Hassan Abdi Dhuhulow, is believed to have participated in the 2013 attack on the Westgate Mall in Nairobi, Kenya,[2] one of the worst terror attacks the country has ever suffered.

Al-Shabaab's attractiveness for the diaspora has significantly waned. As long as the group is active, however, the danger remains that it could again appeal to the diaspora. Understanding travellers can help governments prevent that from happening. Travellers' experiences also offer clues to what an effective Countering Violent Extremism (CVE) programme targeting Islamist radicalization should include, an increasingly urgent task throughout the world.

A Long History

The conflicts in Somalia attracted Western-affiliated foreign fighters well before Al-Shabaab formed. As far back as 1996, a European citizen fought against Ethiopian forces with Al-Ittihad Al-Islami,[3] as did Mogadishu-born Swedish asylee Gouled Hassan Dourad from 1997 until his capture.[4]

The Union of Islamic Courts (UIC), in which Al-Shabaab incubated, also had foreign fighters, including Americans Daniel Maldonado[5] and Omar Hammami. (The latter went on to become the most notorious American member of Al-Shabaab.) There were several prominent UIC leaders from the diaspora, including Swedish citizen Fu'ad Muhammed Qalaf, who became a senior member of Al-Shabaab, and Abdullahi Ali Afrah, a naturalized Canadian citizen.[6] There are credible reports that other Somali-origin citizens of the United Kingdom, Canada, Sweden, and Denmark also joined the UIC.[7]

From its earliest days, Al-Shabaab coveted foreign fighters,[8] and Ethiopia's 2006 military intervention proved a boon in this regard. No precise publicly available count of how many Somali diaspora joined Al-Shabaab exists, but open source reporting almost certainly underestimates the number. Diaspora have told researchers that families did not always inform relevant authorities when a member of their family joined Al-Shabaab,[9] and some governments release only partial information—or no information at all—about the cases of which they are aware. Nevertheless, it is likely hundreds from the Somali diaspora joined Al-Shabaab, perhaps as many as 1,000.[10]

Spreading the Message

Al-Shabaab's message to foreign recruits blended nationalist and religious appeals. The two themes were so intertwined as to be nearly indistinguishable from each other, and the group presented them as mutually reinforcing concepts. Al-Shabaab highlighted what it described as a civilizational struggle between the Muslim and Christian worlds, and frequently invoked various "Christian" countries' military involvement in Somalia as evidence of that struggle. Al-Shabaab propagandists commonly argued that believing Muslims had a responsibility to join the jihad, and described the shame good Muslims should feel living in comfort in an infidel country while their countrymen and Muslim brothers and sisters suffered from an invasion.[11]

Al-Shabaab spread its message to the diaspora through videos, in online chat rooms, and, before its accounts were shut down, on social media platforms such as Twitter. Interacting in real time with a persuasive Al-Shabaab devotee, however, was a critical part of the radicalization process for many who joined Al-Shabaab.[12] This dispersed and decentralized recruitment model, often known as "peer-to-peer" recruitment, tends to feature a popular member of a circle of friends and acquaintances recruiting others within the circle. The result was clusters of people who knew each other—including, in some cases, family members—radicalizing, some of whom travelled together to Somalia.[13] Men such as Mahamud Said Omar, Cabdulaahi Ahmed Faarax—who returned to the United States from fighting with Al-Shabaab to recruit before returning to Somalia—and Abdiweli Yassin in the United States, and Ismail Ahmed Yassin and Fu'ad Muhammed Qalaf from Sweden were influential in attracting recruits from those countries.

Peer-to-peer recruitment partly explains why particular cities and neighbourhoods were recruitment hotbeds. Minneapolis, Minnesota in the United States and the Rinkenby neighbourhood in Stockholm, Sweden are good examples, and Norwegian officials have observed that some of their towns and neighbourhoods produce a disproportionate number of Al-Shabaab fighters.[14]

Al-Shabaab's appeal within the diaspora fell dramatically in the late 2000s, though there is still a trickle of support—in May 2017, Dutch police arrested a man of Somali background suspected of aiding Al-Shabaab.[15] However, Al-Shabaab's support has dried up not because the diaspora has overcome its problems with radicalization. In recent years, they have joined Middle Eastern terrorist organizations in significant numbers, even appearing in propaganda videos which echo the role Somalia diaspora members used to play for Al-Shabaab.

Why Travellers Chose Al-Shabaab

Westerners with no ethnic connection to Somalia have joined Al-Shabaab, but most of Al-Shabaab's Western foreign fighters were diaspora. Understanding why is a critical first step in ensuring Al-Shabaab does not again become an attractive destination for travellers.

First, though, we should note that so many variables affect radicalization that it is impossible to pinpoint the precise reasons for a particular individual's embrace of extremism. Biographical data on travellers are also patchy, so extrapolating trends is difficult. Scholars should continue to test all the following hypotheses as more data on travellers emerge.

The data that are available reveal some broad trends. Most travellers were young, male, of the 1.5 generation, relatively well-educated, and radicalized in their country of birth or host country. This rough demographic profile is in keeping with the findings of other studies of Westerners involved in Islamist terrorism.[16]

Some scholars believe a sense of alienation from mainstream society can facilitate radicalization.[17] The diaspora's experience provides some evidence for this. The 1.5 generation that is so heavily represented among travellers can feel adrift, as they do not strongly identify with their parents' home country or with their new, host country.[18] Members of the diaspora have remarked on just this phenomenon to explain why some of their youth radicalize.[19] It is in keeping as well with research on radicalized members of other diasporas.[20]

There are also particularities of Somali culture and Somalis' recent history that contribute to a heightened sense of alienation among their youth in Western societies. Somali diaspora communities are frequently described as insular[21] and sceptical of the mainstream culture of their host countries, fed in part by the belief among a number of Somalis that they are victims of anti-Muslim and anti-African campaigns.[22] This could heighten the struggle for their young people who may feel torn between the attractions of their new home and a community that insists they remain authentically Somali.

Furthermore, most Somali diaspora now living in the West have spent long periods living as refugees or asylum seekers. From the 1980s on, many spent years or even decades in refugee camps with little opportunity to build the skill sets necessary to thrive in Western-style, advanced economies. This partially explains why Somalis in the West usually have much lower rates of employment, educational achievement, income, and native language acquisition than the native community or other immigrant communities.[23]

The added pressures inherent in emigration might also be relevant. Children frequently integrate better into host cultures than do their parents. This can upend the power dynamics within families and place further pressure on immigrant children, as parents must rely on their children to help them navigate a new country.

The Paradox of Comparatively Well-Integrated Travellers

Yet there is also a paradox. Many travellers appear to be among the least alienated people in their communities. In general, members of the 1.5 generation are usually better integrated into their host countries than are others from their same community.[24] It is rare to read of travellers' acquaintances describing them as isolated or disaffected.[25] An uncle of one traveller described them as "our best kids,"[26] while another traveller was a member of the elite Norwegian Royal Guard military unit before he left for Somalia.[27] In retrospect, one of the warning signs for some of those who later joined Al-Shabaab was their withdrawal from the activities and relationships in which they normally engaged and which were typical of those in their peer group.[28]

The fact that so many attended college or university is also of interest. A total of 67 travellers are identifiable through open source reporting. Of the 23 travellers for whom there is educational information, at least 15 attended college or university. Education does not guarantee assimilation into society, but it does tend to expose students to mainstream culture. College and university education also suggests a positive economic trajectory and the potential for greater inclusion in the mainstream economy.

There are several possible explanations for this paradox. The 1.5 generation might be over-represented among travellers not because of the alienating effects of being of that generation, but because they are over-represented within the diaspora. There is a strong chance that a Somali who grew up in the

West arrived there as a child or was born there to first-generation immigrants simply because of the Somali community's recent emigration history.[29]

Alternatively, other influences might outweigh whatever positive effect integration brings. The youth of many of the travellers is likely relevant. The average age of travellers from the United States, when they first engage in radical activity, is 22.[30] This is consistent with research showing the average age of a sample of recruits to Middle Eastern terrorist groups to be 24.[31] Another study found that the average age of people convicted in the United States of supporting IS was 26.[32]

The most likely explanation for the paradox is that travellers' relatively mainstream lives represented only a superficial commitment to the values of their host countries. The fact that they did not recoil from Al-Shabaab's violent anti-Western rhetoric is compelling evidence that travellers did not have a preeminent loyalty to their host countries.

The Importance of Ideology

A leading researcher has found that ideology primarily motivates foreign fighters who join a jihad far from their normal area of residence.[33] The experience of travellers supports this thesis. A worldview, however repulsive, founded on nationalism and religion was the pillar of Al-Shabaab's propaganda to which travellers responded.

The fact that so many travellers were comparatively well educated further suggests the importance of ideology in the radicalization process. Educational attainment is not a perfect gauge of intellectual curiosity, but it at least suggests a certain aptitude for and openness to ideas. Those likely to pursue higher education may well be the type of person most willing to consider Al-Shabaab's ideas and arguments.[34] This is consistent with other scholarship that found that nearly 50 per cent of extremists from a range of groups had some level of higher education.[35]

Conclusion

As with all hypotheses concerning radicalization, the analysis presented here is not entirely satisfactory. It cannot explain what it is about travellers that made them willing to accept Al-Shabaab's propaganda while most in their immediate peer group—with the same demographic profile, pressures, and access to Al-Shabaab propaganda—did not.

431

It is still useful, however, to note that many of the travellers were comparatively well-integrated, well-educated, and well-adjusted young men. They were not the most vulnerable or weakest-minded within the diaspora. Many were instead on more positive trajectories than others within their community, highlighting the inadequacy of understanding travellers as merely angry, immature, or disaffected youths.

Environmental factors may have added to a sense of alienation that contributed to travellers' radicalization—the fact that travellers accepted Al-Shabaab's message with its virulent anti-Western rhetoric and beliefs is evidence they had not deeply assimilated—but they do not appear to be determinative. Rather, in keeping with other scholarship on foreign fighters, Al-Shabaab's ideology appears to have been the driving force behind travellers' radicalization. Understanding the ideology's appeal is a critical first step in preventing travellers—and other potential recruits drawn to Al-Shabaab's beliefs—from joining the group, and in helping to support Somalia's journey to peace and reconciliation.

Recommendations

The fact that Al-Shabaab's ideology played a primary role in travellers' radicalization should guide policy-makers' CVE efforts. Because travellers find Al-Shabaab's worldview more convincing than alternatives, CVE programs should include two components: discrediting Al-Shabaab's worldview and the ideology that underpins it, and promoting tolerant and pluralistic ideologies and ways of life. To do so, Western countries should:

• Work with local religious and youth leaders to develop counter-narratives to Al-Shabaab's propaganda. Given the risks of radicalization among youth, their rejection of established religious norms and institutions, and the potency of peer-to-peer recruitment, young people must play a central role in developing and spreading counter-narratives. Governments must also be careful not to discredit the process with excessive and overt involvement. They should identify quiet ways to support diaspora religious and youth leaders committed to exposing Al-Shabaab's theological errors. Governments could encourage religious leaders to identify the specific religious claims Al-Shabaab makes and then debunk them point by point with evidence from Islamic sacred texts. The results should be distributed in ways appropriate to the various diaspora communities, with a particular focus on youth.

- Confidently articulate and commend the way of life Al-Shabaab derides. Countries should tout their records of creating peaceful, prosperous societies where laws and values demonstrate their commitment to equality and freedom for all their citizens and residents. Countries should juxtapose this with the authoritarian, violent, and unjust rule Al-Shabaab maintains in areas under its control, and which it aspires to spread throughout the region.
- Promote diaspora attachment to mainstream society. Host countries should encourage Somali diaspora communities to patriotically embrace mainstream values. If these communities are disconnected from the rest of society, it will be hard to promote the sort of deep attachment by diaspora to their host countries that makes extremist propaganda seem repulsive.
- Rigorously test CVE results. Governments around the world are dedicating increased resources to CVE programs as they grapple with the accelerating problem of domestic radicalization. The urgency to deploy these programs and the difficulty of quantifying their results should not deter governments from testing their effectiveness. Not doing so risks wasting limited resources and allowing counterproductive programmes to continue.
- Build trust between law enforcement and the diaspora. Law enforcement only addresses the symptoms of radicalization and not the cause. It is still important, however, to increase domestic law enforcement's capacity to prevent radicalized people from hurting others. Some members of the diaspora have already provided invaluable help fighting radicalization, but law enforcement needs a more trusting relationship with diaspora communities to better combat extremism. Hiring qualified Somali policemen and women is one way to build that kind of trust.

ENGAGING WITH AL-SHABAAB

NEGOTIATIONS WITH AL-SHABAAB

LESSONS LEARNED AND FUTURE PROSPECTS

Harmonie Toros and *Stephen Harley*

Authors

Dr Harmonie Toros, Senior Lecturer in International Conflict Analysis at the University of Kent, is author of numerous books, articles, and policy reports on negotiations with non-state armed groups.

Stephen Harley provides consultancy to the Federal Government of Somalia Office of the President, British Embassy in Mogadishu, King's College London's Department of War Studies, and the NATO Centre of Excellence in Defence Against Terrorism.

Summary

The election of President Mohamed Abdullahi Mohamed "Farmaajo" in Somalia is viewed by key actors as potentially opening up the space for negotiations with Al-Shabaab. This research paper, based on a broad review of the existing literature and numerous in-depth interviews with key Somali and international actors, examines the potential for talks, identifies potential facilitators and spoilers, and highlights lessons to be learned from past dialogues with Al-Shabaab. Three main conclusions are reached.

First, many Somali and international parties agree that there exists some degree of common ground between the Federal Government of Somalia (FGS) and Al-Shabaab. In particular regarding the final political objective, the main actors in Somalia can rally behind the project of better Somali-owned governance that is broadly in accordance with local Islamic traditions.

Second, while Somali elders, business leaders, and Muslim-majority countries have been identified as potential facilitators or initiators of a dialogue with Al-Shabaab, the report notes that such talks require at least non-opposition from key factions in the FGS and Al-Shabaab and more broadly from powerful regional powers who have rejected past agreements.

Third, FGS and international actors need to decide whether they want to maintain their focus on facilitating and promoting defections from Al-Shabaab—with the view of isolating hardliners for them to either surrender or be eliminated militarily—or want to explore the possibility of comprehensive talks with Al-Shabaab aimed at bringing in the entire armed group. These are potentially conflicting goals, and this choice has important implications for Somalia's future[1] and for international peace and security.

Introduction

15 years into the "War on Terror", there is increasing agreement amongst researchers, policy-makers, and practitioners that negotiations and dialogue can offer viable paths to peace and reconciliation even in contexts marked by terrorist violence. In-depth studies of numerous longstanding conflicts across the world[2] have been backed by a large-scale quantitative analysis of "how terrorism ends" carried out by the RAND corporation in 2008,[3] which concluded that the most likely reason for terrorist campaigns to end between 1968 and 2006 was through a political process (43 per cent), far outweighing military responses (7 per cent).

This briefing paper examines the potential for negotiations and dialogue with Al-Shabaab, a designated group, subjected to United Nations sanctions under both the Somalia and Eritrea Security Council resolutions (751, 1907) as well as the so-called Islamic State (IS), Al-Qaida and associated individuals, groups, undertakings and entities resolutions (1267, 1989, 2253). The paper has three principal aims. First, to investigate past examples of talks with Al-Shabaab, potential missed opportunities for engagement, and lessons that may be learned from these; second, to outline how relevant actors on the ground—from the Somali government, to clan elders, to former Al-Shabaab fighters, to international actors—envision the role of negotiations with Al-Shabaab in the current political and security climate; and third, to identify the principal hurdles to negotiations in the current context.

The research is based on primary and secondary data collection, starting with an extensive review of academic research, practitioner and policy reports, and news reports on past negotiations with Al-Shabaab. This was complemented by a series of semi-structured interviews with representatives of the principal actors of Somalia's complex political and security landscape. All participants spoke on the condition they not be named. The project underwent a thorough ethics review by the University of Kent of its data gathering process and its confidentiality provisions.

History of Negotiations with Al-Shabaab

Over its more than ten-year lifespan, starting with the Union of Islamic Courts (UIC), several actors have engaged in numerous formal and informal dialogues directly with Al-Shabaab or actors linked to the group. Negotiations and dialogues are formal and informal, reported and unreported.[4] In this section, we will focus on two key tracks during this period that have been documented: the formal high-level dialogue in 2006 and in 2008–09; and the negotiations between humanitarian actors and Al-Shabaab during and following the 2011 famine.

The most important lessons learned from the high-level talks are the vulnerability of peace agreements to the priorities of regional and international actors, and the need for any agreement to include the key Somali factions on the ground. The failure of the 2006 talks in Khartoum between the Transitional Federal Government (TFG) and the UIC can be attributed to a variety of factors, but central among them is the refusal of regional powers to accept an agreement that was not made under their auspices, leading to suspicion from Somalia's immediate neighbours and culminating in a military intervention by Ethiopia.[5]

Two years later, the more sustained peace process based in Djibouti in 2008–09 suffered from what has been identified in the conflict resolution literature as a key flaw in peace processes: a lack of inclusivity. Indeed, as the Alliance for the Re-Liberation of Somalia (representing the recomposed forces of the UIC including Al-Shabaab leaders) split between "moderates" and "hardliners" and the negotiations only involved the moderates, the agreements lacked the support of key armed actors on the ground who did not buy into the process and successfully undermined it through military activity.[6]

The other track is the negotiations that took place between intergovernmental and non-governmental organizations on the one hand and Al-Shabaab officials on the other during and following the 2011 famine. Although differing accounts of these talks have emerged, their occurrence is uncontested and most research seems to agree that Al-Shabaab, at least in some instances, acted as a working negotiating partner.[7] Al-Shabaab set up a cross-organizational structure of "Humanitarian Coordination Officers" to deal with requests to deliver aid in Al-Shabaab-controlled/patrolled territory and most reports note that access was negotiated primarily at a local level. To engage in these talks, humanitarian actors often distanced themselves from their foreign donors to placate ongoing Al-Shabaab suspicion of being used for intelligence gathering and often sent local Somali employees to negotiate with Al-Shabaab representatives.[8]

Particularly interesting is the fact that humanitarian actors appealed "to Al-Shabaab's image as an alternative to the government by stressing the obligation of local commanders to care for civilians under their control."[9] In terms of lessons learned, it is worth noting that all sides emerged suspicious from these interactions, with Al-Shabaab coming under considerable criticism for restricting access to humanitarian aid and Al-Shabaab supporters accusing the international community, particularly in the post-famine phase, of politicizing aid.

In the future, negotiations to ensure humanitarian access or simply aid delivery could be a chance to establish relationships with Al-Shabaab actors at a local level. Such relationships could offer several advantages, including reversing negative perceptions of international actors and building negotiating habits among Al-Shabaab commanders. It must be noted however that Al-Shabaab is known to often transfer its officials from one region to another to ensure that long-term relationships with local communities are not established.[10] These are all important lessons learned with respect to the current drought and the potential need for authorization and coordination for aid distribution in Al-Shabaab-patrolled areas. Such "technical" dialogues have in other cases led to some degree of trust-building between opposing parties that was used to engage in more comprehensive peace talks.[11]

Current Attitudes to Negotiations with Al-Shabaab

The approaches of four key actors toward negotiations with Al-Shabaab have been investigated: the Somali government; the international community; non-aligned Somali elders; and Al-Shabaab itself.

Somali Government

The position of the Somali government with regard to a negotiated settlement is deliberately vague. Although President Farmaajo publicly offered to talk to Al-Shabaab, "including its leaders," there have been no known steps to engage in high-level talks. His offer was coupled with a fixed, 60-day period of amnesty and a parallel declaration of war.

Discussion of amnesties in other contexts have been part of broader peace overtures with non-state armed groups. In Somalia, an Amnesty Policy was issued in the final days of the previous administration under President Hassan Sheikh Mohamud. This generic policy was justified by the government on the grounds that in the absence of large-scale defections or desertions the process needed to remain flexible. There is some degree of logic to this approach but the result has been a lack of clarity for potential defectors or deserters in terms of how they defect or surrender: where, when, and to whom—and what happens if they do.

International Actors

International actors offered a particular understanding of negotiations that overall excluded the possibility of high-level comprehensive negotiations with Al-Shabaab, at least until the group's strength and reach are considerably reduced. Indeed, as stated by one official, the argument is that "any negotiations (with Al-Shabaab) have to start from a position of strength." Some interlocutors ascribed this to Somali propensity to "respond to military pressure," thus requiring parties to feel they are losing ground before they are willing to negotiate.[12] Overall, international actors—whether in foreign services of relevant states or working for intergovernmental organizations—saw negotiations as a potentially useful means to convince senior and mid-level Al-Shabaab commanders to leave the group.

The aim of such an approach would be to reduce the strength and reach of Al-Shabaab so as to either destroy the group militarily or achieve wide-scale surrender. International actors pointed at internal and external actors as potential allies and intermediaries in this strategy. Somali elders could be convinced to act as conduits for discussions with high- and medium-level would-be defectors or deserters, while certain Muslim countries (several pointed at Turkey, Qatar, and Saudi Arabia) could offer incentives to leaders to leave Al-Shabaab (long-term resettlement or temporary access to holy places in Saudi Arabia). They could also act as guarantors for a more comprehensive agreement with Al-Shabaab, similar to the peace agreement reached in the Philippines with the Moro Islamic Liberation Front, though at present this does not seem likely.

International actors acknowledged the difficulty posed for conflict resolution initiatives by the UN sanctions regime, as well as European Union and national legislation of key states (in particular the United States) barring assistance to designated groups. For instance, "offering expert advice" is prohibited in US law, potentially making even dialogue legally problematic.[13] However, some officials do not see these as insurmountable hurdles.

Finally, it is important to note that international actors viewed some of Al-Shabaab's core goals (the end of foreign interference in Somali politics and an Islam-compliant form of governance) as being shared by most Somalis, thereby at least theoretically allowing for the prospect of an inclusive political process.

Elders and the Business Community

Several scholars have pointed to the ongoing role and prominence of Somali elders in local and national politics and power structures[14] and all actors interviewed for this research stressed the ongoing role of elders and how they may offer a particularly effective pathway toward engagement with Al-Shabaab.

Al-Shabaab is widely understood to rely on some degree of support from elders in areas they control or patrol. Indeed, Somali and international actors noted that Al-Shabaab's reputation as a violent but consistent purveyor of security and justice, less prone to random extortion practices, holds sway with local communities who have been subjected to inefficient, corrupt and also violent governing practices by national and regional forces for decades. International actors thus pointed to the need to convince local elders to stop supporting Al-Shabaab by offering them better governance as practiced by a renewed Somali administration. This is seen as a particularly favourable time considering the new president's own reputation as an anti-corruption figure focused on improving governance. Such a dialogue would fit in the international strategy of chipping away at Al-Shabaab's reach in order to weaken it.

Some elders however have argued that a broader political dialogue could be initiated and mediated by elders. In particular, elders not linked to the electoral process (whom Al-Shabaab has been targeting regularly over 2017) could lead a Somali reconciliation process that "brings in" Al-Shabaab as a whole, rather than try to chip away the more moderate actors. Those advocating for a broader negotiation process with Al-Shabaab shared the argument made by international observers above that some of the group's core goals are compatible with those of other key Somali stakeholders.

The proponents expressed two concerns, however. First, they argued that there needs to be clear support for such an initiative from all international and regional backers of the various military and political actors in the conflict. Second, they believed that a foreign location for such a peace process may be best to ensure participants' security. This is likely to require that some actors be removed from the sanctions list. The elders interviewed for this paper insisted nevertheless that such talks would have to be a Somali process for it to have any prospect of convincing Al-Shabaab to participate.

Several actors have also pointed to business leaders as potential interlocutors or intermediaries to establish a dialogue with Al-Shabaab. Business communities were central in the rise of the UIC[15] and some sectors continue to have strong links with Al-Shabaab to be able to operate in their territory. In particular, telecommunications operators—one of the strongest industries in today's Somalia—need to maintain ties with Al-Shabaab in order to provide coverage in their areas. Individuals from the business community could thus be particularly well-placed to convince Al-Shabaab that a national reconciliation process could increase prosperity throughout Somalia, including for Al-Shabaab-linked communities. As mentioned in the analysis of past humanitarian negotiations with Al-Shabaab, the latter's insistence on being recognized as an alternative governing structure can be used to pressure the group into negotiations on the basis that they will improve the life of those living in their areas.

Al-Shabaab

Al-Shabaab has repeatedly stated that it would not negotiate with the Somali government. Indeed, the offer of talks made by Farmaajo shortly after his election was quickly rejected by the Al-Shabaab leadership through media statements and a sustained increase in attacks.

Senior defectors from Al-Shabaab have noted that the organization puts considerable effort into clan dispute resolution and has a pool of trained negotiators with that specific responsibility (usually coupled with fundraising). The process used by Al-Shabaab sits firmly within the traditional Somali *xeer* system of dispute resolution (although it may seem to be at odds with

Al-Shabaab's claims of being "above" clan) and indicates that Al-Shabaab is certainly capable of agreeing negotiated settlements.

However, the senior defectors also note that members of the Executive Council would be unlikely to engage in negotiation unless they were facing an existential level of military threat or a massive internal split. Senior defectors all mention the appearance of the faction in northern Somalia as potentially creating such a split. Sanctions are also a major discouragement to negotiation. Until that threat exists, therefore, the optimal level for negotiation would instead seem to lie with disaffected clan blocks within Al-Shabaab. Commanders are rotated regularly to avoid them forming bonds with either the local population or the fighters under their command. This means that negotiations would primarily be conducted with individuals, rather than also being with blocs of loyal followers.

Senior defectors finally raised the issue of the younger element and foreign fighters (primarily Kenyan Muslims) as an obstruction to negotiated settlement. If anything, such fighters desire a more vigorous posture by Al-Shabaab, somewhat akin to IS in Iraq and Syria. This group is barely held in check by a combination of ruthless security purges and occasional "indulgences"—in other words, major attacks, specifically against AMISOM positions in the Somali hinterland.

Potential Hurdles

Many potential hurdles and drawbacks exist to any negotiation process, particularly in one aimed at ending a longstanding conflict marked by extreme violence. Several hurdles have already been identified above, including the need to manage potential spoiling behaviour from regional powers, and the risks emerging from divergent views both within the Somali government and within Al-Shabaab. Two further hurdles need be examined here.

First, as noted above, the UN sanctions regime on Somalia (in particular UN Security Council Resolution 1844 and 2182 but also Al-Qaida and foreign fighter-related UNSCRs) has created concerns for those intent on fostering a peace process in Somalia.[16] Unlike humanitarian actors who benefit from some level of exemption, conflict resolution and peacebuilding practitioners worry that they can easily be accused of offering "technical assistance" or training to Al-Shabaab through some of their initiatives. Such concerns are amplified by national legislations, particularly those that are extraterritorial and can target third country citizens.

The second hurdle is the potential contradiction between a negotiation strategy aimed at reducing Al-Shabaab's power and reach by inducing Al-Shabaab commanders to desert or defect, and, at the same time, a strategy aimed at starting comprehensive talks with the armed group as a whole. Reducing the strength and reach of Al-Shabaab, while offering obvious military advantages, may have the effect of isolating the group, rendering them less amenable to persuasion from local communities and less open to initiatives aimed at improving living conditions for these communities. An isolated group led only by those hardliners who refused to defect may thus be less open to negotiations, leaving a military response as the only option available to the Somali government and international actors. The latter need to be certain they have the ability to eliminate the remaining Al-Shabaab hardliners militarily. Otherwise, this strategy could give rise to a group disconnected from local needs and an agenda that may represent a greater security threat to international actors as it may become more focused on a global anti-Western agenda than on the future of Somalia.

Conclusion

Most Somali and international actors interviewed for this report argued that Somalia may currently have a renewed chance of bringing an end to decades of violence and suffering, including by opening up a series of avenues for dialogue with Al-Shabaab. The principal reason for this is the belief that there is considerable common ground between the various key actors in Somalia, with both the government and Al-Shabaab adopting anti-corruption, good governance goals. An initiative of achieving stronger Somali-owned governance that is in accordance with local Islamic traditions is a broad goal around which all parties could at the very least start a dialogue. There are no doubts that there will be very different understandings of what such a project entails, but such differences are not necessarily wider than those that have been overcome in other longstanding conflicts.

How can this opportunity be used? Various channels have been identified here. Elders, particularly those who are not clearly aligned with the government, and business leaders would be natural intermediaries to begin confidence-building talks with Al-Shabaab. This could require an easing of sanctions regimes and national legislations that ban technical assistance and support to Al-Shabaab. The international community can also support these initiatives by offering incentives for talks to Al-Shabaab and possible locations for talks.

Finally, Somali government and international actors need to agree on the aim of negotiations with Al-Shabaab as this makes a considerable difference on how they might be approached. All international actors interviewed for this report currently understand negotiations as aimed at convincing Al-Shabaab fighters to abandon the group with the aim of isolating the "hardliners" for the latter to either surrender or be eliminated militarily. This is based on the premise that the hardliners can be defeated militarily. If this is not the case, all actors need to consider whether negotiations aimed at a comprehensive agreement with Al-Shabaab are more likely to yield a long-term peace process for Somalia rather than a negotiation aimed at weakening the armed group.

Recommendations

1. All parties must recognize the new Federal Government's focus on better governance and reduced corruption as a unique occasion to find common ground around a widely supported programme (including by Al-Shabaab) aimed at better Somali-owned governance that is broadly in accordance with local Islamic traditions.
2. The Somali government, international actors, and private sector actors must ensure that ongoing informal dialogues with Al-Shabaab (such as those surrounding the distribution of humanitarian aid or business interests in Al-Shabaab-patrolled territory) are undertaken in good faith and are used as confidence-building dialogues.
3. National and international actors must identify key Somali elders and business leaders who could initiate exploratory dialogues with Al-Shabaab commanders with the view of building confidence in the prospects of a negotiated process.
4. Somali government and international actors must ensure that the current strategy aimed at facilitating high-level defections from Al-Shabaab takes into account the risk of "emptying out" Al-Shabaab of all moderate leaders thus reducing the possibility of future comprehensive talks and potentially increasing the risk of an outward-focused Al-Shabaab. Making peace without Al-Shabaab or key actors on the ground has failed in the past and led to worsening periods of violence.
5. Any plans for negotiations with Al-Shabaab must include a "spoiler" management component, at national, regional and international levels.

   • Nationally, this means building strategies to ensure that the key actors backing the Somali government and the key factions in Al-Shabaab buy into the process.

- Regionally, it means that regional powers are consulted and, at a minimum, their non-opposition sought, as past experience shows that agreements signed in spite of the objection of regional powers are doomed to fail.

- Internationally, it means ensuring that the international community backs a nascent negotiation process, by offering incentives and dialogue facilitation (for example from Muslim-majority countries such as Saudi Arabia and Turkey) and by ensuring that international sanctions regimes and national legislations are calibrated to allow for negotiations, confidence-building, and negotiations capacity-building initiatives.

COMMUNITY PERSPECTIVES TOWARDS AL-SHABAAB

SOURCES OF SUPPORT AND THE POTENTIAL FOR NEGOTIATIONS

Joanne Crouch and *Abdi Ali*

Authorship

Joanne Crouch is a Research Team Leader and Abdi Ali is a Programmes Adviser with the Somalia/Somaliland programme of the international NGO Saferworld. Joanne has a decade of experience working in conflict-affected states, including five years on issues of good governance, conflict analysis and non-state actors in Somalia. Abdi, a Somalia-born Kenyan, has over 25 years' experience working in Somalia across political, governance, development, and humanitarian sectors.

Summary

This interview-based research sought to gather perspectives from various regions of Somalia on the conflict with Al-Shabaab. Overall, respondents expressed a circumspect view.[1] While they highlighted Al-Shabaab's indiscriminate use of violence, its problematic interpretation of Islam and its harsh controls on movement, speech, and association, they also noted positive aspects of the group's operations. Respondents viewed the conflict as a product of sustained injustice, clannism, inadequate governance, and international interference. Reasons cited for Al-Shabaab's support included the group's transcendence of clannism and perceptions of the provision of justice, equality, fairness, stability and security, especially in contrast to the government's deficits in these areas.

While most respondents supported a military approach to Al-Shabaab, a notable minority opposed this. Most respondents were also supportive of political negotiations to address the conflict. Many lacked confidence that Al-Shabaab would accept a political solution, but said they would support one if it could be reached. Many viewed a hybrid approach combining military action with political negotiations as most likely to create peace. Fewer felt that Al-Shabaab could only be addressed through militarily defeat. Others stated that elections could enable Al-Shabaab to legitimately contest the leadership of the country.

Further research should analyse the foundations of Al-Shabaab's support, including clannist governance. It should assess the feasibility of a negotiated solution with Al-Shabaab, and disaggregate which of Al-Shabaab's modes of operation are purely ideological and unlikely to change, and which are largely in response to the existential military threat Al-Shabaab faces. Where government deficiencies in justice provision were widely seen as a key contributor to support for Al-Shabaab, reforming justice systems to better and more fairly serve the people would be beneficial in winning over people now sympathetic to Al-Shabaab.

Introduction

Many of the approaches towards Al-Shabaab by the government of Somalia and the international community are underpinned by a framing of Al-Shabaab as a violent extremist organization without popular legitimacy. This perspective holds that Al-Shabaab must be addressed through a combination of military action to defeat the armed group, encouragement of defections and reduction of the group's uptake of new militants to reduce its internal capacity. This approach also seeks to address governance deficiencies and increase popular support for the Federal Government. The extent to which this approach is grounded in the perspectives of the Somalis most affected by the conflict is uncertain. Military approaches and efforts to counter radicalism have been attempted for over a decade, and despite some successes, there remains little clarity as to how the conflict could be brought to an end. With a new Federal Government in place, Somalia has reached a suitable juncture to explore alternative options to concluding the conflict, meet popular needs and build upon emerging thinking around political negotiations.

In April and May 2017, Saferworld conducted field research in a number of locations in Somalia to gather popular perceptions of Al-Shabaab within communities, both negative and positive, and to understand why many communities and individuals continue to support the group despite its often-deadly approach and the destructive activities it has conducted. The research also explored popular attitudes toward addressing the conflict with Al-Shabaab, with specific attention to the potential for a negotiated settlement. Field research was conducted in Mogadishu, Kismayo and Nairobi, in addition to telephone interviews with participants in Gedo and Baidoa. In total, 71 key informant interviews (KIIs) were conducted using a combination of qualitative and quantitative methodologies.

Respondents were identified through trusted intermediaries who were tasked with selecting participants from targeted areas. Respondents included people currently living under Al-Shabaab rule, those who were previously under Al-Shabaab rule but are now under formal government institutions, and those who have only lived under the formal government. They included farmers, labourers, teachers, IDPs, civil society leaders, women, youth, elders, and government officials. In addition to field research, this paper also draws upon previously unpublished quantitative data and qualitative research on governance and justice access issues conducted by Saferworld from 2015 to 2017.

Drivers of Conflict

Respondents identified a consistent set of primary conflict drivers, including clannism, injustice, inequality, poor governance, and theft of land and resources. Though respondents cited Al-Shabaab as a conflict actor and criticized its extremist ideology, the group was widely portrayed as a symptom of deeper problems rather than a source of conflict in itself. One respondent stated, "clannism came first, then came the ideology."[2] Similarly, interventions in Somalia by international and regional actors were widely viewed as important sources of conflict. One participant from the business community described the Somali conflict as a proxy war between Western counter-terrorist ideology and the Arab/Islamic world.[3]

Negative and Positive Attitudes Towards Al-Shabaab

A broad and complex range of Somali attitudes towards Al-Shabaab emerged from the research, from outright condemnation to measured appreciation of its perceived positive aspects.

Respondents' dominant negative perception of Al-Shabaab was that the group heavily restricts freedom of speech and movement through the use of fear and threat of sanctions such as arrest, detention and violence. Some respondents had experienced torture first-hand. One recounted how his fingernails were removed with pliers when he was suspected of being a government informant.[4]

Respondents were also highly critical of Al-Shabaab's use of indiscriminate violence, including murder, kidnapping, bombing and assassinations, as well as their severe enforcement of *zakat* (alms-giving) and blockading and expulsion of humanitarian agencies.[5] "During the harsh days of this dry season, they refused borehole drilling in the nearby villages of [...] and [...]. They chased away NGOs who wanted to help the community in these villages."[6]

All respondents disagreed with Al-Shabaab's religious ideology and many doubted their claim to be religious, since they do not adhere to core tenets of Islam, especially prohibitions against killing.

> It has become apparent that whatever they say is not reflected in the Sharia. They have displayed all sorts of extremism. In the beginning, they were not as extreme as they are at this point in time ... Allah doesn't permit the killing of innocent people.[7]

Finally, Al-Shabaab's restriction of people's ability to interact with the government was problematic, including threats to the lives of those who participated in government processes. In the run-up to the 2016 parliamentary selection, Al-Shabaab convened elders in Gedo and explicitly forbade them to be involved as candidates or electors.[8] Participants in Afgoye spoke of an elder who participated in the formation of South West state and was then killed by Al-Shabaab upon his return.

Despite the heavy criticism of their use of violence, nearly all respondents mentioned security and stability as positive aspects of Al-Shabaab's rule. Under Al-Shabaab, many stated that everyone knew what was expected of them and the rules by which they had to abide, while crimes such as theft were unheard of. Al-Shabaab's strict enforcement of these rules created fear among community members, but some respondents valued the confidence they gained that they and their possessions were safe.

Virtually all participants spoke positively about Al-Shabaab's provision of justice, and stated that anyone could refer a case to them without having to pay. Respondents reported that Al-Shabaab conducted investigations, invited disputants to present their cases, identified and prepared witnesses and presided over cases. They felt that Al-Shabaab's justice was swift and broadly fair, that judgements were consistently implemented and that there was no manipulation. Many respondents spoke of how people not living under Al-Shabaab rule would actively seek them out to preside over cases, in the belief that the cases would be dealt with in a much fairer way than in the statutory or customary systems. At the same time, referring a case to Al-Shabaab did not guarantee a positive outcome for the person bringing the case. Similarly, respondents indicated that there was no particular clan preference for taking cases to Al-Shabaab nor any perceived clan bias in Al-Shabaab's rulings.

> In the government system, the cases are endless, and you need to pay—there's a lot of corruption. Al-Shabaab don't waste time—they ask for witnesses, they investigate and they make decisions, which are fair and enforced. There is no automatic ruling in my favour if I bring a case. They don't charge people for presiding over a case. They never ask for money.[9]

Respondents reported that Al-Shabaab ensured resources were distributed either equally or according to need. Clans' political influence was also diminished in Al-Shabaab-controlled areas. Particular clans were not privileged over others and people from different clans could trust one another. Some mentioned how after Al-Shabaab left an area, old clan conflicts often re-emerged. "[Al-Shabaab] create a sense of equality between the natives and the outsiders."[10]

Another positive impact of Al-Shabaab's rule identified by respondents, especially women, was the eradication of *khat* usage, known to be a major contributor to domestic and sexual violence.[11]

Furthermore, respondents broadly characterized Al-Shabaab as less corrupt and more structured in their tax collection than the government. Despite complaints around forceful and excessive collection of *zakat*,[12] respondents specifically noted that travellers only paid road tax once, in contrast to roads not managed by Al-Shabaab, and that Al-Shabaab would issue receipts. Al-Shabaab is also described as resistant to corruption or manipulation.

One humanitarian actor noted that Al-Shabaab occasionally sought out medical staff to provide healthcare to community members, especially during medical emergencies such as cholera epidemics. However, most respondents stated that Al-Shabaab does not provide services such as health, education, or development. Others mentioned that Al-Shabaab expanded the provision of education, though they were concerned that this education was ideologically biased.

Why Al-Shabaab Retains Influence and Support

According to respondents, Al-Shabaab manages to assert influence over large areas of Somalia for two main reasons. Firstly, they have a strong practical capacity to hold territory and govern populations. This perception is centred upon Al-Shabaab's financial, military and administrative abilities. Respondents also cited their highly effective and "ghost"-like intelligence networks.

Community members felt Al-Shabaab was everywhere and knew everything, including in government-held and "liberated" areas. A key interviewee who leads independent evaluations into stabilization interventions in Somalia emphasized the sustained and deep-rooted influence that Al-Shabaab retains in supposedly liberated areas. This means that despite the appearance of liberation, some communities continue to support or cooperate with Al-Shabaab.[13] Other respondents emphasized that communities in areas not formally held by Al-Shabaab would regularly adhere to instructions from Al-Shabaab despite their absence from the community.[14]

Al-Shabaab's influence was reinforced by their ability to collect taxes, lack of corruption, and strong administrative systems. A number of respondents believed that Al-Shabaab received financial and military support from external actors, with suspicions raised against a neighbouring country as a provider of weapons.

Whilst many indicated that youth unemployment and radicalization were to blame for continued support for Al-Shabaab, one participant stated that clan elders often decide whether or not youth join Al-Shabaab.

> As long as injustice continues, it is impossible for young people to come back from Al-Shabaab. If we call back our youth from Al-Shabaab, would there be a guarantee that we would be treated well, that the government would not mistreat or exclude us? Elders could withdraw youth militants if they wanted to, but there is no trust that the government would work for the people.[15]

Participants frequently emphasized that people were treated equally by Al-Shabaab in areas where one particular clan had dominated at the expense of another, which they cited as building trust in and support for Al-Shabaab among community members. Conversely, the perceived failings of formal Somali authorities were believed to increase support for Al-Shabaab. One respondent said, "People support them because they are fairer and less corrupt than the government."[16] Another respondent stated:

> People feel discontented, they feel frustrated, because of corruption and injustice they don't support the current system. It pushes people to support the other armed actor [Al Shabaab] … you have no alternative, you have to support the other side".[17]

There was a strong emphasis on inequality and injustice resulting from government actors' moves to ensure the dominance of their particular clan groups, something that Al-Shabaab was recognized for not doing. According to a respondent in Gedo:

> In the case of the government, once a suspect is arrested, his clan runs after him to get him released. With Al-Shabaab, you can't do that. Al-Shabaab defeated clannism whereas the government is defeated by clannism because government is built upon the clan structure.[18]

Some respondents in Afgoye stated that certain clans supported Al-Shabaab because they needed a political and military counter to the unequal and oppressive policies implemented by the clan-dominated district commission and military in the region, with one respondent noting that "communities provide financial support or offer their youth to join because of this anger."[19]

Ambivalent Perspectives

In general, respondents offered multifaceted views of Al-Shabaab. Despite Al-Shabaab's use of fear and violence as tools of control, respondents noted that the government was also guilty of these tactics even if they offered greater freedoms. Some saw little difference between Al-Shabaab and other Somali leaders.

> When the Mad Mullah was ruling in the north, people asked him why he killed people, and he said 'Who can rule Somalis without killing them?' [Al-Shabaab] has that philosophy and Siad Barre was the same. So if Al-Shabaab kills people, what difference does it make in comparison to the past?[20]

> It is the same with [Jubbaland President] Ahmed Madobe as it is with Al-Shabaab—there is fear of punishment, which means people do not do bad things.[21]

Many respondents speculated that if Al-Shabaab ceased its harsher actions, such as indiscriminate killings, and tempered its ideological rigidity and hard-line interpretations of Islam, the group would be more acceptable to the public.

People get relieved when they enter into an Al-Shabaab area. If Al-Shabaab were not slaughtering people, I think everyone would become an Al-Shabaab member. Their problem is the senseless explosions and killing of civilians.[22]

They need to stop the wrong ideology. If they dropped their ideology they would be the same as any other political actor vying for power.[23]

Some even spoke of their desire for Al-Shabaab to return to areas "liberated" by government forces.

I sometimes wish [Al-Shabaab] would come back. There are cases, these guys were controlling that area, people thought they were suffering; then the government came and things got worse. So people want the religious group to come back.[24]

When Al-Shabaab says something, it does it. The government is like a paper tiger—it's there, but in reality, it is not really there.[25]

Although Al-Shabaab was generally viewed as an abhorrent actor that is ideologically extreme and violent towards community members, there was also a widespread sense that Al-Shabaab has been affected and made more violent by sustained conflict with the government. Some argued that it isn't inherently Al-Shabaab's presence that generates violence, but rather the conflict between the two opposing sides, with community members and elders caught in the middle, facing risks to their lives if they are perceived to support one side or the other. "Ordinary people are on a double-edged sword, walking on a danger line between the government and Al-Shabaab."[26]

Addressing the Conflict with Al-Shabaab

Many respondents described the military approach to Al-Shabaab as limited and often hampered by the presence of AMISOM. Neighbouring states were widely deemed problematic actors, thought to be arming Al-Shabaab or providing other forms of support to advance their own interests. Many saw AMISOM as an obstacle to peace, and asserted that requisite investment into the Somali military could enable it to tackle Al-Shabaab alone, without AMISOM.

There was also a widely shared view that the government's current approach to Al-Shabaab is not only ineffective, but is causing suffering.

The government's fight against Al-Shabaab is counterproductive. An area captured from Al-Shabaab is lost a few days later. Civilians are made to suffer. If the government can't consolidate its gains, it should not make people suffer.[27]

While some respondents spoke of the need to encourage defections, there was a sense the current approach was not effective. On one hand, there were few avenues for employment after defecting, while on the other was a sense of fear that defectors would be arrested and even tortured.

> People who are part of Al-Shabaab are anxious about exiting—what happens to them if they run away? Are they killed? Are they captured? We hear stories of them being tortured by the CIA.[28]

Participants were invited to comment on four proposed strategies to address the conflict: military engagement, strengthening governance, creating youth employment, and political negotiations, and were able to add their own proposals as well.

Nearly all participants felt that youth employment and strengthening governance were essential to resolving the conflict. Some emphasized the importance of addressing corruption, and most spoke of the importance of equality and fairness in governance institutions and the institution of justice.

Military Approaches

76 per cent of participants felt that a military approach of some sort was necessary, while 24 per cent felt that a military approach was the only way to address Al-Shabaab. Many emphasized the importance of a unified and rebuilt Somali National Army (SNA), and many felt that AMISOM needed to leave Somalia or change its role. Some emphasized the need for a military approach to be used in conjunction with other tools, including negotiations, facilitating defections, and promoting a Somali interpretation of Islam to compete with Al-Shabaab's radical ideology.

24 per cent of respondents did not think the military approach should be used at all. Their reasons included a lack of faith that this approach could work, that it requires Somalis to fight their own people, and that the Somali way is through dialogue.

> There is an overarching sense that the military approach has been exhausted. The question, then, is why continue in this vein?[29]

> Al-Shabaab—they are locals, they are natives, they are part of the people. A military approach would be to target ourselves.[30]

Negotiation

76 per cent of participants supported a negotiated solution. The overwhelming perspective was that Somalis were tired of the conflict and would support anything that ended it.

It would be better for the government to extend its hand to negotiate and bring Al-Shabaab closer instead of chasing them away.[31]

[The] government has to sit and talk with these guys. I am confident that some of them will resort to non-violent means if there is a proper and genuine dialogue with them.[32]

When interviewers sought to clarify whether respondents envisioned Al-Shabaab joining government, many expressed openness to this. One stated, "There are butchers in government already—what difference would a few more make?"[33] Others stated that as long as Al-Shabaab renounced the use of violence, they should be welcomed into politics.

People would welcome Al-Shabaab in government if it solved the conflict and solved other problems such as freedom of movement and freedom of speech.[34]

I believe that should they come to the negotiating table, they should be offered positions in government. If there is true democracy and true justice, in the areas they control, maybe those people believe in them. If they elect them, then we have to accept it.[35]

This was tempered by caution, as many respondents believed that Al-Shabaab would never be open to negotiations, and had rejected previous attempts at peaceful engagement.

Conclusion

Respondents strongly criticized approaches used to date in combating Al-Shabaab, with many feeling that the government and regional actors are not wholly committed to the battle. Respondents heavily emphasized that approaches to Al-Shabaab must be Somali-led, and appeared to favour a "carrot-and-stick" approach combining military pressure with opening avenues for political negotiations. Respondents demonstrated acceptance that the end result may be the inclusion of Al-Shabaab members in the government, providing that Al-Shabaab is receptive to negotiations.

Given indications that Al-Shabaab could be perceived as a legitimate political actor if they change certain forms of behaviour, it may be useful to analyse which problematic behaviours are inherent to Al-Shabaab, their ideology and their ultimate objectives, and whether some, including escalating repression and indiscriminate attacks on civilians, are the product of the existential military threat Al-Shabaab faces[36] and may change should the terms of conflict change.[37] This analysis could improve understanding of whether communities would support or accept Al-Shabaab as a political actor should military conflict eventually segue into non-violent political contestation. These concerns, however, remain hypothetical in the absence of any clear strategy by either side to shift from a military conflict to political negotiations.

Finally, it would be useful to clarify the ultimate objective of the current conflict. Is it to eradicate and defeat Al-Shabaab, or to end the group's use of violence as a political tool and shift the contestation of politics to non-violent democratic means? Clarity on this front would assist in influencing approaches.

Recommendations

The Somali Federal Government and international forces should clarify the end goals of the conflict with Al-Shabaab. This should determine the approaches to be taken and the results to be pursued. These determinations should be based on Somalis' needs and perspectives together with a broad consideration of approaches that go beyond eradicating or defeating Al-Shabaab.

Deeper comparative analysis should be conducted on whether and how military insurgents change their behaviour and political beliefs as a result of the removal of an existential military threat. There should also be more extensive analysis of Al-Shabaab's objectives to determine whether they would respond to political engagement.

The FGS should also consider community perceptions of its war against Al-Shabaab and assess the feasibility of political negotiations. Though intractable ideologies may make this difficult at Al-Shabaab's leadership level, there may be greater openings at lower levels, where top-line jihadist ambitions may be seen as less urgent than localized political and development concerns.

In addition to their commitments to strengthen the Somali National Army to tackle Al-Shabaab, the Federal Government and the Federal Member States should also make greater investments to identify and apply locally-acceptable forms of justice that are free from manipulation and based on firm principles of equality and fairness. The government also needs to strengthen its institutions of governance in ways that are accountable and accessible to all Somalis, and not beholden to clan influence. This would enable Somalis to have greater confidence in the government and would reduce support for Al-Shabaab.

AL-SHABAAB ATTITUDES TOWARDS
NEGOTIATIONS

Anneli Botha and *Mahdi Abdile*

Authors

Dr Anneli Botha is a Senior Lecturer at the Department of Political Studies
and Governance at the University of the Free State in Bloemfontein, South
Africa. Mahdi Abdile is Head of Secretariat, Network for Religious and
Traditional Peacemakers.

Summary

This paper draws on two separate field research missions conducted in 2016
to see whether there is interest on the part of Al-Shabaab leaders to disengage
and pursue political dialogue with the Somali Federal Government. It also
considers the conditions in which they will negotiate, where negotiations
could take place and who could participate in negotiations. The data are based
on interviews conducted with 17 mid-ranking Al-Shabaab leaders currently
part of the organization, including field commanders with several hundred
soldiers under their command.[1] Analysis of the research findings suggests that
Al-Shabaab's leadership is willing to pursue conditional political dialogue with
the Somali government as long as certain conditions are met.

The data suggest that:

1. Family and friends might play an important role in convincing Al-Shabaab members to desist from insurgent activity, as might elders and religious leaders. In contrast, the Somali government was not seen as having an important role in convincing respondents to abandon fighting and/or apply for amnesty.

2. Two of the most critical conditions for negotiations were identified as the withdrawal of foreign forces and a general amnesty for those who want to re-join society. This was followed by the formation of security forces that consisted of all parties, full implementation of Sharia law, the establishment of a new government that consists of all parties, and the securing of employment for Al-Shabaab members.

3. Representatives from Qatar and Saudi Arabia were seen by respondents as potential facilitators of talks.

4. The negative sentiment directed at AMISOM contributing countries was reflected in the widely held view of respondents that they should be excluded from negotiations.

5. In addition to Somalia itself, Qatar, Saudi Arabia, Sudan, and Turkey were identified as potential venues for negotiations.

Introduction

Finding a lasting peaceful solution to the conflict in Somalia has eluded both national and international actors since the fall of the Siad Barre regime. Confronted with different cycles of violence, the current Al-Shabaab campaign has its own set of actors and associated challenges. In recent years Al-Shabaab has faced serious problems. Many of its key founders are dead and major funding sources have been lost. Consequently, internal dissent has been growing for some time and is likely to grow as the national and regional governments of Somalia improve their service delivery. Yet, although Al-Shabaab is under pressure, it retains powerful operational capabilities.

The objective of this paper is to assess the possibilities for negotiations with Al-Shabaab. Instead of approaching Al-Shabaab as an organization, individual mid-ranked leaders within Al-Shabaab were interviewed. The aim was to:

- Identify the best strategy to engage with Al-Shabaab members willing to disengage;
- Assess potential openings for a negotiated solution;

- Identify with whom and under what circumstances Al-Shabaab might be willing to negotiate;
- Obtain a better understanding of the topics Al-Shabaab may be willing to negotiate and what type of process design may be suitable; and
- Identify potential mediators.

We of course recognize that Al-Shabaab's top leaders may oppose political negotiations, believing that they could be excluded or prosecuted, or because talks would involve "apostate" governments.

In addition to the 17 interviews with mid-ranking members of Al-Shabaab, mainly commanders,[2] the paper also draws on 52 interviews conducted during 2016 with rank and file former members of Al-Shabaab at the Rehabilitation Centre and prison in Baidoa. (In this paper, the two groups are referred to as "leaders" and "members", respectively.)

First of all the paper briefly considers the motivations of Al-Shabaab leaders and ordinary members, why they remained committed to the organization and, where relevant, what motivated them to leave. The paper then addresses: the prospects for a settlement, potential participants in a process, conditions for negotiations, and external involvement.

Joining Al-Shabaab

Most respondents interviewed as part of the leaders sample for this study were older than 30 years of age at the time of joining the organization: 59% were between the ages of 30 and 35, followed by 35% older than 35 years of age (see Figure 1). In comparison, respondents who were part of the rank and file sample were younger, with the largest segment (41%) between the ages of 20 and 25, 28% between the ages of 16 and 19 and 13% between the ages of 10 and 15.

When asked to identify the primary personal reasons as opposed to the overall strategic reasons why they joined the group, 52 per cent of leaders and 15 per cent of members cited religious ideas as the main reason for joining (Figure 2). In contrast to the leadership sample, most ordinary members joined for personal reasons (63 per cent).

Commitment to Al-Shabaab and Disengagement

A key question is why individuals who joined Al-Shabaab remained in the organization. As illustrated in Figure 3, leaders referred to the following fac-

Figure 1: At what age did you decide to join Al-Shabaab?

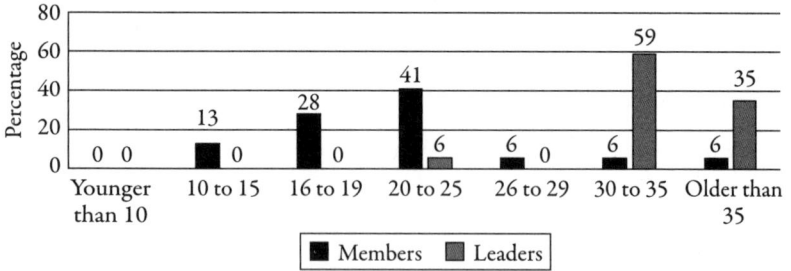

Figure 2: Principle reason for joining Al-Shabaab

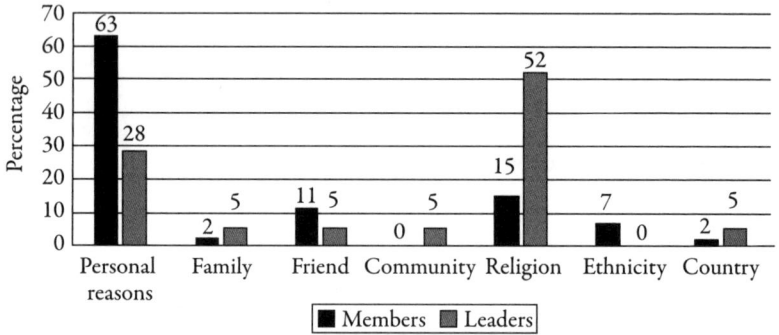

Figure 3: If/when you remained in Al-Shabaab, why did you stay?

tors: standing up for their beliefs (16 per cent), responsibility for their tasks within Al-Shabaab, achieving change, and fear of retaliation for desertion or defection. In contrast, 20 per cent of the rank and file remained in Al-Shabaab to defend Islam, and 18 per cent said it was because they were standing up for something they believe in (speaking to the same level of commitment).

It is interesting to note that security associated with being an Al-Shabaab member was rated higher amongst the leaders (11 per cent) than the members (3 per cent). The financial benefits of being a member of Al-Shabaab did not rate highly amongst the leaders and ordinary members, and nor did the opportunity for adventure or sense of belonging.

These data suggest that encouraging disengagement amongst leaders should involve calling on their sense of responsibility towards Somalia and its people, while securing the necessary protection from retaliation. Among members, a disengagement strategy needs to start with countering the perception that Al-Shabaab represents Islam and provides protection against the perceived enemies of Islam. The organization has capitalized on nationalist and religious sentiments by portraying itself as defending Islam against foreign military intervention by "Christian invaders" of Ethiopia and other AMISOM contributing countries. Yet, if the UN or AMISOM were to try to counter this argu-

Figure 4: If you willingly surrendered or applied for amnesty, select the primary reason for your decision

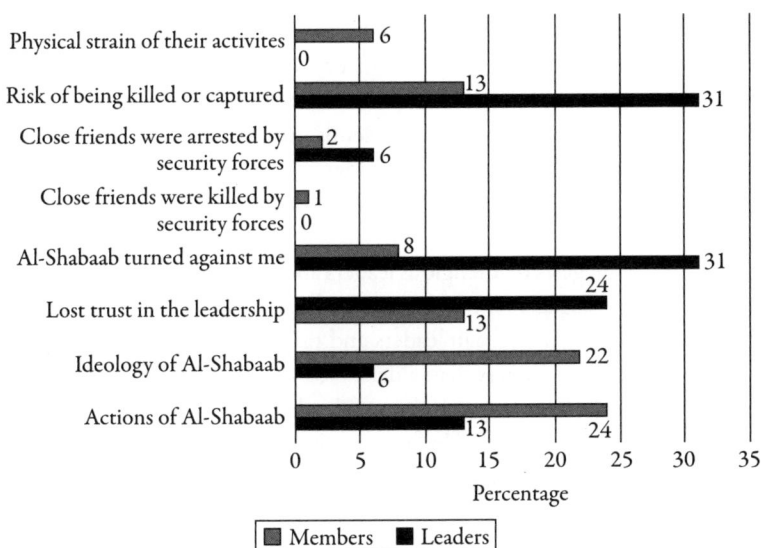

ment, it might prove self-defeating. Equally, according to our interviews the Somali government would not be trusted in its attempts to explain the involvement of the UN or AMISOM. Instead, as noted below, Muslim countries, most notably Qatar, Saudi Arabia, Sudan, and Turkey, would be more trusted messengers for refuting Al-Shabaab's portrayal of the UN and AMISOM.

Respondents were asked what factors or circumstances were most likely to influence their decision to leave Al-Shabaab and apply for amnesty. They were also asked who was most likely to positively influence this decision. The answers are displayed in Figure 4.

There were two main factors for leaders: if Al-Shabaab turned against the person concerned (31 per cent) and if they feared being killed or captured (31 per cent). This observation appears to be borne out by the experience of Al-Shabaab during the leadership of Ahmed Abdi Godane, alias Mukhtar Abu al-Zubayr, before he was killed in September 2014. Due to a leadership struggle within Al-Shabaab and military challenges by Somali and AMISOM forces, a large number of Al-Shabaab members disengaged, including high-ranking leaders. During this period the government exploited Al-Shabaab's difficulties by offering an amnesty for deserters.

Separately, it is important to note that for ordinary Al-Shabaab members, a loss of trust in the leadership of Al-Shabaab or the threat of Al-Shabaab turning against the respondent were more likely to lead to disengagement from the group, than the fear of being killed or captured.

In addition to creating favourable circumstances, the involvement of key actors to facilitate disengagement should not be underestimated. Although not an extensive list, leaders believed disengagement could be initiated by elders or family and friends. Members somewhat preferred elders (41 per cent), followed by family and friends, to initiate discussions to facilitate disengagement. In contrast to members, the leadership sample did not exhibit the same level of trust in the Somali government for initiating disengagement (see Figure 5).

Our research suggests that religious leaders and local elders could play a positive role in the disengagement process. Asked about the degree to which they trusted such figures, Al-Shabaab leaders and rank and file members expressed more trust in religious leaders than elders. Notwithstanding this, rank and file members of Al-Shabaab expressed considerably more trust in elders than expressed by the group's leaders.[3] In fact, a majority of respondents thought clan elders should play an important role in any talks, especially in providing guidance to the community on reintegration (73 per cent), facilitating community meetings (69 per cent), and providing guidance to individuals (67 per cent).

Figure 5: Identify the primary actor to possibly facilitate your surrender

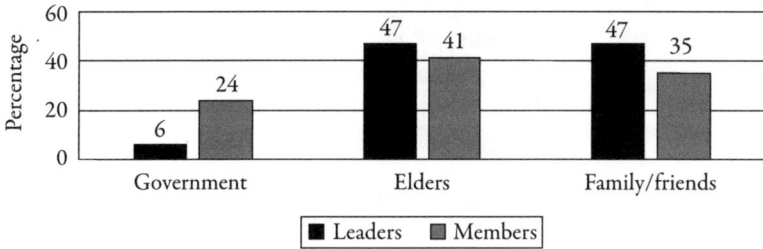

The Prospects for a Political Settlement

A key objective of the research was to understand what it would take for Al-Shabaab to seek political settlement with the government and how that could be brought about. The following section therefore focuses exclusively on answers provided by the leadership sample of the study.

Strikingly, our data show that Al-Shabaab commanders appear to be willing to resolve the ongoing conflict through mediation and an overwhelming majority of respondents said they were in favour of talking to the government. Instead of referring to a military defeat of the Somali government, 80 per cent of respondents referred to negotiations as "extremely important" for resolving the conflict, 85 per cent expressed the same sentiment towards amnesty and 90 per cent considered national reconciliation as "extremely important" (see Figure 6). This shows that although religion is a major motivating factor in joining and staying with the group, most Al-Shabaab military leaders interviewed were not simply extremists with a global jihadist agenda.

Rather, the data suggest that Al-Shabaab leaders have nationalistic goals, reflected in their willingness to look for a negotiated settlement and to bring about national reconciliation to heal the wounds caused by the ongoing conflict. This is reinforced by the fact that 92 per cent of respondents said that the withdrawal of AMISOM was extremely important for resolving the conflict, while 67 per cent of respondents attached the same level of importance to the withdrawal of UNSOM.

In order to bring about talks to resolve the conflict, respondents also called for:

• An increase in citizen participation in the policy-making and constitution-making process. Al-Shabaab appears to believe that citizen participation

Figure 6: Rate the importance of the following solutions to deal with the conflict

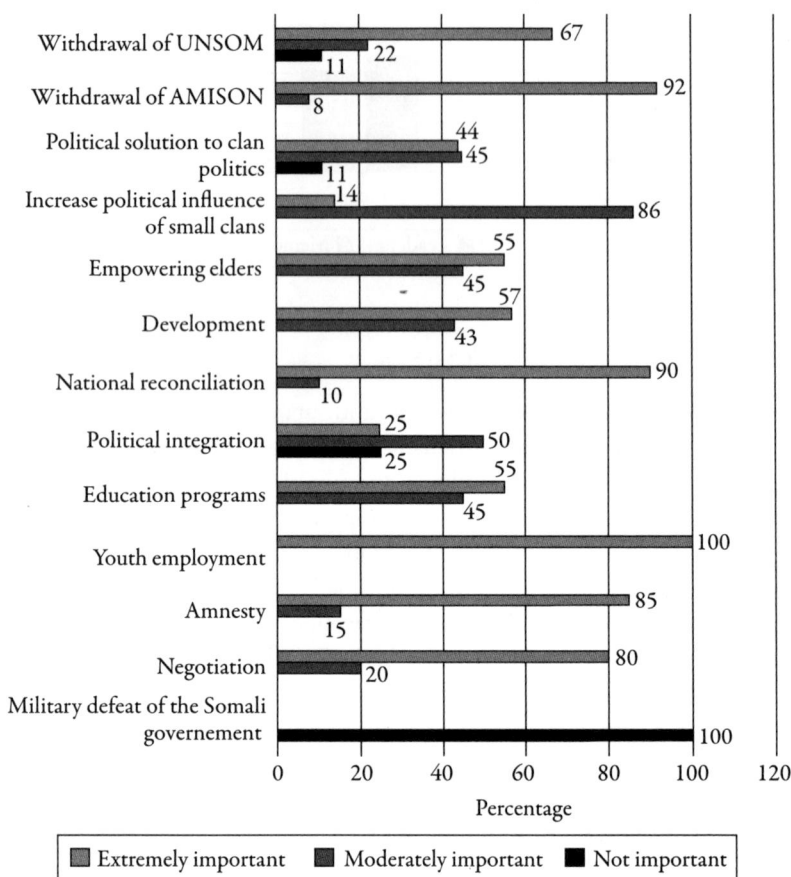

will bolster their claim for a strict Islamic constitution, which will ultimately give them considerable say in all Somalia's political affairs.

- The opening of rehabilitation centres for youth to learn vocational skills.
- Efforts by civil society and the Somali government to advocate for unity among Somalis.
- The rehabilitation and reintegration of Al-Shabaab fighters.

Leaders were also asked to identify those whom the government would be most likely to include in the negotiation process. The results are shown in Figure 7 below, which indicates that leaders assume the process should be

Figure 7: Who do you think Government will be most willing to have included in and to benefit from the negotiation process?

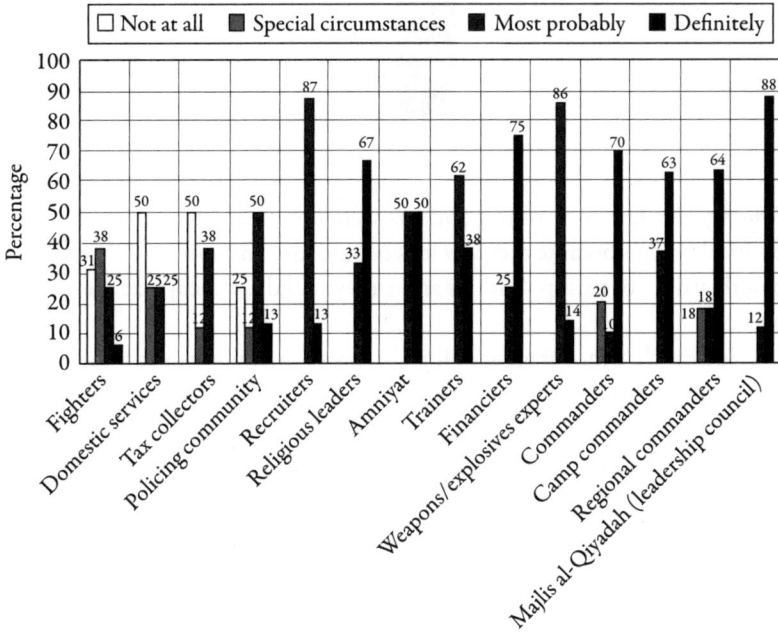

centred around members of the leadership council, financiers, commanders and religious leaders.

Participation in a Political Process

Following up on respondents' views about potential solutions to the conflict in Somalia (Figure 6), we asked leaders and members of Al-Shabaab about their willingness to participate in a future political process and what would cause them not to participate. Interestingly, 91 per cent of the ordinary members, but 53 per cent of the leadership sample, indicated that they were willing to participate in such a process (see Figure 8).

To understand why 47% of leaders and 9% of members would be reluctant to participate in the political process, respondents were asked to rate the main reasons for this. Of Al-Shabaab members, who had already disengaged, 34% said that the unwillingness was because politicians only represent themselves, followed by 33% who believed the political process is not free and fair.

Figure 8: Future participation in the political process

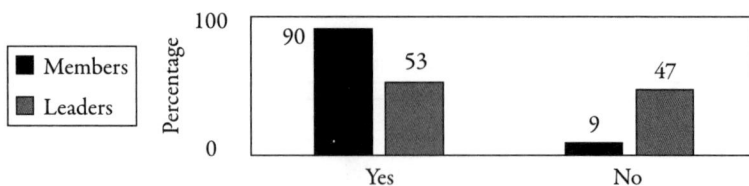

Amongst leaders, 57% of respondents were not willing to participate in the political process because they saw it as being a foreign concept; 29% indicated that they did not trust politicians and 14% said did not recognize the political process.

It is clear that encouraging political expression in non-violent ways should be a government priority. Yet, before this can happen, the legitimacy of the new government needs to be recognized by Al-Shabaab. Similarly, government officials need to be willing to recognize the existence and claims of other parties to the conflict. It should also be recognized that democracy and elections are foreign concepts in Somali political culture. Looking towards national reconciliation, considering that many members and leaders joined Al-Shabaab in response to foreign intervention, perhaps nationalism can serve as a bridge between the different parties.

Conditions Facilitating Negotiations

Respondents were asked about what conditions would be required for negotiations (although respondents may also have considered conditions as required outcomes). Two of the most critical conditions were identified as the withdrawal of foreign forces (100%) and general amnesty (100%) for those who want to rejoin society (see Figure 9 below). This was followed by the formation of security forces that consist of all parties (75%), the full implementation of Sharia law (72%), the formation of a new government consisting of all parties (69%), and securing the employment of Al-Shabaab members (67%).

External Involvement

While being open to the involvement of not only Somali nationals in the negotiation process, respondents called for the exclusion of foreign donors (100%), neighbouring countries (83%) and the African Union (67%). In

Figure 9: Identity the most important conditions for negotiations

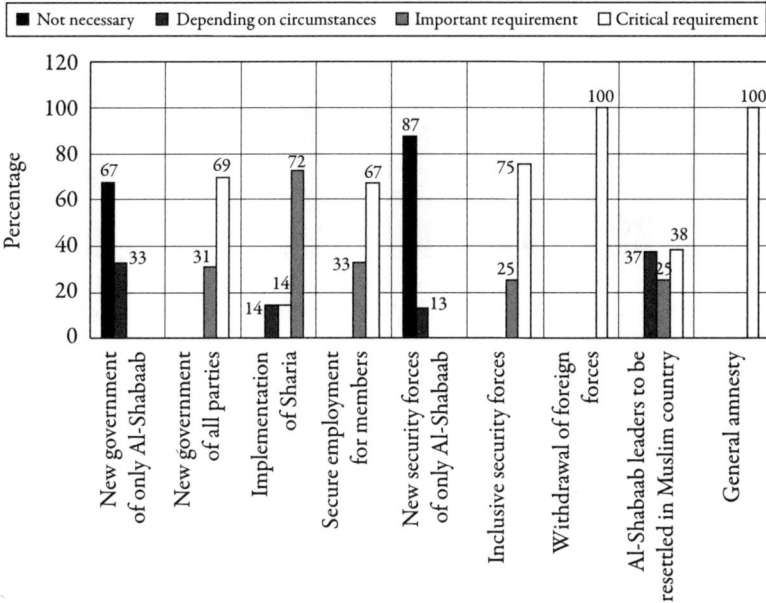

contrast, 67% of respondents were open to the involvement of Middle Eastern countries; a smaller proportion was open to the involvement of the United Nations (31%) (see Figure 10).

Asked about facilitation, the majority of respondents in the leadership sample said that representatives from Qatar and Saudi Arabia could potentially facilitate talks. Predictably, they believed that AMISOM troop-contributing countries should be excluded from the negotiations process. A few respondent leaders also believed the UN and all foreign actors should be excluded from talks. Respondents identified Qatar, Saudi Arabia, Sudan and Turkey, in addition to Somalia, as potential venues for negotiations, given the prominence and importance of Islam in their societies.

Conclusion

History suggests that negotiations are the most effective strategy to address the underlying drivers of conflict. This strategy will often require a series of negotiations to convince different parties to the conflict to lay down their weapons as part of a lasting settlement.

Figure 10: Parties to the negotiation process

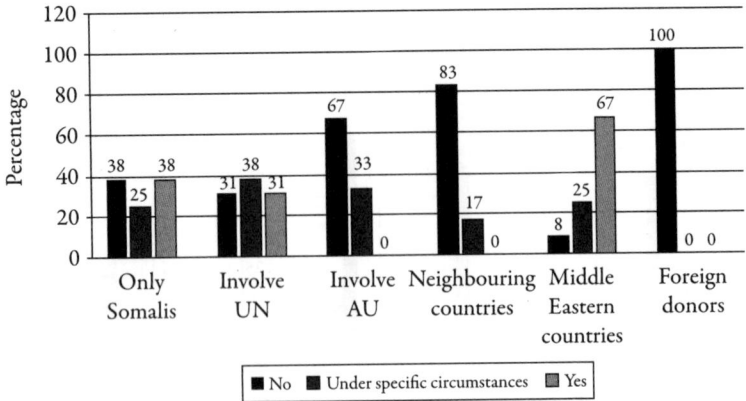

Elders have long been facilitating direct or indirect contacts between Al-Shabaab and their adversaries. For instance, elders mediated the release of individuals kidnapped by Al-Shabaab. When first Al-Shabaab and later the Somali government and Ethiopian forces took control over certain areas of Somalia, locals were forced to make difficult decisions. Whether they joined Al-Shabaab or sided with the Somali government and Ethiopian forces, they could always be suspected of working for the "enemy." Consequently, elders can play a constructive role facilitating the disengagement of prominent Al-Shabaab members willing to negotiate, not only for themselves, but also for those under their control and possibly the broader organization.

Reaching a peaceful solution to the conflict in Somalia will not happen overnight, nor will it happen without visionaries on all sides of the conflict. Considering who would participate and under what circumstances negotiations could take place is the first step in establishing a process. Our research suggests that for Al-Shabaab respondents, successful negotiations would involve the withdrawal of foreign forces from Somalia and the implementation of Sharia. The latter condition and the importance of religion in driving individuals to Al-Shabaab suggest it will be important to determine to what extent Al-Shabaab's leadership recognizes the existing Somali constitution.

Clearly, there are huge differences between the parties. However, instead of focusing on differences, a constructive starting point for dialogue could be to concentrate on what it means to be Somali and the sense that after decades of conflict, the parties to the conflict owe it to their countrymen to search for a peaceful settlement.

Recommendations

1. The data collected suggest that many Al-Shabaab mid-level leaders might be willing to join the political process if there are credible alternative options in place.

2. If such leaders are willing to join the political process with their fighters to seek a political settlement, Al-Shabaab itself could be considerably weakened.

3. Instead of the Somali government convincing Al-Shabaab members to desert, defect or apply for amnesty, this study suggests that family and friends, religious leaders and clan elders are more credible intermediaries.

4. Eventual negotiations might include multiple actors, most notably parties directly involved in the conflict—in this case Al-Shabaab, the Somali Federal Government and AMISOM contributing countries—but also secondary actors within the broader international community, which could be the focus of further study.

5. Even if a settlement with Al-Shabaab were reached, careful planning is required to ensure that Somalia does not fall back to earlier conditions that facilitated the emergence of Al-Shabaab in the first place.

6. The risk of being killed or captured played a prominent role in encouraging Al-Shabaab leaders to disengage. Therefore, continuing to put pressure, or possibly increasing military pressure, on Al-Shabaab, could facilitate increased disengagement.

7. The Somali government should frame Al-Shabaab's tactics as harmful to fellow Somalis, and should consider the impact of their alignment with AMISOM or Western countries.

8. To assess the true potential of negotiations, it is essential to increase the sample size of studies of this kind and to research the views of other parties to the conflict.

AID, BUSINESS AND RECONCILIATION

COLLABORATING FOR PEACE

AN ANALYSIS OF NETWORKS
OF COOPERATION IN SOMALIA

Dominik Balthasar and *Anja Osei*

Authors

Dr Dominik Balthasar is a senior researcher at Swisspeace's statehood pro-gramme and lecturer at the University of Basel, working on issues pertaining to conflict, fragility, and development. He has held fellowships with a range of university institutes and think tanks, and consulted with the UN and World Bank, among others.

Dr Anja Osei is a senior research fellow and lecturer at the Chair of International Politics and Conflict Management, University of Konstanz. Her work focuses on elite sociology, democratization, and conflict studies. She holds an MA and PhD in African Studies.

Summary

Peace and reconciliation are fundamentally about cooperation. Understanding the nature and shape of actors' networks allows us to draw important infer-ences about the degree and kind of cooperation. Denser and more decentralized networks enable a faster flow of information and more inclusive decisions. Denser networks also help to increase mutual trust among network participants, which is crucial for fostering peace and reconciliation.

This research project sets out to capture and analyse the web of national and international networks of cooperation in Somalia. Applying social network analysis to identify patterns of cooperation among international as well as between international and national actors central to the delivery and implementation of humanitarian and development assistance, the project's objective is to better understand prevailing practices of cooperation and their implications for peace and reconciliation.

In order to uncover patterns of cooperation, this project collected primary data through a voluntary online survey among international actors with a mandate to support Somali reconstruction. One of the key findings is that networks of cooperation remain—despite a considerable longevity and plurality of national and international aid organizations—surprisingly sparsely connected. Another major finding concerns the fact that even international non-governmental organizations seem to collaborate more with the host government than with civil society counterparts.

Given the confined scope of both the research project and the survey response rate, caution should be exercised in drawing conclusions about policy recommendations. Nonetheless, the research findings do suggest a need for, and opportunity to bring about, enhanced collaboration between the plethora of national and international actors in order to increase the impact of international aid toward supporting peace and reconciliation in Somalia. Furthermore, cooperation does not necessarily need to take on a formal character. Informal networks may, in fact, be at least as effective in enhancing trust and cooperation, and therefore contributing to peace and reconciliation.

Introduction

Having been labelled the "quintessential failed state",[1] and having consistently featured prominently in diverse fragile states rankings,[2] Somalia has drawn significant international attention. Consequently, the country has been marked by multidimensional involvement on the part of the international community, spanning from humanitarian aid to counter-terrorist interventions. The proliferation of donors and the fragmentation of aid, which has advanced particularly over the course of the past quarter century, has led to repeated calls for the need of increased coordination. These calls have been well-received in an environment in which donors and recipients alike have expressed support for improved aid coordination in order to enhance aid effectiveness and accountability.[3] Moreover, it is recognized that achieving peace and reconciliation in Somalia inherently hinges on cooperation.

This briefing paper provides some initial insights into patterns of contemporary cooperation in Somalia. Applying social network analysis methodology to international aid cooperation in Somalia, this paper asks how current national and international networks of cooperation take shape. What does inter-agency collaboration look like in Somalia? Gaining a better understanding of prevailing networks of cooperation is crucial to improve aid effectiveness and to uncover how problem-framing and decision-making are shaped.

A greater understanding of networks of cooperation also helps us to identify ways of enhancing joint efforts to build peace and stability. Peace and reconciliation processes, by definition, require collaboration, which in turn is affected by the nature of social networks. Broadly speaking, dense and decentralized networks allow a faster flow of information, greater mutual understanding and more effective problem-solving. Such networks are also more inclusive, encompassing diverse stakeholders, which is critical for trust-building and reconciliation.

Networks of Cooperation in Somalia

International Aid in Somalia

Somalia provides a challenging operating context for international aid agencies. Efforts undertaken by the international community to support Somalia in rebuilding a more peaceful and stable state have drawn much criticism. Thereby, internationally brokered peace conferences have generated accusations of a self-interested "aid-industry" that has, for most parts, operated in a "remote control" modus operandi from Nairobi, Kenya. Particularly, Somalis have tended to remain critical of and sceptical toward external assistance. This is partly due to historical experiences, when large quantities of aid were diverted to warlords, militias, or a confined group of elites.

Somalia obtains significant amounts of international aid. According to World Bank data, the Horn of Africa nation received US$1.25 billion in net official development assistance and official aid in 2015.[4] According to the Aid Coordination Unit (ACU) within the Office of the Prime Minister of Somalia, the country's international development partners reported US$675 million in aid for development for 2015.[5] Accompanied by nearly US$593 million in humanitarian aid, official development assistance reached US$1.3 billion in 2015 (which excludes military aid and peacekeeping contributions).[6] Major development partners, in terms of financial contributions, are the UN and the World Bank (multilateral) and the United Kingdom and Norway (bilateral). The significant increase of aid over the course of the past decade (up from approximately US$400 million in 2007) renders aid coordination and thus, agency cooperation, crucial—for reasons of both efficiency and effectiveness.

Somalia has witnessed a range of coordination mechanisms. The country is part of the G7+ and the New Deal for Engagement in Fragile States, both of which are designed to enhance the alignment of official development assistance. There is a range of coordination mechanisms in place in order to facilitate cooperation and coordination.[7] Official development finance has increasingly been channelled through the Somalia Development and Reconstruction Facility (SDRF), a financing architecture that provides strategic guidance for development activities in Somalia. While an assessment of the effectiveness of these coordination instruments promises to be insightful, it is beyond the scope of this paper to do so. Rather, this briefing paper seeks to document and analyse de facto networks of cooperation "on the ground" in order to foster a critical debate about current levels of national and international cooperation, as well as about how collaboration among diverse actors could be improved. The fundamental rationale is that increased cooperation not only results in more effective aid but also fosters greater mutual understanding.

Conceptual Framework

While the dominant canon of scholarship on peacebuilding and state-building centres on the role of institutions, an incremental realization of the need of "bringing agency back in" has taken hold. Drawing on a wide scholarship— particularly in African studies—that emphasizes the role of informal, often clientelistic, relationships that coexist with formal institutions,[8] a buoying literature points towards the importance of clientelism in particular[9] and actor relationships more generally[10] in order to understand state trajectories. In other words, networks have increasingly been recognized as being of crucial importance in coming to grips with state performance.[11]

Acknowledging the significance of political networks for national development, this research project adapts a network lens to the sphere of international cooperation. The fundamental argument is that the effectiveness of international assistance significantly hinges on networks of cooperation that international actors entertain with national counterparts. While it has been acknowledged that actors and their relations can be crucial for the success of state-building endeavour,[12] our empirical insights in these structures have often remained limited. We argue that the mapping of international actor relationships adds an important and empirically grounded actor-centric aspect to the prevailing literature of state-building.

In order to identify and analyse national and international networks of cooperation, this paper uses the method of social network analysis (SNA). Social networks consist of nodes, which are usually the actors, and links or ties, which denote the relationships between them. The network itself consists of chains of interconnected dyads. The ties in a network can be directed, meaning that one node is a sender of something that flows through a network (such as information or resources) while another node acts as a receiver. A range of network measures enable analysis of the quality and nature of such webs of relationships.

In this paper, we use a number of measures to describe the structure of the network. The density measure is a basic description of the global interconnectedness of all nodes. Density is calculated by dividing the number of ties present in a network by the number of theoretically possible ties. The density measure takes on values between zero (when no ties exist at all) and one (for a complete network in which every actor is connected to every other actor). Degree centrality simply looks at the absolute number of connections that a node has. It can be further distinguished between in-degree centrality which relates to the number of ties a node receives and out-degree centrality, which relates to the number of ties that a node transmits. "Betweenness" centrality measures how often a node lies on the shortest path between two other nodes. Actors with high betweenness centrality scores are usually powerful actors that can control and dominate the flow of resources in a network. Centralization, as a property of whole networks, looks at the differences between the centrality scores of the most central node and those of all other points.

Research

Methodology

This briefing paper is based on an online survey conducted among international actors active in Somalia. On the basis of a list of agencies provided by the United Nations, we contacted some 120 international actors, of whom 31 filled out the questionnaire. The response rate, thus, stands at roughly 25%, which puts some limitations on the survey's explanatory power (see below). About half of all responses to the survey request were provided for by international non-governmental organizations (NGOs, 47%), followed by UN agencies and other multilateral organizations (26%), with research organizations/think tanks (9%), bilateral donors (7%), and others (11%) following suit. In terms of the organizations' field of activity as indicated by the respondents themselves, some 37% of all respondents are active in the field of development cooperation, 14% in humanitarian aid, and 12% in political assistance, with the remainder classifying as research (5%), security (2%), and other (30%).

With a view to the questionnaire, the respondents were asked to name all organizations with which they cooperate, followed by a number of questions on the nature and extent of their cooperation. From these ego networks, the global structure of cooperation was constructed (see Figure 1). In order not to unduly expose the specific networks of cooperation a particular organization maintains, the subsequent graphs are displayed without attributing organizations' names to the respective nodes.

Figure 1: Networks of cooperation

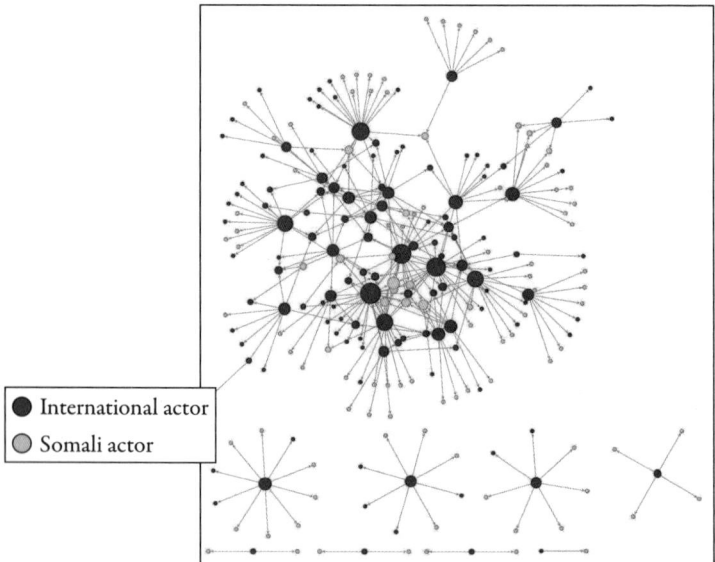

International actor
Somali actor

Findings

A number of findings follow from the research data generated. Taking the entirety of the network composed of national and international actors as a unit of analysis, what emerges is that it is composed of a more integrated core of international organizations that is surrounded by a less densely connected periphery of national counterparts (see Figure 1). Interestingly, all those actors marked by a high degree of centrality are representatives of the international community, with no Somali actor taking a more central position in the prevailing web of relationships. While the data do need to be taken with a pinch of salt, this finding opens up a number of questions with regard to the respective roles played by national and international actors. Although the New Deal for Engagement in Fragile States seeks to put national counterparts into the driving seat, it appears that much humanitarian aid and development assistance coordination happens without their participation.

When confining the scope of analysis to the network of cooperation among international actors (see Figure 2), the data suggest that only 2.4 per cent of all possible connections are realized within the network. While this density is somewhat greater as compared to the network of cooperation between international actors and their national counterparts (see below), it points toward a

Figure 2: Type of networks of cooperation among international actors

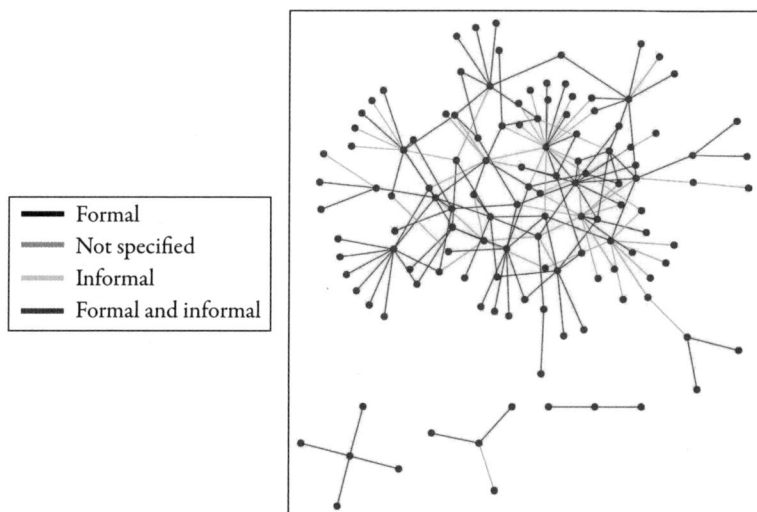

- Formal
- Not specified
- Informal
- Formal and informal

sparsely developed network. Moreover, it is interesting to note that the information provided by the survey respondents indicates that there are no reciprocal ties—although actors are connected with one another via third parties, direct reciprocal ties are missing. Moreover, the centrality measure of 13 per cent suggests that the network, which consists of four distinct components, is rather decentralized in nature. In contrast to highly centralized networks in which a few actors are able to control the flow of information and other resources, decentralized networks point toward more even and inclusive relationships. The actor with the highest measures for in-degree, out-degree, and betweenness centrality is the United Nations Assistance Mission in Somalia (UNSOM), which constitutes the most critical actor within the web of international actors' cooperation. Remarkably, however, while UNSOM takes centre stage when it comes to the network of cooperation among international actors, UNSOM is—according to this dataset—much less present when it comes to collaborations with Somali counterparts.

When considering the network of cooperation between international actors and national counterparts (see Figure 3), one of the most pronounced findings is that this network is relatively sparse. According to the respective density measure, and due to the fact that the average actor exhibits only two ties, the network relies on only 1.5 per cent of all possible connections. What is more, the network is little centralized, but relatively fragmented, constituting itself out of 17 distinct components. According to our survey data, the network's most central actors are the Federal Government of Somalia, followed by the regional governments. This indicates that the public authorities at national and regional level constitute the most important cooperation partners for the collectivity of international actors.

Conversely, Somali civil society organizations appear to be the least important cooperation partners for international actors—indicated by much lower density measures within this network. In light of the fact that nearly half of all survey respondents are international NGOs, this is somewhat surprising, though it can be taken as an indication that international NGOs also rely significantly on cooperation with national and regional public bodies.

Moreover, the data suggest that nearly two-thirds of all cooperation between international actors and Somali counterparts flows along formal mechanisms of cooperation, whereas informal cooperation and the combination of formal and informal cooperation make up for 16 per cent and 18 per cent of relationships, respectively. There is no clear pattern in the distribution of formal and informal ties; many actors have both formal and

Figure 3: Type of networks of cooperation between international and Somali actors

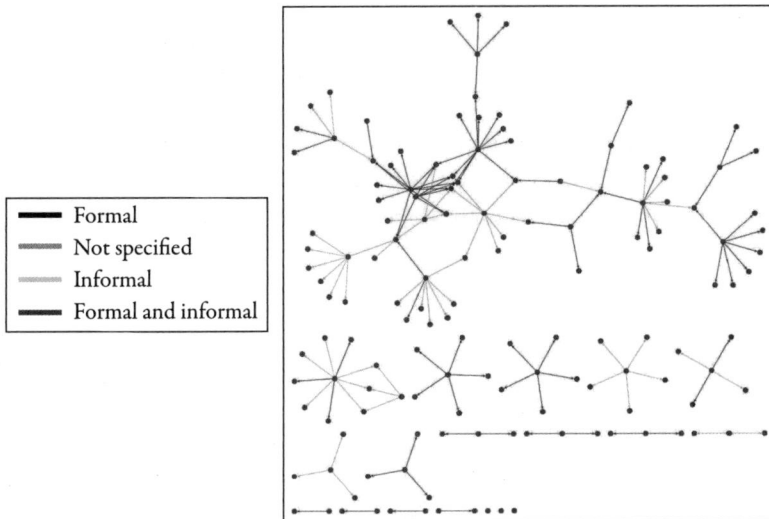

Formal
Not specified
Informal
Formal and informal

informal ties. This indicates that the type of cooperation depends on the particular situations in which actors decide to link up with others in one or the other way. That said, these insights into patterns of formal and informal cooperation are strongly shaped by the survey respondents. If so-called non-traditional donors, local staff, or Somali organizations were to constitute part of the respondents, the resulting data would likely differ in important ways.

A number of additional findings are worth highlighting. First, the data also show that there is no consensus among the international actors of which (individual or collective) actor most decisively shapes the future of Somalia. Yet, among the 71 distinct entries made in the context of this question, the Federal Government of Somalia leads the chart with nine mentions—followed by the UN (seven) and AMISOM, donor community, and President Farmaajo (each six). Thus, according to the perception of representatives of the international community, the UN are accorded a significant role in shaping the future of Somalia. Second, the survey also indicates that international aid agencies remain very open to cooperation with a broad range of actors. The question about which Somali partners international agencies would not consider working with hardly triggered any response. That said, the fact that the question about potential Somali cooperation partners also triggered only few answers may point to either a saturation or lack of imagination when it comes to broadening networks of cooperation. Third, and here finally, our data show that none of the respondents mentioned the Aid Coordination Unit (ACU) at the Office of the Prime Minister and the Ministry of Planning and International Cooperation,[13] the Somali Federal Government's main bodies engaged in promoting the coordination and management of official development finance. While the possibility that this body was not mentioned roots in the nature of the questionnaire, it is telling that this coordination mechanism does not feature at all in the responses given by the survey participants.

Caveats

Although these findings provide some instructive insights into the nature of cooperation in Somalia, the underlying research exhibits a number of caveats. First, at roughly 25 per cent, the response rate remained confined, unfortunately, rendering the data gathered incomprehensive, limiting its representativeness. Second, the survey results are not guarded against self-selection bias among the respondent organizations, as participation was voluntary rather than obliged. Third, the data rely on information provided for by international aid agencies, thus being indicative of the "international community's" subjective viewpoint, rather than a more objective and holistic assessment of the state of affairs. A more comprehensive follow-up project will need to take these caveats into consideration in order to allow for a more detailed and precise assessment of national and international networks of cooperation in Somalia.

Conclusions

Suggesting that networks of cooperation in Somalia remain deficient, this briefing paper concludes that national and international actors should consider enhancing and diversifying their relationships. In view of the general emphasis put on donor and aid coordination[14] at policy level, it remains astonishing that the networks of cooperation in a donor-dependent country such as Somalia remain so confined.

Scholarship on social networks agrees that different kinds of networks exert different influences on actors' ability to exchange information, build mutual understanding and trust, and coordinate their activities in order to develop solutions to challenges they face.[15] Dense networks facilitate cooperation, because an increase in connectivity leads to faster and better solutions in coordination simulations.[16] More tightly connected networks are likely to enhance the effectiveness of measures taken by national and international actors in response to conflict and fragility in Somalia. Such networks are also likely to contribute to trust-building and the emergence of behavioural norms, which are crucial elements of state-building.

Yet, as this research shows, there seems to be a dearth of cooperative networks among and between national and international actors in Somalia. Given the positive implications that dense networks have for cooperation, and for peace and reconciliation, the prevailing situation in Somalia does not appear to be conducive for peacebuilding.

Recommendations

This analysis has provided some initial insights into networks of cooperation in Somalia, and the implications for peacebuilding. While the limited scope of both the research project and the survey response rate do not justify a wide range of policy recommendations, it is clear that much remains to be explored. It is therefore recommended that a more comprehensive quantitative analysis of cooperation in Somalia is undertaken, as well as a more qualitative analysis of its nature. If a more encompassing study, depicting national and international networks of cooperation, were to be carried out, a clearer picture would emerge as to which actors need to be connected in order to enhance the prospects for peace and reconciliation in Somalia.

Three further recommendations can be made. First, given the various advantages of denser networks, national and international actors supporting Somalia's transition out of conflict and fragility should enhance their collaboration and seek to strengthen their respective networks. Second, as trust-building tends to operate at an individual rather than an institutional level, greater efforts should be made to strengthen informal networks of cooperation. Third, international actors should improve collaboration with Somali civil society organizations, which might include an intensification of existing ties, as well as the formation of new partnerships with a broader range of organizations.

INSIGHTS FROM NETWORK ANALYSIS IN SOMALIA

Mircea Gherghina, Sandra McNeill, and *Khadir Abdi*

Authors

Mircea Gherghina holds an MSc in Social Science Research Methods from the University of Bristol. He has an interest in computational methods and economic sociology. Khadir Abdi and Sandra McNeill work for Transparency Solutions (TS), a Somali-led research and development consultancy based in Hargeisa. Together, TS and Gherghina have recently pioneered the use of network analysis in Somalia and are exploring its potential uses in post-conflict states and the wider development field.

Summary

The use of network analysis in the case of Somalia offers insightful new perspectives for peace and reconciliation. By generating data that uncover dynamic links and often concealed ties between individuals, network link analysis reveals intricate power relationships between key actors in Somalia. These relationships, which have implications for peace and reconciliation, might otherwise remain obscure.

In the Somali context, loose and informal power networks are long said to have played a role in the politics of peace and security. This case study models an interpretation of a random sample network between business and state actors. The relationships uncovered span a diverse cross-section of political, economic, and civil society actors. The data expose the extent and depth of the private sector–government links and reveal key influencers who are proactively engaged in peace negotiations, in this case, primarily between Somalia and Somaliland at state level. However, these networks are informal, unstructured and are mostly unnoticed.

The business communities' ability to mobilize networks, share information and foster cooperation, as demonstrated by this case study, is encouraging but it is just one example. The model of network analysis could be applied to understanding other relationships in peace and reconciliation, such as those between armed actors, business and the state, which perpetuate conflict and instability. This would require time and resources but would shed light on the drivers of conflict, the motivations of spoilers, and their leverage.

This study concludes that network link analysis can be used as a research tool to identify different openings, opportunities and pressure points in a network to advance Somali peace and reconciliation.

This briefing paper makes two recommendations:

- The use of network analysis to be expanded as a tool to evaluate the full nature and strength of relationships between actors who already play a role or who could play a role within peace and reconciliation.
- Key private sector and state actors, already informally embedded into peace and reconciliation processes, must be acknowledged and supported to develop existing interventions which routinely occur between key business influencers and state representatives. The process must continue to be Somali-led and, in the short-term at least, must respect the need for interventions to be conducted in private.

Introduction

The primary benefit of network analysis is that it can be used to reveal intricate power relations within networks. For this reason, network analysis as a research method is extensively used in policy research and whilst it has often focused on formal relationships, there is a growing body of literature that uses network analysis to better understand informal relations. However, there is very little literature on its usage and application in policy-making in post-conflict states such as Somalia.

In the case of Somalia, the prolonged civil war fostered cooperation, in the form of loose networks between the private sector and those holding power.[1] Following the collapse of the state, the private sector stepped in to provide essential social services and innovated to ensure the continuation of domestic and international trade. This resulted in investors and entrepreneurs in the private sector aligning themselves with whichever political or military forces were in the ascendant at any time. What is less known is the extent to which these informal networks exist, the nature and impact of such networks, and their relevance to peace and reconciliation.

This paper seeks to explore the benefits of using network analysis techniques to identify the current interplay between actors in business, political elites and armed groups. It will explore whether network analysis can help uncover informal relationships not necessarily otherwise exposed. By modelling an interpretation of the information which can be generated in this way, it will consider the interactions between key actors and show how network analysis can map a topology of those interactions to unravel how groups interact or diverge in terms of ideological positions or different interests.

Through the process of modelling an anonymized network, we first assess the method itself and the often-concealed ties as they exist or otherwise. By adding context and analysis from qualitative methods, we assess the implications and applications of the data and finally we present recommendations for ways to apply the findings to policy-making.

Informal Networks

The idea that networks are sociological tools that convey social structures rose to prominence after Granovetter's[2] seminal paper which discovered that the strength of the weak ties reveals the "cohesive power" of loosely connected actors in networks. He successfully argued that weak ties bridge different networks and facilitate information diffusion.

Networks are projections of formal or informal relationships between social actors. Not all networks are formal. In fact, some argue that even perceived formal networks have a degree of informality embedded into them. These are the hidden relations between actors that are not necessarily on public record. For example, friendship networks between political groups might cross the boundaries of ideological groups. In liberal democracies, where political parties exert power over voting behaviours, there are instances in which negotiated majorities change the expected turnout. This happens due to the "bridges" or weak ties between apparently ideologically divergent groups.

The informality is even more pronounced in political or organizational systems that lack enforcement mechanisms. Network analysis could be one of the most effective methodologies to map informal relationships, not least because of its reliance in the data collection process on survey methods. Surveying is arguably the only method for eliciting information from social actors that are not constrained by any political or institutional mechanisms to have public accountability. In systems where friendship/kinship networks are the most important, network analysis can be used as a tool to formalize power relations and reveal hidden actors that account for most of the ideological support for various factions.

Survey Method of Data Gathering

Before a network is mapped and projected, the data gathering process takes place, often via means of survey.[3] The data are gathered by asking participants in a virtual network to whom they are connected and, in a step-by-step approach, the survey reveals the links between actors and the strength of their relationships. This method does have shortcomings. One is that the reliability of the data is dependent on the quality of the responses. Moreover, the network is often incomplete because the data are bounded by the number of participants in a survey. In Somalia, that information is not as widely available as it is in Western democracies.[4]

The issue of data scarcity contributes to a reliance on survey methods of network data gathering, and yet, in Somalia, data sources cannot be cross-checked with public records which simply do not exist. We therefore adjusted the political or sociological basis of the research in two ways. First, we returned to the primary source of the network data and conducted an in-depth interview to explore areas of interest. Second, we worked with credible political economy experts, who are themselves embedded into Somali society, for verification and added context.

Modelling the Data

The data gathering process began with a survey of one participant whom we label the primary contact. Adam has business interests in Somalia and Somaliland as well as in East Africa and the Middle East. He self-selected a random sample of 33 associates, labelled key contacts. He then ranked them according to the strength of the relationship:

- Seven were close/trusted.
- 12 were good/professional.
- 13 were well-known acquaintances.

The next step was to survey the top three associates of each of the key contacts. This generated a further 105 secondary contacts, which gave a total cohort of 138. It must be emphasized that the network is a random snapshot and is not intended to be representative.

Interpreting the Data

Table 1: Distribution of key contacts and secondary contacts by sector

Politics	(56.19%)
Business associate	(31.43%)
Friend	(2.86%)
Security	(1.9%)
Social	(1.9%)
Media	(0.95%)
Financial sector	(0.95%)
Civil society	(0.95%)
Businessman	(0.95%)
Military	(0.95%)

The data reveal the diversity of connections held by business people investigated in this survey, illustrated in Table 1, above. It is perhaps not surprising that the expanded network of a prominent businessman would contain strong business connections but what is striking is the number of connections to individuals in political life. In almost any nation, one can easily find examples where business and politics intersect, from powerful lobbyists to corporate donations, although not necessarily to the same degree.

We were also interested to know the geographical distribution of the network and included in the survey where the contacts are domiciled, beginning with Adam, who is based in Hargeisa. We did not include additional places of residence outside of Somalia, although many of the contacts hold foreign passports and have second nationalities as well as Somali.[5] The results are illustrated below in Table 2.

Table 2: Distribution of key contacts and secondary contacts by residence

	Hergeisa	(54.29%)
	Mogadishu	(36.19%)
	Garawe	(3.81%)
	Bosaaso	(1.9%)
	Qahiro	(0.95%)
	Bosaso	(0.95%)
	Galkacyo	(0.95%)
	Somaliland	(0.95%)

That the greatest number of contacts in the network are based in the same city as the primary contact might be expected but there is a significant percentage in Mogadishu and some in Puntland. What the data show is that many of the individuals in this network regularly transcend regions and borders.

Rendering the Network

We rendered the network using the Gephi software programme, which generated the giant component. The presentation of the data is visualized as a sociogram (Figure 1, below). The nodes represent individuals; and ties are shown as lines connected to the nodes.

In this sample model, we apply the colour code used in Table 1. The most connected and thereby the most influential node in the sociogram is Adam, represented by the central grey node. Immediately we can visualize his connections. What we see is the emergence of two clusters. The denser of the two is on the left-hand side. Interestingly, this cluster includes two of the most powerful politicians in the 2012–16 Somalia government. Based on these results, we can confidently predict that an expanded survey would contain many more nodes and ties, and the clusters would be more apparent. In both emergent clusters, the black nodes represent individuals, working in security manage-

Figure 1: The large component network, distributed by key contacts and secondary contacts

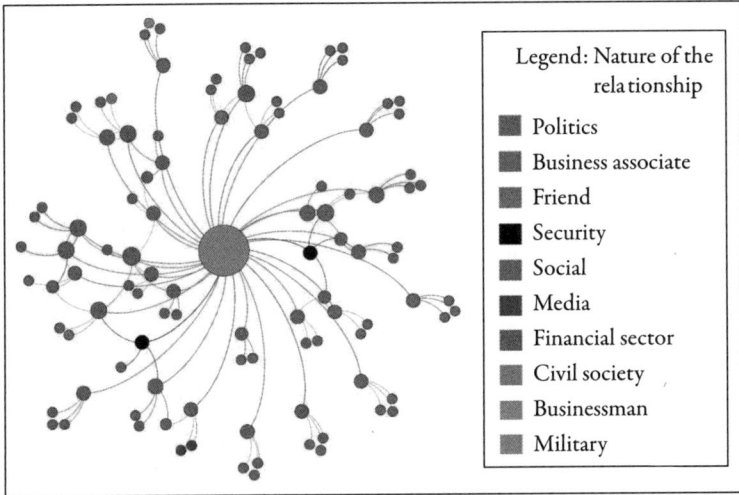

ment, who connect two adjacent networks. While the relevance of these bridge nodes is discussed below, it is important to note that they are the key to connecting two or more groups in a social network.

Evie Browne and Jonathan Fisher,[6] academics from Birmingham University who have produced several papers on a range of contemporary Somali political issues, observe that in Somalia, power is heavily concentrated in individuals rather than institutions. This is corroborated by the data. There are comparatively fewer green nodes, representing business actors, and from this we see the importance of having access to political power.

The relative stability of the private sector contrasts with a succession of weak governments. When biographical data are factored in, we observe the longevity of the business actors compared to the politicians. An example is Mohamed, a Somali Member of Parliament with several ties in the network. He was relatively unknown prior to his selection into the Somali Parliament in 2012 but the necessity of achieving clan balance meant he was given a senior post and quickly assumed power and influence. This is reflected by his relatively higher number of ties. Following the 2016–17 electoral process and a change of administration, his influence is less significant. If the survey were to be repeated after the 2020 elections, the private sector actors would likely stay constant but their ties to political actors would reflect changes in the configuration of power. A key benefit of network analysis is that it shows dynamic relationships, but it needs to be repeated to ensure continued relevance. Network evolution might include actors who move between networks and emerge in a different capacity. Throughout the world there are politicians with business interests and business people with political ambitions. Somalia is no different but understanding the connections and applying context can add new insights. For example, one business contact, Kasim, is a recently elected MP and is known to have political ambitions. Within the network he has a high degree of influence. He has a large business portfolio with interests in several sectors, and yet like others in the network, he is largely unknown. He is also one of the founding members of an emerging political party. Organized political groupings are gaining traction, especially as a multi-party system is a prerequisite of universal suffrage for 2020. Both Dajir and Damajidad, two emerging political groupings,[7] are beginning to resemble political parties as they are understood in more established democracies. Whilst there continues to be a high degree of movement between networks based on shared ideology or self-interest, it is starting to lessen. The implication is that some networks may start to become more formal.

We discover too a high degree of interplay between business and state actors. What then are the drivers of this? First are pragmatic reasons. Business must continue working despite the absence of a functioning state. For example, a business registered in Somaliland is not recognized in Mogadishu and vice versa. Acquiring a licence to operate is extremely difficult without the support of a powerful politician. Equally, there are contracts to be won (invariably with little transparency) and in a largely unregulated society, simply keeping businesses functioning requires considerable time and resources, which is made easier by being able to call on favours.

There are also factors relating to security that explain the high level of interaction between business and state actors. A stable and prosperous Somalia is arguably in the best interests of the private sector, which means there is a vested interest in peacekeeping.[8] What is discovered when we add qualitative data is the extent of the business actors, which is both frequent and significant. For example, when clan fighting breaks out, it is often the business community who is called upon, in many cases by the government, to facilitate peace talks. The state simply has limited capacity and resources to resolve conflict. One example was an outbreak of violence between neighbouring Somali clans on the Ethiopian border. The sultan of one clan, who was deemed essential to the peacemaking process, was in Hargeisa with no means to return. The business community arranged for a vehicle to transport him. The business role in maintaining security also extends to helping to maintain law and order. A recent incident in Garowe involved the theft of US$200,000. The individual concerned attempted to flee the country but was captured and detained after the business community mobilized its networks.

The most significant role of private sector actors in peace and reconciliation however is in information-sharing. Business people have the means to move freely across internal and international borders and they also have trusted relationships with the most powerful political actors. These two critical factors mean they can play a substantial role facilitating peace and reconciliation talks between Somalia and Somaliland. This takes different forms, such as conveying messages from a minister in one region to his or her counterpart in another, or arranging face-to-face talks, although always outside of the country and usually in Djibouti, the Middle East, or Turkey. Such efforts are generally conducted in secret and are bound by confidentiality.

An example of this is enhanced cooperation between the directors of Somalia's and Somaliland's intelligence services. Primarily driven by the need for security, what began as a series of personal messages led to face-to-face talks, facilitated by members of the business community. This culminated in an arrangement to share information on suspected terrorists. Seven months later, the international community, keen to establish information-sharing between the two organizations, suggested talks should be convened, only to discover a functioning mechanism was already in place.

Altruism is another driver of interaction between business and state actors. We have acknowledged the role of the private sector in providing essential services, but we also found examples of businesses using their influence and connections to support cultural and religious activities. Completing the Hajj Pilgrimage is a religious and cultural obligation for most Somalis. Vast numbers, however, do not have passports. Using their networks, business actors worked with their political associates to find a workable solution and now annually facilitate the travel of hundreds of Somalis to the Hajj.

Network data also reveal actors that are hidden or missing (known as structural holes). In this network, there is a notable absence of known links to Al-Shabaab or armed actors. The two "bridge" nodes mentioned earlier are both state actors with responsibility for national security, again emphasizing the importance of peace and stability to the business communities and politicians alike.

If we were to penetrate the network more deeply, we may well uncover illicit and corrupt practices within the network, but they do not appear to be the dominant feature. There are networks where business and state actors do collude with armed actors, and this is sometimes born out of necessity. For example, a study assessing the political economy of roadblocks in Somalia[9] revealed a network of brokers, known locally as "*maqaalas*", who act as go-betweens for transport companies and those in control of roadblocks—including Al-Shabaab—to facilitate safe and speedy passage through occupied territories. The charcoal trade is an example where the trade cycle comprises networks of all three. Rendering those networks could generate data of interest with the potential to inform policy-making.

Conclusion

We first assess the process and benefits of network analysis. It is possible to generate and present a robust network, despite the limitations, most significantly a lack of organized data. To do so, however, it is also necessary to adjust the precepts of data gathering. Essentially, this adjustment involved sitting and talking at length with a small sample of the cohort; collecting and verifying biographical data; and contextualizing the results through a political economy lens. The desk research and expert analysts ensured academic rigour and accuracy. A drawback of this method is that it is time-consuming but the benefits are significant. In fact, the use of network analysis in the case of Somalia is insightful. Visualizing even a small sample network with few ties and connections has unravelled what would otherwise be an opaque web of connections and instead presents with clarity a cast of actors, the majority of whom are unknown to the wider world, who play an important but hidden role in the peace and reconciliation process.

Second, we consider the results of the data itself. Of significance is the interaction between political and business networks where boundaries are blurry and often overlap. With no formal rules to govern those relations, the political reality is the emanation of networks that control strategy and strategic resources. A key aspect is the active pursuit of peace and reconciliation initiatives between business and state actors, largely driven by pragmatic motivations, aligned more closely with business interests than political ones, although importantly, not to the exclusion of the latter. As a result, any achievements and progress resulting from this interaction, if they are recognized at all, are acknowledged in isolation rather than as part of a planned, cohesive process.

The evidence suggests that if we were to expand the network analysis considerably, penetrate more deeply or even consider specific networks, such as the charcoal trade, it is likely that as well as revealing shapers and influencers of positive change, we would uncover and better understand the relationships between individuals who view the continuation of a state of instability to be in their best interests, whether for personal, economic, political or ideological gain.

Recommendations

1. Expand the use of network analysis to support peace and reconciliation.

This pilot of network analysis has demonstrated utility and it is recommended that its use is expanded. Possible groups which could be explored using network analysis methodology include spoiler networks, institutions, women, youth, clans or official actors. Specific public or private sectors could be explored such as justice or health, oil or fishing. Understanding who can influence networks, both positively or negatively, who can bridge networks and act as champions, who can disseminate information, identifying structural holes, all have the potential to improve the peace and reconciliation processes.

2. Acknowledge the role of the private sector in peace and reconciliation and support the development of a more cohesive strategy.

The business network sampled, especially its mechanisms and activities, reveals the actual and potential participation by business actors in peace and reconciliation at local clan level and at national level, between Somaliland and Somalia. There is a significant opportunity to develop a more coordinated, locally-led approach which acknowledges the role of the business community, and preserves the adaptive and responsive nature of peace and reconciliation efforts. It is recommended that the findings of this paper are shared and discussed with selected contacts identified within this sample network together with key Somali and international stakeholders. Such discussions could improve communication and coherence between key actors in the private sector, government and international community when planning and implementing interventions that could advance peace and reconciliation.

BUSINESS-LED PEACEBUILDING IN SOMALIA

Bahar Ali Kazmi and *Faisa Abdi Loyaan*

Authors

Dr Bahar Ali Kazmi is a co-founder and research director of the NGO Applied Management Research and Teaching Unit, Aston Business School (UK) and publishes in the areas of corporate social responsibility, human rights, and business-NGO partnerships/alternative organizations.

Faisa Abdi Loyaan is a director of Creative Alternatives Now (CAN) and works as an independent consultant with expertise in conflict analysis, peacebuilding, civil society participation and governance in East Africa.

Summary

- The political environment in which Somali businesses operate is affected by extreme insecurity, weak national and regional political institutions and unfavourable international political circumstances.
- Somali businesses are essentially defensive in relation to the political aspect of peace and reconciliation as they focus on the success of their businesses and in so doing utilize a range of methods of minimizing risk. In some cases these practices work against peacebuilding objectives.
- Somali businesses see themselves as apolitical and socially responsible organizations. They provide employment, skills, higher education, and support

to small businesses and contribute to humanitarian and development assistance. However, there are concerns about levels of inclusivity, accountability, and competition.

• Somali businesses can play a strategic role in the peace and reconciliation process by developing social partnerships with Somali NGOs, establishing a voluntary code of ethics for regulating their operations, leading the process of formulating an anti-corruption framework for business activities, and supporting, in collaboration with international organizations, new social and environmentally sustainable enterprises.

Introduction

This briefing paper assesses the potential of Somali businesses to engage in the peace and reconciliation process in Somalia. The findings, conclusions and recommendations are based on the thematic analysis of semi-structured interviews with selected and accessible chief executive officers of large and medium Somali companies, the leadership of the Somalia Chamber of Commerce and Industries, Somalia-based NGOs and an examination of the newspaper reports, business reports, websites, academic papers, and non-profit sector reports dealing with business and conflict/peace in Somalia (published in the last five to seven years).

Central to the observations presented in this paper is the understanding that businesses—both local and international—can assist in creating sustainable peace. This viewpoint, broadly seen as Corporate Social Responsibility (CSR), has become an important area of international policy. Since 1999, the United Nations has been leading it by mobilizing businesses and producing a range of policy initiatives such as the Global Compact (1999); the UN Security Council working group on the role of Business in Conflict Prevention, Peacekeeping, and Post-Conflict Peace-Building (2004); and more recently the United Nations "Protect, Respect and Remedy" Framework, known as the Guiding Principles on Business and Human Rights (2011). These and other similar initiatives such as the Organisation for Economic Cooperation and Development (OECD) Guidelines for Multinational Enterprises have formalized the international policy environment for developing a better understanding of business activities that prevent political violence and promote sustainable peace.

While the contribution of businesses in promoting peace has been discussed in other regions such as Colombia and Sri Lanka, limited effort is being made to systematically discuss the activities of Somali businesses. The study, therefore, is by necessity exploratory and aims to fill this gap by focusing on the Somali business activities that directly or indirectly contribute to peace and reconciliation.

The breakdown of the state in 1991 in Somalia has produced a hyper-liberalized economy driven by entrepreneurial innovation, competition, and a globally networked private sector.[1] This process has produced two types of private sectors—licit and illicit.[2] This paper focuses on the former, which includes businesses that operate in livestock, hides and skin, bananas, wood charcoal, construction, mining, transportation, security services, manufactured goods such as textiles, electronics, basic household items, telecommunications, and remittances.

As a case study, the Somali business sector is extraordinary: it is not only the backbone of Somalia's economy but also the main source of employment, services, and goods.[3] In the absence of effective state institutions, businesses can be viewed as "performing public roles" and therefore can potentially play a strategic role in the peace and reconciliation process.[4] The paper focuses on this aspect of Somali businesses.

In the next section, the paper focuses on two areas of business activity in Somalia. First, it considers the political environment in which Somali businesses operate because it is this environment which creates opportunities as well as constraints for them to engage with the peace and reconciliation process. Second, it sketches the organization of business activity which Somali businesses have set up to produce and exchange goods and services. This analysis is essential to grasp the dynamics of business activity and conflict or peace. Against the activities presented in that section, the third section concludes the discussion. The final section lists recommendations which aim to improve the contribution of Somali businesses in the peace and reconciliation process.

Somali Businesses in Peace and Reconciliation

Since 1991, Somalia has experienced ongoing violence, massive population displacement, and cycles of drought and famine, resulting in extreme insecurity, exacerbated by fragmented and transitory political arrangements. The regions of Somalia have dealt with this insecurity differently and have together produced a distinct business environment which is "interconnected and integrated into a globalized economy".[5]

South-central region has tried repeatedly to establish a functioning political framework, but it has still been unable to improve security. Somaliland has solid political institutions and has achieved security. Puntland also has produced a functioning but weaker political system which has improved security to a certain extent, but like south-central region, it is still troubled by food, employment, and income insecurity which is exacerbated due to the problems in law enforcement.

International companies are reluctant to work with Somali businesses because of the concern that they might unwittingly become involved in supporting extremist groups. This situation hinders the operation and growth of Somali businesses that seek to operate in international markets or depend on the international network of investors for the continuity and performance of their businesses.[6]

The political environment in which Somali businesses operate is affected by extreme insecurity, weak national and regional political institutions, and unfavourable international political circumstances. This peculiar business environment can be viewed as a constraint for the growth of Somali businesses. But it also seems to be inspiring Somali businesses to develop innovative ways of doing business which are intricately linked with both peace and reconciliation, and political violence.[7]

Somali businesses have been engaged in developing innovative business processes, growth strategies and products to minimize insecurity. Nonetheless they are still exposed to the shifting political landscape which constantly breeds violence and disrupts their business operations. Interviewees involved in businesses inside Somalia emphasized that their contribution to peace and reconciliation must be judged by considering the political environment in which they operate. They insist that, by doing business innovatively, they have been improving the economic conditions and opportunities that are critical for achieving the objectives of peace and reconciliation.

By providing employment, skills, higher education, and supporting small businesses, they have been keeping a significant segment of young people out of war and illicit activities. Interviewees who are involved in large businesses frequently refer to their innovative business approaches and claim that their businesses are embedded in the cultural and social fabric of Somali society and maintain privileged social access and influence which cross-cut the clan communities, needed for the protection of their business operations.

This business approach is observable in telecommunications, financial services and food livestock sectors, which are intimately connected and play a major role in the social and economic lives of Somalis both inside and outside Somalia. The telecommunication companies—Hormuud in south-central

Somalia, Golis in Puntland and Telesom in Somaliland—have organized themselves differently to minimize the impact of conflict on their operations. For example, Hormuud has created local shareholders and employment opportunities rooted in the cultural and political dynamics of different Somali regions. This arrangement has not only helped the company to secure investment and consumers' loyalty, but also shielded the company from the conflict. In addition, recently, Hormuud has established a Sharia–compliant bank called Salaam Somali Bank. It acts as a venture capital enterprise to assist new business projects. Likewise, Telesom has introduced the mobile money platform Zaad, which became widely popular in Somaliland because it addresses an important need of that region.

In the absence of a national banking sector, Somali businesses have established an extensive and efficient money transferring system, known as "*hawala*". This de facto banking system is a lifeline for 40 per cent of the population which count on the financial support provided by the diaspora for their production, consumption, and humanitarian or development activities in Somalia. The United Nations Development Programme states in its 2011 report "Cash and Compassion" that the diaspora provides US$130–200 million for humanitarian/development activities and US$1.3 and US$2 billion per year for private consumption.[8] The World Bank, in 2016, reports an even higher figure and states that the remittances constitute 23 per cent of the Somali GDP amounting to US$1.4 to US$1.6 billion in 2015. There are many registered money transfer operators (MTOs) in Somalia, not least Dahabshiil Money Transfer, Kaah Express, Tawakal Express and Juba Express. The largest is Dahabshiil, which is used by the United Nations and international NGOs.[9] There are many unregistered transfer operators as well.

The international cross-clan outreach and influence of large telecommunication companies and MTOs, on the one hand, guarantees the survival and growth of communities inside Somalia but it perhaps also contributes to a business-driven sense of identity, which some entrepreneurs are uneasy about. An interviewee who runs a medium-size business in Mogadishu declared that: "we are a nation under Hormuud and Dahabshiil." The comment, to an extent, confirms the emerging evidence that the Somali private sector may have reached its structural limits, promoting monopolistic business, oligopolistic trends, creating entry barriers for new businesses and limiting the growth of small- and medium-size businesses.[10]

Somali businesses are essentially defensive in relation to the political aspect of peace and reconciliation, as they focus on the success of their businesses and in so doing utilize a range of methods of minimizing risk. Interviewees involved in large or small businesses frequently stressed that they could only provide financial support to peace and reconciliation. Their direct involvement in the political aspect of peace could endanger their business operations and increase personal and commercial risk.

Even though the interviewees engaged in large and medium-size businesses were reluctant to talk about their interaction with Al-Shabaab, they nonetheless accepted that they had been spending an enormous amount of money on their personal and commercial security. An interviewee engaged in a large financial business affirmed, "more than 100 employees in Mogadishu are engaged in security. This means almost 10 per cent of employees are security staff". An interviewee engaged in managing a humanitarian organization said that, "it is hidden or not discussed that most companies pay 'tax' to Al-Shabaab in order to continue operating in Al-Shabaab-held territories. This would certainly appear to be a way of contributing to conflict." It therefore appears that the approach which Somali businesses have developed to protect their businesses does not always work in favour of peacebuilding goals.

Notwithstanding this, Somali businesses say they are regulated by Somali customary law which provides them with the necessary framework for resolving commercial disputes and regulating their operations. Looking ahead, some interviewees involved in large businesses stressed the importance of Somalia eventually establishing a standard system of taxation, an effective police force, reliable judiciary system, and national army. They see these political structures from a strategic perspective. In other words, they would minimize the cost of strategizing taxation across different regions, retaining and managing private security companies, and maintaining relationships with multiple sub-clans.

Even though some Somali companies provide small voluntary payments to the Somali public sector[11] and are engaged in the Public–Private Dialogue (PPD), initiated and organized by the World Bank Group, interviewees managing large- and medium-size businesses, however, are still concerned about public-sector corruption.

Somali businesses see themselves as apolitical and socially responsible organizations. Interviewees managing large- and medium-size businesses assert that they have been proactively contributing to humanitarian and development assistance.[12] They see this contribution as a part of their religious duty and believe in "quiet giving."[13]

They have contributed to the provision of health services, water, and, communication services during emergency relief periods (floods, drought, and famine). In so doing, they say they often find ways of delivering relief in conflict-affected areas of Somalia. Some large Somali companies have annual budgets for humanitarian and development assistance. For example, Dahabshiil reports that 10 per cent of its profits goes to hospitals, schools, and community facilities, while during the current humanitarian crisis Hormuud claims that it has provided US$800,000 and Telesom says it has provided US$500,000 for drought relief. Somali businesses are increasingly involved in philanthropy and many interviewees involved in businesses see it as a part of their leadership role and plan to extend it by also increasing their activities to promote environmental sustainability.

Furthermore, some interviewees engaged in large- and medium-size businesses claim that they offer socially responsible role models for youth as they are not involved in "immoral" activities. However, their approach to philanthropy and socially responsible behaviour is ad hoc and to an extent spontaneous. It therefore may have limited long-term social impact.[14]

Moreover, claims of social responsibility were contested by some interviewees. An interviewee engaged in managing a humanitarian organization maintained that, "Somalia is awash with imported stuff; the entire nation has become a commercial hub concerned only with how to make money. There was no thought of contributing to peacebuilding because these men right away cash their money". A female entrepreneur declared that, "most of them [the big companies] profit from the *burburki* [conflict]" adding that in the absence of state regulation large companies were not held accountable or subject to competition.

Women interviewees involved in medium and small businesses insist that the current business environment is highly conservative and does not allow women to enter large commercial enterprises. Some large Somali companies do not recruit women and the contribution of women entrepreneurs to the peace and reconciliation process is unrecognized and in some cases completely ignored and mocked.

Conclusion

There is no doubt that Somali businesses are indirectly contributing to peace and reconciliation. However, their behaviour is driven by the strategic and security interests of their businesses and they are unwilling to go beyond this defensive approach, which does not always work in favour of peace.

In some cases they have shown socially responsible leadership in the areas of humanitarian and development assistance and in this sense, they have continuously been reducing the risk of deprivation which can potentially aggravate conflict, displacement, and violence.

However, their approach to socially responsible management is embedded in Somali culture and faith and may obstruct the realization of human rights of culturally marginalized groups, including women, in Somalia's business environment.

Finally, it is important to note that Somali businesses have structured their own business environment without a statist regulatory framework and institutions. This environment functions efficiently for them and therefore many medium and large Somali businesses do not see the Somali state and its institutions as the solution to accomplish sustainable peace. Some of them, however, do consider the strategic potential of statist institutions and can therefore be persuaded to undertake activities in support of state-building.

Recommendations

The recommendations for policy-makers are aimed at enhancing the contribution of Somali businesses in peace and reconciliation. Their role, however, should be framed within the context of the strategic and security needs of Somali businesses.

Promoting and establishing socially responsible Somali business organizations

- Promote social partnerships between Somali businesses and NGOs aimed at delivering humanitarian and development projects. Social partnership is an effective tool of exchanging complementary resources and achieving strategic and social objectives. Somali businesses operate through extensive cross-clan networks and shareholder relationships with elders and the wider community, and have the capacity and resources to run national and international operations. Businesses can provide resources and outreach to Somali NGOs to achieve their social objectives, while NGOs can improve their social performance and status nationally and internationally by providing the knowledge and expertise needed to address social issues and by strategically bridging their relationship with international community.
- Establish a business social responsibility and sustainability function within the Somali Chamber of Commerce and Industries (SCCI) aimed at developing a national level code of ethics for large- and medium-size businesses. Somali businesses regulate themselves through customary law and

it can provide a starting point to integrate international voluntary codes such as the Global Compact[15] and the UN Guiding Principles on Business and Human Rights, implementing the "Protect, Respect and Remedy" Framework. The United Nations can provide the necessary knowledge and linkages to SCCI.

- Establish a working group of business leaders within the Somali Chamber of Commerce and Industries aimed at leading the process of formulating an anti-corruption framework for business activities. The UN and other bilateral donors can provide the necessary knowledge to the working group and help them with developing a better understanding of international business standards.

- Strengthen and expand the enterprise development programme initiated by Somali businesses and NGOs by providing them with resources and skills to support entrepreneurs who initiate social and environmentally sustainable enterprises and help them with developing access to international markets. Develop specific programmes for women entrepreneurs to be part of the larger business networks and promote them within the current business structures. Establish a non-profit national institution to lead and develop this programme in collaboration with Somali businesses, NGOs, and international organizations.

NOTES

INTRODUCTION

1. Michael Keating is the Special Representative of the United Nations Secretary-General for Somalia and head of the United Nations Assistance Mission in Somalia (UNSOM). Before assuming his current role, he was Associate Director of Chatham House—The Royal Institute of International Affairs and Senior Advisor to the UN Envoy for Syria. He has previously served as Deputy Special Representative of the Secretary-General and United Nations Resident and Humanitarian Coordinator in Afghanistan. He has had numerous assignments with the United Nations, including Resident Coordinator in Malawi. He was also previously Executive Director of the Africa Progress Panel, chaired by former UN Secretary-General Kofi Annan. Matt Waldman is Adviser to the Special Representative of the UN Secretary-General for Somalia. He is also Director of the Center for Empathy in International Affairs and an Associate Fellow at Chatham House. Waldman has served as an Adviser to the UN Special Envoy for Syria and the UN Special Representative for Afghanistan. He has also undertaken mediation work in the Middle East and Africa with the European Institute of Peace and Inter Mediate. Previously, he was a Fellow in the Kennedy School of Government at Harvard University.
2. Readers wishing to obtain Somali translations should contact UNSOM.

LOOMA DHAMA: POLITICAL INCLUSIVITY IN THE SOMALI URBAN CONTEXT

1. Warsan Cismaan and Abdulliziz Ali Ibrahim 'Xildhibaan' argue that the expression *looma dhamma* was first popularized by General Mohamed Farah Aidid to discredit a peace conference to which he was not invited. They note that "this phrase has been used time and again to dismiss peace agreements and justify continued conflict." See Warsan Cismaan and Abdulliziz Ali Ibrahim 'Xildhibaan', "Somali Peace Agreements: Fuelling Factionalism," in Mark Bradbury and Sally Healy, eds.,

Whose Peace is it Anyway: Connecting Somali and International Peacemaking (London: Conciliation Resources, Issue 21, 2010) http://www.c-r.org/downloads/Accord%2021_9Somali%20peace%20agreements_2010_ENG.pdf

2. This follows the conclusion reached by Charles Call, who notes that exclusion is not "a globally applicable objective level of political participation" but is instead "subjective perceptions among former warring factions ... Actions that may not be formally proscribed in an agreement can constitute a violation of expected inclusionary behavior." See Charles Call, *Why Peace Fails: The Causes and Prevention of Civil War Recurrence* (Washington DC: Georgetown University Press, 2012), pp. 4–5.

3. Ibid., p. 5.

4. World Bank, *World Development Report 2011: Conflict, Security, and Development* (Washington DC: World Bank, 2011 pp. 12–13.

5. Jonathan Di John and James Putzel, "Political settlements: Issues paper" (Governance and Social Development Resource Centre, University of Birmingham, 2009), p. 4.

6. Douglass North, John Wallis, Steven Webb, and Barry Weingast, "Limited Access Orders: Rethinking the Problems of Development and Violence," (2011) https://web.stanford.edu/group/mcnollgast/cgi-bin/wordpress/wp-content/uploads/2013/10/Limited_Access_Orders_in_DW_-II_-2011.0125.submission-version.pdf

7. Ibid., p. 5.

8. The pastoral democracy narrative is not entirely accurate—women, and members of low status social groups, were not part of these otherwise open assemblies.

9. Lidwien Kaptiejns, *Clan Cleansing in Somalia: The Ruinous Legacy of 1991* (Philadelphia: University of Pennsylvania Press, 2014).

10. Lee Cassanelli and Catherine Besteman, eds., *The Struggle for Land in Southern Somalia: The War Behind the War* (Boulder: Westview Press, 1997).

11. For a recent study of the political impact of exclusion of refugee returnee in major Somali cities, see Ken Menkhaus, "Dadaab Returnee Conflict Assessment" (Nairobi: Danish Demining Group, August 2017).

12. Ibid.

13. UN Habitat and Geneva Peacebuilding Platform, "Reviewing the State of Safety in World Cities," (Geneva: 6–8 July 2016).

NEITHER INEVITABLE NOR ACCIDENTAL: THE IMPACT OF MARGINALIZATION IN SOMALIA

1. United Nations High Commissioner for Refugees, *Protection and Return Monitoring Network Drought Displacement Report*, 23 June 2017.

2. United Nations Office for the Coordination of Humanitarian Affairs, *Drought Response Situation Report No. 12*, 13 June 2017: http://reliefweb.int/report/

somalia/somalia-drought-response-situation-report-no-12-13-june-2017 (accessed 7 September 2017); note that cholera is often a proxy indicator with respect to the collapse, or non-availability, of services.

3. *Inter-Agency Standing Committee* (IASC), *Principal's Statement on the Centrality of Protection in Humanitarian Action*, 2013; IASC, *Policy on Protection in Humanitarian Action*, 2016; *The Centrality of Protection: Practical Steps for Humanitarian Coordinators and Humanitarian Country Teams*, November 2016.

4. Rift Valley Institute and Heritage Institute for Policy Studies, *Land Matters in Mogadishu: Settlement, ownership and displacement in a contested city*, 78 (2017); Crisis Group Africa Briefing No. 125, *Instruments of Pain (III): Conflict and Famine in Somalia*, May 2017, which states that "[i]n some of the camps, so-called gatekeepers masquerading as camp elders manipulate aid deliveries and extort bribes.' See also Human Rights Watch, *Hostages of the Gatekeepers: Abuses against Internally Displaced in Mogadishu Somalia* (2013).

5. Transparency International, *Collective Resolution to Enhance Accountability and Transparency in Emergencies, Southern Somalia Report*, 20, 2016.

6. See Ken Menkhaus, "No Access: Critical Bottlenecks in the 2011 Somali Famine", *Global Food Security 1* (2012): 29–35; Peter D. Little, "Livelihoods, Assets and Food Security in a Protracted Political Crisis: The case of the Jubba Region, southern Somalia", *Beyond Relief: Food Security in Protracted Crises* (2013): 107–126; Daniel Maxwell and Nisar Majid, *Famine in Somalia: Competing Imperatives, Collective Failure 2011–2012* (London: Hurst, 2016).

7. Maxwell and Majid, op. cit.

8. Priya Gajraj, Shonali Sardesai, and Per Wam, *Conflict in Somalia: Drivers and Dynamics*, World Bank, 2005. The document states that "the report has not undergone review accorded to official World Bank publications. The findings, interpretations, and conclusions expressed ... are those of the author(s) and do not necessarily reflect the views of International Bank for Reconstruction and Development/the World Bank".

9. Ibid. See also Nisar Majid and Stephen McDowell, "Hidden dimensions of the Somalia Famine", *Global Food Security 1* (2012): 1.

10. See Menkhaus, op. cit., note 6, 29–30.

11. Daniel Maxwell, Nisar Majid, Guhad Adan, Khalif Abdirahman, Jeeyon Janet Kim, "Facing Famine: Somali Experiences in the Famine of 2011", *Food Policy 65* (2016): 63–73.

12. Nisar Majid and Stephen McDowell, op. cit., note 9. See also Christian Webersik, "Differences that matter: the structure of the marginalised in Somalia", *Africa 74* (2004): 516–533; Mohamed Haji Mukhtar, "The Plight of the Agro-Pastoral Society of Somalia", *Review of African Political Economy*, (1996): 543–553.

13. UNICEF, Emergency Nutrition Situation Update, October 2016 (on file with authors).

14. UNHCR, op. cit., note 1.
15. https://www.humanitarianresponse.info/en/operations/somalia (accessed 7 September 2017).
16. Crisis Group Africa Briefing No. 125, op. cit., note 4 (observing that "[i]n many instances, predatory/criminal clan militias as well as rogue security elements belonging to the federal states exploit these localised conflicts, erecting checkpoints on major routes to serve as 'toll stations' as a means of extracting money.")
17. Interviews, June 2017; UN Internal Report, 2016.
18. In April 2017 in Balcad, Middle Shabelle, it was reported that Abgaal-dominated Middle Shabelle Regional Administration security forces killed a Somali Bantu man and burned most of the houses (a reported 753) in three predominantly Bantu villages: Jameeco Misra Weyn, Misra Yarey and Kulmis. Local Bantu Somali MPs also approached AMISOM for support for the IDPs following the attack. Most of the 5,000 odd residents fled to neighbouring villages, Jowhar area, and Mogadishu. On 7 June 2017, Abgaal/Hawiye clan militia captured five Somali Bantu men who were travelling in a produce truck from Xawaadley area to Mogadishu and executed them. Middle Shabelle authorities did not comment on the incidents and no action was taken to investigate. While Bantu community leaders held clan negotiations with Abgaal clan elders, no significant outcome was achieved to end hostilities. The violence against the Bantu community has continued. There are indications of active participation of security forces in the attacks despite the insistence of the regional administration that this is an inter-clan issue whereby Abgaal/Hawiye pastoralists lead their cattle to graze in the Bantu farming areas.
19. The Agreement stated *inter alia* that the two warring clans decided to observe a ceasefire and resolve their differences through peaceful means. It was agreed that "there was no need to shed more blood, as it would not bring any solution." The elders from the two sub-clans also agreed to engage in a dialogue in the presence of the elders of the Shidle and Abgaal clans as observers. The elders of the two clans should refer to the mediation committee on any disagreement that may arise and there be accountability in the event that the agreement is violated.
20. In a letter to UNSOM, they alleged that AMISOM supported Biyomaal clan militia with heavy artillery fire, during an attack on Habar Gidir farms at Barire on 3 December 2016.
21. Since 2013, UNSOM documented at least eight major peace and reconciliation agreements signed by clans in Lower Shabelle, Middle Shabelle, Hiraan and Mudug. In addition, there was another agreement between Somaliland and Khatumo in December 2016. Lack of implementation characterizes all of these agreements.
22. The Afgooye Agreement committed the parties to lifting and banning roadblocks, moving military camps away from civilian areas, and accountability for capital crimes.

23. The Lower Shabelle Governor has been engaged in parallel initiatives to resolve local conflicts and promote social cohesion. Although the Governor's efforts have had positive impacts in other districts of Lower Shabelle, negotiations that he undertook in April 2016, aimed at relocating clan militia to specific locations in Marka and enabling a joint force of AMISOM, SNA and NISA to patrol the town centre, proved unsuccessful. A separate reconciliation initiative, led by the Deputy Minister of Defence and Minister of State for Finance in former Federal President Hassan Sheikh Mohamud's cabinet, who were respectively Biyomaal and Habar Gidir, aimed to engage the business community as well as elders of the two clans but did not progress beyond a preparatory meeting in July 2016.

24. The Chairperson, Abdullahi Waafo, is the paramount Biyomaal militia leader and the nominal commander of the South West Special Police Force (SWSPF), which has no presence in Lower Shabelle. Other leaders of the Guard included former Marka District Commissioner Yarisow, who leads the Biyomaal militia at Ayub and Sirjaale; Abdighani Yusuf, the former Afgooye District Commissioner, from the Geledi clan; and Sheikh Salah, a Somali Bantu militia leader believed to retain links with Al-Shabaab.

25. *Report on the Right to the Freedom of Expression: Striving to Widen Democratic Space in Somalia's Political Transition*, United Nations Mission in Somalia and the Office of High Commissioner for Human Rights, 2016.

26. Human Rights Watch op. cit., note 4, 51.

27. http://www.globalprotectioncluster.org/en/tools-and-guidance/protection-cluster-coordination-toolbox.html (accessed 7 September 2017).

28. Kate Holt, "Famine in Somalia: Twice in six years? A commentary from 10 leading academics and humanitarian professionals", *IRIN* (2017). The article notes that "73 per cent of children arriving in Ethiopia during January and February were found to be in a state of severe or moderate acute malnutrition", however, there is no information as to which communities the children were from.

GOVERNING ENDEMIC CRISES: VIOLENCE AND LEGITIMACY IN THE LIVES OF SOMALIS

1. Max Weber, *Economy and Society: An Outline of Interpretive Sociology (Ed, by Guenther Roth and Claus Wittich)* (Berkeley, Los Angeles, London: University of California Press, 1922/1978).

2. Peter L. Berger and Thomas Luckmann, *The Social Construction of Reality: A Treatise in the Sociology of Knowledge* (Harmondsworth: Penguin, 1967).

3. Ibid., 110f.

4. Thomas Luckmann, "Comments on Legitimation", *Current Sociology* 35, no. 2 (1987): 109–17.

5. Michael Pickering, "Experience as Horizon: Koselleck, Expectation and Historical Time", *Cultural Studies* 18, no. 2–3 (2004).

6. Berger and Luckman, op. cit. 118–19.
7. Henrik Vigh, "Crisis and Chronicity: Anthropological Perspectives on Continuous Conflict and Decline," *Ethnos* 73, no. 1 (2008): 5–24.
8. A bias is introduced by the fact that none of the respondents still supported Al-Shabaab. Al-Shabaab supporters may be more likely to remain in Somalia, and less willing to talk to a Western researcher.
9. Interviews were copy-edited.
10. Stephen C. Lubkeman, *Culture in Chaos: An Anthropology of the Social Condition in War By* (Chigaco and London: University of Chicago Press, 2008), here chap. 6.
11. With respect to terror see Michael Taussig, "Culture of Terror—Space of Death. Roger Casement's Putumayo Report and the Explanation of Torture", *Comparative Studies in Society and History* 36, no 3 (1984): 467–97.
12. With respect to gender, see for example Judy El-Bushra and Judith Gardner, "The Impact of War on Somali Men: Feminist Analysis of Masculinities and Gender Relations in a Fragile Context", *Gender & Development* 24, no. 3 (2016); Judith Gardner and Judy El-Bushra, *Somalia—the Untold Story: The War through the Eyes of Somali Women* (London: Pluto Books, 2004).

REMEDYING THE LEGACY OF STATE COLLAPSE: THINKING
THROUGH AND BEYOND SOMALI CIVIL WAR VIOLENCE

1. Lidwien Kapteijns, *Clan Cleansing: The Ruinous Legacy of 1991* (Philadelphia: University of Pennsylvania Press, 2013), 71–95.
2. Ibid. pp. 88–89. That the Barre government was the cradle of the violence that followed is well documented and generally acknowledged.
3. The term "clan cleansing" is used in parallel to that of "ethnic cleansing" adopted in the Final Report of the Commission of Experts established pursuant to Security Council Resolution 780 (1992) to report on evidence of grave breaches of the Geneva Conventions and other violations of international humanitarian law committed in the territory of the former Yugoslavia (S/1994/674). It defined ethnic cleansing as "rendering an area ethnically homogeneous by using force or intimidation to remove from a given area persons of another ethnic or religious group" (p. 33). See http://www.icty.org/x/file/About/OTP/un_commission_of_experts_report1994_en.pdf.
4. Ibid.131–191.
5. Ibid. 91 ff. It also used clan-based violence against civilians in the areas of Zeila and Borama (idem p. 158).
6. Thus the USC welcomed Xuseen Kulmiye Afrax, Vice-President of the Barre regime from beginning to end, with a large ovation. Idem, 103, 108, 133–134.
7. Ibid. 153–158.
8. Ibid. 161 ff.
9. Ibid. 135–146.

10. Ibid. 203–223.

11. Ibid. 211–218.

12. This concept is comparable to René Lemarchand's "mythico-histories" in Burundi: Ethnocide as Discourse and Practice (Washington, D.C.: Woodrow Wilson Press, 1994): 19, and Ben Lieberman's "mythical national hate narratives" in "Nationalist Narratives, Violence Between Neighbours and Ethnic Cleansing in Bosnia-Herçegovina: A Case of Cognitive Dissonance," *Journal of Genocide Research* 8, 3 (2006): 295–309. Kapteijns, *Clan Cleansing*, 206–208.

13. Ibid. 210–213.

14. Ibid. 213–214.

15. Bambi Ceuppens and Peter Geschiere, "Autochthony: Local or Global? New Modes in the Struggle over Citizenship and Belonging in Africa and Europe," *Annual Review of Anthropology* 34 (2005): 385–407.

16. Kapteijns, *Clan Cleansing*, 214–216.

17. Ibid. 79, 211, 279.

18. See ibid. 236–240.

19. The term is that of Maryanne Yerkes, "Facing the Violent Past: Discussions with Serbia's Youth," *Nationalities Papers* 32, 4 (2004): 933.

20. See for example, Jelena Subotic, "Expanding the scope of post-conflict justice: Individual, state and societal responsibility for mass atrocity," *Journal of Peace Research*, 48, 2 (2011): 157–169.

ENDING IMPUNITY: FOSTERING REDRESS AND ACCOUNTABILITY IN SOMALIA

1. The authors contributed in equal parts to the research and writing of this paper.

2. This paper draws on our longstanding research on politics, violence, and law in the Somali territories as well as 12 semi-structured interviews with key informants working in the fields of human rights, law and religion based in Mogadishu, Nairobi, Baidoa, and Garowe respectively. We are indebted to all of our interlocutors for sharing their analysis with us. All errors of fact or interpretation are our sole responsibility.

3. Amnesty International had, by the late 1980s, already described Somalia as a "long-term human rights crisis". Amnesty International, *Somalia: A Long-term Human Rights Crisis* (London: Amnesty International, 1988).

4. By abuses and atrocities we refer to war crimes, violations of international humanitarian law as well as direct and structural violence that kills, tortures, or humiliates individuals and groups.

5. An extensive review of human rights abuses in Somalia by state and non-state actors in the past half-century is beyond the scope of this paper.

6. Amnesty International, *Somalia*.

7. Africa Watch, *Somalia: A Government at War With its Own People* (New York: Africa Watch Committee 1990), p. 2.

8. Mark Bradbury, *The Somali Conflict: Prospects for Peace* (Oxford: Oxfam Working Paper, 1995), p. 2.

9. Africa Watch, *Somalia*, Jutta Bakonyi, "Moral Economies of Mass Violence: Somalia 1988–1991," *Civil Wars* 11(4) (2010), pp. 434–54, Robert Gersony, *Why Somalis Flee: Synthesis of Accounts of Conflict Experience in Northern Somali Refugees, Displaced Persons and Others* (Washington DC: US Department of State, 1989).

10. Bradbury, *The Somali Conflict*.

11. Alex de Waal, "US War Crimes in Somalia," *New Left Review* 30 (1998): pp. 131–44.

12. Human Rights Watch, *Shell-Shocked: Civilians Under Siege in Mogadishu* (Washington DC: Human Rights Watch, 2007); Human Rights Watch, *So Much to Fear: War Crimes and the Devastation of Somalia* (Washington DC: Human Rights Watch, 2008); Anna Lindley, "Leaving Mogadishu: Towards a Sociology of Conflict-related Mobility," *Journal of Refugee Studies* 23(1) (2010), pp. 2–22; Ken Menkhaus, "The Crisis in Somalia: Tragedy in Five Acts," *African Affairs* 106(204) (2007): pp. 357–90.

13. Amnesty International, *Routinely Targeted: Attacks on Civilians in Somalia* (London: Amnesty International, 2008), p. 9.

14. United Nations, *Report of the Monitoring Group on Somalia pursuant to Security Council resolution 1724 (2006)*, S/2007/436 (New York: United Nations, 2007), p. 12.

15. Hamza Mohammed, "AU Troops Gun-Down Unarmed Civilians in Somalia", *Al-Jazeera*, 21 July 2015.

16. Human Rights Watch, "Somalia: AU Should Release Investigation into 14 Civilian Deaths", 25 January 2017.

17. Allehone Mulugeta Abebe, "Al-shabaab's Responsibility to Protect Civilians in Somalia," *Forced Migration Review* 37 (2011): pp. 27–28.

18. Abdi Guled, "Mogadishu Attack: 20 Killed as Al-shabaab Gunmen Storm Somalia Beachfront Restaurant", *The Independent*, 22 January 2016, "Somalia Restaurant Siege: 17 Died as Gunmen Take Hostages in Mogadishu," *The Guardian*, 14 June 2017.

19. Human Rights Watch, *World Report 2015: Events of 2014* (Washington DC: Human Rights Watch, 2015), pp. 383–4.

20. Campaign for Innocent Victims in Conflict, *Civilian Harm in Somalia: Creating an Appropriate Response* (Washington DC: CIVIC, 2011), p. 18.

21. World Health Organization, "Somalia Health Cluster Bulletin," July 2011, p. 1.

22. Human Rights Watch, *You Don't Know Who to Blame: War Crimes in Somalia* (Washington DC: Human Rights Watch, 2011), p. 1.

23. Martin Hill, *No Redress: Somalia's Forgotten Minorities* (London: Minority Rights Group International, 2010), United Nations, *Somalia: Sexual Violence in Conflict: Report of the Secretary-General*, UN's General Assembly 67 Session Agenda Item 33 Prevention of Armed Conflict, New York, March 14, 2013, Vol A/67/792 S/2013/149, p. 14.

24. Amnesty International, "Somalia Human Rights Violations and Abuses Persist," Amnesty International Submission to the UN Universal Periodic Review, January—February 2016 (London: Amnesty International, 2016), p. 6.

25. Amnesty International, "Somalia Human Rights Violations".

26. Sherene Razack, "From the 'Clean Snows of Petawawa': The Violence of Canadian Peacekeepers in Somalia," *Cultural Anthropology* 15(1) (2000): pp. 127–63, Center for Justice and Accountability, "Somalia: Atrocities Under the Siad Barre Regime": http://cja.org/where-we-work/somalia/ (accessed 3 July 2017). The excavation of mass graves in Somaliland's capital Hargeisa represents another first step at dealing with the past.

27. Tobias Hagmann, *Stabilization, Extraversion and Political Settlements in Somalia* (London: Rift Valley Institute, 2016).

28. Lidwien Kapteijns, *Clan Cleansing in Somalia: The Ruinous Legacy of 1991* (Philadelphia: Pennsylvania University Press, 2013).

29. Interview with traditional leader, Mogadishu, 22 April 2016.

30. Ken Menkhaus, "Traditional Conflict Management in Contemporary Somalia", in *Traditional Cures for Modern Conflicts: African Conflict 'Medicine'*, ed. I. W. Zartman (Boulder: Lynne Rienner, 2000), pp. 183–99, Andre le Sage, *Stateless Justice in Somalia: Formal and Informal Rule of Law Initiatives* (Geneva: Centre for Humanitarian Dialogue, 2005), Mohammed Mealin Seid and Zewdie Jotte, "Alternative Dispute Resolution in Somali Regional State" (Addis Ababa: Centre Français d'Études Éthiopiennes, 2004), p. 36, Gunter Schlee, "Customary Law and the Joys of Statelessness: Idealised Traditions Versus Somali Realities," *Journal of East African Studies* 7(2) (2013).

31. Transitional Federal Government of Somalia & African Union, *Status of Mission Agreement (SOMA)* (2007). Mimeo.

32. Rakiya A. Omaar, "Justice for the Atrocities of the 1980s: The Responsibility of Politicians and Political Rarties," *Somaliland Times* Issue 52, 18 January 2003.

33. David Bloomfield, Teresa Barnes and Luc Huyse, *Reconciliation After Violent Conflict: A Handbook* (Stockholm: International Institute for Democracy and Electoral Assistance, 2003), Jamal Benomar, "Justice After Transition," *Journal of Democracy* 4(1) (1993), pp. 3–14, Richard J. Goldstone, "Justice as a Tool for Peace-Making: Truth Commissions and International Criminal Tribunals," *N. Y. U. Journal of International Law and Politics* 28 (1995–1996), pp. 485–501, Nick Grono and Adam O'Brien, "Justice in Conflict? The ICC and Peace Processes" in *Courting Conflict? Justice, Peace and the ICC in Africa*, eds. Nicholas

Waddell and Phil Clark (London: Royal African Society, 2008), pp. 13–20; Lekha Sriram, *Confronting Past Human Rights Violations: Justice vs. Peace in Times of Transition* (London: Frank Cass, 2004).

34. Alex de Waal, *The Real Politics of the Horn of Africa: Money, War and the Business of Power* (Cambridge: Polity Press, 2015).

35. Human Rights Watch, *Harsh War, Harsh Peace: Abuses by al-Shabaab, the Transitional Federal Government, and AMISOM in Somalia* (Washington DC: Human Rights Watch, 2010). Attempts to establish internal and external oversight over Somali police forces are currently underway, according to what the authors were told in a Skype interview with a UN official, 4 May 2017.

36. During its short existence some of the petitioners to the Union of Islamic Courts were able to reclaim stolen property including real estate.

37. Civil and military courts are often biased in favour of individuals from stronger clans. The Somali judicial system remains fragmented, underfunded and understaffed. It is not uncommon for judges to work without salary for prolonged time periods, prompting the Somali Attorney General to refer to the judiciary as "an institution just by name". Interview with Ahmed Ali Dahir, Mogadishu, 1 May 2017.

38. Somalia ranks at the bottom of Transparency International's Corruption Perceptions Index 2016: https://www.transparency.org/country/SOM (accessed 3 July 2017).

39. Consecutive UN Special Rapporteurs on the Human Rights situation in Somalia produced some 15 reports between 1993 and 2009 on behalf of the Commission on Human Rights. These independent experts often had little analytical or research capacity to draw on, but instead worked with their government counterpart. More substantial reporting that often covered human rights violations was undertaken by the UN Somalia and Eritrea Monitoring Group.

40. This narrative will draw on customary, religious, and universal legal categories.

ACHIEVING LOCAL RECONCILIATION IN SOMALIA

1. See: www.worldometers.info/world-population/somalia-population/; in confirmation with UNFPA estimate of 2014.

2. Peace and Development Research Center, *Somali Customary Law and Traditional Economy* (Garowe: PDRC, 2003), p. 71.

3. Mohamud Haji Yousuf, Dean of East Africa University, Garowe branch, 18 March 2017.

4. Interview with Elder Khaliif Aw-Ali, Garowe, March 2017.

STATE-BUILDING AMIDST CONFLICT: THE URGENCY OF LOCAL
RECONCILIATION

1. "A New Deal for Somalia", United Nations in Somalia, 2013: http://so.one.un.org/

content/unct/somalia/en/home/what-we-do/new-deal-for-somalia.html (accessed 29 May 2017).

2. Marcus Manuel, Alastair McKechnie, Gregory Wilson and Rima das Pradhan-Blach, "The new deal in Somalia: An independent review of the Somali Compact, 2014–2016", Overseas Development Institute, London, April 2017: https://www.odi.org/sites/odi.org.uk/files/resource-documents/11466.pdf (accessed 29 May 2017).

3. See this November 2016 map: https://ichef-1.bbci.co.uk/news/624/cpsprodpb/102ED/production/_92658266_updated_somalia_control_624_v2.png

4. The 4.5 clan power-sharing system splits political representation among the four major clans, the Darood, Digil Mirifle, Dir and Hawiye, with the remaining allocation distributed between a set of smaller clans.

5. Considered a moderate Sufi Muslim group, ASWJ mainly operates in Galmudug region and parts of Bakool and Hiiraan. Led by Sh Mohamed Shakir Ali Hassan and with Maleem Mohammed as its spiritual leader, it has an uneasy relationship with the Galmudug state government, despite being part of the wider governance and cultural structures in Galmudug. It is reported to have 2,200 to 4,500 well-armed soldiers and wields considerable religious influence. Stanford University, "Ahlu Sunna Wal Jama", Mapping Militant Organizations, 18 June 2016: http://web.stanford.edu/group/mappingmilitants/cgi-bin/groups/view/109 (accessed 29 May 2017).

6. "Summary Report," *Peacebuilding and Statebuilding: 2008*, Interpeace Partners Forum, 2008: http://www.interpeace.org/2008/11/peacebuilding-and-statebuilding-2008-interpeace-partners-forum-examined-the-nexus-between-them/ (accessed 29 May 2017).

7. Ken Menkhaus, "Reassessing Protracted State Collapse in Somalia" in Ken Menkhaus, *Somalia: State Collapse and the Threat of Terrorism* (Abingdon: Routledge, 2004), p. 18.

8. "A Framework for Mutual Accountability and Accelerated Progress", *London Somalia Conference 2017: New Partnership for Somalia for Peace, Stability and Prosperity* (London: Department for International Development, 2017): http://reliefweb.int/report/somalia/london-somalia-conference-2017-new-partnership-somalia-peace-stability-and-prosperity (accessed 29 May 2017).

9. The head of regional security, the chief of security of Merka district, the head of SNA's 5th brigade, the regional humanitarian aid coordinator and the head of the 3rd unit of the military's 5th brigade were all from the same clan. According to the Biyamal clan, the resident clans in Lower Shabelle region are Wa'dan, Digil, Biyamal, Hintire and 12 Koofi. Information gathered in LPI and Somali civil society partners' consultations with community members, April 2017.

10. Lower Shabelle was controlled by an Ayr clan Islamic court from Mogadishu (1998–99); the Transitional National Governments of Presidents Abdikassim

Salat Hassan (2000–04) and Abdullahi Yusuf (2004–06); and the Islamic Courts Union in 2006, succeeded by Al-Shabaab (2008–12). Except for Abdullahi Yusuf, who tried to establish forces commanded by local clans, these administrations were invariably dominated by Habar Gidir/Ayr forces.

11. "Somalia: Fighting between two clans gets into the third day", *Waaga Cusub Media*, 2013: http://waagacusub.net/articles/95/SomaliaFighting-between-two-clans-gets-into-the-third-day (accessed 29 May 2017). Also: "Clans clash in Somalia's Lower Shabelle", *Irin News*, 2014: http://www.irinnews.org/report/100196/clans-clash-somalia%E2%80%99s-lower-shabelle (accessed 29 May 2017).

12. "Announcement of Lower Shabelle People's Guard", Press release issued by Abdiqani A. Yusuf, spokesman of the Lower Shebelle People's Guard, 10 October 2016: http://www.puntlandes.com/?p=28288 (accessed 30 May 2017). Also, interviews with Biyamal elders, April 2017.

13. "Warring clans agree to uphold peace in Marka", AMISOM, 2016: http://amisom-au.org/so/2016/09/warring-clans-agree-to-uphold-peace-in-marka/ (accessed 29 May 2017).

14. Based on consultations between LPI, Somali civil society partners and local community members.

15. "AMISOM Accused of Involvement in Lower Shabelle Clan Fighting", Radio Dalsan, 2016: https://www.radiodalsan.com/2016/12/26/exclusive-amisom-accused-of-involvement-in-lower-shabelle-clan-fighting/ (accessed 29 May 2017).

16. S. Y. Agnon, "Al-Shabaab Combatants Executes Elder Involved in Election", Strategic Intelligence Service, 2017: http://intelligencebriefs.com/al-shabaab-combatants-executes-elder-involved-in-election/ (accessed 29 May 2017).

17. Sacad, Saleban, Ayr, Murusade, Duduble, but also Dir and Darod-Marehan.

18. "Gaalkacyo Conflict: Drivers, Contributors and Potential Solutions", *Heritage Institute*, December 2016, p. 4: http://www.heritageinstitute.org/wp-content/uploads/2016/12/Gaalkacyo-Conflict-Drivers-Contributors-and-Potential-Solutions-.pdf (accessed 29 May 2017).

19. The Mudug region consists of five districts. While Gaalkacyo district is administered by both regional authorities, Puntland and Galmudug each control two districts. Administratively, the region is divided into two administrations. This leaves Galmudug controlling one and a half regions—short of the constitutionally required two regions. However, Galmudug claims more territory than Puntland in the Mudug region. In Galmudug, politicians and citizens alike express a desire to see Galmudug administer the entire Mudug region, including Galdogob and Jariiban districts, the home-bases of Abdullahi Yusuf and Ali Ismail who signed the Galkayo accord with Aidid in 1993.

20. "OCHA Somalia Flash Update #3 Humanitarian impact of fighting in Gaalkacyo", United Nations Office for the Coordination of Humanitarian Affairs, 10 November 2016: http://reliefweb.int/report/somalia/ocha-somalia-flash-update-3-human-itarian-impact-fighting-gaalkacyo-10-november-2016 (accessed 29 May 2017).

21. "Gaalkacyo Conflict: Drivers, Contributors and Potential Solutions", *Heritage Institute*, December 2016, p. 3: http://www.heritageinstitute.org/wp-content/uploads/2016/12/Gaalkacyo-Conflict-Drivers-Contributors-and-Potential-Solutions-.pdf (accessed 29 May 2017).

22. "Puntland, Galmudug, ASWJ, and the Somali Government Set to Face Off over Federalism Disputes", Somali Newsroom, 10 July 2015: https://somalianewsroom.com/2015/07/10/puntland-galmudug-aswj-and-the-somali-government-set-to-face-off-over-federalism-disputes/ (accessed 30 May 2017).

23. "Somalia: UN envoy calls Islamist militia to withdraw from Central town", *Horseed Media*, 2015: http://horseedmedia.net/2015/06/09/somalia-un-envoy-calls-islamist-militia-to-withdraw-from-central-town/ (accessed 29 May 2017). Also: "Sheik Ahmed Shakir elected to be the president of Galmudug State of Somalia", Radio Shacab, 2015: http://radioshacab.com/articles/2216/Sheik-Ahmed-Shakir-elected-to-be-the-president-of-Galmudug-State-of-Somalia (accessed 29 May 2017).

24. "Puntland, Galmudug, ASWJ, and the Somali Government Set to Face Off over Federalism Disputes", Somalia Newsroom, 2015: https://somalianewsroom.com/2015/07/10/puntland-galmudug-aswj-and-the-somali-government-set-to-face-off-over-federalism-disputes/ (accessed 29 May 2017).

25. The state now has a Hawadle president, a Galje'el speaker and an Abgal vice-president.

26. "Joint Press Statement: International Partners Welcome the Conclusion of the State-Formation Process for the New Hirshabelle Administration", United Nations Assistance Mission in Somalia, 2016: https://unsom.unmissions.org/international-partners-welcome-conclusion-state-formation-process-new-hirshabelle-administration (accessed 29 May 2017).

27. Letter written by elders Hassan Khaliif, Ali Hassan and Ali Hassan Shufeeh of Hiran, reproduced at: "Disgruntled clans in Hiiraan seek UN intervention in Hiiraan/Middle Shabelle state formation deadlock", Goobjoog News, 2016: http://goobjoog.com/english/disgruntled-clans-in-hiiraan-seek-un-intervention-in-hiiraanmiddle-shabelle-state-formation-deadlock/ (accessed 29 May 2017).

28. "Thematic Studies for Somalia: Study on Regional Forces", Itad/Altai Consulting, 8 May 2017.

SUPPORTING LOCAL RECONCILIATION: LESSONS LEARNED ACROSS THE UN SYSTEM

1. In preparing this paper, the author drew directly from staff, former staff and internal documents from a range of peace operations, including MINUSMA, UNSMIL, MONUSCO, UNAMID, UNMISS, UNAMA, UNAMI, and Headquarters staff in DPA and DPKO. In addition, the paper drew on the unpublished "Study of Practice: The Role of UN Peace Operations in Addressing Inter-Communal

Conflict," written by Sara Rendtorff-Smith for the UN's Department for Policy Evaluation and Training. The final version of this paper was consulted with the Chief of Civil Affairs in UN Headquarters in May 2017.

2. This paper does not include analysis of engagement with jihadi groups as a separate issue, as it is instead focused on drawing broad lessons from a range of settings. Nor does this paper address the issue of political engagement in a non-permissive setting, such as in Somalia. Where relevant, however, this paper does point to particular settings that may have parallels with Somalia on these issues.

3. See, for example, J.P. Lederach, *Building Peace: Sustainable Reconciliation in Divided Societies* (Washington, DC: US Institute of Peace Press, 1997), "the greatest resource for sustaining peace in the long term is always rooted in the local people and their culture"; K. Rupesinghe, *Conflict Transformation* (New York: St. Martin's Press, 1995), argues for a focus on "local peacemakers" in addressing conflict-prone societies; B. Fetherston and C. Nordstrom, "Overcoming Habitus in Conflict Management: UN Peacekeeping and War Zone Ethnography," *Peace and Change* Vol. 20, no. 1 (1995), "given that peacekeepers interact extensively with communities in conflict, a reorientation that integrates macro- and micro-level activity aimed at long-term transformation is necessary." Also see Stathis Kalyvas, *The Logic of Violence in Civil War* (Cambridge: Cambridge University Press, 2006).

4. For example, Hutu and Nande parliamentarians in Kinshasa have a well-documented history of manipulating their respective communities in eastern DRC against each other to control resources and maintain power. Similarly, President Kabila's 2015 decision to double the number of states in DRC (so-called "decoupage") caused enormous rifts between communities affected by the new administrative boundaries.

5. For example, in South Sudan the 2013 outbreak of civil war between the Government and the opposition led to a severe deepening of the longstanding tensions between the Dinka and Nuer populations, with a significant increase in local-level violence between these communities outside of the central conflict.

6. See Severine Autesserre, *Peaceland* (Cambridge: Cambridge University Press, 2014), arguing that the international community's focus on national elections in DRC rather than resolving inter-communal violence directly impacted the stabilization of the country; see also A. Schou, "Conflict Resolution Attempts in Self-determination Disputes: The Significance of Local Minority Groups," *Ethnic and Racial Studies* Vol. 37, no. 2 (2014), noting that the failure to include local power-sharing arrangements undermined the broader peace deals in Sri Lanka in 2002 and the Philippines in 2008.

7. A. Odendaal, *A Crucial Link: Local Peace Committees and National Peacebuilding* (Washington, DC: United States Institute of Peace Press, 2013), drawing on case studies from Nicaragua, Nepal, South Africa and Northern Ireland to argue that local peace efforts are crucial in implementing national peace agreements. See also

the Mali example, where longstanding inter-communal tensions directly led to the outbreak of the 2012 crisis, and continued local violence has threatened the national peace process.

8. In this paper, local conflict resolution is defined as any engagement with local, national or international actors designed to resolve conflict at a sub-national level. In many instances, UN engagement in local conflict resolution has been in the context of a peacekeeping operation, with implications for how the mission deploys and uses both force and police. This paper will largely ignore approaches involving force and police, given the makeup of UNSOM, though some points may be of use for the Mission's work with the AU on the ground in Somalia.

9. These forms of conflict are often latent in societies and are not in themselves a cause for intervention by the UN. However, when a local conflict erupts into violence that risks the lives of a significant number of civilians, or when violence levels threaten national political processes, the Security Council has increasingly seen reason to mandate UN engagement.

10. UNMISS's mandate in S/RES/2155, 27 May 2014, para 4(a); UNAMID's mandate in S/RES/1769, 31 July 2007, re-affirms S/RES/1674, 28 April 2006; MINUSCA's mandate in S/RES/2127, 5 December 2013, para 19.

11. MINUSMA's mandate in S/RES/2227, 29 June 2015, para 14(b); UNOCI's mandate in S/RES/2226, 25 June 2015, para 19(b); MONUSCO's mandate in S/RES/2147, 28 March 2014, para 5(b).

12. MINUSCA's mandate in S/RES/2149, 10 April 2014, para 30(b).

13. MINUSMA's mandate in S/RES/2227, 29 June 2015, para 14(c).

14. The mandate of the United Nations Operation in Côte d'Ivoire S/RES/2000, 27 July 2011, para 7(f); MONUSCO's mandate in S/RES/2147, 28 March 2014, para 5(a).

15. The Misrata/Tawergha conflict is illustrative in this case. UNSMIL's mandate calls for the mission to exercise mediation and good offices in support of the Libyan political agreement's implementation, but its mandate does not explicitly or implicitly call for local conflict resolution. Nonetheless, UNSMIL has facilitated and supported reconciliation efforts between the Misrata and Tawergha, and the two sides came to an agreement for the return of the displaced Tawerghans. Terms of the agreement include compensation for killed and missing persons, compensation for personal property, the outlining of a judiciary process to hold those responsible for violations accountable, and it also sets a date of return for the Tawerghans: http://unsmil.unmissions.org/Portals/unsmil/Documents/MT_ Agreement_31–8–2016_EN.pdf

16. See, for example, UNDP's mandate to support local reconciliation in Iraq: http:// www.iq.undp.org/content/iraq/en/home/ourwork/Stabilization.html

17. The United Nations Regional Centre for Preventive Diplomacy (UNRCCA), created 10 December 2007; and the United Nations Office for West Africa and

the Sahel (UNOWAS), created 28 January 2016; joining the United Nations Office for West Africa (established in 2002) with the Office of the Special Envoy for the Sahel, (S/2016/89). UNOWAS' mandate calls for it to consolidate peace and democratic governance in countries emerging from conflict or political crises. Examples of their engagement include Guinea (2009), Burkina Faso (2015), and Kyrgyzstan (2011).

18. In a parallel set of research regarding non-military approaches to protection of civilians, a similar set of elements has been identified, which may be instructive for the Somalia team as well: http://collections.unu.edu/eserv/UNU:3214/unu_cpr_nonmilitary_poc.pdf

19. Or indeed to NGOs in non-mission settings.

20. For example, in UNMISS a typical local mapping would identify risk factors such as disputes over cattle ownership, migration routes, water access and traditional inter-communal tensions, without including sufficiently in-depth analysis of how national actors may manipulate local ones (the national/local dynamic being arguably the one of the most relevant issues in the current civil war).

21. See also UNAMA's 2013 People's Dialogue process in Afghanistan in support of national-level political goals, based on an analysis of conflict drivers following more than 187 focus group discussions, and interviews with more than 3,700 Afghans and 800 local stakeholders. (Internal UNAMA evaluation of 2013 local reconciliation processes, on file with author.)

22. One such case is Burundi, where land disputes are central to local conflict dynamics, but rarely referred to in UN approaches to the recurrent conflicts since 1993. See, for example, Mathijs van Leeuwen, "Crisis or Continuity? Framing land disputes and local conflict resolution in Burundi," *Land Use Policy* Vol. 27, Issue 3 (July 2010): pp. 753–762: http://www.sciencedirect.com/science/article/pii/S0264837709001525

23. See, for example, *Why Dialogue Matters for Conflict Prevention and Peacebuilding,* UNDP, 2009: http://www.undp.org/content/dam/undp/library/crisis%20prevention/dialogue_conflict.pdf

24. See, for example, *Natural Resources and Conflict: A Guide for Mediation Practitioners,* UNEP, 2015: http://postconflict.unep.ch/publications/UNDPA_UNEP_NRC_Mediation_full.pdf

25. For example, in Darfur in 2008 there was discussion of hiring a senior economic adviser to better understand the decentralization law and the fiscal transfers required to support local institutions. This was discarded as too far outside the Mission's mandate, though in retrospect it could have provided invaluable information to support the Mission's work to address local conflict dynamics. In contrast, MONUSCO has employed a dedicated natural resources expert in the front office of the SRSG for several years. While this role was previously underutilized, there is recent evidence that the expertise has been usefully incorporated into mis-

sion planning for engagement at the national and local level. MONUSCO has developed cross-cutting strategies for addressing the risks posed by armed groups, all of which include mapping of natural resources. The natural resources expert has provided in-depth reports to the senior leadership on these links, in turn feeding back into the Mission's strategies.

26. For example, former head of office in Mopti, Mali, interviewed 22 May 2017.

27. Mary B. Anderson, *Do No Harm: How Aid Can Support Peace—or War* (Boulder: Lynne Rienner, February 1999).

28. The full UNICEF checklist is available here: https://www.unicef.org/csr/files/ Child_rights_and_Security_Checklist_ENG.pdf

29. Collaborative for Development Action, *The Do No Harm Handbook (The Framework for Analyzing the Impact of Assistance on Conflict)* (2014), available at http://www.globalprotectioncluster.org/_assets/files/aors/protection_main-streaming/CLP_Do_No_Harm_Handbook_2004_EN.pdf

30. NB: this methodology is also being used to underpin the ongoing World Bank/ United Nations flagship study on prevention (to which UNU-CPR is a contributing author).

31. See also, for example, UNAMID and UNDP addressed a structural driver of conflict in Darfur by rehabilitating roughly 100 water points along seasonal migration routes, thus easing a longstanding source of tension between herders and farmers; and UNSMIL's engagement to resolve the Misrata-Tawergha conflict in Libya was driven by the need for reparations for the displacement of the Tawerghan community at the hands of the Misratans, but was also geared at creating an institutional mechanism for support by the national government.

32. NB: this reconciliation process is a longstanding and unfinished one; therefore, no concrete conclusions can be drawn about the success of combining the national and local levels, as yet.

33. Iraq's National Reconciliation Commission contains representatives for each province (including Anbar). However, UNDP chose to invite the head of the Commission instead of the Anbar representative due to the fact that the Anbar representative was affiliated to a key stakeholder opposed to the governor of the province. This is an example of an effective use of in-depth knowledge of the relationships between actors to ensure that local sensitivities and political dynamics are carefully negotiated, and the best players are found to facilitate reconciliation. Interview with UNDP Iraq, 17 April 2017.

34. Interview with UNDP Iraq, 17 April 2017.

35. For example, in Darfur, the UN built a reconciliation process around farmers and herders associations disseminating messages of peaceful coexistence. In eastern DRC, MONUSCO Civil Affairs organized inter-communal social dialogues to agree on joint messages of co-existence and peace, looking to break down stereotypes across communities via public messaging. Both MINUSMA and

MONUSCO train local journalists in techniques to report on local conflict in a way that avoids raising tensions. In all cases, communications are central to the reconciliation processes.

36. See, "UN boosting aid delivery to refugees as more people flee fighting in Mali," *UN News Centre* (17 February 2012): http://www.un.org/apps/news/story. asp?NewsID=41280#.WNIf_FV96Uk

37. Madamombe, Itai, "Darfur crisis challenges Africa, world," *Africa Renewal* (January 2005): http://www.un.org/africarenewal/magazine/january-2005/darfur-crisis-challenges-africa-world

38. Interview with UNDP Iraq (17 April 2017) regarding local reconciliation process in Anbar province, where some returnees and their families are stigmatized by unverified association with ISIS. Inter-tribal agreements on these families mean that they are shunned and exiled everywhere; many of them can only go to areas controlled by ISIS.

39. Nichols, Michelle, "UN Security Council sanctions Islamist ADF in Congo," *Reuters Africa* (1 July 2014): http://af.reuters.com/article/topNews/idAFK-BN0F63BT20140701

40. One example is Special Envoy de Mistura's refusal to call the Assad government a "regime" despite several instances where reporters prompted him to; Staffan de Mistura, "Note to Correspondents," transcript of press conference (22 February 2017): https://www.un.org/sg/en/content/sg/note-correspondents/2017-02-22/ note-correspondents-transcript-press-conference-staffan-de

41. Interview with UNDP Iraq, 17 April 2017.

42. S. Anderlini, "Mainstreaming Gender in Conflict Analysis," *Social Developments Paper Conflict Prevention and Reconstruction*, World Bank paper no. 33 (2006).

43. See Economic and Social Commission for Western Asia, *White Paper: Mainstreaming a Gender Perspective in Research*, June 2014, E/ESCWA/ OES/2014.Technical Paper 1.

44. See Fred Strasser, "From Nazis to ISIS: Women's Roles in Violence," *USIP* (2 March 2017): https://www.usip.org/publications/2017/03/nazis-isis-womens-roles-violence

45. See Adam Azzain Mohamed, "From Instigating Violence to Building Peace: The Changing Role of Women in Darfur Region of Western Sudan," *ACCORD* (2 June 2004): http://www.accord.org.za/ajcr-issues/%EF%BF%BCfrom-instigating-violence-to-building-peace/

46. See The Republic of Rwanda's National Unity and Reconciliation Commission, *The Role of Women in Reconciliation and Peace Building in Rwanda: Ten Years after Genocide 1994–2004* (May 2005): http://unpan1.un.org/intradoc/groups/public/documents/un/unpan031033.pdf

47. "Women and Peacemaking in Yemen: Mapping the Realities," *Crisis Management Initiative* (September 2015): http://cmi.fi/wp-content/uploads/2016/04/ Women_and_Peacemaking_in_Yemen_EN.pdf

48. See, for example, Conflict Research Unit, "Summary: Women's Roles in Conflict Prevention, Conflict Resolution and Post-Conflict Reconstruction," *Clingendael: Netherlands Institute of International Relations* (1 November 2002): https://www.clingendael.nl/sites/default/files/20021101_cru_bouta.pdf

49. For example, marriage norms in South Sudan require young men to provide large cattle dowries in order to be married. When the civil war drove up the dowry price, it led to an increase in cattle raiding, resulting in higher inter-communal tensions. In this context, reconciliation efforts needed to be tailored to address the inflated dowry price for young men. M. Sommers and S. Schwartz, "Dowry and Division: Youth and Statebuilding in South Sudan," *United States Institute for Peace* (November 2011): https://www.usip.org/sites/default/files/SR_295.pdf

50. The Youth Action for Community Development and Peace (ADECOP) was founded in 2002. It established a network of Youth Clubs for young people to become involved in their communities, focusing on social cohesion, communication, advocacy and community resilience. The Youth Clubs also help with the social re-integration of young former soldiers and combatants, including them in the building and regeneration of their communities: www.congoyouthaction.org

51. Farah Al Ataa was founded in 1985. Farah Al Ataa's recreational "peace camps", for children aged 7–15, bring together children from diverse areas and communities from all over Lebanon. In 2013 it established a school in Kfifan for Syrian refugees: https://www.insightonconflict.org/conflicts/lebanon/peacebuilding-organisations/farah-al-ataa/

52. The Grassroots Relief & Development Agency (GREDA) was founded in 2010 and it receives funding from the UN Democracy Fund (UNDEF). It runs projects to help restore social bonds, trust and confidence among disparate communities. It promotes peaceful co-existence, good governance and dialogue. GREDA also has a programme of micro-credit revolving loans whereby small loans are given to widows, single mothers, youth, disabled persons, returnees and IDPs in order to help them become self-reliant: http://www.gredasouthsudan.org/projects.html

53. Information provided by UNAMA, March 2017 (on file with author).

54. See, for example, Overseas Development Institute, *Assessing the Need to Manage Conflict in Community Based Natural Resource Projects* (1998); Bertram Spector, "Negotiation Readiness in the Development Context: Adding Capacity to Ripeness", in Ho-Won Jeong (ed.), *Approaches to Peacebuilding* (London: Palgrave Macmillan, 2002).

55. Information provided by UNAMA, March 2017 (on file with author).

56. For example, an early example of this is the United Nations Verification Mission in Guatemala (MINUGUA) in 1994: the Mission established eight disarmament camps in the areas within Guatemala known for the highest incidents of fighting. Two concentric rings were placed around the camps; the innermost ring was exclusively for URNG forces, and the outer ring was a boundary area where only local

529

police forces could enter. Guatemalan military forces could be present anywhere outside of the camp boundary areas. The separation of combatants provided a sufficient level of trust for the opposition forces to feel comfortable turning their weapons and ammunition over to MINUGUA peacekeepers, a key condition for the negotiation process to begin. See M. Beach et al., "Civilian Protection and Conflict Resolution: Good Practices at the Local Level," *Stimson Center* (May 2016).

57. For example, part of the UN-brokered 2015 Algiers Agreement for Peace and Reconciliation in Mali was the creation of joint patrols with former rebels and the Malian army deployed to Gao, Kidal and Taoudenit—regions with long histories of fighting—in order to deter al-Qaeda activity.

58. For example, in 2015, United Nations Interim Security Force for Abyei (UNISFA) organized a meeting between the Misseriya and Ngok Dinka traditional leaders in Abyei, to discuss their longstanding disputes over land and migration rights. UNISFA offered to help re-establish a joint trading market between the communities, allowing both sides to profit from contact and begin to rebuild trust between the communities. On the basis of this, the reconciliation process was initiated, allowing for the first direct contact between the tribal leaders in several years.

59. Quick Impact Projects are frequently used in this regard. For example, UNAMID partnered with UNICEF to build a primary school for the IDP community in Dorti camp in 2014, which brought together several local tribes that were in conflict. The school, with associated water points, constituted both shared space and mutually managed resources, contributing to improved relations. It is worth noting that the school had an additional benefit of being a shared space for Quranic teachings, which were used to promote messages of peace.

60. For example, in MONUSCO and some other missions, a multi-donor trust fund was set up to maintain dependable funds to be used for a variety of reconciliation-related activities.

61. For example, a former Head of Office in Mali pointed out: "One element I found always very important in Mali was to link local conflict resolution and reconciliation to concrete projects. There was a tendency in Mali to overdo local conflict resolution and reconciliation conferences, which produced nice words and agreements, but changed little on the ground. I found it much more effective to link such conferences (which often produce the per diem incentive) with a project that is managed by two communities that are at odds. For example, a new well that is jointly managed. This requires some skill to ensure that it does not create new conflicts over those resources, but if you have broad community involvement, especially of women, broader benefits for the community will win over competition over the projects/resource you put in." 22 May 2017.

62. Former Chief of Human Rights UNSMIL, March 2017.

63. For example, a human rights organization called "Le Centre d'études pour la pro-

motion de la paix, la démocratie et les droits de l'homme" (CEPHADO) in eastern DRC is a past partner for MONUSCO in local reconciliation efforts, but was dropped in 2016 when it became evident that the leadership was seen as allied with the ruling party in Kinshasa.

64. For example, MINUSCA's credibility reached a low when it was reported that peacekeepers allegedly killed at least 18 civilians between December 2013 and June 2015, without facing punishment. In October 2016, the Civil Society Reflection Group organized a protest march in Bangui where the slogan was "MINUSCA Out," during which four people were killed: http://www.bbc.com/news/world-africa-37751664

65. For example, in DRC, a local NGO called Initiative for a Cohesive Leadership (ILC) has developed a strong reputation for bringing together conflicting communities in a dynamic and impartial manner, often in a way that would be impossible for MONUSCO given the widespread perception in many communities that the mission is too closely aligned with the government. In 2007, MONUSCO set up a discreet trust fund for ILC through which donors and the Mission could invisibly support the organization. Similarly, in 2016 MONUSCO developed an ad hoc mechanism to provide logistical support and funds to ILC to convene conferences between the Hutu and Nande communities in North Kivu.

66. For example, UNAMID has on several occasions transported the tribal shura councils to locations in Darfur to help resolve inter-communal conflicts; UNMISS transported the Nuer prophet to avoid escalating tensions between the Lou Nuer tribe and its neighbours; and MONUSCO has provided transportation to many traditional leaders to conduct inter-communal dialogue sessions.

67. Interview with former Mopti Head of Office, 22 April 2017.

68. Interview with UNDP Iraq, 17 April 2017.

69. For example, in Libya, the reconciliation process between the Misratans and the Tawerghans required a reparations programme to consolidate the agreement between the two sides. Though the government was supportive in principle, it was unable to commit to funding the reparations program after the UNSMIL-facilitated process. As such, the reconciliation was not provided with any nationally-owned follow-up and it fell apart.

70. For example, President Kabila's decision to divide each state in DRC into two in 2016 resulted in a series of disputes between governors, their respective communities, and chieftancies. Resolving such disputes at the local level required that the outcomes be recognized in Kinshasa.

71. For example, the conflict between the Misseriya and the Ngok Dinka in Abyei was fuelled in part by the government in Khartoum, which supplied the Misseriya with weapons and often infiltrated the Misseriya migration with armed elements to foment violence. For any agreement between the Misseriya and the Ngok Dinka leadership to be sustainable, it would require some kind of blessing from Khartoum.

72. For example, the International Security and Stabilization Support strategy (ISSSS) was set up in eastern DRC following the 2008 Goma accords and the 2009 Peace Agreements between: the DRC government, the National Congress for the Defence of the People and 14 local armed groups. The ISSSS supports the DRC governments' Stabilization and Reconstruction Plan for War-Affected Areas (STAREC) and it has programs for: security; political processes; restoration of state authority; return, reintegration and recovery; and combating sexual violence. The ISSSS project is coordinated by the Stabilization Support Unit (SSU) of MONUSCO, and also receives UN funding via the Peacebuilding Support Office, the Peacebuilding Fund and UNDP.

73. For example, one of the provisions of the UN-brokered 2015 Agreement for Peace and Reconciliation in Mali was the direct election of local representatives from the north into national institutions. This includes more seats in the National Assembly and also seats for traditional leaders in a new Senate, allowing for enhanced, guaranteed, local participation in national level politics.

74. For example, in Afghanistan, the UN-brokered Bonn Agreement of 2001 called for an Afghan Constitutional Commission to be established to draft a new constitution in consultation with the public via a *loya jirga* (a traditional council mechanism for community decision making) within 18 months of the establishment of the Afghan Transitional Administration (which in turn had been established by an emergency *loya jirga* in June 2002). A *loya jirga* involving 502 delegates convened in Kabul on 14 December 2003. After much disagreement, a constitution was finally endorsed on 4 January 2004.

75. For example, the 1996 Guatemala Accord for a Firm and Lasting Peace included sections on judicial and police reform. A Commission on the Strengthening of the Justice System and new Judicial Training School were set up, and the judiciary expanded its geographic presence and increased the number of linguistic interpreters to improve access to justice and address the varied multi-lingual needs of the Guatemalan population. In 1997, Congress established a new National Civil Police (PNC) along with an Office of Professional Accountability, but police reform was ineffective and MINUGUA confirmed the involvement of PNC officers in human rights violations including torture, excessive uses of force and extrajudicial killings.

76. Examples of this are widespread and underpin nearly every major conflict in the world today. For example, the local-level conflicts in South Sudan are frequently exacerbated by lack of state authority at the subnational level, disputes between chieftancies that cannot be addressed by the government, and resources that are doled out in a partial way (often favouring Dinkas over Nuer, for example). In Syria, the unwillingness of the Assad government to implement the decentralization law that would have given greater autonomy and resources at the municipal level was a key driver of grievances in the lead up to the civil war (exacerbated by

a drought that made financial shortfalls more acute in many peripheries in Syria). In places like Somalia, Mali, CAR, DRC and Libya, lack of state authority outside the capital has allowed for non-state actors to proliferate and thrive, undermining rule of law and fomenting local conflict dynamics. In these cases, the UN has frequently focused on extending state authority into the peripheries, to support sustainable solutions to local dynamics and provide better service delivery.

77. There are many examples of this, but few which have resulted in sustained efforts. In Sudan, the Comprehensive Peace Agreement of 2005 stipulated that fiscal transfers would be made from Khartoum to many states, including the three Darfurian ones. This would have allowed for significant funds and capacity to be built in the judiciaries and other rule of law institutions in Darfur. Khartoum's unwillingness to implement these transfers further stripped the local capacity to deliver rule of law, contributed to a sense that local actors needed to pursue their own means of justice, and undermined sustained local-level reconciliation efforts. In Mali, the UN-brokered 2015 Agreement for Peace and Reconciliation created elected regional assemblies for the northern Tuareg population and also called for investment in the economic development of the north. These attempts to decentralize the political and economic power in Mali have been successful in appeasing the historically socio-economically marginalized northern periphery. However, the agreement failed to include communities in the central region of Mali, resulting in ongoing local violence by those actors who were not afforded a seat at the table.

78. For further descriptions of a do-no-harm approach, see *The Civil Affairs Handbook*, United Nations Department of Peacekeeping Operations, available at http://www.un.org/en/peacekeeping/documents/civilhandbook/Civil_Affairs_Handbook.pdf

LOCAL RECONCILIATION IN SOMALIA: THE PROSPECTS FOR SUSTAINABLE PEACE

1. John P. Lederach, *Building Peace: Sustainable Reconciliation in Divided Societies* (Washington, DC: United States Institute of Peace Press, 1997), p. 40.

2. CfPAR's Interview with a former Somali diplomat, Mogadishu, 22 May 2017.

3. Ibid.

4. CfPAR's Interview with a current official in Baraawe District, Lower Shabelle.

5. Fuad Ahmed, "Somalia: Lower Shabelle Clan Conflict Rages on Despite Government Mediation," *All Africa* (26 June 2014): http://allafrica.com/stories/201406270230.html (accessed 16 May 2017).

6. Global Protection Cluster, "Conflict and Protection Analysis," June 2016: http://www.globalprotectioncluster.org/_assets/files/field_protection_clusters/Somalia/files/pc-cp-analysis-lower-shabelle-june-20161.pdf (accessed 16 May 2017).

7. "Somalia: Puntland Confirms Peace Agreement with Galmudug," *Garowe Online*

(2 November 2016): http://www.garoweonline.com/en/news/puntland/soma-lia-puntland-confirms-peace-agreement-with-galmudug (accessed 16 May 2017).

8. "Galmudug Plans to Hold Talks with Ahlu Sunna Wal Jama'a," *Goobjoog News* (28 August 2016): http://goobjoog.com/english/we-will-negotiate-with-ahlu-sunna-waljamaa-galmudug-mp-says/ (accessed 17 May 2017).

9. "Galmudug-ASWJ Talks to Begin on Saturday in Mogadishu," *Goobjoog News* (15 April 2017): http://goobjoog.com/english/galmudug-aswj-talks-begin-sat-urday-mogadishu/ (accessed 17 May 2017).

10. "Warring Clans Agree to Uphold Peace in Marka," *ReliefWeb* (25 September 2016): http://reliefweb.int/report/somalia/somalia-warring-clans-agree-uphold-peace-marka (accessed 17 May 2017).

11. CfPAR's Interview with a former official in the Benaadir Regional Administration (BRA), Mogadishu, 26 May 2017.

12. Anonymous comment from a participant of CfPAR's Local Reconciliations Survey.

13. Joanne Crouch and Oliver Chevreau, "Forging Jubbaland: Community Perspectives on Federalism, Governance and Reconciliation," *SaferWorld* (April 2016).

EXPLOITATION OF NATURAL RESOURCES AS A DRIVER OF CONFLICT: CASE STUDY ON MINING IN BAKI DISTRICT, SOMALILAND

1. The Mayor of Baki district.

2. US Department of Health and Human Services public health service agency for toxic substances and disease registry, September 2002, toxicological profile for beryllium.

3. A chief traditional elder from Reer Mohamed.

4. A chief traditional elder of the Simodi community.

5. A clan sultan.

6. One of the traditional elders of the constituent community.

7. US Department of Health and Human Services public health service agency for toxic substances and disease registry, September 2002 toxicological profile for beryllium.

8. A participant in the FGD for youth groups.

9. An interview with a diaspora member from the UK.

10. Pastoralist.

11. One of the participants for the focus groups held for mining artisans.

12. A mining artisan among the participants in the focus group discussions for mining artisans.

13. Interview with the Mayor of Baki.

14. The Vice-Minister of Minerals and Energy.

15. The Director-General of the Ministry of Mineral Resources and Energy.

16. An expert in local mining industry.
17. See: https://www.hiiraan.com/news4/2015/Jan/97670/somalia_expels_chinese_firm_for_illegal_mining.aspx

TRADITIONAL PEACEMAKING IN SANAAG REGION, SOMALILAND

1. Marlen Renders and Ulf Terlinder, "Negotiating Statehood in a Hybrid Political Order: The Case of Somaliland", *Development & Change* 41:4 (2010): pp. 723–746, p. 729.
2. APD (Academy for Peace and Development)/Interpeace, *Peace in Somaliland: An Indigenous Approach to State-Building* (Hargeisa: Academy for Peace and Development/Interpeace, 2009).
3. Mark Bradbury, *Becoming Somaliland* (Oxford: James Currey, 2008), p. 79.
4. A. Y. Farah and I. M. Lewis, "Making Peace in Somaliland", *Cahiers d'Études africaines* 37:146 (1997), pp. 349–377.
5. APD (Academy for Peace and Development)/Interpeace, *Peace in Somaliland*, esp. p. 17.
6. Ibid.
7. Renders and Terlinder, "Negotiating Statehood in a Hybrid Political Order", p. 730.
8. Bradbury, *Becoming Somaliland*, p. 52.
9. Farah and Lewis, "Making Peace in Somaliland".
10. Ibid, p. 123.
11. Ibid, p. 366.
12. APD (Academy for Peace and Development)/Interpeace, *Peace in Somaliland*, esp. p. 13.
13. Ibid, p. 15.
14. Ibid, p. 15.
15. Ibid, p. 66.
16. Interview with Osman Ali Abdi, a traditional leader from Sanaag region, Erigavo, 26 April 2017.
17. Interview with Abdi Egal Jama, a traditional leader from Sanaag region, Erigavo, 25 April 2017.
18. Interview with Ali Mohamoud Adan, a traditional leader from Sanaag region, Erigavo, 25 April 2017.
19. Ibid.
20. Interview with Osman Ali Abdi, a traditional leader from Sangaad region, Erigavo, 26 April 2017.
21. Interview with Jama Abdi Mohamed, a traditional leader from Sanaag region, Erigavo, 25 April 2017.
22. Interview with Asiya Abdullahi Omar, a women's rights activist from Sanaag region, Erigavo, 26 April 2017.

23. Interview with Mohamoud Gulleid Du'alle (Ateye), a traditional elder from Sanaag region, Erigavo, 26 April 2017.
24. Interview with Adan Hassan Egge, an elder from Sanaag region, Erigavo, 26 April 2017.
25. Interviews with traditional leaders, religious figures, and business people from Sanaag region, Erigavo, 25–26 April 2017.
26. Ibid.

THE SHARIA COURTS OF MOGADISHU: LESSONS FOR PEACE AND RECONCILIATION

1. See Cedric Barnes and Harun Hassan, "The Rise and Fall of Mogadishu's Islamic Courts", *Journal of Eastern African Studies* 1, no. 2 (2007): pp. 151–160.
2. For a very good example of this approach to Islam in Africa see, Evers E. Rosander and David Westerlund (eds), *African Islam and Islam in Africa: Encounters between Sufis and Islamists* (Athens: Ohio University Press, 1997). For a critique of such an approach see B. F. Soares and R. Otayek (eds), *Islam and Muslim Politics in Africa* (New York: Palgrave Macmillan, 2007).
3. See Tobias Hagmann and Markus V. Hoehne. "Failures of the State Failure Debate: Evidence from the Somali Territories", *Journal of International Development* 21 (2009): pp. 42–57; Kenneth J.Menkhaus, *Somalia: State Collapse and the Threat of Terrorism* (London and New York: Routledge, 2006); Robert Rotberg (ed.), *Battling Terrorism in the Horn of Africa* (Washington, DC: Brookings Institution Press, 2005); Alex de Waal (ed.), *Islamism and its Enemies in the Horn of Africa* (London: Hurst & Co., 2004).
4. It is a well-established position in academia now that the Sharia shouldn't be equated with "law" in the modern sense of this term. See Talal Asad, *Genealogies of Religion: Discipline and Reasons of Power in Christianity and Islam* (Baltimore, MD: Johns Hopkins University Press, 1993); Wael B. Hallaq, *Sharia: Theory, Practice, Transformations* (Cambridge: Cambridge University Press, 2009); Brinkley Messick, *The Calligraphic State: Textual Domination and History in a Muslim Society* (Berkeley and Los Angeles: University of California Press, 1993).

DETERMINANTS OF SUCCESS: ANALYSIS OF PEACE INITIATIVES IN SOUTH-CENTRAL SOMALIA

1. For instance, Djibouti Talks of 1991, Addis Ababa National Reconciliation Talks of 1993, Sodere Conference of 1996, Cairo Conference of 1997, Arta Peace Conference of 2000 and Mbagathi Conference of 2002 in Kenya.
2. Gunther Schlee, "Customary Law and the Joys of Statelessness: Idealized traditions versus Somali realities", *Journal of Eastern African Studies* (2013).
3. Ibrahim Ali Amber, "Community-based Peace Processes in South-central Somalia", *Interpeace and Center for Research and Dialogue* (2008).

4. Gunther Schlee, op. cit.

5. Ibrahim Ali Amber, op. cit.

6. Ralph Sundberg, Kristine Eck and Joakim Kreutz, "Introducing the UCDP Non-State Conflict Dataset", *Journal of Peace Research* (March 2012).

7. The limited number of salient cases of peace initiatives identified in this study might be attributed to the limits of the databases I used to check the history. UCDP database covers the period between 1990 and 2012 and only records conflicts with annual deaths of 25 or more. This may mean that parties to peace agreement had armed clashes but the conflict failed to result in 25 deaths. ACLED records all conflicts including low-intensity ones, but only starting from 1997 which means it misses cases before that year.

8. Inter-clan refers to any affair *between* major clans of Hawiye, Darood, Dir, Isaaq and Digil Mirifle. Intra-clan refers to any affair between sub-clans *within* the major clans.

9. Unfortunately, literature on the duration of peace agreements at very local context is limited to several case studies, which were useful in identification of possible determinants.

10. Ibrahim Ali Amber, op. cit. Nduwimana Donatien, "Local Capacity for Peace Building in Somalia", *International Peace Support Training Center, Issue Brief 8* (December 2013). Mark Bradbury and Sally Healy, "Whose peace is it anyway? Connecting Somali and international peacemaking", *Accord, Issue Brief 21* (2010).

11. Caroline Hartzell and Matthew Hoddie, "Institutionalizing Peace: Power Sharing and Post-Civil War Conflict Management", *American Journal of Political Science* (April 2003); Stathis N. Kalyvas, "The Logic of Violence in Civil War: Theory and Preliminary Results", *Estudio/Working Paper* (2000); David T Mason, Mehmet Gurses, Patrick T. Brant, Jason M. Quinn, "When Civil Wars Recur: Conditions for Durable Peace after Civil Wars", *International Studies Perspective* (2011); Jason M. Quinn, David Mason and Mehmet Gurses, "Sustaining the Peace: Determinants of Civil War Recurrence", *International Interactions* (January 2007).

12. For the coding rule of the peace duration, please see the "Data Description" section.

13. A governmental body that ruled Somalia between 1969 and 1976. The Council's chairman was Siad Barre. Later it was renamed the Somali Revolutionary Socialist Party.

14. Mohamed Haji Mukhtar, "The Plight of the Agro-Pastoral Society of Somalia", *Review of African Political Economy* (December 1996).

15. Ibrahim Ali Amber, op. cit.

16. Mohamed Haji Mukhtar, op. cit.

17. Alex de Waal, "Class and Power in a Stateless Somalia", *Social Science Research Council* (February 2007). Bronwyn Bruton, "Clan and Islamic Identity in Somalia", *CEADS Papers, volume 2, Center for Security Armed Forces and Society of the Royal Military College of Canada* (March 2012); Mohamed Haji Mukhtar, op. cit.

18. Kenneth R. Rutherford, "The US and UN Intervention in Somalia", *Kumran Press* (2008).

19. Hartzell, Caroline and Matthew Hoddie, op. cit.

20. Gunther Schlee, op. cit.

21. "From the Bottom Up: Perspectives through Conflict Analysis and key Political Actors' Mapping of Gedo, Middle Juba, Lower Juba, and Lower Shabelle", *Conflict Early Warning Early Response Unit* (December 2013).

AMISOM: CHALLENGES OF INFLUENCE, IMPARTIALITY AND DISENGAGEMENT

1. "AMISOM Military Component", AMISOM, 2017: http://amisom-au.org/mission-profile/military-component/ (accessed 29 May 2017).

2. Such as the Ras Kamboni Brigade in control of Jubaland (RKB) and the Ahlu Sunna wal Jama'a.

3. "London Somalia Conference 2017: Security Pact", *London Somalia Conference 2017: New Partnership for Somalia for Peace, Stability and Prosperity*, United Kingdom Department for International Development, 2017: http://reliefweb.int/report/somalia/london-somalia-conference-2017-security-pact (accessed 29 May 2017).

4. For a detailed review of interventions, see: P.D. Williams and A. Hashi, "Exit Strategy Challenges for the AU Mission in Somalia", *The Heritage Institute for Policy Studies*, 2017: http://www.heritageinstitute.org/wp-content/uploads/2016/02/Exit-Strategy-Challenges-for-the-AU-Mission-in-Somalia.pdf (accessed 29 May 2017).

5. "More authority to act in Somalia would be 'very helpful': U.S. general", *Reuters* (2017): http://www.reuters.com/article/us-usa-somalia-military-idUSKBN16V2OO?il=0 (accessed 29 May 2017).

6. Some fundamental challenges include the constitutional review process, which is still unfinished, and the disputes over the division of power between the FGS and member states. The structure and distribution of Somali National Army remains uncertain. Above all, insecurity is pervasive with Al-Shabaab challenging the legitimacy of the government.

7. AMISOM, 2017, op. cit.

8. "A Question of Trust: The African Union and the Somali Army", Danish Institute for International Studies, 2015: http://pure.diis.dk/ws/files/310783/PB_AMISOM_SNA_WEB.pdf (accessed 29 May 2017).

9. S. Suri, "Barbed wire on our heads: Lessons from counter-terror, stabilisation and statebuilding in Somalia," Saferworld, 2016: http://www.saferworld.org.uk/resources/view-resource/1032-barbed-wire-on-our-heads (accessed 29 May 2017).

10. B.E. Bruton and P.D. Williams, *Counterinsurgency in Somalia: Lessons Learned*

from the African Union Mission in Somalia, 2007–2013 Report 14–5 (Florida: JSOU Press, 2014).

11. C.H. Wiklund, "The Role of the African Union Mission in Somalia: AMISOM— Peacekeeping Success or Peacekeeping in Regress?" Swedish FOI, 2013: https://www.foi.se/download/18.7920f8c915921957088a937/1484125405393/foir_3687.pdf (accessed 29 May 2017).

12. "A New Deal for Somalia", United Nations in Somalia, 2013: http://so.one.un.org/content/unct/somalia/en/home/what-we-do/new-deal-for-somalia.html (accessed 29 May 2017).

13. Reports estimate 32 to 36 US drone strikes in Somalia between 2001 and 2016. The most deadly killed about 150 suspected Al-Shabaab militants in March 2016. But some strikes hit the wrong targets, such as a September 2016 strike that killed more than a dozen soldiers from one of Somalia's regional administrations, mistaken for Al-Shabaab. In the past two years, however, raids involving US special forces have usually been conducted in tandem with Somali commando units, notably the *Danab* battalion. For further information, see: "Somalia: Reported US Covert Actions 2001–2016", The Bureau of Investigative Journalism, 2016: https://www.thebureauinvestigates.com/drone-war/data/somalia-reported-us-covert-actions-2001–2017 (accessed 29 May 2017). Also see: "U.S. Airstrike Stirs Conflict in Somalia", *Somalia Newsroom*, 2016: https://somalianewsroom.com/2016/10/01/photo-timeline-u-s-airstrike-stirs-conflict-in-somalia/ (accessed 29 May 2017).

14. UNSCR 2297 lays down parameters for AMISOM support to non-United Nations security forces. "AMISOM forces receive pre-deployment training through the DoS Global Peace Operations Initiative's Africa Contingency Operations Training and Assistance (ACOTA) program. U.S. forces support and complement ACOTA activities with specialized training in skills that have played a critical role in enhancing the operational success of AMISOM forces, including intelligence analysis and countering improvized explosive devices. To date, the forces of five AMISOM troop contributing countries (Burundi, Djibouti, Kenya, Sierra Leone, and Uganda) were trained through the ACOTA program": https://appropriations.house.gov/uploadedfiles/hhrg-113-ap02-wstate-rodriguezg-20130425.pdf (accessed 29 May 2017).

15. "U.S. air strike in Somalia killed local militia, not al Shabaab", *Reuters* (2016): http://www.reuters.com/article/us-usa-somalia-idUSKBN13526O (accessed 29 May 2017).

16. "A Navy SEAL was killed in Somalia. Here's what you need to know about U.S. operations there", *The Washington Post*, 2017: https://www.washingtonpost.com/news/monkey-cage/wp/2017/05/08/a-navy-seal-was-killed-in-somalia-heres-what-you-need-to-know-about-u-s-operations-there/?utm_term=.6a419847b8e1 (accessed 29 May 2017).

17. United Kingdom Department for International Development, 2017, op. cit.

18. Ugandan troops are deployed in Sector 1, which comprises the regions of Banadir, including Mogadishu, and Lower Shabelle. Kenyan forces are responsible for Sector 2 that covers Lower and Middle Jubba, mainly in support of the regional administration of Jubbaland. Sector 3, comprising Bay and Bakool as well as Gedo (Sub Sector 3), comes under Ethiopian command. Djiboutian forces oversee Sector 4, which covers Hiiraan and Galgaduud, while Burundian forces control Sector 5, which covers the Middle Shabelle region. In addition, Sierra Leone forces are in charge of Sector Kismayo, covering the port city and its surrounding areas.

19. S. Salaad, "Backing rival clans led to the defeat in El Adde", *The Star*, 2016: http://www.the-star.co.ke/news/2016/03/01/backing-rival-clans-led-to-the-defeat-at-el-adde_c1303693 (accessed 31 May 2017).

20. C. Barnes, "Somalia's Al-Shabaab Down but Far from Out", International Crisis Group, 2016: http://blog.crisisgroup.org/africa/somalia/2016/06/27/somalias-al-shabaab-down-but-far-from-out/ (accessed 29 May 2017).

21. "Explaining Ethiopia's Curious Strategy in Somalia", *Somalia Newsroom*, 2013: https://somalianewsroom.com/2013/04/01/explaining-ethiopias-curious-strategy-in-somalia/ (accessed 29 May 2017).

22. See: "Somalia report of the Monitoring Group on Somalia and Eritrea submitted in accordance with resolution 2182", UN Letter S/2015/801, Somalia, 6, 2015: http://www.un.org/ga/search/view_doc.asp?symbol=S/2015/801 (accessed 29 May 2017).

23. K. Menkhaus, "Al-Shabaab and Social Media: A Double-Edged Sword", *World Affairs* xx, Issue 11, (2014), p. 315: https://www.brown.edu/initiatives/journal-world-affairs/sites/brown.edu.initiatives.journal-world-affairs/files/private/articles/Menkhaus.pdf (accessed 31 May 2017).

24. "Ethiopian Troop Withdrawals in Somalia Raise Concern of Al-Shabaab Resurgence", *Voice of America*, 2016: http://www.voanews.com/a/somlaia-al-Shabaab-in-comeback-as-ethiopia-pulls-troops/3568528.html (accessed 31 May 2017).

25. "Somali President pledges to work with AMISOM to defeat Al-Shabaab", AMISOM, 2017: http://amisom-au.org/2017/02/somali-president-pledges-to-work-with-amisom-to-defeat-al-shabaab/ (accessed 29 May 2017).

26. "Somali president pledges to work with AMISOM to defeat Al-Shabaab", AMISOM Press Release, 2017: http://amisom-au.org/so/2017/02/somali-president-pledges-to-work-with-amisom-to-defeat-al-shabaab/ (accessed 31 May 2017).

27. United Kingdom Department for International Development, 2017, op. cit.

28. Ibid.

29. Ibid.

30. The existing SNA sectors shall be redrawn to align with FMS boundaries to reflect

the political developments in the country/federal system. This task shall be completed within three (3) months, starting from 1 June 2017.

31. "A New Policing Model for Somalia", United Nations Assistance Mission in Somalia, 2016: https://unsom.unmissions.org/new-policing-model-somalia (accessed 29 May 2017).

32. United Kingdom Department for International Development, 2017, op. cit.

33. P.D. Williams and A. Hashi, 2017, op. cit.

34. "Parliament approves security architecture with few amends", *Goobjoog News* (2017): http://goobjoog.com/english/parliament-approves-security-architecture-amends/ (accessed 29 May 2017).

35. "Ways to Improve Somalia's Plans to Take Over Security from Foreign Troops", *Somalia Newsroom*, 2017: https://somalianewsroom.com/2017/05/25/ways-to-improve-somalias-plans-to-take-over-security-from-foreign-troops/ (accessed 29 May 2017).

36. See: "Parliament approves security architecture with few amends", *Goobjoog News* (2017): http://goobjoog.com/english/parliament-approves-security-architecture-amends/ (accessed 29 May 2017). Also: "Somalia: Police forces vacate posts in Adado town to protest unpaid salaries", *Garowe Online*, 2017: http://www.garoweonline.com/en/news/somalia/somalia-police-forces-vacate-posts-in-adado-town-to-protest-unpaid-salaries (accessed 29 May 2017).

37. Somalia Newsroom, 2017, op. cit.

RECONCILIATION IN SOMALIA: REFORM, REPRESENTATION AND RESPONSIBILITY

1. David Bloomfield, "Rehabilitating reconciliation", *Making Peace with the Past: Transforming Broken Relationships*, Accord Insight 3, Conciliation Resources, 2016.

2. Alexander Ramsbotham and Zahbia Yousuf, *Making Peace with the Past: Transforming Broken Relationships*, Accord Insight 3, Conciliation Resources, 2016.

3. Graeme Simpson, "Foreword", Accord Insight 3, Conciliation Resources, 2016.

4. Conciliation Resources, *Whose Peace is it Anyway: Connecting Somali and International Peacemaking*, Accord 20 Policy Brief, 2010.

5. Mark Bradbury and Sally Healey (eds), *Whose Peace is it Anyway: Connecting Somali and International Peacemaking*, Accord 21, Conciliation Resources, 2010; Sue Unsworth, "The State's Legitimacy in Fragile Situations: Unpacking Complexity", OECD, 2010.

6. Unsworth, op. cit.

7. Bradbury and Healey, op. cit.

8. Bradbury and Healey op. cit; Unsworth, op. cit.

9. Bradbury and Healey op. cit.

10. Christine Bell and Kimana Zulueta-Fülscher, *Sequencing Peace Agreements and*

Constitutions in the Political Settlement Process, Policy Paper No. 13, November, International IDEA, 2016.

11. Zakaria Yousuf and Abdul Khalif, "Galkayo and Somalia's Dangerous Faultlines", International Crisis Group, 2015: http://blog.crisisgroup.org/africa/somalia/2015/12/10/galkayo-and-somalias-dangerous-faultlines/

12. "New 'Breakaway' Administration Forms in Somalia In Latest Federalism Dispute", Somalia Newsroom, 2015: https://somalianewsroom.com/2015/12/29/new-breakaway-administration-forms-in-somalia-in-latest-federalism-dispute/

13. Peacebuilding Organisations' Joint Statement on the UK Conference on Somalia, 11 May 2017.

14. Bell and Zulueta-Fülscher, op. cit.

15. Accord, Whose Peace is it Anyway: Connecting Somali and International Peacemaking, Accord 21 Policy Brief, 2010.

16. Conciliation Resources, Accord 20 Policy Brief, 2010.

17. Rufa Cagoco-Huiam, Grounding Reconciliation: Transforming Relationships in Mindanao, Accord Insight 3, Conciliation Resources, 2016.

LAUNCHING RECONCILIATION IN SOMALIA

1. This paper does attempt to present a comprehensive, in-depth analysis. It sets out the key analytical reasons why reconciliation is still a vital requirement to solve the Somali predicament and outlines how a reconciliation process could unfold.

2. Ken Menkhaus et al., A History of Mediation in Somalia since 1988 (The Centre for Research and Dialogue, May 2009); Tobias Hagman, Stabilization, Extraversion and Political Settlements in Somalia (Rift Valley Institute, 2016).

3. Barry Buzan, People, States and Fear: The National Security Problem in International Relations (ECPR Press, 1983).

4. Report of the Monitoring Group on Somalia and Eritrea pursuant to Security Council Resolution 2111 (2013): Somalia, 10 October 2014.

5. This section draws upon Joakim Gundel, The Predicament of the 'Oday': The Role of Traditional Structures in Security, Rights, Law and Development in Somalia (November 2006).

6. The Rahanwein speak Af-Maay, which is not immediately intelligible with the "national language" of af-Maxitirii, which is the language of the predominant nomadic people the Darood, Hawiye and Isaak clans. The Rahanwein culture is agro-pastoralist, and hence in many ways different from the pastoralists.

7. They are known as Gosha, Makane, Shiidle etc. These people also speak different languages, have quite different cultures, and are agriculturalists.

8. Martin Hill, No Redress: Somalia's Forgotten Minorities (Minority Rights Group International, November 2010).

9. These "minority" populations are not minorities as such, as they outnumber the pastoralists in the regions they live. But the dominant clans have successfully made

the international community believe in their representation of the Bantus as a minority, as their number is most likely far higher than stated in official statistics. The pastoralist clans have successfully occupied and dominated the Bantus since 1990, and still control their land. They are also systematically being denied a representative participation in politics through the informal application of the 4.5 system, a fact that is consistently ignored by the international community. Only Minority Rights and other minority rights groups have emphasized these facts, but to no avail.

10. This mistrust has a long history, which, however, was deepened and entrenched thanks to the civil war. Hence, many Darood still have grievances over their displacement from Mogadishu and other regions, and the experience of being hunted down and killed by primarily Hawiye militias. Clearly, this was not just a reflection of the rivalry between these two main clans, but a process initiated by their political elites who manipulated the clans for their political and military pogroms.

11. A process sponsored by funds originating in the Arab oil states. There are non-militant Wahhabi-associated groups with significant political influence in Somalia, including Al-Islah and Dam ul-Jadiid.

12. Warsuge, Barnes & Kiepe (eds.), *Land Matters in Mogadishu: Settlement, Ownership and Displacement in a Contested City* (Rift Valley Institute, 2017).

13. Abdihakim Ainte, in *Somalia: Another Paradigm Shift?* (Al Jazeera Centre for Studies, 11 May 2017).

14. As Abdihakim Ainte (op. cit.) clearly points out: "This political crisis has its roots, primarily, in Somalia's provisional constitution, which vests great power and authority in the hands of the unelected prime minister over the elected president. Second, there is a political element to the crisis. Under the current system, the political practice and culture is far more important than the constitutional rules. In the absence of effective rule of law and political parties, crises are settled through political bargaining between the stakeholders and elites. Without clear checks and balances, the provisional constitution provides both the president and prime minister with excessive power to abuse for their own gain."

15. The prevalent corruption is evidenced elsewhere. See for instance *2016 State of Accountability in Somalia* (Marqaati, February 2017).

16. Gundel, Berg & Ibrahim, *Political Economy of Justice in Somalia* (World Bank, 2016).

17. AMISOM, the Somali army and other local forces such as the Ras-Kamboni and Ahlu-Sunna Wal-Jamaa now control almost all major cities and towns in southern and central Somalia, but Al-Shabaab remains far from defeated, and still controls big parts of the countryside and towns like Buale in Middle Jubba region.

18. Furthermore, as Ainte (op. cit.) points out, the international coalition—AMISOM, US, UK, and other foreign troops—have made virtually no effort to find a political solution to the perpetual war and have prioritized military solutions over diplo-

macy. This narrow focus on counterinsurgency has created fatigue among the foreign troops.

19. It is widely believed that Somali forces are built along clan lines and lack allegiance to the Federal Government. Moreover, they are heavily reliant on external support for salaries, training, and equipment. Cognizant of this, President Farmajo has promised to improve the quality of Somalia National Army and re-establish a competent, capable, and well-disciplined national force. The recently adopted plan for a new Somali national security architecture was an important step in that process, but requires political buy-in from the various regional administrations and other competing actors.

20. Somaliland is a case in point, where an army was built upon the basis of reconciliation and clan consensus rather than a top-down merger of brokered de facto "warlord" business-controlled militias/security forces. See Brickhill & Bryden, *Disarming Somalia: Lessons in Stabilisation from a Collapsed State* (Conflict, Security & Development, April 2010).

21. There are positive precedents for the application of participatory action research methods in Somalia. See for example Allen & Gundel, *Enhancing District-Level Governance & Accountability in Somalia: A Case Study on the Citizen-Directed Negotiated Accountability Project* (KATUNI Consult & IAAAP, February 2017).

22. See http://theelders.org/

23. Joakim Gundel, *The Predicament of the 'Oday': The Role of Traditional Structures in Security, Rights, Law and Development in Somalia* (Danish Refugee Council & Novib/Oxfam, November 2006).

STATE-BUILDING AND PEACEBUILDING IN SOMALIA: LESSONS FROM OTHER PEACE AND TRANSITION PROCESSES

1. Since 1992, Dr Paffenholz has supported peace and transition processes in nineteen countries, including Somalia between 1996 and 2000 as Peacebuilding Advisor to the EU Special Envoy. She was awarded the Wihuri International Prize in 2015.

2. Constance Dijkstra holds an MSc in Conflict Studies from the London School of Economics and Political Science (LSE) as well as a BA in Politics and International Relations from Royal Holloway, University of London.

3. Dr Hirblinger holds a PhD from the University of Cambridge, an MA in International Conflict Studies from King's College in London and a BA in African Studies from Humboldt Universität in Berlin.

4. Emeric Rogier, "Democratic Republic of Congo: Problems of the Peacekeeping Process" in Oliver Furley and Roy May (eds), *Ending Africa's Wars: Progressing to Peace* (New York: Routledge, 2006), pp. 99–114, p. 111.

5. Hussein Solomon and Gerrie Swart, "Conflict in the DRC: A Critical Assessment of the Lusaka Ceasefire Agreement", *South African Institute of International Affairs*

Report no. 40 (SAIIA: Johannesburg, 2004): http://www.eprpinformation.org/files/peaceprocesses/ceasefires/a-critical-assessment-of-the-lusaka-ceasefire-agreement-2of2.pdf (accessed 20 April 2017).

6. Laura David and Priscilla Hayner, "Difficult Peace, Limited Justice: Ten Years of Peacemaking in the DRC", *International Center for Transitional Justice* 36 (2009).

7. William I. Zartman, "Negotiating with Terrorists", *International Negotiations* 8, 3 (2003): pp. 443–450: http://booksandjournals.brillonline.com/content/journals/10.1163/1571806031310815 (accessed 20 April 2017).

8. Thomas H. Johnson, "Afghanistan's post-Taliban Transition: The State of State-building after War", *Central Asian Survey*, 25:1–2 (2006): pp. 1–26.

9. Barnett R. Rubin and Humayun Hamidzada, "From Bonn to London: Governance Challenges and the Future of Statebuilding in Afghanistan", *International Peacekeeping*, 14:1 (2007): pp. 8–25.

10. "Taliban and Afghanistan restart secret talks in Qatar", *The Guardian* (18 October 2016): https://www.theguardian.com/world/2016/oct/18/taliban-afghanistan-secret-talks-qatar

11. "Afghanistan: Hezb-i-Islami armed group signs peace deal", *Al-Jazeera* (22 September 2016): http://www.aljazeera.com/news/2016/09/gulbuddin-hekmatyar-group-signs-afghan-peace-deal-160922093420326.html

12. April Alley, "Yemen Changes Everything... And Nothing", *Journal of Democracy* 24:4 (October 2013): pp. 74–85: https://muse.jhu.edu/article/523087 (last accessed 17 April 2017).

13. Charles Schmitz, "Yemen's National Dialogue", *MEI Policy Paper 2014–1* (February 2014): http://www.mei.edu/sites/default/files/publications/Schmitz%20Policy%20Paper.pdf (accessed 17 April 2017).

14. Timor Sharan, "The Dynamics of Elite Networks and Patron-Client Relations in Afghanistan", *Europe-Asia Studies*, 63:6 (2011): pp. 1109–1127, p. 1110.

15. Ibid., p. 1123.

16. Ibid., p. 1124.

17. Jennifer C. Seely, "A Political Analysis of Decentralisation: Coopting the Tuareg Threat in Mali", *The Journal of Modern African Studies* 39:3 (September 2001): 499–524, pp. 511–512.

18. Morten Bøås, "Crime, Coping, and Resistance in the Mali-Sahel Periphery", *African Security* 8:4 (2015): pp. 299–319.

19. Morten Bøås, "Castles in the Sand: Informal Networks and Power Brokers in the Northern Mali Periphery" in Mats Utas (ed.), *African Conflicts and Informal Power: Big Men and Networks* (London: Zed Books, 2012), pp. 119–136.

20. Susanna D. Wing, "Briefing Mali: Politics of a Crisis", *African Affairs* 112/448 (2013): pp. 476–485: https://academic.oup.com/afraf/article/112/448/476/124663/Mali-Politics-of-a-crisis (accessed 20 April 2017).

21. "Yemen's Imposed Federal Boundaries", Middle East Research and Information

Project (MERIP), 20 July 2015: http://www.merip.org/yemens-imposed-federal-boundaries

22. Tobias Thiel, "After the Arab Spring: Power Shift in the Middle East? Yemen's Arab Spring: From Youth Revolution to Fragile Political Transition", *IDEAS Reports* (London: LSE IDEAS, 2012): https://www.lse.ac.uk/IDEAS/publications/reports/pdf/SR011/FINAL_LSE_IDEAS__YemensArabSpring_Thiel.pdf (accessed 21 April 2017).

23. "Yemen's Imposed Federal Boundaries": http://www.merip.org/yemens-imposed-federal-boundaries

24. Astri Suhrke, Kristian Berg Harpviken, and Arne Strand, "Conflictual Peacebuilding: Afghanistan Two Years after Bonn", *Chr. Michelsen Institute Report 2014* 4 (2014): https://www.cmi.no/publications/file/1763-conflictual-peace-building.pdf (accessed 24 April 2017).

25. Ebrahim Afsah and Alexandra H. Guhr, "Afghanistan: Building a State to Keep the Peace", *Max Planck Yearbook of United Nations Law* 9 (2005): pp. 373–456, p. 427.

26. Suhrke et al, "Conflictual Peacebuilding".

27. Susanna D. Wing, *Constructing Democracy in Africa: Mali in Transition* (New York: Palgrave, 2008), p. 71.

28. Ousmane Sy, Ambroise Dakouo, and Kadari Traoré, "Dialogue National au Mali: Leçons de la Conférence Nationale de 1991 pour le processus de sortie de crise", *Etude de Cas* (August 2016).

29. Seely, "A Political Analysis of Decentralisation", p. 511.

SOMALI NATIONAL RECONCILIATION: EXPLORING A COMPREHENSIVE APPROACH

1. The Somali political elite constitutes Islamists and non-Islamists. The first conflict was among non-Islamists competing for power and resources which provoked clan wars. The second was between Islamists and non-Islamists disagreeing on the nature of the state, which became violent as evidenced by the emergence of Al-Shabaab.

2. Sidney Waldron and Naima A. Hasci, "State of the Art Literature Review on Somali Refugees in the Horn of Africa", Refugees Studies Programme Authority, Oxford University and the Swedish International Development Authority, 1994. Exceptions are few, but include Virginia Luling and Friederike Teutsch. See Friederike Teutsch, *Collapsing Expectation: National Identity and Disintegration of the State in Somalia* (Edinburgh: Centre of African Studies, Edinburgh University, 1999), p. 4.

3. It could be said these conferences started in Djibouti in 1991, which involved the participation of factions such as SSDF, SPM, USC, SAMO, SNU, SDM and ended in Djibouti in 2009 between TFG, ARS-Djibouti. The chronology of these conferences and their participants refer to Interpeace, Somali Programme, "A History

of Mediation in Somalia Since 1988", edited by Pat Johnson (2009): http://3n589z370e6o2eata9wahfl4.wpengine.netdna-cdn.com/wp-content/uploads/2009/05/2009_Som_Interpeace_A_History_Of_Mediation_In_Somalila_Since_1988_EN.pdf (accessed 18 May 2017).

4. The current use of the term "transitional justice" dates to 1995, but its mechanisms were used earlier. For instance, the Conquest of Mecca (11 January 630) offers a good example of transitional justice in Islam. The term transitional justice was defined by The International Centre for Transitional Justice as follows: "Transitional Justice refers to the ways countries emerging from periods of conflict and repression address large scale or systematic human rights violations so numerous and so serious that the normal justice will not be able to provide as adequate response": https://www.ictj.org/about/transitional-justice (accessed 30 April 2017).

5. For the concept of Sharia-based transitional justice and its applicability in Somalia, see Abdurahman Abdullahi, *Recovering the Somali State: Islam, Islamism and Transitional Justice* (London: Adonis & Abbey Co., 2017), pp. 97–139.

6. The adoption of the federal system may be considered an early attempt in this direction. However, the process of their formation was haphazard and lacked required legitimacy in most federal state members.

7. Many countries were involved in the internal Somali conflict. In particular, Ethiopia hosted, trained, and equipped armed factions who toppled the state in 1991, continuing their support afterwards. Ethiopia also hosted the alliance of warlords who opposed the Transitional National Government established in Arta, Djibouti in 2000, and supported the Abdullahi Yusuf administration militarily. Thus, Ethiopian involvement is a part of the Somali conflict and must also be addressed. Other countries include Eritrea, Egypt, and Kenya.

8. The elitist approach overcomes the methodological challenge for it permits a high degree of integration of the two levels of analysis. Elite theory starts with two basic assumptions: (1) in every society, the distribution of political power is unequal; and (2) in every system, some people have more power than others. People who have more power (economic, political, religious) within every society may be either one person (a political leader) or a small group (the elites). See Abdurahman Abdullahi, "Tribalism, Nationalism and Islam: The Crisis of Political Loyalty in Somalia", MA Thesis submitted to the Islamic Institute, McGill University, 1992, p. 7.

9. Early armed factions included the Somali Salvation Democratic Front (SSDF), the Somali National Movement (SNM), United Somali Congress (USC), and the Somali Patriotic Movement (SPM).

10. Abdurahman Abdullahi, *The Islamic Movement in Somalia: A Case Study of Islah Movement (1950–2000)* (London: Adonis & Abbey Co., 2015), pp. 215–231.

11. Human Rights Watch, *Somalia: A Government at War with its Own People, Testimonies About the Killings and Conflict in the North* (1990): https://www.hrw.org/sites/default/files/reports/somalia_1990.pdf (accessed 10 May 2017).

12. New World Encyclopaedia, "Somali Revolution (1986–1992)": http://www.new-worldencyclopedia.org/entry/Somalian_Revolution_(1986%E2%80%931992) (accessed 20 April 2017).

13. Anna Simons, *Networks of Dissolution: Somalia Undone* (Boulder, CO: Westview Press, 1995), p. 79.

14. Ibid.

15. See Mohamed Sahnoun, "Somalia: The Missed Opportunities" (paper delivered to the United State Institute of Peace, 1994), p. 11.

16. The total cost of lives was never fully tallied. Lewis provides a statistic of 300,000 See I.M. Lewis, *A Modern History of the Somali: Nation and State in the Horn of Africa*, Revised/Fourth Edition (Columbus: Ohio University Press, 2003), p. 265. See also Kenneth Rutherford, *Humanitarianism under Fire: The US Intervention in Somalia* (West Hartford, CT: Kumerian Press, 2008), p. 38; and Ahmed Samatar (ed.), *The Somali Challenge*, p. 3.

17. Abdullahi, *Recovering the Somali State*, p. 146.

18. For instance, the mandate of the African Union Mission in Somalia does not include a transitional justice component. See Margherita Suin, "A Model for Transitional Justice for Somalia", *PRAXIS, The Fletcher Journal of Human Security* Vol XXIII, (2008).

19. Somali warlords participated in all political reconciliation conferences. While alleged human rights violations were examined as one of the criteria for participation, many of these warlords still remain members of the Somali Parliament.

20. Menkhaus, "Mediation Efforts for Somalia", *Africa Mediators Retreat*, p. 41.

21. This is a conventional anthropological interpretation, originating from the structural-functionalist school, rather than a contemporary approach.

22. Abdurahman Abdullahi, *Making Sense of Somali History* (London: Adonis & Abbey Co., 2017), p. 20.

23. Accordingly, clan elders have monopolized representation of the clans after the collapse of the state.

24. The "state versus clan" model promotes hegemony of the majority clans and excludes minorities and naturalized Somalis who do not belong to any clan.

25. Said S. Samatar, "Unhappy Masses and the Challenges of Political Islam in the Horn of Africa": www.wardheernews.com/March_05/05 (accessed 2 February 2017).

26. Abdi I. Samatar, "Destruction of State and Society in Somalia: Beyond the Tribal Convention", *The Journal of Modern African Studies* 30 (1992): pp. 625–641.

27. The *diya*-paying group is the smallest clan unit who take collective responsibility in making or receiving reparation for killed or injured individuals.

28. State–society relations can be described in six possible scenarios ranging from extreme cooperation to extreme conflict. These are mutual collaboration, mutual engagement, conflictual engagement, mutual disagreements, enforced disengage-

ment, and resistance-revolutionary disengagement. See Abdurahman Abdullahi and Ibrahim Farah, "Reconciling the State and Society: Reordering Islamic Work and the Clan System": www.scribd.com/document/15327358/Reconciling-the-State-and-Society-in-Somalia (accessed 2 May 2017).

29. Abdullahi, *The Islamic Movement in Somalia*, p. 231.
30. Al-Itihad al-Islami in the 1990s and Al-Shabaab of today are examples of the militancy of some Islamic organizations.
31. For the rationale of adopting the terminology of "non-Islamist" which means not Islamic activist as an alternative to the term "secularist" refer to Abdurahman Abdullahi, *Reconverting the Somali State: Islam, Islamism and Transitional Justice* (Adonis &Abbey, 2017), 28.
32. Ibid.
33. Abdullahi, "Tribalism, Nationalism and Islam", pp. 92–100.
34. It is important to address the four major violations of human rights that occurred during the military regime, and, in particular, to address Somaliland grievances.

CHALLENGES AND OPPORTUNITIES: POLITICAL DIALOGUE BETWEEN THE FEDERAL GOVERNMENT OF SOMALIA AND SOMALILAND

1. For the text of the Chevening Agreement: https://www.qurbejoog.com/somalil-and-and-somalia-talks-Chevening-house-declaration
2. Mohamed A. Omar (Foreign Minister, Somaliland), "Somaliland did not surrender sovereignty by attending the London Conference": http://africanarguments.org/
3. "Turkey in Somalia: Shifting Paradigms of Aid", *SAIIA Research Report No. 24* (November 2016).
4. Cooperation on airspace management was agreed upon but never implemented.

BEYOND PRINCIPLES: THE INCLUSION OF SOMALI WOMEN IN PEACEMAKING

1. In early 2016, LPI, in partnership with its local partner the Somali Women's Solidarity Organization (SWSO), launched a women-centred dialogue process in Kismayo. As part of this project the author worked with LPI, SWSO and Peace Direct to carry out research in Kismayo to deepen understanding of how to enhance women's participation in peace processes. This briefing paper draws on this research. Please note that validation processes for this research have not taken place at the time of this briefing paper.
2. This assertion is made on the basis of personal communication with several external actors, professionals involved in peace negotiations, including the Mbgathi Peace Process. Globally, evidence also comes from the fact that the gender dimensions of

peace governance are not fully articulated in the Sustainable Development Goals— despite the evidence of the relationship between women's participation and sustainable peace and despite high-level lobbying by women movement. For a critique of the current situation see: "Global Review of UN SCR 1315+15 years on", UN Women, 2015: http://wps.unwomen.org/ (accessed 29 May 2017).

3. Unless otherwise indicated, all quotes are drawn from the LPI-SWSO-Peace Direct Kismayo study.

4. See for example: A.M. Warsame, "Queens Without Crowns: Somaliland Women's Changing Roles and Peacebuilding", *Life & Peace Institute* (2002); Judith Gardner and Judy El Bushra (eds), *Somalia—The Untold Story* (London: Pluto Press, 2004); J.M. Faiza, "Somali Women and Peacebuilding" in Mark Bradbury and Sally Healy (eds), *Whose Peace is it Anyway? Connecting Somali and International Peacemaking* (Conciliation Resources ACORD Issue 21, 2010).

5. For one of the highest-quality explanations of relational gender analysis, see: Carol Cohn, *Women and Wars: Contested Histories, Uncertain Futures* (Oxford: Polity Press, 2012).

6. For more on the concept of war as a gendered social construction see ibid.

7. Findings do suggest women from marginalized groups have different experiences of the war but a more targeted study would be needed to identify whether specific groups or types of women are more or less likely than others to have engaged in conflict and in what type of ways—reactive or pro-active, for example.

8. This "admission" echoes the words of Somalia's award-winning environmentalist and peace activist, Fatima Gibreel, who when speaking to women at a peace conference in 1997 is reported as having said, "Let us not pretend innocence...Women have empowered and encouraged their husbands, their leaders and their militia to victimize fellow countrymen'. Cited in: Matt Bryden and Martina Steiner, "Somalia Between Peace and War: Somali Women on the Eve of the 21st century", *African Women for Peace Series*, UNIFEM (1998).

9. See, for example, Gardner and El Bushra, *Somalia* (op. cit.). And as recorded in women's poetry from the 1950s independence struggle, these roles have been played by women in support of change in the past.

10. See for example: Cohn, *Women and Wars* (op. cit.), Laura Sjoberg, *Mothers, Monsters, Whores—Women's Violence in Global Politics* (London: Zed Books, 2007), Megan H. MacKenzie, *Female Soldiers in Sierra Leone—Sex, Security and Post-Conflict Development* (New York: New York University Press, 2012), p. 138.

11. See: Judith Gardner and Judy El Bushra, "The Impact of War on Somali Men and its Effects on the Family, Women and Children", Rift Valley Institute, 2016: http://riftvalley.net/publication/impact-war-somali-men-and-its-effects-family-women-and-children#.WS19CevyjIU (accessed 29 May 2017).

12. Male respondents gave several accounts of how women have judged and humiliated men who are unwilling, or unable, to fight including forcing one man to wear women's clothing and marking others out as cowards with coloured ink.

13. Male respondents discussed at length their protective responsibilities towards their sisters, for example, "If your sister says, 'a man has insulted me or beat me' you will go and fight straight away."

14. The killing of the wounded from rival clans appears to have been a role designated to or taken on by women. Material from another LPI set of consultations with men confirms it is a role women have played in the war.

15. "Winning" in the context of Kismayo apparently meant, "they wanted (their clan/family) to remain and rule the town" but in other localities it could mean "to capture land".

16. Hawa Tako, a Somali heroine from the independence struggle died in 1948 leading a violent protest against the Italian police in Mogadishu.

17. Somali inter-clan warfare used to be conducted with spears and other hand-thrown weapons for which young males trained from an early age. In her Masters study on Somali women in conflict, Saadia Mohamed postulates that the ready availability of small arms and light weapons has changed the gendered nature of combat within the Somali community, women and children being physically equally capable of wielding a gun as a man. Saadia Mohamed, "The Role of Somali Women in Conflict: The case of the Degodia and Ajuran Clans of Wajir County, 1964–1984", University of Nairobi, 2013: http://erepository.uonbi.ac.ke/handle/11295/58823 (accessed 29 May 2017). Others have also made this point, for instance, see: MacKenzie, *Female Soldiers in Sierra Leone* (op. cit.).

18. Respondents noted "many girls have fought" but more research is needed to understand the details (including questions around whether they are with clan militia and/or Al-Shabaab) and to confirm if their engagement has been voluntary or involved forced recruitment. The Report of the Secretary-General on children and armed conflict in Somalia (December 2016) notes a resurgence in numbers of children (under 18s) recruited by armed groups. According to its figures girls comprise around 10 per cent of those recruited.

19. Asked what roles their clansmen did expect them to play, women listed everything shown in Table 3.4, except the armed combat roles. When men were asked the same question, they said the same as the women.

20. At the time of the study and writing this report there are reportedly no active clan militia in Jubbaland.

21. Unlike the Kurdish women's wing fighting in Syria, for instance.

22. "Technical" refers to a light improvised fighting vehicle, typically an open-backed civilian pickup truck or four-wheel drive vehicle mounting a gun.

23. More research would be needed to confirm or refute this claim.

24. For an example from Erigavo of how women's peace-building activism involves transcending clan divisions and presenting a collective bulwark against it, see Gardner and El Bushra, *Somalia* (op. cit.).

25. For instance, as evidenced by LPI-SWSO women-centred dialogues.

26. See for example: Siham Rayale, "Narrating Peace: Somaliland Women's Experiences", 50:50 Inclusive Democracy, 5 Sept 2012: https://www.opendemocracy.net/5050/siham-rayale/narrating-peace-somaliland-women%E2%80%99s-experiences (accessed 8 August 2017); Faiza Jama, "Somali Women and Peacebuilding", in Bradbury and Healy, *Whose Peace Is It Anyway?* (op. cit.); Abdisalam Sheikh Ali, "The Role of Somali Women On Peacebuilding": http://www.academia.edu/7846027/The_Role_of_Somali_women_on_peace_building (accessed 8 August 2017); Gardner and El Bushra, *Somalia* (op. cit.).

27. The exogamous marriage preference—marriage between members of different kinship groups—that has been widely practiced both facilitates and motivates women to build peace, as it is so central in the causes of their suffering. See details of gendered nature of clan identity and exogamous marriage in Gardner and El Bushra, *Somalia* (op. cit.).

28. A *diya* group is an alliance formed by related lineages within a clan by means of a contract, in which the rights and duties of members of the group with respect to the burdens of payment and the distribution of receipts of blood compensation are stated.

29. See: Gardner and El Bushra, "The Impact of War on Somali Men and its Effects on the Family, Women and Children" (op. cit.) for findings on the normative characteristics associated with male leadership.

30. This refers to the customary calculation whereby 100 camels is compensation sought for the loss of one man's life.

31. It was noted by women that sometimes "the men from the rival clans cannot fight unless accompanied by women … they ululate and motivate the men to fight".

32. For example: Tobias Hagmann, "Stabilisation, Extraversion and Political Settlements in Somalia", Rift Valley Institute, 2016: http://riftvalley.net/publication/stabilization-extraversion-and-political-settlements-somalia#.WS1-XevyjIU (accessed 29 May 2017); and Markus V. Hoehne, "Political Representation in Somalia: Citizenship, Clannism and Territoriality" in Bradbury and Healy, *Whose Peace Is It Anyway?* (op. cit.).

33. See footnote 24 in Gardner and El Bushra, *Somalia* (op. cit.). Women describe how intra- and inter-clan conflict places them at the "centre of suffering" as the conflict literally tears families apart.

FROM THE MARGINS TO THE CENTRE: SOMALI WOMEN IN PEACEBUILDING

1. The inspiration for this title is credited to bell hooks: *Feminist Theory: From Margin to Centre* (Boston, MA: South End Press, 1984).

2. The women interviewed were selected for their knowledge and to provide a wealth of deeper insights on the particular ways women negotiate and influence peace. They are either leaders or members of women's organizations that advance peace

and reconciliation and actively lobby to make political space for women. The field-work for this qualitative research was conducted in Mogadishu and Garowe in May 2017. The research sites were selected to gather contextually local informa-tion to reflect the diversity in the socio-political and gender dynamics as well as the intersections of gender, politics, and peace building.

3. *Xeer* has been defined as a set of customary laws that have provided general rules and created order and continuity in the traditional Somali society. For a good dis-cussion on Somali customary law see Ali Moussa Iye, *Le Verdict de l'arbre (Go'aankii Geedka): Le Xeer Issa Etude d'une Democratie Pastorale*. While there are similari-ties in principle and purpose in these customary laws, there are considerable vari-ations among the approaches of the different regions.

4. Ali Moussa Iye, "Traditional Democratic Systems and New Political Challenges: Revisiting the Issa Xeer".

5. Hassan A. Keynan, "Male Roles and the Making of the Somali Tragedy: Reflections on Gender, Masculinity and Violence in Somali Society" in Muddle Suzanne (ed.) and Lilius, *Variations on the Theme of Somaliness* (Turku: Centre for Continuing Education, Abo Akademi University, 1998), p. 246.

6. See Lidwien Kapteijns, "Gender Relations and the Transformation of the Northern Somali Pastoral Tradition", *The International Journal of African Historical Studies* Vol. 28, No. 2. (1995): pp. 241–259; and Mussa Galal, "Some Observations on Somali Culture", *Perspectives on Somalia* (Mogadishu: Somali Institute of Public Administration, 1968).

7. See: Amina Adan, "Women and Words", *Ufahamu*, vol. 10, no. 3 (Spring 1998): pp. 115–142; Christine Choi Ahmed, "Finely Etched Chattel: The Invention of a Somali Woman", in Ali Jimale Ahmed (ed.), *The Invention of Somalia* (Lawrenceville, NJ: The Red Sea Press Inc., 1995), pp. 157–189; and Hilarie Kelly, "The Potential Role of Women's Groups in Reconstruction", in Hussein M. Adam and Richard Ford, *Mending Rips in the Sky: Options for Somali Communities in the 21st Century* (Lawrenceville, NJ: The Red Sea Press Inc., 1997), pp. 359–369.

8. Raqiya Haji Dualeh, "Women in Somali Society: Roles and Images", Paper pre-sented at a UNDP conference in Hargeisa, Somalia, 1997, p. 2.

9. Ibid.

10. Ali Moussa Iye, "Traditional Democratic Systems and New Political Challenges: Revisiting the Issa Xeer."

11. Hussein Adam, "Somalia: International versus Local Attempts at Peace building", in Taisier Mohamed Ahmed Ali and Robert O. Matthews (eds), *Durable Peace: Challenges for Peacebuilding in Africa* (Toronto: University of Toronto Press, 2004), pp. 253–281.

12. Ibid.

13. Keynan, op. cit. 1998, p. 244.

14. As one interviewee put it, "the tragedy we see today has nothing to do with the old system. Being old, man and with red beard doesn't make a person a leader."

15. While *xeer* is an important indigenous institution with traditional mechanisms to regulate and moderate conflicts and "established surprising rules of war that some analysts consider as an early model of the Geneva Convention", it is a product of its time. This means it does not have proper mechanisms to include women. One could compare it to the Bill of Rights, when this brilliant document was developed women were disenfranchised and most blacks were in slavery. However, with the civil rights movement and continued pressures for civil rights, it has evolved and continues to evolve.
16. See: http://www.cdacollaborative.org/media/45058/Women-Gender-and-Peacebuilding-Do-Contributions-Add-Up.pdf
17. See: http://lifepeace.org/making-resolution-1325-the-norm-not-an-exception/
18. See: http://www.cdacollaborative.org/media/45058/Women-Gender-and-Peacebuilding-Do-Contributions-Add-Up.pdf
19. http://repository.upenn.edu/cgi/viewcontent.cgi?article=1156&context=curej
20. See: http://www.cr.org/downloads/Accord%2021_19Somali%20women%20and%20peacebuilding_2010_ENG.pdf
21. Held in Arta, Djibouti, in 2000 and in Mbagathi, Kenya, in 2004 respectively are the only two (of nearly 20 regionally and internationally facilitated) Somali peace conferences where women participated in the negotiations formally.
22. Faiza Jama, "Somali Women and Peacebuilding."
23. See: http://www.iwm.at/iwmauthor/brigitte-bargetz/
24. See: https://www.usip.org/sites/default/files/pwks24.pdf
25. Important gains are made thanks to these lobbying strategies. For example, there is a record high number of women cabinet ministers; the highest in Somali history in fact. Also, five out of the 15 District Commissioners in Mogadishu are women.

BETWEEN A ROCK AND A HARD PLACE: YOUNG SOMALI MEN TODAY

1. Judith Gardner and Judy El-Bushra (eds), *Somalia—the Untold Story: The War through the Eyes of Somali Women* (London: Pluto Press, CIIR, 2004).
2. Judith Gardner and Judy El-Bushra, "The Impact of War on Somali Men: Report of an Inception Study", *LOGiCA/RVI* (2015).
3. Ibid.
4. See for example: Lidwien Kapteijns, *Clan Cleansing in Somalia: The Ruinous Legacy of 1991* (Pennsylvania: University of Pennsylvania Press, 2012).
5. The same can result if a youth lacks a father for example, or if their father is unknown or has offended his clansmen for whatever reason, or if they live displaced and far from their own clansmen.
6. See RVI's briefing paper, Judith Gardner and Judy El-Bushra, "Somalia: A state of male power, insecurity and inequality", Rift Valley Institute briefing paper, 2017.

7. See David Duriesmith on the concept of "good men", for example: "Manly States And Feminist Foreign Policy: Revisiting The Liberal State As An Agent Of Change", University of Melbourne conference paper, 2017.

8. The Report of the Secretary-General on children and armed conflict in Somalia (December 2016) notes a resurgence in numbers of children (under 18s) recruited by armed groups. Boys comprise more than 90 per cent of those recruited, and possibly half of all Al-Shabaab's forces.

9. See for example: Introduction of *Somalia the Untold Story* and in this series, "Beyond Principles—Why Somali women must be seen as primary peacebuilding actors, findings from a Life and Peace Institute and Peace Direct study in Kismayo".

10. See Nimo Ilhan-Ali, "Going on Tahriib: The Causes and Consequences of Somali Youth Migration to Europe", *RVI Research Paper* 5 (2016).

11. In a separate, unpublished study from 2012 on drivers of conflict, RVI research from Somaliland found male youth's own sense of powerlessness is perceived by others in society to be a threat to peace and stability.

12. Finding from research conducted for the Gender Profile of Somalia update, EC Somalia 2014.

ADDRESSING THE GAP: PROMOTING YOUTH INCLUSION IN SOMALI PEACE AND RECONCILIATION

1. Federal Government of Somalia, *The Somalia National Development Plan (SNDP)— Towards Recovery, Democracy And Prosperity 2017—2019* (2016): http://mopic. gov.so/wp-content/uploads/2016/11/SOMALIA-NATIONAL-DEVELOPMENT-PLAN-2017–2019.pdf.16

2. Johan Galtung, "Violence, Peace, and Peace Research", *Journal Of Peace Research* 6/3 (1969): pp. 183, 190; Interview 12B; Interview 5K; Interview 13B.

3. Clare Magill and Brandon Hamber, "'If They Don't Start Listening To Us, The Future Is Going To Look The Same As The Past': Young People and Reconciliation in Northern Ireland and Bosnia and Herzegovina", *Youth & Society* 43/2 (2010): pp. 523–524.

4. Interview 8K.

5. Ken Menkhaus, "The Crisis in Somalia: Tragedy in Five Acts", *African Affairs* 106/424 (2007): pp. 357–390.

6. Altai Consulting, *Youth, Employment And Migration In Mogadishu, Kismayo and Baidoa* (Mogadishu: IOM Somalia, 2016): https://www.iom.int/sites/default/files/country/docs/IOM-Youth-Employment-Migration-9 Feb2016.pdf; United Nations Development Programme, *Somalia Human Development Report 2012: Empowering Youth For Peace And Development* (2012): http://www.hdr.undp.org/sites/default/files/reports/242/somalia_report _2012.pdf

7. Alexander Cárdenas, *Sport, Conflict and Reconciliation: Exploring the Use of Sports for Peacebuilding and Conflict Resolution*, Working Paper Series N°1 (Liverpool:

Archbishop Desmond Tutu Centre for War and Peace Studies, Liverpool Hope University, 2012): http://tutu.hope.ac.uk/media/microsites/tutucentre/documents/Exploring%20the%20Use%20of%20Sports%20for%20Peacebuilding%20and%20Conflict%20Resolution.pdf

8. "Overview", *United Nations Office on Sport for Development and Peace* (2014): https://www.un.org/sport/content/why-sport/overview

9. Kofi Annan, "We Must Use the Power of Sport as an Agent of Social Change". Speech, SportAccord International Convention (2010).

10. Broadcasting Board of Governors, *Media Use In Somalia* (2013): https://www.bbg.gov/ wp-content/media/2013/11/gallup-somalia-brief.pdf

11. BBC World Service Trust, *An Analysis of the Somali Media Environment* (2011): http://downloads.bbc.co.uk/rmhttp/mediaaction/pdf/AnAnalysisOfTheSomaliMediaEnvironment.pdf

12. Ken Menkhaus, "Al-Shabaab and Social Media: A Double-Edged Sword" *Brown Journal of World Affairs* XX/II (2014).

13. *Global Forum on Youth, Peace and Security*, Amman (2015): http://www.un.org/en/peace building/pbso/pdf/Final%20Report%20%20Global%20Forum%20on%20Youth%20Peace%20%20Security%2011.11.2015.pdf

14. "Wakiil", 2017: https://www.wakiil.org/#!/

15. Interview 6H; Interview 3K; Interview 5K.

16. 1H, 6H, 7H, 9H, 9K.

17. Interview 6K; Interview 15K.

18. Interview 11K.

19. Interview 8H.

20. Interview 14K.

21. Interview 12H; Interview 4K; Interview 10K.

22. Interview 11B; Interview 12B; Interview 13B; Interview 5K.

23. Interview 1B; Interview 13B.

24. Altai Consulting, *Youth, Employment and Migration in Mogadishu, Kismayo and Baidoa* (Mogadishu: IOM Somalia, 2016): https://www.iom.int/sites/default/files/country/docs/IOM-Youth-Employment-Migration-9Feb2016.pdf

25. "About Somalia", *United Nations Development Programme* (2014): http://www.so.undp. org/content/somalia/en/home/countryinfo.html

26. Interview 7K.

27. Federal Government of Somalia, *The Somalia National Development Plan (SNDP)—Towards Recovery, Democracy and Prosperity 2017—2019* (2016): http://mopic.gov.so/wp-content/uploads/2016/11/SOMALIA-NATIONAL-DEVELOPMENT-PLAN-2017–2019.pdf

28. Interview 1B; Interview 4B; Interview 5B; Interview 15B; Interview 13K.

29. Anneli Botha and Mahdi Abdile, "Radicalisation and Al-Shabaab Recruitment in Somalia", *ISS Paper* 266 (Institute for Security Studies, 2014): https://issafrica.s3.amazon aws.com/site/uploads/Paper266.pdf; Interview 12B

30. Diab M. Al-Badayneh "Social Causes of Terrorism in Arab Society", in Suleyman Ozeren, Ismail Dincer Gunes, and Diab M. Al-Badayneh (eds), *Understanding Terrorism: Analysis of Sociological and Physiological Aspects* (Amsterdam: IOS Press, 2007), p. 139.

31. Interview 5K.

32. Interview 9B, Interview 4K.

33. Interview 12B.

34. Interview 5B; Interview 11B; Interview 6K; Interview 9K; Interview 12K; Interview 14K; Interview 15K.

35. Interview 12B; Interview 14B; Interview 15B.

36. Interview 1B; Interview 12B; Interview 11K.

37. "Wakiil", 2017: https://www.wakiil.org/#!/; Wakiil is an online resource for Somalis to find out about their elected representatives and MPs with the goal of encouraging democracy and accountability.

38. "Wakiil", 2017: https://www.wakiil.org/#!/

SOMALIA'S SOUTHERN WAR: THE FIGHT OVER LAND AND LABOUR

1. Lee V. Cassanelli, "The Ending of Slavery in Italian Somalia: Liberty and the Control of Labor, 1890–1935," in Suzanne Miers and Richard Roberts (eds), *The End of Slavery in Africa* (Madison: University of Wisconsin Press, 1988), pp. 308–331. See also Catherine Besteman, "The Invention of Gosha: Slavery, Colonialism, and Stigma in Somali History," in Ali Jimale Ahmed (ed.), *The Invention of Somalia* (Lawrenceville, NJ: The Red Sea Press, 1995), pp. 43–62; Kenneth J. Menkhaus, "Rural Transformation and the Roots of Underdevelopment in Somalia's Lower Jubba Valley" (Ph.D. diss, University of South Carolina, 1989).

2. Daniel Van Lehman and R. Proehl, "Population Estimates of Somali Bantu with East African Slave Ancestry", *Journal of Somali Studies* 2:1 & 2 (2015): pp. 47–66.

3. M. A. Eno, *The Bantu Jareer Somalis: Unearthing Apartheid in the Horn of Africa.* (London: Adonis & Abbey Publishers Ltd, 2008), p. 224. See also M. Hill, *No Redress: Somalia's Forgotten Minorities* (London: Minority Rights Group International, 2010); M. A., Eno, M. H. Ingiriis, and O. A. Eno, "Discrimination and Prejudice in the Nucleus of African Society: Empirical Evidence from Somalia", *African Renaissance* 10: 3–4, (2013), pp. 13–36; M. A. Eno and A. M. Kusow, "Racial and Caste Prejudice in Somalia", *Journal of Somali Studies* 1: 2, (2014): pp. 91–118.

4. A. Botha and M. Abdile, "Radicalisation and al-Shabaab recruitment in Somalia", *Institute for Security Studies*, ISS paper 266 (2014): p. 6; Abdul-Ahad Ghaith, "How Somalia's Civil War became a New Front in the Battle against al-Qaida," *The Guardian*, 7 June 2010.

5. Human Rights Watch, *Hostages of the Gatekeepers: Abuses against Internally Displaced in Mogadishu, Somalia* (New York: Human Rights Watch, 2013), p. 6.

6. Catherine Besteman, *Unraveling Somalia* (Philadelphia: University of Pennsylvania Press, 1999).
7. Lee V. Cassanelli, *Victims and Vulnerable Groups in Southern Somalia* (Ottawa: Canadian Immigration and Refugee Board, 1995), p. 8.
8. Human Rights Watch, *Hostages*, p. 11.

WHY THEY FIGHT AND WHY THEY QUIT: AN ANALYSIS OF INTERVIEWS WITH CURRENT AND FORMER AL-SHABAAB FIGHTERS

1. Leaders are defined as people who are decision makers and independent actors within the overall structure and strategy of Al-Shabaab.
2. Conducted for this study.
3. Unavailable publicly but shared with TGSN.
4. Anneli Botha and Mahdi Abdile, "Radicalisation and Al-Shabaab Recruitment in Somalia", *Institute for Security Studies Paper 266* (26 Sept 2014): https://issafrica. org/research/papers/radicalisation-and-al-shabaab-recruitment-in-somalia
5. A separate study by Anneli Botha found 87 per cent of respondents gave a religious reason for joining: http://eip.org/en/news-events/why-do-people-join-terrorist-organisations
6. The Serendi camp holds ex-Al-Shabaab fighters who are classified as "low risk" by Somalia's National Intelligence and Security Agency.
7. European Institute for Peace, "Interview with Mahdi Abdile", June 2016: http:// eip.org/en/news-events/why-do-people-join-terrorist-organisations
8. See: https://unsom.unmissions.org/ex-al-shabaab-combatants-celebrate-start-new-life-following-graduation-baidoa-rehabilitation-center

YOUTH RADICALIZATION: CAUSES, CONSEQUENCES AND POTENTIAL SOLUTIONS

1. Senior official at Somali Federal Government, 15 February 2017, Mogadishu, Somalia.
2. Al-Shabaab also do not allow other agendas to undermine their dominance, hence their efforts to subdue inter- and intra-clan conflicts.
3. Raffaello Pantucci and A.R. Sayyid, "Foreign Fighters in Somalia and al-Shabaab's Internal Purge", *The Jamestown Foundation Terrorism Monitor* Volume, 11 Issue: 22 (December 2013).
4. A chief security official in Middle Shabelle region has warned people against seeking justice in Al-Shabaab strongholds. See: http://www.jowhar.com/2017/07/13/taliyaha-nabadsugida-shdhexe-oo-u-digay-dadka-u-doonta-garsoorka-deegaanada-al-shabaab/
5. Robert Pape, *Dying to Win: The Strategic Logic of Suicide Terrorism* (New York: Random House, 2016).

6. See: http://www.criminaljusticedegreesguide.com/features/10-most-corrupt-police-forces-in-the-world.html

AL-SHABAAB'S YOUTH RECRUITMENT PROJECT

1. Sirkku Hellsten, "Radicalisation and Terrorist Recruitment among Kenya's Youth", The Nordic Africa Institute, February 2016; and Alexander Meleagrou-Hitchens, "ICSR Insight—Al-Shabaab: Recruitment and Radicalisation in Kenya", ICRS, Department of War Studies, 2014. One exception is Anneli Botha and Mahdi Abdile, "Radicalisation and al-Shabaab recruitment in Somalia", *Institute for Security Studies Paper 266* (September 2014).

2. Anneli Botha, "Political Socialization and Terrorist Radicalization among Individuals who Joined Al-Shabaab in Kenya", *Studies in Conflict & Terrorism* 37/11 (2014): pp. 895–919; and Paul Joosse, Sandra M. Bucerius and Sara K. Thompson, "Narratives and Counternarratives: Somali-Canadians on Recruitment as Foreign Fighters to Al-Shabaab", *British Journal of Criminology* 55 (2015): pp. 811–832.

3. David Keen, "The Economic Functions of Violence in Civil Wars", *Adelphi Paper* 320 (London: Oxford University Press for the International Institute for Strategic Studies, 1998).

4. One should be cautious: often stories provided by Al-Shabaab defectors cannot be wholly depended on for research study or other purposes unless employing critical analysis or using triangulation.

5. Stig Jarle Hansen, *Al-Shabaab in Somalia: The History and Ideology of a Militant Islamist Group, 2005–2012* (London: Hurst, 2013); and Roland Marchal, "A Tentative Assessment of the Somali *Harakat Al-Shabaab*", *Journal of Eastern African Studies* 3/3 (2009), pp. 381–404.

6. Hellsten, "Radicalisation"; Meleagrou-Hitchens, "ICSR Insight"; and *Sunday Nation*, "How Poverty and Search for Identity Drive Youth into Terrorism", 10 August 2014.

7. Hansen, *Al-Shabaab in Somalia*, pp. 2, 9, 19, 28 & 45.

8. *Wajaale News*, "Dhalinta Maanta Dalkeena ma dhalan dhoolka Tahriibka ayaa u miciina, Qalinkii Sacad Faysal", 30 March 2015; and *Waxsansheeg*, "Halkan Ka Daawo: Wasaarada Dhalinyarada SOMALILAND oo Ka Hadashay Tahriibka Dhalinta", 20 April 2016: http://waxsansheeg.com/?p=66214 (accessed 15 May 2017).

9. Fieldwork ethnographic observations in Hargeisa (Somaliland), July–August 2016.

10. Anonymous, "Banana Wars in Somalia", *Review of African Political Economy* 22/64 (1995): pp. 274–275. See also Peter D. Little, *Somalia: Economy without State* (Oxford: James Currey, 2003); Roland Marchal, "Monetary Illegalism and Civil War: The Case of Somalia", in Jean-Louis Briquet and Gilles Favarel-Garrrigues (eds), *Organized Crimes and States: The Hidden Faces of Politics* (New York:

Palgrave Macmillan, 2010), pp. 221–146; and Jamil A. Mubarak, "The 'Hidden Hand' Behind the Resilience of the Stateless Economy of Somalia", *World Development* 25/12 (1997): pp. 2027–2041.

11. Roland Marchal, "La Guerre à Mogadiscio", *Politique Africaine* 46 (1992), pp. 120–125.

12. Jutta Bakonyi, "Between Protest, Revenge and Material Interests: A phenomenological analysis of looting in the Somali war", *Disasters* 34/2 (2010): pp. 238–255.

13. Hansen, *Al-Shabaab in Somalia*; and Marchal, "A Tentative Assessment".

14. Interview with Al-Shabaab defectors, Mogadishu, Somalia, April–May 2016. Markus Hoehne noted that there are "many young people who have been lured into joining the group based on religious rhetoric as well as forcibly recruited ones and others who joined for the sake of getting a regular salary. There is also a core of more dedicated fighters, some of who[m] are Somali, others are foreigners". Markus Virgil Hoehne, "No Intervention! The Way Forward in Somalia", *Horn of Africa Bulletin* 24/2 (2012): pp. 8–11, p. 8. As Marchal noted, forced recruitment is the exception not the norm. Roland Marchal, "The Rise of a Jihadi Movement in a Country at War: Harakat al Shabaab al Mujaheddin in Somalia", CERI Research Paper, Sciences Po, Paris, March 2011, p. 40.

15. *Jariiban News*, "Wiil Ka Mid ah Maxaabiistii Deegaanka Garacad", https://www.youtube.com/watch?v=DTbMRCDXTCQ (accessed 9 May 2017).

16. Nicasius Achu Check, "Radical Movements and their Recruitment Strategies in Africa: Some Theoretical Assumptions", *Africa Insight* 46/3 (2016): pp. 67–82; and Tedd R. Gurr, *Why Men Rebel* (Princeton: Princeton University Press, 1970).

17. Marchal, "A Tentative Assessment", p. 394. See also Matt Bryden, "The Reinvention of Al-Shabaab: A Strategy of Choice or Necessity?", Washington, DC: CSIS, February 2014.

18. Stig Jarle Hansen, "Somalia—Grievance, Religion, Clan, and Profit", in Stig Jarle Hansen, Atle Messoy and Tuncay Kardas (eds), *The Borders of Islam: Exploring Samuel Hunting's Faultlines, From Al-Andalus to the Virtual Ummah* (London: Hurst, 2009), pp. 127–138. See also John Duckitt and Chris G. Sibley, "Personality, Ideology, Prejudice, and Politics: A dual-process motivational model", *Journal of Personality* 78/6 (December 2010): p. 1869.

19. ICG, "The Islamic State Threat in Somalia's Puntland State", International Crisis Group, Africa Briefing, 26 October 2016: https://www.crisisgroup.org/africa/horn-africa/somalia/islamic-state-threat-somalias-puntland-state (accessed 6 May 2016).

20. Interview with Al-Shabaab defectors, Mogadishu, Somalia, 4 May 2016; and interview with Al-Shabaab defectors, Mogadishu, Somalia, 6 May 2016. *YouTube*, "Daawo warbixin cajiib ah: Taariikhda Axmed Godane iyo mustaqbalka Al-Shabaab dilkiisa kadib", https://www.youtube.com/watch?v=YQsGz-ReQA4 (between min. 13:00 and 13:27), accessed 6 May 2016. For theoretical under-

standing of the will to die for a killing, see Mia Bloom, *Dying to Kill: The Allure of Suicide Terror* (New York: Columbia University Press, 2005).

21. Interview with Al-Shabaab defectors, Mogadishu, Somalia, 4 May 2016; and interview with Al-Shabaab defectors, Mogadishu, Somalia, 6 May 2016.

22. Fieldwork ethnographic observations, Do'oleey, central Somalia, 1 June 2015.

23. *New Vision*, "Lack of Ideology is Somalia's Problem", 3 November 2016. On counter-ideological attempts, see Walid Jumblatt Abdullah, "Merits and Limits of Counter-ideological Work Against Terrorism: A Critical Appraisal", *Small Wars & Insurgencies* 28/2 (2017): pp. 291–308.

24. *Madasha Barbaarta TV*, "Deg deg waano cajiib ah oo ka timi dhalinyaro kuna socota dhalinyarada", https://www.youtube.com/watch?v=Xb7xAIwuWPQ (accessed 7 May 2017).

25. *YouTube*, "YUSRA ABRAAR OO CADEEYSEY LACAGTA SOMALI LOOGU TALAGALEY MEELAHA AY KU BAXDO Q 1AAD", https://www.youtube.com/watch?v=sP1bI6I16z8 (accessed 12 May 2017).

26. Fund for Peace, "Fragile States Index", Washington, DC, 2016.

27. James Ferguson, *The Anti-Politics of Machine: Development, Depoliticization, and Bureaucratic Power in Lesotho* (Cambridge: Cambridge University Press, 1990).

28. Interview with Al-Shabaab defectors, Mogadishu, Somalia, 4 May 2016; and interview with Al-Shabaab defectors, Mogadishu, Somalia, 6 May 2016.

29. Interview with C. A. H., Afgooye, via IMO from Afgooye, Somalia, 8 March 2017.

30. Interview with A.T., London, 18 June 2017.

31. Muhsin Hassan, "Understanding Drivers of Violent Extremism: The Case of Al-Shabab and Somali Youth", *CT Sentinel* 5/8 (2012): pp. 18–20; and Roland Marchal, "Joining Al-Shabaab in Somalia", in Jeevan Deol & Zaheer Kazmi (eds), *Contextualising Jihadi Thought* (London: Hurst and Co., 2012), pp. 259–274.

32. Interview with A. A. M., Mogadishu, Somalia, 4 May 2016.

33. *WARSOM*, "Ciidamo Iyo Gaadiid Ka Soo Baxsaday Dowlad TFG-da Oo U Goostay Xarakada Al-shabaab", 17 September 2011: http://warsom.com/wararka/2011/09/ciidamo-iyo-gaadiid-ka-soo-baxsaday-dowlad-tfg-da-oo-u-goostay-xarakada-al-shabaab/ (accessed 12 May 2017).

34. *Caasimada*, "Sawir: Ciidamo ka tirsan Dowlada FS oo isku dhiibay Kooxda al-Shabaab", 13 April 2017: http://www.caasimada.net/ciidamo-ka-tirsan-dowlada-fs-oo-isku-dhiibay-kooxda-al-shabaab/ (accessed 12 May 2017).

35. This delineation is not a clear-cut, though. There are many within the "powerful" clans who feel marginalized within the government system.

RIVALS IN GOVERNANCE: CIVIL ACTIVITIES OF AL-SHABAAB

1. Karen DeYoung, "U.S. Strike in Somalia Targets Al-Qaeda Figure", *Washington Post*, 8 January 2007.

2. Stig Jarle Hansen, *Al-Shabaab in Somalia: The History and Ideology of a Militant Islamist Group 2005–2012* (Oxford: Oxford University Press, 2013).

3. Madawi al-Rasheed, *Contesting the Saudi State: Islamic Voices from a New Generation* (Cambridge: Cambridge University Press, 2007).

4. Roland Marchal, "Lower Shabelle in the Civil War: Historical Dynamics of Land Conflicts in a Somali Region", Mogadishu/Nairobi/Paris (forthcoming).

5. Roland Marchal, "The rise of a Jihadi Movement in a Country at War: Harakat al-Shabaab al-Mujahidin", Nairobi, March 2011.

6. This practice already existed within clan factions in the 1990s and has a long history in some agricultural regions, such as Lower Shabelle and Lower Jubba.

7. *Huduud* is an Islamic term referring to punishments which under Islamic law (the Sharia) are mandated and fixed by God. *Huduud* punishments range from public lashing to publicly stoning to death, amputation of hands, and crucifixion.

CAN AL-SHABAAB DELIVER? REALITY AND RHETORIC IN THE STRUGGLE FOR POWER

1. Interviews were carried out with two dozen Somalis in Police, NISA, Office of the President, Ministry of Information, Ministry of Internal Security, youth groups and other NGOs, as well as with foreign academics, communications experts, observers and officials.

2. https://qz.com/995127/al-shabaab-overtook-boko-haram-as-the-most-deadly-terror-group-in-africa-in-2016/

3. "They are Not Welcome—they shall burn in their fire", issued in Arabic, English, Somali and Swahili: http://www.longwarjournal.org/archives/2017/05/shabaab-claims-us-is-satan-of-our-time-praises-al-qaedas-leadership.php

4. "Labayk ya Osama" (At your Service Osama) issued in September 2009.

5. Al-Shabaab has mounted attacks outside Somalia—or has attempted to do so—in Djibouti (2014), Ethiopia (2013, 2014), Kenya (2013, 2014, 2015, 2016), Tanzania (2015), and Uganda (2010, 2014).

6. See: http://english.alarabiya.net/en/News/africa/2014/03/11/Al-Shabaab-leader-urges-Somalisto-battle-old-enemy-Ethiopia.html

7. The attempt by an Al-Shabaab suicide bomber to bring down Daallo Airlines flight 159 between Mogadishu and Djibouti, on 2 February 2016, was described by Al-Shabaab as an attack on "Western intelligence officials" and the "Western and apostate [Somali] intelligence infrastructure", so casting it in a national context.

8. Despite its claim that "Islamic" identity is the only relevant identity, Al-Shabaab has nonetheless appealed to Somali national pride, for example by highlighting the persecution of ethnic Somalis inside Kenya and Kenya's suzerainty over historically Somali regions.

9. See: https://www.ctc.usma.edu/posts/an-in-depth-look-at-al-shababs-internal-divisions

10. See: https://www.crisisgroup.org/africa/horn-africa/somalia/somalia-s-al-sha-baab-down-far-out

11. Approximately 30 per cent of the newly elected MPs are also affiliated with Islamist-leaning groups, including Salafi movements and the Muslim Brotherhood. See: https://www.crisisgroup.org/africa/horn-africa/somalia/regional-risks-soma-lias-moment-hope

12. See: https://www.ctc.usma.edu/posts/an-in-depth-look-at-al-shababs-internal-divisions

13. See: http://www.africanews.com/2017/04/21/al-shabaab-cautions-parents-over-non-islamic-education//

IS ANYBODY LISTENING? AL-SHABAAB'S COMMUNICATIONS

1. Al-Shabaab officials, 2007 to the present.

2. Somali government minister, April 2017.

3. Director of Somali NGO, April 2017.

4. European Union official, May 2017.

5. British military official, May 2017.

6. See, for example, the daily briefings from the Albany Associates' Communications Adviser to the Office of the President of Somalia.

7. Member of Somali NGO, February 2017.

8. Non-Somali communications consultants based in Mogadishu, 2013–17.

9. Director of Somali NGO, May 2017.

10. Christopher Anzalone, "Continuity and Change: The Evolution and Resilience of Al-Shabaab's Media Insurgency, 2006–2016", *Hate Speech International* (November 2016); Peter Chonka, "Spies, stonework and the suuq: Somali nationalism and the narrative politics of Harakat Al-Shabaab Al Mujaahidiin's online propaganda", *Journal of Eastern African Studies* 10/2 (2016): pp. 247–265; Mary Harper, *Getting Somalia Wrong? Faith, War and Hope in a Shattered State* (London: Zed Books, 2012); Mary Harper, "Somalia's Al-Shabaab launches 'Twitter war'," BBC, 8 December 2011: http://www.bbc.co.uk/news/world-africa-16091751

11. Sympathizers of Al-Shabaab and similar groups, London, June 2017.

12. Government official, Baidoa, April 2017.

13. University student, Mogadishu, April 2017.

14. People who have recently fled Al-Shabaab. The interviews were conducted in Baidoa, Mogadishu, Hargeisa, and London.

15. Phone calls, text messages and emails from Al-Shabaab, 2007 to the present.

16. Journalists covering Somalia for local, regional and international media, May 2017.

17. See, for example, Operational Guidance Notes on High Profile Attacks provided by the Albany Associates' Communications Adviser to the Office of the President of Somalia.

18. Somali journalists working in Somalia, Kenya, Uganda, Ethiopia, the UK, and the US.

19. Somali journalist, May 2017.

20. Somali journalist, April 2017.

21. Abdinoor Aden, "Profile: Al-Shabaab journalist Hassan Hanafi", BBC, 11 April 2016: http://www.bbc.co.uk/news/world-africa-35725716

22. The author is aware of at least two Somali journalists who work/have worked for international broadcasters who have expressed sympathy for Islamist extremism of the kind espoused by Al-Shabaab.

23. The author has seen a number of these discussions on Twitter and Facebook.

24. Forthcoming Palgrave Macmillan publication on the Somali media based on the PhD thesis of the Somali academic, Idil Osman.

25. Oxford University workshop on the Somali media, August 2011.

26. See for example the HD video "Beyond the Shadows", produced in 2014 by Al-Shabaab's Al Kataib Foundation.

27. See for example the Al Furqaan film of Eid celebrations in Brava, 2013: https://www.youtube.com/watch?v=Erik6x_lcPg

28. Businesswoman, Mogadishu, April 2017.

29. Member of the returned diaspora, Mogadishu, April 2017.

30. Oxford University workshop on the Somali media, August 2011.

31. Jamal Osman, "Somali journalists are dying from corruption as much as conflict", *The Guardian*, 11 October 2012: https://www.theguardian.com/commentis-free/2012/oct/11/somali-journalists-dying-corruption-conflict; the author has witnessed multiple instances of Somali journalists demanding money for reports to be published or broadcast or to be removed from websites, and of Somali and non-Somali actors paying for positive and biased media coverage.

32. An exception is the Netherlands-based Somali journalist Dahir Alasow, who has faced court action.

33. Harper, *Getting Somalia Wrong?*

34. "Somali Perceptions Survey", Parts 1 and 2, USAID, 14 February 2017; Idil Osman, Forthcoming publication on the Somali media.

35. "Somali Perceptions Survey", Parts 1 and 2.

36. Somali human rights activist and academic in Hargeisa.

37. Somali student in Hargeisa who recently moved there from the UK.

38. The Hargeisa International Book Fair was threatened by the religious community in 2015. Some guests (Somali and non-Somali) left the territory early or confined themselves to their hotels as a result.

39. Recent defector from Al-Shabaab, Baidoa, April 2017.

40. "The Jihadis Next Door", Channel 4, 2016: http://www.channel4.com/programmes/the-jihadis-next-door

41. Author visits to madrasas in IDP camps and other parts of Mogadishu, and in Nairobi and Hargeisa.

42. "A Memo for Somalia's New Leaders on the Priorities of Citizens", *Heritage Institute of Policy Studies* (April 2017).

ANATOMY OF COUNTER-JIHAD: COMMUNITY PERSPECTIVES ON REHABILITATION AND RECONCILIATION

1. Pumla Gobodo-Madikizela, "Trauma, Forgiveness and the Witnessing Dance: Making public spaces intimate," *Journal of Analytical Psychology* 53, no. 2 (2008): pp. 169–188.
2. Stig Jarle Hansen, Stian Lid, and Omondi Okwany, *Countering Violent Extremism in Somalia and Kenya: Actors and Approaches* (Oslo: NIBR-Rapport, 2016), p. 20. See also David Kilcullen, *The Accidental Guerrilla: Fighting Small Wars in the Midst of a Big One* (Oxford: Oxford University Press, 2009).
3. Stig Jarle Hansen, *Horn, Sahel and Rift: Fault-Lines of the African Jihad* (London: Hurst, 2019—forthcoming).
4. Hansen et. al., *Countering Violent Extremism*, p. 20.
5. For more on the widespread sense of insecurity, see Center for Research and Dialogue, "In Pursuit of Peace: Challenges and opportunities in the central regions" (Pillars of Peace: Somalia Program, 2012): http://3n589z370e6o2eata9wahfl4. wpengine.netdna-cdn.com/wp-content/uploads/2012/08/2012_08_28_SomSC_ Pillars_Of_Peace_ENG.pdf (accessed 15 June 2017); Observatory of Conflict and Violence Prevention (OCVP), "Briefing on community perceptions of security, justice and governance in Baidoa district" (2014): http://ocvp.org/docs/2015/SC. pdf (accessed 15 June 2017).

AL-QAIDA AND AL-SHABAAB: A RESILIENT ALLIANCE

1. Michael C. Horowitz and Philip B. K. Potter, "Allying to Kill Terrorist Intergroup Cooperation and the Consequences for Lethality", *Journal of Conflict Resolution* 58, no. 2 (2014): pp. 199–225; Victor Asal and R. Karl Rethemeyer, "The Nature of the Beast: Organizational Structures and the Lethality of Terrorist Attacks", *The Journal of Politics* 70, no. 2 (2008): pp. 437–49; Victor Asal et al., "With Friends Like These ... Why Terrorist Organizations Ally", *International Public Management Journal* 19, no. 1 (2016): pp. 1–30; Victor H. Asal, Gary A. Ackerman, and R. Karl Rethemeyer, "Connections Can Be Toxic: Terrorist Organizational Factors and the Pursuit of CBRN Weapons", *Studies in Conflict & Terrorism* 35, no. 3 (2012): pp. 229–54; Brian J. Phillips, "Terrorist Group Cooperation and Longevity", *International Studies Quarterly* 58, no. 2 (2014): pp. 336–47.
2. Michael N. Barnett and Jack S. Levy, "Domestic Sources of Alliances and Alignments: The Case of Egypt, 1962–73", *International Organization* 45 (1991): p. 370; Stephen Walt, "Enduring Questions in a Changing Time," *Realism and the Balancing of Power: A New Debate* (2003), p. 12.

3. Daniel Byman, "Buddies or Burdens? Understanding the Al Qaeda Relationship with Its Affiliate Organizations", *Security Studies* 23, no. 3 (2014): p. 434.

4. Bardia Rahmani and Andrea Tanco, "ISIS's Growing Caliphate: Profiles of Affiliates", *Wilson Center Blog*, February 2016: https://www.wilsoncenter.org/article/isiss-growing-caliphate-profiles-affiliates

5. A number of the interviewees preferred not to be named specifically in the paper because of the sensitivity of this issue; therefore, we have used descriptions for all of interviewees to preserve anonymity.

6. Mustafa Hamid and Leah Farrall, *The Arabs at War in Afghanistan* (London: Hurst, 2015), p. 188.

7. Ibid., p. 187–8.

8. "Interview with Abu Jandal Part III", *Al-Quds Al-'Arabi*, 2 April 2005.

9. For Al-Qaida correspondence on the situation in Somalia and its activities in the 1990s, see: "AQ-MSLF-D-000–126", *Conflict Records Research Center*, March 1993, pp. 1–13; Saiful-Islam, "AQ-MSLF-D-000–260", *Conflict Records Research Center*, October 1993, p. 1; Salih 'Abd-al-Wahid, "AQ-POAK-D-000-052", *Conflict Records Research Center*, December 1993, pp. 1–3; "AQ-POAK-D-000-060", *Conflict Records Research Center*, estimated 1993, pp. 1–4; Saif Al-Adel, "AQ-POAK-D-000-104", *Conflict Records Research Center*, January 1994, pp. 1–6; Abu Hafs, "AQ-POAK-D-000-171", *Conflict Records Research Center*, 1994, pp. 1–18; Shaykh 'Abdul Rahman al-Sadiq al-Qayidi, "AQ-SHPD-D-000–001", *Conflict Records Research Center*, Estimated 1993, pp. 1–4. Also see: Hamid and Farrall, *The Arabs at War in Afghanistan*, pp. 188–89; Stig Jarle Hansen, *Al-Shabaab in Somalia: The History and Ideology of a Militant Islamist Group, 2005–2012* (Oxford: Oxford University Press, 2013), pp. 17, 24; Jacqueline Page, "Jihadi Arena Report: Somalia—Development of Radical Islamism and Current Implications", *International Institute for Counter-Terrorism* (2010): https://www.ict.org.il/Article/1071/Jihadi%20Arena%20Report%20Somalia%20-%20Development%20of%20Radical%20Islamism%20and%20Current%20Implications; David Shinn, "Al Shabaab's Foreign Threat to Somalia", *Orbis* 55, no. 2 (2011): pp. 204–5; Clint Watts, Jacob Shapiro, and Vahid Brown, *Al-Qaida's Misadventures in the Horn of Africa* (West Point, VA: Countering Terrorism Center at West Point, 2007).

10. "Interview with Abu Jandal," *Al-Quds Al-'Arabi*, 20 March 2005.

11. United Nations Al-Qaida Sanctions Committee, "Narrative Summaries for Reasons of Listing: Al Ittihad Al Islamiyah": https://www.un.org/sc/suborg/en/sanctions/1267/aq_sanctions_list/summaries/entity/al-itihaad-al-islamiya/aiai; Page, "Jihadi Arena Report", p. 8; Shinn, "Al Shabaab's Foreign Threat", p. 205.

12. Hansen, *Al-Shabaab in Somalia*, p. 24. Stig Jarle Hansen, "Shabab central—Africa's 'Taliban' grows more unified," *Janes Intelligence Review* 22, no. 8 (July 2010): pp. 18–21; Congressional Research Service, "Terrorism and Violent Extremism

in Africa", *Congressional Research Service Report* (2016), p. 6: https://www.every-crsreport.com/files/20160714_R44563_044e4e8d7e8401469235bb33afa9961 6dd43b688.pdf

13. David H. Shinn, "Al-Qaeda in East Africa and the Horn", *The Journal of Conflict Studies* 27, no. 1 (2007).

14. Rob Wise, "Al Shabaab", *Center for Strategic & International Studies, AQAM Futures Project Case Study Series: Case Study Number 2* (2011), p. 7; Page, "Jihadi Arena Report," p. 8.

15. Hansen, *Al-Shabaab in Somalia*, p. 41.

16. Ibid., pp. 43–44, 55; Hansen, "Shabab central—Africa's 'Taliban'"; Nelly Lahoud, "The Merger of Al-Shabab and Qa'idat al-Jihad", *CTC Sentinel* 5, no. 2 (2012): pp. 1–5, 3.

17. Hansen, "Shabab central—Africa's 'Taliban,'" p. 2.

18. Atiyatallah (Atiyah Abd al-Rahman), "Letter to Mujahidin in Somalia dtd 28 December 2006," *Office of the Director of National Intelligence Bin Laden's Bookshelf*, 20 May 2015: https://www.dni.gov/files/documents/ubl/english2/ Letter%20to%20Mujahidin%20in%20Somalia%20dtd%2028%20December%20 2006.pdf; Hansen, *Al-Shabaab*, p. 62; Lahoud, "The Merger", pp. 2–3.

19. Lahoud, "The Merger", p. 2; American Enterprise Institute Editors, "Al Shabaab Leadership Profiles", (2011): https://www.aei.org/publication/Al-Shabaab-leadership-profiles/

20. "Letter to Abu 'Abdallah al-Hajj", *Office of the Director of National Intelligence Bin Laden's Bookshelf*, 20 May 2015, p. 1: https://www.dni.gov/files/documents/ubl/ english/Letter%20to%20Abu%20Abdallah%20al-Hajj.pdf

21. Usama bin Laden, "SOCOM-2012–0000005", *Countering Terrorism Center at West Point*, 3 May 2012: https://www.ctc.usma.edu/posts/letters-from-abbot-tabad-bin-ladin-sidelined

22. Zamaray (Usama bin Laden), "Letter to Abu Yahya", *Office of the Director of National Intelligence Bin Laden's Bookshelf*, 19 January 2017, pp. 1–2: https:// www.dni.gov/files/documents/ubl2017/english/Letter%20to%20Abu%20Yahya. pdf; "Letter about efforts in other regions," *Office of the Director of National Intelligence Bin Laden's Bookshelf*, 19 January 2017, pp. 1–3: https://www.dni. gov/files/documents/ubl2017/english/Letter%20about%20efforts%20in%20 other%20regions.pdf; Azmarai (Usama bin Laden), "Letter dtd 07 August 2010", *Office of the Director of National Intelligence Bin Laden's Bookshelf*, 20 May 2015, pp. 1–4: https://www.dni.gov/files/documents/ubl/english/Letter%20dtd%20 07%20August%202010.pdf; Abu 'Abdullah (Usama bin Laden), "SOCOM-2012–0000010", *Countering Terrorism Center at West Point*, 3 May 2012, p. 6: https://www.ctc.usma.edu/posts/letters-from-abbottabad-bin-ladin-sidelined

23. Mahmud (Atiyah Abd al-Rahman), "Letter dtd 5 April 2011", *Office of the Director of National Intelligence Bin Laden's Bookshelf*, 20 May 2015, p. 4: https://www.

dni.gov/files/documents/ubl/english/Letter%20dtd%205%20April%202011.
pdf; Mahmud (Atiyah Abd al-Rahman), "Letter to Shaykh Abu Abdallah dtd
17 July 2010", *Office of the Director of National Intelligence Bin Laden's Bookshelf,*
20 May 2015, pp. 2–3: https://www.dni.gov/files/documents/ubl/english2/
Letter%20to%20Shaykh%20Abu%20Abdallah%20dtd%2017%20July%202010.
pdf

24. Your Beloved Brother (Ayman al-Zawahiri), "SOCOM-2012–0000006",
Countering Terrorism Center at West Point, 3 May 2012, pp. 1–2: https://www.
ctc.usma.edu/posts/letters-from-abbottabad-bin-ladin-sidelined

25. American Enterprise Institute Editors, "Al Shabaab Leadership Profile"; "Shabaab
Spokesman Comments on Zawahiri as New al-Qaeda Leader", *Site Intelligence,*
20 June 2011: https://news-siteintelgroup-com.proxyau.wrlc.org/Groups-Pledge-
Allegiance-to-Zawahiri/shabaab-spokesman-comments-on-zawahiri-as-new-al-
qaeda-leader.html

26. "Letter to Uthman," *Office of the Director of National Intelligence Bin Laden's
Bookshelf,* 20 May 2015, p. 8: https://www.dni.gov/files/documents/ubl/english/
Letter%20to%20Uthman.pdf

27. "Letter to Abu 'Abdallah al-Hajj", p. 1; "Dear brother Abu-'Abdallah al-Haj
'Uthman", *Office of the Director of National Intelligence Bin Laden's Bookshelf,*
1 March 2016, pp. 1–3: https://www.dni.gov/files/documents/ubl2016/english/
Dear%20brother%20Abu-%E2%80%98Abdallah%20al-Haj%20
%E2%80%98Uthman.pdf; "Gist of conversation Oct 11", *Office of the Director of
National Intelligence Bin Laden's Bookshelf,* 20 May 2015, pp. 2–4: https://www.
dni.gov/files/documents/ubl/english/Gist%20of%20conversation%20
Oct%2011.pdf; "Letter Addressed to Atiyah", *Office of the Director of National
Intelligence Bin Laden's Bookshelf,* 20 May 2015, p. 3: https://www.dni.gov/files/
documents/ubl/english/Letter%20Addressed%20to%20Atiyah.pdf; Azmarai
(Usama bin Laden), "Letter dtd 07 August 2010", pp. 1–6.

28. Western Government Analyst, interview by Tricia Bacon, Washington, DC,
20 December 2016; International Crisis Group, "Somalia: Al-Shabaab—It Will
Be a Long War", *Crisis Group Africa Briefing* no. 99 (June 2014): pp. 10–11:
https://d2071andvip0wj.cloudfront.net/somalia-Al-Shabaab-it-will-be-a-long-
war.pdf; Matt Bryden, "The Reinvention of Al-Shabaab: A Strategy of Choice or
Necessity?" *Center for Strategic & International Studies Africa Program* (2014),
p. 1; American Enterprise Institute Editors, "Al Shabaab Leadership Profiles."

29. Matthew J. Thomas, "Exposing and exploiting weaknesses in the merger of
Al-Qaeda and Al-Shabaab", *Small Wars & Insurgencies* 24, no. 3 (2013): pp. 413–
435, 417.

30. Western Government Official A, interview by Tricia Bacon, Washington, DC,
28 April 2017.

31. Peter Dörrie, "Al-Shabab: A Close Look at East Africa's Deadliest Radicals", *World*

Politics Review, 19 August 2014: http://www.worldpoliticsreview.com/articles/14005/al-shabab-a-close-look-at-east-africa-s-deadliest-radicals; Stig Jarle Hansen, "An In-Depth Look at Al-Shabaab's Internal Division", *CTC Sentinel* 7, no. 2 (2014): p. 11.

32. "Shabaab Appoints New Leader After Death of Godane, Renews Pledge to Zawahiri," *Site Intelligence*, 6 September 2014: https://news-siteintelgroup-com. proxyau.wrlc.org/Jihadist-News/shabaab-appoints-new-leader-after-death-of-godane-renews-pledge-to-zawahiri.html; Thomas Jocelyn, "Shabaab names new emir, reaffirms allegiance to al Qaeda", *Long War Journal*, September 2014: http://www.longwarjournal.org/archives/2014/09/shabaab_names_new_em.php

33. For example, Al-Qaida has criticized Al-Shabaab's attacks as harming too many Muslims and questioned its target selection after the Al-Shabaab attack in Uganda in 2010.

34. 'Atiyah (Atiyah Abd al-Rahman), "Letter from 'Atiyah to Abu Basir", *Office of the Director of National Intelligence Bin Laden's Bookshelf*, 19 January 2017, p. 2: https://www.dni.gov/files/documents/ubl2017/english/Letter%20from%20 Atiyah%20to%20Abu%20Basir.pdf; "SOCOM-2012–0000016", *Countering Terrorism Center at West Point*, 3 May 2012, p. 2: https://www.ctc.usma.edu/posts/letters-from-abbottabad-bin-ladin-sidelined; UN Monitoring Group on Somalia and Eritrea, *Report of the Monitoring Group on Somalia and Eritrea pursuant to Security Council resolution 2244* (October 2016), p. 53; Western Government Analysts, interview by Tricia Bacon, Washington, DC, 13 December 2016; Western Diplomat based in Nairobi, interviewed by Tricia Bacon & Daisy Muibu, Nairobi, 12 January 2017; Private Security Firm Operating in Mogadishu A, interview by Tricia Bacon, Washington, DC, 26 April 2017; Western Government Official A, interview by Tricia Bacon, Washington, DC, 28 April 2017; Bryden, "The Reinvention of Al-Shabaab", p. 11; Ken Menkhaus, "Al-Shabaab's Capabilities Post-Westgate", *CTC Sentinel, Special Issue* 7, no. 2 (2014): p. 7; Congressional Research Service, "Terrorism and Violent Extremism in Africa", p. 7; Western Analyst Based in Nairobi, interview by Tricia Bacon & Daisy Muibu, Nairobi, 23 May 2017; Former UN official Based in Nairobi, interview by Tricia Bacon & Daisy Muibu, Nairobi, 22 May 2017; East African Journalist, interview by Tricia Bacon, Nairobi, 25 May 2017; Matthew J. Thomas, "Exposing and exploiting", p. 421.

35. Al-Shabaab has sometimes expressed public support for the other affiliates and received public statements of support from them as well. See for example: "AQIS Gives Eulogy for Former Shabaab Leader, Reminds that U.S. Must be Fought", *Site Intelligence*, 5 November 2014: https://news-siteintelgroup-com.proxyau. wrlc.org/Jihadist-News/aqis-gives-eulogy-for-former-shabaab-leader-reminds-that-u-s-must-be-fought.html; "Shabaab Mourns Scholars and Fighters Executed by Saudi Arabia, Applauds AQIM for Burkina Faso Attack", Site Intelligence,

24 January 2016: https://news-siteintelgroup-com.proxyau.wrlc.org/Jihadist-News/shabaab-mourns-scholars-and-fighters-executed-by-saudi-arabia-applauds-aqim-for-burkina-faso-attack.html

36. Western Government Analysts, interview by Tricia Bacon, Washington, DC, 13 December 2016.

37. Graham Turbiville, John Meservey and James Forest, "Countering the Al-Shabaab Insurgency in Somalia: Lessons for U.S. Special Operations Forces", *Joint Special Operations University Report* 14, no. 1 (February 2014): p. 54; UN Monitoring Group on Somalia and Eritrea, *Report of the Monitoring Group*, pp. 40, 51–53.

38. Hansen, *Al-Shabaab in Somalia*, p. 43.

39. Atiyah (Atiyah Abd al-Rahman), "Letter from 'Atiyah to Abu Basir", pp. 1–2.

40. Western Government Analyst B. interview by Tricia Bacon, Washington, DC, 2 May 2017. See for example: "AQAP Gives Condolences to Afghan Taliban, Shabaab for Death of Scholars", *Site Intelligence*, 9 November 2015: https://news-siteintelgroup-com.proxyau.wrlc.org/Jihadist-News/aqap-gives-condolences-to-afghan-taliban-shabaab-for-death-of-scholars.html; "AQAP Gives Eulogy for Deceased Shabaab Official Hassan Hersi", *Site Intelligence*, 9 June 2015: https://news-siteintelgroup-com.proxyau.wrlc.org/Jihadist-News/aqap-gives-eulogy-for-deceased-shabaab-official-hassan-hersi.html; "AQAP Official Nasser bin Ali al-Ansi Speaks on al-Qaeda's War with the U.S., Death of Shabaab Leader, Creation of AQIS", *Site Intelligence*, 7 November 2014: https://news-siteintelgroup-com.proxyau.wrlc.org/Jihadist-News/aqap-official-nasser-bin-ali-al-ansi-speaks-on-al-qaeda-s-war-with-the-u-s-death-of-shabaab-leader-creation-of-aqis.html

41. Western Government Official A. interview by Tricia Bacon, Washington, DC, 28 April 2017.

42. Hansen, *Al-Shabaab in Somalia*, p. 74; Federal Bureau of Investigation New York Office, "Guilty Plea Unsealed in New York Involving Ahmed Warsame, a Senior Terrorist Leader and Liaison Between al Shabaab and al Qaeda in the Arabian Peninsula, for Providing Material Support to Both Terrorist Organizations", 25 March 2013: https://archives.fbi.gov/archives/newyork/press-releases/2013/guilty-plea-unsealed-in-new-york-involving-ahmed-warsame-a-senior-terrorist-leader-and-liaison-between-Al-Shabaab-and-al-qaeda-in-the-arabian-peninsula-for-providing-material-support-to-both-terrorist-organizations

43. Private Security Firm Operating in Mogadishu A, interview by Tricia Bacon, Washington, DC, 26 April 2017; Rob Wise, "Al Shabaab", p. 8.

44. Hansen, *Al-Shabaab in Somalia*, pp. 121–4; Western Government Analyst B, interview by Tricia Bacon, Washington, DC, 2 May 2017; Abdirahman "Aynte" Ali, "Anatomy of Al-Shabaab", Unpublished Paper (July 2010), p. 5; "Al Shabaab Urges Muslims to Support Yemeni Qaeda", *Hiiraan Online*, 1 January 2010: https://www.hiiraan.com/news2/2010/jan/al_shabaab_urges_muslims_to_support_yemeni_qaeda.aspx; Martin Plaut, "Somalia and Yemen 'swapping militants'",

BBC, 17 January 2010: http://news.bbc.co.uk/2/hi/8463946.stm; Gabriel Koehler-Derrick, "A False Foundation? AQAP, Tribes and Ungoverned Spaces in Yemen", *Countering Terrorism Center at West Point* (September 2011), pp. 50–1.

45. "Letter about efforts in other regions", pp. 1–3; East African Defense Official, interview by Tricia Bacon & Daisy Muibu, Nairobi, 5 January 2017; Think Tank Analyst Based in Nairobi A, interview by Tricia Bacon & Daisy Muibu, Nairobi, 9 January 2017; AMISOM Official Based in Mogadishu, interview by Tricia Bacon, Mogadishu, 19 May 2017; UN Official Based in Mogadishu, interview by Tricia Bacon, Mogadishu, 18 May 2017.

46. David Shinn, "Neither Desperate Nor Stronger: The Adaptation of Al Shabaab", *E-International Relations* (July 2015): http://www.e-ir.info/2015/07/03/neither-desperate-nor-stronger-the-adaptation-of-Al-Shabaab/; Western academic, interview by Tricia Bacon & Daisy Muibu, Nairobi, 4 January 2017; Analyst Based in Nairobi, interview by Tricia Bacon & Daisy Muibu, Nairobi, 10 January 2017; Roland Marchal, *The Rise of a Jihadi Movement in a Country at War: Harakat Al-Shabaab al Mujaheddin in Somalia* (Paris: SciencesPo/CERI, 2011), pp. 67–69.

47. Nir Rosen, "Somalia's Al-Shabaab: A Global or Local Movement?" *Time*, 20 August 2010: http://content.time.com/time/world/article/0,8599,2010700,00.html; Turbiville, Meservey, and Forest, "Countering the Al-Shabaab Insurgency in Somalia", pp. 14–16.

48. See, for example, "Al-Qaeda Draws Awareness to Drought in Somalia, Urges Muslims to Provide Support", *Site Intelligence*, 26 March 2017: https://news-site-intelgroup-com.proxyau.wrlc.org/Jihadist-News/al-qaeda-draws-awareness-to-drought-in-somalia-urges-muslims-to-provide-support.html; "Call to Support the Shabaab-Vanguards of Khorasan, Issue 19", *Site Intelligence*, 16 September 2011: https://news-siteintelgroup-com.proxyau.wrlc.org/Jihadist-News/call-to-support-the-shabaab-qvanguards-of-khorasanq-issue-19.html

49. Stig Jarle Hansen, "The Islamic State is Losing in Africa", *Foreign Policy*, 13 December 2016; Western government official based in Nairobi, interview by Tricia Bacon, Nairobi, 16 May 2017.

50. Dörrie, "Al-Shabab"; Researcher with an NGO, interview by Tricia Bacon & Daisy Muibu, Nairobi, 24 May 2017; Western Government Official A. interview by Tricia Bacon, Washington, DC, 28 April 2017; Hansen, "An In-Depth Look at Al-Shabaab's Internal Divisions", pp. 9–10; Christopher Anzalone, "The Resilience of Al-Shabaab", *CTC Sentinel* 9:4 (2016), p. 13.

51. See for example, "Shabaab Calls for Lone-Wolf Attacks on Interests of Jews, Israel, Allies", *Site Intelligence*, 11 October 2015: https://news.siteintelgroup.com/Jihadist-News/shabaab-calls-for-lone-wolf-attacks-on-interests-of-jews-israel-allies.html; "Shabaab Gives Eulogy for Zawahiri's Deputy in Syria, Threatens Revenge", *Site Intelligence*, 6 March 2017: https://ent.siteintelgroup.com/Statements/shabaab-gives-eulogy-for-zawahiri-s-deputy-in-syria-threatens-revenge.html

52. Hansen, *Al-Shabaab in Somalia*, p. 72.

53. AMISOM Official Based in Mogadishu, interview by Tricia Bacon, Mogadishu, 19 May 2017; Western academic, interview by Tricia Bacon & Daisy Muibu, Nairobi, 4 January 2017.

54. Western Government Official A. interview by Tricia Bacon, Washington, DC, 28 April 2017; Western Analyst Based in Nairobi, interview by Tricia Bacon & Daisy Muibu, Nairobi, 23 May 2017.

55. Somali Analysts Based in Nairobi, interview by Tricia Bacon, Nairobi, 25 May 2017.

56. Think Tank Analyst Based in Nairobi A, interview by Tricia Bacon & Daisy Muibu, Nairobi, 9 January 2017; Think Tank Analyst Based in Nairobi B, interview by Tricia Bacon & Daisy Muibu, Nairobi, 12 January 2017; UN Monitoring Group on Somalia and Eritrea, *Report of the Monitoring Group*, p. 52; Somali Analyst Based in Mogadishu, interview by Tricia Bacon, Mogadishu, 16 May 2017; UN Official Based on Mogadishu, interview by Tricia Bacon, Mogadishu, 18 May 2017; Western Analyst Based in Nairobi, interview by Tricia Bacon & Daisy Muibu, Nairobi, 23 May 2017.

57. Dan Milton and Muhammad al-'Ubayd, "Pledging Baya'a: A Benefit or a Burden?" *CTC Sentinel* 8, no. 3 (March 2015): p. 3.

58. Of note, Al-Qaida's leaders have sworn *bayah* to the Afghan Taliban's leaders.

59. Think Tank Analyst Based in Nairobi B, interview by Tricia Bacon & Daisy Muibu, Nairobi, 12 January 2017.

60. Milton and al-'Ubayd, "Pledging Baya'a", p. 3; J. M. Berger, "The Islamic State vs. al Qaeda: Who's winning the war to become the jihadi superpower?" *Foreign Policy*, 2 September 2014.

61. Hansen, "The Islamic State is Losing in Africa"; East African Defense Official, interview by Tricia Bacon & Daisy Muibu, Nairobi, 5 January 2017; Western Government Official A. interview by Tricia Bacon, Washington, DC, 28 April 2017; Intergovernmental Authority on Development (IGAD), *Al-Shabaab as a Transnational Security Threat* (IGAD Security Sector Program and Sahan Foundation, 2016), p. 11; East African Journalist, interview by Tricia Bacon, Nairobi, 25 May 2017.

62. Former Western diplomat, interview by Tricia Bacon, Washington, DC, 30 December 2016.

63. Leah Farrall, "Will Al-Qaida and Al-Shabaab Formally Merge?", *CTC Sentinel* 4:73 (July 2011): pp. 10–12.

64. East African Defense Official, interview by Tricia Bacon & Daisy Muibu, Nairobi, 5 January 2017.

65. Ibid.

66. IGAD, *Al-Shabaab as a Transnational Security Threat*, pp. 12–13; Western government official based in Nairobi, interview by Tricia Bacon, Nairobi, 16 May

2017; Somali Analyst Based in Mogadishu, interview by Tricia Bacon, Mogadishu, 16 May 2017, Private Security Firm Operating in Mogadishu B, interview by Tricia Bacon, Mogadishu, 18 May 2017; East African Defense Official, interview by Tricia Bacon & Daisy Muibu, Nairobi, 5 January 2017; Former UN official Based in Nairobi, interview by Tricia Bacon & Daisy Muibu, Nairobi, 22 May 2017; Roland Marchal, "Book Review: Al-Shabaab in Somalia: The History and Ideology of a Militant Islamist Group", *The Journal of Modern African Studies* (Sep 2014): pp. 502–3.

67. IGAD, *Al-Shabaab as a Transnational Security Threat*, p. 12; East African Defense Official, interview by Tricia Bacon & Daisy Muibu, Nairobi, 5 January 2017; Somali Analysts Based in Nairobi, interview by Tricia Bacon, Nairobi, 25 May 2017.

68. UN Official Based in Nairobi B; International Crisis Group, "Somalia: Al-Shabaab", pp. 10–11; Western Government Analyst, interview by Tricia Bacon, Washington, DC, 20 December 2016.

69. UN Official Based on Mogadishu, interview by Tricia Bacon, Mogadishu, 18 May 2017; AMISOM Official Based in Mogadishu, interview by Tricia Bacon, Mogadishu, 19 May 2017.

70. Western Aid Official, interview by Tricia Bacon, Nairobi, 12 May 2017; UN Official Based in Mogadishu, interview by Tricia Bacon, Mogadishu, 18 May 2017; Western Analyst Based in Nairobi, interview by Tricia Bacon & Daisy Muibu, Nairobi, 23 May 2017; Researcher with an NGO, interview by Tricia Bacon & Daisy Muibu, Nairobi, 24 May 2017.

71. "IS Condemns Shabaab for Murdering Sudanese Killer of U.S. Diplomat in Naba 33", *Site Intelligence*, 3 June 2016: https://news-siteintelgroup-com.proxyau.wrlc. org/Jihadist-News/is-condemns-shabaab-for-murdering-sudanese-killer-of-u-s-diplomat-in-naba-33.html; "IS Gives Biography of Slain Shabaab Defector Hussein Abdi Gidi in al-Naba", *Site Intelligence*, 18 May 2016: https://news-siteintelgroup-com.proxyau.wrlc.org/Jihadist-News/is-gives-biography-of-slain-shabaab-defec-tor-hussein-abdi-gidi-in-al-naba.html; "IS Reports on Circumstances of Shabaab Defector's Assassination, Engaging Shi'ites in War of Attrition in al-Naba Newspaper", *Site Intelligence*, 28 April 2016: https://news-siteintelgroup-com. proxyau.wrlc.org/Jihadist-News/is-reports-on-circumstances-of-shabaab-defec-tor-s-assassination-engaging-shi-ites-in-war-of-attrition-in-al-naba-newspaper. html; "Shabaab Defector to IS Abdul Qadr Mu'min Condemns Shabaab's Pursuit, Killing of Pledgers", *Site Intelligence*, 12 December 2015: https://news-siteintel-group-com.proxyau.wrlc.org/Jihadist-News/shabaab-defector-to-is-abdul-qadr-mu-min-condemns-shabaab-s-pursuit-killing-of-pledgers.html

72. Asal et al., "With Friends Like These ... Why Terrorist Organizations Ally", pp. 10–11, 21–22.

73. Gary Ackerman and Jeffrey Bale, "Where the Extremes May Touch: Islamist

Networks, Extremism, and Terrorism", Unpublished Paper, University of Maryland (2010): p. 22.

74. Tricia Bacon, "Hurdles to International Terrorist Alliances: Lessons From Al Qaeda's Experience", *Terrorism and Political Violence* 29, no. 1 (2017): pp. 79–101.

75. Al-Qaida even trusted Al-Shabaab sufficiently to consider sending one of its operatives planning for attacks in the West (Sheikh Yunis)—its highest priority activity—to Somalia. See Mahmud (Atiyah Abd al-Rahman), "Letter dtd 5 April 2011", p. 4.

76. See Azmarai (Usama bin Laden), "Letter dtd 07 August 2010", for an example of Al-Qaida's critiques of Al-Shabaab's targets. The US publicized intercepted communications between Al-Qaida and Al-Qaida in Iraq that revealed their strife. See Ayman al-Zawahiri, "Zawahiri's Letter to Zarqawi," *Combating Terrorism Center at West Point*, October 2005: https://www.ctc.usma.edu/posts/zawahiris-letter-to-zarqawi-english-translation-2; Atiyah Abd al-Rahman, "'Atiyah's Letter to Zarqawi", *Combating Terrorism Center at West Point*, October 2006: https://www.ctc.usma.edu/posts/atiyahs-letter-to-zarqawi-english-transcatlation-2

AL-SHABAAB AS A TRANSNATIONAL SECURITY THREAT

1. In 2010 the group staged its first major external operation, in Kampala, Uganda, and issued its first propaganda video in the Swahili language.

2. Djibouti, Ethiopia, Kenya, Somalia, Uganda, and Tanzania. Of these, only Tanzania has not been targeted, while an attempted suicide attack in Ethiopia ended when the bombers accidentally blew themselves up without causing any other casualties.

3. In August 2015, the Federal Government of Somalia expressed an interest in joining this initiative.

4. Titled traditional leader.

5. Religiously-mandated taxation.

6. In Lower Jubba, for example, Awrmale pastoralists presented armed resistance to Al-Shabaab attempts to tax their herds, leading to an armed conflict involving Jubbaland authorities. Ultimately, some elements of the community decided that they had no choice but to pledge allegiance to Al-Shabaab. Similarly, in South West State (SWS), the local Al-Shabaab commander raised taxes on local herders, leading to conflict. In this instance Al-Shabaab was forced to enter into reconciliation talks with the herders and return the animals that they had confiscated.

7. Despite the fact that over half of the IED attacks in 2016 targeted AMISOM and SNA security forces, more civilians were killed and wounded by IEDs than members of AMISOM and the SNA combined. According to available figures, civilians constituted 40% of the IED-related deaths—compared to 22% from AMISOM and 15% from SNA—and 55% of all IED-related injuries: more than the 21% from SNA and 15% from AMISOM combined. These figures clearly illustrate that

civilians have borne the brunt of Al-Shabaab's use of IEDs within Somalia during the course of the 2016 calendar year.

8. Figures include victims of complex attacks in which IEDs were used, regardless of whether death/injury was the direct result of the blast.

9. Close to 50 per cent of the total IED-related deaths in Somalia in 2016 occurred in attacks in Mogadishu, with 54 per cent of IED-related injuries taking place within the capital as well.

10. DFCs have been recovered from Afmadow, Middle Jubba (28 March 2016); Bussar, Gedo (23 June 2016); and in Mogadishu (28 June 2016).

11. While a sedan car or minivan could carry approximately 100–200 kg of explosives, a truck can transport up to several tons of material depending on the model. The large SVBIED used against Peace Hotel on 2 January 2017 held the blast equivalent of at least 500 kilos of explosives.

12. Major IED attacks in 2016 included a complex operation involving both VBIEDs and suicide gunmen against the Beach View Hotel in January 2016,[12] a similar attack on the Naaso Hablood Hotel in June 2016,[12] and a large VBIED attack against the Somali Youth League Hotel in August 2016.

13. Such ambushes generally involve the use of one or more IEDs to stop the convoy, in combination with infantry using small arms and rocket-propelled grenades to cause as much damage as possible within the chosen "kill zone".

14. The availability of TNT extracted from munitions has decreased in Mogadishu, but it remains available to Al-Shabaab from Siad Barre-era regime ammunition stores and from attacks on SNA and AMISOM bases.

15. The main importers of fertilizer into Mogadishu bring in over 320 tons a month from each of Kenya, India, and the UAE.

16. In a video message recorded by one of the suicide bombers who attacked Kampala in July that year, "Salman Al-Muhajir" warns his audience that Al-Shabaab includes fighters from across the region who know their own countries' vulnerabilities intimately. See undated video message entitled "Final Message of the Kampala Attack Warrior".

17. Available evidence strongly indicates that Jaysh Ayman largely consists of Swahili-speaking East Africans, notably from Kenya, Tanzania, and Uganda. In 2015, Al-Shabaab released a series of videos featuring members of its Jaysh Ayman force. In one video, it claimed a Somali fighter, Abdifataah Hersi "Umar" Nadheer had been killed in an attack in on the coast of Kenya. Abdifataah was from the Majerteen clan and born and raised in Bossaso, Puntland. See also: http://www.mirror.co.uk/news/world-news/thomas-evans-horrifying-footage-shows-5942555

18. Especially following Operation Linda Boni launched in September 2015.

19. The Kenyan authorities have closely monitored suspected Jaysh Ayman sympathizers in Malindi and Mombasa. One of Kenya's most wanted terrorist suspects, Mohammed Juma Mwamuraji, was killed during a confrontation with police in

Msambweni, Kwale county, on 26 February 2017. See "Anti-Terror Detectives Gun Down An Al-Shabaab Returnee, Recover Grenade In Kwale", SIS, 27 February 2017: http://intelligencebriefs.com/anti-terror-detectives-gun-down-an-al-sha-baab-returnee-recover-grenade-in-kwale/ (accessed 30 March 2017). It is unknown if Mwamuraji had been directed to return to Kenya to carry out an attack or if he aspired to do so independently of Al-Shabaab.

20. Kunow (aka Ga'amadheere), who hailed from Garissa, was most notorious for his alleged role as the mastermind of the attack on a university in Garissa in 2015 that killed almost 150. See "Garissa university attack plotter Mohamed Kuno 'dead'", BBC News, 1 June 2016: http://www.bbc.com/news/world-africa-36427289 (accessed 29 March 2017).

21. In one of the boldest cross-border attacks of 2016, Al-Shabaab operatives attacked Hamey Police Station in Garissa Country on 22 September 2016, killing six offi-cers and returning to Somalia with over a thousand rounds of ammunition, as well as a police vehicle and an unknown number of uniforms. See "Two policemen still missing after Al-Shabaab gunmen attacked Hamey police post", Standard Digital, 26 September 2016: https://www.standardmedia.co.ke/article/2000217299/two-policemen-still-missing-after-al-shabaab-gunmen-attacked-hamey-police-post (accessed 29 March 2017). A similar attack took place on a Kenyan police base in Arabia, Mandera County, during the night of 1 February 2017, when Al-Shabaab captured a police land cruiser and a motorcycle along with weapons, ammunition, and uniforms. See "Militants raid Kenyan police camp in Mandera", Africa Review, 2 February 2017: http://www.africareview.com/news/Militants-raid-Kenyan-police-camp-Mandera/979180–3796694–118ulqjz/ (accessed 29March 2017).

22. The seizure of Kenya police equipment, vehicles, and uniforms potentially aug-ments the group's ability to infiltrate targets in northern Kenya, disguised as secu-rity officials. Arms and ammunition seizures also provide the group with new weapons and possibly explosive materials needed for IED construction.

23. On 6 October 2016 Al-Shabaab attacked a residential compound known as the Jalane Hotel in Mandera County, Kenya, just a few kilometres from the Somali border. See "Al-Shabaab attack: Six dead in Kenya after militants strike at residen-tial area in Mandera", *The Telegraph*, 6 October 2016: http://www.telegraph.co.uk/news/2016/10/06/al-shabaab-attack-six-dead-in-kenya-after-militants-strike-at-re/; later that month, on 25 October 2016, Al-Shabaab attacked the Bishaaro Guest House in Mandera town, killing over a dozen and wounding many more. See "Al Shabaab launch three attacks in Kenya, France24, Somalia", 25 October 2016: http://www.france24.com/en/20161025-kenya-somalia-shabaab-attacks (accessed 29 March 2017).

24. Aimed at interrupting mobile phone service in and around areas where Al-Shabaab operates—especially during periods when raids are planned.

25. Some of the group's most serious losses include Musa Osodo, the group's former

Nairobi "Amir", key operatives Jeremiah Okumu, Steven Mwanzi Osaka, and Aboud Rogo, the latter designated by the UNSC in 2012 for his role as Al-Hijra's ideological leader and a key supporter of Al-Shabaab. Yet arguably the most damaging loss to Al-Hijra was the shooting of Abubakar Shariff Ahmed "Makaburi" a.k.a. "Buda" by unidentified gunmen in a Mombasa street in 2014. Makaburi was both an ideologue and an operational leader, whose influence extended beyond Al-Hijra to members of the "Ansar movement" in Tanga, Tanzania (Ansar Muslim Youth Centre) and to remnants of Al-Qaeda's East Africa (AQEA).

26. Especially the Rift Valley (mainly Eldoret, Naivasha, and Nakuru) and Western Kenya.

27. Evidence pointing to the increased use of prisons to recruit for Al-Shabaab-related activities has been found.

28. Evidence obtained by the Kenyan authorities in 2015 identified two recruiting cells who had together enlisted at least 30 potential recruits aspiring to join ISIS.

29. Historically, members of the Ansar Muslim Youth Centres in Tanzania have been operationally linked to other affiliates like Al-Hijra. While during the current reporting period, there have been publicized cases of an "Al-Shabaab-linked group" in Tanzania, credibility of this information has not yet been fully assessed.

30. Electronic surveillance conducted by a government agency of members of an Al-Hijra cell between February and August 2015.

31. Observations of the network suggest it has procured explosives and small arms for Al-Hijra for a fee. This is also apparent from the network's criminal background and access to the fishing and mining sectors across Tanzania, according to a former Al-Hijra operative with direct links to the organization.

32. http://english.alarabiya.net/en/News/africa/2014/03/11/Al-Shabaab-leader-urges-Somalis-to-battle-old-enemy-Ethiopia.html

33. A member of the Darood / Ogaden / Reer Isaaq / Reer Haarun clan.

34. Including figures such as Ahmed Nuur Sheikh Mohamed Muhumed (a.k.a. "Sandheere" a.k.a. "Ukaash") or Yusuf Deeq (a.k.a. Ismaa'il).

35. One from Somaliland via Tog Wajaale, one from Somaliland via Dhegahbur, and one from Kismayo and Bardheere via Dolow.

36. See: http://www.coastweek.com/3834-AMISOM-and-Somali-troops-welcomed-after-liberating-Diinsoor.htm

37. NSP NGO Safety Programme, "Daily Security Report", 21 July 2015.

38. See: http://amisom-au.org/kenya-kdf/

39. See: http://www.hiiraan.com/news4/2012/July/24886/kdf_troops_formally_join_amisom.aspx

40. Interview with KFD officials, October 2015.

41. See: http://www.ibtimes.com/possible-al-shabab-attack-foiled-kenya-authorities-arrest-terrorist-suspects-garissa-2064592

42. See: http://www.the-star.co.ke:8080/news/security-chiefs-launch-operation-linda-boni-forest-flush-out-al-shabaab

43. See: http://www.intelligencebriefs.com/kenyan-security-forces-arrest-4-al-shabaab-suspects-in-dadaab-seize-weapons/

FOREIGN FIGHTER INFLUENCE IN AL-SHABAAB: LIMITATIONS AND FUTURE PROSPECTS

1. In addition, some foreign fighters in Somalia reportedly opted to return home during the Arab Spring uprisings.

2. For foreign fighter motivations, see, for example, the works of Daniel Byman and Jeremy Shapiro, *Be Afraid, Be a Little Afraid: The Threat of Terrorism from Western Foreign Fighters in Syria and Iraq* (Foreign Policy at Brookings, 2014), pp. 12–13; Kylie Baxter and Renee Davidson, "Foreign Terrorist Fighters: Managing a twenty-first century threat", *Third World Quarterly* 37:8 (2016): p. 1301; Norma Costello, "What draws foreign fighters to Iraq and Syria?" *Al Jazeera*, 27 July 2016: http://www.aljazeera.com/news/2016/07/draws-foreign-fighters-iraq-syria-160718104739660.html; For the threat posed by returnees see Matt Bryden, *The Reinvention of Al-Shabaab: A Strategy of Choice or Necessity?* (Center for Strategic & International Studies Africa Program, 2014); Jeanine de Roy Zuijdewijn and Edwin Bakker, *Returning Western Foreign Fighters: The Case of Afghanistan, Bosnia and Somalia* (Hague: International Centre for Counter-Terrorism, 2014).

3. See, for example, Sudarsan Raghavan, "Foreign fighters gain influence in Somalia's Islamist al-Shabab militia", *Washington Post*, 8 June 2010: http://www.washingtonpost.com/wp-dyn/content/article/2010/06/07/AR2010060704667.html

4. "Somalia: The Forgotten Story", *Al Jazeera*, 2 November 2016: http://www.aljazeera.com/programmes/aljazeeraworld/2016/10/somalia-forgotten-story-161027115655140.html

5. Thomas Hegghammer, "The Rise of Muslim Foreign Fighters: Islam and the Globalization of Jihad", *International Security*, 35:3 (2011): pp. 57–58.

6. Of note, we are primarily focused on foreign fighters operating as part of Al-Shabaab in Somalia. By definition, if these individuals operate in their home country or return home, they are no longer foreign fighters. For an excellent discussion of Al-Shabaab's efforts to create affiliates in Kenya and Ethiopia, see Intergovernmental Authority on Development (IGAD), *Al-Shabaab as a Transnational Security Threat* (IGAD Security Sector Program and Sahan Foundation, 2016).

7. Barak Mendelsohn, "Foreign Fighters—Recent Trends", *Orbis* 55:2 (2011): p. 194.

8. Roland Marchal, *The Rise of a Jihadi Movement in a Country at War: Harakat Al-Shabaab al Mujaheddin in Somalia* (SciencesPo/CERI, 2011), p. 56; AMISOM Official Based in Mogadishu, interview by Tricia Bacon, Mogadishu, 19 May 2017; UN Official Based on Mogadishu, interview by Tricia Bacon, Mogadishu, 18 May 2017; Western Analyst Based in Nairobi, interview by Tricia Bacon & Daisy Muibu,

Nairobi, 23 May 2017; David Shinn, "Al Shabaab's Foreign Threat to Somalia", *Orbis* 55:2 (2011): p. 211.

9. A number of the interviewees preferred not to be named specifically in the paper because of the sensitivity of this issue; therefore, we have used descriptions for all of interviewees to preserve anonymity.

10. Marchal, *The Rise of a Jihadi Movement in a Country at War*, p. 16.

11. "Wareysi Qaybtii 2aad: Sheekh Cali Dheere—Interview Part 2: Sheekh Cali Dheere", *Dalsoor*, 10 January 2017, YouTube: https://www.youtube.com/watch? v=S9OjzeTw66s&feature=youtu.be; American Enterprise Institute Editors, "Al Shabaab Leadership Profiles", 2011: https://www.aei.org/publication/Al-Shabaab-leadership-profiles/; AMISOM Official Based in Mogadishu, interview by Tricia Bacon via Skype, 13 January 2017.

12. Stig Jarle Hansen, *Al-Shabaab in Somalia: The History and Ideology of a Militant Islamist Group* (New York: Oxford University Press, 2016), p. 135. Al-Shabaab's members are accused of looking down on East Africans, despite the group's efforts to portray itself as overcoming such xenophobic tendencies. Think Tank Analyst Based in Nairobi B, interview by Tricia Bacon & Daisy Muibu, Nairobi, 12 January 2017.

13. They frame the conflict as one between Islam and the West. See David Malet, "Why Foreign Fighters? Historical Perspectives and Solutions", *Orbis* 54:1 (2010): pp. 97–114. Of note, some foreign fighters were attracted to Somalia because of the Islamic Courts Union, prior to the clear emergence of Al-Shabaab. See Hansen, *Al-Shabaab in Somalia*, pp. 42–4.

14. Marchal, *The Rise of a Jihadi Movement in a Country at War*, p. 8; Think Tank Analyst Based in Nairobi B, interview by Tricia Bacon & Daisy Muibu, Nairobi, 12 January 2017; AMISOM Official Based in Mogadishu, interview by Tricia Bacon via Skype, 13 January 2017.

15. Kristen Bakke, "Help Wanted? The Mixed Record of Foreign Fighters in Domestic Insurgencies," *International Security* 38:4 (2014): pp. 150–152. Of note is that this influence can either strengthen or weaken the indigenous group, depending on how well foreign fighters' introductions accord with the local environment.

16. IGAD, *Al-Shabaab as a Transnational Security Threat*, p. 12. On 23 May, the Islamic State-aligned group in Puntland conducted its first suicide operation, striking at a security checkpoint in Bosaso and killing five. The Islamic State declared responsibility for the attack and several prior actions by the group in Puntland through its official outlet, *Amaq News Agency*, which signals that the two groups are cooperating. However, the Islamic State has not recognized the group in Puntland as a *wilayat*, or province, i.e. the official representative of the Islamic State in Somalia. See Caleb Weiss, "Islamic State claims suicide bombing in Somalia", *Long War Journal*, 25 May 2017: http://www.longwarjournal.org/archives/2017/05/islamic-state-claims-suicide-bombing-in-somalia.php; Conor Gaffey,

"ISIS Claims Somali Suicide Attack as it Vies with Al-Shabaab for Recognition", *Newsweek*, 24 May 2017: http://www.newsweek.com/isis-somalia-Al-Shabaab-suicide-bombing-614666

17. UN Official Based in Nairobi B, interview by Tricia Bacon, Nairobi, 11 May 2017; Western Government Official A. interview by Tricia Bacon, Washington, DC, 28 April 2017; "IS Condemns Shabaab for Murdering Sudanese Killer of U.S. Diplomat in Naba 33", *Site Intelligence Group*, 3 June 2016: https://news-siteintelgroup-com.proxyau.wrlc.org/Jihadist-News/is-condemns-shabaab-for-murdering-sudanese-killer-of-u-s-diplomat-in-naba-33.html; "IS Gives Biography of Slain Shabaab Defector Hussein Abdi Gidi in al-Naba", *Site Intelligence Group*, 18 May 2016: https://news-siteintelgroup-com.proxyau.wrlc.org/Jihadist-News/is-gives-biography-of-slain-shabaab-defector-hussein-abdi-gidi-in-al-naba.html; "IS Reports on Circumstances of Shabaab Defector's Assassination, Engaging Shi'ites in War of Attrition in al-Naba Newspaper", *Site Intelligence Group*, 28 April 2016: https://news-siteintelgroup-com.proxyau.wrlc.org/Jihadist-News/is-reports-on-circumstances-of-shabaab-defector-s-assassination-engaging-shi-ites-in-war-of-attrition-in-al-naba-newspaper.html

18. Somali Civil Society Activists Based in Nairobi, interview by Tricia Bacon, Nairobi, 12 May 2017; Western Government Official A, interview by Tricia Bacon, Washington, DC, 28 April 2017; Ken Menkhaus, "Al-Shabaab's Capabilities Post-Westgate", *CTC Sentinel, Special Issue* 7:2 (2014): p. 7; IGAD, *Al-Shabaab as a Transnational Security Threat*, p. 21–3; Shinn, "Al Shabaab's Foreign Threat to Somalia", p. 210; East African Journalist, interview by Tricia Bacon, Nairobi, 25 May 2017. The estimates of the number of East African foreign fighters provided to the authors range significantly, from dozens to thousands.

19. Researcher with an NGO, interview by Tricia Bacon & Daisy Muibu, Nairobi, 24 May 2017; Think Tank Analyst Based in Nairobi A, interview by Tricia Bacon & Daisy Muibu, Nairobi, 9 January 2017.

20. See for example Maimuna Shinn Mohamud, "Somalia-Yemen links: refugees and returnees", *Forced Migration Review* (May 2016): pp. 55–6; Theodore Karasik, "Historical Links between the Arabian Peninsula and Somali Peninsula: A Regional Response Based on Partnership" (paper presented at UAE Counter-Piracy Conference, Dubai, June 2012); Graham Turbiville, Josh Meservey, and James Forest, "Countering the Al-Shabaab Insurgency in Somalia: Lessons for U.S. Special Operations Forces", *Joint Special Operations University Report* 14–1 (February 2014): p. 54.

21. AMISOM Official Based in Mogadishu, interview by Tricia Bacon, Mogadishu, 19 May 2017; UN Official Based in Mogadishu, interview by Tricia Bacon, Mogadishu, 18 May 2017.

22. Hansen, *Al-Shabaab in Somalia*, p. 63. This is a reference to Al-Qaida in Iraq's deceased leader Abu Musab al-Zarqawi. Of note, Al-Qaida leaders expressed res-

ervations to Zarqawi about a foreigner taking on such a visible leadership role in Iraq, because they feared it would alienate local Iraqis. See Ayman al-Zawahiri, "Zawahiri's letter to Zarqawi", *Countering Terrorism Center at West Point*, October 2005: https://www.ctc.usma.edu/v2/wp-content/uploads/2013/10/Zawahiris-Letter-to-Zarqawi-Translation.pdf

23. Western Government Analysts, interview by Tricia Bacon, Washington, DC, 13 December 2016.

24. Somali Analyst Based in Mogadishu, interview by Tricia Bacon, Mogadishu, 16 May 2017; Western Analyst Based in Nairobi, interview by Tricia Bacon & Daisy Muibu, Nairobi, 23 May 2017; Western Government Analyst, interview by Tricia Bacon, Washington, DC, 20 December 2016. This stands in contrast to the 2006–11 timeframe, during which the 85-member executive council of Al-Shabaab reportedly consisted of 42 Somalis and 43 foreigners. See Shinn, "Al Shabaab's Foreign Threat to Somalia", p. 209.

25. Think Tank Analyst Based in Nairobi B, interview by Tricia Bacon & Daisy Muibu, Nairobi, 12 January 2017.

26. Former Western diplomat, interview by Tricia Bacon, Washington, DC, 20 December 2016.

27. Think Tank Analyst Based in Nairobi B, interview by Tricia Bacon & Daisy Muibu, Nairobi, 12 January 2017. Hansen, *Al-Shabaab in Somalia*, pp. 28, 39–40, 55.

28. Hansen, *Al-Shabaab in Somalia*, 43.

29. Counterterrorism pressure targeted and eliminated a number of the more influential and capable foreign fighters, including some of the East African Al-Qaida operatives.

30. Bryden, *The Reinvention of Al-Shabaab*, p. 5; "Somalia: Open Letter to Al-Shabaab Leader Reveals—'Yes, There Are Problems'", *Hiiraan Online*, 1 May 2013: http://www.hiiraan.com/news4/2013/May/29139/somalia_open_letter_to_al_shabaab_leader_reveals_yes_there_are_problems.aspx; Stig Jarle Hansen, "An In-Depth Look at Al-Shabaab's Internal Divisions" *CTC Sentinel, Special Issue* 7:2 (2014): p. 10; Rashid Nuune, "Al Qaeda, Al-Shabaab Pledge Allegiance…Again", *Somalia Report*, 9 February 2012: http://piracyreport.com/index.php/post/2749/Al_Qaeda_Al-Shaabab_Pledge_AllegianceAgain; Abdulkador Khalif, "Al-Shabaab foreign fighters flee Somalia", *Daily Nation*, 24 February 2012, http://www.nation.co.ke/news/Al-Shabaab-foreign-fighters-flee-Somalia-/1056-1334572-sibysbz/index.html; Menkhaus, "Al-Shabaab's Capabilities Post-Westgate", p. 5.

31. Researcher with an NGO, interview by Tricia Bacon & Daisy Muibu, Nairobi, 24 May 2017; Western Analyst Based in Nairobi, interview by Tricia Bacon & Daisy Muibu, Nairobi, 23 May 2017; Menkhaus, "Al-Shabaab's Capabilities Post-Westgate", p. 20; Anneli Botha and Mahdi Abdile, "Radicalisation and Al-Shabaab Recruitment in Somalia", *Institute for Security Studies* (ISS Paper 266: September 2014): pp. 13, 16; Hansen, *Al-Shabaab in Somalia*, p. 126; Private Security Firm

Operating in Mogadishu A, interview by Tricia Bacon, Washington, DC, 26 April 2017.

32. Researcher with an NGO, interview by Tricia Bacon & Daisy Muibu, Nairobi, 24 May 2017; Western Analyst Based in Nairobi, interview by Tricia Bacon & Daisy Muibu, 23 May 2017; Think Tank Analyst Based in Nairobi C, interview by Tricia Bacon and Daisy Muibu, Nairobi, 12 January 2017; AMISOM Official Based in Mogadishu, interview by Tricia Bacon via Skype, 13 January 2017; Hansen, *Al-Shabaab in Somalia*, p. 128.

33. Think Tank Analyst Based in Nairobi B, interview by Tricia Bacon & Daisy Muibu, Nairobi, 12 January 2017; AMISOM Official Based in Mogadishu, interview by Tricia Bacon via Skype, 13 January 2017; Somali Analyst Based in Mogadishu, interview by Tricia Bacon, Mogadishu, 16 May 2017; UN Official Based in Mogadishu, interview by Tricia Bacon, Mogadishu, 18 May 2017.

34. IGAD, *Al-Shabaab as a Transnational Security Threat*, p. 15.

35. Marchal, *The Rise of a Jihadi Movement in a Country at War*, pp. 54–56; Western government official based in Nairobi, interview by Tricia Bacon, Nairobi, 16 May 2017; Hansen, *Al-Shabaab in Somalia*, pp. 44, 55; Western Government Official B, interview by Tricia Bacon, Washington, DC, April 2017; Analyst Based in Nairobi, interview by Tricia Bacon and Daisy Muibu, Nairobi, 10 January 2017; Shinn, "Al Shabaab's Foreign Threat to Somalia", p. 210.

36. Marchal, *The Rise of a Jihadi Movement in a Country at War*, p. 54.

37. Think Tank Analyst Based in Nairobi B, interview by Tricia Bacon & Daisy Muibu, Nairobi, 12 January 2017, Analyst Based in Nairobi, interview by Tricia Bacon and Daisy Muibu, Nairobi, 10 January 2017.

38. Western Government Analyst B, interview by Tricia Bacon, Washington, DC, 2 May 2017.

39. Private Security Firm Operating in Mogadishu B, interview by Tricia Bacon, Mogadishu, 18 May 2017.

40. Mark Hosenball, "Suspect tied to African, Yemen militants pleads guilty to U.S. charges," *Reuters*, 25 March 2013: http://www.reuters.com/article/us-usa-somalia-militant-idUSBRE92O0RF20130325; UN Monitoring Group on Somalia and Eritrea, *Report of the Monitoring Group on Somalia and Eritrea pursuant to Security Council Resolution 2244* (October 2016): pp. 53, 202; AMISOM Official Based in Mogadishu, interview by Tricia Bacon, Mogadishu, 19 May 2017; Western Government Official based in Nairobi, interview by Tricia Bacon, Nairobi, 16 May 2017; Western Government Analyst B. interview by Tricia Bacon, Washington, DC, 2 May 2017; Think Tank Analyst Based in Nairobi C, interview by Tricia Bacon and Daisy Muibu, Nairobi, 12 January 2017.

41. UN Monitoring Group on Somalia and Eritrea, *Report of the Monitoring Group*, p. 203; Western Government Analyst B, interview by Tricia Bacon, Washington, DC, 2 May 2017; Private Security Firm Operating in Mogadishu A, interview by Tricia Bacon, Washington, DC, 26 April 2017.

42. Western Government Official A, interview by Tricia Bacon, Washington, DC, 28 April 2017: Think Tank Analyst Based in Nairobi A, interview by Tricia Bacon & Daisy Muibu, Nairobi, 9 January 2017; Marchal, *The Rise of a Jihadi Movement in a Country at War*, p. 22.

43. Think Tank Analyst Based in Nairobi A, interview by Tricia Bacon & Daisy Muibu, Nairobi, 9 January 2017; UN Monitoring Group on Somalia and Eritrea, *Report of the Monitoring Group*, p. 203.

44. Western Government Analyst, interview by Tricia Bacon, Washington, DC, 20 December 2016; Think Tank Analyst Based in Nairobi B, interview by Tricia Bacon & Daisy Muibu, Nairobi, 12 January 2017; Researcher with an NGO, interview by Tricia Bacon & Daisy Muibu, Nairobi, 24 May 2017.

45. UN Official Based in Mogadishu, interview by Tricia Bacon, Mogadishu, 18 May 2017.

46. Hansen, *Al-Shabaab in Somalia*, p. 129; Christopher Anzalone, "Kenya's Muslim Youth Center and Al-Shabaab's East African Recruitment," *CTC Sentinel* 5:10 (2012), p. 10; AMISOM Official Based in Mogadishu, interview by Tricia Bacon, Mogadishu, 19 May 2017; Think Tank Analyst Based in Nairobi A, interview by Tricia Bacon & Daisy Muibu, Nairobi, 9 January 2017.

47. Think Tank Analyst Based in Nairobi A, interview by Tricia Bacon & Daisy Muibu, Nairobi, 9 January 2017; Christopher Anzalone, "The Resilience of Al-Shabaab," *CTC Sentinel* 9:4 (2016): p. 15. See for example: "Shabaab Official Calls Muslims to Immigrate to Somalia for Jihad in Video", *Site Intelligence Group*, 7 August 2015: https://news-siteintelgroup-com.proxyau.wrlc.org/Jihadist-News/shabaab-official-calls-muslims-to-immigrate-to-somalia-for-jihad-in-video.html; "Female Jihadist Releases Second Issue of Swahili Magazine for Women", *Site Intelligence Group*, 29 October 2015: https://news-siteintelgroup-com.proxyau.wrlc.org/Jihadist-News/female-jihadist-releases-second-issue-of-swahili-magazine-for-women.html; "Shabaab Supporters Release 'Special Edition' of Gaidi Mtaani Magazine Featuring Last Speech of Former Shabaab Leader", *Site Intelligence Group*, 24 November 2014: https://news-siteintelgroup-com.proxyau.wrlc.org/Jihadist-News/shabaab-supporters-release-special-edition-of-gaidi-mtaani-magazine-featuring-last-speech-of-former-shabaab-leader.html

48. IGAD, *Al-Shabaab as a Transnational Security Threat*, p. 20; East African Journalist, interview by Tricia Bacon, Nairobi, 25 May 2017.

49. Anzalone, "The Resilience of Al-Shabaab", p. 15.

50. Western Government Analysts, interview by Tricia Bacon, Washington, DC, 13 December 2016.

51. Think Tank Analyst Based in Nairobi A, interview by Tricia Bacon & Daisy Muibu, Nairobi, 9 January 2017.

52. Menkhaus, "Al-Shabaab's Capabilities Post-Westgate", p. 5.

53. Hansen, *Al-Shabaab in Somalia*, p. 44.

54. Roland Marchal, "A tentative assessment of the Somali Harakat Al-Shabaab", *Journal of Eastern African Studies* 3:3 (2009): p. 389; Mohamed Sheikh Nor and Katharine Houreld, "Somali defector reveals foreigners' role in war", *Washington Times*, 2 March 2011: http://www.washingtontimes.com/news/2011/mar/2/somali-defector-reveals-foreigners-role-in-war/; Hansen, *Al-Shabaab in Somalia*, pp. 74–5.

55. For example, prior to his death in the June 2016 attack on an AMISOM forward operating base manned by Ethiopian troops in Halgan, Khattab al-Masri functioned as a trainer for Al-Shabaab. See UN Monitoring Group on Somalia and Eritrea, "Report of the Monitoring Group", p. 13; UN Official Based in Nairobi B, interview by Tricia Bacon, Nairobi, 11 May 2017.

56. Think Tank Analyst Based in Nairobi A, interview by Tricia Bacon & Daisy Muibu, Nairobi, 9 January 2017; East African Journalist, interview by Tricia Bacon, Nairobi, 25 May 2017.

57. Think Tank Analyst Based in Nairobi A, interview by Tricia Bacon & Daisy Muibu, Nairobi, 9 January 2017; Researcher with an NGO, interview by Tricia Bacon & Daisy Muibu, Nairobi, 24 May 2017; Hansen, *Al-Shabaab in Somalia*, p. 134.

58. Western Analyst Based in Nairobi, interview by Tricia Bacon & Daisy Muibu, Nairobi, 23 May 2017; IGAD, *Al-Shabaab as a Transnational Security Threat*, pp. 22–5; United States of America versus Maalik Alim Jones, "Sealed Complaint," *Southern District of New York*, pp. 8–9: https://www.justice.gov/opa/file/812381/download; UN Monitoring Group on Somalia and Eritrea, "Report of the Monitoring Group", pp. 17–8.

59. Thomas Joscelyn, "Shabaab spokesman calls on Kenyan jihadists to form an 'army'", *Long War Journal*, 22 May 2017: http://www.longwarjournal.org/archives/2017/05/shabaab-spokesman-calls-on-kenyan-jihadists-to-form-an-army.php

60. Western Analyst Based in Nairobi, interview by Tricia Bacon & Daisy Muibu, Nairobi, 23 May 2017; Advocate with a local NGO, interview by Daisy Muibu, Mombasa, 26 May 2017.

61. Shinn, "Al Shabaab's Foreign Threat to Somalia", p. 211; "Shabaab Video Focuses on Recruitment of Foreign Fighters", *Site Intelligence Group*, 23 November 2012: https://news-siteintelgroup-com.proxyau.wrlc.org/Multimedia/shabaab-video-focuses-on-recruitment-of-foreign-fighters.html; Advocate with a local NGO, interview by Daisy Muibu, Mombasa, 26 May 2017.

62. Western academic, interview by Tricia Bacon & Daisy Muibu, Nairobi, 4 January 2017.

63. AMISOM Official Based in Mogadishu, interview by Tricia Bacon via Skype, 13 January 2017; Private Security Firm Operating in Mogadishu A, interview by Tricia Bacon, Washington, DC, 26 April 2017; Researcher with an NGO, interview by Tricia Bacon & Daisy Muibu, Nairobi, 24 May 2017. The need to weigh local and clan considerations more heavily increased when the group gained ter-

ritory and thus was required to engage in governance. See Hansen, *Al-Shabaab in Somalia*, p. 72.

64. Western Government Official A, interview by Tricia Bacon, Washington, DC, 28 April 2017; AMISOM Official Based in Mogadishu, interview by Tricia Bacon, Mogadishu, 19 May 2017; Somali Analyst Based in Mogadishu, interview by Tricia Bacon, Mogadishu, 16 May 2017; Hansen, *Al-Shabaab in Somalia*, p. 137.

65. AMISOM Official Based in Mogadishu, interview by Tricia Bacon, Mogadishu, 19 May 2017; Think Tank Analyst Based in Nairobi A, interview by Tricia Bacon & Daisy Muibu, Nairobi, 9 January 2017; Western Government Analyst, interview by Tricia Bacon, Washington, DC, 20 December 2016; Former Western diplomat, interview by Tricia Bacon, Washington, DC, 30 December 2016; UN Official Based in Mogadishu, interview by Tricia Bacon, Mogadishu, 18 May 2017; Think Tank Analyst Based in Nairobi C, interview by Tricia Bacon and Daisy Muibu, Nairobi, 12 January 2017, "Shabaab Claims Resolving Tribal Conflict in Lower Shabelle", *Site Intelligence Group*, 28 April 2016: https://news.siteintel-group.com/Jihadist-News/shabaab-claims-resolving-tribal-conflict-in-lower-sha-belle.html

66. Clint Watts, Jacob Shapiro, and Vahid Brown, *Al-Qaida's Misadventures in the Horn of Africa* (West Point, VA: Countering Terrorism Center at West Point, 2007); Western Government Analyst, interview by Tricia Bacon, Washington, DC, 20 December 2016; Nir Rosen, "Somalia's Al-Shabaab: A Global or Local Movement?" *Time*, 20 August 2010: http://content.time.com/time/world/arti-cle/0,8599,2010700,00.html; UN Official Based in Mogadishu, interview by Tricia Bacon, Mogadishu, 18 May 2017.

67. Raffaello Pantucci, "Bilal al-Berjawi and Shifting Fortunes of Foreign Fighters in Somalia", *CTC Sentinel* 6:9 (2013): p. 17; Erroll Southers and Justin Hienz, *Foreign Fighters: Terrorist Recruitment and Countering Violent Extremism (CVE) Programs in Minneapolis-St. Paul* (National Center of Excellence for Risk and Economic Analysis of Terrorism Events, University of Southern California, 2015), pp. 15–6, 39; Western Analyst Based in Nairobi, interview by Tricia Bacon & Daisy Muibu, Nairobi, 23 May 2017.

68. Think Tank Analyst Based in Nairobi B, interview by Tricia Bacon & Daisy Muibu, Nairobi, 12 January 2017; Think Tank Analyst Based in Nairobi A, interview by Tricia Bacon & Daisy Muibu, Nairobi, 9 January 2017; Western Analyst Based in Nairobi, interview by Tricia Bacon & Daisy Muibu, Nairobi, 23 May 2017; Somali Analysts Based in Nairobi, interview by Tricia Bacon, Nairobi, 25 May 2017.

69. AMISOM Official Based in Mogadishu, interview by Tricia Bacon via Skype, 13 January 2017; Western Analyst Based in Nairobi, interview by Tricia Bacon & Daisy Muibu, Nairobi, 23 May 2017.

70. Dominic Wafula, "Al Shabaab kill Kenyan fighters over spying suspicion", *Standard Digital*, 2 April 2017: https://www.standardmedia.co.ke/article/2001234749/

Al-Shabaab-kill-kenyan-fighters-over-spying-suspicion; Jeremy Scahill, "The Purge: How Somalia's Al Shabaab Turned Against Its Own Foreign Fighters", *The Intercept*, 19 May 2015: https://theintercept.com/2015/05/19/somalia-Al-Shabaab-foreign-fighter-cia/; Western Government Analyst, interview by Tricia Bacon, Washington, DC, 20 December 2016; "Shabaab Executes Two Accused Spies for Kenyan, Foreign Intel Agencies", *Site Intelligence Group*, 11 June 2016: https://news-siteintelgroup-com.proxyau.wrlc.org/Jihadist-News/shabaab-executes-two-accused-spies-for-kenyan-foreign-intel-agencies.html

71. Western Analyst Based in Nairobi, interview by Tricia Bacon & Daisy Muibu, Nairobi, 23 May 2017.

72. Daniel Byman, "What's Beyond the Defeat of ISIS?" *Brookings Institution Blog*, 27 September 2016: https://www.brookings.edu/blog/markaz/2016/09/27/whats-beyond-the-defeat-of-isis/

73. Martin Chulov, Jaime Grierson, and John Swaine, "Isis faces exodus of foreign fighters as its 'caliphate' crumbles", *The Guardian*, 26 April 2017: https://www.theguardian.com/world/2017/apr/26/isis-exodus-foreign-fighters-caliphate-crumbles

74. Peter Neumann, "Foreign fighter total in Syria/Iraq now exceeds 20,000; surpasses Afghanistan conflict in the 1980s", *International Centre for the Study of Radicalisation and Political Violence Blog*, 26 January 2015: http://icsr.info/2015/01/foreign-fighter-total-syriairaq-now-exceeds-20000-surpasses-afghanistan-conflict-1980s/

75. Thomas Hegghammer, "Should I stay or should I go? Explaining Variation in Western Jihadists' Choice between Domestic and Foreign Fighting", *American Political Science Review* 1–15 (2013): p. 1.

76. Menkhaus, "Al-Shabaab's Capabilities Post-Westgate", p. 7; IGAD, *Al-Shabaab as a Transnational Security Threat*, p. 21.

77. Hansen, *Al-Shabaab in Somalia*, p. 11; Western Government Official A, interview by Tricia Bacon, Washington, DC, 28 April 2017.

78. "Somalia: Hizbul Islam Group Withdraws Allegiance, Says 'Al Shabaab Is Weakened'", *All Africa*, 25 September 2012: http://allafrica.com/stories/201209261141.html

TRAVELLING FOR AN IDEA: THE APPEAL OF AL-SHABAAB TO DIASPORA IN THE WEST

1. "Countering the Terrorist Threat in Canada: An Interim Report", Standing Senate Committee on National Security and Defence, 2015: https://sencanada.ca/Content/SEN/Committee/412/secd/rep/rep18jul15-e.pdf

2. Christopher Dickey, "Nairobi Mall Attack: Al Shabaab's Scandinavian Connection", *The Daily Beast*, 19 October 2013: http://www.thedailybeast.com/nairobi-mall-attack-al-shabaabs-scandinavian-connection

3. Evan F. Kohlmann, "Shabaab Al-Mujahideen: Migration and Jihad in the Horn of Africa", The NEFA Foundation, May 2009: https://web-beta.archive.org/web/20100601062036/http://www.nefafoundation.org/miscellaneous/FeaturedDocs/nefashabaabreport0509.pdf

4. Office of the Director of National Intelligence, "Biographies of High Value Terrorist Detainees Transferred to the US Naval Base at Guantanamo Bay", Press release, 6 September 2006: https://www.dni.gov/files/documents/Newsroom/Press%20Releases/2006%20Press%20Releases/DetaineeBiographies.pdf

5. Jerome P. Bjelopera, "American Jihadist Terrorism: Combating a Complex Threat", Congressional Research Service, 23 January 2013: https://fas.org/sgp/crs/terror/R41416.pdf

6. Michelle Shephard, "Top Islamist Ponders Return to Toronto", Thestar.com, 8 January 2007: https://www.thestar.com/news/2007/01/08/top_islamist_ponders_return_to_toronto.html

7. Stewart Bell, "Somali-Canadians Joined Fight in Horn of Africa: Report", National Post, 25 July 2007: http://circ.jmellon.com/docs/view.asp?id=1142; Michael Taarnby and Lars Hallundbaek, "Al-Shabaab: The Internationalization of Militant Islamism in Somalia and the Implications for Radicalisation Processes in Europe", February 2010: http://www.justitsministeriet.dk/sites/default/files/media/Arbejdsomraader/Forskning/Forskningspuljen/2011/2010/alshabaab.pdf; See also "Swedes Reported Dead in Somalia", The Local, 30 January 2007: https://www.thelocal.se/20070130/6245; See also James Brandon, "Islamist Movements Recruiting in the West for the Somali Jihad" Terrorism Monitor 7, Issue 1 (9 January 2009): https://jamestown.org/program/islamist-movements-recruiting-in-the-west-for-the-somali-jihad/ (accessed 31 May 2017).

8. Kohlmann, "Shabaab Al-Mujahideen".

9. Erroll Southers and Justin Hienz, "Foreign Fighters: Terrorist Recruitment and Countering Violent Extremism (CVE) Programs in Minneapolis-St. Paul", USC CREATE Homeland Security Center, April 2015: http://securitydebrief.com/wp-content/uploads/2015/04/Foreign-Fighters-Terrorist-Recruitment-and-CVE-in-Minneapolis-St-Paul.pdf

10. Christopher Anzalone, "Al-Shabaab Recruits in Somalia's Diaspora", The Daily Star, 6 September 2011: http://www.dailystar.com.lb/Opinion/Commentary/2011/Sep-06/147995-al-shabaab-recruits-insomalias-diaspora.ashx

11. For a variety of excerpts from al-Shabaab propaganda videos highlighting these themes, see Kohlmann, "Shabaab Al-Mujahideen"; See also Alexander Meleagrou-Hitchens, Shiraz Maher, and James Sheehan, "Lights, Camera, Jihad: Al-Shabaab's Western Media Strategy", The International Centre for the Study of Radicalisation and Political Violence, 2012: http://icsr.info/wp-content/uploads/2012/11/ICSR-Lights-Camera-Jihad-Report_Nov2012_ForWeb-2.pdf

12. Southers and Hienz, "Foreign Fighters"; Michael Taarnby and Lars Hallundbaek,

"Al-Shabaab: The Internationalization of Militant Islamism in Somalia and the Implications for Radicalisation Processes in Europe", February 2010: http://www. justitsministeriet.dk/sites/default/files/media/Arbejdsomraader/Forskning/ Forskningspuljen/2011/2010/alshabaab.pdf

13. Examples include the so-called "Somali Six" who left Canada in 2009 to join Al-Shabaab, and three German brothers of Somali descent—identified in press reports only as Abdullah, Abdulsalam, and Abdiwahid W.—who travelled to Somalia in 2013 to join Al-Shabaab. Colin Freeze and Joe Friesen, "Why the Canadian Pipeline to al-Shabaab Has Dried Up", *The Globe and Mail*, 30 September 2013: https://www.theglobeandmail.com/news/world/why-the-canadian-pipe-line-to-al-shabab-has-dried-up/article14620270/; See also "Germany Jails Five Men for Fighting with Somali Shabaab", World Bulletin, 7 July 2016: http://www. worldbulletin.net/europe/174695/germany-jails-five-men-for-fighting-with-somali-shabaab

14. Andrew Higgins, "A Norway Town and Its Pipeline to Jihad in Syria", *The New York Times*, 4 April 2015: https://www.nytimes.com/2015/04/05/world/europe/ a-norway-town-and-its-pipeline-to-jihad-in-syria.html

15. "Dutch Arrest Suspected Shabab Extremist", *Arab News*, 3 May 2017: http://www. arabnews.com/node/1093596/world

16. Frazer Egerton and Alexandre Wilner, "Militant Jihadism in Canada Prosecuting the War of Ideas", Report, February 2009: http://canada.metropolis.net/pdfs/ militant_jihadism_in_canada_e.pdf

17. "Violent Islamic Extremism: Al-Shabaab Recruitment in America", 111th Cong., 1 (2009) (testimony of Ken Menkhaus): https://webcache.googleusercontent. com/search?q=cache:u6RZaRk8H7kJ:https://www.hsgac.senate.gov/downloa d/031109menkhaus+&cd=1&hl=en&ct=clnk&gl=us

18. Integrated Threat Assessment Centre, "Al Shabaab's Recruitment of Youths from Canada", 29 March 2010: http://wpmedia.news.nationalpost.com/2010/07/ alshababreport.pdf; See also United Kingdom General Intelligence and Security Service, "Recruitment for the Jihad in the Netherlands", 2002: https://english. aivd.nl/publications/publications/2002/12/09/recruitment-for-the-jihad-in-the-netherlands

19. Taarnby and Hallundbaek, "Al-Shabaab".

20. "Recruitment for the Jihad in the Netherlands: from Incident to Trend", General Intelligence and Security Service Ministry of the Interior and Kingdom Relations, December 2002: https://english.aivd.nl/publications/publications/2002/12/09/ recruitment-for-the-jihad-in-the-netherlands

21. Dina Temple-Raston, "Minnesota Trial Offers Window on Jihadi Pipeline", NPR, 10 October 2012: http://www.npr.org/2012/10/10/162663573/court-minn-man-recruited-somalis-for-terrorism; See also Janel Smith et al., "Exploring the Impacts of Conflicts Abroad on Diaspora Communities in Canada", SCG Working

Papers No. 1 April 2017, Security Governance Group for Public Safety Canada: https://secgovgroup.com/wp-content/uploads/2017/04/Working-Paper-1-Exploring-the-Impacts-of-Conflicts-Abroad-on-Diaspora-Communities-in-Canada. pdf

22. "Violent Islamic Extremism: Al-Shabaab Recruitment in America", 111th Cong., 1 (2009) (testimony of Ken Menkhaus): https://webcache.googleusercontent. com/search?q=cache:u6RZaRk8H7kJ:https://www.hsgac.senate.gov/downloa d/031109menkhaus+&cd=1&hl=en&ct=clnk&gl=us

23. "The Road is Long", *The Economist*, 17 August 2013: http://www.economist.com/ news/britain/21583710-somalis-fare-much-worse-other-immigrants-what-holds-them-back-road-long; See also David Frum, "America's Immigration Challenge", *The Atlantic*, 11 December 2015: http://www.theatlantic.com/politics/archive/ 2015/12/refugees/419976/; See also Emily Woodgate, "Somalis Face Prejudice and Exclusion", Newsinenglish.no, 11 December 2013: http://www.newsinenglish.no/2013/12/11/somalis-face-prejudice-and-exclusion/

24. Hassan Sheikh and Sally Healy, *Somalia's Mission Million: The Somali Diaspora and Its Role in Development* (UNDP Somalia, March 2009): www.undp.org/content/dam/somalia/docs/undp_report_onsomali_diaspora.pdf and *Somalis in European Cities* (New York: Open Society Foundations, 2015): https://www. opensocietyfoundations.org/reports/somalis-european-cities-overview (accessed 31 May 2017).

25. See, for instance, friends' description of Mohamoud Ali Hassan in Laura Yuen, "Fifth Minn. Man Dies in Somalia", MPRNews, 5 September 2009: https://www. mprnews.org/story/2009/09/04/somali-death

26. Andrea Elliott, "A Call to Jihad, Answered in America", *The New York Times*, 11 July 2009: http://www.nytimes.com/2009/07/12/us/12somalis.html.

27. Christopher Dickey, "Nairobi Mall Attack: Al Shabaab's Scandinavian Connection", *The Daily Beast*, 19 October 2013: http://www.thedailybeast.com/nairobi-mall-attack-al-shabaabs-scandinavian-connection

28. Raveena Aulakh, "Somali Canadians Grapple with Terrorism's Appeal to Youth", Thestar.com, 8 April 2011: https://www.thestar.com/news/gta/2011/04/08/ somali_canadians_grapple_with_terrorisms_appeal_to_youth.html

29. For instance, more than 50 per cent of Somalis living in the US are 24 years old or younger: Southers and Hienz, "Foreign Fighters".

30. The author identified in open source reporting 33 travellers from the US Data on their ages at first radical activity was available for 27 of them.

31. Peter Bergen, Courtney Schuster, and David Sterman, *ISIS in the West: The New Faces of Extremism* (New America, November 2015): https://static.newamerica. org/attachments/11813-isis-in-the-west-2/ISP-Isis-In-The-West-v2.b4f2e9e3a7c-94b9e9bd2a293bae2e759.pdf

32. Lorenzo Vidino and Seamus Hughes, *ISIS in America: From Retweets to Raqqa*

(Washington, DC: Program on Extremism at George Washington University, December 2015): https://cchs.gwu.edu/sites/cchs.gwu.edu/files/downloads/ISIS%20in%20America%20-%20Full%20Report.pdf (accessed 31 May 2017).

33. Thomas Hegghammer, "The Rise of Muslim Foreign Fighters: Islam and the Globalization of Jihad", *International Security* 35, No. 3 (Winter 2010/11): pp. 53–94: http://www.mitpressjournals.org/doi/pdf/10.1162/ISEC_a_00023 (accessed 31 May 2017).

34. Frank Furedi, "Are 'Terrorist Groomers' Warping Our Kids?" Sp!ked, 6 November 2007: http://www.spiked-online.com/newsite/article/4050#.WS9hN2jyvcs

35. This was a dramatically higher rate of university-level education than the average in the Middle East and North Africa region that produced the recruits. Diego Gambetta and Steffen Hertog, "Engineers of Jihad", Working Paper No. 2007–10, University of Oxford, Department of Sociology, Oxford, UK: https://www.sociology.ox.ac.uk/materials/papers/2007–10.pdf

NEGOTIATIONS WITH AL-SHABAAB: LESSONS LEARNED AND FUTURE PROSPECTS

1. This report recognizes that there are many other elements to a comprehensive peace and reconciliation process in Somalia that go well beyond an end to Al-Shabaab violence.

2. Harmonie Toros, *Terrorism, Talking and Transformation: A Critical Approach* (Abingdon: Routledge, 2012); Harmonie Toros, *Terrorism, Counterterrorism, and Conflict Resolution: Building Bridges* (Ankara: NATO Centre of Excellence—Defence Against Terrorism, 2015).

3. Seth G. Jones and Martin C. Libicki, *How Terrorist Groups End: Lessons for Countering al Qa'ida* (Arlington, VA: RAND Corporation, 2008).

4. Toros, *Terrorism, Talking and Transformation*, pp. 42–64.

5. International Crisis Group, "Somalia: To Move Beyond the Failed State", Africa Report #147 (ICG, 2008), p. 33: https://www.crisisgroup.org/africa/horn-africa/somalia/somalia-move-beyond-failed-state (accessed 2 May 2017).

6. Stig Jarle Hansen, *Al-Shabaab in Somalia: The History and Ideology of a Militant Islamist Group* (London: Hurst, 2016); see also Meredith Preston McGhie, "Mediating Djibouti," in Mark Bradbury and Sally Healy (eds), *Whose Peace is it Anyway? Connecting Somali and International Peacemaking: Accord* Issue 21 (London: Conciliation Resources, 2010), pp. 20–23.

7. Joe Belliveau, "Red Lines and al-Shabaab: Negotiating Humanitarian Access in Somalia", (NOREF: Norwegian Peacebuilding Resource Centre, 2015), p. 4; Ashley Jackson and Abdi Aynte, "Talking to the Other Side: Humanitarian Negotiations with Al-Shabaab in Somalia", HPG Working Paper, 2013: www.odi.org/sites/odi.org.uk/files/odi-assets/publications-opinion-files/8744.pdf (accessed 20 March 2017).

8. Jackson and Aynte, *Talking to the Other Side*, p. 8.

9. Ibid., p. 9.

10. Belliveau, *Red Lines and al-Shabaab*, p. 4.

11. Toros, *Terrorism, Talking and Transformation*, pp. 158–168.

12. The notions of "ripeness" and "mutually hurting stalemate" have been put forward by key negotiation scholars outside the Somali context. See I. William Zartman, "Dynamics and Constraints in Negotiations in Internal Conflicts" in I. William Zartman (ed.) *Elusive Peace: Negotiating an End to Civil Wars* (Washington: Brookings Institution, 1995), pp. 3–29.

13. Sophie Haspeslagh, "'Listing Terrorists': The Impact of Proscription on Third-Party Efforts to Engage Armed Groups in Peace Processes—A Practitioner's Perspective", *Critical Studies on Terrorism* 6, no. 1 (April 2013): p. 193.

14. See for example Ken Menkhaus, "Traditional Conflict Management in Contemporary Somalia" in I. William Zartman (ed.), *Traditional Cures for Modern Conflicts: African Conflict "Medicine"* (Boulder, CO: Lynne Reinner, 1999), pp. 183–200 and Ken Menkhaus, "Diplomacy in a Failed State" in Bradbury and Healy (eds), *Whose Peace is it Anyway?*, pp. 16–19.

15. Aysha Ahmad, "The Security Bazaar: Business Interests and Islamist Power in Civil War Somalia", *International Security* 39, no. 3 (Winter 2014–2015): pp. 89–117.

16. Louise Boon-Kuo, Ben Hayes, Vicki Sentas and Gavin Sullivan, *Building Peace in Permanent War: Terrorist Listing and Conflict Transformation* (London: International State Crime Initiative, 2015); Teresa Dumasy and Sophie Haspeslagh, "Proscribing Peace: The Impact of Terrorist Listing on Peacebuilding Organisations", Conciliation Resources Briefing Paper, 2016: http://www.c-r.org/downloads/Conciliation_Resources_Counter-terrorism_brief.pdf (accessed 26 February 2017).

COMMUNITY PERSPECTIVES TOWARDS AL-SHABAAB: SOURCES OF SUPPORT AND THE POTENTIAL FOR NEGOTIATIONS

1. Officially known as Harakat Al-Shabaab al-Muhijadeen, within this paper they are referred to by the colloquial name of Al-Shabaab.

2. Mogadishu KII 2.

3. Mogadishu KII 7.

4. Kismayo KII 7.

5. Gedo KII ALS.

6. Gedo KII XI—village names redacted for the purposes of security.

7. Gedo KII MKas.

8. Gedo/Mogadishu, KII, candidate in 2016 parliamentary elections.

9. Afgoye KII 4.

10. Afgoye KII 3.

11. Saferworld consultations for UK HMG National Action Plan on Women Peace and Security March 2017.

12. *Zakat* is a payment made under Islamic law on certain types of property; the payments are intended to be used for charitable and religious purposes.

13. KII International independent evaluator to a large stabilization intervention (June 2017).

14. Mogadishu KII 8.

15. Afgoye KII 4.

16. Gedo KII LIN.

17. Afgoye KII 7.

18. Gedo KII GYW.

19. Afgoye KII 8.

20. Afgoye KII 9.

21. Nairobi KII 1—Humanitarian aid manager. Previous research by Saferworld in 2015 indicated that the prevalence of fear about speaking critically of those in charge does not differ dramatically between places such as Eel Wak and Kismayo, overseen by AS and the Jubaland Administration respectively, with survey respondents in both places expressing that it was highly dangerous to speak critically of the ruling power. Similarly, respondents in Dollow, governed under the Jubaland Administration, refused to participate in interviews in 2015 due to fear of punishment if they were found out. One informant spoke fearfully of the Dollow administration, reporting that problematic individuals were "taken to the Ethiopian side." See "Forging Jubaland: Community perspectives on federalism, governance and reconciliation", Saferworld, 2016.

22. Baidoa KII FOD.

23. Kismayo KII 1.

24. Afgoye KII 1.

25. Afgoye KII 6.

26. Baidoa KII AA.

27. Baidoa KII ABD.

28. Nairobi KII 1.

29. Nairobi KII 2.

30. Kismayo KII 3.

31. Baidoa KII ABQ.

32. Baidoa KII FR.

33. Nairobi KII 2.

34. Nairobi KII 2.

35. Kismayo KII 2.

36. Mogadishu KII 8.

37. It would be valuable to think about how other conflicts in other countries with armed insurgents have concluded through peace agreements and how the use of

military action and indiscriminate killings changed following negotiated political agreements.

AL-SHABAAB ATTITUDES TOWARDS NEGOTIATIONS

1. We recognize that this is very small sample as it is intended to be the first phase of a larger research project. We also recognize that some of the research questions may not have translated well into English. However, despite this and the sample's limited size, we believe the results provide valuable insights into the thinking of individuals in leadership positions with respect to the reasons for joining Al-Shabaab and what it will take to bring them to the negotiation table.

2. Of these 17 individuals, five respondents were in other organizations, including Al-Ittihad Al-Islamiyya, Islamic Courts, and Hisbul Islam, although according to the interviews none received training outside Somalia's borders. The sample consisted of field and mid-level commanders, district commanders, trainers, a head of finance, and judges.

3. Leaders expressed more trust in religious leaders with 60% rating their trust at "improving" (in other words, increasing since joining Al-Shabaab) and a further 20% as "excellent". Like the leadership sample, ordinary Al-Shabaab members considered that trust in religious leaders is "improving" (54%), while a further 16% rated religious leaders as "excellent." Separately, 60% of the leadership sample rated their trust in elders as "average" and 19% as "improving." Rank-and-file members interviewed expressed more trust in elders with 44% describing their trust in elders as "average", 39% as "improving" and a further 12% as "excellent." In other words, although elders can play an important role in the disengagement process, both groups expressed more trust in religious leaders.

COLLABORATING FOR PEACE: AN ANALYSIS OF NETWORKS OF COOPERATION IN SOMALIA

1. T. Nenova and T. Harford, *Anarchy and Invention—How Does Somalia's Private Sector Cope without Government?* (Washington, DC: World Bank, 2004), p. 1. See, for example, also M. Angeloni, "Somalia: The Tortuga of the 21st Century", *Transition Studies Review* 16 (2009): pp. 755–67, p. 577; A. Weber, "State Building in Somalia: Challenges in a Zone of Crisis", in E.-M. Bruchhaus and M. Sommer (Eds.), *Hot Spot Horn of Africa Revisited—Approaches to Make Sense of Conflict* (Berlin: LIT, 2008), pp. 14–27, p. 14.

2. See, for example, Fragile States Index.

3. Organisation for Economic Co-Operation and Development, *Supporting Statebuilding in Situations of Conflict and Fragility: Key messages for policymakers* (Paris: OECD, 2011). See for example the Paris Declaration (2005), the Accra Agenda for Action (2008), as well as the Busan Partnership for Effective

Development Cooperation (2011), all of which mention aid coordination as one of the key mechanisms to enhance aid effectiveness.

4. Source: http://data.worldbank.org/indicator/DT.ODA.ALLD.CD?end=2015 &locations=SO&start=2006

5. Source: https://www.somaliampf.org/sites/smpf/files/Aid%20Flows%20in%20 Somalia.pdf

6. Ibid.

7. The UN's top-level coordination structure is headed by the Resident Coordinator, for example, who heads the UN Development Program and leads the UN Country Team, bringing together all UN agencies with operations in a given country. Moreover, the UN also entertains a Humanitarian Mission in Somalia, seeing the Humanitarian Country Team coordinating humanitarian responses across the entire country. The Humanitarian Coordinator reports directly to the UN Emergency Relieve Coordinator at the UN Headquarters in New York.

8. For an overview, see M. Bratton, "Formal versus Informal Institutions in Africa", *Journal of Democracy* 18, 3 (2007): pp. 96–110.

9. See for example Bøås, M., "Crime, Coping, and Resistance in the Mali-Sahel Periphery", *African Security* 8, 4 (2015): pp. 299–319 and D. Koter, "King Makers: Local Leaders and Ethnic Politics in Africa", *World Politics* 65, 2 (2013): pp. 187–232.

10. See A. Barabási, *Linked: The New Science of Networks* (Cambridge, MA: Perseus Publishing, 2002); M. Buchanan, *Nexus: Small Worlds and the Groundbreaking Science of Networks* (New York: Norton & Company, 2002); D. J. Watts, *Six Degrees: The Science of a Connected Age* (New York: Norton & Company, 2003).

11. See for example P. K. MacDonald, *Networks of Domination: The Social Foundations of Peripheral Conquest in International Politics* (Oxford: Oxford University Press, 2014); T. Sharan, *The Network Politics of International Statebuilding: Intervention and Statehood in Post-2001 Afghanistan* (PhD), University of Exeter (2013); P. Staniland, *Networks of Rebellion: Explaining Insurgent Cohesion and Collapse* (London: Cornell University Press, 2014).

12. See for example G. Easter, "Personal Networks and Postrevolutionary State Building: Soviet Russia Reexamined", *World Politics* 48, 4 (1996): pp. 551–578; and A. Jackson, *Seeing Like the Networked State: Subnational Governance in Afghanistan* (Kabul: Secure Livelihoods Research Consortium, 2016).

13. The ACU was set up by the government of President Hassan Sheikh Mohamud in an effort to organize donors on the ground.

14. Whilst donor coordination refers to the specific mechanisms and arrangements agreed within the community of development partners to improve their effectiveness, aid coordination refers to the established mechanisms and arrangements that country governments and their development partners have agreed upon in order to maximize the effectiveness of external aid for development at national or sector levels.

15. H. Song and W. P. Eveland, "The Structure of Communication Networks Matters: How Network Diversity, Centrality, and Context Influence Political Ambivalence, Participation, and Knowledge", *Political Communication* 32 (2015): pp. 83–108; T. S. Van Gunten, "Cohesion, Consensus, and Conflict: Technocratic Elites and Financial Crisis in Mexico and Argentina", *International Journal of Comparative Sociology* 56 (2015): pp. 366–90.

16. M. D. McCubbins, R. Paturi, and N. Weller, "Connected Coordination: Network Structure and Group Coordination", *American Politics Research* 37 (2009): pp. 899–920.

INSIGHTS FROM NETWORK ANALYSIS IN SOMALIA

1. Lee Cassanelli, "Whose Peace is it Anyway? Connecting Somali and international peacemaking", Conciliation Resources Organisation, *Accord* Issue 21 (2010).

2. Mark Granovetter, "The Strength of Weak Ties", 1973.

3. Adam Douglas Henry, Mark Lubell, and Michael McCoy, "Survey-Based Measurement of Public Management and Policy Networks", *Journal of Policy Analysis and Management* 31/2 (2012): pp. 432–52: doi:10.1002/pam.21623

4. Karin Ingold, "Network Structures within Policy Processes: Coalitions, Power, and Brokerage in Swiss Climate Policy", *Policy Studies Journal* 39/3 (2011): pp. 435–59: doi:10.1111/j.1541-0072.2011.00416.x.

5. Survey Data.

6. E. Browne and J. Fisher, "Key Actors Mapping, Somalia", 2013, GSDRC 2.

7. Damajadid, led by Hassan Sheikh Mohamoud, has consolidated its position as the leading political group. However, since his presidential term ended, the group no longer commands the same degree of power and it remains to be seen whether the alliances forged will remain. Daljir party emerged from the Ala Sheikh group. In the 2012–16 parliament, only four MPs were known to be associated with Ala Sheikh. Whilst still relatively small, in the 2016 elections, Daljir outperformed Damajadid in terms of its supporters elected.

8. Various, "Conflict in Somalia, Drivers and Dynamics", World Bank, 2005.

9. Sandra McNeill and Khadir Abdi, "Assessing the political economy of roadblocks in South Central Somalia", *Transparency Solutions* (2016): pp. 64–66.

BUSINESS-LED PEACEBUILDING IN SOMALIA

1. A. Bruzzone, 'Somalia: Recent History', in Iain Frame (ed.) *Africa South of the Sahara 2017*, 46th Edition (London: Europa/Routledge, 2016), pp. 1075–1087. The author considers the origin and development of Somali business.

2. Tobias Hagmann and Finn Stepputat, "Corridors of trade and power: Economy and state formation in Somali East Africa" (DIIS WORKINGPAPER 2016: p. 8) have introduced this distinction. They include piracy, illegal fishing, kidnapping

for ransom, the production of counterfeit money and documents, and trafficking of drugs, arms and people and abuse and corruption of public funds or shady dealings involving international aid agencies and in the category of illicit business.

3. A. Bruzzone, "Somalia: Economy", in Frame, Africa South of the Sahara 2017, pp. 1087–90.

4. The most noticeable feature of the liberal political view of companies is its emphasis on the separation of power and politics that has a direct impact on the protection of human rights. The scholars listed below insist on considering the public roles of (state-like) companies. Dirk Matten and Andrew Crane, "Corporate Citizenship: Toward an extended theoretical conceptualization", *Academy of Management Review* 30, no. 1 (2005): pp. 166–179; Jeremy Moon, Andrew Crane, and Dirk Matten, "Can corporations be citizens? Corporate citizenship as a metaphor for business participation in society", *Business Ethics Quarterly* 15, no. 3 (2005): pp. 429–453.

5. Neil Carrier and Emma Lochery, "Missing states? Somali trade networks and the Eastleigh transformation", *Journal of Eastern African Studies* 7, no. 2 (2013): pp. 334–352 quoted in Hagmann and Stepputat, "Corridors of trade and power".

6. Bruzzone, "Somalia: Economy", pp. 1087–90.

7. See note 1 above.

8. Laura Hammond, Mustafa Awad, Ali Ibrahim Dagane, Peter Hansen, Cindy Horst, Ken Menkhaus, and Lynette Obare, "Cash and Compassion: The role of the Somali diaspora in relief, development and peace-building", UNPD. The report lists ten different categories of diaspora—individual households, local NGOs based in the diaspora, clan-based or home-town associations, professional association, transnational associations, mosques, private investors and shareholders in private businesses, members of boards of trustees, women's group and youth groups—which provide financial, technical and professional support to production, consumption, and development in Somalia. A significant segment (40 per cent) of the Somali population depends on financial support provided by the diaspora.

9. About us; Dahabshiil website: https://www.dahabshiil.com/about-us

10. Bruzzone, "Somalia: Recent History", pp. 1075–87. The author reports the Somali private sector "may reach its structural limits unless reforms are carried out to the business environment to enhance security, access to finance and competition. The lack of sector regulation is favouring the emergence of monopolistic behaviour, thereby hindering the growth of small and medium-size businesses and preventing new companies from entering the market. The absence of proper taxation has also encouraged the development of oligopolistic trends, since the few big businesses in the country are able to pay the ruling élites in order to safeguard their own position and block potential rivals".

11. Progress Report, May 1—December 31, 2016: p. 21. The Multi-Partner Fund Supporting the Somali Compact: The World Bank IBRD.IDA: World Bank

Group. The report offers an analysis of the telecommunication sector and states that the "sector represents an important source of potential revenue for the Somali Government. Although the industry currently makes "voluntary" payments to the Ministry of Finance of around US$ 5 million per year, it should be contributing much more, perhaps as much as twenty times that level".

12. Shabelle Media Network, 10 Jan 2011, and IRIN, 9 February 2010, report that Somali "private business people have been heavily involved in providing humanitarian support to displaced populations and others in need, and their contributions have been encouraged in both TFG and al-Shabaab controlled areas".

13. Hammond et al, "Cash and compassion", states: "Somali businesses are top targets for fund-raising, and many commit to the principle of zakat or tithing. They often allow local managers discretion to contribute to local causes. Businesses have no formal review process of grant requests or personnel dedicated to oversight of their 'corporate philanthropy' but instead assess requests on an ad hoc, case by case basis. They acknowledge that it is difficult to say 'no' in the Somali social setting, but are unable to meet most of the many requests for money they receive. Businesses are reluctant to advertise this donor role, arguing that 'quiet giving' is in keeping with the principle of zakat. Current economic pressures, especially on the remittance companies, have dried up much of their charitable funds".

14. Ibid.

15. For example, the ten normative principles of GC conform to theological (Islamic) moral precepts. This moral synergy can avert a clash of civilizations (Williams et al, 2010). GC also has strong potential to contribute to the realization of women's rights (Kilgore, 2007) and to reduce structural violence that results from political structures and cultural norms (Dubee, 2007). Geoffrey Williams and John Zinkin, "Islam and CSR: A study of the compatibility between the tenets of Islam and the UN Global Compact", *Journal of Business Ethics* 91, no. 4 (2010): pp. 519–533. Maureen A. Kilgour, "The UN Global Compact and substantive equality for Women: revealing a 'well hidden' mandate", *Third World Quarterly* 28, no. 4 (2007): pp. 751–773; Fred Dubee, "Structural violence and productivity: The role of business and the United Nations Global Compact", *International Journal of Productivity and Performance Management* 56, no. 3 (2007): pp. 252–258.

ACKNOWLEDGEMENTS

The United Nations extends its sincere thanks to the experts and researchers who have contributed briefing papers to this Portfolio. We also wish to express our gratitude to the Government of Norway for funding the Initiative, and to the Federal Government of Somalia for its support, advice, and collaboration.

The United Nations acknowledges and thanks many staff members who dedicated time and effort to the Portfolio, including the lengthy process of review and editing, including the SRSG's adviser, special adviser and special assistants, the Deputy SRSG, Political Affairs and Mediation Group, Integrated Analysis Team, copy editor, and translators. We are also grateful to the United Nations Office for Project Services who provided important administrative and operational support to the Initiative.

SOMALI AND ARABIC TERMS

Amniyat	Al-Shabaab's security and intelligence division
Bayah	oath of allegiance
Biri ma geydo	'spared from the spear'—people who are protected in war by Somali custom
Bulsho	society
Darwish	local reserve police forces
Dawa	Islamic preaching
Diya	compensation, under Sharia law, provided to victims of serious crimes
Godobir	practice of exchanging a young girl as a wife, with or without her consent, often as part of a larger exchange to cement a peace agreement between warring parties
Hizba	Al-Shabaab's police force
Huduud	punishments stipulated by Sharia law
Jabha	Al-Shabaab's combat operations division
Looma dhama	not inclusive
Qabiil	clan
Qaran	state
Qorraxjoog	local youth
Qurbojoog	diaspora youth
Shir	council or assembly of elders
Tahriib	illegal immigration
U dhasheey	certain birthrights
Ulema	Islamic scholars
Wilayat	province
Xeer	Somali traditional customary law
Zakat	alms or taxation in Islam

ACRONYMS

AAPOR	American Association for Public Opinion Research
ACLED	Armed Conflict Location and Event Data Project
ACU	Aid Coordination Unit
ADF	Allied Democratic Forces
AFRICOM	United States Africa Command
AIAI	Al-Ittihad Al-Islami
AMISOM	African Union Mission in Somalia
APD	Academy for Peace and Development
AQAP	Al-Qaida in the Arabian Peninsula
ARC	African Resource Corporation
ARPCT	Alliance for the Restoration of Peace and Counter-Terrorism
ASWJ	Ahlu Sunna Wal Jama'a
AU	African Union
BBC	British Broadcasting Company
BBG	Broadcasting Board of Governors
C-IED	Counter-Improvised Explosive Device
CAN	Creative Alternatives Now
CAR	Central African Republic
CfPAR	Centre for Policy Analysis & Research
CIA	Central Information Agency
CLJ	Constitutional Loya Jirga
CNRS	National Centre for Scientific Research
CRD	Center for Research and Dialogue
CSO	Civil Society Organization
CSR	Corporate Social Responsibility
CVE	Countering Violent Extremism

CWIED	Command-Wire Improvised Explosive Device
DDR	Disarmament, Demobilization and Reintegration
DFCs	Directional Fragmentation Charges
DPA	United Nations Department of Political Affairs
DPKO	Department of Peacekeeping Operations
DPW	Dubai Port World
DRC	Democratic Republic of the Congo
ENDF	Ethiopian National Defence Forces
EPLF	Eritrean People's Liberation Front
FAO	Food and Agriculture Organization
FGD	Focus Group Discussion
FGM	Female Genital Mutilation
FGS	Federal Government of Somalia
FMS	Federal Member States
FOI	Totalförsvarets forskningsinstitut
GCC	Gulf Cooperation Council
GDP	Gross Domestic Product
HD	Centre for Humanitarian Dialogue
HIV	Human Immunodeficiency Virus
HME	Home-Made Explosive
HMM	Halima Mohamud Mohamed
ICC	International Criminal Court
IDP	Internally Displaced Person
IED	Improvised Explosive Device
IGAD	Intergovernmental Authority on Development
IOM	International Organization for Migration
IPTI	Inclusive Peace and Transition Initiative
IS	Islamic State of Iraq and the Levant
ISS	Institute for Strategic Studies
ISSP	IGAD Security Sector Programme
ISWA	Interim South West Administration
KII	Key Informant Interview
KNF	Kenya Defence Forces
LPI	Life and Peace Institute
MINUSCA	United Nations Multidimensional Integrated Stabilization Mission in the Central African Republic
MINUSMA	United Nations Multidimensional Integrated Stabilization Mission in Mali

MoD	UK Ministry of Defence
MONUSCO	United Nations Organization Stabilization Mission in the Democratic Republic of the Congo
MOPIC	Somalia's Ministry of Planning and International Cooperation
MP	Member of Parliament
MTO	Money Transfer Operators
MYC	Muslim Youth Centre
NATO	North Atlantic Treaty Organization
NDC	Yemeni National Dialogue Conference
NGO	Non-Governmental Organization
NISA	National Intelligence and Security Agency
NLF	National Leadership Forum
NRC	National Reconciliation Commission
NSO	National Security Office
NSS	National Security Service
OCVP	Observatory of Conflict and Violence Prevention
OECD	Organization for Economic Cooperation and Development
OHCHR	Office of the United Nations High Commissioner for Human Rights
PAR	Participatory Action Research
PBIED	Person-Borne Improvised Explosive Device
PDRC	Peace and Development Research Center
PPD	Public-Private Dialogue
PVE	Preventing Violent Extremism
RAND	Research and Development Corporation
RCD	Royal Canadian Dragoons
RCIED	Radio-controlled Improvised Explosive Device
RST	Rehabilitation Support Team
RVI	Rift Valley Institute
SCCI	Somali Chamber of Commerce and Industries
SDG	Sustainable Development Goal
SDRF	Somalia Development and Reconstruction Facility
SFG	Somali Federal Government
SLPI	Somalia Local Peace Initiatives
SNA	Social Network Analysis
SNA	Somali National Army
SNM	Somali National Movement

SNSF	Somali National and Security Forces
SRSG	Special Representative of the Secretary-General
SSDF	Somali Salvation Democratic Front
SVBIED	Suicide-Vehicle-Borne Improvised Explosive Device
SWSO	Somali Women Solidarity Organization
TFG	Transitional Federal Government
TGSN	The Global Strategy Network
TJRC	Transitional Justice and Reconciliation Commission
TPLF	Tigray People's Liberation Front
TRC	Truth and Reconciliation Commission
TS	Transparency Solutions
TST	Transnational Security Threats
TTPs	Tactics, Techniques, and Procedures
UAE	United Arab Emirates
UCDP	Uppsala Conflict Data Program
UIC	Union of Islamic Courts
UK	United Kingdom
UN	United Nations
UNAMA	United Nations Assistance Mission in Afghanistan
UNAMI	United Nations Assistance Mission for Iraq
UNAMID	African Union/United Nations Assistance Mission in Darfur
UNDP	United Nations Development Programme
UNEP	United Nations Environment Programme
UNHCR	United Nations High Commissioner for Refugees
UNICEF	United Nations Children's Fund
UNITAF	Unified Task Force
UNMIS	United Nations Mission in Sudan
UNOCHA	United Nations Office for the Coordination of Humanitarian Affairs
UNOPS	United Nations Office for Project Services
UNOSOM	United Nations Operation in Somalia
UNSCOL	Office of the United Nations Special Coordinator for Lebanon
UNSCR	United Nations Security Council Resolution
UNSMIL	United Nations Support Mission in Libya
UNSOM	United Nations Assistance Mission in Somalia
US	United States
USC	United Somali Congress